ASSESSMENT AND DIAGNOSIS
IN CHILD PSYCHOPATHOLOGY

ASSESSMENT AND DIAGNOSIS IN CHILD PSYCHOPATHOLOGY

Edited by

MICHAEL RUTTER
A. HUSSAIN TUMA
IRMA S. LANN

THE GUILFORD PRESS
New York   London

Printed in the United States of America

Last digit is print number: 9 8 7 6 5 4 3 2 1

Library of Congress Cataloging-in-Publication Data

Assessment and diagnosis in child psychopathology.

Includes bibliographies and index.
1. Psychology, Pathological—Classification.
2. Mental illness—Diagnosis. 3. Child psychopathology.
I. Rutter, Michael. II. Tuma, A. Hussain. III. Lann,
Irma S. [DNLM: 1. Mental Disorders—classification.
2. Mental Disorders—diagnosis. 3. Psychopathology—in
adolescence. 4. Psychopathology—in infancy & childhood.
WS 350 A846]
RJ503.5.A85   1988   618.92′89075   87-12180
ISBN 0-89862-699-4

CONTRIBUTORS

Thomas M. Achenbach, PhD, Department of Psychiatry, College of Medicine, University of Vermont, Burlington, Vermont

David V. Baldwin, PhD, Oregon Social Learning Center, Eugene, Oregon

Russell A. Barkley, PhD, Department of Psychiatry, University of Massachusetts Medical Center, Worcester, Massachusetts

Harry N. Bawden, PhD, Department of Psychology, Isaak Walton Killam Hospital for Children, Halifax, Nova Scotia, Canada

Dennis P. Cantwell, MD, Department of Child Psychiatry, University of California, Neuropsychiatric Institute, Center for the Health Sciences, Los Angeles, California

Anthony J. Costello, MD, Department of Psychiatry, University of Massachusetts Medical Center, Worcester, Massachusetts

Eric Courchesne, PhD, Neuropsychology Research Laboratory, Children's Hospital Research Center, San Diego, California, and Neurosciences Department, University of California at San Diego, La Jolla, California

Thomas J. Dishion, MA, Oregon Social Learning Center, Eugene, Oregon

Craig Edelbrock, PhD, Department of Psychiatry, University of Massachusetts Medical Center, Worcester, Massachusetts

H. Bruce Ferguson, PhD, Departments of Psychology, Carleton University and Royal Ottawa Hospital, Ottawa, Ontario, Canada

Madelyn S. Gould, PhD, MPH, New York State Psychiatric Institute and Division of Child Psychiatry, Columbia University College of Physicians and Surgeons, New York, New York

Theodore Jacob, PhD, Division of Child Development and Family Relations, University of Arizona, Tucson, Arizona

Gerald R. Patterson, PhD, Oregon Social Learning Center, Eugene, Oregon

John B. Reid, PhD, Oregon Social Learning Center, Eugene, Oregon

Helmut Remschmidt, MD, Klinik und Poliklinik für Kinder und Jugendpsychiatrie, Marburg, West Germany

Michael Rutter, CBE, MD, FRCP, FRCPsych, FRS, Department of Child and Adolescent Psychiatry, University of London Institute of Psychiatry, London, England

Eric Schopler, PhD, Department of Psychiatry, University of North Carolina Memorial Hospital, Chapel Hill, North Carolina

David Shaffer, MB, BS, MRCP, FRCPsych, New York State Psychiatric Institute and Division of Child Psychiatry, Columbia University College of Physicians and Surgeons, New York, New York

Claire Sturge, MB, BS, MRCPsych, Department of Child Psychiatry, Northwick Park Hospital, Harrow, Middlesex, England

Eric Taylor, MA, MB, FRCP, MRCPsych, Department of Child and Adolescent Psychiatry, University of London Institute of Psychiatry, London, England

Daniel L. Tennenbaum, PhD, Department of Psychology, Kent State University, Kent, Ohio

A. Hussain Tuma, PhD, Western Psychiatric Institute and Clinic, University of Pittsburgh, Pittsburgh, Pennsylvania

Rachel Yeung-Courchesne, Neuropsychology Research Laboratory, Children's Hospital Research Center, San Diego, California

PREFACE

Over the past decade both clinicians and researchers have come to appreciate the need for a reliable and valid system of diagnosis and classification that is generally accepted and used in a uniform, comparable fashion. The World Health Organization (1978) scheme, ICD-9, differed from its predecessors in its greater reliance on scientific findings and on its use of field trials to test new and old aspects of the system. ICD-9 departed markedly from ICD-8 in its introduction of a range of codings specifically devised to cover child psychiatric disorders. The American Psychiatric Association (1980) scheme, DSM-III, followed shortly afterwards. In many respects its psychiatric categories paralleled those in ICD-9 but it broke significant new ground in many key features. Most crucially of all, it constituted the first comprehensive psychiatric classification to use research diagnostic criteria that lay down precise rules to be followed in making each coding. Also, it made even greater use of field trials and put on an "official" basis a multiaxial system that built on the experimental scheme developed earlier through the World Health Organization for the child psychiatric section of the classification scheme. It is fair to say that DSM-III has had a broad acceptance that exceeds that of any previous psychiatric classification scheme.

Nevertheless, it was clear from the outset that neither ICD-9 nor DSM-III was entirely satisfactory. As Spitzer wrote in the introduction to DSM-III, "this final version of DSM-III is only one still frame in the ongoing process of attempting to better understand mental disorders" (1980, p. 12). The evaluative studies of both systems have revealed serious problems as well as major successes.

In order to facilitate research that might lead to improved systems of classification in the future and more generally to improved research in child and adolescent psychopathology, the National Institute of Mental Health sponsored a workshop that brought together researchers from both the United States and Europe who had worked with ICD-9 and DSM-III. Several other investigators with research expertise in the theories and methodologies of measurement of psychopathology and whose work does not focus on the DSM-III and ICD-9 systems also participated. Many of the chapters in this book were first presented in draft form at that meeting but extensive revisions were undertaken to prepare them for this volume; in addition, several new chapters were added in order to provide a more comprehensive coverage of key topics and issues.

The first section begins with three chapters that provide an overview of the evidence on the strengths and weaknesses of the currently available classification systems. Dennis Cantwell reviews the concepts underlying DSM-III, the evidence deriving from the field trials, and the theoretical issues that have been highlighted in the literature. Madelyn Gould, David Shaffer, Michael Rutter, and Claire Sturge provide new findings from the British studies of ICD-9, sponsored by the World Health Organization, and Helmut Remschmidt outlines the evidence from the German studies of the same scheme. It is striking that the problems concerning the classification of child psychiatric disorders are closely similar in DSM-III and ICD-9, reflecting in both systems rather well our current knowledge as well as ignorance. Both systems stand in need of substantial data-based revision, as recognized by the recent publication of DSM-III-R (since the chapters were written) and the distribution of a draft version of ICD-10. A brief postscript following the final chapter takes note of the changes introduced by DSM-III-R.

To an important extent, the strength of any diagnostic scheme must rely on the quality of the data on which the system is based and also on the information used in making the diagnoses. There have been major developments during recent years in the better measurement of different aspects of child and adolescent psychopathology. Accordingly, the second section of the book contains a series of NIMH commissioned reviews of currently available assessment methodologies. Some of these relate rather directly to the measurement of child behaviors that must be taken into account in diagnosis. Thus, Craig Edelbrock and Anthony Costello survey structured psychiatric interviews for children; Russell Barkley appraises behavioral ratings scales; and John Reid, David Baldwin, Gerald Patterson, and Thomas Dishion consider the role for observational methods. However, it would be unduly narrow to focus exclusively on behavioral measures; in the future diagnosticians may well come to make much greater use of psychobiological laboratory measures. These are reviewed by H. Bruce Ferguson and Harry Bawden and by Eric Courchesne and Rachel Yeung-Courchesne. Children spend much of their growing years in the context of their family and many child disorders both impinge on the family and are influenced by the interactions of family members. Theodore Jacob and Daniel Tennenbaum review some of the systematic measures that reflect family perspectives of psychopathology in the index child. Finally, in this section, Thomas Achenbach considers the integration of assessment and taxonomy. Throughout these chapters there is an awareness that a variety of perspectives and measurement approaches are required. Some of these rely on dimensional concepts that put morbidity and psychopathology on a continuum; others use categorical distinctions that imply a discontinuity between normality and clinical disorders.

The problems that are inherent in psychiatric classification are by no means confined to the technology of assessment, however. There is an equally pressing need to consider the theoretical elements by which a disorder is defined and to decide how best to test the respective merits of differing approaches to diagnosis and classification. Obviously, it would be impractical to discuss the issues that arise with respect to the total range of child psychiatric conditions. Instead, we selected just three groups of disorders that exemplify many of the concerns that also apply to other diagnostic categories. Michael Rutter reviews some of the issues and concepts applicable to depressive disorders in young people; Eric Taylor tables issues that arise with respect to attention deficit and conduct disorder syndromes; and Michael Rutter and Eric Schopler perform a parallel service for autism and the pervasive developmental disorders.

The book ends with a brief epilogue by Michael Rutter and A. Hussain Tuma that looks to the tasks ahead. It is clear that we are far from having solved all the problems, but the range of questions posed attest to the major progress achieved over the past few years and provide promise of even greater accomplishments in the years ahead. We hope that by reviewing and summarizing the extant diagnostic and assessment methods in child and adolescent psychopathology, this volume may stimulate and facilitate further progress in this field. This in turn can contribute to improved case identification and homogeneity in samples selected for studies of etiology, course, and treatment of mental disorders in children and adolescents.

We are most grateful to the authors of all chapters for their thoughtful and knowledgeable critiques, as well as for being so patient with our requests to clarify, expand, or shorten sections of their work.

The Editors

REFERENCES

American Psychiatric Association. (1980). *Diagnostic and statistical manual of mental disorders* (3rd ed.). Washington, DC: Author.

World Health Organization. (1978). *International classification of diseases* (9th ed.). Geneva: Author.

CONTENTS

III. PROBLEMS OF SYNDROME DEFINITION AND VALIDATION

ASSESSMENT AND DIAGNOSIS IN CHILD PSYCHOPATHOLOGY

I

EVALUATION OF DSM-III AND ICD-9

1

DSM-III STUDIES

DENNIS P. CANTWELL

INTRODUCTION

This chapter reviews studies of the classification of the psychiatric disorders of childhood according to the third edition of the *Diagnostic and Statistical Manual of Mental Disorders* (DSM-III), a publication of the American Psychiatric Association (1980). It ends with a discussion of what is needed for improved systems of classification in the future.

The topic of psychiatric diagnosis in childhood includes at least three separate but interrelated areas. The first concerns the overall system of classification, that is, the grouping and organization of diagnoses. The second concerns the diagnostic process itself, a process that involves a series of questions, only one of which relates to the particular diagnostic category used.

A third issue applies to the diagnostic instruments involved—interviews with the parent, interviews with children, rating scales, psychobiologic measures, and so forth. In addition, some consideration must be given to the process by which a clinician assimilates the information collected by these instruments to make a specific diagnosis.

THE DIAGNOSTIC PROCESS AND DIAGNOSTIC CLASSIFICATION IN CHILD PSYCHIATRY

The diagnostic process has been conceptualized as answering a number of important questions:

1. Does the child have any type of psychiatric disorder? That is, does he or she have a problem in behavior, emotions, relationships, or cognition that is of sufficient severity and duration to cause distress, disability, or disadvantage? ·

2. If there is a disorder, does the clinical picture fit that of a recognized

Dennis P. Cantwell. Department of Child Psychiatry, University of California, Neuropsychiatric Institute, Center for the Health Sciences, Los Angeles, California.

clinical syndrome? In DSM-III terms that means: does he or she have a condition that meets the criteria for one or more of the DSM-III diagnoses?

3. What are the various roots of that disorder in terms of intrapsychic, family, social–cultural and biological factors; and what are the relative strengths of each of these root causes in this particular patient?

4. What forces are maintaining the problem?

5. What forces are facilitating the child's normal development?

6. What are the strengths and competencies of the child and of the family?

7. Untreated, what is the likely outcome of the child's disorder(s)? Obviously, this depends heavily on the syndrome that is present. If the syndrome is well recognized and well studied (say, infantile autism or attention deficit disorder), there is likely a body of knowledge on the untreated natural history. On the other hand, if there is an unrecognized mixture of symptoms, little may be known on prognosis. Moreover, diagnosis is not the sole determining factor of outcome. Some children with attention deficit disorder with hyperactivity do well; others do very poorly. There is a complex interaction of individual, social, environmental, and family factors that partially determine the untreated natural history.

Questions number 8 and 9 involve intervention.

8. Is intervention necessary in this case?

9. What types of intervention are most likely to be effective?

The answers to these questions depend heavily on syndrome diagnosis. If the child has a disorder, such as an anxiety disorder, that tends to pass with time and leaves little or no residual effect, then intervention is much less likely to be urgently needed than in the case of a disorder such as infantile autism, which is usually disabling. The literature on effectiveness of different forms of intervention is organized around diagnostic problems. A solid scientific base for selecting therapeutic intervention is most likely to be available for well-established syndromes. Only one of these nine questions involves making a specific categorical diagnosis. In the cases described in DSM-III it should be added that some disorders (such as avoidant disorder) lack a literature on natural history or therapeutic interventions, so diagnosis does not aid greatly in treatment planning. Much more is involved in the diagnostic formulation than simply selecting a classificatory diagnostic coding.

Diagnostic Assessment Tools

Six major types of instruments are generally available in the diagnostic process: an interview with the parents about the child (this may include family interviews and may include interviews with significant others who are in a position to observe the child's behavior on a daily basis); interviews with the child himself or herself; behavior rating scales completed by parents, teacher, and significant others in the child's life; physical examination, neurological examination; and laboratory studies. Laboratory studies include not only the traditionally medical (e.g., X rays and blood tests) but also reliable and valid psychological tests. Only in rare cases will a physical or neurological examination and laboratory studies, including psychological testing, contribute to the making of a specific diagnosis. Nevertheless, cognitive testing is necessary for the diagnosis of mental retardation and of specific developmental disorders (e.g., of language). Projective tests have not been shown to contribute significantly to diagnosis (Gittelman, 1980). Of course, projective testing and neurological examinations may be important in answering other questions in the diagnostic process. The making of a specific diagnosis will usually be done on the basis of interviews with parents and children, possibly associated with behavior rating scales.

In general, the diagnostic process in child psychiatry involves collecting information from multiple sources, weighing their significance, and making a diagnostic formulation. There are very few studies of the differential value of these sources of information for diagnosis. In the classic Isle of Wight study (Rutter, Tizard, & Whitmore, 1970) this was undertaken for parent and child interviews and for parent and teacher questionnaires with respect to a crude distinction between psychiatrically ill or not ill. When the individual instruments were examined, it was found that the parental interview was distinctly the best instrument when used alone (as validated against overall psychiatric judgment). It was also found that the child interview by itself was probably the least useful in terms of detecting a disorder that had been missed on the other measures. On the other hand, the child interview did tend to pick up certain types of disorders (such as minor depressive episodes) that the other instruments did not and also helped to make a distinction between *types* of disorders.

The data from the parent rating scale and the teacher rating scale were equally interesting. It was found that they were about equally effective in picking out children who were considered to be psychiatrically well or psychiatrically ill on the basis of all information combined. However, there was little overlap between the two. That is, the parent rating scales tended to pick up certain children, and the teacher rating scales tended to pick up others. The implication is that many children have disorders that are relatively situation-specific (i.e., largely confined to home or school).

Basic Principles of Classification in Child Psychiatry

The basic principles of classification have been outlined by Spitzer and Cantwell (1980). The first principle is that in our current state of knowledge there is no right or natural way to classify psychiatric disorders of childhood. In the past, official classification systems have been categorical systems—and DSM-III carries on that tradition. Dimensional systems offer a real alternative, but for a variety of reasons it was decided that DSM-III should be categorical.

Second, etiology is not necessarily the best basis for classification. Thus DSM-III is a phenomenologic system. Although it is often assumed that etiology offers the best basis for classification, there are many areas of medicine in which this is not true. In infectious diseases, etiology is crucial for classification because knowledge on the specific pathogenic agent provides a good guide to treatment. However, this is not so, for example, in the case of fractures. A phenomenologic–descriptive classification of simple versus compound tells us much more about what needs to be done with that fracture than whether the fracture was caused by a particular etiologic agent such as a football injury or an auto accident.

The third principle is that classification should be based on facts rather than theory. Psychoanalysts differ from learning theorists on the etiology of phobias, but they can agree on whether or not a child has a phobia. However, a classification based on either theory would fail to serve the purpose of communication between the two groups because they would not agree on the concepts essential for a theory-based diagnosis. Accordingly, the fundamental purpose of classification—namely, to provide an agreed language for communication—would be lost. It was recognized by the DSM-III committee that child psychiatry lacks adequate knowledge on many syndromes and that there is much dispute on many "facts." A successful classification must be based on the common core of facts that are accepted by people with different theoretical orientations.

Attention was given to the issue of reliability. Information, observation, interpretation and criterion variance all contribute as sources of unreliability in psychiatric diagnosis, regardless of the system of classification. However, criterion variance can be minimized by the use of specific diagnostic criteria. The Research Diagnostic Criteria (RDC) served as the starting point for adult disorders in DSM-III. However, there were no RDC for child disorders on which to build. Thus, some of the criteria in DSM-III are decidedly arbitrary and at best derive from a literature that is not as substantial as that available in adult psychiatry.

A categorical system generally begins with the description by experienced clinicians of the supposedly essential features for a particular diagnosis. When these are agreed by clinicians working in different settings, the category has *face validity*. At present, many of the categories in DSM-III have only this type of validity. Some of them, in addition, have *descriptive validity*; that is, they are characterized by symptoms not commonly seen in persons with other types of mental disorders or in individuals with no mental disorders. This justifies the assumption that this particular disorder indeed represents a distinct behavioral syndrome rather than a random collection of clinical features. For *predictive validity*, the differentiation on one basis must predict differences in other areas. Thus, a categorization based on phenomenology should be associated with differences between syndromes on features such as natural history, biological correlates, family pattern, and response to treatment. In child psychiatry such knowledge is limited, and many of the categories newly introduced nto DSM-III (such as avoidant disorder) lack predictive validity.

Another basic principle is that disorders rather than children should be classified. There is inevitable heterogeneity within any group of children with a particular psychiatric disorder. Moreover, children with one type of disorder when young may be free of disorder or show some different condition later in life.

DSM-III sought to provide adequate differentiation and adequate coverage. If the system were ideal, every child would have just one disorder included somewhere within the classification. Perhaps a quarter of psychiatrically ill adults receive a diagnosis of "undiagnosed" mental disorder if one uses strict diagnostic criteria. It is likely that very young children, who have a limited repertoire of behaviors, will include an even higher proportion with disorders that do not fulfill the specific criteria for any single syndrome.

A perfect system would also provide adequate differentiation between the syndromes. This was a major weakness of the DSM-II categories such as adjustment reaction of childhood. Some 80% of the children in child psychiatry clinics received that diagnosis. It provided tremendous coverage, but it was useless for differentiation between patients presenting with syndromes that required differential types of intervention or that would have different outcomes without treatment.

The DSM-III committee recognized that there are conditions that are normal at one time of life but may yet be pathological at other ages (e.g., bedwetting at age 2 vs. bedwetting at age 16). The same symptom may have very different implications at different age periods. School refusal in the early years of schooling generally reflects separation anxiety. School refusal presenting for the first time in high school often has very different origins—such as incipient schizophrenia or major depressive disorder. All psychiatrists must contend with the question of distinguishing normality from abnormality. However, child psychiatrists have the added problem of defining normality for different ages at different developmental levels. Thus, child psychiatric classification systems must attempt to have a developmental framework. This lack may be one of the major weaknesses of the DSM-III.

Finally, DSM-III had to meet multiple uses. Most important, it had to be practically and clinically useful in everyday practice.

Elements of the DSM-III System

Because many child psychiatric disorders lack predictive validity and because it would not be acceptable to have a general system that failed to classify many disorders, it was decided that DSM-III should include conditions for which there was only face validity. At the same time, it was clear that it was essential to conduct further research to establish descriptive and predictive validity. As we move toward DSM-IV it will be necessary to demand high levels of validity if conditions are to retain their places in the classification. For example, in DSM-III there is a breakdown between attention deficit disorder with hyperactivity and attention deficit disorder without hyperactivity. This was done strictly on clinical grounds because it was felt that there were patients who had inattentiveness and impulsivity but who were not motorically overactive. It was decided to include these as two separate disorders even though it was not known (and still is not known) whether the distinction has any clinical meaning. Indeed, we do not even know the frequency of either diagnosis. Nevertheless the inclusion in DSM-III of this differentiation will allow the collection of data to test its validity.

DSM-III is almost completely atheoretical because there are so few psychiatric disorders for which etiology or pathophysiological process has been demonstrated.

Previous official classification systems, such as DSM-I, DSM-II, and ICD-9, did not provide diagnostic criteria to specify which symptoms are required for diagnosis. There were only general descriptions of the disorders. In DSM-III specific diagnostic criteria are outlined for each disorder in the childhood section. This is true in other sections of the manual as well, with the exception of schizo-affective disorder. Although the term "operational" is often used to describe these diagnostic criteria, it is literally an incorrect term. The criteria in DSM-III are specific in that they spell out which criteria *must* be present for the diagnosis to be made. However, they are not truly operational in that they do not spell out what operations must be made in order to make the diagnosis.

The text of DSM-III systematically describes psychiatric disorders under the following major headings: essential features, associated features, age of onset, course, impairment, complications, predisposing factors, prevalence, sex ratio, familial pattern, and differential diagnosis. For some of the disorders a substantial amount of information is listed under each heading. For other disorders, especially those that were created for the first time in DSM-III, there may be only one line or a statement that no knowledge was available on this particular issue at the time the text was drafted. With the exception of etiology and treatment, then, DSM-III systematically describes much of what one would like to know about each of the psychiatric disorders of infancy, childhood, and adolescence.

In addition to the main body of the text, DSM-III contains a number of appendices. Some of these describe the field trials and interrater reliability obtained for various diagnostic categories; and one contains decision trees for differential diagnosis. There is also a glossary, which has been updated, describing technical terms used in the text and an annotated comparative listing of DSM-II and DSM-III. The latter appendix contains explanations for the major changes made and for new categories added with references justifying the change. The decision tree approach to differential diagnosis is described in some detail with respect to many common symptoms.

Only rarely were reliability and validity studies done on the disorders described in DSM-I and DSM-II even after the classification system had been fully established and was out in use. However, during the development of DSM-III, once preliminary diagnostic criteria and preliminary systematic description of the various disorders had been drafted, a preliminary version of the manual was completed and was sent to a variety of individuals across the country. Field tests were carried out prior to the completion of the document. During these field tests the document was used repeatedly by clinicians in many different diagnostic settings. This led to revisions of diagnostic criteria. In some cases it led to the addition of diagnostic categories that had not previously been considered for the document. Also, in many cases less ambiguous wording was drafted. The formal reliability trials were also conducted at many settings, and the results of these are described in one of the appendices at the end of the DSM-III manual as described above.

One of the more innovative aspects of the DSM-III diagnostic system is its multiaxial aspect. A complete diagnosis will require codings on all five axes of DSM-III. Axis I codes all clinical psychiatric syndromes except the specific developmental disorders and the personality disorders (which are on Axis II). In general, Axis I provides the principal diagnosis, but Axis II may do so if there is no Axis I diagnosis or if some developmental or personality disorder is predominant. The reasons for separating these first two axes were entirely practical, not theoretical. Systematic studies have indicated that if acute psychiatric and personality disorders are on the same axis, the latter tend to be overlooked when coding. There is an analogous situation in childhood with developmental disorders. Thus, reading disorder that is strongly associated with a conduct disorder may be overlooked if the clinician is not forced to look at Axis II to see whether a developmental disorder is present.

Axis III allows the clinician to code all physical disorders and conditions that are current and potentially relevant to the understanding or management of a particular disorder. For example, if a child has a long-standing temporal lobe seizure disorder that is followed by a psychotic episode, it would be important to code the epilepsy because of its probable etiological role. Equally, however, if an adolescent with a conduct disorder has diabetes, it would be important to note the diabetes because it influences management even though it did not cause the conduct disturbance.

Axis IV codes severity of psychosocial stressors on a seven-point rating scale, for those considered to be significant contributors to the etiology or exacerbation of an Axis I or an Axis II condition. The manual provides anchor points for each level, with severity based on expected reaction for an average individual. Psychosocial stressors may be coded in terms of the type of stress, its severity, both type and severity, or the degree of threat or stress for this particular individual. The way chosen to code severity of psychosocial stressors in DSM-III is not necessarily consistent with what is known about the relationships between psychosocial stress and psychiatric disorder (see below).

Axis V codes the highest level of adaptive functioning that the patient has experienced in the past year for at least a few months' duration. Adaptive functioning is conceptualized as consisting of a composite of three major areas, social relationships, use of leisure time, and occupational or school functioning. As with Axis IV, there is a seven-point rating scale with anchor points.

A complete description of each of the disorders described in the DSM-III section, "Disorders Usually First Evident in Infancy, Childhood and Adolescence," is beyond the scope of this chapter. They can be read in the DSM-III manual (see also Cantwell, 1980; Spitzer & Cantwell, 1980). Many children present with symptoms for evaluation to a child psychiatrist that are not part of a diagnosable psychiatric disorder using DSM-III criteria. In these cases one can use a diagnosis of "unspecified mental disorder" and, if desired, can describe the predominant features of the disorder. It is also recognized that children may be presented for evaluation to a child psychiatrist with conditions that do not warrant the diagnosis of a mental disorder at all. There are "V" codes at the end of the diagnostic classification system (such as "parent–child problem" or "other specified family circumstance") for use in such situations.

This section of the manual includes disorders that usually are first manifest in childhood. However, these are not the only diagnoses in DSM-III that are appropriate for this age group. Simple phobic or obsessive–compulsive disorders may occur in childhood. Since these conditions often arise in adult life as well, they are not included in the childhood section of DSM-III. These general codes should be used when such disorders occur in childhood.

Arbitrary decisions had to be made about certain types of problems that regularly occur. The first of these involves the diagnosis of well-recognized syndromes that occur in adults (such as schizophrenic disorder and affective disorders) and that *may* arise for the first time in childhood, even though usually they do not. Research findings suggested that the crucial features are essentially the same in children and adults. Accordingly, there are no special categories of childhood depression, childhood mania, or childhood schizophrenia. These diagnoses should be used when the criteria are met regardless of the age of the individual. The rationale was that in medicine we do not have special categories for illness according to age of onset. Pneumonia is pneumonia regardless of the age of the individual; there is not pneumonia of childhood. However, it was recognized that in many cases, especially in the case of affective disorders, there may be age-specific *associated* features. In the text of the DSM-III these associated features have been described for infants, children, and adolescents. However, they do not affect the essential diagnostic criteria, nor do they affect where in the classification scheme these disorders are placed.

A different problem arises in cases where there is a known relationship between a particular disorder in childhood and a particular disorder in adult life—but not a one-to-one relationship between the two. An example is antisocial personality disorder of adult life and conduct disorder in childhood. There are innumerable studies to show that an antisocial personality disorder in adult life rarely develops without previous manifestations of conduct disorder in childhood and adolescence (Robins, 1966, 1978). However, only some 40% to 50% of children with a diagnosable conduct disorder will carry a diagnosis of antisocial personality disorder in adult life. Others will carry no diagnosis; some will become schizophrenic and some will show other conditions. At our current level of knowledge, there is no way of conclusively predicting which individual child with a conduct disorder will show an antisocial personality disorder in adult life. Thus, one overall category was not used for children and adults in this case. Antisocial personality disorder is coded on Axis III. Conduct disorder (with several subgroups) is included in the section on child psychiatric disorders if the individual is under the age of 18, but after that age personality disorder, antisocial type, is diagnosed arbitrarily.

Likewise, some of the anxiety disorders in childhood may have a relationship with comparable adult diagnoses. However, even more fragmentary is the evidence on which children will go on to show anxiety disorders in adult life. Thus, certain specific anxiety disorders of childhood are coded in the childhood section, whereas the adult diagnoses are elsewhere in the manual.

A different problem arises when a condition that regularly arises for the first time in childhood persists into adult life in a modified form. A clear example is provided by attention deficit disorder with hyperactivity. For cases like this, there is a "residual" category for the adult form.

CRITIQUES OF DSM-III

Many critiques were written about DSM-III prior to its being published and after its publication (see Achenbach, 1980; Cantwell, 1980; Gittelman, 1980; Rutter & Shaffer, 1980; Spitzer & Cantwell, 1980). One asked why DSM-III had to be created in the first place rather than using the ninth edition of the *International Classification of Diseases* (ICD-9) for psychiatric diagnosis in the United States as it is used elsewhere. A second related to the lack of an overall definition of mental disorder in DSM-III and to the guidelines as to what constitutes a disorder. The third area of criticism concerned the multiaxial system, with queries about the number and types of axes, the lack of mental retardation as a separate axis, and the specific types of codings on Axis IV and Axis V. The fourth criticism was on the reliability of the diagnostic categories. A fifth referred to the validity of the categories and especially to what was perceived as an excessive subdivision of the psychiatric disorders of childhood. The final criticism related to the use of specific diagnostic criteria.

Rutter and Shaffer (1980) pointed out that the ICD-9 has a solid research background behind it. They questioned why a separate diagnostic system was needed for use in the United States. The DSM-III Committee claimed that the ICD-9 did not meet their needs in many areas. Only systematic research can answer which of the systems is better. Indeed, there is a great deal of overlap between them, the major differences being in the use of diagnostic criteria, the multiaxial system, and certain changes in terminology.

ICD-9 does not contain a definition of mental disorder, nor did DSM-I or DSM-II. On theoretical grounds, this is certainly a problem. If DSM-III purports to be a classification system of mental *disorders*, then there should be an overall definition of what these are. If there is not, there is a lack of any criterion for the decision on whether or not any particular disorder should be included in the classification system. For a variety of reasons it was decided that no generally accepted satisfactory definition of mental disorder could be formulated. However, the introduction to DSM-III states that mental disorders are conceptualized first as clinically significant behavioral or psychological syndromes. These patterns must be associated with either distress (such as a painful symptom) or disability (impairment in one or more areas of functioning). Finally, there must be a behavioral, psychological, or biological dysfunction that does not reside solely in the relationship between the individual and society. This falls short of a definition of mental disorder, but it does provide guidelines.

There have been multiple critiques about the multiaxial classification scheme. Field studies conducted by the World Health Organization (WHO) and by Cantwell and colleagues (Cantwell, Mattison, Russell, & Will, 1979; Cantwell, Russell, Mattison, & Will, 1979; Mattison, Cantwell, Russell, & Will, 1979; Russell, Cantwell, Mattison, & Will, 1979) do support the idea that mental retardation is more reliably diagnosed when it is on a separate axis. Although retardation was not placed on a separate axis, I agree that it should have been. The major reason why it was not was to avoid an undue proliferation of axes. The number and type of potential axes are almost innumerable, and some practical cutoff point had to be made. The American Association on Mental Deficiency now has a rather extensive multiaxial system, with one axis for level of IQ and another for the level of adaptive behavior (Grossman *et al.*, 1983). Since the DSM-III definition of mental retardation requires concurrent impairment of both adaptive behavior *and* intellectual functioning, it seems logical that there should be codings for the severity of each of these two dimensions of retardation. Up until now all systems, including DSM-III, have a severity coding that is based only on the level of IQ. In individual cases the severity of IQ impairment and of adaptive behavior impairment are not necessarily congruent. Thus, if one argues for mental retardation on a separate axis, one should logically argue further for separate levels of impairment of adaptive behavior and intellectual function. The emphasis on impairment of adaptive behavior is not as great in the ICD-9 diagnosis of mental retardation.

More substantial criticism on the Axis IV coding is justified. This is based solely on severity as it applies to the average person; it does not consider the type of psychosocial stressor or the severity of the stressor as it applies to the particular individual. It is clear that the same stressor may have very different impacts on different individuals; the expectation of a rather uniform impact is not reasonable. The criticism that DSM-III did not take into account some important advances in methodology of stress research is certainly justified. Needless to say, a coding of type and severity of stressor as it applied to the individual would have involved more methodological problems, but probably more useful data would have been collected.

The coding on Axis III, highest level of adaptive functioning within the past year, also raises particular problems. I believe that it should have carried a dual coding—one code for impairment level produced by the current episode of illness and one for highest previous level of adaptive functioning obtained by the individual. The restriction to a period of within a year of the time that the individual is seen for an Axis I or Axis II condition necessarily means that the adaptive level coding cannot be taken as a measure of premorbid functioning. Thus the coding will have a different meaning for individuals whose disorder lasts for longer than a year than for those whose disorder is episodic and of a shorter duration. Thus, a child with a chronic attention deficit disorder may have had a significant drop in impairment in adaptive functioning in the 3 months prior to evaluation. However, it is probable that the child's functioning was always suboptimal no matter how far one goes back. On the other hand, it is likely that a child with no preexisting disorder who presents with an acute episode of depression lasting for 6 weeks will have a level of adaptive functioning 1 year ago that was higher than that for a child with a dysthymic disorder, one in which, by definition, the duration must exceed 1 year.

The DSM-III Committee did consider reliability to be of primary importance. It is unfortunate that there have not been more systematic studies of the reliability of this particular section of DSM-III. Nevertheless, some childhood disorders in DSM-III have adequate or better reliability, although others do not. The overall level of reliability of the entire system should be improved for DSM-IV.

The issues with regard to the validity and possible excessive subdivision of categories in the childhood section are much more complex. DSM-III is a categorical system. Traditionally, categorical systems have been validated by such parameters as response to treatment, natural history without treatment, biological correlates, and family pattern of illness. Since many of the categories of DSM-III were new, such data were not available. This was not the case in other areas of the manual. The Feighner criteria and RDC had some degree of established validity. Since they constituted the starting point for many of the adult categories, more data on validity were available. DSM-III took a "splitter" rather than a "lumper" approach, despite the evidence from previous studies that there tends to be better agreement on broad categories of disturbance than on the finer subdivisions of emotional disorder and conduct disorder.

The splitter approach meant in practice that conditions were included in DSM-III if clinicians agreed that they could be described, even if no validity other than face validity had been demonstrated. In their critique of the childhood section of DSM-III, Rutter and Shaffer (1980) argued that codings should have been confined to broader categories of conduct disorder, emotional disorder, and so forth unless there was empirical justification for finer subdivision. It was suggested that such justification did not exist for the finer subdivisions proposed in DSM-III.

DSM-III requires separate diagnoses to be made when a child presents with overlapping disorders. For example, a child presenting with anxiety and conduct disturbance would get both diagnoses in DSM-III. Rutter and Shaffer (1980) felt that the inclusion of mixed types, such as a mixed disturbance of conduct and emotions, would have been more practical and more fruitful than the use of separate diagnostic categories. Quay (1986) has also thoughtfully reviewed the issue of validity of the childhood section of DSM-III. He correctly pointed out that there are no infallible criteria for validity against which the DSM-III categories can be compared. He suggested, however, that one approach would be to validate the categorical DSM-III disorders against mathematically derived dimensional systems of classification. He suggested that there is such empirical validation for certain DSM-III syndromes but not others. The same point was made by Achenbach (1980). Multivariate dimensional systems are not entirely empirical, however. The results will depend upon what methods are used to collect data, whether or not certain specific symptoms are present in the parent and teacher rating scales, whether the "meaning" of these symptoms is correctly interpreted, the nature of the population studied (i.e., psychiatrically disordered vs. general population; inpatient vs. outpatient), and the various types of statistical techniques utilized (Quay, 1986). Different statistical techniques may give different results even with the same data. Generally, user judgment has constituted the final step of deciding which is the correct "solution." The effects of the data collection instruments and of the meaning of specific symptoms has often been underemphasized by proponents of the multivariate dimensional classification system.

It is clear that there are well-recognized syndromes such as infantile autism that do not turn up in dimensional studies (Quay, 1986). This is because most of the symptoms that describe the syndrome are not present on the parent and teacher rating scales used in the analyses and because a sufficient number of patients with the disorder were not included in the samples studied. However, there are other syndromes where that seems to be true. As Quay pointed out, there is little empirical evidence from the multivariate literature to suggest a separation between distinct syndromes of anxiety and depression. These tend to load on one factor. However, Puig-Antich and colleagues (Puig-Antich, 1983; Puig-Antich, Chambers, & Tabrizi, 1983) have clearly demonstrated that there is a categorical diagnosis of depressive disorder occurring in children that is a phenomenologically similar one that occurs in adults and has a similar history, a similar response to tricyclic antidepressants, and similar biological correlates (such as the dexamethasone suppression test, other measures of hypothalamic–pituitary function, and sleep parameters). Whether a categorical system can truly be validated by a dimensional system or whether these are complementary to each other remains an issue for further research.

Another criticism of DSM-III centers around the use of specific diagnostic criteria. Some critics pointed out that since there is little or no evidence for the predictive validity of finer subdivisions of the diagnostic categories in DSM-III, there is little or no evidence on which to base specific criteria to make the diagnosis. On the face of it, this is a sound argument. If there are no studies demonstrating descriptive and predictive validity, these subdivisions cannot be used to provide inclusion and exclusion criteria for diagnosis.

The counterargument is that without specific diagnostic criteria, it is valid to lump together conditions that appear similar but in reality are different. If these criteria were not spelled out in the initial system, they could not be used to assess descriptive and predictive validity. The DSM-III Committee recognized that many of the specific diagnostic criteria were taken from clinicians' descriptions. Quay did not necessarily question the use of specific criteria but he did question why they were not arrived at empirically. It was his view that some form of statistical analysis should be used to pinpoint exclusion and inclusion criteria. Since the DSM-III diagnostic criteria were not arrived at empirically, Quay believes they cannot increase validity substantially. This concept has been further discussed by Finn (1982).

STUDIES OF THE CHILDHOOD SECTION OF DSM-III

Studies of psychiatric diagnosis in childhood include investigations of diagnostic instruments, the diagnostic process, criteria for disorders, validity of disorders, reliability, and the utility of the diagnostic system. One study of diagnostic instruments was done as part of the Isle of Wight investigations by Rutter and his colleagues et al. (1970). Here a "best-estimate" diagnosis was made using information from four instruments (interview with the parents, interview with the child, parent rating scale, and teacher rating scale) and then the utility of each of the individual instruments in making a diagnosis of either psychiatrically ill or well was compared. One important finding was that diagnoses that are made without the benefit of systematic information from the school are likely to be skewed. There seem to be children whose disorder primarily manifests itself in the school and, without systematic information from the school, exclusive reliance on the child and/or the parent may produce a different set of diagnoses.

Diagnostic Process

A second type of study concerns the *diagnostic process itself*. How are the data collected and how are they synthesized to make a particular diagnosis or set of diagnoses? Costello's (1982) research was designed to tackle these questions with respect to the assumptions that underlie the DSM-III classification system. The children were referred to Western Psychiatric Institute and Clinic in Pittsburgh, Pennsylvania, and were given a 1-day assessment in which they and their family were seen by many clinicians: one interviewed the child, one interviewed the family members, an educational assessment was conducted by a psychologist, and a physical examination was completed by a pediatric nurse practitioner or a pediatrician. The clinicians briefed the psychiatrist, who then spent 30 minutes with the child. Following this, a diagnostic conference took place, which was attended by everyone who had taken part in the diagnostic process. The clinicians shared information and the decisions taken by the team. On the basis of these decisions, one or more DSM-III diagnoses on Axis I were made. Where relevant, diagnoses were made on other axes. The Costello study focused only on the Axis I diagnoses.

The data base for her study were the tape recordings of these diagnostic conferences; in addition, brief assessments of the accuracy of the diagnosis were made by the clinicians in the form of a confidence judgment. The clinicians reduced the great amount of information collected by each to a mean of 171 items communicated to one another during the conference. The median number of Axis I diagnosis made per child was 2, with a range from 0 to 3 emerging from 0 to 12 hypotheses about diagnoses being discussed.

The first question Costello asked was: "Do clinicians first assemble information and then generate and test hypotheses about the diagnoses?" The information generated in the conference was divided into quartiles, and Costello's data made it clear that hypotheses actually began to appear very early in the process of collecting information—within the first quartile in two-thirds of the cases. In only 5% of the cases was the hypothesis generation delayed until the last quartile. However, in no case was the diagnosis suggested in the first quartile adopted as a final diagnosis.

Hypotheses that led to final diagnoses typically appeared in the third and fourth quartile. Costello concluded that clinicians did not wait until all of the data were available to them to generate diagnostic hypotheses.

However, early ideas on diagnosis were heavily influenced by later data presented.

The next question Costello asked was: "Once hypotheses are generated about diagnoses, how are they tested?" Somewhat to the investigators' surprise, the number of cues used was very much lower than had been predicted—an average of 20 per case or about 3.8 per hypothesis. Of these, only 10% were disconfirmatory. Cues were thus used to confirm an adopted hypothesis, not to disconfirm those rejected. Those cues initially suggesting a diagnostic hypothesis were mainly just dropped when something more promising came along as more data were presented.

A third issue investigated was the extent to which actual DSM-III criteria were used in making DSM-III diagnoses. Costello found three strategies. One was the orthodox strategy, in which there was an explicit checking of patient symptoms against DSM-III criteria. A second strategy was an implicit one. Clinicians agreed that certain items of information indicated that the child met criteria even though no specific evidence was presented. The implicit strategy was used for 28% of diagnoses, the orthodox strategy for 16%.

A third strategy Costello called impression matching. The patient was not compared with DSM-III criteria but rather with a more global clinical impression of what a child with attention deficit disorder, conduct disorder, depression, or some other disorder would look like, even though the child may not have a clinical picture that met strict DSM-III criteria. This approach was used in about 50% of Axis I diagnoses.

Finally, Costello looked at the extent to which the clinicians followed the DSM-III flowchart example, proceeding logically through a hierarchy of possibilities of children presenting with a certain set of clinical symptoms. It was clear that they did not. Several differentials of a particular problem were eliminated entirely by default. For example, organic conditions, mental retardation, psychosis, and intermittent explosive disorder were not discussed in any of the cases of overt behavioral problems as possible differential diagnoses. Moreover, Costello found that the reasons for selecting one diagnosis over another in the differential were rarely consistent with the flowchart of the DSM-III type at the end of the DSM-III manual.

In summing up, this sample of highly trained clinicians acted strictly in conformity with DSM-III assumptions with regard to differential diagnosis in only about 50% of the cases. This study has major implications for the analysis of any reliability study of the DSM-III or any other system. The clinical process of information collection is not likely to produce interrater reliabilities higher than those described in the later sections of this report. Thus, in the study of any diagnostic system, what may be revealed is not anything about the system itself but rather the differences that are inherent in the way different clinicians go about synthesizing certain sets of data.

Diagnostic Validity

Studies of the diagnostic system might more properly be considered in terms of the validity of the disorders within the system, a major concern of the DSM-III Committee. The validation of diagnostic categories in psychiatry has proved to be a difficult task.

The approach taken in DSM-III relied heavily on the papers of Robins and Guze (1970), who put forward the basic principle that acceptance of any disorder requires demonstrated reliability and validity (including internal validation or consistency as well as external validation). They proposed a five-stage model for creating valid diagnostic categories for certain psychiatric disorders of adulthood.

The first step is a careful description of the clinical picture in terms of symptoms and demographic data. This step establishes (usually only with correlational statistics) symptoms that comprise the essential diagnostic criteria.

The second step involves validation by external criteria such as laboratory data, follow-up findings, or family features (Robins & Guze, 1970). This approach led to the development of a set of research criteria (the Feighner criteria) for a limited number of psychiatric disorders of adults, later expanded by Spitzer, Endicott, and Robins (1978) into the Research Diagnostic Criteria (RDC).

This particular model was expanded and modified somewhat by Cantwell (1975) into a six-stage model for validation of psychiatric disorders of childhood, comprising (1) description of the clinical picture, (2) physical and neurologic factors, (3) laboratory studies, (4) family studies, (5) natural history studies, and (6) treatment studies. Only a few child psychiatric disorders have been studied in this way; probably the most extensive data are available for the attention deficit disorder with hyperactivity. Nevertheless, even here we lack adequate data to establish diagnostic validity (Cantwell, 1983).

Kovacs and her colleagues (Kovacs, Feinberg, Crouse-Novak, Paulauskas, & Finkelstein, 1984; Kovacs, Feinberg, Crouse-Novak, Paulauskas, Pollack, & Finkelstein, 1984) have conducted a seminal study of the validity of the DSM-III affective disorders as they apply to children. In the context of a longitudinal prospective study, they examined the characteristics and diagnostic validity of three conditions: major depressive disorder, dysthymic disorder, and adjustment disorder with depressed mood. They were able to show that the three conditions diagnosed by specific diagnostic criteria, as specified in the DSM-III manual, were also distinguishable in other areas. These areas include age of onset and the longitudinal course of recovery. The adjustment disorder group had the most favorable recovery pattern; that is, 90% of them remitted during 9 months. On the other hand, the dysthymic disorder group has a remission rate of 89% over a 6-year period. The major depressive group was somewhat in between.

Major depressive disorder and dysthymic disorder both had high rates of concurrent nonaffective disorders associated with them, whereas adjustment disorder with depressed mood did not. For both major depressive disorder and dysthymic disorder an early age of onset was predictive of a longer period of illness. In addition, both major depressive disorder and dysthymic disorder were associated with a high risk of a new bout of depressive disorder. For the 40% of children who recovered from their first episode of major depressive disorder and then had a second episode, the "well" period did not exceed 2 years.

Children with major depressive disorder who also had an underlying dysthymic disorder were more likely than those with major depressive disorder without an underlying dysthymic disorder to have a second episode. Adjustment disorder with depressed mood differed from both major depressive disorder and dysthymic disorder in terms of a minimal risk for a subsequent episode of major depressive disorder. Thus, the DSM-III criteria identified three separate subgroups (major depressive disorder, dysthymic disorder, and adjustment disorder with depressed mood) for which there was some external validation.

Several studies have looked at attention deficit disorder without hyperactivity, a new disorder in DSM-III. In a child psychiatry clinic Maurer and Stewart (1980) examined 297 patients with an IQ over 55 and without psychosis or a definite history of brain damage or convulsive disorder. Of these, 17% had attention deficits in the absence of hyperactivity—on parental history of short attention span and difficulty finishing school work or projects, but without the DSM-III requirement of impulsivity. Children who also met criteria for undersocialized conduct disorder, aggressive subtype were eliminated; this excluded 31 out of 52 children. Eleven of the remaining 22 children had specific psychiatric diagnoses, including depression, socialized conduct disorder, adjustment reaction, probable autism, probable schizophrenia, and anxiety secondary to hyperactivity. Five of these had definite delays in development. Some had specific reading retardation. The remaining four had neither a DSM-III diagnosable psychiatric disorder nor any evidence of developmental delay. Impulsivity was present in only one of these nine children.

The authors felt that impulsivity was a common symptom in their clinic population and that it was a mistake to make impulsivity a criterion for attention deficit disorder without hyperactivity. They concluded that their data do not support the idea of attention deficit disorder without hyperactivity as an independent syndrome. However, it should be noted that they did not use DSM-III criteria to make the diagnosis, and hence the data do not test the diagnostic validity of the DSM-III category.

Lahey, Schaughency, Strauss, and Frame (1984) also compared attention deficit disorder with and without hyperactivity and concluded that probably these were different disorders. However, this diagnosis was based on a dimensional cutoff score rather than DSM-III criteria for a categorical diagnosis. Thus, only the Kovacs study could be considered a definitive study of certain aspects of diagnostic validity of disorders *as diagnosed by DSM-III criteria.* If one is to come to any conclusions about the validity of DSM-III syndromes, it seems axiomatic that DSM-III criteria must be used to form the original group.

It may be that for some disorder there is agreement about its existence and probable validity but yet disagreement about the specific diagnostic criteria in DSM-III. The depressive disorders seen in childhood should be the same as in adult life.

In contrast, Weinberg, Rutman, Sullivan, Penick, and Dietz (1973) proposed specific criteria for childhood that were modified from the Feighner adult criteria and differed from those in DSM-III. As part of a study of 102 randomly selected children presenting for evaluation to the UCLA Neuropsychiatric Institute, Carlson and Cantwell (1982) compared the Weinberg and DSM-III criteria. Using both sets of criteria applied to data obtained from systematic interviews with parents and children and from parent and teacher rating scales, five groups of children could be obtained: (1) those who met DSM-III criteria for one of the affective disorders; (2) those who met the Weinberg criteria for depression on the basis of parental data (the original Weinberg criteria include "a change from previous function"; thus these children met the criteria for acute symptomatology and were called the "acute parent Weinberg group"); (3) those who met the Weinberg criteria on the basis of child data (the "child Weinberg group"); (4) those who met the Weinberg criteria on both parent and child data (this group was called "both Weinberg"); (5) those for whom parent data met the Weinberg criteria except that there was no discrete onset or that the duration exceeded 3 years (the "chronic parent Weinberg group").

Out of 102 children, 28 met DSM-III criteria for some affective disorder; 14 had a primary depression—that is, a depression in the absence of any preexisting psychiatric disorder—and 14 had a secondary depression, with some preexisting psychiatric disorder. All but 5 of these 28 children also fell into one of the above Weinberg groups. Thus, 17.8% of the 28 children meeting DSM-III criteria did not meet any of the Weinberg criteria. Nine (or 32%) were in both the acute parent and the child Weinberg group. Five (or 17.8%) were in the child Weinberg group criteria. Four (or 14.2%) were in the acute parent Weinberg group alone. Three (or 10.7%) were in the chronic parent Weinberg group alone. Two (or 7.1%) were in the chronic parent group and not the acute child Weinberg group criteria. Of the five children who did not meet any of the Weinberg criteria, two had reoccurring depression, and three denied feeling depressed but admitted to a loss of pleasure in usual activity.

In contrast, a total of 34 of the 102 children met Weinberg criteria as described by Weinberg himself—including the criteria that the symptoms had to involve a change from usual functioning. However, there were an additional 28 patients whose parents described chronic depressive symptomatology in their children. Only 3 of these 28 children met simultaneous DSM-III criteria for affective disorder compared with 20 of the 34 children of the acute parent Weinberg group. However, it is significant that of the latter group, only 20 out of 34 met DSM-III criteria, leaving 14 (or 41%) who did not do so. In these 14 children there was a mixture of behavior disorders, anxiety disorders, undiagnosed mental disorders, and 1 case of childhood pervasive developmental disorder. Thus, it seems clear that the Weinberg criteria and the DSM-III criteria identify largely different groups of children with only some overlap. The great majority of children who meet DSM-III criteria will also meet Weinberg criteria. However, there is a substantially large number of children who meet Weinberg criteria but not DSM-III criteria. Thus, if one were to use the two sets of criteria to identify depressed patients in a study of biological correlates or family history, one would likely obtain different results. Kovacs (1983) also looked at DSM-III criteria and found that the sensitivity and specificity of cardinal depressive symptoms different between major depression, dysthymia, and adjustment disorder. For example, depressed mood was a highly sensitive indicator of the diagnosis of major depressive disorder, but it was not specific to that condition.

If dysthymic disorder and adjustment disorder with depressed mood are used as the comparison groups, the symptom of depressed mood has a true negative rate of only 20% in the diagnosis of major depressive disorder. On the other hand, both anhedonia (which is included as a core feature of the DSM-III criteria of major depressive disorder) and social withdrawal (which DSM-III does not consider a pathognomonic sign of major depression) have considerable sensitivity and specificity for major depressive disorder in the Kovacs group.

A positive symptom of anhedonia correctly identified 86% of the children with major depressive disorder, and its absence correctly identified 9% of the cases with the other two depressive conditions as not having a major depressive disorder. Using major depressive disorder as the index disorder and the other two conditions (dysthymic disorder and adjustment disorder with depressed mood) as the comparison group revealed that the symptom of social withdrawal had a 73% true positive rate and a true negative rate of 93%. Kovacs concluded that social withdrawal should be one of the essential criteria for the diagnosis of major depressive disorder in children.

Irwin (1981) examined DSM-III criteria for anorexia nervosa in children with 13 female patients under the age of 13 who were hospitalized between 1960 and 1980 with a diagnosis of anorexia nervosa. He made a presumptive diagnosis of anorexia based on the patient having the following symptoms and history: (1) excessive fear of becoming obese; (2) distorted body image; (3) weight loss of 15% or more of initial body weight; (4) voluntary restriction of food intake with refusal to maintain body weight and hydration of minimal levels; (5) no known medical illness that would account for the weight loss; and (6) no evidence of schizophrenia or primary affective disorder.

Seven of these did not meet DSM-III criteria for anorexia nervosa. Four of them did not meet the criteria because they had not lost 25% or more of their body weight (which is criterion 3 for anorexia nervosa in DSM-III). Three of the children generalized their restriction of food intake to refusing fluid. Irwin suggests that the 25% total weight loss required by DSM-III may be unrealistic and that the pediatric adjustment allowed by DSM-III is negligible.

Cantor and her colleagues (Cantor, Evans, Pearce, & Pezzot-Pearce, 1981) in a similar vein have looked at the issue of "childhood schizophrenia" and suggested that the pervasive developmental disorder and the schizophrenia criteria, as outlined in DSM-III, leave a group of patients unaccounted for anywhere.

It is clear that the DSM-III criteria, if strictly applied, will leave out some children who probably have the disorder in question even though they do not meet the specific criteria. This will always occur when diagnostic criteria are specified. Future studies should help identify which criteria are appropriate for which age group, and it may be that for certain disorders different criteria will have to be specified for preschool, grade school, and the adolescent age range population.

Diagnostic Reliability

Several different types of studies, mainly focusing on reliability and practical utility, have been done on "real-world" populations of children using various drafts of DSM-III. The first to be considered are the *DSM-III field trials* that were conducted as part of the construction of DSM-III. The results are described in several publications by Spitzer and his colleagues (1979) and also appear as Appendix F in the DSM-III manual. It should be noted that the draft of DSM-III, dated *January 15, 1978*, was used for phase one of these NIMH-sponsored field trials, and for phase two this draft was supplemented by a set of revised criteria. Clinicians were invited to participate in the field trials through notices appearing in several publications. Each clinician was asked to participate in four reliability evaluations, and these were to be done after each clinician had already had experience using DSM-III to evaluate at least 15 patients. Each patient was evaluated on each of the five axes of DSM-III.

Spitzer, Forman, and Nee (1979) stated that they gave detailed instructions to the clinicians on how to avoid possible biases. In addition, the two clinicians evaluating the same individual were to have access to the same material whether in the form of interviews, case records, outside information, information from the family, or whatever. Both clinicians could be present at the same evaluation interview, or they could arrange to do separate evaluations as close together as possible. In phase one, approximately 60% of child and adolescent diagnostic assessments were done separately, and in phase two approximately two-thirds were done separately. Eighty-four clinicians evaluated a total of 126 child and adolescent patients, half of whom were below the age of 11.

Several tables in Appendix F of the DSM-III manual present the interrater reliability for diagnostic classes and subclasses using the kappa statistic. It is noteworthy that the overall reliability of the diagnostic classes for children and adolescents in phase one was the same as that for adults. However, the reliabilities in phase two were lower, which is the opposite of what happened with adults. The same pattern occurred for intraclass reliability coefficients for Axis IV and Axis V for children and adolescents. That is, these coefficients were higher with adults in phase two than in phase one but were lower with children.

Table 2 in Appendix F of the DSM-III manual presents the kappa coefficients of agreement for Axis I and Axis II diagnostic classes for children and adolescents. The overall kappa for all of the Axis I disorders in the child section was .69, with mental retardation and stereotyped movement disorders achieving a kappa of 1.0, pervasive developmental disorders a kappa of .85, other disorders .79, eating disorders .66, and conduct disorder .61. Somewhat surprisingly the kappa for attention deficit disorder was only .58. The anxiety disorders received a kappa of .25. These did not change substantially in phase two, with the exception of pervasive developmental disorders, which went down considerably. Adjustment disorder had a kappa of .66, but affective disorders as a group had a kappa of only .53, with the specific types of affective disorders being considerably lower. Overall kappa for the specific developmental disorders on Axes II was .77. All of these were phase one kappas. As described above, the kappas went down in phase two. The intraclass reliability coefficients for Axes IV and V are presented in Table 3 of Appendix F, that for Axis IV being .75 and Axis V being .77 in phase one, dropping to .59 and .52, respectively, in phase two.

As Rutter and Shaffer (1980) have pointed out, however, there are many problems with the interpretation of these data. The reliability concerned agreement between clinicians who were close colleagues, and these clinicians had an unknown data base that, though the same for each pair, differed from pair to pair. Moreover, there were no controls over the "detailed instructions" that were provided to the clinician participants by the authors of the field trial.

In the study by Strober, Green, and Carlson (1981) conducted at UCLA, the patient population was composed of adolescents referred by inpatient care at the UCLA Neuropsychiatric Institute. Ninety-five consecutive first admissions took part in the study of interrater agreement. The only exclusion criteria were: no evidence of organic brain disease, inadequate cooperation, and lack of consent to be interviewed and be accompanied by parent who could provide relevant background information. Within the week following admission, the patient and relative were interviewed jointly by two raters using an interviewer–observer paradigm, the role of the primary interviewer rotating on a case-by-case basis. Structured interviews were conducted using the Schedule for Affective Disorders and Schizophrenia, which was supplemented by questions that probed physical health, school adjustment, social and interpersonal relationships, early developmental functioning, maladaptive personality and behavior traits, and precipitating circumstances related to the present admission.

Prior to the interview, the two raters independently reviewed all available information. This could include school records, case reports, referral notes, and detailed observations from the nurses during the initial days of UCLA hospitalization. After completion of the interview and reviewing all of the accumulated data, each rater independently assigned a DSM-III diagnosis taken from the April 15, 1977, draft of DSM-III.

Certain conventions were followed in the study. The primary diagnosis was the one felt to be most descriptive of the current episode. Since the statistical analyses were confined to this primary diagnosis, the reliability of multiple diagnoses in one patient could not be tested. When there was a close overlap between several diagnoses, precedence was given to the disorder having the earliest age of onset.

Personality disorder was diagnosed only when there was an absence of a corresponding category in the childhood section of the manual, and when disorder had to be present for at least 1 year. Whenever there was vague, ill-defined, or paradoxical symptomatology, the category of undiagnosed illness was used. Three statistically different measures on interrater reliability were used: (1) overall agreement, which is the percentage of agreement on diagnosis present and absent; (2) specific agreement, which is the proportion of positively concordant cases among all cases in which a particular diagnosis was given by at least one rater; and (3) kappa, which corrected for chance agreement.

The results indicated that the percentage of the overall agreement statistic yielded a consistently high level of agreement for each category. The kappa coefficient of reliability was very satisfactory for most of the 14 categories used. Complete diagnostic agreement was reached in 73 of 95 patients, an overall kappa of .74. Three coefficients fell below .6. Eight had values of .7 or better. Three categories (undiagnosed illness, dissociative disorder, and anxiety disorders of childhood and adolescence) had kappas of less than .5. The reliability for the anxiety disorders of childhood and adolescence seem to involve a lack of consensus on whether primary consideration should be given to anxiety symptoms as opposed to depressive symptoms, which intermingled in these cases. This would suggest that the subtypes of the anxiety disorders of childhood need refinement. Subtypes of schizophrenic disorders, personality disorders, and conduct disorders had kappas that ranged from adequate to very good, with the exception of socialized conduct disorder. Kappa for socialized conduct disorder was .46; for undersocialized–unaggressive it was .59; for unsocialized–aggressive it was .85. The overall kappa for conduct disorder was .75.

The authors suggested that in the explicit symptomatic criteria and rules of diagnostic assessment in DSM-III, were one of the major reasons for high diagnostic agreement as well as the use of structured interviews and uniformity of data base used by each of the raters. In addition, the range of degree of psychiatric abnormality in the patients that were evaluated and the uniform training and clinical experience of the raters in the study probably played a role as well.

A similar study was conducted by Werry and his colleagues in New Zealand (Werry, Methven, Fitzpatrick, & Dixon, 1983). A case history and case presentation were given to a series of clinicians over a 2-year period of successive admissions to an inpatient unit; diagnoses were assigned by one or more of five clinicians who varied in background and seniority. There were two senior child psychiatrists, one fellow in child psychiatry, one fellow in behavioral pediatrics, and one clinical psychologist. The diagnosis was made on the basis of the presentation of the case at the ward rounds in the week of each patient's admission to the unit. Thus the same data base was used by each of the raters. There were 168 cases in which two or more diagnostic raters made a particular diagnosis. The median age of the sample was 10.5 years; two-thirds were male.

The kappa coefficient for unequal numbers of raters per subject requires independence of judgments from subject to subject. However, it has been pointed out that the error created is minimal if the total number of different judges is at least twice the mean number of judges per subject. Thus, Werry was able to use the kappa statistic.

The overall DSM-III system proved to be of satisfactory reliability, with a kappa value of .71. For different major categories, reliabilities varied greatly. Seven categories were quite reliable: substance use, eating, adult anxiety, other physical disorders, organic disorders, attention deficit disorders, and schizophrenic disorders. The child anxiety disorder and mental retardation had kappas between .60 and .69. The conduct disorder, the psychotic disorder, and somatoform disorders had kappas between .45 and .60, which were moderately unreliable. All the others proved highly unreliable.

Subcategories were looked at in several different ways. Attention deficit disorder with hyperactivity, separation anxiety, anorexia nervosa, enuresis, encopresis, obsessive–compulsive disorder, and delirium were subcategories with good reliability. Overanxious disorder, adjustment disorder with depressed mood, substance use, and mixed or unspecified borderline had kappas between .49 and .70. However, all of the other categories had kappas below .5 and were considered to be unreliable. These were found within all major categories except the category of "other physical."

Werry et al. (1983) also looked at the extent to which subcategorization either improved the reliability of a major category or impaired it. The schizophrenic, psychotic, and substance use categories as major categories had their reliabilities lowered by subcategorization. No subcategory of any of these major categories had a reliability even close to that of the major category. In one instance, adjustment disorder with depressed mood (an individual subcategory) had a higher reliability than the major category of adjustment disorder per se. In the categories of other physical and childhood anxiety disorders, reliabilities of the subcategories were all nearly similar to that of the parent category. However, the majority of categories in Werry's study revealed only one subcategory that had a reliability similar to the major category, whereas all other subcategories had reliabilities far less than those of the major categories.

The sources of disagreement when there was a majority diagnosis were also included. The reliability of schizophrenia, for example, was diminished by a disagreement on the duration of the illness. If it was 6 months or greater, the diagnosis is supposed to be schizophrenia, according to DSM-III; if 6 months or less, the diagnosis is schizophreniform disorder even though the clinical picture is the same. Oppositional disorder constituted a source of disagreement in a number of different diagnostic categories. When oppositional and conduct disorders were combined, there was a marked improvement in signal-to-noise ratio for this combined category. Since oppositional disorder appeared in DSM-III from an attempt to describe severity criteria for conduct disorder (i.e., a mild conduct disorder), the result is not surprising.

One interesting aspect of the Werry study is the reliability of the subcategories of the anxiety disorders and conduct disorders. Separation anxiety and overanxious disorder maintained high degrees of reliability even though neither was as good as the overall category of anxiety disorder. Obsessive–compulsive disorder was one of the most robust. However, the subtypes of conduct disorder presented a different picture. The reliability of conduct disorder as a whole was much greater than that of any of the subcategories.

Inasmuch as both the Strober and the Werry study involved inpatients only, the generalizability of these findings to a broader patient population of outpatients is not justified. Child psychiatry remains primarily an outpatient specialty. As in the Strober study, an early draft of DSM-III was used in the Werry study.

Two other investigators have looked at the utility of the DSM-III system. Earls (1982) reported on the use of DSM-III criteria with 3-year-old children. There were 100 children who were diagnosed by parent interviews and a 1-hour play developmental session. Teacher reports were obtained for less than half the sample and were not used systematically in making diagnostic decisions. Fourteen percent of the 100 children were found by two independent judges to have a behavior problem serious enough to warrant a full diagnostic evaluation. Earls used DSM-III criteria to make diagnoses of the 14 children. He found that 20 categories were acceptable for use with 3-year-old children. Of the 14 children, all could be assigned DSM-III diagnoses. Thirteen children had at least one Axis I diagnosis. One child had only an Axis II diagnosis, and two children had both Axis I and Axis II diagnoses.

He also found that each of the remaining three DSM-III axes were useful in further categorizing the diagnostic picture.

The diagnostic judgments made in the Earls study were made on the basis of written, edited, data protocols. Nevertheless, DSM-III was found to be a useful system with this preschool age group. It is likely that a fuller diagnostic evaluation including reports from the school, a more extensive evaluation of the child, and more extensive interview of the parent might produce even better results.

Russell, Mattison, and Cantwell (1983) examined the clinical utility of DSM-III by examining its inclusiveness, its correspondence to DSM-II diagnoses, and difficulties in its use in evaluation of 108 children referred to the UCLA Neuropsychiatric Institute. First- and second-year child fellows were given an overview of the project and were provided with an April 1977 draft of DSM-III along with a brief orientation to its use. There was no extensive training, however, and the child fellows had to learn it through becoming acquainted with it. They were asked to fill out a questionnaire on each new patient evaluated during the subsequent 6 months. The questionnaire asked the raters to code a DSM-II diagnosis, the DSM-III diagnoses on Axes I to V and the types of difficulties they encountered in using DSM-III. They were also asked to indicate which of the two diagnostic systems they preferred.

Most major categories and a wide variety of individual subcategories were used with both DSM-II and DSM-III. There was no large accumulation of DSM-III diagnoses in any major specific category. Thus, apparently there was no overall wastebasket category used by raters. Comparison of DSM-II and DSM-III correspondence indicated that DSM-III did lead to greater specificity. This was particularly evident when looking at the use of the DSM-II categories of childhood schizophrenia, withdrawing reaction and special symptoms. In approximately half of the children with DSM-III diagnosis of specific developmental disorder, the diagnosis was not coded when the raters used the DSM-II diagnostic system.

When the raters were asked to specify difficulties encountered on using each axis, the most common difficulty reported was "no suitable DSM-III diagnosis" noted in 14% of cases on Axis I and 10% on Axis II. Unclear, too restrictive, and too inclusive criteria, as well as insufficient information, were each reported in 4% of the cases. Problems with differential diagnosis was reported in 8% of the cases. A mean difficulty rating of 1.95 on a scale of 1 (no difficulty) to 5 (extreme difficulty) was obtained. Thus, the great majority of cases were found to be of only mild difficulty. DSM-III was preferred as the diagnostic system in 51% of the cases, and the two systems (DSM-II and DSM-III) were equally useful in 31% of the cases.

Mezzich and Mezzich (1985) examined the suitability and utility of DSM-III compared to DSM-II by asking a randomly selected group of clinical psychologists and child psychiatrists to rate 27 case histories. They were then asked to fill out a questionnaire comparing various aspects of the suitability and utility of DSM-II and DSM-III based on their experience in using both systems.

DSM-III was rated higher than DSM-II by both psychiatrists and psychologists in its conceptual value and its definitional clarity of psychiatric syndromes. DSM-III was thought to have greater utility of certain DSM-III categories, especially because of the enhanced descriptive differentiation that was available by the greater numbers of disorders in childhood and adolescence described in DSM-III compared to DSM-II and also the inclusion of the separate Axis II for coding specific developmental disorder and personality disorder. However, DSM-II was rated higher on its manageability and efficiency. It should be pointed out that the raters were more familiar with DSM-II than with DSM-III. This may have played a role, along with the greater complexity of the DSM-III manual. Somewhat surprisingly, the DSM-III decision trees were not rated very useful as aids in the diagnostic process.

Axis V was rated the highest in both its conceptual appropriateness and clarity even though there might be stronger alternative formats for this axis. Axis IV was rated relatively low, particularly in conceptual appropriateness. Specific concerns about Axis IV included definition of stressors at different developmental levels, acute versus chronic stressors, and the demand imposed by the system on the rater to consider social–cultural factors in the diagnostic formulation.

The Russell study thus rated the utility of DSM-III compared to DSM-II in real-life clinical work, whereas the Mezzich study rated its utility in the diagnosis of prepared case histories. The results of both studies suggest that DSM-III is rated as the more useful system in most regards and was well accepted in both studies.

A different type of reliability study was done by Cantwell and his colleagues (Cantwell, Mattison, et al., 1979; Cantwell, Russell, et al., 1979; Mattison et al., 1979; Russell et al., 1979). The investigators selected 24 case histories to provide a broad range of diagnostic possibilities using a preliminary draft of DSM-III (current as of December 1976). Each case history was prepared in a standard format. Each rater was given the standard DSM-III manual and a packet of DSM-III diagnostic materials, including instructions on how to make a diagnosis on each axis, an outline of numerical codings for all of the DSM-III diagnostic categories, a complete draft of the childhood and adolescent section, and drafts of several pertinent adult sections, such as schizophrenia and affective and anxiety disorders. Each rater was asked to complete a standardized questionnaire for each case. They were asked to make a diagnosis according to DSM-II and according to Axes I to V of DSM-III. Up to three diagnoses could be made on Axis I and Axis II of DSM-III. On Axis IV, up to three psychosocial stressors could be coded. Severity of the stressors were not rated. On Axis V, the raters were asked to rate the degree of impairment of adaptive functioning at the time of the illness, and finally, to address the usability of DSM-III and the difficulties that were encountered with it by the raters.

The raters were 20 volunteers for the UCLA Department of Child Psychiatry: 8 child psychiatry faculty, 2 third-year, 4 second-year, and 6 first-year fellows in child psychiatry. All were using DSM-III for the first time and without prior instructions, and each rater diagnosed each case independently.

The first issue looked at was agreement with the "expected diagnosis." The expected diagnosis was the diagnosis agreed upon is the most likely diagnosis or diagnoses according to DSM-III by the three investigators. Group A consisted of four cases in which "psychotic" disorders were the expected diagnosis. This included infantile autism, two cases of schizophrenia, and one case of pervasive developmental disorder and mental retardation. Agreement with the expected diagnosis was perfect in three out of four cases; that is, the most common diagnosis of the raters was the same as the expected diagnosis in three out of four cases. One case of a child with clear-cut schizophrenia was diagnosed as pervasive developmental disorder. However, the interrater agreement ranged from 45% to 100% with the number of diagnoses in each case ranging from 1 (the infantile autism case) to 10.

In Group B, the expected diagnosis were various types of affective disorder. Again in three cases out of four, the most common diagnosis was the correct diagnosis. The one case of depressive disorder, single episode, was diagnosed most commonly as adjustment disorder with depressed mood. The interrater agreement in this group ranged from 35% to 50%, with the number of different diagnoses ranging from 7 to 15.

Group C comprised three anxiety disorders (obsessive–compulsive, separation anxiety, and conversion disorder). In two cases, the most common diagnosis was the expected one. For the separation anxiety disorder case, the most common diagnosis was depressive disorder, single episode, with only 15% of the raters agreeing with the expected diagnosis compared to 39% in Group B and 55% in Group A. In Group C, the number of different diagnosis ranged from four to seven.

In Group D, there were three cases with attention deficit disorder or conduct disorder. One case was attention deficit disorder and mental retardation. In all three cases, the most common diagnosis was the expected one. In the case of the undersocialized disorder, conduct disorder, aggressive type, there were 11 different diagnoses used, and the interrater agreement was only 30%. Overall, this group had a 58% interrater agreement with expected diagnoses.

Group E contained cases with mental retardation and various organic diagnoses. Case 1 was mental retardation and pervasive developmental disorder. The most common diagnosis was the same in mental retardation, with 90% interrater agreement, but only 50% made the diagnosis of pervasive developmental disorder, and 25% made both correct diagnoses. Ten different diagnoses were used. In a case with attention deficit disorder and mental retardation, again mental retardation was diagnosed by 90% of the raters; attention deficit disorder by 75% of the raters. Only 65% made both diagnoses, and there were six different diagnoses used. The third case was a case of an organic brain syndrome and mild mental retardation. Here, 75% of the raters diagnosed mental retardation, 35% diagnosed the organic brain syndrome, and 25% diagnosed both, with 12 different diagnoses used. The rater agreement with the expected diagnosis in this group using the one most common diagnosis for each case was 72%, but it was considerably lower than it would have been if *both* correct diagnoses were looked at as the standard.

Group F contained "miscellaneous" cases. One was a case of Tourette's syndrome, or motor–verbal tic disorder, and although the rater agreement with expected diagnosis was 80%, the number of different diagnoses used was eight. The next case was elective mutism, which at the time did not exist as a separate syndrome in the draft of DSM-III. The most common diagnosis used was avoidant disorder, with interrater agreement being 60% and 10 different diagnoses being used. Many of the raters commented on the need for an elective mutism category, which appeared in later drafts of DSM-III. Categories such as regressive disorder, asocial disorder, and emancipation disorder of adolescence had low rates of agreement with the expected diagnosis. Some of these were later dropped from the final draft of DSM-III.

The last group of three cases contained two that had no mental disorder diagnosed on Axis I, and one was a case in which the investigators felt did not meet the criteria for any diagnosis. The agreement with the expected diagnosis in the no-mental-disorder cases were 50% and 30%, respectively, although it was the most common diagnosis. From seven to nine different diagnoses were used in the three cases. Intermittent explosive disorder was the most common diagnosis in the undiagnosable case, with 30% interrater agreement and two different diagnoses being used.

In looking at the broad diagnostic groupings (A through to G), only the mental retardation group had a very high level of agreement within any group. In Group A, the level of agreement ranged from a low of 25% to a high of 100%. The overall level of rater agreement with expected diagnosis was 49%.

The next issue was the issue of interrater agreement. For all cases, the raters made 620 diagnoses with DSM-II and 605 diagnoses with Axis I of DSM-III. However, 112 of the DSM-II diagnoses were in the major category of "special symptoms," which are essentially equivalent to the Axis II specific developmental disorders in DSM-III. Thus, if these are subtracted from the total DSM-II diagnosis, almost 100 more diagnoses were made with Axis I of DSM-III than with DSM-II. The average interrater agreement was slightly less for the DSM-III diagnoses than for the DSM-II diagnoses (57% for DSM-II and 54% for Axis I of DSM-III).

In breaking the cases down into five major groupings (psychotic disorders, depressive disorders, anxiety disorders, attention deficit and conduct disorders, mental retardation and organic disorders), along with miscellaneous disorders, and cases without an Axis I diagnosis, it was found that there was good agreement in cases of psychosis, conduct disorder, hyperactivity, and mental retardation, with DSM-III slightly better in these cases. There was a good deal of disagreement among the raters in both DSM-II and DSM-III systems for subtyping anxiety disorders, subtyping depression and complex cases with multiple clinical features. For example, using the DSM-III system, the interrater agreement for the expected psychotic cases was 76%. It was 63% for the attention deficit disorder and conduct disorder, 85% for the mental retardation and organic disorders, 37% for the cases without an Axis I diagnosis, 48% for the miscellaneous disorders, 42% for the depressive disorders, and 50% for the anxiety disorders. The figures were broadly comparable to the British WHO study (see Gould, Shaffer, Rutter, & Sturge, Chapter 2, this volume) of 17 case histories provided to child psychiatrists in comparing ICD-8 and ICD-9. The anxiety disorders seemed to be much better diagnosed in the WHO study than they were in the Cantwell *et al.* study.

Concerning the issue of multiple diagnoses on Axis I and Axis II, the multiaxial system of DSM-III did seem to lead to more complete and reliable diagnosis of complex cases. Medical disorders and psychosocial stressors were coded with relatively good levels of interrater agreement. However, both correct diagnoses were diagnosed relatively uncommonly in a fairly large number of cases, even with DSM-III, although the results were considerably better with DSM-II. The data indicate that in every case involving a specific developmental disorder, the DSM-III multiaxial system led to a more frequent recording of both the Axis I disorder and a developmental disorder. Also, there were four cases in which it was vital for the understanding of the psychiatric condition to code an appropriate medical or neurological disorder. This was done much better with DSM-III than it was with DSM-II.

Overall, the raters reported few difficulties using DSM-III and consistently preferred it over DSM-II as the more useful system. Considering the fact that the trainees and faculty were using DSM-III for the first time without any special training and that an early draft was used, the results were considered by the authors to be encouraging. However, considerable refinement would be necessary before DSM-III could be considered to be a reliable document.

Mezzich, Mezzich, and Coffman (1985) also conducted a comparative study of the reliability of DSM-III and DSM-II. They took geographic random samples of child psychiatrists and clinical child psychologists from the western states of the United States and used either DSM-II or DSM-III to diagnose 27 children and adolescent case histories, which were prepared in standard format.

In contrast to the study by Cantwell and his colleagues (Cantwell, Mattison, *et al.*, 1979; Cantwell, Russell, *et al.*, 1979; Mattison *et al.*, 1979;

Russell *et al.*, 1979), each clinician rated a particular case using only DSM-II or DSM-III (1978 draft). Three case histories per clinician were used. The raters were asked to read carefully each of the three case histories that were sent to them, consulting closely the diagnostic manual (either DSM-II or DSM-III) in order to complete a diagnostic report for each case history. The reliabilities of DSM-II and each of the five axes of DSM-III were computed for psychologists, psychiatrists, and both groups combined. This was done in every case by first computing the reliability value for each block of three case histories and then averaging the value across the nine blocks. The reliability value for each block was computed in terms of a kappa coefficient for either categorical or nominal axes and intraclass correlation coefficient for dimensional or quantitative axes.

Among psychologists and psychiatrists, the reliability values for DSM-II and for all axes of DSM-III were statistically significantly greater than chance, except for Axis IV. There were no differences between psychologists and psychiatrists. Among DSM-II categories, the highest kappa values were obtained for mental retardation, schizophrenia, and the category of behavior disorders of childhood and adolescence. Out of the eight diagnostic categories frequently used in DSM-II, six had kappa values significantly above zero. For the specific categories in DSM-III, Axis I, the highest kappa values were for mental retardation, enuresis, pervasive developmental disorder, and conduct disorder. Among the eight diagnostic categories frequently used in DSM-III, Axis I, seven had kappa values significantly above zero. Most of the corresponding categories had higher kappas for the DSM-III, Axis I, system than for DSM-II. The average of the kappas for the most frequently mentioned categories of DSM-III, Axis I, was .45; for DSM-II it was .33.

Very few specific diagnostic categories for DSM-III, Axes II and III, were frequently mentioned. None of them obtained reliability values significantly above chance levels. Thus, the reliabilities in the Mezzich study for DSM-II and for Axis I and Axis II of DSM-III, while significantly above chance level, were modest at best and were quite similar to each other. The findings are quite similar to the Cantwell *et al.* study.

RECOMMENDATIONS FOR THE FUTURE

DSM-III was not meant to be the final statement on psychiatric classification. The expectation of the committee was that future years would lead to major refinements and that DSM-IV and future editions would reflect ever-increasing sophisticated knowledge about psychiatric classification of childhood disorders. However, upon reviewing the research that has been done on the DSM-III childhood section, one has to be disappointed both in the number of studies and in their results, particularly in the area of reliability.

Earlier in the chapter I discussed the basic principles of classification that underlie the DSM-III system. It would seem that much more research is needed in some areas. For example, it was stated that there is no right way to classify the psychiatric disorders of childhood. One way to decide upon the preferred system is to compare DSM-III with alternative methods of classification on the same group of children in order to determine which serves best for which purposes. For example, comparison of DSM-III categorical diagnoses with diagnoses made in a dimensional fashion by factor and cluster analysis would provide much information. For example, it would be important to know whether the DSM-III category of attention deficit disorder with hyperactivity is more strongly associated with a positive response to stimulant medication than is membership in a patient cluster formed by factor analysis and cluster analysis. To date, no significant study of this type has been done.

Another basic principle was that the system had to have reliable categories. The results to date do not demonstrate great reliability. Some of these studies have been done with live interviews and some with case reports. Reliability in the DSM-III field trials that compared reliability of psychiatric diagnosis done by live interviews and from case summaries on the same patients by the same clinicians indicated that major diagnostic classes of DSM-III had higher reliability when diagnoses were made from live interviews than they were from case summaries (Hyler, Williams, & Spitzer, 1982). This must be kept in mind when looking at reliability studies.

Diagnostic reliability is affected by criterion variance, observation and interpretation variance, and information variance. The DSM-III system attempts to affect only criterion variance. However, there have been very few studies on the specific diagnostic criteria used in DSM-III. Those that have been done suggest that some of the criteria probably need to be modified. However, this modification should be based on empirical research and not simply on continuing debate followed by personal statements of opinion and then a vote. There should be ways of empirically studying which symptoms of what severity are necessary for the diagnosis of attention deficit disorder to give the greatest predictive validity for outcome and response to treatment. Similar studies can be done with other disorders. However, information variance and observation variance will not be affected by the system per se. Rather, these will require modification in other aspects of the diagnostic process—modifications in data collection instruments and in the way people assimilate and interpret the data they collect. There is room for research on exactly how interviews with parents, interviews with children, parent and teacher rating scales, psychobiologic measures, and other data collection instruments fit into the diagnostic process. As the Costello (1982) study shows, we need to know a great deal more about how people actually use data to arrive at a diagnosis according to a specific system.

A further basic principle is that categories have to be valid. Again, there have been very few studies of the validity of the DSM-III diagnostic categories—particularly those introduced for the first time (such as attention deficit disorder without hyperactivity and avoidant disorder). This is a disappointing state of affairs.

The DSM-III system, like all systems, was meant to provide differentiation between disorders and good coverage of the disorders presented by groups of children with psychiatric problems. The data suggest that the DSM-III system does provide better differentiation than DSM-II and probably better coverage. The system seems to be accepted by those raters who have used it, and is relatively easily learned. However, without validity studies, we are not clear as to whether the differentiation among disorders is really meaningful, particularly among subcategories of disorders. Is the differentiation between attention deficit disorder with hyperactivity and conduct disorder a meaningful one in terms of predictive validity? Only future research will answer this and related questions.

If a multiaxial system is to be used, we need to know more about how many axes there should be, what is to be coded on the various axes, the type of information that each axis should carry, and so forth. It is quite clear that Axis IV not only is unreliable but also presents information in a way that is not consistent with the most modern concepts and research data on psychosocial stressors. If specific diagnostic criteria are to be used, a greater amount of consideration will be needed with regard to a more developmental framework. It may be that different criteria will have to be used for the same disorder for preschool children, grade school children, and adolescent age range children.

It is hoped that the next 10 years of research will produce by the 1990s the kind of information necessary to answer the major questions that were raised by the introduction of DSM-III.

REFERENCES

Achenbach, T. (1980). DSM-III in light of empirical research on the classification of child psychopathology. *Journal of the American Academy of Child Psychiatry, 19*, 395–412.

American Psychiatric Association. (1980). *Diagnostic and statistical manual of mental disorders* (3rd ed.). Washington, DC: Author.

Cantor, S., Evans, J., Pearce, J., & Pezzot-Pearce, T. (1981). Childhood schizophrenia: Present but not accounted for. *American Journal of Psychiatry, 139*, 758–762.

Cantwell, D. P. (1975). A model for the investigation of psychiatric disorders of childhood—Its application in genetic studies of the hyperkinetic syndrome. In E. J. Anthony (Ed.), *Explorations in child psychiatry* (pp. 57–79). New York: Plenum.

Cantwell, D. P. (1980). The diagnostic process and diagnostic classification in child psychiatry—DSM-III. *Journal of the American Academy of Child Psychiatry, 19*, 345–355.

Cantwell, D. P. (1983). Diagnostic validity of the hyperactive child (attention deficit disorder with hyperactivity) syndrome. *Psychiatric Developments, 1*, 277–300.

Cantwell, D. P., Mattison, R., Russell, A. T., & Will, L. (1979). A comparison of DSM-II and DSM-III in the diagnosis of childhood psychiatric disorders. IV. Difficulties in use, global comparison, and conclusions. *Archives of General Psychiatry, 36*, 1227–1228.

Cantwell, D. P., Russell, A. T., Mattison, R., & Will, L. (1979). A comparison of DSM-II and DSM-III in the diagnosis of childhood psychiatric disorders. I. Agreement with expected diagnosis. *Archives of General Psychiatry, 36,* 1208–1213.

Carlson, G. A., & Cantwell, D. P. (1982). Diagnosis of childhood depression: A comparison of the Weinberg and DSM-III criteria. *Journal of the American Academy of Child Psychiatry, 21,* 247–250.

Costello, E. J. (1982, October). *Clinical decision making in child psychiatry.* Paper presented at the 29th Meeting of the American Academy of Child Psychiatry, Washington, DC.

Earls, F. (1982). Application of DSM-III in an epidemiological study of preschool children. *American Journal of Psychiatry, 139,* 242–243.

Finn, S. E. (1982). Base rates, utilities, and DSM-III: Shortcomings of fixed-rule systems of psychodiagnosis. *Journal of Abnormal Psychology, 91,* 294–302.

Gittelman, R. (1980). The role of psychological tests for differential diagnosis in child psychiatry. *Journal of the American Academy of Child Psychiatry, 19,* 413–438.

Grossman, H. G., Begab, M. J., Cantwell, D. P., Clements, J. D., Eyman, R. K., Meyers, C. E., Tarjan, G., & Warren, S. A. (Eds.). (1983). *Classification in mental retardation.* Washington, DC: American Association on Mental Deficiency.

Hyler, S. E., Williams, J. B. W., & Spitzer, R. L. (1982) Reliability in the DSM-III field trials. Interview v. case summary. *Archives of General Psychiatry, 39,* 1275–1278.

Irwin, M. (1981). Diagnosis of anorexia nervosa in children and the validity of DSM-III. *American Journal of Psychiatry, 138,* 1382–1383.

Kovacs, M. (1983, December). *DSM-III criteria for depressive disorders in children.* Paper presented at the American Psychiatric Association Conference to Evaluate DSM-III, Washington, DC.

Kovacs, M., Feinberg, T. L., Crouse-Novak, M. A., Paulauskas, S. L., & Finkelstein, R. (1984). Depressive disorders in childhood. I. A longitudinal prospective study of characteristics and recovery. *Archives of General Psychiatry, 41,* 229–237.

Kovacs, M., Feinberg, T. L., Crouse-Novak, M., Paulauskas, S. L., Pollack, M., & Finkelstein, R. (1984). Depressive disorders in childhood. II. A longitudinal study of the risk for a subsequent major depression. *Archives of General Psychiatry, 41,* 643–649.

Lahey, B. B., Schaughency, E. A., Strauss, C. C., & Frame, C. L. (1984). Are attention deficit disorders with and without hyperactivity similar or dissimilar disorders? *Journal of the American Academy of Child Psychiatry, 23,* 302–309.

Mattison, R., Cantwell, D. P., Russell, A. T., & Will, L. (1979). A comparison of DSM-II and DSM-III in the diagnosis of child psychiatric disorders. II. Interrater agreement. *Archives of General Psychiatry, 36,* 1217–1222.

Maurer, R. G., & Stewart, M. A. (1980). Attention deficit without hyperactivity in a child psychiatry clinic. *Journal of Clinical Psychiatry, 41,* 232–233.

Mezzich, A. C., & Mezzich, J. E. (1985). Perceived suitability and usefulness of DSM-III vs. DSM-II in child psychopathology. *Journal of the American Academy of Child Psychiatry, 24,* 281–285.

Mezzich, A. C., Mezzich, J. E., & Coffman, G. A. (1985). Reliability of DSM-III vs. DSM-II in child psychopathology. *Journal of the American Academy of Child Psychiatry, 24,* 273–281.

Puig-Antich, J. (1983). Neuroendocrine and sleep correlates of prepubertal major depressive disorder: Current status of the evidence. In D. P. Cantwell & G. A. Carlson (Eds.), *Affective disorders in childhood and adolescence—An update* (pp. 211–227). New York: Spectrum Publications.

Puig-Antich, J., Chambers, W. J., & Tabrizi, M. A. (1983). The clinical assessment of current depressive episodes in children and adolescents: Interviews with parents and children. In D. P. Cantwell & G. A. Carlson (Eds.), *Affective disorders in childhood and adolescence—An update* (pp. 157–179). New York: Spectrum Publications.

Quay, H. C. (1986). A critical analysis of DSM-III as a taxonomy of psychopathology in childhood and adolescence. In T. Millon & G. L. Klerman (Eds.), *Contemporary directions in psychopathology: Toward the DSM-IV* (pp. 151–165). New York: Guilford.

Robins, E., & Guze, S. B. (1970). Establishment of diagnostic validity and psychiatric illness: Its application to schizophrenia. *American Journal of Psychiatry, 126,* 983–987.

Robins, L. N. (1966). *Deviant children grown up.* Baltimore: Williams & Wilkins.

Robins, L. N. (1978). Sturdy predictors of adult antisocial behavior: Replications from longitudinal studies. *Psychological Medicine, 8,* 611–622.

Russell, A. T., Cantwell, D. P., Mattison, R., & Will, L. (1979). A comparison of DSM-II and DSM-III in the diagnosis of childhood psychiatric disorders: III. Multiaxial features. *Archives of General Psychiatry 36,* 1223–1226.

Russell, A. T., Mattison, R., & Cantwell, D. P. (1983). DSM-III in the clinical practice of child psychiatry. *Journal of Clinical Psychiatry, 44,* 86–90.

Rutter, M., & Shaffer, D. (1980). A step forward or back in terms of the classification of child psychiatric disorders? *Journal of the American Academy of Child Psychiatry, 19,* 371–394.

Rutter, M., Tizard, J., & Whitmore, K. (Eds.). (1970). *Education, health, and behavior.* London: Longmans. (Reprinted 1981. New York: Krieger.)

Spitzer, R. L., & Cantwell, D. P. (1980). The DSM-III classification of the psychiatric disorders of infancy, childhood, and adolescence. *Journal of the American Academy of Child Psychiatry, 19,* 356–370.

Spitzer, R. L., Endicott, J., & Robins, E. (1978). Research diagnostic criteria: Rationale and reliability. *Archives of General Psychiatry, 35,* 773–782.

Spitzer, R. L., Forman, J. B., & Nee, J. (1979). DSM-III field trials: II. Initial experience with the multiaxial system. *American Journal of Psychiatry, 136,* 818–820.

Strober, M., Green, J., & Carlson, G. (1981). Reliability of psychiatric diagnosis in hospitalized adolescents—Interrater agreement using DSM-III. *Archives of General Psychiatry, 38,* 141–145.

Weinberg, W. A., Rutman, J., Sullivan, L., Penick, E. C., & Dietz, S. G. (1973). Depression in children referred to an educational diagnostic center: Diagnosis and treatment. *Journal of Pediatrics, 83,* 1065–1072.

Werry, J. S., Methven, R. J., Fitzpatrick, J., & Dixon, H. (1983). The interrater reliability of DSM-III in children. *Journal of Abnormal Child Psychology, 11,* 341–354.

World Health Organization. (1978). *International classification of diseases* (9th ed.). Geneva: Author.

2

UK/WHO STUDY OF ICD-9

MADELYN S. GOULD   **MICHAEL RUTTER**
DAVID SHAFFER   **CLAIRE STURGE**

INTRODUCTION

There is no doubt that there have been great advances in the classification of child psychiatric disorder in recent years. The two most notable advances have been the third edition of the *Diagnostic and Statistical Manual of Mental Disorders* (DSM-III) of the American Psychiatric Association (1980) and a version of the ICD-9 classification scheme sponsored by the World Health Organization (Rutter, Shaffer, & Sturge, 1975). These classifications have provided a multiaxial framework yielding rules as to what and how many categories should be used. Moreover, these classification have greatly elaborated and differentiated the childhood categories. However, problems still remain. A critique of DSM-III has been published by Rutter and Shaffer (1980). A number of the unresolved issues and questions that need further review and deliberation is the focus of this chapter, dealing with the UK/WHO study of the reliability and validity of ICD-9. These questions include: (1) To what extent do children assigned a similar or different diagnosis resemble or differ from one another (discriminant validity), and are these discriminations made reliably? (2) How should we deal with the group of mixed disorders in which both emotional disturbance and conduct disorder are evident? (3) To what extent can broad diagnostic categories be subdivided? (4) Can psychiatric categories be grouped hierarchically to yield better reliability? (5) What is the value of a descriptive glossary? (6) What difficulties have been noted in employing the ICD-9 classification scheme? The UK/WHO study examined the reliability and validity of the five axes of the ICD-9; however, only information pertaining to Axis I, clinical psychiatric syndrome, will be reviewed in this chapter.

Madelyn S. Gould and David Shaffer. New York State Psychiatric Institute and Division of Child Psychiatry, Columbia University College of Physicians and Surgeons, New York, New York.

Michael Rutter. Department of Child and Adolescent Psychiatry, University of London Institute of Psychiatry, London, England.

Claire Sturge. Department of Child Psychiatry, Northwick Park Hospital, Harrow, Middlesex, England.

METHOD

A project to examine the properties of the child diagnostic codes in ICD-9 was announced at a professional meeting of British child psychiatrists. Participation in the project was invited, and 52 child psychiatrists, representing a broad cross section of practicing British child psychiatrists, volunteered to take part. Most worked in a hospital or medical school and all had received postgraduate certification in psychiatry. Their training and fields of practice were diverse and, although the number included trained psychoanalysts and family therapists, the majority would have used phenomenological criteria and prevailing diagnostic concepts in their everyday clinical work. Their clinical practices were generally mixed, although a small number were primarily engaged in such subspecialities as forensic child psychiatry. Thirteen of the raters had had prior experience with both the new ICD codes and a glossary (Rutter, Shaffer, & Sturge, 1975). None of the other raters had had prior experience with the new codes or access to the glossary.

Design Considerations

The study had two principal goals: (1) to examine the reliability of the ICD-9 as it is applied to childhood disorders, and (2) to examine the discriminant validity of categories. In other words, do the ICD-9 categories differentiate between disorders in a reliable and meaningful way? A third goal was to determine the effects of a glossary on diagnostic reliability.

In order to examine these different questions, several strategies were employed. Interrater agreement was assessed by a case history exercise. In this exercise, each rater was exposed to similar clinical material presented in a uniform way. In order to examine the homogeneity of patient characteristics within a given diagnostic category and to examine the extent to which patients within such categories differed from patients within other categories, it was necessary to examine a large number of different patients in a naturalistic setting. A field study was designed for that purpose. The field study also allowed examination of the rate of the use of the codes as a means of testing whether the codes were being used discriminately.

The measurement of a glossary effect called for a comparison between rates of agreement among raters who had and who did not have a glossary at their disposal at the time of their diagnostic assessments.

Sequence

The study was divided into three discrete stages.

1. *First case history exercise.* Four groups of 13 psychiatrists gathered together and were provided with 14 case histories to rate during the course

of a single day's meeting. Instructions were given to participants not to discuss the case history material or exchange information, and seating arrangements were made so that adjacent raters would not be considering the same case history at the same time. One subgroup had access to the glossary during this exercise.

2. *The field study*. At the end of the first case history exercise, all participants were provided with rating forms and were asked to diagnose and describe ten consecutive new cases from their clinical practice. This constituted the "field sample." Fifty-one of the raters took part in this study. The clinicians who participated were given a glossary at the time of the field exercise with the exception of one subgroup who acted as a control and had access to the coding system but not to the glossary.

The clinical cases included approximately 62% males. Fifteen percent of the sample were younger than 6 years. The remaining 85% were equally divided among 6- to 11-year-olds and those 12 years or older.

3. *Second case history exercise*. Several months after the first exercise and after the participants had completed rating their clinic cases, the groups reconvened to rate a further 14 case histories. All 52 psychiatrists participated in this exercise.

Case Histories

Twenty-two case histories were abstracted from actual case records available at the Maudsley Hospital. An additional six case histories were abstracted from cases sent by psychiatrists from Europe so that an international characteristic would be included in the reliability exercise. The 28 case history abstracts were prepared from the full history and background, description of present symptoms and problems, an interview of the child, and results of testing. Particular attention was given to details that were likely to be helpful in diagnosis. These included the timing and nature of the onset of the problem, a full description of the clinical features, and results of psychometric and laboratory testing at the time of the initial diagnostic assessment. Examples of behavior and, where possible, a description of the situations that appeared to make the clinical condition better or worse were given, and jargon terms were edited out. In addition, a full description of the family situation, an outline of family interactions and child rearing attitudes, and the family's social situation were provided.

Ratings

In addition to providing ratings of psychiatric and medical diagnosis (Axes I and IV), the participants coded developmental disorders and intellectual level (Axes II and III) and indicated up to three abnormal psychosocial situations (Axis V) coded in order of clinical importance. The participants also indicated the presence or absence of 35 different symptoms, the duration of the disorder before assessment, whether they considered the onset of the disorder to be related to the experience of acute or chronic stress, whether the disorder was situation-specific or cross-situational, and finally whether they had experienced one of a number of different difficulties in using any component of the multiaxial system or glossary.

RESULTS

Reliability of ICD-9 Diagnoses

The interrater reliability of Axis I diagnoses (at the three-digit level) is presented in Table 2-1. Kappa was employed as the summary measure of reliability of the major three-digit diagnoses. Neurotic disorders (code 300)

TABLE 2-1. Reliability of Axis I Three-Digit Diagnoses (Summary of κ Statistics)

Clinical psychiatric syndrome	Number of cases on which used (by any rater)[a]	Percentage use ($N = 1456$) (28 cases × 52 raters)	κ (total sample)
299 Psychoses specific to childhood	7	8.5%	.66
300 Neurotic disorders	23	12.9%	.37
307 Special symptoms or syndromes not elsewhere classified	9	9.2%	.67
309 Adjustment reaction	24	17.8%	.23
312 Disturbance of conduct, not elsewhere classified	17	21.7%	.48
313 Disturbance of emotions specific to childhood and adolescence	23	11.7%	.17
314 Hyperkinetic syndrome of childhood	6	6.1%	.63

Note. Overall $\kappa = .38$ (eight-category variable).
[a]The sum of this column exceeds the total number of cases because any one case could receive several different diagnoses from the total group of 52 raters.

($\kappa = .37$), adjustment reaction (309) ($\kappa = .23$), and disturbance of emotions specific to childhood and adolescence (313) ($\kappa = .17$) were used rather indiscriminately, as indicated by the large number of cases in which they were employed and their low kappas. Reliabilities were good for psychoses specific to childhood (299) ($\kappa = .66$), special symptoms of syndromes not elsewhere classified (307) ($\kappa = .67$), and hyperkinetic syndrome of childhood (314) ($\kappa = .63$). Disturbance of conduct (312) had a moderate reliability ($\kappa = .48$). The poorer kappas resulted not from the lower frequency of use of the particular diagnostic category, but rather from a greater frequency of indiscriminate use. The present levels of agreement are quite similar to those reported for Axis I diagnoses of DSM-III (Mattison, Cantwell, Russell, & Will, 1979; Strober, Green, & Carlson, 1981; Werry, Methven, Fitzpatrick, & Dixon, 1983; Mezzich, Mezzich, & Coffman, 1985). A consistent finding is that the agreement for attention deficit disorder or hyperactivity and conduct disorder is good, whereas the reliability for adjustment disorder is quite poor. With the exception of the study by Werry et al. (1983), anxiety disorders have been found to be employed unreliably. The overall reliability for ICD-9 Axis I diagnoses ($\kappa = .38$) is similar to that obtained by Mezzich et al. (1985) for DSM-III ($\kappa = .37$), using the same case histories as those in the present study. However, Strober et al. (1981), in a study of successive first admissions, reported an overall reliability for DSM-III Axis I ($\kappa = .74$) that was higher than that found in the present study.

Four psychiatric diagnoses (three-digit level) accounted for 70% of the clinic cases. Disturbance of conduct (312) was the most frequently diagnosed (25% of cases). Adjustment reaction (309) and disturbance of emotions (313) were the next most frequent diagnoses (17% and 15.8%, respectively) followed by neurotic disorders (300) used in 12% of the cases. Among each of these four most frequent three-digit diagnoses, the following four-digit diagnoses were coded most often: unsocialized disturbance of conduct (312.0) (13.2%); adjustment reaction with mixed disturbance of emotions and conduct (309.4) (5.3%); adjustment reaction with predominant disturbance of other emotions (309.2) (5.1%); disturbance of emotions with anxiety and fearfulness (313.0) (5.5%); and neurotic depression (300.4) (4.5%).

It appears that the diagnoses of adjustment reaction (309), disturbance of emotions (313) and neurotic disorders (300) were being applied indiscriminately, as indicated by their low reliabilities in the case history exercise and their frequent use in the clinic exercise.

Discriminant Validity of ICD-9 Categories

In the following analyses of the discriminant validity of the diagnostic categories only those clinicians with access to the glossary ($N = 377$) were included. Moreover, only the main 12 symptoms (out of 35) were statistically examined for their value in differential diagnosis so as not to capitalize on chance findings.

Emotional Disorder (313) versus Conduct Disorder (312)

One of the least stringent tests of the usefulness of the classification scheme would be to show that discrimination at the three-digit level between symptom patterns in children with conduct disorders and those with emotional disorders. Since overwhelming evidence already exists for the differentiation of conduct and emotional disorders (Quay, 1979; Rutter & Gould, 1985), the present comparison of emotional and conduct disorders is presented as a baseline for evaluating the remaining comparisons. These two broad groups differed significantly on the majority of symptoms and in a variety of background features including family problems (see Table 2-2). Children with emotional disorder were more likely to show familial overinvolvement, an associated speech or language delay, and situation specificity, whereas those with conduct disorders included a higher proportion with discordant intrafamilial relationships and inadequate or inconsistent parental control, as well as with lower levels of intelligence. Nevertheless, there were a few symptoms, such as depressed mood, that might seem to form part of one or other of the categories, but which did not discriminate between the two conditions.

TABLE 2-2. Conduct and Emotional Disorders of Childhood

	Conduct 312 (N = 102)		Emotional 313 (N = 59)		χ^2	p
	N	%	N	%		
Demographic						
Age						
≤ 5 years	12	11.8	10	16.9		
6–11 years	27	36.3	30	50.8	5.91	.052
12 + years	53	52.0	19	32.2		
Sex (male)	73	71.6	38	64.4	NS	
Symptoms						
Short attention span	36	35.6	17	28.8	NS	
Overactivity	16	15.7	4	6.8	2.73	.098
Generalized anxiety	19	18.6	21	35.6	5.76	.016
Somatic symptoms	11	10.8	16	27.6	7.44	.006
Depressed mood	28	27.5	15	25.4	NS	
Tempers or tantrums	59	57.8	21	35.6	7.40	.006
Antisocial behavior (nondelinquent socially disapproved behavior)	78	76.5	25	42.4	18.85	.0001

TABLE 2-2. (cont.)

	Conduct 312 (N = 102)		Emotional 313 (N = 59)			
	N	%	N	%	χ^2	p
Solitary delinquency	42	41.2	7	11.9	15.17	.0001
Delinquency with others	32	31.7	1	1.7	20.46	.0001
Disturbed family relationships	84	82.4	38	64.4	6.56	.01
Disturbed peer relationships	57	55.9	30	50.8		NS
Educational retardation	43	43.4	17	28.8		NS
Duration (< 6 months)	2	2.1	4	7.0		NS
Situation specificity	26	25.1	26	44.1	5.90	.015
Current social impairment	67	66.3	41	69.5		NS
Family situation						
Mental disturbance in family	25	24.5	18	30.5		NS
Discordant intrafamilial relationships	44	43.1	15	25.4	5.05	.037
Familial overinvolvement	14	13.7	18	30.5	6.61	.01
Inadequate or inconsistent parental control	35	34.3	10	16.9	5.59	.018
Parental living situation (both natural parents)	56	54.9	35	59.3		NS
Specific delays in development (Axis II)						
No delay	82	80.4	41	69.5		NS
Reading	9	8.8	7	11.9		NS
Speech/language	4	3.9	8	13.6	5.03	.025
Mixed	4	3.9	2	3.4		NS
Intellectual level (Axis III)						
Retardation	10	10.0	1	1.7	3.88	.048

Emotional Disorder (313) versus Neurotic Disorder (300)

It remains uncertain whether more than one main heading for emotional disorders is justified and, if multiple categories are required, how they should be defined. In ICD-9 the three-digit category of emotional disorders is differentiated from another three-digit code (300) for children who show emotional disorders of types similar to those found in adults. The following analyses tackle the question of whether emotional disturbance and neurosis in childhood are the same condition or can be differentiated.

The reliability of a combined syndrome of disturbance of emotions and neurotic disorder ($\kappa = .38$) was significantly higher than the reliability of the disturbance of emotions category alone ($\kappa = .17, p < .05$) and approximately equal to neurotic disorder ($\kappa = .37$). This pattern of reliabilities indicates that there was a fair amount of overlap in the use of the two categories in the reliability exercise. However, it must be noted that the diagnosis of disturbance of emotions was confused with other disorders as well.

Despite the overlap and the poor reliabilities, the children diagnosed with emotional disorder and the neurotic disorder group differ somewhat in clinical practice (see Table 2-3). Those with emotional disorder were younger, were more likely to have associated antisocial behavior, inattentiveness, developmental delay, and disorder of longer duration. The neurotic disorder group exhibited more anxiety, more somatic symptoms, and more depression. The family situations of the two groups were equivalent.

TABLE 2-3. Neurotic and Emotional Disorders of Childhood

	Neurotic 300 ($N = 40$)		Emotional 313 ($N = 59$)			
	N	%	N	%	χ^2	p
Demographic						
Age						
≥ 5 years	2	5.0	10	16.9		
6–11 years	13	32.5	30	50.8	9.57	.008
12 + years	25	62.5	19	32.2		
Sex (male)	20	50.0	38	64.4		NS
Symptoms						
Short attention span	4	10.0	17	28.8	11.95	.0005
Overactivity	1	2.5	4	6.8		NS
Generalized anxiety	21	52.5	21	35.6	2.79	.09
Somatic symptoms	24	60.0	16	27.6	10.70	.001
Depressed mood	29	72.5	15	25.4	21.39	.0001
Tempers or tantrums	12	30.0	21	35.6		NS
Antisocial behavior (nondelinquent socially disapproved behavior)	6	15.0	25	42.4	8.30	.007
Solitary delinquency	3	7.5	7	11.9		NS
Delinquency with others	0	0.0	1	1.7		NS
Disturbed family relationships	26	65.0	38	64.4		NS

TABLE 2-3. (cont.)

	Neurotic 300 (N = 40)		Emotional 313 (N = 59)			
	N	%	N	%	χ^2	p
Disturbed peer relationships	19	47.5	30	50.8		NS
Educational retardation	10	27.0	17	28.8		NS
Duration (< 6 months)	14	35.9	4	7.0	12.68	.0003
Situation specificity	5	12.5	26	44.1	11.04	.0009
Current social impairment	27	67.5	41	69.5		NS
Family situation						
Mental disturbance in family	12	30.0	18	30.5		NS
Discordant intrafamilial relationships	8	20.0	15	25.4		NS
Familial overinvolvement	15	37.5	18	30.5		NS
Inadequate or inconsistent parental control	4	10.0	10	16.9		NS
Parental living situation (both natural parents)	24	60.0	35	59.3		NS
Specific delays in development (Axis II)						
No delay	38	95.0	41	69.5	9.6	.001
Reading	1	2.5	7	11.9	2.81	.02
Speech/language	1	2.5	8	13.6	3.53	.06
Mixed	0	0.0	2	3.4		NS
Intellectual level (Axis III)						
Retardation	1	2.5	1	1.7		NS

Hyperkinetic Syndrome (314) versus Conduct Disorder (312)

Both ICD-9 and DSM-III have separate categories for attention deficit or hyperkinetic syndromes. Over a decade of controversy surrounds this syndrome. There is evidence, such as cognitive correlates and outcome (Schachar, Rutter, & Smith, 1981), suggesting that there may be justification for a separate main heading. However, the differentiation between these syndromes from conduct disturbance is not clear-cut (Rutter & Shaffer, 1980). Quay (1980) argued against the existence of hyperactivity as a primary diagnosis, citing high correlations between hyperactivity and conduct problem scales in the factor analytic literature. On the other hand, Trites and Laprade (1983) provide evidence for an independent syndrome of hyperactivity. Since the findings do not yet yield firm conclusions on the validity of the distinction between hyperactivity and conduct disorder, additional relevant data from the present UK/WHO study are presented. Taylor (Chapter 12, this volume) addresses this issue in greater detail.

Both the hyperkinetic syndrome and disturbance of conduct were used with good reliability in the case history exercise (see Table 2-1). Combining the syndromes yielded an interrater reliability ($\kappa = .52$) that was significantly lower than that for hyperkinesis ($\kappa = .63$, $p < .05$) and approximately equal to the reliability of disturbance of conduct ($\kappa = .48$). This pattern of reliabilities indicates that there was no more confusion between hyperkinesis and conduct disorder than existed between conduct disorder and other diagnoses or between the hyperkinetic syndrome and other disorders. However, it should be noted that the diagnosis of hyperkinetic syndrome in this study followed the narrower ICD-9 definition rather than the broader DSM-III approach.

TABLE 2-4. Conduct Disorder and Hyperkinetic Syndrome

	Conduct 312 (N = 102)		Hyperkinesis 314 (N = 11)		χ^2	p
	N	$\%$	N	$\%$		
Demographic						
Age						
≥ 5 years	12	11.8	2	18.2		
6–11 years	27	36.3	8	72.7	13.60	.001
12 + years	53	52.0	1	9.1		
Sex (male)	73	71.6	8	72.7		NS
Symptoms						
Short attention span	36	35.6	11	100	17.11	.0001
Overactivity	16	15.7	11	100	38.80	.0001
Generalized anxiety	19	18.6	0	0		NS
Somatic symptoms	11	10.8	0	0		NS
Depressed mood	28	27.5	0	0	4.01	.045
Tempers or tantrums	59	57.8	8	72.7		NS
Antisocial behavior (nondelinquent socially disapproved behavior)	78	76.5	6	54.5	2.50	.11
Solitary delinquency	42	41.2	0	0	7.21	.007
Delinquency with others	32	31.7	0	0	4.81	.028

TABLE 2-4. (cont.)

	Conduct 312 (N = 102)		Hyperkinesis 314 (N = 11)			
	N	%	N	%	χ^2	p
Disturbed family relationships	84	82.4	8	72.7		NS
Disturbed peer relationships	57	55.9	7	63.6		NS
Educational retardation	43	43.4	6	54.5		NS
Duration (< 6 months)	2	2.1	1	10.0		NS
Situation specificity	26	25.1	2	18.2		NS
Current social impairment	67	66.3	9	81.1		NS
Family situation						
Mental disturbance in family	25	24.5	2	18.2		NS
Discordant intrafamilial relationships	44	43.1	2	18.2	2.56	.10
Familial overinvolvement	14	13.7	1	19.1		NS
Inadequate or inconsistent parental control	35	34.3	3	27.3		NS
Parental living situation (both natural parents)	56	54.9	7	63.6		NS
Specific delays in development (Axis II)						
No delay	82	80.4	6	54.5	3.85	.05
Reading	9	8.8	0	0		NS
Speech/language	4	3.9	0	0		NS
Mixed	4	3.9	5	45.5	23.37	.0000
Intellectual level (Axis III)						
Retardation	10	10.0	4	36.4	4.94	.03

In the field sample many differences were found between the children diagnosed as having hyperkinesis and those with conduct disorder (see Table 2-4). By the definition of the categories we would have expected the significant differences that were found on inattentiveness, overactivity, and antisocial and delinquent behavior. Deliquent behaviors were not manifested by any of children diagnosed as hyperkinetic. Inattentiveness, overactivity, and nondelinquent antisocial behavior were not restricted to one group. The children with conduct disorders tended to be older, have an associated depressed mood, and were more likely to have discordant intrafamilial relationships. The children with hyperkinesis showed associated delays in development and a greater likelihood of retardation. Thus, although symptoms of inattentiveness, overactivity, and antisocial behavior may coexist in the two groups, the two syndromes can be differentiated. However, this cross-sectional analysis cannot rule out the possibility that hyperkinesis is a precursor of conduct disorder. The children diagnosed as hyperkinetic may start showing conduct problems as they get older and later be diagnosed as having a conduct disorder.

For cases in which the hyperkinetic syndrome is associated with marked conduct disturbance, ICD-9 provides a diagnosis of hyperkinetic conduct disorder (314.2). By definition, cases are excluded from this diagnosis if an associated developmental delay exists. Presumably, the expectation is that such cases in which the hyperkinetic syndrome is associated with conduct disturbance *and* a developmental delay should be given a different four-digit subcategorization of hyperkinetic disorder, namely 314.8 (other). Unfortunately, the glossary remains quite ambiguous as to the procedure to follow in this situation and it could be that clinicians would instead put the cases into the category of disturbance of conduct. To determine the extent to which these misclassifications might be occurring we examined the conduct disorder cases within the clinic sample to find out whether the presence of attention deficit and overactivity were associated with developmental delay. Only ten cases of conduct disorder (9.8%) had an associated developmental delay with concurrent symptoms of overactivity or a short attention span. Moreover, for cases with a conduct disorder there was no significant association between an associated developmental delay and either overactivity or an attentional problem. Therefore, it appears that few of these artifactual misclassifications occurred.

Mixed Disorder

There is uncertainty as to how to deal with mixed disorders in which there is a marked disturbance of emotions in addition to socially disapproved behavior. DSM-III deals with mixed disorders by allowing for multiple diagnoses. ICD-9, which allows only a single choice on the first axis, has included mixed disorders as separate subcategories within the main groupings of conduct disturbances and adjustment reaction. Their inclusion in separate categories was based on the frequency with which emotional and conduct problems occur together and the lack of evidence to support their inclusion in any diagnostic group. To date, there is insufficient information to evaluate the relative merits of the alternative solutions of DSM-III and ICD-9.

The interrater reliability of the mixed disturbance codes in ICD-9 is given in Table 2-5. The reliability of the mixed category in both the adjustment reaction (309.4) and disturbance of conduct (312.3) diagnostic groups

TABLE 2-5. Reliability of a Mixed Disturbance of Conduct and Emotions

		Number of cases on which used	Percentage use ($N = 1456$)	κ
309.4	Adjustment reaction—mixed	16	5.8	.16
312.3	Disturbance of conduct—mixed	16	8.5	.18
309.4	Adjustment reaction—mixed and			
312.3	Disturbance of conduct—mixed	20	14.3	.25

TABLE 2-6. Mixed Disorders in Comparison with Other Conduct Disorders

	Mixed 312.3 + 309.4 ($N = 52$)		Other conduct 312.0 + 312.1 + 312.2 + 312.8 ($N = 59$)			
	N	%	N	%	χ^2	p
Demographic						
Age						
≥ 5 years	2	3.8	11	15.9		
6–11 years	20	38.5	26	37.7	4.78	.09
12 + years	30	57.7	32	46.4		
Sex (male)	29	55.8	52	75.4	5.14	.02
Symptoms						
Short attention span	15	28.8	23	33.8		NS
Overactivity	9	17.3	10	14.5		NS
Generalized anxiety	16	30.8	7	10.1	8.19	.004
Somatic symptoms	10	19.2	6	8.7	2.87	.09
Depressed mood	29	55.8	9	13.0	25.13	.0000
Tempers or tantrums	33	63.5	38	55.1		NS
Antisocial behavior (nondelinquent socially disapproved behavior)	40	76.9	52	75.4		NS
Solitary delinquency	19	36.5	28	40.6		NS
Delinquency with others	12	23.1	22	32.4		NS
Disturbed family relationships	45	86.5	53	76.8		NS
Disturbed peer relationships	29	55.7	36	52.2		NS

TABLE 2-6. (cont.)

	Mixed 312.3 + 309.4 (N = 52)		Other conduct 312.0 + 312.1 + 312.2 + 312.8 (N = 59)			
	N	%	N	%	χ^2	p
Educational retardation	19	38.0	28	41.2		NS
Duration (< 6 months)	6	12.2	2	3.0	3.68	.054
Situation specificity	15	28.8	26	26.1		NS
Current social impairment	36	69.2	41	60.3		NS
Family situation						
Mental disturbance in family	13	25.0	20	29.0		NS
Discordant intrafamilial relationships	28	53.8	24	34.8	4.39	.036
Familial overinvolvement	10	19.2	8	11.6		NS
Inadequate or inconsistent parental control	11	21.2	26	37.7	3.82	.05
Parental living situation (both natural parents)	29	55.8	39	56.5		NS
Specific delays in development (Axis II)						
No delay	45	86.5	54	78.3		NS
Reading	4	7.7	6	8.7		NS
Speech/language	0	0.0	4	5.8	3.118	.07
Mixed	2	3.8	3	4.3		NS
Intellectual level (Axis III)						
Retardation	2	3.9	9	13.2	3.01	.08

was very poor. When the two codes were combined into one mixed disturbance category, the reliability increased slightly ($\kappa = .25$) but still indicated an unacceptable level of agreement.

The extent to which the mixed syndrome can be differentiated from other conduct disorders and emotional disorders is presented in Tables 2-6 and 2-7. Children exhibiting a mixed syndrome appear equally distinct from both groups. When compared with children having other conduct disorders, the mixed syndrome group, not surprisingly, resembles children with emotional disorders. Likewise, when compared with children with emotional

TABLE 2-7. Mixed Disorders and Emotional Disorder

	Mixed 312.3 + 309.4 (N = 52)		Emotional 313 (N = 59)			
	N	%	N	%	χ^2	p
Demographic						
Age						
≥ 5 years	2	3.8	10	16.9		
6–11 years	20	38.5	30	50.8	9.39	.009
12 + years	30	57.7	19	32.2		
Sex (male)	29	55.8	38	64.4		NS
Symptoms						
Short attention span	15	28.8	17	28.8		NS
Overactivity	9	17.3	4	6.8	2.96	.08
Generalized anxiety	16	30.8	21	35.6		NS
Somatic symptoms	10	19.2	16	27.6		NS
Depressed mood	29	55.8	15	25.4	10.64	.001
Tempers or tantrums	33	63.5	21	35.6	8.59	.003
Antisocial behavior (nondelinquent socially disapproved behavior)	40	76.9	25	42.4	13.60	.0002
Solitary delinquency	19	36.5	7	11.9	9.38	.002
Delinquency with others	12	23.1	1	1.7	12.22	.0005
Disturbed family relationships	45	86.5	38	64.4	7.18	.0074
Disturbed peer relationships	29	55.7	30	50.8		NS
Educational retardation	19	38.0	17	28.8		NS
Duration (< 6 months)	6	12.2	4	7.0		NS
Situation specificity	15	28.8	26	44.1	2.75	.09
Current social impairment	36	69.2	41	69.5		NS
Family situation						
Mental disturbance in family	13	25.0	18	30.5		NS
Discordant intrafamilial relationships	28	53.8	15	25.4	9.41	.002
Familial overinvolvement	10	19.2	18	30.5		NS
Inadequate or inconsistent parental control	11	21.2	10	16.9		NS
Parental living situation (both natural parents)	29	55.8	35	59.3		NS

TABLE 2-7. (cont.)

	Mixed 312.3 + 309.4 ($N = 52$)		Emotional 313 ($N = 59$)		χ^2	p
	N	%	N	%		
Specific delays in development (*Axis II*)						
No delay	45	86.5	41	69.5	4.60	.03
Reading	4	7.7	7	11.9		NS
Speech/language	0	0.0	8	13.6	7.60	.005
Mixed	2	3.8	2	3.4		NS
Intellectual level (*Axis III*)						
Retardation	2	3.9	1	1.7		NS

disorder, the mixed syndrome group resembles children with conduct disturbances. However, the mixed disorder group appears distinct from both groups with respect to some characteristics; they tend to be older, are more depressed, and have a greater proportion of discordant intrafamilial relationships and less associated developmental delays than the children with either "pure" conduct disorders or emotional disorders.

Subclassification

There has been a proliferation of subcategories in both ICD-9 and DSM-III. The question remains as to how far broad diagnostic categories can be subdivided. In general, the level of agreement at the fourth-digit level was poor. The average agreement for four-digit diagnoses was 45.7%. Twenty of the 28 cases had less than 51% of the raters agreeing on the modal fourth-digit diagnosis. Fifty-one percent to 80% of the raters agreed on the modal fourth-digit diagnosis on 4 cases and the level of agreement was greater than 80% for only 4 of the 28 case histories. Therefore, at the fourth-digit level the Axis I diagnoses were not used reliably. This is consistent with other studies of both ICD-9 and DSM-III in showing poor reliability for these fine diagnostic distinctions (Remschmidt, Chapter 3, this volume; Werry et al., 1983; Strober et al., 1981). For 57% of the cases, the second most common diagnoses was still within the same three-digit diagnostic category. As expected, at the three-digit level of diagnosis the level of agreement improved, the average agreement increasing to 60%.

It is beyond the scope of this chapter to review the reliability and discriminant validity of all of the fourth-digit level diagnoses. Instead, we have addressed the question of what subcategories of conduct disorder and emotional disorder are reliable or valid.

Conduct Disorder (313)

ICD-9 and DSM-III both discriminate within the conduct disorder group. The main distinction has been between unsocialized and socialized delinquency. The literature is in disagreement about whether children who have a "socialized" conduct disorder—that is, those who despite committing antisocial acts of behavior seem capable of forming good peer relationships, expressing guilt, and so on—differ from those children who are judged to be more isolated and less "capable of guilt" (Quay, 1979).

The reliability of the subcategory of socialized conduct disorder ($\kappa = .49$) was as high as the reliability of the three-digit conduct disorder category ($\kappa = .48$). This is comparable to the level of reliability that Strober et al. (1981) reported for socialized nonaggresssive conduct disorder in DSM-III. However, the unsocialized disturbance of conduct (312.0) subcategory had a poor level of interrater reliability ($\kappa = .27$) and appeared to be used indiscriminantly in the case history exercise. Strober et al. (1981) found higher levels of agreement for undersocialized conduct disorders.

There were virtually no symptomatic differences between the groups with the exception of whether or not the delinquency was performed with other peers and only a nearly significant difference on disturbed peer relationships (Table 2-8). As judged by the titles of the subcategories it might be

TABLE 2-8. Fourth-Digit Conduct Disorder Categories

	Unsocialized 312.0 (N = 52)		Socialized 312.1 (N = 14)			
	N	%	N	%	χ^2	p
Demographic						
Age						
$\geq$ 5 years	9	17.3	0	0.0		
6–11 years	21	40.4	4	28.6	4.76	.092
12 + years	22	42.3	10	71.4		
Sex (male)	37	71.2	14	100.0	5.23	.022
Symptoms						
Short attention span	21	41.2	2	14.3	3.47	.062
Overactivity	9	17.3	1	7.1	NS	
Generalized anxiety	5	9.6	2	14.3	NS	

TABLE 2-8. (cont.)

	Unsocialized 312.0 (N = 52)		Socialized 312.1 (N = 14)			
	N	%	N	%	χ^2	p
Somatic symptoms	4	7.7	2	14.3	NS	
Depressed mood	9	17.3	0	0.0	2.81	.093
Tempers or tantrums	29	55.8	6	42.9	NS	
Antisocial behavior (nondelinquent socially disapproved behavior)	41	78.8	10	71.4	NS	
Solitary delinquency	23	44.2	5	35.7	NS	
Delinquency with others	9	17.6	13	92.9	27.75	.0001
Disturbed family relationships	41	78.8	10	71.4	NS	
Disturbed peer relationships	31	59.6	5	35.7	NS ($p = .11$)	
Educational retardation	22	43.1	6	42.9	NS	
Duration (<6 months)	1	2.0	0	0.0	NS	
Situation specificity	14	26.9	4	28.6	NS	
Current social impairment	34	66.7	6	42.9	NS	
Family situation						
Mental disturbance in family	16	30.8	4	28.6	NS	
Discordant intrafamilial relationship	20	38.5	4	28.6	NS	
Familial overinvolvement	6	11.5	2	14.3	NS	
Inadequate or inconsistent parental control	16	30.8	9	64.3	5.27	.021
Parental living situation (both natural parents)	30	57.7	7	50.0	NS	
Specific delays in development (Axis II)						
No delay	43	82.7	9	64.3	NS	
Reading	3	5.8	3	21.4	3.27	.07
Speech/language	3	5.8	0	0.0	NS	
Mixed	2	3.8	1	7.1	NS	
Intellectual level (Axis III)						
Retardation	7	13.5	2	28.5	NS	

supposed that there should have been a more clear-cut differentiation between socialized and unsocialized disturbances of conduct in terms of the quality of peer relationships. The fact that this was not found almost certainly implies that the glossary seems to place equal emphasis on the solitary nature of delinquent activities, the presence of aggression and destructive behavior, and disturbed relationships with others. In keeping with this, perhaps, there was a tendency for the unsocialized group to exhibit more inattentiveness and depression. There were few differences for the remaining factors, with the exception that the socialized group was all male and had more inadequate or inconsistent parental control. The findings do not necessarily indicate that there could be no reliable differentiation between these two subcategories of conduct disorder. However, the results do emphasize that if the differentiation is to be reliable, the coding instructions must be more explicit on which features are to be taken into account in making the differentiation.

Disturbance of Emotions (313)

The subclassification of emotional disorder in childhood presents considerable problems. The way this was dealt with in ICD-9 was to separate emotional disorders into those that show predominantly anxiety symptoms (313.0), a predominantly depressive group (313.1), a group with shyness or social withdrawal symptoms (313.2), and one that shows predominantly relationship difficulties. It should be emphasized that there is no empirical basis for categorizing emotionally disturbed children in this way, but nevertheless it is a classification system that would probably be accepted by many clinicians as reasonable and in conformity with their own clinical experience.

The subcategories of disturbance of emotions could not be rated reliably. Three subcategories—with anxiety (313.0), depression (313.1), and relationship problem (313.3)—had a level of agreement no greater than chance. The kappa of the remaining subcategory—social withdrawal (313.2) ($\kappa = .26$)—indicated very poor interrater reliability.

Children diagnosed in the different subcategories differed remarkably little from each other (see Table 2-9). The groups differed on only four variables. The anxious group had more somatic symptoms than the group with relationship difficulties and had more mental disturbance in the family; the groups with predominantly depression and relationship difficulties had more temper tantrums than the other groups; and the group with relationship difficulties were more likely to have disturbed family relationships. There were no significant differences in predominant sex, age, the majority of the symptoms, family situation, intellectual level, and whether or not there was an associated developmental delay. Thus the UK/WHO study provides no evidence to support this subdivision of disturbances of emotions.

TABLE 2-9. Fourth-Digit Emotional Disorder Category

	(a) Anxious 313.0 (N = 20)		(b) Depression 313.2 (N = 4)		(c) Withdrawn 313.3 (N = 12)		(d) Relationship problems 313.3 (N = 17)		χ^2	p
	N	%	N	%	N	%	N	%		
Demographic										
Age										
≤ 5 years	2	10.0	0	0.0	2	16.7	6	35.3		NS
6-11 years	9	45.0	3	75.0	6	50.0	8	47.1		
12 + years	9	45.0	1	25.0	4	33.3	3	17.6		
Sex (male)	15	75.0	1	25.0	7	58.3	11	64.7		NS
Symptoms										
Short attention span	6	30.0	0	0.0	2	16.7	5	29.4		NS
Overactivity	2	10.0	0	0.0	0	0.0	2	11.8		NS
Generalized anxiety	10	50.0	1	25.0	5	25.0	4	23.5		NS
Somatic symptoms	10	50.0	0	0.0	4	36.4	2	11.8	8.29	.04
Depressed mood	6	30.0	2	50.0	4	33.3	1	5.9		NS
Tempers or tantrums	2	10.0	2	50.0	2	16.7	11	64.7	14.68	.002 ab, ad, cd
Antisocial behavior (nondeliquent socially disapproved behavior)	6	30.0	2	50.0	3	25.0	10	58.8		NS
Solitary delinquency	1	5.0	0	0.0	3	25.0	3	17.6		NS
Delinquency with others	1	5.0	0	0.0	0	0.0	0	0.0		NS
Disturbed family relationship	11	55.0	3	75.0	5	41.7	15	88.2	7.86	.049 ad, cd

	n	%	n	%	n	%	n	%	Statistic	p
Disturbed peer relationships	8	40.0	3	75.0	6	50.0	10	58.8		NS
Educational retardation	7	35.0	0	0.0	5	41.7	2	13.3		NS
Duration (<6 months)	1	5.0	1	25.0	1	8.3	1	6.3		NS
Situation specificity	11	55.0	0	0.0	4	33.3	10	58.8		NS
Current social impairment	13	65.0	4	100.0	8	66.7	11	64.7		NS
Family situation										
Mental disturbance in family	10	50.0	1	25.0	2	16.7	2	11.8	7.75 ad, ac	.05
Discordant intra-familial relationship	3	15.0	2	50.0	1	8.3	7	41.2	6.63	.08
Familial overinvolvement	8	40.0	0	0.0	3	25.0	6	35.3		NS
Inadequate or inconsistent parental control	5	25.0	0	0.0	1	8.3	3	17.6		NS
Parental living situation (both natural parents)	13	65.0	1	25.0	7	58.3	11	64.7		NS
Specific delays in development (Axis II)										
No delay	14	70.0	4	100.0	8	66.7	12	70.6		NS
Reading	2	10.0	0	0.0	2	16.7	1	5.9		NS
Speech/language	3	15.0	0	0.0	1	8.3	4	23.5		NS
Mixed	0	0.0	0	0.0	1	8.3	0	0.0		NS
Intellectual level (Axis III)										
Retardation	0	0.0	0	0.0	1	8.3	0	0.0		NS

Hierarchical Grouping

The possibility that the reliability of psychiatric diagnosis might be improved by grouping similiar three-digit and four-digit diagnoses together into broader "umbrella" categories (see Table 2-10) was examined. The three-digit diagnoses were combined on an a priori basis using clinical judgment (D.S. and M.R.).

The interrater reliability of the umbrella categories is presented in Table 2-11. The reliability of the emotional disorder umbrella ($\kappa = .50$) was considerably higher than the reliability of the two major three-digit diagnoses that comprised this umbrella: disturbance of emotions (313) ($\kappa = .17$) and neurotic disorders (300) ($\kappa = .37$). The emotional disorder umbrella was also more reliable than the combined emotions and neurotic syndrome ($\kappa = .38$). The conduct disorder umbrella did not have a significantly higher reliability ($\kappa = .52$) than the three-digit diagnosis of disturbance of conduct (312) ($\kappa = .48$). The only other umbrella category that had a kappa of above .50 was the depression umbrella. This reliability was considerably higher than its component parts (see Table 2-12). The reliabilities of the remaining umbrella categories—adaptation reaction, mixed, anxiety, and mixed psychosis—were still quite poor. Thus, a hierarchical grouping of similar three-digit and four-digit diagnosis is most advantageous for the emotional and depressive disorders.

TABLE 2-10. Umbrella Categories

Umbrella 1—Adaptation reaction

308   Acute reaction to stress
309   Adjustment reaction

Umbrella 2—Conduct disorder

301.3   Personality disorders—explosive
301.7   Personality disorders—sociopathic
309.3   Adjustment reaction—conduct disturbance
312.0   Disturbance of conduct—unsocialized
312.1   Disturbance of conduct—socialized
312.2   Disturbance of conduct—compulsive
312.8   Disturbance of conduct—other
312.9   Disturbance of conduct—unspecified
314.2   Hyperkinetic—conduct disorder

Umbrella 3—Emotional disorder

300   Neurotic disorders
313   Disturbance of emotions
311   Depressive disorder
308.0   Acute reaction to stress—disturbance of emotions
309.0   Adjustment reaction—brief depressive reaction
309.1   Adjustment reaction—prolonged depressive reaction
309.2   Adjustment reaction—disturbance of other emotions
309.8   Adjustment reactions—other

TABLE 2.10. (cont.)

Umbrella 4—Depressive

296-   Affective psychoses
311-   Depressive disorder
298.0   Other nonorganic psychoses—depressive type
300.4   Neurotic disorders—depression
309.0   Adjustment reaction—brief depressive reaction
309.1   Adjustment reaction—prolonged depressive reaction
313.1   Disturbance of emotions—with misery and unhappiness

Umbrella 5—Mixed

309.4   Adjustment reaction—mixed
312.3   Disturbance of conduct—mixed
308.4   Acute reaction to stress—mixed

Umbrella 6—Anxiety

300.0   Neurotic disorders—anxiety
300.2   Neurotic disorders—phobic
309.2   Adjustment reaction—other emotions
313.0   Disturbance of emotions—anxiety
313.2   Disturbance of emotions—sensitivity

Umbrella 7—Mixed psychosis

295   Schizophrenic psychoses
297   Paranoid states
298[a] Other nonorganic psychoses (except depressive type)

[a]Except 298.0.

TABLE 2-11. Reliability of Umbrella Categories

	Number of cases on which used	Percentage ($N = 1456$)	κ
Adaptation reaction	25	18.8	.22
Conduct disorder	17	19.2	.52
Emotional disorder	24	33.1	.50
Depression	19	15.3	.54
Mixed	20	14.5	.26
Anxiety	20	9.2	.18
Mixed psychosis	2	1.0	.14

TABLE 2-12. Reliability of Diagnostic Components of Depression
Umbrella Category

		Number of cases on which used	Percentage use $(N = 1456)$	κ
296	Affective psychoses	3	0.5	.04
311	Depressive disorder	1	0.1	.00
298.0	Other nonorganic psychoses— depressive type	5	0.7	.26
300.4	Neurotic disorder—depression	12	6.9	.29
309.0	Adjustment reaction—brief depressive reaction	7	1.8	.08
309.1	Adjustment reaction—prolonged depressive reaction	8	2.3	.13
313.1	Disturbance of emotion—with misery and unhappiness	15	3.1	.05

Glossary Effects

ICD-9 uses a descriptive glossary as a guide to coding, whereas DSM-III employs precise, operationally defined diagnostic criteria. It may be that the use of diagnostic criteria in DSM-III is an improvement over the general descriptions in ICD-9. At the present time, however, there has not been enough research with many child psychiatric disorders to warrant the delineation of precise criteria.

Information on the extent to which the descriptive glossary increases the reliability of the ratings of clinical psychiatric syndromes in ICD-9 should be valuable in deciding on which strategy might be employed in a future classification scheme.

A comparison between the rates of agreement among raters who had and who did not have a glossary is presented in Table 2-13. The use of the glossary did improve the overall reliability of the diagnoses. There was a tendency for the glossary to improve the reliability of the diagnoses that had very poor reliability without the glossary—that is, disturbance of emotion (313) ($p < .05$), neurotic disorder (300), and adjustment reaction (309). It appears that specific descriptions of these three diagnostic categories may be required before they can be used with even moderate reliability. The use of the glossary did not make much difference in increasing the reliability of the syndromes that had good interrater agreement without the glossary—psychoses specific to childhood (299), special symptoms (307), and hyperkinetic syndrome (314).

For the case histories where the modal psychiatric diagnosis differed depending on whether the raters had access to the glossary there was a tendency for the diagnosis of adjustment reaction (309) to be used less

TABLE 2-13. Reliability of Axis I Three-Digit Categories as a Function of Use of Glossary (Summary of κ Statistics)

Clinical psychiatric syndrome	Glossary	No glossary	
299 Psychoses specific to childhood	.64	.71	
300 Neurotic disorders	.46	.33	
307 Special symptoms	.69	.66	
309 Adjustment reaction	.33	.22	
312 Disturbance of conduct	.56	.44	
313 Disturbance of emotion	.31	.06	$p < .05$
314 Hyperkinetic syndrome	.65	.68	
Overall κ	.45	.35	$p < .05$

frequently by those raters with the glossary. Instead, the raters with the glossary used the diagnoses neurotic disorder (300) and disturbance of emotions (313). It appears that the glossary yielded a more discriminating use of these three categories.

Difficulties in Coding ICD-9

Each time that a case was rated, the participants were asked to comment on difficulties experienced in using Axis I and the other axes. The percent of raters reporting difficulties on each case history ranged from 3% to 68% (see Table 2-14). The most prevalent difficulty was that the condition could be

TABLE 2-14. Difficulties in Coding

Nature of difficulty	Number of cases on which difficulty is specified	Range within 28 cases (percentage of raters)	Percentage use ($N = 1456$)
Any difficulty in making an Axis I diagnosis	28	3.1–68.0	48.3
Condition could be coded on more than one category	28	4.0–54.0	34.1
No appropriate category available	28	2.0–36.0	18.4
Category used for this case too narrow	26	0.0–28.8	13.6
Category used for this case too broad	26	0.0–11.5	5.4

TABLE 2-15. Difficulties in Coding within Three-Digit Diagnosis

	Percentage of column							
	Psychoses 299 (N = 122)	Neurotic disorder 300 (N = 185)	Special symptoms 307 (N = 133)	Adjustment reaction 309 (N = 257)	Conduct disorder 312 (N = 313)	Emotions 313 (N = 168)	Hyperkinesis 314 (N = 88)
Difficulties with Axis I	21.3%	44.6%	50.4%	58.4%	45.7%	63.1%	40.9% $\chi^2 = 64.7$ $p < .001$
Condition could be coded on more than one category	18.5	35.6	36.4	39.2	35.9	43.9	28.4 $\chi^2 = 23.6$ $p < .001$
No appropriate category available	8.4	14.1	17.8	23.2	13.4	28.7	10.2 $\chi^2 = 35.1$ $p < .001$
Category used for this case too narrow	4.2	14.1	15.5	15.2	11.8	17.1	18.2 $\chi^2 = 14.1$ $p < .05$
Category used for this case too broad	0	5.6	1.6	6.0	6.9	10.4	2.3 $\chi^2 = 21.4$ $p < .01$

coded on more than one category, a finding similar to that for DSM-III (Cantwell, Mattison, Russell, & Will, 1979). The next most frequent complaint was that no appropriate category was available. Similar rates of difficulties were reported in coding the clinical cases. Overall, difficulties in coding psychiatric syndromes were reported for approximately 45% of the cases. There was no significant differences in the rates of difficulties reported by raters with or without the glossary.

The rates of difficulties are presented within three-digit diagnoses for the reliability exercise in Table 2-15. The greatest amount of difficulty was cited within the diagnosis disturbance of emotions (313). The diagnosis with the least difficulties was psychoses specific to childhood (299). It is of interest to note that, in general, those diagnoses with the most difficulties in coding had the lowest kappas—for example, disturbance of emotions and adjustment reaction. Conversely, those diagnoses with the least difficulties in coding had the highest kappas—for example, psychoses specific to childhood, hyperkinetic syndrome, and special symptoms.

CONCLUSIONS

The results of the present study indicate that reliable and valid differentiations can be made between many of the principal clinical psychiatric syndromes on Axis I. However, there are diagnoses that appear to be causing confusion—neurotic disorders, adjustment reaction, and disturbance of emotions. The glossary ameliorates the unreliability in these diagnoses somewhat, but further work is required on the conceptualization and definition of these categories. One possible strategy might be to group the similiar three-digit and four-digit diagnoses to form broader "umbrella" categories. This vastly improved the reliability of the emotional disorder category.

A separate category for the hyperkinetic syndrome was justified by its good reliability and clinically useful differentiation from conduct disturbance in the current ICD-9 trials. The justification for a mixed disorder was less clear-cut. The reliability of this category was quite poor, yet some meaningful distinctions emerged.

Overall, the reliability of the subcategories at the four-digit level were unsatisfactorily low. This was particularly evident for the subclassification of disturbance of emotions. Because this subcategorization also did not show validity, it must be concluded that it lacked justification. However, some evidence was found for the discrimination within the conduct disorder group.

Although the UK/WHO study of the ICD-9 has provided valuable information on the reliability and discriminant validity of the diagnostic codes, it should be emphasized that it is difficult to evaluate the differentiation of codes on cross-sectional data alone. A thorough evaluation will require studies on the response to treatment, follow-up studies of outcome, and biological studies.

Overwhelming similarities exist between the present results of ICD-9, the German study of ICD-9 (see Remschmidt, Chapter 3, this volume), and the studies on DSM-III (Mattison *et al.*, 1979; Mezzich *et al.*, 1985; Strober *et al.*, 1981; Werry *et al.*, 1983; see also Cantwell, Chapter 1, this volume). The overall level of reliability of Axis I diagnoses, the reliabilities of the specific diagnoses, and the difficulties in coding the systems are consistent across studies. The overall interrater agreement in the present study was 59%. The rate reported in the German study of ICD-9 was 62.2% and Mattison *et al.* (1979) reported an average interrater agreement of 54% for Axis I of DSM-III. The specific diagnoses posing a problem in ICD-9, such as adjustment disorder and anxiety disorders, were the same diagnoses that were unreliable in DSM-III, and ICD-9 and DSM-III share their most prevalent difficulty—that the condition could fit within more than one diagnoses (Cantwell *et al.*, 1979).

Thus there are few classification system-specific problems. Problems in the reliability and validity of diagnoses appear to stem from problems of measurement or psychiatric conceptualization rather than from difficulties in a particular classification system. Both ICD-9 and DSM-III include a much more detailed subcategorization of disorders than could be justified on the basis of findings regarding either reliability or validity. There is a need for simplification of both classification schemes. Doubtless, too, other improvements in the structure of the two schemes or the instructions on their usage are possible. Nevertheless, the main conclusion to derive from the studies of both classification schemes that have been undertaken is that there is a pressing need for more basic research into the diagnostic categories themselves. Other chapters in this volume consider such needs with respect to depressive disorders (Rutter, Chapter 11), attention deficit and conduct disorder syndromes (Taylor, Chapter 12), and pervasive developmental disorders (Rutter & Schopler, Chapter 13). However, the findings from the UK/WHO study of ICD-9 indicate that there is an equal need for further research into other types of psychiatric problems, especially the fields of emotional disturbances and of adaptation and stress reaction. In all these diagnostic areas it is crucial that the research be concerned as much with the validity of diagnostic distinctions (see Rutter & Gould, 1985) as with the reliability of psychiatrists' diagnostic categorizations.

REFERENCES

American Psychiatric Association. (1980). *Diagnostic and statistical manual of mental disorders* (3rd ed.). Washington, DC: Author.

Cantwell, D. P., Mattison, R., Russell, A. T., & Will, M. A. (1979). A comparison of DSM-II and DSM-III in the diagnosis of childhood psychiatric disorders: IV. Difficulties in use, global comparison, and conclusions. *Archives of General Psychiatry, 36*, 1227–1228.

Mattison, R., Cantwell, D. P., Russell, A. T., & Will, M. A. (1979). A comparison of DSM-III and DSM-III in the diagnosis of childhood psychiatric disorders: II. Interrater agreement. *Archives of General Psychiatry, 36*, 1217–1222.

Mezzich, A. D., Mezzich, J. E., & Coffman, G. A. (1985). Reliability of DSM-III vs. DSM-II in child psychopathology. *Journal of the American Academy of Child Psychiatry, 24*, 273–280.

Quay, H. (1979). Classification. In H. C. Quay & J. S. Werry (Eds.), *Psychopathological disorders of childhood* (2nd ed.). New York: Wiley.

Quay, H. C. (1980, September). *Comments on conduct disorder, attention deficit disorder and hyperactivity.* Paper presented at the Annual Meeting of the American Psychological Association, Montreal.

Rutter, M., & Gould, M. (1985) Classification. In M. Rutter & L. Hersov (Eds.), *Child psychiatry: Modern approaches* (2nd ed.). Oxford: Blackwell.

Rutter, M. & Shaffer, D. (1980). DSM-III: A step forward or back in terms of the classification of child psychiatric disorders. *Journal of the American Academy of Child Psychiatry, 19*, 371–393.

Rutter, M., Shaffer, D., & Sturge, C. (1975). *A guide to a multiaxial classification scheme for psychiatric disorders in childhood and adolescence.* London: Institute of Psychiatry.

Schachar, R., Rutter, M., & Smith, A. (1981). The characteristics of situationally and pervasively hyperactive children: Implications for syndrome definition. *Journal of Child Psychology and Psychiatry, 22*, 375–392.

Strober, M., Green, J., & Carlson, G. (1981). Reliability of psychiatric diagnosis in hospitalized adolescents: Interrater agreement using DSM-III. *Archives of General Psychiatry, 38*, 141–145.

Trites, R. L., & Laprade, K. (1983). Evidence for an independent syndrome of hyperactivity. *Journal of Child Psychology and Psychiatry, 24*, 573–586.

Werry, J. S., Methven, R. J., Fitzpatrick, J., & Dixon, H. (1983). The interrater reliability of DSM-III in children. *Journal of Abnormal Child Psychology, 11*, 341–354.

3

GERMAN STUDY OF ICD-9

HELMUT REMSCHMIDT

INTRODUCTION

In child psychiatry, classification of disorders is necessary for several reasons. First, progress in understanding psychiatric disorders depends on the ability to differentiate behavior according to important categories (such as symptomatology, similarity and dissimilarity of symptoms, age, developmental stage, etc.). This is a general requirement in all sciences. Second, different disorders require different diagnostic procedures and different treatments. Third, meaningful discussion between child psychiatrists from different countries is possible only if they have a clearly defined and agreed-upon terminology. Fourth, collaborative multicenter studies are possible only on the basis of such agreements.

The criteria for an adequate classification of child psychiatric disorders have been summarized by Rutter and his colleagues (Rutter, 1965; Rutter *et al.*, 1969; Rutter & Gould, 1985: Rutter, Shaffer, & Shepherd, 1975) as follows:

1. The classification must be based on facts, not concepts, and it must be defined in operational terms;
2. The aim is to classify disorders or problems—*not* to classify children as persons;
3. There should not be different classifications for different age periods, although there must be provision for disorders that arise only at a particular age;
4. The classification must be reliable, meaning that terms should be used in the same way by different clinicians;
5. The classification must provide adequate differentiation between disorders;
6. The classification must provide adequate coverage, so that important disorders are not omitted;

Helmut Remschmidt. Klinik und Poliklinik für Kinder und Jugendpsychiatrie, Marburg, West Germany.

7. The differentiation should have validity;
8. There should be logical consistency, so that the system will be based on a constant set of principles with a clear-cut set of precise rules;
9. The classification must convey information that is relevant to the clinical situation and helps in making clinical decisions;
10. The classification must be practicable in ordinary clinical practice.

There is a huge body of experience in the field of classification of child psychiatric disorders, and these endeavors have also stimulated progress in child psychiatry in several fields, including epidemiology, diagnosis, therapy, and rehabilitation. Nonetheless, there are some methodological problems that should be mentioned in this context.

Problems of Sampling

Empirically derived classification systems depend upon samples of individuals. In this field, errors are, of course, possible. A good classification system must be able to introduce disorders from several different samples—for instance, from clinical and epidemiological studies. In this connection we have the problem of a "spectrum of psychopathology," ranging from clear-cut psychopathological states to normality.

Selection of Marker Variables

The selection of key variables that are typical for the disorder discussed is important for an adequate classification of psychiatric disorders. A good example of this problem is provided by the hyperkinetic syndrome. There are different opinions on whether hyperactivity, attention deficit, or impulsivity should be looked upon as the "key symptom." These differences are recognized in the classification system described in the third edition of the *Diagnostic and Statistical Manual of Mental Disorders* (DSM-III) of the American Psychiatric Association (1980).

Complexity of the Disorder

Classification systems always include disorders that differ according to their complexity. Classifications can be made on the level of symptoms or syndromes, which may have different correlations with each other.

Etiology

The best classification system should be based on a clear etiology of the disorder. However, the history of classification systems shows that etiology is no longer the central point of classification. Several reasons are responsible for this development. On the one hand, the etiology of many child psychiatric disorders is not yet clear; on the other hand, there are only a few conditions in which there is a single etiologic factor. Most child psychiatric disorders are multifactorial in origin. The exclusion of etiologic aspects does not mean that etiology is unimportant, but it facilitates a discussion that is not hampered by fruitless theoretical disputes that are unresolvable in the present state of knowledge.

CLASSIFICATION SYSTEMS IN CHILD PSYCHIATRY

Classification systems in child psychiatry may be subdivided into three groups: unidimensional systems, multiaxial systems of clinical origin, and statistically derived multidimensional classification systems.

Unidimensional Systems

The eighth and ninth editions of the World Health Organization's *International Classification of Diseases* (ICD-8 and ICD-9) provide examples of unidimensional systems. ICD-8 (1965) covered the classical psychiatric diagnoses such as psychosis (ICD 290–299), neurosis and personality disorders (ICD 300–316), and mental retardation (ICD 310–315). There were no special categories for child psychiatry and the system was not adequate for the classification of child psychiatric disorders.

ICD-9 (1978) brought a remarkable progress in several aspects. First of all, the classification of depression was better and more finely differentiated. Second, child psychiatric disorders were separately included, with an introduction of the following categories:

- Psychosis with an onset specific to childhood (ICD 299)
- Disturbances of emotions, specific to childhood and adolescence (ICD 313)
- Hyperkinetic syndrome of childhood (ICD 314)
- Specific delays in development (ICD 315)
- Adjustment reaction (ICD 309)
- The not very convincing category "special symptoms or syndromes not elsewhere classified" (ICD 307)

There was also progress in other categories in comparison to ICD-8.

Multiaxial Classification Systems of Clinical Origin

For some time it has been evident that unidimensional classifications in child psychiatry imply a very narrow approach to the process of diagnosis. Developmental factors, intelligence, and psychosocial circumstances are all important for the clinical picture of child psychiatric disorders. Bearing in mind these arguments, an international group under the chairmanship of Michael Rutter began to classify child psychiatric disorders in terms of a multiaxial approach. Meanwhile, the American counterpart, DSM-III, also uses a multiaxial approach derived from clinical experience.

Multiaxial Classification Scheme (MAS)

This classification system was originally conceived as a three-axis system, then extended to a system with four axes, and finally, in 1976, to a multiaxial system with five axes. Axis I was devoted to the clinical psychiatric syndrome using ICD-9 categories; Axis II, developmental lags; Axis III, intelligence; Axis IV, somatic disorders, including neurological conditions; and Axis V, abnormal psychosocial situations. The multiaxial system was introduced into a large number of child psychiatric institutions all over Europe. The experience with the systems in clinical practice, as well as in research, are encouraging. It is also a very good tool for the training of child psychiatrists because it promotes in a remarkable way differential diagnostic thinking and sensibility for the diagnostic process. Remschmidt and Schmidt (1983) have summarized the results and experiences with the multiaxial approach with special reference to the MAS.

Diagnostic and Statistical Manual of Mental Disorders (DSM-III)

Since 1952, the American Psychiatric Association has been engaged in unifying classification systems, a process that led to DSM-III which for the first time uses a multiaxial approach. Table 3-1 shows that there are several similarities to the MAS. In both systems Axis I deals with the clinical psychiatric syndrome and (for children) Axis II is concerned with developmental lags. For adults Axis II is devoted to personality disorders. Axis III shows a difference between the two systems: whereas the MAS introduces intelligence within Axis III, such a category is not included in DSM-III. Both systems, however, include classifications concerning somatic disorders and psychosocial circumstances. In addition, DSM-III includes a judgment of the adaptation level of the patient during the past year. According to Spitzer (1980) and Cantwell (1980), the progress of DSM-III can be seen with respect to the following aspects: a good definition and description of psychiatric disorders; a descriptive approach that is free from etiologic preoccupations; a comprehensive and systematic description of every disorder; the existence of standardized diagnostic criteria; and a multiaxial approach.

TABLE 3-1. Comparison of the Multiaxial Classification Scheme for Psychiatric Disorders in Childhood and Adolescence (MAS) and DSM-III

MAS (1966, 1977)	DSM-III (1980)
I. *Clinical psychiatric syndrome* Categories of ICD-9, including specific child psychiatric categories: 299, psychoses with origin specific to childhood; 300, neurotic disorders; 307, special symptoms or syndromes; 309, adjustment reactions; 312, disturbances of conduct; 313, disturbances of emotions specific to childhood and adolescence; 314, hyperkinetic syndrome of childhood	I. *Clinical psychiatric syndrome* Very differentiated categories partly including ICD-9 with a new chapter on "Disorders usually first evident in infancy, childhood, or adolescence," such as attention deficit disorder (314), anxiety disorders of childhood or adolescence (309.21, 313.21, 313.00), pervasive developmental disorders (299.0x, 299.9x, 299.8x), other disorders of infancy, childhood, or adolescence (313.—)
II. *Specific delays in development* 0, no specific delay; 1, specific reading retardation; 2, specific arithmetic retardation; 3, other specific learning difficulties; 4, developmental speech–language disorders; 5, specific motor retardation; 6, mixed developmental disorders	II. *Specific developmental disorders (for children and adolescents)* 315.00, developmental reading disorder; 315.10, developmental arithmetic disorder; 315.31, developmental language disorders; 315.39, developmental articulation disorder; 307.6, enuresis; 307.7, encopresis; 315.50, mixed specific and 315.90, atypical specific developmental disorders
III. *Intellectual level* Nine categories plus one supplementary (IQ as reference, either measured or estimated)	III. *Physical disorders and conditions* ICD-categories for physical disorders of any kind
IV. *Medical conditions* Categories of ICD-9	IV. *Psychosocial stressors* Presumable specificity of psychosocial stressors as contributors to the development or exacerbation of the current disorder and judgment of their overall severity
V. *Associated abnormal psychosocial situations* 18 heterogeneous psychosocial situations with significant categories such as 01, mental disturbance in other family members; 02, discordant intrafamilial relationships; 03, lack of warmth . . . ; 07, inadequate living conditions; 09, anomalous family situations; 15, persecution or adverse discrimination	V. *Highest level of adaptive functioning past year* 1, superior; 2, very good; 3, good; 4, fair; 5, poor; 6, very poor; 7, grossly impaired; 0, unspecified These categories of adaptive functioning refer to social relations, occupational functioning, and the use of leisure time

Comparison between MAS and DSM-III

Both multiaxial systems have made important progress in classification, but both also have weak points. For example, the ICD-9 group 307 (special symptoms or syndromes not elsewhere classified) comprises an extremely heterogeneous mixture of disturbances, including stammering, anorexia nervosa, tics, sterotyped repetitive movements, specific disorders of sleep, enuresis, encopresis, and psychalgia. A weak point of DSM-III is the absence of a special axis for intelligence factors. Rutter and Shaffer (1980) were critical of several aspects of DSM-III but they expressed the opinion that DSM-III might constitute a milestone in the historical development of classification systems.

Evaluation studies of the multiaxial system (Rutter, Shaffer, & Shepherd, 1975; Remschmidt, Schmidt, & Goebel, 1982, 1983) and of DSM-III (Cantwell, Mattison, Russell, & Will, 1979; Cantwell, Russell, Mattison, & Will 1979; Mattison, Cantwell, Russell, & Will, 1979; Russell, Cantwell, Mattison, & Will, 1979) have given rise to very similar findings. They show that the agreement of experts in classifying global diagnostic categories is fairly good, whereas the agreement diminishes when special subgroups are to be classified. On the whole, both systems can be looked upon as important steps in the direction of an empirically derived classification system in child psychiatry.

Multidimensional Classifications Derived from the Multivariate Statistical Approach

Several attempts have been made to classify behavior disorders on the basis of multivariate statistical procedures, usually applied to rating scales or questionnaires. Factor analysis, cluster analysis, and discriminant functions analysis have all been used. Both Quay (1979) and Achenbach (1980) have reviewed findings on this approach. The studies are in general agreement with respect to six dimensions of behavior (according to Quay, 1979): (1) conduct disorders, (2) symptoms of anxiety and withdrawal, (3) syndromes of immaturity; (4) socialized–aggressive disorders; (5) psychotic syndromes and autism; and (6) syndromes of hyperactivity and hyperkinesis.

There is considerable evidence for the cross-cultural generality of conduct disorders and anxiety–withdrawal symptoms, whereas the generality of immaturity syndromes and socialized–aggressive disorders is less certain (Quay, 1979).

A comparison of these "dimensions of behavior" with categories of the MAS and DSM-III shows important differences (as well as similarities). It will be an important task for the research in the field of classification to bring together the results of these different methodological approaches.

EVALUATION OF THE MULTIAXIAL
CLASSIFICATION SCHEME

Aims of the Study

In 1977 we introduced the WHO multiaxial classification scheme (ICD-8) to German child psychiatry and began to classify all our patients according to this system (Remschmidt & Schmidt, 1977). In order to evaluate this system and the glossary published by Rutter and his colleagues we carried out a study using 28 child psychiatric case histories, which had to be classified by 21 experts during two sessions. The aims of our investigations were as follows:

1. Evaluation of the child psychiatric categories in ICD-9.
2. Evaluation of the categories with reference to the dimension of development (Axis II).
3. Evaluation of the categories concerning abnormal psychosocial circumstances (Axis V).
4. Evaluation of the glossary.

Methodology

This study was carried out during two sessions, one in Berlin (June 30, 1978) and one in Mannheim (November 11, 1978), with the participation of 21 experts, all of whom were qualified child psychiatrists or child psychiatrists in training from the Federal Republic of Germany and West Berlin. The majority of the experts had more than 6 years of experience in child psychiatry. Fourteen of the experts had finished a psychotherapeutic training and three more were receiving such training. All came from child psychiatric institutes—most of them from clinical settings, some from child guidance clinics, and one from private practice.

Table 3-2 shows the design for the evaluation and reliability study, which is identical with the design for the British group. In order to compare our results with those of the British study, we used the same 28 cases, which had been translated into German.

During the first session, all experts received a table including the categories of the multiaxial classification scheme (all axes). None of the experts had had any previous experience with the multiaxial classification scheme or with other schemes using a multiaxial framework.

During the second session, all experts had access to the complete glossary, with clear definitions of the diagnostic categories. The experts were then subdivided into two groups (group A and group B, with 10 and 11 experts respectively). Each group had to classify 14 cases and make symptom ratings. The 14 cases provided to group A in the first session were given to

TABLE 3-2. Design for the Reliability Study

		Trial 1	Trial 2
Group A	Experts 1–11	Cases 1–14	Cases 50–63
Group B	Experts 12–22[a]	Cases 50–63	Cases 1–14

[a]Expert 19 is missing in this trial.

group B in the second session, and vice versa. There was a gap of 5 months between the first and the second sessions. During this time, the experts were asked to classify ten consecutive cases according to the categories of the multiaxial classification scheme in order to gain experience with the system for the second session. There was control over this exercise by the agreement of the experts to send us all the sheets of the ten patients whose disorders had been classified.

Results

Symptomatology

For all of the 28 cases the experts were asked to record the symptoms of the child, using the following categories: 0, symptom not present; 1–3, severity of the symptom; 8, not applicable; and 9, unknown. For each of the cases and each of the items we developed a measure of agreement, based on information theory, redundancy, and entropy. This measure, R, had the value 0 in the case of total nonagreement and the value 1 in the case of complete agreement of all experts. There was a very high interrater agreement concerning "objective items" on the symptom list. Such items included: encopresis (.97 during the first session and .95 during the second session); enuresis (.84 and .86); drug abuse (.97 and .97); delinquency (.97 and .98); and sexual deviations (.92 and .89).

The interrater agreement was lower with respect to items of a more subjective character. Such items included phobias of objects or situations (.38 and .38), disturbed relationships with peers (.36 and .37), and disturbed intrafamilial relationships (.34 and .35). As expected, the results of the first and the second sessions were closely similar.

Axis I (Clinical Psychiatric Syndrome)

The coding of the first axis proved to be the most difficult. The average agreement of all experts concerning fourth-digit ICD codings was 42.4% in the first session and 43.2% in the second session. Of course, there were enormous differences between cases. For instance, there was a very high agreement (more than 90%) on a case of the hyperkinetic syndrome, but a very low agreement on one of disintegrative psychosis.

The reduction of the complexity of the classification process to three-digit ICD codings led to a better interrater agreement, with 53.5% agreement in the first and 62.2% in the second session. A further reduction of the diagnostic categories from the three-digit codes to five global categories (neurotic disorders, psychotic disorders, disturbances of psychosocial behavior, emotional disorders, and hyperkinetic syndromes) led to a still higher interrater agreement. The total interrater agreement, including all five global categories, was 76.2% without the glossary and 78.6% with the glossary. The highest agreement was found for social disorders (87.6% before and 92.0% after using the glossary). The lowest figures concerned the emotional disorders (62.4% before and 66.5% after using the glossary). Of course, it would have been possible to get still higher interrater agreements if one used "pure cases." The interrater agreement goes down if "mixed disorders" or those with "mixed symptomatology" are to be classified.

Axis II (*Specific Delays in Development*)

The mean value of the agreement of all experts concerning all cases was 80.7% for the first session and 75.1% for the second session. Table 3-3 summarizes the findings on agreement concerning the second axis for the first and second sessions. On the whole, there was a good agreement, but it was low in those cases where the developmental factors could not be clearly integrated with the clinical picture.

Axis III (*Intellectual Level*)

For Axis III, too, there was a high interrater agreement in both sessions (see Table 3-4). Of course, high agreement was to be expected in view of the availability of 10 scores in most cases. But there were some cases where intellectual level was not quite clear because the children could not be tested;

TABLE 3-3. Agreement of the Experts Rating the 28 Cases on Axis II (Developmental Impairments)

	Session 1	Session 2
<30%	2	0
31%–50%	1	7
51%–80%	7	7
81%–99%	4	1
100%	14	13
Total	28	28

TABLE 3-4. Agreement of the Experts Rating the 28 Cases on Axis III (Intellectual Level)

	Session 1	Session 2
< 70%	2	0
70%–79%	2	2
80%–89%	1	2
90%–99%	4	9
100%	16 + 3	12 + 3
Total	28	28

hence the experts had to judge the intellectual level according to other information from the case history.

Axis V (Abnormal Psychosocial Situations)

There was relatively good interrater agreement for 18 of the 28 cases. The other 10 cases gave rise to greater disagreement. Comparison of the first and second sessions showed that the glossary did not help, but the glossary did lead to a reduction in the number of categories used per case, dropping from 1.98 to 1.73 between the first and the second trial ($p < .05$). The results for Axis V are not very encouraging. This has to do not only with the complexity of the categories, but also with the definitions, which do not differentiate the categories very clearly. Further development of this axis seems to be very important.

Problems of Coding

All experts reported difficulties during the first session. There was no case that could be classified without any difficulties. Most of the problems concerned the first axis, followed by the problems with Axis V.

Effects of the Glossary

On the whole the glossary had the effect of reducing the number of problem codings between the first and the second trial. In the first trial the experts reported difficulties in 62.1% of instances; in the second, only 45.7%. There were problems with Axis V in 25.9% of instances in the first session and 15.7% in the second.

A very interesting result concerning the glossary involved the relationship between duration of clinical practice in child psychiatry and a specially devised rater score that reflected the extent to which each rater's score agreed. Table 3-5 gives the correlations between the rater scores before and after the knowledge of the glossary with the duration of clinical practice.

TABLE 3-5. Correlations of the Rater Scores with the Experts' Professional Experience in Child and Adolescent Psychiatry in Three- and Four-Digit Classifications (b) before and (a) after Knowing the Glossary

	Four-level classification		Three-level classification	
Correlations	Practice	Significance	Practice	Significance
1 b	.2164	NS	.1734	NS
1 a	−.5730	(.003)	−.7012	(.001)
2 b	.1556	NS	.0156	NS
2 a	−.6250	(.001)	−.6424	(.001)
3 b	.1149	NS	−.0276	NS
3 a	−.5352	(.006)	−.5641	(.004)
4 b	.1087	NS	−.0227	NS
4 b	−.5373	(.006)	−.5881	(.003)

It is evident that before knowledge of the glossary there was a low positive correlation between the rater score and the duration of clinical practice; however, *after* knowledge of the glossary, the correlation was highly negative.

This result is analyzed in a more detailed way in Table 3-6, which shows the mean values of the rater scores with respect to the number of ratings of the experts with shorter practice (less than 6 years) and longer practice (more than 6 years) before and after knowing the glossary.

TABLE 3-6. Mean Values of the Rater Scores (Axis I, Four-Digit Classifications) with Respect to the Number of Ratings of the Experts with Shorter and Longer Practice (b) before and (a) after Knowing the Glossary.

Number of ratings	Practice < 6 years				Practice > 6 years	
	b		a		b	a
1	3.0709			← NS →	3.4416	
	↑	.048		‖	↑	NS
	.002		3.9571	← .038 + →		.000 3.4196
	↓		↑	‖	↓	↑
	3.7218		.001	← NS + →	3.9416	.003
2	↑	.010	↓	‖	↑	NS ↓
	.002		4.6071	← .012 + →		.012 4.0315
	↓		↑	‖	↓	↑
	3.9587		.000	← NS + →	4.0942	.001
3	↑	.002	↓	‖	↑	NS ↓
	NS		4.8417	← .035 + →		NS 4.3143
	↓		↑	‖	↓	↑
	4.0099		.027	← NS + →	4.1118	NS
4		.002	↓	‖		NS ↓
			4.8799	← .028 + →		4.3334

Note. Significance according to the *t* test for dependent and independent samples (+).

There is a very clear difference between the first and the second session for the experts with a shorter clinical experience, which is not true for those experts with a long clinical experience (more than 6 years). This result shows that there is a very good learning effect for those colleagues with a shorter duration of clinical experience. This result applies for the four-digit as well as for the three-digit classifications.

Conclusions

At first glance, the results concerning the interrater agreement on Axis I of the multiaxial classification scheme might not seem very encouraging. There was an overall interrater agreement of under 45% in both the first and second sessions. The interrater agreement could be increased by reduction of the categories to three-digit codings. There was a good agreement concerning Axis II (developmental delays) and on the Axis III (intelligence), with a low agreement on the Axis V (abnormal psychosocial situations). The glossary led to a more specific classification. Thus, there was a shift from the category "neurosis" (ICD 300) to "specific emotional disorders" (313). The glossary also led to a reduction in the number of categories used, which might be interpreted as a gain in adequate diagnostic ability. Also, in the training of young child psychiatrists, the multiaxial classification system and the glossary have proved to be very good instructional instruments, as underlined by the results of our study.

The further development of the multiaxial classification seems to be very important and should be carried out on the basis of the available empirical data. Most of the problems concern Axes I and V. Concerning Axis I (clinical psychiatric syndrome), conclusions should be drawn from the numerous studies on both MAS and DSM-III. It is necessary to compare very carefully the categories of both systems and to come up with some unifying solution based on empirical evidence and clinical practicability.

A recent reliability study was carried out by Goor-Lambo (1984) on Axis V (abnormal psychosocial situations), in which 100 case studies (all taken by the same individual) on children seen at a child psychiatric institution were judged by six raters each, and 40 of the histories were also rated by the history taker. Each of the six raters rerated 20 cases histories after an interval of at least 3 months.

It was found that the level of reliability was adequate for only a few codes and that the differences in reliability were greater between the codes than between the raters. This would indicate that more reliable scoring could be achieved primarily by improving the descriptions for each code that are provided in the glossary. Such an improvement of the description is especially necessary for the categories 02, 03, 04, 05, 06, 08, and 13 (see Figure 3-4 for definitions).

MULTIAXIAL CLASSIFICATION IN BERLIN, MANNHEIM, AND ZURICH

Methodology

In 1979 the child and adolescent psychiatric departments of the universities of Berlin, Mannheim, and Zurich classified all patients according to the multiaxial classification scheme for psychiatric disorders in childhood and adolescence (Rutter, Shaffer, & Sturge, 1979) using its German adaptation (Remschmidt & Schmidt, 1977). Basic data on histories and symptoms, psychopathological and somatic findings, treatment, and prognosis were also available. For the year 1979, a comparable documentation was available on the patient populations of all three departments. Possible reasons for the differences in the incidence of disorders in the three departments included differences in the use of the classification as well as different referral patterns or different populations served in the three catchment areas. The study was carried out in collaboration with Robert Corboz and Martin Schmidt and is reported fully in Remschmidt and Schmidt (1983).

Age Distribution and Social Class

Figure 3-1 shows the age distribution of the patients from the three departments. There was a predominance of adolescents in the Mannheim clinic but

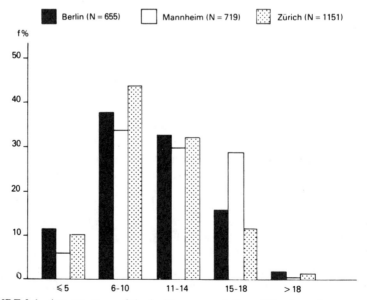

FIGURE 3-1. Age structure of the incidence population of the three departments in 1979 ($\chi^2 = 95.23$; $df = 6$; $p \leq .0001$).

more younger children in Zurich. Social class data were available only for Berlin and Mannheim. In Berlin, there were more patients from the upper classes (12.7% vs. 1.1% for Mannheim). The two clinics did not differ significantly in the proportion from lower social groups (52.6% in Berlin and 54.4% in Mannheim), but Mannheim had more middle-class children (44.5% vs. 34.8%).

Clinical Psychiatric Syndrome (Axis I)

Figure 3-2 gives the distribution of clinical psychiatric syndromes (Axis I) in the three departments. The fact that there were important differences in some categories may reflect variations in habits of classification and interpretation of the glossary, due to different clinical concepts (e.g. the high rate of neurotic disorders in Zurich).

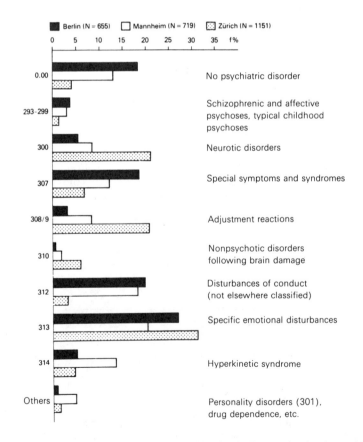

FIGURE 3-2. Distribution of clinical psychiatric syndromes in the three child psychiatric departments in 1979.

Specific Delays in Development (Axis II)

Whereas Berlin and Zurich had closely comparable figures for the presence of some developmental disorder and for subtypes, developmental delays were much less frequently reported at Mannheim (see Table 3-7). It is likely that this pattern was a consequence of the use of the same diagnostic measures for defining developmental delays in Berlin and Zurich, but not in Mannheim.

Intellectual Level (Axis III)

There were no marked differences in intellectual level between the three clinics (see Figure 3-3). As might be expected, in all three there was a slight excess of those with an IQ below 70 compared with an IQ exceeding 130.

Abnormal Psychosocial Situations (Axis V)

Figure 3-4 shows a comparison of the classifications on Axis V for the three incidence populations. There were differences between the three centers for some categories and the question arises as to their origin. This question cannot easily be answered because, although it is known that there are some demographic differences between the three cities, many Axis V categories are not very clearly defined. For example, the rate of divorce/separation in the parents of child psychiatric clinic patients was about 30% for West Berlin, 22% for Mannheim, and 7% for Zurich (Corboz, Schmidt, Remschmidt, Schieber, & Goebel, 1983). Of course, this is reflected also in category 09 (anomalous family situations), which shows a clear difference between the three centers. On the other hand, perhaps it is not so likely that the excess of family members with mental disturbances (category 01) in Zurich was real. Axis V remains a weak point in the multiaxial classification system (see Goor-Lambo, 1984).

TABLE 3-7. Specific Delays in Development

	Code[a]						
	0	1	2, 3	4	5	6	Σ
Berlin	423	58	12	42	25	89	649
	65%	9%	2%	6%	4%	14%	100%
Mannheim	661	26	0	20	1	11	719
	92%	3%	0%	3%	0%	2%	100%
Zurich	745	74	23	64	41	200	1147
	64%	7%	2%	6%	4%	17%	100%

[a]Codes: 0 = no specific delay; 1 = specific reading retardation; 2 = specific arithmetic retardation; 3 = other specific learning diffculties; 4 = developmental speech–language disorder; 5 = specific motor retardation; 6 = mixed developmental disorders.

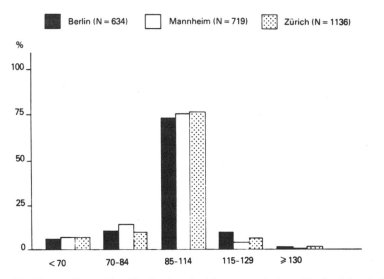

FIGURE 3-3. Intellectual level in the three incidence populations (Berlin, Mannheim, Zurich) in 1979.

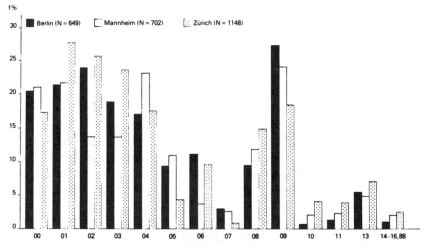

FIGURE 3-4. Abnormal psychosocial situations (fifth axis) in the incidence populations in the three departments in 1979. 00 = no significant distortion or inadequacy of the psychosocial environment; 01 = mental disturbance in other family members; 02 = discordant intrafamilial relationships; 03 = lack of warmth in intrafamilial relationships; 04 = familial overinvolvement; 05 = inadequate or inconsistent parental control; 06 = inadequate social, linguistic, or perceptual stimulation; 07 = inadequate living conditions; 08 = inadequate or distorted intrafamilial communication; 09 = anomalous family situation; 10 = stresses or disturbance in school or work environment; 11 = migration or social transplantation; 13 = other intrafamilial psychosocial stress; 14–16, 88 = others.

CONCLUSIONS

The study has shown that artifacts in classification occur in spite of a glossary that defines the categories. Problems of case definition remain, with consequent difficulties in interpreting nosologic and etiologic findings from different clinics. Similarly, there are difficulties in relating findings on Axes I and V. Investigators cannot generalize from abnormal psychosocial situations to the clinical psychiatric syndrome.

The study showed that artifacts might be produced not only by unclear glossary definitions but also by preoccupations of the investigators, especially concerning more "introspective" diagnoses. Finally the incidence of certain diagnoses is also dependent on the interests of the investigators. If one is looking for certain syndromes, one will find more of them. On the other hand, if people know that there is a special treatment for certain disorders available at a particular clinic, more of them will be likely to use that clinic.

Naturally, there are also real differences between the three clinical institutions. For instance, disturbances of conduct seem to be less prevalent in Switzerland than in Germany.

On the basis of our study, the following general statements are appropriate.

1. Multiaxial classification systems have been widely introduced into clinical practice and research in child psychiatry all over the world.
2. This development implies a great progress for training and mutual understanding of child psychiatrists in different countries. It promotes general knowledge about psychiatric disorders in children and adolescents and facilitates transcultural multicenter studies.
3. There are differences between findings based on clinically derived multiaxial systems and those based upon multivariate statistical approaches.
4. The evaluation of both multiaxial systems (MAS and DSM-III) as well as the studies using the multivariate statistical approach are encouraging, but much remains to be done to improve systems of classification.

REFERENCES

Achenbach, T.M. (1980). DSM-III in the light of empirical research on the classification of child psychopathology. *Journal of Child Psychiatry, 19,* 395–412.
American Psychiatric Association. (1980). *Diagnostic and statistical manual of mental disorders* (3rd ed.). Washington, DC: Author.
Cantwell, D. P., (1980). The diagnostic process and diagnostic classification in child psychiatry—DSM-III. Introduction. *Journal of Child Psychiatry, 19,* 345–355.
Cantwell, D. P., Mattison, R., Russell, A. T., & Will, L. (1979). A comparison of DSM-II and DSM-III in the diagnosis of childhood psychiatric disorders. IV. Difficulties in use, global comparison, and conclusions. *Archives of General Psychiatry, 36,* 1227–1228.

Cantwell, D. P., Russell, A. T., Mattison, R., & Will, L. (1979). A comparison of DSM-II and DSM-III in the diagnosis of childhood psychiatric disorders. I. Agreement with expected diagnosis. *Archives of General Psychiatry, 36*, 1208–1213.

Corboz, R., Schmidt, M., Remschmidt, H., Schieber, P., & Gobel, D. (1983). Multiaxiale Klassifikation in Berlin, Mannheim und Zurich. In H. Remschmidt & M. Schmidt (Eds.), *Multiaxiale Diagnostik in der Kinder- und Jugendpsychiatrie*. Bern-Stuttgart-Wien: Huber.

Goor-Lambo, G. van. (1984). Wie zuverlassig ist die Achse V? Eine intersubjektive und intra-subjektive Zuverlassigkeitsuntersuchung der Achse V des multiaxialen Klassifikations-schemas und deren Konsequenzen. *Zeitschrift für Kinder- und Jugendpsychiatrie, 12*, 62–78.

Mattison, R., Cantwell, D. P., Russell, A. T., & Will, L. (1979). A comparison of DSM-II and DSM-III in the diagnosis of childhood psychiatric disorders. II. Interrater agreement. *Archives of General Psychiatry, 36*, 1217–1222.

Quay, H. C. (1979). Classification. In H. D. Quay & J. S. Werry (Eds.), *Psychopathological disorders of childhood*. New York: Wiley.

Remschmidt, H., & Schmidt, M. (Eds.). (1977). *Multiaxiales Klassifikationsschema für psychia-trische Erkrankungen im Kindes- und Jugendalter nach Rutter, Shaffer und Sturge*. Bern-Stuttgart-Wien: Huber.

Remschmidt, H., & Schmidt, M. (Eds.). (1983). *Multiaxiale Diagnostik in der Kinder- und Jugendpsychiatrie*. Bern-Stuttgart-Wien: Huber.

Remschmidt, H., Schmidt, M., & Goebel, D. (1982, July). *Evaluation and reliability study on the multiaxial classification scheme for psychiatric disorders in children and adolescents*. Paper presented at the 10th Congress of the IACAP and AP, Dublin.

Remschmidt, H., Schmidt, M., & Goebel, D. (1983). Erprobungs- und Reliabilitatsstudie zum multiaxialen Klassifikationsschema für psychiatrische Erkrankungen im Kindes- und Jugendalter. In H. Remschmidt & M. Schmidt (Eds.), *Multiaxiale Diagnostik in der Kinder- und Jugendpsychiatrie*. Bern-Stuttgart-Wien: Huber.

Russell, A. T., Cantwell, D. P., Mattison, R., & Will, L. (1979). A comparison of DSM-II and DSM-III in the diagnosis of childhood psychiatric disorders. III. Multiaxial features. *Archives of General Psychiatry, 36*, 1223–1226.

Rutter, M. (1965). Classification and categorization in child psychiatry. *Journal of Child Psychology and Psychiatry, 6*, 71–83.

Rutter, M., & Gould, M. (1985). Classification. In M. Rutter & L. Hersov (Eds.), *Child and adolescent psychiatry: Modern approaches* (2nd ed.). Oxford: Blackwell.

Rutter, M., Lebovici, S., Eisenberg, L., Sneznevskij, A. V., Sadoun, R., Brooke, E., & Lin, T.-Y. (1969). A triaxial classification of mental disorders in childhood. *Journal of Child Psychology and Psychiatry. 10*, 41–61.

Rutter, M., & Shaffer, D. (1980). DSM-III. A step forward or back in terms of the classification of child psychiatric disorders? *Journal of the American Academy of Child Psychiatry, 19*, 371–394.

Rutter, M., Shaffer, D., & Shepherd, M. (1975). *A multi-axial classification of child psychiatric disorders*. Geneva: World Health Organization.

Rutter, M., Shaffer, D., & Sturge, C. (1979). *A guide to a multiaxial classification scheme for psychiatric disorders in childhood and adolescence*. London: Institute of Psychiatry.

Spitzer, R. L. (1980). Classification of mental disorders and DSM-III. In H. I. Kaplan, A. M. Freedman, & B. J. Sadock (Eds.), *Comprehensive textbook of psychiatry*. Baltimore: Williams & Wilkins.

World Health Organization. (1965). *International classification of diseases* (8th ed.). Geneva: Author.

World Health Organization (1978). *International classification of diseases* (9th ed.). Geneva: Author.

II

MEASUREMENT INSTRUMENTS

4

STRUCTURED PSYCHIATRIC INTERVIEWS FOR CHILDREN

CRAIG EDELBROCK
ANTHONY J. COSTELLO

INTRODUCTION

There has been considerable effort in the past few years toward improving psychiatric interviewing procedures for children and adolescents. The development of structured interviewing procedures has been motivated to a large extent by dissatisfaction with the reliability and validity of traditional child diagnostic procedures. Efforts in the child area have been spurred by the development of structured interview schedules for adults, which have been found to boost diagnostic reliability substantially (Endicott & Spitzer, 1978; Robins, Helzer, Croughan, & Ratcliff, 1981). The development of more differentiated taxonomies of child disorders and more explicit diagnostic criteria has also demanded a more standardized approach to the assessment of child symptoms. Examples of these criteria include those described in the third edition of the *Diagnostic and Statistical Manual of Mental Disorders* (DSM-III) of the American Psychiatric Association (1980), and the ninth edition of the *International Classification of Diseases* (ICD-9) of the World Health Organization (1978), as well as Research Diagnostic Criteria (RDC).

Structured interviewing has certain advantages over other assessment methods such as direct observation, psychological testing, and paper-and-pencil questionnaires. Face-to-face interviews are useful for establishing rapport with the respondent and they are generally good at maintaining interest. They also provide a means of clarifying misunderstandings, resolving ambiguous responses, and documenting the context and chronicity of child symptoms. Interviewing is also one way of obtaining self-report data from children. Although the assessment of child psychopathology still depends

Craig Edelbrock and Anthony J. Costello. Department of Psychiatry, University of Massachusetts Medical Center, Worcester, Massachusetts.

heavily on data from adults, children are now viewed as valuable informants regarding their own feelings, behaviors, and social relationships. Anamnestic and symptom-oriented interviews have proved feasible with children, including children too young to complete written self-report measures.

Several psychiatric interview schedules for children and adolescents are available, but few have reached a stage of development acceptable for clinical research. Compared to other assessment procedures, structured interviewing in child psychiatry is relatively new. The development of structured interviews for children can be traced to early efforts by Lapouse and Monk (1958) and Rutter and Graham (1968), but most of the work in this area has been in the last decade. Current interview schedules for children are also undergoing constant revision and refinement. None has reached final form, and all face unsolved conceptual, methodological, and technical problems and issues.

The handful of structured interview procedures showing promise as research tools vary widely, and there are few grounds for direct comparison. All provide a list of target behaviors, symptoms, and events to be covered, and guidelines for conducting the interview and recording responses. However, the nature of the target phenomena to be assessed, and the degree of structure imposed on the interviewer varies. Some interviews are *semistructured* in that they provide only general and flexible guidelines for conducting the interview and recording information. Others are *highly structured* in that they specify the exact order, wording, and coding of each item. Degree of structure is closely related to interviewer training and the degree of clinical inference involved in the assessment process. Because they permit greater latitude in phrasing questions, pursuing alternative lines of inquiry, and interpreting responses, semistructured interviews are usually designed for clinically sophisticated interviewers. Highly structured interviews, on the other hand, minimize the role of clincial inference in the interview process and can be administered by lay interviewers having only instrument-specific training.

Interview schedules also differ in information yield. Most procedures yield information about the presence, absence, severity, onset, and/or duration of individual symptoms. Others yield quantitative scores in symptom areas, or global indices of maladjustment or psychopathology. A few were designed to yield psychiatric diagnoses. Most interview schedules are designed for parents, but many have parallel formats for parent and child and few are designed exclusively for interviewing children. Structured interviews differ in many other ways, including item content and coverage, age range, and applications.

The purpose of this chapter is to review and compare structured psychiatric interviews for children and adolescents. The focus is on interview schedules that have reached an advanced stage of development and show promise in clinical research. Our discussion of each interview will cover four broad areas: *description, information yield, psychometric properties*, and *applications*.

We aim first to describe each interview, including its length, organization, style, and format; coding and response scaling; degree of structure; informant; training requirements; adminstration time; and recommended age range. The information yield of each procedure will be discussed, including the presence/absence, severity, and duration of individual symptoms; scores for various dimensions, symptom clusters, or syndromes; global indices of maladjustment or psychopathology; and diagnoses according to a specific taxonomic system such as DSM-III, ICD-9, or RDC.

The psychometric properties of each interview schedule, including reliability and validity, will be reviewed. Unfortunately, direct comparisons among interviews are limited by the use of different reliability procedures and validity criteria. Even when the same type of reliability is reported, there are often major statistical and procedural differences which preclude comparative analyses. Test–retest reliability, for example, often entails different statistics (percent agreement, kappa, correlations), retesting intervals (days, weeks, or months), interviewers (same or different), informants, levels of analysis (i.e., symptoms, summary scores, or diagnoses) and interviewing procedures. Likewise, validation procedures vary widely. It is possible, for example, to discuss the *sensitivity* and *specificity* of most interview schedules, but only in relation to vastly different criteria such as referral for mental health services, psychiatric diagnosis, or clinical judgments of psychiatric impairment. Nevertheless, it seems worthwhile to report what is known about the performance of each interview schedule, as long as we add cautions about the potential for misleading conclusions regarding relative performance. That is, the subject samples, reliability procedures and validity criteria vary so widely from study to study that meaningful comparisons among measures are often precluded. Last, we will review applications such as screening and identification of disturbed children, selection of subjects for research, differential diagnosis, and the assessment of change over time and in response to treatment.

REVIEW OF INTERVIEW SCHEDULES

Behavioural Screening Questionnaire

The Behavioural Screening Questionnaire (BSQ) was developed as a means of identifying psychiatrically disturbed preschool-age children (Richman & Graham, 1971) (see Table 4-1). The BSQ is a parent interview comprising approximately 60 questions concerning the health, behavior, and development of the child. The time frame varies from item to item and ranges from "now" to the previous year. The BSQ can be considered a semistructured interview. The items are designed to be read as written, but can be supplemented "until the interviewer feels comfortable about the rating" (Richman & Graham, 1971, p. 7). As such, the BSQ has been administered by trained

TABLE 4-1. Behavioural Screening Questionnaire

Description	
Item content:	60 items covering the behavior, health, and development of the child; 12-item behavior scale used for screening
Response scaling:	0–1–2 (absent/sometimes or mild/frequent or severe)
Administration time:	20–30 minutes for entire interview; 10–20 minutes for 12-item behavior scale
Degree of structure:	Semistructured
Informant:	Parent (usually the mother)
Age range:	Preschool (3–5 years)
Interviewer:	Advanced clinical
Training:	Brief orientation, practice
Alternate forms:	Rating scale format for 12-item behavior scale
Information yield	
Individual symptoms:	Present/absent; frequency/severity
Summary scales:	12-item behavior scale
Diagnoses:	N/A
Psychometric properties	
Reliability:	
Test–retest:	$r = .77$ (different interviewers)
Interrater:	$r = .94$ (videotaped interviews)
Interinformant:	N/A
Other:	N/A
Validity:	Discriminates significantly between clinically referred ($n = 20$) and nonreferred ($n = 57$) groups Sensitivity: 70%; specificity: 91.2% Correlates significantly with clinicians' ratings of psychiatric status
Applications	
Primary:	Screening and early identification
Secondary:	Measurement of change

clinicians, rather than lay interviewers. Parents' responses are rated on a scale of 0–2, where 0 indicates that the behavior is *absent*; 1, that it occurs sometimes or to a mild degree; and 2, that it occurs frequently or to a marked degree. The wording of BSQ items is simple, and questions are readily understood by most parents. The BSQ requires about 20–30 minutes for the typical child.

The behavior scale of the BSQ was constructed from the 12 items that discriminated best between clinically referred and nonreferred groups. Interrater reliability of the behavior scale was $r = .77$ for separate interviews of parents by two clinicians and $r = .94$ for independent ratings of taped interviews. Individual items were moderately reliable (average $r = .44$, range $I = .15-.77$). Validity of the BSQ has been explored by comparing 20 children referred for psychiatric services with 57 normal controls. A cutoff score of 11 out of a possible 24 points on the behavior scale yielded a sensitivity of 70% and a specificity of 91.2%. Richman (1977) has also developed a parallel paper-and-pencil version of the BSQ which rivals the interview version in reliability and screening efficiency.

The validity of the BSQ has been supported in numerous studies (Earls, 1980a, 1980b; Earls, Jacobs, Goldfein, Silbert, Beardslee, & Rivinus, 1982; Earls & Richman, 1980a, 1980b; Richman, 1977; Richman, Stevenson, & Graham, 1975). Earls *et al.* (1982), for example, found that BSQ scores correlated $r = .69, .57$, and $.58$ with averaged clinicians' ratings of severity of psychiatric disorder, need for intervention, and prognosis, respectively. However, the clinicians' ratings were based in part on a summary of the BSQ interview, so to some degree these correlations reflect shared information. Using clinicians' ratings of moderate to severe psychiatric disorder as the criterion for psychopathology, a cutoff score of 11 yielded a sensitivity of 64% and a specificity of 98% for a sample of 70 preschoolers. Dropping the cutoff score to 8 boosted sensitivity to 100% but reduced specificity to 70% (see Earls *et al.*, 1982, p. 54).

In sum, the BSQ has a limited age range and information yield but can be recommended as a means of screening preschool-age children for broad-spectrum behavioral deviations. The interview version, however, appears to have no advantages over the rating scale version which is much less costly and time consuming to administer in large-scale screening efforts.

Child Screening Inventory

The Child Screening Inventory (CSI) was developed by Langner *et al.* (1976) as a means of assessing psychiatric impairment in children aged 6–18 (see Table 4–2). The 35-item screening measure was developed from a 2- to 3-hour structured interview administered to parents of more than 2,000 children residing in Manhattan. The initial pool of 654 items was reduced to 287 items by eliminating low-frequency items and pooling items of similar content. Factor analysis yielded seven factors, which were labeled Self-Destructive Tendencies, Mentation Problems, Conflict with Parents, Regressive Anxiety, Fighting, Delinquency, and Isolation. Only the five highest-loading items were retained for each of the seven factors, producing a 35-item inventory that requires only 15–20 minutes to administer.

Test–retest and interinterviewer reliabilities were not reported. The scales have mediocre internal consistency (coefficient alpha averaged .49). Total scores correlated $r = .69$ with total impairment ratings derived from the entire interview, but correlated only $r = .33$ with psychiatrists' ratings of psychiatric impairment based on direct examination of the child, and only

TABLE 4-2. Child Screening Inventory

Description	
Item content:	35 items covering emotional and behavioral problems
Response scaling:	Varies (present/absent; frequency; severity)
Administration time:	15–20 minutes
Degree of structure:	Semistructured
Informant:	Parent
Age range:	6–18 years
Interviewer:	At least some training in psychology or social work
Training:	Brief orientation, practice
Alternate forms:	N/A
Information yield	
Individual symptoms:	Present/absent; frequency; severity
Summary scales:	7 factor-based scales; total score
Diagnoses:	N/A
Psychometric properties	
Reliability:	
Test–retest:	Not reported
Interrater:	Not reported
Interinformant:	Not reported
Other:	Internal consistency (alpha) averaged .46
Validity:	Total score correlated $r = .33$ with psychiatrists' ratings of psychiatric impairment and $r = .49$ with treatment referral
	Discriminates significantly between normal children and children judged by psychiatrists to have marked or severe psychiatric impairment
	Sensitivity: 38.5–67.2%; specificity: 91.8–95.9%
Applications	
Primary:	Descriptive tool (not recommended as a screening device)
Secondary:	N/A

$r = .49$ with treatment referral status. Taking psychiatrists' ratings of "marked or severe psychiatric impairment" as the criterion for child psychopathology, total score had a sensitivity of 67.2% and specificity of 91.8% in a cross-sectional sample of 1,034 randomly selected children. For a welfare sample of 1,000 children, total score had specificity of 95.9%, but sensitivity was only 38.5%. In other words, the CSI produce numerous false negatives. The authors have therefore recommended that this measure be used as a descriptive tool, rather than as a screening device (Langner *et al.*, 1976, p. 286).

The CSI is unique among structured interviews in having factor-based behavior problem scales. Beyond that distinction, however, the CSI has several weaknesses that preclude its use as a screening device. Test–retest and interinterviewer reliability data are lacking and validation is weak. The CSI was developed as a screening procedure, but cannot be recommended for that purpose due to weak validation and low sensitivity. It may have some utility as a descriptive tool, but as such it may be inferior to more rigorously developed and standardized behavior checklists and rating scales.

Kiddie-SADS

The Kiddie-SADS (Puig-Antich & Chambers, 1978) (see Table 4-3) is a semistructured diagnostic interview for children aged 6–17 modeled after the Schedule for Affective Disorders and Schizophrenia (SADS) designed for adults (Endicott & Spitzer, 1978). The Kiddie-SADS (or K-SADS) covers current psychopathology and is scorable in terms of DSM-III diagnostic criteria and Research Diagnostic Criteria for major affective disorders, as well as other disorders of childhood. It is administered by clinically sophisticated interviewers who are familiar with RDC and the DSM-III and have received extensive interview-specific training.

The standard procedure is to interview the parent first about the psychiatric status of the child. During the subsequent interview of the child, the interviewer attempts to resolve any discrepancies between parent and child. The first 15–20 minutes of the K-SADS is an unstructured interview designed to establish rapport, obtain a history of the present illness, and determine current symptoms, their severity and chronicity. Onset of the current disorder is described and previous treatment is noted. The interviewer then begins the more structured sections of the K-SADS, which are focused on specific symptoms. This portion takes about 30–40 minutes with clinically referred children.

Each section includes an item to be rated (e.g., depressed mood) on a 1–6 scale ranging from not at all to very extreme. Prompts are provided (e.g., Have you felt sad? Have you cried?) as guidelines for the interviewer. Interviewers have considerable flexibility in choosing the line of inquiry and the wording of questions. They are also encouraged to ask as many questions as needed to substantiate symptom ratings. The K-SADS also embodies a skip structure, which substantially reduces interviewing time with children having few symptoms. If the response to an initial screening question or "probe" is negative, subsequent questions can be skipped. After completing the structured sections, the interviewer rates 11 observational items (e.g., appearance, affect, attention, motor behavior) and rates the reliability and completeness of the entire interview. The interviewer then completes a global assessment scale reflecting overall level of functioning.

The K-SADS yields information on the presence and/or severity of 49

TABLE 4-3. Kiddie-SADS

Description	
Item content:	More than 100 items cover 49 symptom areas (onset, severity, and duration); primary focus is on major affective disorders 11 observational items; Global Assessment Scale
Response scaling:	Symptoms are rated 1 (not at all) to 6 (extreme)
Administration time:	Unstructured portion takes 15–20 minutes, structured portion takes 30–40 minutes
Degree of structure:	Semistructured
Informant:	Parent and child
Age range:	6–16 years
Interviewer:	Advanced clinical
Training:	Very extensive clinical and instrument-specific training required
Alternate forms:	Same format for parent and child Epidemiologic version (K-SADS-E) covers past and current episodes of psychopathology
Information yield	
Individual symptoms:	Present/absent; severity
Summary scales:	12 summary scales; Global Assessment Scale
Diagnoses:	Covers RDC and DSM criteria for major affective disorders and other child disorders
Psychometric properties	
Reliability:	
Test–retest:	Short-term (2- to 3-day) reliabilities averaged .55 for items (intraclass correlation), .68 for summary scales Reliabilities ranged from .24 to .70 for diagnoses (kappa statistic)
Interrater:	Not reported
Interinformant:	Parent–child agreement (intraclass correlation) averaged .53 for symptoms (range = −.08–.96)
Other:	Internal consistency (alpha) averaged .66 for 12 summary scales (range = .25 to .86)
Validity:	Strong content validity; presumptive evidence of ability to identify children with major affective disorders; preliminary evidence suggests may be useful in elucidating biological correlates of major depression in children and in monitoring treatment effects
Applications	
Primary:	Diagnostic tool used for selecting research subjects meeting specific diagnostic criteria
Secondary:	Measurement of change (some items)

core symptoms: 23 pertain to primary depressive syndrome and 9 to clinical features associated with depression (e.g., suicidal ideation, social withdrawal). The remaining 16 areas cover somatization, nondepressive neurotic disorders, conduct disorder, and psychotic disorder. The K-SADS also yields 12 scores on summary scales, 4 of which are hierarchically related depression scales comprising 2, 9, 12, and 17 items. Five additional scales have been adapted from the SADS (depressed mood and ideation, endogenous features, depression-associated features, suicidal ideation and behavior, anxiety). The three remaining scales reflect somatization, emotional disorder, and conduct disorder. The K-SADS data can also be translated into RDC or DSM-III diagnostic criteria for major and minor depressive disorder, conduct disorder, and neurotic disorder. Diagnoses are based on a diagnostician's overview of the interview responses, as opposed to computer algorithms applied to K-SADS data.

The short-term (2- to 3-day) test–retest reliability of the K-SADS has recently been evaluated on a sample of 52 psychiatrically referred children aged 6–17 (Chambers *et al.*, 1985). Individual symptom items were moderately reliable (average intraclass correlation = .55, range = .09–.89). Higher reliabilities were obtained for the 12 summary scales (average intraclass correlation = .68, range = .41–.81). The reliability of diagnoses ranged from .24 to .70 (kappa statistic).

The K-SADS has strong content validity in that it was designed to tap prespecified diagnostic criteria. Its primary use has been in selecting children who meet criteria for major affective disorders (Puig-Antich, Blau, Marx, Greenhill, & Chambers, 1978). Two preliminary investigations also suggest that the K-SADS may be useful for elucidating biological correlates of child depression and for detecting treatment effects. Children meeting RDC for major depression have reportedly demonstrated overnight and 24-hour cortisol hypersecretion—a neuroendocrine abnormality seen in approximately 50% of adult depressed patients (Puig-Antich, Chambers, Halpern, Hanlon, & Sachar, 1979). However, these provocative findings were based on only four subjects; only two showed the abnormality, and only one of those two had been diagnosed using the K-SADS. The K-SADS has also been shown to be sensitive to the effects of imipramine treatment of affective disorders in prepubertal children (Puig-Antich, Perel, *et al.*, 1979). However, treatment effects were seen only for the two-item depression summary score, and statistical significance was obtained only in post hoc analyses of a selected subsample of treated patients (i.e., nondelusional depressives). Both of these preliminary findings require further extension and replication.

An epidemiologic version of the K-SADS (K-SADS-E) has been developed to assess lifetime psychopathology in children aged 6–17 (Orvaschel, Puig-Antich, Chambers, Tabrizi, & Johnson, 1982). The K-SADS-E parallels the K-SADS, except that most questions are worded "Have you *ever* done X?" Diagnoses based on the K-SADS-E have been compared with diagnoses of current status (K-SADS) completed 6 months to 2 years earlier.

Of 17 patients, 16 obtained the same diagnosis with the K-SADS-E as with the previous K-SADS interview.

In sum, the K-SADS was developed as a means of selecting subjects for research on childhood depression, and it serves that purpose well. To the extent that it taps symptoms in other areas, it could also be useful in differential diagnosis. Reliability is adequate in most areas. Validation is preliminary and limited primarily to the area of child depression. A major strength of the K-SADS is the high degree of precision and detail in assessing child symptoms, their onset, severity, duration, and associated impairments. It is limited, however, in its focus on affective disorders and it requires extensive clinical and instrument-specific training. Explicit diagnostic algorithms have not been developed, so diagnoses are formulated by expert judgment.

Diagnostic Interview for Children and Adolescents

The Diagnostic Interview for Children and Adolescents (DICA) was developed by Herjanic and her colleagues at Washington University in St. Louis (see Table 4-4). The DICA is a highly structured diagnostic interview in which the order, wording, and coding of all items are specified. It can be administered to parents or children age 6 and older and takes approximately 30–40 minutes to complete. It can be administered by clinicians and lay interviewers having extensive instrument-specific training. The interview covers the frequency and duration of a broad range of child symptoms. The version for parents includes questions about developmental history, family history, and socioeconomic status.

Symptom items are designed to be coded either "yes" or "no," and ambiguous responses (e.g., "sometimes") can be resolved by considering subsidiary questions about frequency, onset, duration, severity, and functional impairment. Most of the interview is organized thematically (e.g., behavior at school, behavior at home, relationships with peers), but some parts cover specific content areas (e.g., drug and alcohol abuse) and other sections are organized around psychiatric syndromes (e.g., depression, mania, anxiety). Like the K-SADS, the DICA employs a skip structure to reduce interviewing time with children having few symptoms.

The DICA yields information on the presence/absence of 185 symptoms, as well as their onset, duration, severity, and associated impairments (Herjanic & Reich, 1982). The interview also yields summary scores reflecting number of symptoms in six content areas: relationship problems, school behavior, school learning, neurotic symptoms, somatic symptoms, and psychotic symptoms (Herjanic & Campbell, 1977). Additionally, DICA responses have been translated into categorizations that parallel ICD-9 diagnoses (Reich, Herjanic, Weiner, & Gandhy, 1982) and recent revisions of the interview have been cross-indexed against the DSM-III.

Two interrater reliability studies using videotaped interviews have been

TABLE 4-4. Diagnostic Interview for Children and Adolescents

Description	
Item content:	Approximately 200 items covering child symptoms, onset, duration, and impairments
Response scaling:	Most symptoms involve three steps (no/sometimes/yes)
Administration time:	30–40 minutes
Degree of structure:	Highly structured
Informant:	Parent or child
Age range:	6 years and older
Interviewer:	Clinicians or lay interviewers
Training:	Extensive instrument-specific training
Alternate forms:	N/A
Information yield	
Symptoms:	Approximately 200 symptom items
Scales:	Has been scored in six content areas: relationship problems, school behavior, school learning, neurotic symptoms, somatic symptoms, and psychotic symptoms
Diagnoses:	ICD-9 (early versions), DSM-III
Psychometric properties	
Reliability:	
Test–retest:	N/A
Interrater:	85%–89% agreement on child symptoms rated from vidoetapes
Interinformant:	Parent–child agreement on child symptoms averaged .22 (kappa)
Other:	N/A
Validity:	Discriminated significantly between matched samples of pediatric and psychiatric referrals
Applications	
Primary:	Epidemiologic surveys
Secondary:	Symptom inventory in clinical research

published (Herjanic & Reich, 1982). In the first study, ten interviewers independently coded two taped interviews with children. Agreement on symptom items averaged 85%. In the second study, five psychiatrists coded the same child interview twice, over a 2- 3-month interval. Within-interviewer agreement on individual symptoms averaged 89% (range = 80%–95%). Parent–child agreement on DICA items has also averaged about 80% (Herjanic, Herjanic, Brown, & Wheatt, 1975). These figures are misleading, however, because most DICA items refer to symptoms that are rare. High percentages of agreement are expected by chance and they primarily reflect agreement regarding the absence, rather than presence, of any problems. The statistic kappa (Cohen, 1960) corrects for chance level of agreement and provides a more realistic picture of level of agreement. For 168 DICA items tapping psychiatric symptoms, parent–child agreement averaged only .22 (Herjanic & Reich, 1982). Parent–child agreement on diagnoses was only slightly better, with the majority being below .40 (Reich et al., 1982).

The validity of the DICA is supported by its ability to discriminate significantly between matched samples of children referred to either pediatric or psychiatric clinics ($n = 50$ for each group). Summary scores for relationship problems and academic problems provided the best discrimination between criterion groups, whereas scores in the areas of neurotic and somatic symptoms provided the poorest discrimination (Herjanic & Campbell, 1977). The groups also overlapped considerably on symptom scores. This was particularly true among children aged 6–8. For relationship problems, which provided the best discrimination, sensitivity was 72% and specificity was 76%. These results are also limited by the fact that scores were derived from a composite interview combining parent and child responses in different areas. Parent data were used in the areas of relationship problems, school behavior, and academic problems, whereas child data were used in the areas of neurotic, somatic, and psychotic symptoms. Thus, it is impossible to determine the discriminative power of either informant alone, and better discrimination might have been obtained by combining parent and child data in a more statistically rigorous way (e.g., multiple discriminant analysis).

The DICA has broad diagnostic coverage, and its high degree of structure and minimal training requirements make it suitable for large-scale epidemiologic studies. Interrater reliability seems adequate, but test–retest data are lacking. Validation is weak and rests primarily upon one study comparing pediatric and psychiatric referrals. Even in that study, the sensitivity and specificity of the DICA were mediocre. Further validation is needed before the DICA can strongly be recommended for use in clinical reasearch.

Mental Health Assessment Form

The Mental Health Assessment Form (MHAF) was developed by Kestenbaum and Bird (1978) as a means of recording the results of a semistructured interview with children aged 7–12 (see Table 4-5). The 168-item MHAF is loosely structured and is organized in two parts: (1) a mental status exam covering appearance, speech, motor behavior, relatedness, affect, language, and thinking, and (2) a symptom section dealing with affective symptoms, relationships, dreams and fantasies, self-concept, conscience, and level of adaptation. Most items are rated on a 1 to 5 scale reflecting *no deviation* to *marked deviation* from expected. Guidelines for expected behaviors and responses are provided, but the interview requires a high degree of clinical judgment and inference and is recommended only for clinically trained personnel. Little is known about the reliability and validity of the MHAF.

TABLE 4-5. Mental Health Assessment Form

Description	
Item content:	168 items covering mental status and symptoms
Response scaling:	Symptom items are rated 1–5 (no deviation from expected to marked deviation)
Administration time:	Not reported
Degree of structure:	Semistructured
Informant:	Child
Age range:	7 to 12 years
Interviewer:	Advanced clinical
Training:	Not reported
Alternate forms:	N/A
Information yield	
Symptoms:	Each symptom rated on 1–5 scale
Scales:	Symptoms organized into affective, relationships, dreams and fantasies, self-concept, conscience, and level of adaptation
Diagnoses:	N/A
Psychometric properties	
Reliability:	
Test–retest:	Not reported
Interrater:	*r* averaged .72 for videotaped interviews
Interinformant:	N/A
Other:	N/A
Validity:	Unknown
Applications	
Primary:	Clinical assessment
Secondary:	N/A

Reliability has been explored using 35 videotaped interviews that were rated by three child psychiatrists. Interrater reliability for symptom ratings ranged from $r = .43$ to .94 and averaged .72—which is low for taped interviews. Overall, the MHAF has had little empirical testing and cannot be recommended at this time. Reliability data are inadequate, and validity is largely undocumented. The MHAF represents no technical innovations in structured interviewing, and the information yield does not compare well with alternative interview schedules.

Interview Schedule for Children

The Interview Schedule for Children (ISC) (Kovacs, 1982) is a semistructured symptom-oriented interview for children aged 8–17 (see Table 4-6). It is designed to be administered by clinicians familiar with the ISC items and

TABLE 4-6. Interview Schedule for Children

Description	
Item content:	43 core symptoms, 12 observational items
Response scaling:	0–8 (none to severe)
Administration time:	40–60 minutes
Degree of structure:	Semistructured
Informant:	Parent and child
Age range:	8–17 years
Interviewer:	Advanced clinical
Training:	Very extensive
Alternate forms:	Same form for parent and child, separate forms for initial versus follow-up evaluations
Information yield	
Symptoms:	43 core symptoms rated 0–8
Scales:	N/A
Diagnoses:	DSM-III
Psychometric properties	
Reliability:	
Test–retest:	Not reported
Interrater:	Intraclass correlations averaged .89 for symptoms rated by two interviewers rating the same live interview
Interinformant:	Parent–child agreement averaged .61 for child symptoms
Other:	N/A
Validity:	Strong face validity and utility in selecting subjects for research in child depression
Applications	
Primary:	Differential diagnosis, subject selection
Secondary:	Clinical assessment device, symptom inventory

rating procedures and with DSM-III diagnostic criteria. Interviewers must have advanced clinical training and very extensive interview-specific training and experience. Two forms of the ISC are available—one for initial evaluation and the other for follow-up assessments. The ISC is focused primarily on current depressive symptomatology, although diagnostic addenda have been developed to tap additional diagnoses such as overanxious disorder and attention deficit disorder. The ISC is designed for separate interviews of parent and child and takes about 40–60 minutes.

Like the K-SADS, the ISC begins with an unstructured interview intended to establish rapport and determine the nature of the current disorder. This is followed by a more structured symptom-oriented interview. The ISC covers the severity of the current condition and 43 core symptoms (e.g., depressed mood, irritability, suicidal ideation) which are rated on a 0–8 scale ranging from none to severe. Points along the 0–8 continuum are anchored by descriptive text. For dysphoric mood, for example, a rating of minimal (1 or 2) corresponds to "infrequent, occasional sadness, but transient and not marked; not problem." A rating of severe (7 or 8) corresponds to "pronounced dysphoria almost constantly; or acute dysphoric episodes that entail little or no response to affection/distraction; wretchedness is prominent; pronounced impairment in social functioning." Following the symptom section, the interviewer rates eight mental status items, 12 observational items (e.g., impaired concentration, psychomotor agitation), two developmental milestones (dating and sexual behavior), and five clinical impressions (e.g., grooming, social maturity).

The ISC has been carefully and thoughtfully designed and has several technical assets. For one, the order of questions may vary, depending on whether the respondent spontaneously mentions symptoms covered by the interview schedule. The ISC also employs "double-check" questions designed to confirm children's initial responses before making a final rating. This procedure is particularly useful when interviewing young children because their initial replies are occasionally inappropriate or misleading. The ISC also employs standard prompts, which are abbreviated on the interview form. This necessitates more extensive interviewer training and practice, but results in a fairly standardized and smoothly flowing interview once these prompts are mastered.

The validity of the ISC rests primarily on strong content validity and utility in research in child depression (Kovacs, Feinberg, Crouse-Novak, Paulauskas, & Finkelstein, 1984). Reliability was recently explored for a sample of 75 child psychiatric outpatients aged 8–13 (Kovacs, 1983). Interrater reliability was evaluated by having pairs of interviewers participate in a concurrent interview: one conducted the ISC examination, while the other observed and made ratings independently. For 39 symptoms having sufficent variability, intraclass correlations averaged .89 (range = .64–1.00). Intraclass correlations averaged .86 for mental status items, .78 for observational items, and .77 for clinical impressions. Interrater agreement was perfect for developmental milestones pertaining to dating and sexual behavior. Parent–child agreement was also examined for the same sample of 75 outpatients. For 38 core symptoms having sufficient variability, parent–child agreement averaged $r = .61$ (range = .02–.95). Agreement was highest for fairly overt, easily observable behaviors, such as temper tantrums, encopresis, enuresis, and school refusal, and was lowest for affective and cognitive symptoms, such as pessimism, feelings of guilt, and thoughts of wanting to die.

In sum, the ISC is similar to the K-SADS in that it is focused on symptoms related to depression and it requires a high degree of clinical expertise and very extensive instrument-specific training. Along with the K-SADS, the ISC can be recommended for purposes of selecting subjects for research on affective disorders in childhood, and as an aid in differential diagnosis. The ISC is highly refined in the area of depressive symptoms and appears to have adequate interrater reliability. Test–retest reliability is lacking, and validation is weak. Diagnoses are formulated from the ISC via group conference, and explicit diagnostic rules have not been developed. The ISC has also been used exclusively with clinically referred children and may not be suitable for nonreferred community samples.

Child Assessment Schedule

The Child Assessment Schedule (CAS) (Hodges, Kline, Stern, Cytryn, & McKnew, 1982: Hodges, McKnew, Cytryn, Stern, & Kline, 1982) is a semistructured interview for children aged 7–12 (see Table 4-7). It was originally designed for direct interview of the child only, but a parallel parent version has been developed recently (Hodges, personal communication). The CAS is intended for trained clinical interviewers and requires about 45–60 minutes to administer. It comprises 75 questions about school, friends, family, self-image, behaviors, mood, and thought disorder. The responses are coded yes/no/ambiguous/no response/not applicable. The interview is organized thematically beginning with questions about family and friends, followed by feelings and behaviors, and ending with items about delusions, hallucinations, and related psychotic symptoms. Following the completion of the child interview, the interviewer rates 53 items (e.g., insight, grooming, motor behavior, activity level, and speech).

The CAS was designed to facilitate evaluation of the child's functioning in various areas and to aid in the formulation of diagnostic impressions. It is less structured than other interview schedules and provides an outline of target phenomena to be assessed, suggested questions, and a simple format for recording the presence or absence of symptoms. A considerable degree of clinicial judgment and inference is required in administering and scoring CAS items. The interpretation of CAS data is also quite flexible and requires clinical expertise. Although many CAS items parallel DSM-III diagnostic criteria, the interview was not originally designed to yield DSM diagnoses. Instead, the CAS yields scores in 11 content areas (e.g., school, friends, activities, family) and nine symptom areas corresponding to diagnostic constructs (e.g., attention deficit disorder, conduct disorder, overanxious, oppositional). A total score reflecting number of symptoms present is also obtained.

More recently, a diagnostic index has been developed that indicates the correspondence between CAS items and DSM criteria. This index is intended as an aid in formulating diagnoses from CAS data, but many CAS items do not correspond to DSM criteria, and some DSM criteria are not represented in the CAS. Moreover, the original CAS did not address symptom onset and duration, which are essential for many DSM diagnoses. To remedy this, a separate section has been developed for covering onset and duration of

TABLE 4-7. Child Assessment Schedule

Description	
Item content:	75 items about school, friends, family, self-image, behavior, mood, and thought disorder
Response scaling:	Yes/no/ambiguous/no response/not applicable
Administration time:	45–60 minutes
Degree of structure:	Semistructured
Informant:	Parent or child
Age range:	7–12 years
Interviewer:	Advanced clinical
Training:	Moderate instrument-specific training
Alternate forms:	Separate forms for parent and child
Information yield	
Symptoms:	Presence/absence of 75 symptoms: appendix covers onset and duration
Scales:	11 content areas and 9 symptom complexes
Diagnoses:	DSM-III diagnostic index available
Psychometric properties	
Reliability:	
Test–retest:	Not reported
Interrater:	$r = .90$ for total symptom score, .73 for content areas, .69 for symptom clusters rated from videotapes
Interinformant:	N/A
Other:	N/A
Validity:	Discriminated significantly between inpatient, outpatient, and normal groups; correlated significantly with several other measures of child psychopathology
Applications	
Primary:	Clinical assessment, diagnostic aid
Secondary:	Symptom inventory in clinical research

selected symptoms. This complicates and lengthens the interview, since the interviewer must review responses to the symptom part of the CAS, then inquire about onset and duration of certain symptoms and/or disorders. Nevertheless, the modified CAS yields sufficient information to address a range of child diagnoses, including attention deficit disorders, conduct disorder, anxiety disorders, schizoid disorder, oppositional disorder, enuresis, encopresis, and affective disorders.

Interrater reliability, based on independent ratings of videotapes of 53 interviews, was $r = .90$ for total symptom score, and averaged $r = .73$ for content areas and $r = .69$ for symptom complexes. Interrater reliabilities were somewhat higher for hyperactivity and aggression (average $r = .80$) than for fears, worries, and anxiety (average $r = .60$). For selected pairs of raters, reliability of individual items averaged .57 (kappa statistic). The reliability of DSM diagnoses derived from the CAS has not yet been addressed.

The validity of the CAS is supported by several findings. Total score has been found to discriminate significantly between inpatient, outpatient, and normal groups, and to correlate significantly ($r = .53$, $p < .001$) with total behavior problem score derived from the Child Behavior Checklist (CBCL) completed by mothers. Scores on the overanxious scale correlated ($r = .54$, $p < .001$) with Spielberger's (1973) State–Trait Anxiety Inventory for Children. CAS depression scores also correlated significantly ($r = .53$, $p < .001$) with the Child Depression Inventory. Using referral for inpatient or outpatient psychiatric services as a criterion for psychopathology, total CAS score achieved a sensitivity of 78% and a specificity of 83.8% based on discriminant analysis (Hodges, Kline, *et al.*, 1982, p. 184). In comparison, the CBCL achieved higher sensitivity (86.7%) and specificity (94.6%) on the same sample. Combining the CAS and CBCL in one discriminant analysis yielded 93.3% sensitivity and 100% specificity (no false positives). This suggests that combining parent and child data (or, alternatively, interview and rating scale data) may have advantages in case identification. In addition, Hodges, McKnew, Burbach, and Roebuck, (1984) have recently explored concordance between the CAS and K-SADS for major diagnostic groups. The analyses are preliminary, but the results suggest high agreement between these two interviews.

Overall, the CAS can be tentatively recommended as a descriptive tool and diagnostic aid. It is useful with children as young as 7 years of age and it has a very simple format. The age range is limited, however, and test–retest reliability is lacking. The parallel form for parents is an important addition, but it is in need of further research on reliability and validity. The CAS also involves a relatively high degree of clinical training and inference, and symptom coverage is somewhat narrower than other interviews. A diagnostic index has been developed to assist in translating CAS data into DSM diagnoses, but explicit diagnostic algorithms have not been developed.

Diagnostic Interview Schedule for Children

The Diagnostic Interview Schedule for Children (DISC) was developed by NIMH for use in epidemiologic studies of psychopathology in children aged 6–18 (Costello, Edelbrock, Kalas, Kessler, & Klaric, 1982) (see Table 4-8). It is similar in purpose to the Diagnostic Interview Schedule (DIS) developed for surveying adult disorders (Robins *et al.*, 1981). The DISC is a highly structured diagnostic interview in which the order, wording, and coding of all items are prespecified. Like the DICA, the DISC employs an explicit skip structure that reduces interviewing time with children having few symptoms. It can be administered by clinicians or lay interviewers having 2–3 days of instrument-specific training. Parallel versions of the interview have been

TABLE 4-8. Diagnostic Interview Schedule for Children

Description

Item content:	264 items (child interview), 302 items (parent interview) Covers a broad range of child symptoms and behaviors
Response scaling:	Most symptoms are rated 0–1–2 (no/somewhat or sometimes/yes)
Administration time:	40–60 minutes (child); 60–80 minutes (parent)
Degree of structure:	Very highly structured
Informant:	Parent or child
Age range:	6–18 years
Interviewer:	Clinician or lay interviewer
Training:	Moderate instrument-specific training
Alternate forms:	Separate forms for parent and child

Information yield

Symptoms:	Presence/absence, onset, duration, impairment
Scales:	27 symptom scales corresponding to diagnostic constructs
Diagnoses:	Wide range of DSM-III diagnoses

Psychometric properties
Reliability:

Test–retest:	One-week test–retest interval; r averaged .76 (parent) and .43 (child) for symptom scores; kappa averaged .55 (parent) and .37 (child) for DSM diagnoses.
Interrater:	r averaged .98 for symptom scores rated from videotapes
Interinformant:	Parent-child agreement averaged $r = .27$ for symptom scores (range = $-.03$–.68).
Other:	Test–retest and parent–child correlations were strongly related to age of child and were higher for children aged 10 and older than those aged 6–9
Validity:	Discriminated very well between matched samples of pediatric and psychiatric referrals Correlated significantly with parent and teacher ratings of child behavior problems

Applications

Primary:	Epidemiologic surveys
Secondary:	Symptom inventory in clinical research

---

developed for separate interviewing of parents (DISC-P) and children (DISC-C). The child version has 264 items and takes about 40–60 minutes to complete with clinically referred children. The parent version includes 302 items and takes about 60–70 minutes to administer. A time frame of the past year applies to most items, and more specific information about onset and duration is obtained for many symptoms.

The DISC has a high information yield. It covers a very broad range of child behaviors and symptoms as well as their onset, duration, severity, and associated impairments. Most symptom items are coded 0–1–2, where 0 corresponds to no or never, 1 corresponds to somewhat, sometimes, or a little, and 2 corresponds to yes, often, or a lot. Descriptions and examples offered by the respondent are recorded verbatim for later data editing. The interviews were designed to assess diagnostic criteria set forth in the DSM-III. and they cover almost all diagnoses applied to children and adolescents. In areas where the child's report may be questionable or unavailable (e.g., pica, autism), diagnoses are based on the parent interview alone. Diagnoses are generated by the application of computer algorithms to DISC data. The DISC-C and DISC-P also yield quantitative severity scores in 27 symptom areas that correspond to diagnostic constructs (e.g., overanxious, conduct disorder, obsessions–compulsions). Administration and scoring of the DISC requires very little clinical training, although interpretation of the computer-generated output may require clinical expertise.

Interrater reliability has been examined by comparing symptom scores for ten videotaped child interviews, independently coded by three lay interviewers (Costello, Edelbrock, Dulcan, Kalas, & Klaric, 1984). Reliabilities averaged $r = .98$ for symptom scores (range = .94–1.00). Test–retest reliability has been determined on a sample of 242 clinically referred children and their parents (Edelbrock, Costello, Dulcan, Kalas, & Conover, 1985). Parent and child were interviewed separately and were assessed twice at a median interval of 9 days. For the parent interview, test–retest reliability was .90 for total symptom score (intraclass correlation), and averaged .76 for the remaining 26 symptom clusters (range = .44–.86). For the child interview, test–retest reliability was strongly related to age and averaged .43, .60, and .71 for children aged 6–9, 10–13, and 14–18, respectively. Total symptom score was much more reliable among children aged 14–18 (ICC = .81), than children aged 10–13 (ICC = .55) and 6–9 (ICC = .39). For 21 DSM diagnoses having sufficient prevalence, reliability of the parent interview averaged .56 (kappa statistic) and ranged from .35 to .81. Reliabilities of diagnoses derived from the child interview averaged .36 (range = .12–.71).

Parent–child agreement has been examined for 299 dyads (Edelbrock, Costello, Dulcan, Conover, & Kalas, 1986). Correlations between symptom scores derived from separate interviews with parents and children were significant in 23 of 27 symptom areas ($p < .05$), but were modest in magnitude (average $r = .27$). Parent–child agreement was much higher for behavior/conduct problems than affective/neurotic symptoms. In addition, agreement was substantially higher among children aged 14–18 than those aged 10–13 and 6–9. Across all age groups, parents reported significantly more behavior/conduct problems than their children, whereas children reported significantly more affective/neurotic problems and alcohol/drug abuse than their parents.

Validity of the DISC-C and DISC-P were recently explored by comparing 40 pediatric referrals and 40 psychiatric referrals aged 7–11 (Costello,

Edelbrock, & Costello, 1985). For the DISC-P, psychiatric referrals scored significantly higher in 21 symptom areas, with total symptom score providing the greatest discrimination (paired t tests $=$ 7.5, $p < .001$). For DISC-C interviews, psychiatric referrals scored higher in 21 symptom areas, and scores in the area of simple fears provided the greatest separation between criterion groups (paired t tests $= 4.1$, $p < .001$). Based on the parent interview, the psychiatric referrals received 51 diagnoses of severe disorders, compared to only two in the pediatric group. Combining symptom scores derived from both parent and child interviews in one multiple discriminant analysis yielded a sensitivity of 95% and a specificity of 98%.

Concurrent validity of the DISC interviews has also been supported by significant correlations with the parent and teacher versions of the Child Behavior Checklist (Costello *et al.*, 1984). Total symptom score derived from the DISC-R, for example, correlated .70 ($p < .001$) with total behavior problem score derived from the parent CBCL. The DISC-C has shown weaker ($r = .30$, $p < .01$), but significant, relations to the CBCL. Children receiving different DISC diagnoses have also been found to have significantly different patterns of scores on the parent and teacher versions of the Child Behavior Profile. Children diagnosed attention deficit disorder with hyperactivity, for example, obtained significantly higher scores on the inattentive and nervous–overactive scales of the teacher profile. Children meeting criteria for conduct disorder obtained significantly higher scores on the aggressive scale of teacher profile and the aggressive and delinquent scales of the parent profile (Edelbrock, 1984).

SUMMARY AND CONCLUSIONS

Structured psychiatric interviewing with children is relatively new, and the interview schedules reviewed here are in early stages of development. Much more work is needed before structured interviews can be recommended as assessment and diagnostic tools. All of the currently available interviews are in need of more thorough studies of reliability and validity. Structured interviews appear somewhat less reliable than other assessment methods such as direct observation, psychological testing, and behavioral ratings. Interjudge agreement on videotaped or concurrent interviews has generally been high ($> .90$), but these types of reliability tests sidestep major sources of variability inherent in the assessment process (i.e., interviewer differences, temporal instability of the interviewee's responses, variation in symptoms over time). It seems likely therefore that the levels of reliability reported for many interviews is much higher than would be obtained in actual practice. *In vivo* test–retest and interinterviewer reliabilities have been only moderately high for both symptom scores (intraclass correlations average .70–.80) and diagnoses (kappas average .40–.60).

The validation of existing interview schedules is weak and rests primarily on content validity and ability of global indices to discriminate between vastly different groups. The most common step in validating interviews has been to compare groups of children considered "disturbed" and "normal" on the basis of other criteria—usually clinical referral. The interviews tested in this way have discriminated significantly between criterion groups, but their sensitivity and specificity has usually been no better (and has often been much worse) than simpler and more cost-effective checklists and rating scales.

Very little research on the etiology, course, prognosis, and treatment responsiveness of child disorders has involved structured interviews, probably because of their short history in the child area. One exception is the provocative but preliminary work relating the K-SADS to biological parameters and to treatment response. Of course, validation of structured diagnostic interviews ultimately depends upon progress in the field in general. One cannot expect a diagnostic procedure to be more valid than the taxonomic system on which it is based. The interview schedules designed to operationalize the DSM-III, for example, have inherent weaknesses due to the questionable validity of the diagnostic system itself. Nevertheless, research based on structured interviews may in turn accelerate the revision and refinement of diagnostic categories and criteria applied to children.

No single interview has emerged as superior for all purposes, and all interviews have strengths and weaknesses. Neither the Child Screening Inventory nor the Mental Health Assessment Form can be recommended for research applications because of low reliability and weak validation. The interview version of the Behavioural Screening Questionnaire has proved useful in screening preschool-age children for behavioral disorders, but the rating scale version appears equally good and the Preschool Behavior Questionnaire—a paper-and-pencil scale (Behar, 1977)—has broader symptom coverage, high reliability, strong validation, and good screening efficiency. The Child Assessment Schedule can be tentatively recommended as a descriptive tool, particularly because of the recent addition of a parallel form for parents, the lack of which was a previous limitation. However, it has a narrower age range, symptom coverage, and diagnostic range than measures such as the DISC and DICA, and the reliability of CAS diagnoses has not been established.

The remaining four interview schedules can be recommended for specialized purposes. The K-SADS and the Interview Schedule for Children were developed to select subjects for research on child depression, and both serve this purpose well. Their symptom coverage is much more comprehensive in the area of affective disorders than other disorders. Both yield extremely precise and detailed information about affective symptoms, and both have acceptable reliability in this area These interviews are semistructured and require extensive instrument-specific training. Both are intended for clinically sophisticated interviewers, which limits their applications in large-scale studies.

The last two interview schedules, the DICA and the DISC, are quite opposite to the K-SADS and ISC. They are very highly structured diagnostic interviews designed primarily for epidemiologic surveys of nonreferred populations. They do not have a particular diagnostic focus, but cover an extremely broad range of child behaviors, symptoms, and events. Both the DICA and the DISC can be administered by trained lay interviewers, and they involve a minimum of clinical inference. At the current time both the DICA and the DISC can be recommended as descriptive and epidemiologic tools. They seem best suited to screening and identification of children at risk for psychiatric disorder and for producing "best-estimate" diagnoses in survey studies. The DICA was the first highly structured diagnostic interview schedule for children and it has undergone many revisions, including alterations of the item content to address DSM-III criteria. In fact, the DICA has evolved to the point where much of the early research on its reliability and validity may be obsolete. The DISC is the more recently developed of the two interviews and it has more extensive reliability and validity data. However, it is closely tied to the DSM, which itself is currently undergoing revisions in the child area.

Overall, we conclude that considerable work is needed before any structured interview for children can be unconditionally recommended for clinical research. Most interview schedules are relatively new, and they are subject to major revisions, some of which may render earlier research on their reliability and validity obsolete. Additionally, interview schedules for children are undergoing constant revision and refinement. Any review of such "moving targets" is itself obsolete when completed.

At minimum, we can state that there are two distinct types of structured interviews being developed—those, such as the CAS, ISC, and K-SADS, that depend and capitalize on clinical judgment and inference, and those, such as the DICA and DISC, that have greatly reduced the role of clinical judgment. Determining the optimal degree of clinical inference in structured interviewing will involve much debate, and it is likely that no one solution is possible or desirable. Different types of structured interviews will be suitable for different purposes and populations.

One formula for choosing an interview may involve the relative emphasis placed on *sensitivity* versus *specificity*. It is obviously desirable to maximize both the sensitivity and specificity of a diagnostic tool, but in practice there is almost always a trade off between one and the other. At the current time, interviews that involve a high degree of clinical inference appear to have emphasized specificity of diagnoses in that the items and interviewing procedures are rigorous and require considerable clinical training and judgment. The diagnostic thresholds are "high," meaning that few children will fulfill the rigorous criteria for a given disorder. This emphasis seems reasonable in that interviews such as the ISC and K-SADS were developed primarily for use with clinically referred children who have already been identified as "cases," and the focus is on differential diagnosis and selection of highly homogenous groups of subjects for research.

In contrast, the DICA and DISC appear to maximize sensitivity of diagnoses. They depend to a greater extent on the face validity of simply worded items that involve less clinical insight and inference. The interviewing procedures involve considerably less training, and the diagnostic thresholds are relatively "low" in that many children may fulfill the minimum diagnostic criteria for a given disorder. Moreover, diagnoses produced by such measures are termed "provisional" or "best estimate" and they may or may not correspond to final clinical diagnoses. Emphasizing the sensitivity of a diagnostic tool seems appropriate, however, when a large, nonreferred community population is being surveyed, and the essential task is often case identification rather than precise differential diagnosis or the identification of homogeneous groups of disturbed children.

REFERENCES

American Psychiatric Association. (1980). *Diagnostic and statistical manual of mental disorders* (3rd ed.). Washington, DC: Author.

Behar, L. (1977). The Preschool Behavior Questionnaire. *Journal of Abnormal Child Psychology 5*, 265–295.

Chambers, W., Puig-Antich, J., Hirsch, M., Paez, P., Ambrosini, P. J., Tabrizi, M. A., & Davies, M. (1985). The assessment of affective disorders in children and adolescents by semi-structured interview: Test-retest reliability of the K-SADSA-P. *Archives of General Psychiatry, 42,* 696–702.

Cohen, J. A. (1960). A coefficient of agreement for nominal scales. *Educational and Psychological Measurement, 20,* 37–46.

Costello, E. J., Edelbrock, C., & Costello, A. J. (1985). The validity of the NIMH Diagnostic Interview Schedule for Children: A comparison between pediatric and psychiatric referrals. *Journal of Abnormal Child Psychology, 13,* 579–595.

Costello, A. J., Edelbrock, C., Dulcan, M. K., Kalas, R., & Klaric, S. H. (1984). *Development and testing of the NIMH Diagnostic Interview Schedule for Children in a clinic population.* Final report (Contract No. RFP-DB-81-0027). Rockville, MD: Center for Epidemiologic Studies, National Institute of Mental Health.

Costello, A. J., Edelbrock, C., Kalas, R., Kessler, M. D., & Klaric, S. H. (1982). *The NIMH Diagnostic Interview Schedule for Children (DISC).* Unpublished interview schedule, Department of Psychiatry, University of Pittsburgh.

Earls, F. (1980a). The prevalence of behavior problems in three-year-old children: A cross-national replication. *Archives of General Psychiatry, 37,* 1153–1157.

Earls, F. (1980b). The prevalence of behaviour problems in three-year-old children: Comparison of mothers and fathers. *Journal of the American Academy of Child Psychiatry, 19,* 439–452.

Earls, F., Jacobs, G., Goldfein, D., Silbert, A., Beardslee, W., & Rivinus, T. (1982). Concurrent validation of a behavior problem scale for use with three-year-olds. *Journal of the American Academy of Child Psychiatry, 21,* 47–57.

Earls, F., & Richman, N. (1980a). Behaviour problems of preschool children of West Indian-born parents: A re-examination of family and social factors. *Journal of Child Psychology and Psychiatry, 21,* 108–117.

Earls, F., & Richman, N. (1980b). The prevalence of behaviour problems in three-year-old children of West Indian-born parents. *Journal of Child Psychology and Psychiatry, 21,* 99–107.

Edelbrock, C. (1984, October). *Relations between the NIMH Diagnostic Interview Schedule for Children (DISC) and the Child Behavior Checklist and Profile.* Paper presented at the annual meetings of the American Academy of Child Psychiatry, Toronto.

Edelbrock, C., Costello, A. J., Dulcan, M. K., Conover, N. C., & Kalas, R. (1986). Parent–child agreement on child psychiatric symptoms assessed via structured interview. *Journal of Child Psychology and Psychiatry, 27,* 181–190.

Edelbrock, C., Costello, A. J., Dulcan, M. K., Kalas, R., & Conover, N. C. (1985). Age differences in the reliability of the psychiatric interview of the child. *Child Development, 56,* 265–275.

Endicott, J., & Spitzer, R. L. (1978). A diagnostic interview: The Schedule for Affective Disorders and Schizophrenia. *Archives of General Psychiatry, 35,* 837–844.

Herjanic, B., & Campbell, W. (1977). Differentiating psychiatrically disturbed children on the basis of a structured interview. *Journal of Abnormal Child Psychology, 5,* 127–134.

Herjanic, B., Herjanic, M., Brown, F., & Wheatt, T. (1975). Are children reliable reporters? *Journal of Abnormal Child Psychology, 3,* 41–48.

Herjanic, B., & Reich, W. (1982). Development of a structured psychiatric interview for children: Agreement between child and parent on individual symptoms. *Journal of Abnormal Child Psychology, 10,* 307–324.

Hodges, K., Kline, J., Stern, L., Cytryn, L., & McKnew, D. (1982). The development of a child assessment interview for research and clinical use. *Journal of Abnormal Child Psychology, 10,* 173–189.

Hodges, K., McKnew, D., Burbach, D. J., & Roebuck, L. (1984). *Diagnostic concordance between two structured interviews for children: The Child Assessment Schedule and the Kiddie-SADS.* Paper presented at the annual meetings of the American Psychological Association, Toronto.

Hodges, K., McKnew, D., Cytryn, L., Stern, L., & Kline, J. (1982). The Child Assessment Schedule (CAS) diagnostic interview: A report on reliability and validity. *Journal of the American Academy of Child Psychiatry, 21,* 468–473.

Kestenbaum, C. J., & Bird, H. R. (1978). A reliability study of the Mental Health Assessment Form for school-age children. *Journal of the American Academy of Child Psychiatry, 7,* 338–347.

Kovacs, M. (1982). *The Interview Schedule for Children (ISC).* Unpublished interview schedule, Department of Psychiatry, University of Pittsburgh.

Kovacs, M. (1983). *The Interview Schedule for Children (ISC): Interrater and parent–child agreement.* Unpublished manuscript.

Kovacs, M., Feinberg, T. L., Crouse-Novak, M. A., Paulauskas, S. L., & Finkelstein, R. (1984). Depressive disorders in childhood: I. A longitudinal prospective study of characteristics and recovery. *Archives of General Psychiatry, 41,* 229–237.

Langner, T., Gersten, J., McCarthy, E. D., Eisenberg, J. G., Greene, E. L., Herson, J. H., & Jameson, J. D. (1976). A screening inventory for assessing psychiatric impairment in children aged 6–18. *Journal of Consulting and Clinical Psychology, 44,* 286–296.

Lapouse, R., & Monk, M. A. (1958). An epidemiologic study of behavior characteristics of children. *American Journal of Public Health, 48,* 1134–1144.

Orvaschel, H., Puig-Antich, J., Chambers, W., Tabrizi, M. A., & Johnson, R. (1982). Retrospective assessment of prepubertal major depression with the Kiddie-SADS-E. *Journal of the American Academy of Child Psychiatry, 21,* 392–397.

Puig-Antich, J., Blau, S., Marx, N., Greenhill, L. I., & Chambers, W. (1978). Prepubertal major depressive disorder: A pilot study. *Journal of the American Academy of Child Psychiatry, 17,* 695–707.

Puig-Antich, J., & Chambers, W. (1978). *The Schedule for Affective Disorders and Schizophrenia for school-aged children.* Unpublished interview schedule, New York State Psychiatric Institute.

Puig-Antich, J., Chambers, W., Halpern, F., Hanlon, C., & Sacher, E. J. (1979). Cortisol hypersecretion in prepubertal depressive illness: A preliminary study. *Psychoneuroendocrinology, 4,* 191–197.

Puig-Antich, J., Perel, J. M., Lupatkin, W., Chambers, W., Shea, C., Tabrizi, M. A., & Stiller, R. L. (1979). Plasma levels of imipramine (IMI) and desmethylimipramine (DMI) and clinical response in prepubertal major depressive disorder: A preliminary report. *Journal of the American Academy of Child Psychiatry, 18*, 616–627.

Reich, W., Herjanic, B., Welner, Z., & Gandhy, P. R. (1982). Development of a structured psychiatric interview for children: Agreement on diagnosis comparing parent and child. *Journal of Abnormal Child Psychology, 10*, 325–336.

Richman, N. (1977). Short-term outcome of behavioral problems in preschool aged children. In P. Graham (Ed.), *Epidemiological approaches in child psychiatry*. London: Academic Press.

Richman, N., & Graham, P. (1971). A behavioural screening questionnaire for use with three-year-old children: Preliminary findings. *Journal of Child Psychology and Psychiatry, 12*, 5–33.

Richman, N., Stevenson, J., & Graham, P. (1975). Prevalence of behaviour problems in three-year-old children: An epidemiologic study in a London borough. *Journal of Child Psychology and Psychiatry, 16*, 277–287.

Robins, L., Helzer, J. E., Croughan, J., & Ratcliff, K. S. (1981). National Institute of Mental Health Diagnostic Interview Schedule: Its history, characteristics, and validity. *Archives of General Psychiatry, 38*, 381–389.

Rutter, M., & Graham, P. (1968). The reliability and validity of the psychiatric assessment of the child: Interview with the child. *British Journal of Psychiatry, 11*, 563–579.

Spielberger, C. D. (1973). *Manual for the state–trait anxiety inventory for children*. Palo Alto, CA: Consulting Psychologists Press.

World Health Organization (1978). *International classification of diseases* (9th ed.). Geneva: Author.

5

CHILD BEHAVIOR RATING SCALES AND CHECKLISTS

RUSSELL A. BARKLEY

INTRODUCTION

Numerous rating scales and checklists exist for use in research on child psychopathology. They range in length from 10 to 600 items and yield from 1 to 33 subscale scores. Item content ranges from highly specific behaviors to highly abstract qualities of personal or social functioning, and from highly specific constructs (e.g., activity level) to broad categories of psychopathology (e.g., externalizing behaviors). They vary in quality, in research available on their psychometric properties, and the research purposes for which they are best suited. It is the purpose of this review to critique a number of the many rating scales employed. Those chosen represented the most widely available, most promising, or most frequently cited within the U.S. literature on child psychopathology. A few others were selected because they were typical of the abundant number available in the commercial marketplace. Only rating scales completed by parents or teachers and assessing dimensions of child psychopathology are reviewed. A number of issues involved in the use of rating scales and checklists in research will be considered first, followed by a critique of specific instruments.

Assumptions Underlying the Use of Checklists and Rating Scales

Cairns and Green (1979) have described a number of important assumptions underlying the use of behavior rating scales:

1. The informant shares with the researcher some common understanding of the attribute or behavior to be rated. The more abstract the concept, the greater the discrepancy that may exist between what the investigator intended to have rated and what the informant actually rated.

Russell A. Barkley, Department of Psychiatry, University of Massachusetts Medical Center, Worcester, Massachusetts.

2. The informant shares an understanding of which behaviors of the child actually represent the attribute on the scale. Behaviors that are relevant to a given scale item may vary due to developmental, situational, or demographic variables, and it is assumed that the rater and investigator share a similar perception of which aspects of these behaviors are to be considered in responding to the item.

3. The rater is capable of extracting from the "stream of everyday-life activities" of the child those behaviors relevant to the quality or attribute being rated. Informants must decide not only whether the attribute being rated has occurred but whether that occurrence qualifies for inclusion in the item being rated.

4. The informant and investigator share the same concept of the reference points for the scaling along which the item is to be rated. The informant and investigator may or may not share the same perception of the base rates of the behavior being rated and hence what constitutes such scale anchor points as "just a little" or "very much." Interrater reliability of scales depends greatly upon this shared understanding of scale reference points. For instance, Ross and Ross (1982) provided college-educated parents with the four response choices from the Conners Parent Rating Scale along with three items from the scale and asked these mothers how many times within the past month the child would have had to show the behavior in that item for her to use each point on the response scale (not at all, just a little, pretty much, very much). The resulting responses were surprisingly varied. Frequencies of behavior for the response of "not at all" ranged from 0 to 15, for "just a little" from 1 to 120, and for "very much" from 5 to 300. One cannot always assume, then, that rater and investigator share the same notion of quantity or quality of behavior reflected in an item's response scale.

The extent to which most or all of these assumptions are valid for particular rating scales, populations of raters or of children, or types of psychopathology is open to considerable question.

Issues Related to Using Behavior Rating Scales

The validity or reliability of child behavior rating scales can also be compromised by numerous other conceptual or practical problems in their construction, use, or interpretation. One is the nature of those sources of variation contributing to the ratings on a scale. Many studies interpret scale findings as if they represented only the actual behavior of the children being rated. Yet, characteristics of the informant, their education, intelligence, emotional status at the time the ratings were conducted, and their tendency toward response biases all contribute to some degree to the particular ratings on a scale (Bond & McMahon, 1984). Other sources of variation come from the manner in which the scale has been constructed, the specificity of its wording, the time period over which the ratings are to be made, and the breadth of response scaling provided—as well as those factors (developmental, demographic, contextual, etc.) creating actual situational variation in the child's behavior.

A second problem is the dilemma of deciding what other types of measures will be used to assess the construct validity of the scale. Using direct behavioral observations of specific behaviors within specific natural or analogue settings is helpful in providing more direct and objective assessments of the behavior or construct for comparison with ratings obtained on a scale. But such ratings may not be completely comparable to the behavioral category being recorded. Behavioral observations often focus upon highly molecular behavioral units in very specific situations and over short time intervals. In contrast, rating scales require the rater to collapse observations across longer time intervals (weeks to months) and numerous situations (in the home, in the community, etc.) resulting in substantial methodological differences in how the two measures of the same construct are obtained.

Ratings and direct observational measures may also disagree or fail to correlate highly for many other reasons, such as: (1) ratings are often more vaguely defined than observations; (2) they are more influenced by variables affecting the informant; and (3) raters are not usually trained to anywhere near the extent that observers using direct observational methods are (Mash & Terdal, 1981). Although the information derived from each methodology certainly overlaps to some extent, each also offers unique sources of information not obtained by the other. As a result, complete agreement between these two approaches to assessment cannot be expected. This limits the degree to which the construct validity of a rating scale can be established by such comparisons. Similar problems afflict the use of psychometric tests or laboratory instruments as other means of establishing a scale's construct validity.

Many scale developers employed various types of factor analyses to develop subscales reflecting dimensions of child psychopathology. Such subscales are then labeled as reflecting a certain construct or dimension of child behavior (e.g., aggression, social withdrawal). However, those interpreting such subscale scores or dimensions must consider that they only partially reflect the actual child behaviors they are meant to represent. Factors derived from these analyses depend heavily upon the type, nature, content, and number of items entering the analysis, their scaling, situation specificity, and the informant from whom the ratings are obtained, as well as the nature of the sample from which the ratings were taken. As a result, such factors may or may not represent real dimensions of child behavior; however, they undoubtedly reflect more than simply child behavior, given the assumptions and issues already noted (Mischel, 1973). It is essential, therefore, that research establish the construct validity of these subscales by anchoring them to measures of the same construct taken by other means before they can be interpreted as truly reflecting that quality or attribute of child behavior.

Advantages of Behavior Rating Scales

Despite the problems inherent in the use and interpretation of rating scales, they offer numerous advantages over other methods and, for these reasons, will increasingly be used in research in child psychopathology (see Edelbrock & Rancurello, 1985; Mash & Terdal, 1981; McMahon, 1984; O'Leary, 1981). Some of the many advantages are that ratings: (1) have the capability of gathering information from informers with many years of experience with the child across diverse settings and circumstances; (2) permit the collection of data on behaviors that occur extremely infrequently and are likely to be missed by *in vivo* measures; (3) are inexpensive to collect and efficient in the time needed to complete the scales; (4) may have normative data for establishing the statistical deviance of child behavior ratings; (5) exist in a variety of forms focusing on a diversity of dimensions of child psychopathology; (6) incorporate the opinions of significant people in the child's natural environment who are responsible for the care, management, and ultimately the therapeutic treatments a child will receive; (7) filter out situational variation, thereby achieving the most stable and enduring characteristics of the child; and (8) permit quantitative distinctions to be made concerning qualitative aspects of child behavior that are often difficult to obtain through direct observational methods.

Scales may also serve a variety of useful functions (see Achenbach & Edelbrock, 1983), such as in epidemiologic research, subgrouping of children into more homogeneous clusters, further exploration of etiologic hypotheses about certain disorders, and determination of prognosis of clinical groups of children followed over long time intervals. Some scales have demonstrated great sensitivity to change, such as that rendered by various treatments, making them indispensable in treatment outcome studies. Others provide sufficient breadth of coverage of child psychopathology as to permit the development of a taxonomy of psychopathological disorders using profile analysis or the evaluation of mental health programs and their efficacy in addressing the initial presenting complaints (ratings) of children participating in those programs. Given such advantages, rating scales will continue to have an important role in research on child psychopathology.

A number of parent and teacher rating scales of child behavior will now be reviewed. The structure, scaling, factorial content, and procedure for obtaining each scale will be briefly presented in tabular form, along with an indication of whether information on various forms of reliability and validity are available. Indications of yes or no after each category of reliability and validity serve only to note that information of this sort is or is not available in the literature. It does not indicate the adequacy of those findings. Whether or not normative data are available is also specified, along with the ages of the children for whom those data are appropriate. A brief commentary provides more specific information on reliability and validity of the scale, if available, and addressing the strengths or weaknesses of the scale as appropriate.

PARENT RATING SCALES

Conners Parent Rating Scales

There are three versions of the Conners Parent Rating Scale currently in common use: (1) the original 93-item scale (Conners, 1970); (2) the 48-item revised version (Goyette, Conners, & Ulrich, 1978); and (3) the 10-item Abbreviated Symptom Questionnaire.

Original Conners Parent Rating Scale

The original Conners Parent Rating Scale (CPRS) (see Table 5-1) appears to have satisfactory utility where the focus of research is to assess briefly a broad array of psychopathological symptoms, such as hyperactivity, depression, and aggression. The majority of items, however, assess conduct problems or externalizing disorders more than neuroses or internalizing disorders. The scale is widely used and has a substantial research literature concerning its psychometric properties. Two-month test–retest reliabilities have been generally satisfactory, averaging .85, but they vary considerably across the factor scores (O'Conner, Foch, Sherry, & Plomin, 1980). Declines in scores from first to second administrations have been reported (Werry & Sprague, 1974) on several of the factors (hyperactivity, antisocial, and learning problems) suggesting a possible practice effect comparable to that noted for the teacher version of the rating scale to be discussed later. It is therefore recommended that the scale be administered twice before use in assessing changes in ratings due to treatment so as to reduce the confounding of the results with this apparent practice effect (Conners, 1985). Interrater

TABLE 5-1. Original Conners Parent Rating Scale

Developer: C. Keith Conners

Where to obtain: C. Keith Conners, PhD, Department of Psychiatry, Children's Hospital National Medical Center, 111 Michigan Ave. N.W., Washington, DC 20010

Cost: None   Copyrighted: No

Items: 93   Scaling: 0–3   Ages: 6–14 years

Completion time: 10–15 minutes   Scoring software: Yes

Reliability information available:
    Test–retest: Yes   Interrater: No   Internal consistency: No

Validity data available:
    Construct: Yes   Discriminant: Yes   Concurrent: Yes
    Predictive: Yes   Treatment sensitive: Yes

Normative data: Yes (ages 6–14 years; $N = 683$)

Factors assessed: Conduct disorder, fearful–anxious, restless–disorganized, learning problem–immature, psychosomatic, obsessional, antisocial, hyperactive–immature (Conners & Blouin, 1980)

Bibliography: Yes; more than 260 references, from developer

---

reliability between parents has not been reported for the CPRS. Normative data have been reported by Conners and Blouin (1980).

Factor analytic studies have also been conducted with speech- and language-impaired children (Mattison, Cantwell, & Baker, 1980). O'Conner *et al.* (1980) reported intraclass correlations on factors derived for a 73-item version of this scale for identical versus fraternal twins which ranged from .67 to .91 for the former and .15 to .56 for the latter. Glow and her colleagues (Glow, 1979; Glow, Glow, & Rump, 1982) have developed an Adelaide (Australia) version of the scale, with normative data available on 1,919 children. This slightly modified version also has adequate test–retest reliability and internal consistency.

The original CPRS shows adequate concurrent validity. Research has shown it to correlate significantly with ratings from the Werry–Weiss–Peters Activity Rating Scale (Broad, 1982), the Child Behavior Checklist (Achenbach & Edelbrock, 1983; Mash & Johnson, 1983), the Behavior Problem Checklist (Arnold, Barneby, & Smeltzer, 1981; Campbell & Steinert, 1978) and its revised version (Quay & Peterson, 1983), and the Davids Hyperactivity Index (Arnold *et al.*, 1981). The ratings also correlate significantly with those of infant temperament (Weissbluth, 1984), parent reported stress and self-esteem (Mash & Johnston, 1983), and the results of semistructured interviews (Hodges, Kline, Stern, Cytryn, & McKnew, 1982). Substantial research supports the discriminant validity of the scale in separating groups of hyperactive and normal children (Prior, Leonard, & Wood, 1983; Ross & Ross, 1976, 1982), clinic-referred from nonclinic-referred children (Conners, 1970), neurotic from conduct problem clinic-referred children (Conners, 1970), depressed from nondepressed children (Leon, Kendall, & Garber, 1980), and speech- and language-impaired from purely speech-impaired children (Baker, Cantwell, & Mattison, 1980). Studies of various interventions, such as stimulant drugs, or dietary management, with hyperactive children have found the scale to be useful (Barkley, 1977; Cantwell & Carlson, 1979; Harley *et al.*, 1981). However, the scale appears to have little utility in predicting stimulant drug responding in hyperactive children (Barkley, 1976).

Conners Parent Rating Scale—Revised

Conners revised the original CPRS (CPRS-R) in 1978, reducing the number of items to 48 and slightly rewording those that were retained to simplify administration and interpretation (Goyette *et al.*, 1978) (see Table 5-2). Those items assessing internalizing or neurotic disorders appear to have been greatly reduced in number, making the revised scale more useful for assessing conduct problems (aggression, hyperactivity, etc.) as opposed to the more internalizing disorders of depression, psychosomatic disorders, and so forth. Hence the revised scale (CPRS-R) would seem most useful where a brief evaluation of conduct problems or hyperactivity is of interest. Norma-

TABLE 5-2. Conners Parent Rating Scale—Revised

Developer: Same
Where to obtain: Same
Cost: None   Copyrighted: No
Items: 48   Scaling: 0–3   Ages: 3–17 years
Completion time: 5–10 minutes   Scoring software: No

Reliability information available:
    Test–retest: No   Interrater: Yes   Internal consistency: No

Validity information available:
    Construct: Yes   Discriminant: No   Concurrent: No
    Predictive: No   Treatment sensitive: Yes

Normative data: Yes (ages 3–17 years; $N = 570$)

Factors assessed: Conduct problems, learning problems, psychosomatic,
    impulsive–hyperactive, anxiety

tive data on the scale are reported in the paper by Goyette *et al.* (1978) for boys and girls aged 3 to 17 years. Where normative data are important, investigators may wish to use this version over the original as the norms are provided for a wider age range of subjects and are broken down by sex. Ratings between mothers and fathers were not found to differ significantly, with agreement ranging between .46 and .57 across the five factors. Not unexpectedly, agreement between the parent and teacher ratings was somewhat lower, ranging between .33 and .45. Test–retest reliability information could not be located for this scale. Nevertheless, it would appear prudent to assume that this scale will demonstrate the same practice effects as the original scale, making it important for the CPRS-R to be administered at least twice before use in any research assessing treatment effects.

The validity of the CPRS-R has not been as well studied as the original scale. Given the similarity of items assessing conduct problems between the two scales, data on the validity of the externalizing factors, such as hyperactivity and conduct problems, for the original scale would appear to be applicable to the comparable factors on the revised version. Nevertheless, additional research using the CPRS-R would seem useful to establish its discriminant, concurrent, construct, and predictive validity. Recent research has shown the scale to be sensitive to stimulant drug effects (Barkley, Fischer, Newby, & Breen, 1985), parent training in child management (Pollard, Ward, & Barkley, 1983), and self-control training of hyperactive children (Horn, Ialongo, Popovich, & Peradotto, 1984).

Conners Abbreviated Symptom Questionnaire

The Conners Abbreviated Symptom Questionnaire (ASQ) (see Table 5-3) comprises the 10 most frequently endorsed items by parents of hyperactive

TABLE 5-3. Conners Abbreviated Symptom Questionnaire

Developer: Same
Where to obtain: Same
Cost: None   Copyrighted: No
Items: 10   Scaling: 0–3   Ages: 3–17 years
Completion time: 3–5 minutes   Scoring software: No

Reliability information available:
       Test–retest: No   Interrater: Yes   Internal consistency: No

Validity information available:
       Construct: No   Discriminant: Yes   Concurrent: No
       Predictive: Yes   Treatment sensitive: Yes

Normative data: Yes (ages 3–17 years; $N = 570$)

Factors assessed: Not factor analyzed

---

children and is often referred to as the Hyperactivity Index. The items were believed to measure "core psychopathology" in these children and to provide a convenient means of assessing change in behavior due to treatment (Conners, 1985). Several different versions of the ASQ exist (Ullmann, Sleator, & Sprague, 1985), but Conners recommends that the 10-item index described in the paper on the CPRS-R by Goyette *et al.* (1978) be used. The ASQ items scored using the template provided by Abbott Laboratories are incorrect, according to Conners, and should not be confused with other versions of the index. Normative data for the ASQ can be found in the report by Goyette *et al.* (1978). No test–retest reliability information could be located for the parent version of the ASQ, but interparent agreement (.55–.71) and parent–teacher agreement (.49) have been reported as satisfactory (Goyette *et al.*, 1978; Mash & Johnston, 1983). Again, the scale is likely to show declines from first to second administrations in an apparent practice effect and so should be administered at least twice before being used in research on intervention.

The ASQ has been used extensively for selecting children as hyperactive for research. However, Ullmann *et al.* (1985) report that the scale actually assesses a mixture of conduct problem and hyperactivity symptoms, and so will result in a mixed conduct problem–hyperactive sample when used in this fashion. Considering the importance shown in recent research of distinguishing between pure hyperactive children and those having both hyperactivity and conduct problems (Paternite & Loney, 1980), investigators interested in selecting the former type of hyperactive child should not use this scale. Interestingly, the ASQ has not been found to correlate significantly with actometer measures of activity level taken in a clinical playroom (Barkley & Cunningham, 1980) or to be predictive of stimulant drug responding in hyperactive children (Barkley, 1976). Significant correlations have been found between parent ASQ ratings in the home and clinic playroom measures of child compliance and mothers' directiveness in hyperactive children

(.38–.48), further supporting the aforementioned point that this scale most likely assesses interaction conflicts and conduct problems in children.

Child Behavior Checklist

Investigators interested in employing the Child Behavior Checklist (CBCL) (see Table 5-4) should thoroughly peruse the manual (Achenbach & Edelbrock, 1983), from which most of the information on reliability and validity were obtained. The 138 items on the CBCL are broken down into 20 items that assess social competence and 118 items that comprise the behavior problems scale. The social competence scale generates three scores: activities (sports, hobbies, etc.), social (organizations, friendships, etc.), and school (performance, problems, etc.). These are then plotted on one of six profiles, depending on the age (4–5 years, 6–11 years, and 12–16 years) and sex of the child. The profiles provide unique and informative aspects of the scale, as opposed to other scales that yield little or no information on social competence. The remaining 118 items comprise the behavior problems scale. Factor analyses of the responses to these items for 2,300 clinic-referred children revealed a different set of factors for males and females and for three separate age groupings (4–5 years, 6–11 years, and 12–16 years). The profiles generated for each grouping consist of eight or nine factors. Norms for the factor scales were collected on 1,300 normal children well stratified regarding socioeconomic class and ethnic composition. The percentage of children receiving a positive endorsement by each item is reported in Achenbach and Edelbrock (1981). The developers suggest that parents completing the scale have at least a fifth-grade reading level, while linguistic analysis of the items indicates a mean reading complexity level of 8.2 (Harrington & Follett, 1984).

TABLE 5-4. Child Behavior Checklist

Developers: Thomas Achenbach and Craig Edelbrock (1983)
Where to obtain: Thomas M. Achenbach, PhD, Department of Psychiatry,
    University of Vermont, Burlington, VT 05401
Cost: $5.00 for sample kit; $18.00 for manual   Copyrighted: Yes
Items: 138   Scaling: 0–2   Ages: 4–16 years
Completion time: 15–20 minutes   Scoring software: Yes

Reliability information available:
    Test–retest: Yes   Interrater: Yes   Internal consistency: Yes

Validity information available:
    Construct: Yes   Discriminant: Yes   Concurrent: Yes
    Predictive: Yes   Treatment sensitive: Yes

Normative data: Yes (4–16 years; $N = 1,300$)

Factors assessed (dependent on age): Social withdrawal, depressed, immature, somatic complaints, sex problems, schizoid, aggressive, delinquent, hyperactive, uncommunicative, obsessive–compulsive

Bibliography: Yes; see manual

Reliability information from the manual indicates 1-week test–retest coefficients of .95 (behavior problems) and .99 (social competence) by the intraclass computation method. Test–retest coefficients over a 3-month interval were .84 (behavior problems) and .97 (social competence). Pearson coefficients ranged from .61 to .96 across factors and age by sex groupings. Stability coefficients of .53 for clinician's reports and .59 for mother's reports over a 6-month period have been noted. Estimates of stability over 3 months, 6 months, and 18 months are reported in the manual. Interparent agreement on a clinic sample of children was .978 for social competence and .985 for behavior problems. Across factors, the range of agreement between parents was .26–.78 for those on the behavior problems profile and .44–.81 on the social competence profile. Satisfactory interparent agreements were also reported by Mash and Johnston (1983).

Although less research exists on this scale than on that for the Conners scales or the Behavior Problem Checklist because of its more recent development, this situation is quickly changing. Large numbers of current research projects are using the Child Behavior Checklist and so ample published research on the validity of the scale will be forthcoming very soon. Concurrent validity has been established by demonstrating significant correlations of like factors between CBCL and Conners scales and the Revised Behavior Problem Checklist (see Achenbach & Edelbrock, 1983; Kazdin & Heidish, 1984; Mash & Johnston, 1983), the Werry–Weiss–Peters Activity Rating Scale (Mash & Johnston, 1983), and a semistructured psychiatric interview, the Diagnostic Interview Schedule for Children—Parent Report (DISC-P) (Costello & Edelbrock, 1985). The CBCL has shown adequate discriminant validity in distinguishing between clinic-referred and nonreferred children (see manual), hyperactive and normal children (Barkley, 1981; Edelbrock & Rancurello, 1985; Mash & Johnston, 1983), children of maritally distressed versus nondistressed mothers (Bond & McMahon, 1984), depressed and nondepressed children (Seagull & Weinshank, 1984), adopted and nonadopted children (Brodzinsky, Schechter, Braff, & Singer, 1984), and maltreated versus control children (Salzinger, Kaplan, Pelcovitz, Samit, & Krieger, 1984). The instrument has shown some usefulness as a screening measure for psychopathology in a primary-care pediatric setting (Costello & Edelbrock, 1985), and for assessing changes in conduct problems following a parent training program in child management skills (Webster-Stratton, 1984). Research has also been done developing profile typologies for a variety of childhood disorders (Edelbrock & Achenbach, 1980).

There can be little doubt that this is the most well-developed, empirically derived behavior rating scale currently available for assessing psychopathology and social competence in children. The item content is sufficiently broad to capture the majority of internalizing or externalizing disorders, to assess social competence, and to evaluate a diversity of psychopathological disturbances upon which to base an empirical taxonomy of childhood disorders. The developers respect their findings that different types of profiles of psychopathology exist for the different sexes and different age groupings of children and provide for this in the scoring of the instrument. The availability of an equally well-developed teacher report form for the CBCL (see below), as well as a youth report form now being standardized and normed, further commend the use of these scales where multiple informants are desired.

Personality Inventory for Children

The Personality Inventory for Children (PIC) (see Table 5-5) is not merely a child behavior rating scale like most others reviewed here. Rather, as its name implies, it is more of an inventory of child personality characteristics. An assumption of most rating scales is that their items and the adult responses thereto are face valid, representing a generally truthful reporting of the actual characteristics or behaviors described in the item. Such an assumption is not necessarily the case with the PIC, inasmuch as its items were chosen based on how well they discriminated groups of children rather than on their construct validity. In fact, two methods of item development were employed: the Darlington (1963) method, where items are selected by how well they correlate with a criterion group, and the rational strategy, where items are nominated by four experienced judges. Nonetheless, the recent revision of the inventory such that it now has factor analytically based scales makes these scales similar to the others reviewed here and so it is discussed.

TABLE 5-5. Personality Inventory for Children

Developers: Robert D. Wirt, David Lachar, James K. Klinedinst, and Phillip D. Seat (1984)

Where to obtain: Western Psychological Services, 12031 Wilshire Blvd., Los Angeles, CA 90025

Cost: $125   Copyrighted: Yes

Items: 131–600 (four versions)   Scaling: 0–1   Ages: 6–16 years

Completion time: 20 minutes to 2 hours   Scoring software: Yes

Reliability information available:
    Test–retest: Yes   Interrater: Yes   Internal consistency: Yes

Validity data available:
    Construct: Yes   Discriminant: Yes   Concurrent: Yes
    Predictive: No   Treatment sensitive: No

Normative data: Yes (3–16 years; $N = 2,390$)

Scales: Achievement, intellectual screening, development, somatic concern, depression, family relations, delinquency, withdrawal, anxiety, psychosis, hyperactivity, social skills

Factors assessed: Undisciplined/poor self-control, social incompetence, internalization/somatic symptoms, cognitive development

Bibliography: Yes; 70 references, from David Lachar, PhD, Institute of Behavioral Medicine, Good Samaritan Medical Center, 111 East McDowell Rd., P.O. Box 2989, Phoenix, AZ 85062

Scores for each scale are plotted on a profile and clinical judgments are then made based upon the T score elevations of each score. Cutoff scores for determining clinical significance are reported in the paper by Lachar and Gdowski (1979a). The more recent revision of the PIC (Lachar, 1982) contains four possible versions for administration. The first section of 131 items permits scoring of the four factorially developed scales and the lie scale (one of three validity scales). Completion of the first 280 items permits these factors to be scored as well as shortened versions of the 12 clinical scales and general adjustment scale. Completion of 420 items permits scoring of all 16 scales plotted on the PIC profile, the four-factor scales, and a full critical-items list. Should all 600 items be used, all of the possible scales can be scored, including a number of supplemental scales. A sixth- to seventh-grade reading level appears to be necessary for completing the scale (Harrington & Follett, 1984).

Reliability information is reported in the PIC manual (Wirt et al., 1984), with test–retest coefficients for a 15-day interval ranging from .46 to .94 (mean .86) across the scales. Interparent agreement ranges from .21 to .79 (mean .57–.69), depending upon the study (see manual). Coefficients for internal consistency were −.03 to .86 for the scales and .81 to .92 for the factor analytically derived scales. Information on validity of the PIC is also reported in the manual and in several more recent reports. Construct validity is difficult to assess given the method of item development, but it appears to be satisfactory for those scales based on factor analysis. The scales significantly differentiate hyperactive, learning-disabled, and normal children (Breen & Barkley, 1983, 1984), learning-disabled versus behavior-disordered children (Goh, Cody, & Dollinger, 1984; Porter & Rourke, 1985; Strang & Rourke, 1985), and depressed and nondepressed children (Lobovitz & Handal, 1985). Several of the clinical scales correlated well with parental ratings of children's adjustment to divorce (Kurdek, Blisk, & Siesky, 1981). Profile typologies and actuarial interpretation of the profiles can be found in the recent report by Lachar, Kline, and Boersma (1986). Some of the PIC scales correlate satisfactorily with parent, teacher, and clinician ratings of child deviance (Lachar & Gdowski, 1979b; Lachar, Gdowski, & Snyder, 1984), the Conners Parent Rating Scale (Leon et al., 1980), and response to stimulant medication in hyperactive children (Voelker, Lachar, & Gdowski, 1983). Software for computer scoring of profiles is available from the publisher as well as from Greene, Martin, Bennett, and Shane (1981).

The 131-item version of the scale appears to be the most useful in research wishing to employ a child behavior rating scale. However, where interest is in family relations, use of one of the longer versions may be of greater value in that it permits scoring of the clinical scale assessing this domain. Nevertheless, several problems exist with the use of this scale in research. The true/false scoring procedure does not yield any specific information on the frequency or severity of the behavior problem or characteristic described in the item. The methods of item development introduce confusion as to just what each item assesses and precludes the use of the items in epidemiological research. The item length of the original PIC is also problematic; for many parents it requires 1 to 2 hours to complete. This has been partially rectified by the more recent availability of four different versions of lesser item length. It is likely that this scale will remain more attractive to clinicians for an evaluation of personality characteristics of individual children than to clinical scientists desiring shorter, more empirically developed scales.

Louisville Behavior Checklist

The Louisville Behavior Checklist (LBCL) (see Table 5-6) contains three separate forms: E-1 for 4- to 6-year-olds, E-2 for 7- to 12-year-olds, and E-3 for 13- to 17-year-olds. Each version can be scored to yield factors similar to those noted above, as well as several additional scales that were developed by means of a rational strategy similar to that used in the PIC described earlier. Normative data are available for forms E-1 and E-2 only, but these are based upon quite small samples of normal children, and hence their representativeness of the general childhood population is questionable. Additional normative data have been reported by Tarte, Vernon, Luke, and Clark (1982). The items on the scale appear to require a tenth-grade reading level for completion (Harrington & Follette, 1984). Additional factor analyses of the items have been done with populations of phobic (Miller, 1976) and emotionally disturbed or delinquent adolescents (Miller, 1980). Reliability information is contained in the manual and indicates test–retest coefficients for form E-2 only of .60–.92 over a 3-month period. Internal consistency of the scales varies from .33 to .97, depending upon the scale and which form was used. No interparent reliability agreements have been reported, but parent–teacher

TABLE 5-6. Louisville Behavior Checklist

Developer: Lovick C. Miller (1984)

Where to obtain: Western Psychological Services, 12031 Wilshire Blvd., Los Angeles, CA 90025

Cost: $79.50   Copyrighted: Yes

Items: 164   Scaling: 0–1   Ages: 4–17 years

Completion time: 30–45 minutes   Scoring software: No

Reliability information available:
    Test–retest: Yes   Interrater: No   Internal consistency: Yes

Validity information available:
    Construct: Yes   Discriminant: Yes   Concurrent: Yes
    Predictive: No   Treatment sensitive: No

Normative data: Yes (ages 4–12 years; $N = 425$)

Factors assessed: Aggression, inhibition, learning disability, infantile aggression, hyperactivity, antisocial behavior, social withdrawal, sensitivity, fear, academic disability, immaturity

Bibliography: Yes; 22 references, see manual

---

agreements of .06–.57 have been described (see manual). Validity of the scales are based primarily upon studies showing differentiation of various clinical and normal groups (Tarte *et al.*, 1982) and significant correlations of the scales with ratings from teachers, ratings of parental hostility in samples of separated and divorced couples, ratings of parental attention to children, and ratings of life stress in children (see manual).

The LBCL has not been widely adopted in research on psychopathology. The availability of a cognitive development or learning disabilities scale is unique to this scale and the PIC, suggesting it may be useful where such domains of development are of interest. Otherwise, there is little to commend this scale over the others reviewed here. The normative samples are quite small, and thus their representativeness is suspect, and test–retest reliability information for forms E-1 and E-3 are lacking. Like the PIC, the true/false response format does not yield information on the frequency or intensity of the problem behaviors described in the items, making the scales of little value for epidemiologic research.

Eyberg Child Behavior Inventory

The Eyberg Child Behavior Inventory (ECBI) (see Table 5-7) is a short rating scale designed to record parent reports of childhood behavioral problems, particularly oppositional behavior and conduct disorders (Eyberg & Ross, 1978). Two scores are obtained: an intensity score, reflecting the sum of the ratings (1–7) across all items, and a problem score, comprised of the number of items endorsed as a problem by the parent. Although normative data are available (Eyberg & Robinson, 1983; Robinson, Eyberg, & Ross, 1980), the samples are more representative of lower-income to lower-middle-income groups; moreover, the sample for the older age group (13–16 years) is quite small and contains a disproportion of females (63%). Furthermore, despite reporting initially significant effects of sex on the norms, the normative data are not broken down by sex but by age alone. Factor analyses (Eyberg & Robinson, 1983; Robinson *et al.*, 1980) suggest that the scale is predominantly assessing conduct problems. However, other factors were discovered but not reported, making interpretation of the scale and its comparison to other rating scales difficult. Computer software for scoring the scale can be found in Holtum, Robinson, and Eyberg (1984).

Reliability information has been reported in several papers. Test–retest coefficients over 21 days were .86 for the intensity score and .88 for the problem score (Robinson *et al.*, 1980). Interparent agreement on ratings for eight adolescents was found to be .79 (Eyberg & Robinson, 1983). Internal consistency coefficients of .98 and split-half reliabilities of .90–.94 have been reported (Eyberg & Robinson, 1983; Robinson *et al.*, 1980).

The validity of the scale has been primarily established through the

TABLE 5-7. Eyberg Child Behavior Inventory

Developer: Sheila M. Eyberg (1980)

Where to obtain: Sheila M. Eyberg, PhD, Department of Clinical Psychology, University of
Florida, Box J-165 JHMHC, Gainesville, FL 32610

Cost: None   Copyrighted: Yes

Items: 36   Scaling: 1–7   Ages: 2–12 years

Completion time: 10 minutes   Scoring software: Yes

Reliability information available:
     Test–retest: Yes   Interrater: Yes   Internal consistency: Yes

Validity information available:
     Construct: Yes   Discriminant: Yes   Concurrent: Yes
     Predictive: No   Treatment sensitive: Yes

Normative data: Yes (ages 2–7 and 13–16 years; $N = 512$ and 102)

Factors assessed: Conduct problems, oppositional behavior

Bibliography: Yes; 19 references, from developer

---

aforementioned factor analytic studies as well as those documenting adequate discrimination between normal, conduct problem, neglected, and other clinic-referred children (Aragona & Eyberg, 1981; Eyberg & Robinson, 1983; Eyberg & Ross, 1978; Robinson et al., 1980). The scores have been found to relate significantly to direct observational measures of noncompliance and negative parent–child interactions, as well as child activity level and temperament (Robinson & Eyberg, 1981; Webster-Stratton & Eyberg, 1982). The scale has been shown to be sensitive to treatment effects from parent training in child behavior management skills (Eyberg & Robinson, 1982; Eyberg & Ross, 1978; Packard, Robinson, & Grove, 1983; Webster-Stratton, 1984).

In summary, where the investigator desires a scale measuring child conduct problems and oppositional behavior, particularly for evaluating the effects of parent training programs, this scale appears quite useful. Its narrowness of item content, however, limits its use where a broad assessment of child psychopathology is desired.

Werry–Weiss–Peters Activity Rating Scale

Two versions of the Werry–Weiss–Peters Activity Rating Scale (WWPARS) (see Table 5-8) currently exist: the longer 31-item version of the developers (see Appendix A of Werry & Sprague, 1968) and the modified 22-item version reported by Routh, Schroeder, and O'Tuama (1974), in which school-related items were deleted (see Barkley, 1981, for this scale). The original WWPARS was developed as a means of quantifying activity level in children, especially as a dependent measure for research in psychopharmacology (Werry & Sprague, 1968). Much debate has occurred over whether

TABLE 5-8. Werry–Weiss–Peters Activity Rating Scale

Developers: John Werry, Gabrielle Weiss, and John Peters (Werry & Sprague, 1968)
Where to obtain: John Werry, MD, Department of Psychiatry, University of Auckland,
    Auckland, New Zealand
Cost: None   Copyrighted: No
Items: 22–31   Scaling: 0–2   Ages: Not reported
Completion time: 5 minutes   Scoring software: No

Reliability information available:
    Test–retest: No   Interrater: Yes   Internal consistency: No

Validity information available:
    Construct: Yes   Discriminant: Yes   Concurrent: Yes
    Predictive: Yes   Treatment sensitive: Yes

Normative data: Yes (ages 2–9 years; $N = 140$)

Factors assessed: Television, bedtime /sleep, mealtime, play behaviors, restlessness

Bibliography: No

---

the scale actually assesses activity level or some other dimension of child psychopathology, such as situationally inappropriate behavior (see Ross & Ross, 1982, for a discussion). The scale has been employed in numerous studies of hyperactive children as a parent-report measure of activity level. The normative data available are for the modified version of the scale (Routh et al., 1974) and are for a small sample of children of above average intelligence from upper-middle-class families and hence are not especially representative of the larger childhood population. Additional normative data for 129 children, ages 2 to 5, were reported by Campbell and Breaux (1983).

No information on test–retest reliability could be located, but interparent agreements of .82 to .90 have been noted (Mash & Johnston, 1983; Werry, Weiss, Douglas, & Martin, 1966). Validity of the scale has been established in studies demonstrating its ability to discriminate hyperactive from normal and clinic-referred nonhyperactive children (Barkley & Ullman, 1975; Campbell, Schleifer, & Weiss, 1978; Prior, Leonard, & Wood, 1983; Routh & Schroeder, 1976; Ullman, Barkley, & Brown, 1978) and its significant correlation with actometer measures of activity level in a day hospital setting (Stevens, Kupst, Suran, & Schulman, 1978). However, others have not found parent ratings in the home on the WWPARS to correlate with clinic playroom measures of activity level or attention (Barkley & Ullman, 1975; Routh & Schroeder, 1976; Routh et al., 1974; Ullman et al., 1978). The scale has been found to correlate significantly with the Davids Hyperkinesis Index (Zentall, 1984), the Behar Preschool Behavior Questionnaire (Campbell & Breaux, 1983), and direct observational measures of mother–child interactions in a clinic playroom (Barkley & Cunningham, 1980). Evidence for some predictive validity of the scale was reported by Campbell et al. (1978) in which WWPARS ratings at age 4.5 years were significantly related to ratings on the Conners Parent Rating Scale at 6.5 years of age, and by Barkley and Cunningham (1980), in which the ratings predicted some improvements in mother–child interactions in response to stimulant medication in hyperactive children.

This scale appears of limited usefulness in cases where parental reports of situationally inappropriate activity are desired. The scale may be of some value in measuring within-subject changes in this behavior in response to interventions since it has been shown to be sensitive to both stimulant drug and parent training programs for hyperactive children (Barkley, 1977; Dubey, O'Leary, & Kaufman, 1983; Pollard et al., 1983). However, because the normative data are not satisfactory, the scale is of little value in circumstances where deviance from normal is of interest. Moreover, as noted by its developer (Werry, 1978, p. 70), the scale appears to be measuring more than simply activity level given its relationship to measures of oppositional behavior and conduct problems reported above.

TEACHER RATING SCALES

Conners Teacher Rating Scales

There are at least four versions of the Conners Teacher Rating Scales in current use: (1) the original Conners Teacher Rating Scale (Conners, 1969, 1973); (2) the revised Conners Teacher Rating Scale (Goyette et al., 1978); (3) the Abbreviated Symptom Questionnaire, or Hyperactivity Index (see Goyette et al., 1978); and (4) the Iowa Conners Teacher Rating Scale (Loney & Milich, 1981). These scales vary primarily in the number of items of the original scale they have retained. The Abbreviated Symptom Questionnaire has also been called the Abbreviated Teacher Rating Scale.

Original Conners Teacher Rating Scale

Developed to assess the effects of stimulant drugs in hyperactive children and to aid in differentiating hyperactive from nonhyperactive children, the original Conners Teacher Rating Scale (CTRS) (see Table 5-9) has become the most widely used rating scale in research on child psychopathology to date. Each of the 39 items is rated on a scale of "not at all," "just a little," "pretty much," and "very much," with these responses assigned credits of 0–3 points, respectively. A total score can be obtained by summing across all items, and factors scores are derived by summing the credits across only those items loading on that factor. The largest sample of normative data, comprising more than 9,500 Canadian children, was collected by Trites, Blouin, and Laprade (1982), although smaller samples of normal children are available for the United States (Kupietz, Bialer, & Winsberg, 1972; Ullmann et al., 1985), New Zealand (Sprague, Cohen, & Werry, 1974),

TABLE 5-9. Original Conners Teacher Rating Scale

Developer: C. Keith Conners (1969)

Where to obtain: C. Keith Conners, PhD, Department of Psychiatry, Children's Hospital
National Medical Center, 111 Michigan Ave. N.W., Washington DC 20010

Cost: None   Copyrighted: No

Items: 39   Scaling: 0–3   Ages: Not reported

Completion time: 5–10 minutes   Scoring software: Yes

Reliability information available:
      Test–retest: Yes   Interrater: No   Internal consistency: Yes

Validity information available:
      Construct: Yes   Discriminant: Yes   Concurrent: Yes
      Predictive: No   Treatment sensitive: Yes

Normative data: Yes (ages 4–12 years; $N = 9,583$)

Factors assessed: Hyperactivity, conduct problem, emotional–overindulgent, anxious–passive,
      asocial, daydreams/attendance problem

Bibliography: Yes; 260 references, from developer

Germany (Sprague, Cohen, & Eichlseder, 1977), Australia (Glow, 1979), French Canada (Trites & Laprade, 1984), Italy (O'Leary, Vivian, & Nisi, 1985), and Great Britain (Taylor & Sandberg, 1984; Thorley, 1983). Nevertheless, despite its wide application and the collection of normative samples, the range of ages for these samples remains limited to the elementary school ages (4 to 12 years). Moreover, different studies have found somewhat different factor structures, making it imperative that investigators identify the source for the factor scores when reporting data on the factors. Conners recommends that the norms collected by Trites et al. (1982) and the factors derived therefrom be employed, inasmuch as they represent the largest sample available.

Reliability information for the original Conners scale has been well established. Test–retest coefficients over a 1-month interval ranged from .70 to .90 across factors (Conners, 1973) and showed satisfactory stability over a 1-year interval, with reliability coefficients ranging from .35 to .57 (Trites, Blouin, Ferguson, & Lynch, 1981). An Australian revision of this scale, the Adelaide version, has also shown excellent stability over a 1-year interval (Glow et al., 1982). Trites et al. (1982) reported interrater (teacher) agreements of .17 to .53 across four of the six factors, with most falling between .44 and .53. Others have found interteacher agreements of .92 for the entire scale, with coefficients ranging from .09 to .89 across the factors (Vincent, Williams, Harris, & Duvall, 1977). As with the Trites et al. (1982) study, lower agreements were found for those factors reflecting neurotic or internalizing characteristics and higher agreements for conduct problems or externalizing symptoms. Agreements between teachers and trained classroom behavioral observers have also been satisfactory, ranging from .39 to .73 (mean .51) across the factors (Kazdin, Esveldt-Dawson, & Loar, 1983).

Information on the validity of the scale comes from a multitude of sources, including the original factor analytic study by Conners (1969) using normal children, and the later work by Trites et al. (1981), Arnold et al. (1981), Glow et al. (1982), O'Leary et al. (1985), Taylor and Sandberg (1984), and Trites and Laprade (1984). Other studies have examined the factor structure of the scale for neurotic and conduct problem children (Conners, 1969), as well as speech- and language-delayed children (Mattison et al., 1980). Various factors from the scale were found to correlate significantly with direct observations of activity level and negative parent–child interactions in the home (Rapoport & Benoit, 1975), inclass behavioral observations and achievement tests (Copeland & Weissbrod, 1978; Lahey, Green, & Forehand, 1980; Kendall & Brophy, 1981), and computerized continuous performance tests (Klee & Garfinkel, 1983). The concurrent validity of the scale has been frequently demonstrated through findings of significant correlations with other rating scales, including the Behavior Problem Checklist (Arnold et al., 1981; Campbell & Steinert, 1978), Davids Hyperactivity Index (Arnold et al., 1981), and the Child Behavior Checklist (Achenbach & Edelbrock, 1983), among others. Numerous studies attest to the ability of the scale to differentiate significantly between various groups of clinic-referred and nonreferred children, such as hyperactive and normal children (Conners, 1969; Sandoval, 1977); conduct problem, normal, and hyperactive children (Taylor & Sandberg, 1984); hyperactive, learning-disabled, and normal children (Ackerman, Elardo, & Dykman, 1979); speech- and language-delayed children (Baker et al., 1980); and other groups of children (King & Young, 1982; Leon et al., 1980; Salzinger et al., 1984). The scale has also proven quite useful as a measure of treatment effects in studies on stimulant medication (see Barkley, 1977, and Cantwell & Carlson, 1979, for reviews), dietary manipulations with hyperactive children (Harley et al., 1981), self-control training (Horn, Chatoor, & Conners, 1983), and classroom behavior modification programs (Abikoff & Gittelman, 1984; O'Leary & Pelham, 1978).

There can be little question that where investigators desire a quick screening measure of psychopathology, particularly conduct problems, the CTRS is a most valuable scale with an enviable record of research on its properties. Although its breadth of item coverage for the neurotic or internalizing disorders is somewhat weak, several factors have been found to reflect these dimensions of psychopathology. Those wishing to use the scale to assess treatment effects should be cautious of demonstrated practice effects wherein reductions in scores are noted to be significant between first and second administrations (Ullmann et al., 1985). Conners suggests that the scale be administered at least twice before assessing pre- and posttreatment effects. Where normative data are of importance, the scale appears to have the largest pool of data available for any rating scale for ages 4 to 12 years (Trites et al., 1982).

Revised Conners Teacher Rating Scale

In 1978 the original 39-item scale was reduced to 28 items, producing the Revised Conners Teacher Rating Scale (CTRS-R) (see Table 5-10). Most of the items retained are similar to those on the original scale with some slight rewording, and the response scaling for each item remains the same. The scale and its psychometric properties and norms are available in the report by Goyette *et al.* (1978). Test–retest reliability coefficients over a 1-week period were found to be .97 for the total score and .94 to .98 for the factors (Edelbrock & Reed, 1984). However, no information on interrater (teacher) agreement or internal consistency coefficients could be located for this revised version. Parent–teacher agreement has ranged from .33 to .45 across factors (Goyette *et al.*, 1978), which is not surprising in view of the different situations and behaviors being rated by each adult. Information on the validity of the revised version is less given its relatively recent development, but given the comparability of the factors with their counterparts on the original scale, the revised version is likely to prove as valid and useful for assessing externalizing or conduct problem symptoms as the original. The factors from the revised version correlate well with comparable factors from the Child Behavior Checklist—Teacher Report Form (Edelbrock & Reed, 1984). Like the original scale, the revised version has also proved useful in assessing behavioral changes in hyperactive children due to stimulant medication (Barkley, Fischer, Newby, & Breen, 1985).

The CTRS-R appears most useful as a quick screening measure for conduct problems and hyperactivity, but not especially useful for evaluating internalizing, neurotic, depressive, and anxious symptoms. It is likely to find its greatest value in assessing stimulant drug effects or other treatment effects where the convenience of teacher completion of the scale is paramount. Once again, however, investigators must be aware of potential practice effects on

TABLE 5-10. Revised Conners Teacher Rating Scale

Developer: C. Keith Conners (see Goyette *et al.*, 1978)
Where to obtain: Same as original scale (see Table 5-9)
Cost: None   Copyrighted: No
Items: 28   Scaling: 0–3   Ages: 3–17 years
Completion time: 5–10 minutes   Scoring software: Yes
Reliability information available:
       Test–retest: Yes   Interrater: No   Internal consistency: No
Validity information available:
       Construct: Yes   Discriminant: No   Concurrent: Yes
       Predictive: No   Treatment sensitive: No
Normative data: Yes (ages 3–17 years; $N = 383$)
Factors assessed: Conduct problem, hyperactivity, inattentive–passive
Bibliography: Yes; see original scale (Table 5-9)

---

the scale over repeat administrations, following the guidelines set forth for the original scale.

Conners Abbreviated Symptom Questionnaire

Although the brief 10-item scale making up the Conners Abbreviated Symptom Questionnaire (ASQ) (see Table 5-11) is one of the most frequently used instruments for selecting hyperactive children for research, investigators should know that at least four versions of this ASQ, or hyperactivity index, have been used (Ullmann *et al.*, 1985). The initial 10 items, like those for the parent ASQ described earlier, were believed to reflect the most frequently endorsed items by teachers in rating hyperactive children. Yet, more recent research suggests the scale is assessing a mixture of hyperactive *and* conduct problem symptoms and so children selected by this instrument will not be purely hyperactive but a mixed group of hyperactive/conduct-disordered children. Conners recommends that the 10-item index cited in the paper by Goyette *et al.* (1978) be used and that investigators state which version of the scale they have employed in their research articles.

The utility of this scale is chiefly in selecting groups of hyperactive children for research and in assessing changes in hyperactive and conduct problem behaviors after intervention, particularly stimulant drug therapy. In doing so, the scale has an abundance of literature available on its psychometric properties and treatment sensitivity. Normative data for the scale are available in the paper by Goyette *et al.* (1978). Test–retest reliabilities of .91 to .98 have been found (Edelbrock & Reed, 1984; Milich, Loney, & Whitten, 1980) over 1-week intervals, and .89 over a 2-week interval (Zentall & Barrack, 1979). Interrater agreement for the ASQ with teachers could not be located, but that cited earlier for the same 10-item scale completed by parents has been satisfactory. Agreement between parent and teachers of .49

TABLE 5-11. Conners Abbreviated Symptom Questionnaire

Developer: C. Keith Conners (see Goyette *et al.*, 1978)
Where to obtain: Same as original scale
Cost: None   Copyrighted: No
Items: 10   Scaling: 0–3   Ages: 3–17 years
Completion time: 3–5 minutes   Scoring software: No

Reliability information available:
     Test–retest: Yes   Interrater: Yes   Internal consistency: No

Validity information available:
     Construct: Yes   Discriminant: Yes   Concurrent: Yes
     Predictive: No   Treatment sensitive: Yes

Normative data: Yes (ages 3–17 years; $N = 383$)

Factors assessed: Hyperactivity, conduct problems

Bibliography: Yes; 260 references, from developer

---

was reported by Goyette *et al.* (1978), which is satisfactory considering the differences between home and school settings and behaviors being rated by these individuals. As with the parent ASQ, validity information has come from research demonstrating significant relationships between the ratings and teacher ratings of impulsivity, laboratory tests of impulse control and distractibility (Brown & Wynne, 1982), teacher records of aggression and hyperactivity, clinic playroom observations of child behaviors, and other rating scales of hyperactivity and conduct problems (Arnold *et al.*, 1981). The scale has proved sensitive to behavioral changes related to stimulant drug treatment (Sprague & Sleator, 1977) and cognitive–behavioral training in self–control strategies with impulsive children (Kendall & Wilcox, 1980; Kendall & Zupan, 1981).

Iowa Conners Teacher Rating Scale

Loney and Milich (1981) selected 10 items from the original CTRS, five of which had high loadings on the conduct problem factor and five on the hyperactivity factor (see Table 5-12). The items were selected for high divergence such that each item loaded only one one factor and not the other. This was done to be able to select purely aggressive versus purely hyperactive children. The 10 items use the same response scaling as the CTRS and separate scores are calculated for the two factors. Normative data are not available on the scale, and its chief use has been in selecting children as either hyperactive, aggressive, or both. Milich, Roberts, Loney, and Caputo (1980) have reported significant stability of ratings on these two factors over a 2-year period. However, other information on the scale's psychometric properties is lacking.

TABLE 5-12. Iowa Conners Teacher Rating Scale

Developers: Richard Milich and Jan Loney (see Loney & Milich, 1981)

Where to obtain: Jan Loney, PhD, Department of Psychiatry, State University of New York at Stony Brook, Stony Brook, NY 11794-8790

Cost: None   Copyrighted: No

Items: 10   Scaling: 0–3   Ages: Not reported

Completion time: 3–5 minutes   Scoring software: No

Reliability information available:
         Test–retest: Yes   Interrater: No   Internal consistency: No

Validity information available:
         Construct: Yes   Discriminant: Yes   Concurrent: No
         Predictive: Yes   Treatment sensitive: No

Normative data: None

Factors assessed: Hyperactivity, aggression

Bibliography: No

Child Behavior Checklist—Teacher Report Form

The Child Behavior Checklist—Teacher Report Form (CBCL-TRF) (see Table 5-13) is quite similar in format and item content to the parent report form described earlier. In place of the social competence profile on the parent form, an adaptive functioning profile has been developed, reflecting the child's work habits, level of academic performance, degree of teacher familiarity with the child, and general happiness of the child. The behavior problem profile, like that for the parent, comprises a number of factorially developed scales spanning a broad range of child psychopathology. These profiles differ according to the age and sex of the child (three age groupings by sex), respecting the changing nature of psychopathology across the developmental span of childhood and adolescence. This is a major advantage of this scale over other teacher rating scales; a further advantage is the excellent normative data available for addressing questions of statistical deviance.

Test–retest reliability was reported to average .89 across the various scores from the measure (range .74–.96) over a 1-week period (Edelbrock & Achenbach, 1984). For a 2-month interval, the mean coefficient was .77 (range .63–.88), while stability coefficients over a 4-month period ranged between .25 and .82 (mean .64), indicating satisfactory test–retest reliability as well as stability of the scores over longer periods. As with most scales, stability of the internalizing scales was generally lower than those for the externalizing scales. However, significant declines were noted in six of the eight behavior problem scale scores over the 4-month interval—a finding of import for studies wishing to measure changes in ratings due to treatment. Interteacher agreements have not yet been reported for this scale, but,

TABLE 5-13. Child Behavior Checklist—Teacher Report Form

Developers: Craig Edelbrock and Thomas Achenbach (1984)

Where to obtain: Thomas Achenbach, PhD, Department of Psychiatry, University of Vermont, Burlington, VT 05401

Cost: $5.00 for sample kit   Copyrighted: Yes

Items: 126   Scaling: 0–2   Ages: 6–16 years

Completion time: 15–20 minutes   Scoring software: Yes

Reliability information available:
    Test–retest: Yes   Interrater: No   Internal consistency: Yes

Validity information available:
    Construct: Yes   Discriminant: Yes   Concurrent: Yes
    Predictive: No   Treatment sensitive: No

Normative data: Yes (ages 6–16 years; $N = 1,100$)

Factors assessed (varies with age and sex): Anxious, social withdrawal, unpopular, self-destructive, obsessive–compulsive, inattentive, nervous–overactive, aggressive; ratings of school performance also provided

Bibliography: Yes; see manual (Achenbach & Edelbrock, 1983)

---

parent–teacher agreements have ranged between .29 (anxiety) and .61 (hyperactivity) (Edelbrock, personal communication).

Due to the recent availability of the scale, information on its various types of validity are not as substantial as for the parent report form described earlier. Nevertheless, what research has been done suggests great promise for this rating scale. Significant correlations between scores on the behavior problem profile and those obtained by direct classroom observations have been obtained (Edelbrock, personal communication; Reed & Edelbrock, 1983), and the factor scores correlate well with their equivalents on the Conners Teacher Rating Scale (Edelbrock & Reed, 1984). The inattention scale as well as several from the adaptive functioning profile have also been found to differentiate significantly between clinic-referred children with attention deficit disorders and those referred for other problems, and to further differentiate between those ADD children with hyperactivity and those without (Edelbrock, Costello, & Kessler, 1984; Kazdin *et al.*, 1983). Another recent study (Harris, King, Reifler, & Rosenberg, 1984) noted significant differences between learning-disabled children and those with emotional disabilities on four of the eight scales from the behavior problem profile. The use of the scale as a measure of treatment effects has not yet been accomplished.

In summary, the CBCL-TRF is still in the process of validation as of this writing, but it offers great promise as an equally useful counterpart to the parent report form of this scale, on which more research has been done. As a measure of general psychopathology in children, as well as of the more commonly found specific dimensions of maladjustment, the scale appears to be quite useful. Its method of development and standardization are without equal within the various scales available for teacher reports of child behavior problems. The availability of the parent report form, youth self-report form (now completing standardization), and direct observation form (see manual) of this same scale further recommends its adoption for research, particularly where multiple informants and sources of information are of interest. With further research on its interrater agreement with teachers and its construct, discriminant, and concurrent validity, this scale should offer great utility to investigators wishing a broad yet conveniently administered method of assessment for child psychopathology, profile analysis of subtypes of psychopathology, and treatment outcome research.

School Behavior Checklist

The School Behavior Checklist (SBC) (see Table 5-14) assesses a wide array of problem behaviors in child psychopathology. Form A-1 (104 items) is for use with children ages 3 to 6 years, whereas form A-2 (96 items) is for ages 7 to 13 years. The items are answered true or false and are scored to yield six factor scores and a total deviance score on form A-2 (see factors above),

TABLE 5-14. School Behavior Checklist

Developer: Lovick C. Miller (1981)
Where to obtain: Western Psychological Services, 12031 Wilshire Blvd., Los Angeles, CA 90025
Cost: $32.50   Copyrighted:Yes
Items: 104/96   Scaling: 0–1   Ages: 3–13 years
Completion time: 20 minutes   Scoring software: No

Reliability information available:
      Test–retest: Yes   Interrater: No   Internal consistency: Yes

Validity information available:
      Construct: Yes   Discriminant: Yes   Concurrent: No
      Predictive: Yes   Treatment sensitive: No

Normative data available: Yes (4–13 years; $N = 5{,}912$)

Factors assessed: Low need achievement, aggression, anxiety, academic disability,
    hostile isolation, extraversion

Bibliography: Yes; see manual

---

while for form A-1 the academic disability factor is now a cognitive disability one. Two additional scores for form A-1 can be scored, these being the rationally developed scales of normal irritability and school disturbance. Normative data by year and sex are available for form A-1 and by sex alone for A-2. The normative sample for form A-2 is substantial (over 5,000 children) and certainly that for form A-1 would appear adequate (greater than 500). A sixth- to seventh-grade reading level would appear to be necessary for completion of the scale.

Reliability information is chiefly found in the manual (Miller, 1981). Test–retest information is provided for form A-2 only. Over a 6-week interval, coefficients of .70–.89 were found. Split-half reliabilities of .58–.95 were found for form A-1 and .44–.93 for A-2. Interteacher agreements were not reported, but parent–teacher agreements of .11–.50 and .06–.57 have been noted for forms A-1 and A-2, respectively.

The validity of the scale has been established by several means, including the original factor analytic studies developing the scales, as well as research showing significant differences among groups of phobic, learning-disabled, aggressive, and normal children (see manual; Miller, 1976). Differences between depressed and nondepressed seventh-grade students have also been reported on several of the SBC scales (Seagull & Weinshank, 1984). The relationship of this scale to other teacher rating scales has not been reported, but the scores have been reported to correlate significantly with measures of intelligence (see manual). The scale has apparently not been used in assessing treatment outcome.

The SBC would appear to have some utility as a measure of child psychopathology in children of ages 4 to 13 years, having adequate test–retest reliability and some information available on its validity. Nevertheless, several limitations exist with the scales. The factorial structure of the scales was obtained for 7- to 13-year-olds on form A-2 and was extrapolated downward to the 3- to 6-year-old group, where a different set of factors might have been obtained had they been analyzed. In addition, the factor structure for form A-2 was developed on normal children and may not reflect that structure likely to have emerged had a clinic referred population served as the subject pool (see Achenbach & Edelbrock, 1983). Norms for form A-1 have an overrepresentation of black and lower-socioeconomic-status children, and despite it being labeled as useful for 3-year-olds, no norms for that age group are reported. These are problems only if normative data are desired.

ADD-H Comprehensive Teacher Rating Scale

The ADD-H Comprehensive Teacher Rating Scale (ACTeRS) (see Table 5-15) was developed for the assessment of children with attention deficit disorders and for monitoring their response to treatment. The four subscales assessed by the ACTeRS were developed through factor analysis, with the oppositional behavior factor accounting for more than 76% of the variance. This factor is quite similar to the conduct problems factor on the Conners Teacher Rating Scale and the aggression factor on the CBCL-TRF. Normative data for a large sample of ages 5 to 12 years are provided in a profile format for easy interpretation of factor scale elevations. However, norms are not reported by age or sex.

Unpublished data are available from Ullmann on the reliability of the instrument. Over a 2-week interval, test–retest coefficients ranged from .68 to .78 for 55 ADD children. Interteacher agreements for 131 children referred for learning disabilities services ranged between .51 and .73. Internal consistency was reported to be .93–.97 (α coefficients).

TABLE 5-15. ADD-H Comprehensive Teacher Rating Scale

Developers: Rina K. Ullmann, Esther Sleator, and Robert L. Sprague (1984a)

Where to obtain: Rina K. Ullmann, PhD, Institute for Child Behavior and Development, 51 Gerty Dr., Champaign, IL 61820

Cost: None   Copyrighted: No

Items: 24   Scaling: 1–5   Ages: 5–12 years

Completion time: 5–10 minutes   Scoring software: No

Reliability information available:
     Test–retest: Yes   Interrater: Yes   Internal consistency: Yes

Validity information available:
     Construct: Yes   Discriminant: Yes   Concurrent: No
     Predictive: No   Treatment sensitive: Yes

Normative data: Yes (ages 5–12 years; $N = 1,347$)

Factors assessed: Oppositional behavior, attention, hyperactivity, social problems

Bibliography: No

The construct validity of the scale rests mainly on its development through factor analysis. Little research is yet available correlating it with other measures or ratings of these same constructs. Moreover, the use of a normal population on which to base the factor analysis of the scale leaves open to question the generality of this factor structure to groups of clinic-referred children. The scale has been noted to significantly differentiate ADD from normal and learning-disabled children (Ullmann, 1984; Ullmann, Sleator, & Sprague, 1984b) and has shown some sensitivity to stimulant drug effects (Ullmann & Sleator, 1984a, 1984b) in research with ADD children.

In general, the chief utility of this scale is in research on children with attention deficit disorders, and particularly where stimulant drug treatment is being studied. Greater research is necessary on the validity of the scale. It is not clear what advantages this scale has over the Conners Teacher Rating Scale, which assesses a somewhat similar factor structure, which has a larger sample of normative data, and on which there is far greater research on its reliability and validity.

MULTI-INFORMANT RATING SCALES

Behavior Problem Checklists

Two versions of this scale presently exist—the original (Quay & Peterson, 1975) and recently revised versions (Quay & Peterson, 1983, 1984). Future research should employ the revised version, since Quay is no longer making the original version of the scale available. Nevertheless, the original version will be discussed here because of the substantial research on its development, reliability, and validity, which, because of many similarities between the scales, can provide some information on these properties with regard to the new scale.

Original Behavior Problem Checklist

The Original Behavior Problem Checklist (BPC) (see Table 5-16) scale is one of the most commonly used behavior rating scales in research, second only to the Conners Teacher Rating Scales. It can be completed by parents, teachers, residential treatment center staffs, or other informants experienced with children. The scale identifies broad dimensions of psychopathology based upon orthogonal factors discovered through factor analysis of the ratings on different clinic populations. The fourth factor (socialized delinquency) emerged during analyses of data on juvenile offenders and appears to be a less stable factor than the other three. Quay suggests caution in its interpretation. Victor and Halverson (1975) developed two additional scales (distractibility and hypersensitivity) for studying normal children. Normative data for children in grades K to 2 (Arnold *et al.*, 1981; Werry & Quay,

TABLE 5-16. Original Behavior Problem Checklist

Developers: Herbert C. Quay and Donald R. Peterson (1975)

Where to obtain: Herbert C. Quay, PhD, Program in Applied Social Sciences,
      University of Miami, P.O. Box 248074, Coral Gables, FL 33124

Cost: $20.00   Copyrighted: Yes

Items: 55   Scaling: 0–2   Ages: Not reported

Completion time: 10–15 minutes   Scoring software: No

Reliability information available:
      Test–retest: Yes   Interrater: Yes   Internal consistency: Yes

Validity information available:
      Construct: Yes   Discriminant: Yes   Concurrent: Yes
      Predictive: Yes   Treatment sensitive: Yes

Normative data: Yes (ages 5–13 years)

Factors assessed: Conduct problems, personality problems, inadequate–immature, socialized
      delinquency

Bibliography: Yes; see Quay (1977)

1971), 3 to 4 (Schultz, Salvia, & Fein, 1974), and 7 to 8 (Quay & Quay, 1965) were reported using teachers as informants. A 36-item version of the scale was also used, for which there are norms on 24,997 children (Stone, 1981) for the conduct and personality problem factors only. Data are also available on various clinical populations such as deaf (Hirshoren & Schittjer, 1979), visually impaired (Schittjer & Hirshoren, 1981), institutionalized retarded (Quay & Gredler, 1981), emotionally disturbed (Quay, Morse, & Cutler, 1966), clinic-referred (Lessing & Zagorin, 1971), and learning-disabled children (Paraskevopolous & McCarthy, 1970). Norms for Oglala Sioux Indian children were reported by O'Donnell and Cress (1975). These studies and others have provided additional information on the factor structure of the scale with various populations (O'Donnell & Van Tuinan, 1979).

Ample evidence exists to support the reliability of the scale. Test–retest reliability over a 2-week period was found to range from .74 to .93 (Evans, 1975) for teachers, and from .46 to .70 for dormitory counselors (Kelley, 1981). Stability of the factors over a 2-year interval with normal children were relatively high (range .28–.74) using teacher ratings (Victor & Halverson, 1976). Interparent agreements between .43 and .83 were noted in several studies (Jacob, Grounds, & Haley, 1982; Quay, Sprague, Schulman, & Miller, 1966) depending upon the factor score and the population being used. Not unexpectedly, lower agreements were found for clinic-referred than for normal children, and for inadequate–immature scores than for the other factors. Studies vary as to whether ratings given by mothers differed significantly from those of fathers (Jacob et al., 1982; Speer, 1971). Agreements between teachers have ranged from .22 to .77 (Quay & Quay, 1965; Peterson, 1961), and from .06 to .68 for dormitory counselors (Kelley, 1981). Information on parent–teacher agreements can be found in the papers by

Quay *et al.* (1966), Emery and O'Leary (1984), and Touliatos and Lindholm (1981). Ratings have been found to vary as a function of age, grade, sex, race, and social class of the children (Eaves, 1975; Speer, 1971; Touliatos & Lindholm, 1975).

The validity of the BPC is well documented in the review by Quay (1966, 1977) and the manual (Quay & Peterson, 1975). Its scales have been found to correlate significantly with measures of activity level (Victor, Halverson, Inoff, & Buczkowski, 1973); recidivism in male criminal offenders (Mack, 1969); peer and teacher ratings of classroom behavior (Harris, Drummond, & Schultz, 1977; Victor & Halverson, 1975); galvanic skin responses (Borkovec, 1970); anemia (Webb & Oski, 1973); equivalent scales on the Conners scales (Arnold *et al.*, 1981; Campbell & Steinert, 1978); the Davids Hyperkinesis Index (Arnold *et al.*, 1981); the Bower–Lambert procedures for identifying emotionally handicapped children (Schultz, Manton, & Salvia, 1972); and the Devereaux scales (Proger, Mann, Green, Bayuk, & Burger, 1975). Others have examined the relationship of the scales to marital discord in the parents of the rated children (Emery & O'Leary, 1982, 1984; Porter & O'Leary, 1980). The BPC has been shown to discriminate significantly between various groups of children, including clinic-referred and normal children (Speer, 1971; Sultana, 1974); aggressive, hyperactive, and withdrawn children (Proger *et al.*, 1975); and epileptic, hyperactive, learning-disabled, and normal children (Campbell, 1974). Several studies used the BPC successfully to evaluate changes following psychotherapy (Aksamit, 1974; Brown, 1975; Zold & Speer, 1971) and stimulant medication (Knights & Hinton, 1969; Millichap, Aymat, Sturgis, Larsen, & Egan, 1969).

Revised Behavior Problem Checklist

The expansion of the BPC to 89 items in the Revised Behavior Problem Checklist (RBPC) (see Table 5-17) has permitted a broader assessment of commonly identified dimensions of psychopathology than did the original version. The addition of several items for assessing psychotic behavior increases the utility of the scale for programs dealing with more severely disturbed children. Normative data can be found in the manual for both parent and teacher ratings on large samples of children between grades K and 12, and also in Aman, Werry, Fitzpatrick, Lowe, and Waters (1983). Those available for parent ratings are on a smaller sample. Additional normative data on parent ratings for a wider age group would be desirable. Although there is less information available on the reliability and validity of this revised version due to its recent development, what is accumulating suggests that the scale will prove as satisfactory in these areas as did the original version. Test–retest coefficients have ranged between .49 and .83. Interteacher agreements have ranged between .52 and .85, while interparent agreements were reported to be between .55 and .93 (Quay & Peterson, 1983, 1984). The scale has been shown to significantly differentiate clinic-referred

TABLE 5-17. Revised Behavior Problem Checklist

Developers: Herbert C. Quay and Donald Peterson (1983, 1984)
Where to obtain: Same as BPC (see Table 5-16)
Cost: $20.00   Copyrighted: Yes
Items: 89   Scaling: 0–2   Ages: 5–17 years
Completion time: 15–20 minutes   Scoring software: No

Reliability information available:
      Test–retest: Yes   Interrater: Yes   Internal consistency: Yes

Validity information available:
      Construct: Yes   Discriminant: Yes   Concurrent: Yes
      Predictive: No   Treatment sensitive: No

Normative data: Yes (ages 5–17 years; for teachers and mothers)

Factors assessed: Conduct disorder, socialized aggression, attention problems–immaturity, anxiety–withdrawal, psychotic behavior, motor tension–excess

Bibliography: Yes; see Quay (1983) and manual (Quay & Peterson, 1983, 1984)

---

and normal children (see manual and Aman & Werry, 1984), and attention deficit disorders with and without hyperactivity (Lahey, Shaughency, Strauss, & Frame, 1984).

Preschool Behavior Questionnaire

The Preschool Behavior Questionnaire (PBQ) (see Table 5-18) was originally developed to identify preschoolers at risk for the development of later emotional problems. Item coverage is limited to the factors noted in Table 5-18, with little content dealing with social withdrawal, psychosomatic symptoms, psychotic or obsessive–compulsive behaviors, or learning and cognitive problems. Although the normative data available are for teacher reports (see Behar & Stringfield, 1974), recent research has used the scale for assess-

TABLE 5-18. Preschool Behavior Questionnaire

Developers: Lenore Behar and Samuel Stringfield (Behar, 1974)
Where to obtain: Lenore Behar, PhD, 1821 Woodburn Rd., Durham, NC 27705
Cost: $10.00   Copyrighted: Yes
Items: 30   Scaling: 0–2   Ages: 3–6 years
Completion time: 5–10 minutes   Scoring software: No

Reliability information available:
      Test–retest: Yes   Interrater: Yes   Internal consistency: No

Validity information available:
      Construct: Yes   Discriminant: Yes   Concurrent: Yes
      Predictive: No   Treatment sensitive: No

Normative data: Yes (ages 3–6 years; $N = 496$, teacher ratings)

Factors assessed: Hostile–aggressive, anxious, hyperactive–distractible

Bibliography: Yes; see Behar (1977)

---

ing parental ratings of child behavior (Campbell & Breaux, 1983). Where establishing the deviance of child behavioral problems in preschool children based upon parental ratings is of interest, use of the Child Behavior Checklist would be more helpful given the availability of better norms for 4- to 5-year-olds.

Test–retest reliability over a 3- to 4-month period was found to range from .60 to .94, and interrater reliability for teacher ratings was .67 to .84 (Behar & Stringfield, 1974). The scale significantly differentiates hyperactive and normal preschool children (Campbell, Szumowski, Ewing, Gluck, & Breaux, 1982; Prior *et al.*, 1983) as well as normal and emotionally disturbed preschoolers (Behar, 1977). Ratings have been found to correlate significantly with observations of classroom behavior and interactions (Behar, 1977; Rubin & Clark, 1983) and ratings from the Kohn Problem Checklist and California Preschool Social Competence Scale (Behar & Stringfield, 1974).

Although at the time of its original development (1973) it was the best rating scale available for preschool children, it has been overshadowed by the development of other ratings scales having better normative data and research on their psychometric properties. The Conners Parent Rating Scales now have norms down to age 3 years, while that for the Child Behavior Checklist extends to age 4 years. The latter scale also has broader item coverage, yielding greater information on more dimensions of psychopathology. However, where a short screening instrument of emotional disturbance in preschoolers is desired using teacher reports, the scale may continue to be of value as other teacher rating scales do not have normative data down to age 3 years.

Self-Control Rating Scale

The Self-Control Rating Scale (SCRS) (see Table 5-19) was developed to assess the narrow constellation of behaviors associated with deficits in

TABLE 5-19. Self-Control Rating Scale

Developers: Phillip C. Kendall and Lance E. Wilcox (1979)

Where to obtain: Phillip C. Kendall, PhD, Department of Psychology, Temple University, Weiss Hall, Fourth Floor, Philadelphia, PA 19122

Cost: None   Copyrighted: No

Items: 33   Scaling: 1–7   Ages: Not reported

Completion time: 5–10 minutes   Scoring software: No

Reliability information available:
    Test–retest: Yes   Interrater: No   Internal consistency: No

Validity information available:
    Construct: Yes   Discriminant: Yes   Concurrent: Yes
    Predictive: No   Treatment sensitive: Yes

Normative data: Yes (ages 8–11 years; $N = 110$, teacher ratings)

Factors assessed: Self-control behavior

Bibliography: No

---

self-control in children and to evaluate changes in this behavior associated with cognitive–behavioral interventions. As such, it seems to have some utility for this prupose, and has shown sensitivity to treatment effects from such interventions (Kendall & Braswell, 1982). Nevertheless, the normative data are quite restricted in sample size and age range, making the scale of little value in establishing statistical deviance of children on this measure. Interrater reliability information is lacking, but test–retest reliability was .84 over a 3- to 4-week interval. Ratings on the scale correlate significantly with the Kagan Matching Familiar Figures Test, Porteus Mazes, teacher ratings on the Child Behavior Checklist, and classroom observations of off-task and disruptive behavior (Kendall, Zupan, & Braswell, 1981; Kendall & Wilcox, 1979). The scale significantly differentiates children referred by teachers for self-control problems versus those who were not so referred (Kendall & Wilcox, 1979) and children referred to mental health clinics versus those referred to medical clinics (Robin, Fischel, & Brown, 1984). Research using parent ratings on the scale has been much more limited (see Kendall & Braswell, 1982). A slightly modified version of this scale is available with normative data on 763 children in the fourth and fifth grades using teacher ratings (Humphrey, 1982).

Fear Survey Schedule

The Fear Survey Schedule (see Table 5-20) was originally developed to evaluate a wide range of potential fears in children and adolescence (Miller et al., 1971). Informants can be parents, teachers, or the children. The scale lacks adequate normative data, but would have some utility in epidemiological surveys of the incidence of children's fears and perhaps in assessing change in highly fearful children as a function of interventions. Little or no research exists on the scale's reliability, validity, and sensitivity to treatment effects.

TABLE 5-20. Fear Survey Schedule

Developers: Lovick C. Miller, Curtis L. Barrett, Edward Hampe, and Helen Noble (1971)
Where to obtain: Lovick C. Miller, PhD, Child Psychiatry Research Center, University of
      Louisville School of Medicine, 608 South Jackson St., Louisville, KY 40202
Cost: None   Copyrighted: No
Items: 81   Scaling: 1–3   Ages: 4–18 years
Completion time: 15–20 minutes   Scoring software: No
Reliability information available:
      Test–retest: No   Interrater: No   Internal consistency: Yes
Validity information available:
      Construct: Yes   Discriminant: No   Concurrent: No
      Predictive: No   Treatment sensitive: No
Normative data: No

Factors assessed: Fear of physical injury/personal loss, fear of natural or supernatural events, psychic distress

DISCUSSION

A vast number of rating scales of child behavior are currently in existence, only a handful of which could be reviewed here. However, it is clear from this review that sufficient scales exist for the purposes of assessing the most common dimensions of psychopathology in children. There is little need for any further development of other general, broad-band behavior rating scales for children. Investigators desiring such scales have only to look to the recent literature to find one that will likely suit most purposes for which such scales are sought. Advancement in this area is likely to come only from further investigations of the properties and utility of those scales already in existence, particularly those that have been well developed and standardized, such as the Child Behavior Checklist (parent and teacher forms), the Revised Behavior Problem Checklist, and the Conners scales.

Such is not the case, however, concerning very narrow-band rating scales assessing highly specific aspects of psychopathology, such as anxiety, depression, psychosomatic complaints, and social skills, where few if any adequate parent and teacher rating scales exist. Although it is possible to utilize the particular subscales evaluating these areas from the broad-band rating scales already in existence, these do not necessarily permit an in-depth assessment of these areas of psychopathology. A few highly specialized scales have already come into existence for self-control, activity level, and fears (see Table 5-20), but more of these scales could certainly be developed, and greater research is definitely required for those already in existence.

A major area of weakness in the literature has been the utility of many of the current rating scales in assessing changes in behavior either due to treatment effects, developmental effects, or eventual adult outcome. Like the literature on child psychopathology in general, that with rating scales has been heavily obsessed with describing dimensions of child behavior rather than evaluating specific interventions for these dimensions. Even though prescriptive research cannot progress until some descriptive research has occurred, the present state of affairs with rating scales is sufficiently lopsided to eliminate this as a credible defense. Rating scales have much to offer by way of subgrouping populations of children into more specific "taxons" and relating this to differential treatment outcomes (Achenbach & Edelbrock, 1983). Such a procedure allows others to replicate the study by employing the same scale and cutoff points for subject classification, the lack of which has created severe problems for research on certain childhood disorders due to the idiosyncratic and subjective criteria now used by many investigators for subject selection (see Barkley, 1982, for a review of this dilemma with attention deficit disorders).

A related problem with the literature on rating scales has been the extent to which such scales are sensitive to practice or regression effects over repeated administrations. Those few scales where the issue has been studied substantiate the likelihood of such effects. This has substantial import for research on developmental trends or treatment effects, inasmuch as such regression effects can clearly confound the interpretation of rating scale data collected over time.

Investigators wishing to employ ratings in treatment research or developmental investigations would do well to consider this problem and perhaps repeat the administration of the scale twice before employing it in the research.

It is difficult, if not impossible, in such a review to reach any determination as to which scale among those considered is "the best." This clearly depends upon the purpose to which the scale is to be put in any specific investigation. Although the Child Behavior Checklists seem to be the best developed and standardized of the multifactor rating scales and would have great value in assessing a broad array of common psychopathological dimensions, they would not be as useful in studies of more rare or highly specialized disorders such as autism, childhood psychosis, or Tourette's syndrome. Their item coverage for these disorders is slim to nonexistent and would therefore miss highly significant aspects of the psychopathology of interest. Similarly, these checklists may not be especially useful in studies of acute treatment effects due to their length, cumbersomeness in repeated administrations over short-time periods, and possible lack of specificity for the treatment effects of interest. In such cases, shorter, more narrowly focused rating scales would be of greater utility, as in the Self-Control Rating Scale for research on behavioral interventions for impulsivity or the revised Conners scales for research on stimulant drug effects in hyperactive children.

In summary, this review has presented general information on the assumptions, advantages, and disadvantages inherent in the use of rating scales in research on child psychopathology. A number of rating scales were reviewed in detail as to their structure and psychometric properties. The result of this review is the demonstration that sufficient broad-band, multidimensional rating scales currently exist to satisfy the needs of researchers for such scales, while such is far from the case for more narrow, specialized scales of rare or understudied disorders. Further advances in this type of assessment methodology are likely to come from greater study of the nature, properties, and utility of those scales currently in existence; the efficacy of these scales for subtyping populations of disturbed children and evaluating their differential outcomes or response to intervention; and the interrelationships of these scales to other measures of the same behavioral dimensions collected by other means. It should not be overlooked that scores on these scales are merely quantified *opinions* and have reality in child behavior only to the extent that they have been anchored to more direct, observable measures obtained by less subjective means.

ACKNOWLEDGMENTS

Preparation of this review was supported by funds from the Center for Studies of Children and Adolescents, National Institute of Mental Health, and the Department of Neurology, Medical College of Wisconsin. Appreciation is expressed to the following individuals and companies for providing materials and instruments for this review or commentaries on the reviews of their respective scales: Thomas Achenbach, C. Keith Conners, Craig Edelbrock, David Lachar, Robert McMahon, Sheila Eyberg, Herbert Quay, Lenore Behar, Ronald Trites, Rina Ullmann, Lovick Miller, Phillip Kendall, and Western Psychological Services. Comments provided by Mariellen Fischer are also gratefully acknowledged.

REFERENCES

Abikoff, H., & Gittelman, R. (1984). Does behavior therapy normalize the classroom behavior of hyperactive children? *Archives of General Psychiatry, 41,* 449–454.

Achenbach, T. M., & Edelbrock, C. S. (1981). Behavioral problems and competencies reported by parents of normal and disturbed children aged four through sixteen. *Monographs of the Society for Research in Child Development, 46* (1).

Achenbach, T. M., & Edelbrock, C. S. (1983). *Manual for the Child Behavior Checklist and Revised Child Behavior Profile.* Burlington, VT: Thomas A. Achenbach.

Ackerman, P. T., Elardo, P. T., & Dykman, R. A. (1979). A psychosocial study of hyperactive and learning disabled boys. *Journal of Abnormal Child Psychology, 7,* 91–99.

Aksamit, D. L. (1974). *Identification and change in the behavior of students placed in special classes for the emotionally disturbed.* Unpublished doctoral dissertation, University of Nebraska.

Aman, M. G., & Werry, J. S. (1984). The Revised Behavior Problem Checklist in clinic attenders and nonattenders: Age and sex effects. *Journal of Clinical Child Psychology, 13,* 237–242.

Aman, M., Werry, J., Fitzpatrick, J., Lowe, M., & Waters, J. (1983). Factor structure and norms for the Revised Behavior Problem Checklist on New Zealand children. *Australian and New Zealand Journal of Psychiatry, 17,* 354–360.

Aragona, J. A., & Eyberg, S. M. (1981). Neglected children: Mothers' report of child behavior problems and observed verbal behavior. *Child Development, 52,* 596–602.

Arnold, L. E., Barnebey, N. S., & Smeltzer, D. J. (1981). First grade norms, factor analysis and cross correlation for Conners, Davids, and Quay–Peterson behavior rating scales. *Journal of Learning Disabilities, 14,* 269–275.

Baker, L., Cantwell, D. P., & Mattison, R. E. (1980). Behavior problems in children with pure speech disorders and in children with combined speech and language disorders. *Journal of Abnormal Child Psychology, 8,* 245–256.

Barkley, R. A. (1976). Predicting the response of hyperactive children to stimulant drugs: A review. *Journal of Abnormal Child Psychology, 4,* 327–348.

Barkley, R. A. (1977). A review of stimulant drug research with hyperactive children. *Journal of Child Psychology and Psychiatry, 18,* 137–165.

Barkley, R. A. (1981). *Hyperactive children: A handbook for diagnosis and treatment.* New York: Guilford.

Barkley, R. A. (1982). Guidelines for defining hyperactivity in children (attention deficit disorder with hyperactivity). In B. Lahey & A. Kazdin (Eds.), *Advances in clinical child psychology* (Vol. 5, pp. 137–180). New York: Plenum.

Barkley, R. A., & Cunningham, C. E. (1980). The parent–child interactions of hyperactive children and their modification by stimulant drugs. In R. Knights & D. Bakker (Eds.), *Treatment of hyperactive and learning disabled children* (pp. 219–236). Baltimore: University Park Press.

Barkley, R. A., Fischer, M., Newby, R., & Breen, M. (1985). *A multi-method clinical protocol for assessing stimulant drug responding in ADD children.* Paper presented at the meeting of the American Psychological Association, Los Angeles.

Barkley, R. A., & Ullman, D. G. (1975). A comparison of objective measures of activity and distractibility in hyperactive and nonhyperactive children. *Journal of Abnormal Child Psychology, 3,* 231–244.

Behar, L. (1974). *Manual for the Preschool Behavior Questionnaire.* Unpublished manuscript, Durham, NC.

Behar, L. (1977). The Preschool Behavior Questionnaire. *Journal of Abnormal Child Psychology, 5,* 265–275.

Behar, L., & Stringfield, S. (1974). A behavior rating scale for the preschool child. *Developmental Psychology, 10,* 601–610.

Bond, C. R., & McMahon, R. J. (1984). Relationships between marital distress and child behavior problems, maternal personal adjustment, maternal personality, and maternal parenting behavior. *Journal of Abnormal Psychology, 93,* 348–351.

Borkovec, T. D. (1970). Autonomic reactivity to sensory stimulation in psychopathic, neurotic, and normal juvenile delinquents. *Journal of Consulting and Clinical Psychology, 35,* 217–222.

Breen, M., & Barkley, R. A. (1983). The Personality Inventory for Children: Its clinical utility with hyperactive children. *Journal of Pediatric Psychology, 8,* 359–366.

Breen, M., & Barkley, R. A. (1984). Psychological adjustment in learning disabled, hyperactive, and learning disabled/hyperactive children using the Personality Inventory for Children. *Journal of Clinical Child Psychology, 13,* 232–235.

Broad, J. C. (1982). Assessing stimulant treatment of hyperkinesis by Bristol Social Adjustment Guides. *Journal of Psychiatric Treatment and Evaluation, 4,* 355–358.

Brodzinsky, D. M., Schechter, D. E., Braff, A. M., & Singer, L. M. (1984). Psychological and academic adjustment in adopted children. *Journal of Consulting and Clinical Psychology, 52,* 582–590.

Brown, J. E. (1975). *A comparison of social casework and behavioral contracting with juvenile delinquents on probation.* Unpublished master's thesis, University of Calgary.

Brown, R. T., & Wynne, M. E. (1982). Correlates of teacher ratings, sustained attention, and impulsivity in hyperactive and normal boys. *Journal of Clinical Child Psychology, 11,* 262–267.

Cairns, R. B., & Green, J. A. (1979). How to assess personality and social patterns: Observations or ratings? In R. B. Cairns (Ed.), *The analysis of social interactions* (pp. 209–226). Hillsdale, NJ: Erlbaum.

Campbell, S. B. (1974). Cognitive styles and behavior problems of clinic boys. *Journal of Abnormal Child Psychology, 2,* 307–312.

Campbell, S. B., & Breaux, A. M. (1983). Maternal ratings of activity level and symptomatic behaviors in a nonclinical sample of young children. *Journal of Pediatric Psychology, 8,* 73–82.

Campbell, S. B., Schleifer, M., & Weiss, G. (1978). Continuities in maternal reports and child behaviors over time in hyperactive and comparison groups. *Journal of Abnormal Child Psychology, 6,* 33–45.

Campbell, S. B., & Steinert, Y. (1978). Comparisons of rating scales of child psychopathology in clinic and nonclinic samples. *Journal of Consulting and Clinical Psychology, 46,* 358–359.

Campbell, S. B., Szumowski, E. K., Ewing, L. J., Gluck, D. S., & Breaux, A. M. (1982). A multidimensional assessment of parent-identified behavior problem toddlers. *Journal of Abnormal Child Psychology, 10,* 569–592.

Cantwell, D. P., & Carlson, G. (1979). Stimulants. In J. Werry (Ed.), *Pediatric psychopharmacology* (pp. 171–207). New York: Brunner/Mazel.

Conners, C. K. (1969). A teacher rating scale for use in drug studies with children. *American Journal of Psychiatry, 126,* 884–888.

Conners, C. K. (1970). Symptom patterns in hyperkinetic, neurotic, and normal children. *Child Development, 41,* 667–682.

Conners, C. K. (1973). Rating scales for use in drug studies with children. *Psychopharmacology Bulletin: Special Issue, Pharmacotherapy with Children,* 24–84.

Conners, C. K. (1985). *The Conners rating scales: Instruments for the assessment of childhood psychopathology.* Unpublished manuscript, Washington, DC.

Conners, C. K., & Blouin, A. G. (1980). *Hyperkinetic syndrome and psychopathology in children.* Paper presented at the meeting of the American Psychological Association, Montreal.

Copeland, A. P., & Weissbrod, C. S. (1978). Behavioral correlates of the hyperactivity factor of the Conners Teacher Questionnaire. *Journal of Abnormal Child Psychology, 6,* 339–343.

Costello, E. J., & Edelbrock, C. S. (1985). Detection of psychiatric disorders in pediatric primary care: a preliminary report. *Journal of the American Academy of Child Psychiatry, 24,* 771–774.

Darlington, R. B. (1963). *Increasing test validity through the use of interitem correlations.* Unpublished doctoral dissertation, University of Minnesota. (*Dissertation Abstracts International, 24,* 477B.)

Dubey, D. R., O'Leary, S. G., & Kaufman, K. F. (1983). Training parents of hyperactive children in child management: A comparative outcome study. *Journal of Abnormal Child Psychology, 11,* 229–246.

Eaves, R. C. (1975). Teacher race, student race, and the Behavior Problem Checklist. *Journal of Abnormal Child Psychology, 3,* 1–9.

Edelbrock, C., & Achenbach, T. M. (1980). A typology of child behavior profile patterns: Distribution and correlates for disturbed children aged 6–16. *Journal of Abnormal Child Psychology, 8,* 441–470.

Edelbrock, C., & Achenbach, T. A. (1984). The teacher version of the Child Behavior Profile: I. Boys aged 6–11. *Journal of Consulting and Clinical Psychology, 52,* 207–217.

Edelbrock, C., Costello, E. J., & Kessler, M. D. (1984). Empirical corroboration of attention deficit disorder. *Journal of the American Academy of Child Psychiatry, 23,* 285–290.

Edelbrock, C., & Rancurello, M. D. (1985). Childhood hyperactivity: An overview of rating scales and their applications. *Clinical Psychology Review, 5,* 429–445.

Edelbrock, C., & Reed, M. L. (1984). *Reliability and concurrent validity of the Teacher Version of the Child Behavior Profile.* Unpublished manuscript, University of Pittsburgh.

Emery, R. E., & O'Leary, K. D. (1982). Children's perceptions of marital discord and behavior problems in boys and girls. *Journal of Abnormal Child Psychology, 10,* 11–24.

Emery, R. E., & O'Leary, K. D. (1984). Marital discord and child behavior problems in a nonclinic sample. *Journal of Abnormal Child Psychology, 12,* 411–420.

Evans, W. R. (1975). The Behavior Problem Checklist: Data from an inner-city population. *Psychology in the Schools, 12,* 301–303.

Eyberg, S. (1980). Eyberg Child Behavior Inventory. *Journal of Clinical Child Psychology, 9,* 22–28.

Eyberg, S. M., & Robinson, E. A. (1982). Parent–child interaction training: Effects on family functioning. *Journal of Clinical Child Psychology, 11,* 130–137.

Eyberg, S. M., & Robinson, E. A. (1983). Conduct problem behavior: Standardization of a behavioral rating scale with adolescents. *Journal of Clinical Child Psychology, 12,* 347–354.

Eyberg, S. M., & Ross, A. W. (1978). Assessment of child behavior problems: the validation of a new inventory. *Journal of Clinical Child Psychology, 7,* 113–116.

Glow, R. A. (1979). Cross-validity and normative data on the Conners Parent and Teacher Rating Scales. In K. Gadow & J. Loney (Eds.), *Psychosocial aspects of drug treatment for hyperactivity.* Boulder, CO: Westview Press.

Glow, R. A., Glow, P. H., & Rump, E. E. (1982). The stability of child behavior disorders: A one-year test–retest study of Adelaide Versions of the Conners Teacher and Parent Rating Scales. *Journal of Abnormal Child Psychology, 10,* 33–60.

Goh, D. S., Cody, J. J., & Dollinger, S. J. (1984). PIC profiles for learning disabled and behavior–disordered children. *Journal of Clinical Psychology, 40,* 837–841.

Goyette, C. H., Conners, C. K., & Ulrich, R. F. (1978). Normative data on Revised Conners Parent and Teacher Rating Scales. *Journal of Abnormal Child Psychology, 6,* 221–236.

Greene, R. L., Martin, P. W., Bennett, S. R., & Shane, J. A. (1981). A computerized scoring system for the Personality Inventory for Children. *Educational and Psychological Measurement, 41,* 233–236.

Harley, J. P., Ray, R. S., Tomasi, L., Eichman, P. L., Matthews, C. G., Chun, R., Cleelund, C. S., & Traisman, E. (1981). Hyperkinesis and food additives: testing the Feingold hypothesis. *Pediatrics, 61,* 818–828.

Harrington, R. G., & Follett, G. M. (1984). The readability of child personality assessment instruments. *Journal of Psychoeducational Assessment, 4,* 37–48.

Harris, J. C., King, S. L., Reifler, J. P., & Rosenberg, L. A. (1984). Emotional and learning disorders in 6–12-year-old boys attending special schools. *Journal of the American Academy of Child Psychiatry, 23,* 431–437.

Harris, W. J., Drummond, R. J., & Schultz, E. W. (1977). An investigation of relationships between teachers' ratings of behavior and children's personality tests. *Journal of Abnormal Child Psychology, 5,* 43–52.

Hirshoren, A., & Schnittjer, C. J. (1979). Dimensions of problem behavior in deaf children. *Journal of Abnormal Child Psychology, 7,* 221–228.

Hodges, K., Kline, L., Stern, L., Cytryn, L., & McKnew, D. (1982). The development of a child assessment interview for research and clinical use. *Journal of Abnormal Child Psychology, 10,* 173–189.

Holtum, J., Robinson, E. A., & Eyberg, S. M. (1984). *Computer administration and scoring of the Eyberg Child Behavior Inventory.* Unpublished manuscript, Oregon Health Sciences University.

Horn, W. F., Chatoor, I., & Conners, C. K. (1983). Additive effects of Dexedrine and self–control training. *Behavior Modification, 7,* 383–402.

Horn, W. F., Ialongo, N., Popovich, S., & Peradotto, D. (1984). *An evaluation of a multi-method treatment approach with hyperactive children.* Paper presented at the 92nd Convention of the American Psychological Association, Toronto.

Humphrey, L. L. (1982). Children's and teachers' perspectives on children's self-control: the development of two rating scales. *Journal of Consulting and Clinical Psychology, 50,* 624–633.

Jacob, T., Grounds, L., & Haley, R. (1982). Correspondence between parents' reports on the Behavior Problem Checklist. *Journal of Abnormal Child Psychology, 10,* 593–608.

Kazdin, A. E., Esveldt-Dawson, & Loar, L. L. (1983). Correspondence of teacher ratings and direct observations of classroom behavior of psychiatric inpatient children. *Journal of Abnormal Child Psychology, 11,* 549–564.

Kazdin, A. E., & Heidish, I. E. (1984). Convergence of clinically derived diagnoses and parent checklists among inpatient children. *Journal of Abnormal Child Psychology, 12,* 421–436.

Kelley, C. (1981). Reliability of the Behavior Problem Checklist with institutionalized male delinquents. *Journal of Abnormal Child Psychology, 9,* 243–250.

Kendall, P. C., & Braswell, L. (1982). Cognitive-behavioral self-control therapy for children: A component analysis. *Journal of Consulting and Clinical Psychology, 50,* 672–689.

Kendall, P. C., & Brophy, C. (1981). Activity and attentional correlates of teacher ratings of hyperactivity. *Journal of Pediatric Psychology, 6,* 451–458.

Kendall, P. C., & Wilcox, L. E. (1979). Self-control in children: Development of a rating scale. *Journal of Consulting and Clinical Psychology, 47,* 1020–1029.

Kendall, P. C., & Wilcox, L. E. (1980). Cognitive-behavioral treatment for impulsivity: Concrete varsus conceptual training in non-self-controlled problem children. *Journal of Consulting and Clinical Psychology, 48,* 80–91.

Kendall, P. C., & Zupan, B. A. (1981). Individual versus group application of cognitive–behavioral self-control procedures with children. *Behavior Therapy, 12,* 344–359.

Kendall, P. C., Zupan, B. A., & Braswell, L. (1981). Self-control in children: Further analyses of the Self-Control Rating Scale. *Behavior Therapy, 12,* 667–681.

King, C., & Young, R. D. (1982). Attentional deficits with and without hyperactivity: Teacher and peer perceptions. *Journal of Abnormal Child Psychology, 10,* 483–496.

Klee, S. H., & Garfinkel, B. D. (1983). The computerized continuous performance task: A new measure of inattention. *Journal of Abnormal Child Psychology, 11,* 487–496.

Knights, R. M., & Hinton, G. G. (1969). The effects of methylphenidate (ritalin) on the motor skills and behavior of children with learning problems. *Journal of Nervous and Mental Disease, 148*, 643–653.

Kupietz, S. S., Bialer, I., & Winsberg, B. G. (1972). A behavior rating scale for assessing improvement in behaviorally deviant children: A preliminary investigation. *American Journal of Psychiatry, 128*, 1432–1436.

Kurdek, L. A., Blisk, D., & Siesky, A. E. (1981). Correlates of children's long-term adjustment to their parents' divorce. *Developmental Psychology, 17*, 565–579.

Lachar, D. (1982). *Personality Inventory for Children (PIC): Revised Format Manual Supplement*. Los Angeles: Western Psychological Services.

Lachar, D., & Gdowski, C. L. (1979a). *Actuarial assessment of child and adolescent personality: An interpretive guide for the Personality Inventory for Children profile*. Los Angeles: Western Psychological Services.

Lachar, D., & Gdowski, C. L. (1979b). Problem-behavior factor correlates of Personality Inventory for Children profile scales. *Journal of Consulting and Clinical Psychology, 47*, 39–48.

Lachar, D., Gdowski, C. L., & Snyder, D. K. (1984). External validation of the Personality Inventory for Children (PIC) profile and factor scales: Parent, teacher, and clinician ratings. *Journal of Consulting and Clinical Psychology, 52*, 155–164.

Lachar, D., Kline, R. B., & Boersma, D. C. (1986). The Personality Inventory for Children: Approaches to actuarial interpretation in clinic and school settings. In H. M. Knoff (Ed.), *The assessment of child and adolescent personality*. New York: Guilford.

Lahey, B. B., Green, K. D., & Forehand, R. (1980). On the independence of ratings of hyperactivity, conduct problems, and attention deficits in children: A multiple regression analysis. *Journal of Consulting and Clinical Psychology, 48*, 566–574.

Lahey, B. B., Shaughency, E. A., Strauss, C. C., & Frame, C. L. (1984). Are attention deficit disorders with and without hyperactivity similar or dissimilar disorders? *Journal of the American Academy of Child Psychiatry, 23*, 302–309.

Leon, G. R., Kendall, P. C., & Garber, J. (1980). Depression in children: Parent, teacher, and child perspectives. *Journal of Abnormal Child Psychology, 8*, 221–235.

Lessing, E. E., & Zagorin, S. W. (1971). Dimensions of psychopathology in middle childhood as evaluated by three symptom checklists. *Educational and Psychological Measurement, 31*, 175–197.

Lobovitz, D. A., & Handel, P. J. (1985). Childhood depression: Prevalence using DSM-III criteria and validity of parent and child depression scales. *Journal of Pediatric Psychology, 10*, 45–54.

Loney, J., & Milich, R. S. (1981). Hyperactivity, inattention, and aggression in clinical practice. In M. Wolraich & D. K. Routh (Eds.), *Advances in behavioral pediatrics* (Vol. 2). Greenwich, CT: JAI Press.

Mack, J. L. (1969). Behavior ratings on recidivist and non-recidivist delinquent males. *Psychological Reports, 25*, 260.

Mash, E. J., & Johnston, C. (1983). Parental perceptions of child behavior problems, parenting self-esteem, and mothers' reported stress in younger and older hyperactive and normal children. *Journal of Consulting and Clinical Psychology, 51*, 68–99.

Mash, E. J., & Terdal, L. G. (Eds.). (1981). *Behavioral assessment of childhood disorders*. New York: Guilford.

Mattison, R. E., Cantwell, D. P., & Baker, L. (1980). Dimensions of behavior in children with speech and language disorders. *Journal of Abnormal Child Psychology, 8*, 323–338.

McMahon, R. J. (1984). Behavioral checklists and rating scales. In T. H. Ollendick & M. Hersen (Eds.) *Child behavioral assessment: Principles and procedures* (pp. 80–105). New York: Pergamon.

Milich, R., Loney, J., & Whitten, P. (1980). *Two-year stability and validity of playroom observations of hyperactivity*. Paper presented at the meeting of the American Psychological Association, Anaheim, California.

Milich, R., Roberts, M. A., Loney, J., & Caputo, J. (1980). Differentiating practice effects and statistical regression on the Conners Hyperkinesis Index. *Journal of Abnormal Child Psychology*, *8*, 549–552.

Miller, L. C. (1976). Method factors associated with assessment of child behavior: Fact or artifact? *Journal of Abnormal Child Psychology*, *4*, 209–219.

Miller, L. C. (1980). Dimensions of adolescent psychopathology. *Journal of Abnormal Child Psychology*, *8*, 161–173.

Miller, L. C. (1981). *School Behavior Checklist Manual*. Los Angeles: Western Psychological Services.

Miller, L. C. (1984). *Louisville Behavior Checklist Manual*. Los Angeles: Western Psychological Services.

Miller, L. C., Barrett, C. L., Hampe, E., & Noble, H. (1971). Factor structure of childhood fears. *Journal of Consulting and Clinical Psychology*, *39*, 264–268.

Millichap, J. G., Aymat, F., Sturgis, L., Larsen, K. W., & Egan, R. (1969). Hyperkinetic behavior and learning disorders. *American Journal of Diseases of Children*, *116*, 235–244.

Mischel, W. (1973). Toward a cognitive social learning reconceptualization of personality. *Psychological Review*, *80*, 252–283.

O'Conner, M., Foch, T., Sherry, R., & Plomin, R. (1980). A twin study of specific behavioral problems of socialization as viewed by parents. *Journal of Abnormal Child Psychology*, *8*, 189–199.

O'Donnell, J. P., & Cress, J. N. (1975). Dimensions of behavior problems among Oglala Sioux adolescents. *Journal of Abnormal Child Psychology*, *3*, 163–169.

O'Donnell, J. P., & Van Tuinan, M. (1979). Behavior problems of preschool children: Dimensions and correlates. *Journal of Abnormal Child Psychology*, *7*, 61–75.

O'Leary, K. D. (1981). Assessment of hyperactivity: observational and rating methodologies. In S. A. Miller (Ed.), *Nutrition and behavior*. Philadelphia: Franklin Institute Press.

O'Leary, K. D., Vivian, D., & Nisi, A. (1985). Hyperactivity in Italy. *Journal of Abnormal Child Psychology*, *13*, 485–500.

O'Leary, S. G., & Pelham, W. E. (1978). Behavior therapy and withdrawal of stimulant medication in hyperactive children. *Pediatrics*, *61*, 211–217.

Packard, T., Robinson, E. A., & Grove, D. C. (1983). The effect of training procedures on the maintenance of parental relationship building skills. *Journal of Clinical Child Psychology*, *12*, 181–186.

Paraskevopoulos, J., & McCarthy, J. M. (1970). Behavior patterns of children with special learning disabilities. *Psychology in the Schools*, *7*, 42–46.

Paternite, C. E., & Loney, J. (1980). Childhood hyperkinesis: relationships between symptomatology and home environment. In C. Whalen & B. Henker (Eds.), *Hyperactive children: The social ecology of identification and treatment* (pp. 105–141). New York: Academic Press.

Peterson, D. R. (1961). Behavior problems of middle childhood. *Journal of Consulting Psychology*, *25*, 205–209.

Pollard, S., Ward, E. M., & Barkley, R. A. (1983). The effects of parent training and ritalin on the parent–child interactions of hyperactive boys. *Child and Family Therapy*, *5*, 51–69.

Porter, B., & O'Leary, K. D. (1980). Marital discord and childhood behavior problems. *Journal of Abnormal Child Psychology*, *8*, 287–295.

Porter, J. E., & Rourke, B. P. (1985). Socioemotional functioning of learning-disabled children: A subtypal analysis of personality patterns. In B. P. Rourke (Ed.), *Neuropsychology of learning disabilities: Essentials of subtype analysis*. New York: Guilford.

Prior, M., Leonard, A., & Wood, G. (1983). A comparison study of preschool children diagnosed as hyperactive. *Journal of Pediatric Psychology*, *8*, 191–207.

Proger, B. B., Mann, L., Green, P. A., Bayuk, R. J., Jr., & Burger, R. M. (1975). Discriminators of clinically defined emotional maladjustment: Predictive validities of the Behavior Problem Checklist and Devereaux Scales. *Journal of Abnormal Child Psychology*, *3*, 71–82.

Quay, H. C. (1966). Personality patterns in preadolescent delinquent boys. *Educational and Psychological Measurement, 16*, 99–110.

Quay, H. C. (1977). Measuring dimensions of deviant behavior: The Behavior Problem Checklist. *Journal of Abnormal Child Psychology, 5*, 277–287.

Quay, H. C. (1983). A dimensional approach to behavior disorder: The Revised Behavior Problem Checklist. *School Psychology Review, 12*, 244–249.

Quay, H. C., & Gredler, Y. (1981). Dimensions of problem behavior in institutionalized retardates. *Journal of Abnormal Child Psychology, 9*, 523–528.

Quay, H. C., Morse, W. C., & Cutler, R. L. (1966). Personality patterns of pupils in special classes for the emotionally disturbed. *Exceptional Children, 32*, 297–301.

Quay, H. C., & Peterson, D. R. (1975). *Manual for the Behavior Problem Checklist.* Unpublished manuscript, University of Miami.

Quay, H. C., & Peterson, D. R. (1983). *Interim manual for the Revised Behavior Problem Checklist.* Unpublished manuscript, University of Miami.

Quay, H. C., & Peterson, D. R. (1984). *Appendix I to the interim manual for the Revised Behavior Problem Checklist.* Unpublished manuscript, University of Miami.

Quay, H. C., & Quay, L. C. (1965). Behavior problems in early adolescence. *Child Development, 36*, 215–220.

Quay, H. C., Sprague, R. C., Shulman, H. S., & Miller, A. L. (1966). Some correlates of personality disorder and conduct disorder in a child guidance clinic sample. *Psychology in the Schools, 3*, 44–47.

Rapoport, J. L., & Benoit, M. (1975). The relation of direct home observations to the clinic evaluation of hyperactive school age boys. *Journal of Child Psychology and Psychiatry, 16*, 141–147.

Reed, M. L., & Edelbrock, C. (1983). Reliability and validity of the Direct Observation Form of the Child Behavior Checklist. *Journal of Abnormal Child Psychology, 11*, 521–530.

Robin, A. L., Fischel, J. E., & Brown, K. E. (1984). The measurement of self–control in children: Validation of the Self-Control Rating Scale. *Journal of Pediatric Psychology, 9*, 165–175.

Robinson, E. A., & Eyberg, S. M. (1981). The dyadic parent–child interaction coding system: Standardization and validation. *Journal of Consulting and Clinical Psychology, 49*, 245–250.

Robinson, E. A., Eyberg, S. M., & Ross, A. W. (1980). The standardization of an inventory of child conduct problem behaviors. *Journal of Clinical Child Psychology, 9*, 22–28.

Ross, D. M., & Ross, S. A. (1976). *Hyperactivity.* New York: Wiley.

Ross, D. M., & Ross, S. A. (1982). *Hyperactivity* (2nd ed.). New York: Wiley.

Routh, D. K., & Schroeder, C. S. (1976). Standardized playroom measures as indices of hyperactivity. *Journal of Abnormal Child Psychology, 4*, 199–207.

Routh, D. K., Schroeder, C. S., & O'Tuama, L. (1974). The development of activity level in children. *Developmental Psychology, 10*, 163–168.

Rubin, K. H., & Clark, M. L. (1983). Preschool teacher ratings of behavioral problems: Observational, sociometric, and social–cognitive correlates. *Journal of Abnormal Child Psychology, 11*, 273–285.

Salzinger, S., Kaplan, S., Pelcovitz, D., Samit, C., & Krieger, R. (1984). Parent and teacher assessment of children's behavior in child maltreating families. *Journal of the American Academy of Child Psychiatry, 23*, 458–464.

Sandoval, J. (1977).The measurement of hyperactive syndrome in children. *Review of Educational Research, 47*, 293–318.

Schnittjer, C. J., & Hirshoren, A. (1981). Factors of problem behavior in visually impaired children. *Journal of Abnormal Child Psychology, 9*, 517–522.

Schultz, E. W., Manton, A. B., & Salvia, J. A. (1972). Screening emotionally disturbed children in a rural setting. *Exceptional Children, 39*, 134–137.

Schultz, E. W., Salvia, J., & Fein, J. (1974). Prevalence of behavioral symptoms in rural elementary school children. *Journal of Abnormal Child Psychology, 2*, 17–24.

Seagull, E. A. W., & Weinshank, A. B. (1984). Childhood depression in a selected group of low-achieving seventh graders. *Journal of Clinical Child Psychology, 13,* 134–140.

Speer, D. C. (1971). The Behavior Problem Checklist (Peterson–Quay): Baseline data from parents of child guidance and nonclinic children. *Journal of Consulting and Clinical Psychology, 36,* 221–228.

Sprague, R. L., Cohen, M. N., & Eichlseder, W. (1977). *Are there hyperactive children in Europe and the South Pacific?* Paper presented at the meeting of the American Psychological Association, San Fransisco.

Sprague, R., Cohen, M. N., & Werry, J. (1974). *Normative data on the Conners Teacher Rating Scale and Abbreviated Scale.* Unpublished manuscript, University of Illinois.

Sprague, R. L., & Sleator, E. K. (1977). Methylphenidate in hyperkinetic children: Differences in dose effects on learning and social behavior. *Science, 198,* 1274–1276.

Stevens, T. M., Kupst, M. J., Suran, B. G., & Schulman, J. L. (1978). Activity level: A comparison between actometer scores and observer ratings. *Journal of Abnormal Child Psychology, 6,* 163–173.

Stone, B. F. (1981). Behavior problems in elementary school children. *Journal of Abnormal Child Psychology, 9,* 407–418.

Strang, J. D., & Rourke, B. P. (1985). Adaptive behavior of children who exhibit specific arithmetic disabilities and associated neuropsychological abilities and deficits. In B. P. Rourke (Ed.), *Neuropsychology of learning disabilities: Essentials of subtype analysis.* New York: Guilford.

Sultana, Q. (1974). *An analysis of the Quay–Peterson Behavior Checklist as an instrument to screen emotionally disturbed children.* Unpublished doctoral dissertation, University of Georgia.

Tarte, R. D., Vernon, C. R., Luke, D. E., & Clark, H. B. (1982). Comparison of responses by normal and deviant populations to Louisville Behavior Checklist. *Psychological Reports, 50,* 99–106.

Taylor, E., & Sandberg, S. (1984). Hyperactive behavior in English schoolchildren: a questionnaire survey. *Journal of Abnormal Child Psychology, 12,* 143–156.

Thorley, G. (1983). *Normative data on the Conners Teacher Questionnaire in two British clinic populations.* Unpublished manuscript.

Touliatos, J., & Lindholm, B. W. (1975). Relationships of children's grade in school, sex, and social class to teachers ratings on the Behavior Problem Checklist. *Journal of Abnormal Child Psychology, 3,* 115–126.

Touliatos, J., & Lindholm, B. W. (1981). Congruence of parents' and teachers' ratings of children's behavior problems. *Journal of Abnormal Child Psychology, 9,* 347–354.

Trites, R. L., Blouin, A. G., Ferguson, H. B., & Lynch, G. W. (1981). The Conners Teacher Rating Scale: An epidemiological inter-rater reliability and follow-up investigation. In K. Gadow & J. Loney (Eds.). *Psychosocial aspects of drug treatment for hyperactivity.* Boulder, CO: Westview Press.

Trites, R. L., Blouin, A. G., & Laprade, K. (1982). Factor analysis of the Conners Teacher Rating Scale based on a large normative sample. *Journal of Consulting and Clinical Psychology, 50,* 615–623.

Trites, R. L., & Laprade, K. (1984). *Traduction et normes pour une version française du Conners Teacher Rating Scale.* Unpublished manuscript, Royal Ottawa Hospital.

Ullman, D. G., Barkley, R. A., & Brown, H. W. (1978). The behavioral symptoms of hyperkinetic children who successfully responded to stimulant drug treatment. *American Journal of Orthopsychiatry, 48,* 425–437.

Ullmann, R. K. (1984). *Teacher ratings useful in screening learning disabled from attention deficit disordered (ADD-H) children.* Unpublished manuscript, University of Illinois.

Ullmann, R. K., & Sleator, E. K. (1984a). *ADD-H children: Which behaviors are helped by stimulants?* Unpublished manuscript, University of Illinois.

Ullmann, R. K., & Sleator, E. K. (1984b). *Are there really any ADD children? Patterns of ACTeRS' ratings at baseline and on medication.* Unpublished manuscript, University of Illinois.

Ullmann, R. K., Sleator, E. K., & Sprague, R. L. (1984a). A new rating scale for diagnosis and monitoring of ADD children. *Psychopharmacology Bulletin, 20,* 160–164.

Ullmann, R. K., Sleator, E. K., & Sprague, R. L. (1984b). ADD children: Who is referred from the schools? *Psychopharmacology Bulletin, 20,* 308–312.

Ullmann, R. K., Sleator, E. K., & Sprague, R. L. (1985). A change of mind: Conners' Abbreviated Rating Scales reconsidered. *Journal of Abnormal Child Psychology, 13,* 553–566.

Victor, J. B., & Halverson, C. F., Jr. (1975). Distractibility and hypersensitivity: Two behavior factors in elementary school children. *Journal of Abnormal Child Psychology, 3,* 83–94.

Victor, J. B., & Halverson, C. F., Jr. (1976). Behavior problems in elementary school children: A follow-up study. *Journal of Abnormal Child Psychology, 4,* 17–29.

Victor, J. B., Halverson, C. F., Jr., Inoff, G., & Buczkowski, H. J. (1973). Objective behavior measures of first and second grade boys' free play and teachers' ratings on a behavior problem checklist. *Psychology in the Schools, 10,* 439–443.

Vincent, J. P., Williams, B. J., Harris, G. E., & Duvall, G. (1977). *Classroom observations of hyperactive children: A multiple validation study.* Paper presented at the meeting of the American Psychological Association, San Francisco.

Voelker, S., Lachar, D., & Gdowski, C. (1983). The Personality Inventory for Children and response to methylphenidate: Preliminary evidence for predictive validity. *Journal of Pediatric Psychology, 8,* 161–169.

Webb, T. E., & Oski, F. A. (1973). Behavioral status of young adolescents with iron deficiency anemia. *Journal of Special Education, 8,* 153–156.

Webster-Stratton, C. (1984). Randomized trial of two parent training programs for families with conduct-disordered children. *Journal of Consulting and Clinical Psychology, 52,* 666–678.

Webster-Stratton, C., & Eyberg, S. M. (1982). Child temperament: Relationship with child behavior problems and parent–child interactions. *Journal of Clinical Child Psychology, 11,* 123–129.

Weissbluth, M. (1984). Sleep duration, temperament, and Conners' ratings of three-year-old children. *Developmental and Behavioral Pediatrics, 5,* 120–123.

Werry, J. S. (1978). Measures in pediatric psychopharmacology. In J. S. Werry (Ed.), *Pediatric psychopharmacology* (pp. 29–78). New York: Brunner/Mazel.

Werry, J., & Quay, H. (1971). The prevalence of behavior symptoms in younger elementary school children. *American Journal of Orthopsychiatry, 41,* 136–143.

Werry, J. S., & Sprague, R. L. (1968). Hyperactivity. In C. G. Costello (Ed.), *Symptoms of psychopathology.* New York: Wiley.

Werry, J. S., & Sprague, R. L. (1974). Methylphenidate in children—Effect of dosage. *Australian and New Zealand Journal of Psychiatry, 8,* 9–19.

Werry, J. S., Weiss, G., Douglas, V., & Martin, J. (1966). Studies on the hyperactive child: III. The effect of chlorpromazine upon behavior and learning ability. *Journal of the American Academy of Child Psychiatry, 5,* 292–312.

Wirt, R. D., Lachar, D., Klinedinst, J. K., & Seat, P. D. (1984). *Multidimensional description of child personality: A manual for the Personality Inventory for Children Revised 1984.* Los Angeles: Western Psychological Services.

Zentall, S. S. (1984). Context effects in the behavioral ratings of hyperactivity. *Journal of Abnormal Child Psychology, 12,* 345–352.

Zentall, S. S., & Barack, R. S. (1979). Rating scales for hyperactivity: Concurrent validity, reliability, and decisions to label for the Conners and Davids Abbreviated Scales. *Journal of Abnormal Child Psychology, 7,* 179–190.

Zold, A. C., & Speer, D. C. (1971). Follow-up study of child guidance patients by means of the Behavior Problem Checklist. *Journal of Clinical Psychology, 27,* 519–524.

6

OBSERVATIONS IN THE ASSESSMENT OF CHILDHOOD DISORDERS

JOHN B. REID   GERALD R. PATTERSON
DAVID V. BALDWIN   THOMAS J. DISHION

INTRODUCTION

According to the third edition of the *Diagnostic and Statistical Manual of Mental Disorders* (DSM-III) (American Psychiatric Association, 1980), there are now several major and minor classes of disordered child behavior. Whether one is a defender or a critic of this particular system, there is a consensus that a reliable system of classification provides a base for the development of a body of systematic knowledge about child disturbances. After three decades of effort (DSM-I was published in 1952), there are now several categories, such as infantile autism, attention deficit, and conduct disorders, that are both clearly defined and of proven clinical significance to warrant a serious examination of the means by which a child is to be classified. Our discussion will focus primarily on the area of conduct disorders. This focus reflects the fact that problems related to antisocial conduct characterize the majority of children referred for diagnosis and treatment. It also reflects the fact that the last decade has witnessed an explosion of empirically based studies encompassing longitudinal designs, field observation studies, and intervention with families of antisocial children.

As a general case, the majority of referrals pose a serious problem for the diagnostician. In that most child services are quite appropriately modeled along the lines of their adult counterparts, arrangements are typically made for diagnostic appointments with the identified problem child and with the parents. During the contacts with the child, someone on the staff may carry out a brief interview and/or play therapy contact in addition to a staff

John B. Reid, David V. Baldwin, Gerald R. Patterson, and Thomas J. Dishion. Oregon Social Learning Center, Eugene, Oregon.

member administering a battery of intelligence, achievement, and personality tests. During contacts with the parents, developmental histories and systematic parent report data are collected. This general approach became standard procedure early in the development of the community child guidance clinics in the 1930s and 1940s. The problem for the diagnostician lies in the fact that interview and assessment information make only very limited contributions toward classifying the disturbed child as having one type of problem or another. Even the best standarized instruments cannot reliably discriminate among, or categorize, children showing various disorders. This is not to say that current assessment batteries do not perform useful functions. The most seriously disturbed children in most categories can be identified, and usually the data provide information for case planning. But beyond classification, the goals for assessment of children are to understand causes and identify needs (Blau, 1979). In his review of the state of the assessment art, Cronbach (1975) pointed out that existing tools do not meet any of these goals. More recent reviews by Ross and Pelham (1981) and Achenbach and Edelbrock (1984) also paint a discouraging picture.

The diagnostic interview is also relatively nonproductive for the bulk of referrals. Although it aids in the identification of, and discrimination among, profound disorders, such cases account for only a tiny fraction of the referrals to most agencies. Office interviews and observations of children with attention deficit and conduct problems are singularly unrevealing. There are no consistent data, to the writers' knowledge, that demonstrate the utility of such interviews for the reliable classification of children within the major DSM-III categories. We would certainly argue that one set of programmatic studies in the area of child assessment should consist of multivariate analyses of existing interview and other assessment devices. One hopes such studies would prove that the writers have overstated the limitations of existing procedures.

The fact that the existing assessment procedures for children lack the necessary validity for classification is hardly news. We believe that a central problem plaguing current attempts at child assessment results from the diagnostic practices that have resulted from our historic marriage to adult assessment procedures. The same format is used to assess children that has been employed with adults; interviews are used in conjuction with reports and observations made in the clinic setting. Unfortunately, while most adults have problems that are usually consistent across time and situations, have a long history that can be used to put those problems into context, and are able to articulate their problems, most children present problems that are inconsistent, have problems that they may not experience as problems (few children are self-referred), and have short histories characterized by rapid change. Nevertheless, the same sorts of assessment strategies are employed: interview, clinic observation, and systematic report data. For the adult, most of the data are provided through interview, observation, and reports by the

FIGURE 6-1. Where do the data come from?

patient, but for children nearly all the data are provided by someone else (see Figure 6-1).

It is perhaps an oversimplification to assert that the vast bulk of the information that leads to the classification of adult patients is based on two major sources: the patients' immediate behavior in the office and self-reports concerning symptoms and history. As shown in Figure 6-1, only a minor portion of the classifying information comes from other informants such as spouse, other family members, relatives, friends, or colleagues. Disrupted or retarded cognitive processes are readily apparent to the diagnostician and are usually reflected in the assessment procedures. The self-reported intensity of negative affect occurring in setting after setting for a prolonged period of time can be a sufficient base for a preliminary diagnosis. An interesting exception to this admitted oversimplification is the need for independent assessment data for some of the personality disorders.

The adult comes to, or is brought to, the diagnostic center where his or her own behavior serves as the primary source of data for classification. We contend that the secondary sources of data provided by significant others contribute little additional variance to reliable classification of most adult patients, but that the reverse is true for classification of disturbed children. Here, very little of the relevant information that goes into an equation for classifying the child currently comes from his or her behavior. The bulk of it comes from parents, and typically it is the report of only one parent that is available. Admittedly, children do not tend to show symptomatic behavior to diagnosticians in clinical settings. Hyperactive children are not always hyperactive in the doctor's office (Loney, 1980); many aggressive boys are not usually aggressive in the reception room or the clinician's office (Patterson, 1964); enuretics and encopretics seldom display symptoms during the diagnostic interview. Immature and anxious or withdrawn children may show their disturbances in clinical settings, but even that remains to be demonstrated. Considering that hyperactive and conduct-disordered children together make up the vast bulk of referrals, and given the limitations of in-office interview and report data for this group, direct observations may have a useful role in the assessment of these children.

THE ROLE OF OBSERVATIONAL ASSESSMENT

As used in this chapter, the term *observational assessment* refers to a data collection system with the following characteristics: an agent uses preset, finite, and specific categories to summarize direct observations in specified settings over specified time periods; the length of the observational time period, though dependent on the base rate of the phenomena of interest, should be such as to minimize the use of memory by the observer; and the system should allow for some procedure to check the accuracy or reliability of the data collected.

Observations by Involved Others

This is by far the most economical observation method. Parents (and potentially teachers or staff at in-patient facilities) can be quickly introduced to the items to be observed. If the behaviors to be observed are restricted to reasonably salient categories, the involved observer can be oriented or trained in about half an hour, and is capable of producing data with acceptable reliability and temporal stability with about 6 to 10 days of data (Chamberlain, 1980). The data can be collected from the observers by daily phone calls or using the mail each day. A number of studies have shown consistent concurrent validity for this type of measure when compared to independent observational assessment (Reid, 1978) or to objective indices of serious problem behavior (Loeber, Dishion, & Patterson, 1984). The measure is also sensitive to treatment effects in intervention studies with conduct disordered and hyperactive children (Chamberlain, 1980; Patterson, 1974; Reid, 1978).

Although it is a relatively inexpensive procedure, it is the most susceptible to bias. If there is any reason to suspect the ability or willingness of the "involved other" to provide veridical data (e.g., child abuse, substance abuse), independent observations are definitely indicated.

Independent Observations

For most childhood disorders there are few, if any, widely used assessment procedures that permit independent evaluation of the behavior outside the child's intimate social system. It is our position that systematic observation by uninvolved agents is one potentially useful strategy to provide such data. In addition, the fact that direct observation permits the precise description of moment-by-moment child behavior should lead to better distinctions and classifications in child disorders; independent, direct observations also permit the possibility of obtaining molecular descriptions of the manner in which specific behaviors of the child interact with those of intimate others in the social system. Thus, in addition to providing an important additional source of assessment data for the classification of children, observations potentially provide a description of child behavior at a different level from that provided by the more global reports of involved others. If it is possible to integrate molar perceptions of the child's behavior, molar information about the characteristics of the child's social environment, and molecular data on the child's moment-by-moment behavior, we think it is quite possible that better and more fruitful classification of children can be accomplished and that more variance in the outcome of children with various problems can be explained. It should be made clear at the outset, however, that although systematic work in the development of observational systems for children has been going on for at least 50 years, such techniques have not been used consistently in combination with other modes of assessment to improve classification or prediction.

Independent Observations in Standardized Settings

As pointed out previously, observation in clinic or laboratory settings is a convenient procedure in that the subjects come to the observer rather than vice versa. The resulting data are also not affected by the individual characteristics of the home or classroom, family or class size, and the like. On the other hand, data reviewed earlier in this chapter suggest that significant differences have been found between children's behavior in laboratory and home settings. Nonetheless, an assessment procedure does not have to reflect typical behavior to be useful. The main issue is the degree to which they make consistent differentiations among children and predict important criteria. However, if factors in the natural enviroment are suspected to be important in a disorder, observations in target settings are indicated.

Independent Observations In Vivo

Though they are expensive, inconvenient, and intrusive, observations in natural settings provide the richest information. Not only is it possible to obtain reliable and valid data on the child behavior (e.g., Reed & Edelbrock, 1983; Reid, 1978), but is is also possible to get data on the reaction of the relevant social system to that behavior (e.g., Taplin & Reid, 1977), and the observers can fill out questionnaire data on a host of variables concerning the setting (e.g., Weinrott, Reid, Bauske, & Brummett, 1981). Observations in the target settings are extremely valuable for disorders that are variable across settings and for those disorders in which parents or teachers may be involved.

CONSIDERATIONS IN THE USE OF
OBSERVATIONAL MEASURES

Costs of Observation

As indicated previously, different observation strategies vary a good deal in cost. Observation systems for use by parents are extremely cheap, involving only about an hour or less to train the observer, and about 15 to 30 minutes each day for a couple of weeks to collect the phone call data. The data can be collected by receptionists, secretaries, or inexperienced assistants. Data are easily scored and used for quantitative analysis. Finally, parents do not appear to dislike the procedure.

In the case of independent observations, the costs increase significantly. For observation systems of any complexity, it takes at least 10 hours to train an observer to acceptable levels of accuracy and reliability (Reed & Edelbrock, 1983; Reid, 1970). In the case of an extremely complex code we are currently developing at our center, it takes about 12 weeks to train observers. Independent observations typically take at least 1 hour per session, and a minimum of three to six sessions are usually required to get stable estimates of behavior rates if social interactional variables are assessed (Reid, 1978). In the case of home observations, one must also expect "dry runs" (i.e., observations canceled at the last minute or family not home when the observer arrives). Depending on the sample studied, we have experienced dry-run rates of about 10% to 30%. In addition, the travel time and costs for observers must be absorbed. In our work, an average completed observation, including dry runs, observer time and travel costs, and summarizing the data, is about $35.00. Thus, for a complete observation and assessment of six sessions, the cost is $210.00—less than the cost of a personality assessment in our community.

Duration of the Assessment Period

It would be extremely desirable to conduct assessment of children over a brief time interval. Children not only develop and change quickly over the course of childhood, but many children also show behavior disorders as a function of a dramatic change in their social environment. Some young children show severe problems on entry to school, others show behavior disorders as a function of divorce (Hetherington, Cox, & Cox, 1981), and still others may show disrupted behavior as a function of physical or sexual abuse. Most data currently used to evaluate such disorders assume a good deal of familiarity with the child (e.g., the Child Behavior Checklist asks parents to rate the youngsters using a 1-year time frame; teacher CBCs also assume relatively thorough knowledge of the child by the teacher). Such a requirement for assessment data for children not only places restrictions on assessment studies (e.g., getting data from recent stepparents or trying to get teacher data on new students at the beginning of the year), but such formats also make treatment research difficult. To what extent, for example, would such a device be useful in assessing the effects of short-term treatment procedures, say an 8-week program, given that the time frame for pre- to postevaluation is 1 year, with the implication that an immediate posttreatment assessment would include reference to behaviors of the child that happened before treatment began?

The use of observation strategies provides a reasonably clear solution to this problem. As pointed out earlier, parent observation systems covering a 2-week period and home observations covering the same period correlated moderately well with checklist data. In a recent study by Reed and Edelbrock (1983), a brief direct observation form of the Child Behavior Checklist for teachers showed that the two instruments were significantly and moderately correlated, and that the independent observation form discriminated significantly between children who were identified by teachers as having marked behavioral problems in the classroom. Given the fact that such observation procedures have been developed only recently, and can probably be further improved, their potential in the field of integrated assessment of children appears to be quite large. In reference to the preceding section, such observational instruments will also provide the opportunity for investigators to make both quantitative and qualitative differentiations between the behavioral topography of children within the same class of disorder from one age period to the next.

Instruments

A variety of methods may be used to record observed behaviors, including audio recording, pencil-and-paper checklists, event recorders, clocks and counters, and digital keyboards. In general, instruments that permit entry of numerical codes by an observer as the behaviors of interest are seen (in sequence) and store each code and record its durations until the next code is entered, will permit more rapid and less costly transfer of the raw data to a form suitable for analysis. Such devices have a higher initial cost, which is eventually offset by their increased efficiency (Holm, 1978, 1981). They include the Datamyte and OS-3.

Measures

Basically, observational data of the sort described can be boiled down to four measures. The occurrence of each behavioral category can be counted (frequency) and timed (duration). Both frequency and duration measures can be made relative to the total observation period; by dividing these measures by total behavior changes or by total observation time, respectively, we obtain probability (or relative frequency) and proportion of the duration of each category. (Additional measures are also possible. See Sackett, Gluck, & Ruppenthal, 1978.) Relative measures must be used if observation sessions are of variable length. Frequency provides information about the child's behavioral repertoire, while duration indicates how the child fills time with these behaviors. In principle, the two measures are independent, and selection of the "best" one depends on the specific research questions. Durations can sometimes yield different results than frequencies because of their greater variability. This is especially true for behaviors of longer and more variable duration.

Sampling Considerations

Additional considerations surround the use of sampling techniques. Continuous sampling means that the observed behavior is recorded as it happens, and thus both frequency and duration information are potentially available for later analysis. In general, continuous sampling is preferred whenever possible (Altmann, 1974). If observation is performed with pencil and paper under demanding or complex conditions (many children actively playing, for example), it may be tempting to resort to a less taxing method of sampling behavior. Interval sampling means recording behavior that occurred within a certain interval (e.g., at the end of a 25-second period). Perhaps the predominant behavior during that interval is recorded, or as many as the observer can remember, or just the most interesting one. This method of sampling is easier for observers than continuous sampling, but at the cost of losing information that can be analyzed (Powell, 1984), particularly accurate information regarding duration (Ary, 1984). A variation on interval sampling is called point (or momentary) sampling. In this method, the behavior occurring at a particular moment in time (e.g., every 30 seconds) is recorded, and behaviors occurring at other points are lost. Relatively brief or infrequent behaviors are likely to be underrepresented when interval sampling methods are used, unless the interval is smaller than the briefest behavior to be observed (Ary & Suen, 1983). If the actual frequencies and durations of a set of behaviors are known, then the measures obtained by various interval methods can be compared with the true figures. In general, the proportion of intervals during which a behavior occurred is fairly closely tied to the actual frequency and is considerably less than the actual duration. Conversely, the point-sampling method corresponds more closely to actual duration than the actual frequency. Both interval methods are more accurate with shorter interval sizes and higher rates of behavior, as one would expect (Rhine & Ender, 1983).

A related question concerns sampling of individual subjects, interacting in groups such as families and classrooms. In focal sampling, a selected (target) individual is observed and the observer codes all interactive behaviors initiated by or directed toward this target; all other interactions in the group are ignored. If there is enough observation time, each member in the group can be observed as the target in turn. The alternatives to focal subject sampling involve simplifying the coding scheme, reducing the size of the group observed, and hiring additional observers, each of whom focuses on a single target subject.

Real Time versus Taping

The availability of audio- or videotaping equipment opens the possibility of altering the speed at which behavior is coded. Real-time recording refers to behavior that is coded as it occurs. In some cases, behavior happens more quickly or more densely than can accurately be recorded in real time. If it is not possible to hire an extra observer or simplify the coding system, then it may still be possible to code that behavior in slower motion using video- or audiotape. The main advantage of taping behavior—that it can be observed again and again until all the information is captured and a consensus can be reached—is also its disadvantage; that is, taping increases the time needed to score an hour's worth of behavior.

On the other hand, there can be advantages in the use of videotaped interactions when two or more different coding systems are used in the same investigation.

Devices such as the OS-3 permit repeated coding of an audio- or videotaped behavioral sequence, as, for example, by different coders using the same or different coding schemes. This requires an audiotrack devoted to a time base written or dubbed on the tape by the device in addition to a separate audio track for talk (if needed). When the tape is played, the OS-3 reads time from this time base, and so allows stopping and rewinding tape for recoding difficult segments. Additionally, two or more different codes may be taken on the same behavior, and then precisely joined together (using the time base information) for analysis of a combined code, which may be too complex to code in one pass.

Setting

Typically, observations will be done in the home, clinic, laboratory, or classroom. The stability of behavior observed across these and other settings is clearly an important issue. In general, rates of behavior may be quite variable across settings (Zangwill & Kniskern, 1982), but there is some evidence for consistency between classroom and school playground when coercive bahavior, for example, is analyzed as a class of combined specific behaviors (Harris & Reid, 1981).

Where consistency is not found, it likely reflects the importance of differing opportunities, individuals, and rewards for specific behaviors across settings. Even when the rate of behaviors across settings is significantly different, correlations of these behaviors across settings may be high (Zangwill & Kniskern, 1982), as for example, if rate of all behavioral activity decreased initially on a visit to a new surrounding, but the move does not alter the child's behavioral repertoire of available responses.

Rather than trying to control for variance in behavior associated with different settings, it may be better to identify how various social and situational agents may be influencing behavior in specific settings. Barkley (1981), discussing behavioral assessment of hyperactive children, noted the potential problem of unrepresentativeness in child problem behavior when the child is observed in the clinic playroom. He believes that assigning structural tasks that include parental commands likely to cause noncompliance will increase the likelihood that problem behaviors can be observed in this analogue setting. For example, a mother whose child generally acts up whenever she is on the phone can receive a phone call in the playroom while the dyad is being observed. Following the observation, the mother might be questioned for her perception of the representativeness of the child's problem behaviors; if necessary, home observation can be arranged to resolve discrepancies between parental reports and clinic observations.

Evaluating the Child in Standardized or Natural Settings

Observation systems relevant to the assessment of a variety of childhood disorders have been developed for use in both laboratory and natural or target settings. In the case of hyperactivity, the system developed by Mash, Terdal, and Anderson (1973) has been used successfully to differentiate hyperactive from normal control children in classroom settings, free play, and structured laboratory settings (e.g., Cunningham & Barkley, 1979). Carlson and Williams (1984) used the home observation code described by Reid (1978) to discriminate hyperactive, conduct-disordered, and normal children in the home setting. Observational instruments have been used to evaluate autistic children in the laboratory and in free-play settings (e.g., Lovaas, Freitag, Gold, & Kassorla, 1965; Lovaas, Koegel, Simmons, & Long, 1973; Strain & Cook, 1976).

Observational instruments that have proven useful in clinic settings have been described by Eyberg and Johnson (1974), Gloglower and Sloop (1976), Tavormina (1975), and Forehand and Peed (1979). Observational systems for such behaviors for use in home settings have also been used with success, and are represented by systems described by Reid (1978), Wahler, House, and Stambaugh (1976), Conger and McLeod (1977), and Wilcox, Goocher, and Grove (1979).

There are obvious pros and cons when deciding between standarized and naturalistic observations. On the one hand, standardized or laboratory–clinic systems allow one to compare a given child's performance with that of children in various reference groups in the same setting and under the same conditions. Because of such standarization of the environment, relevant situational, context, or social interactional factors will be controlled, or variations held to a minimum, as well. In the case of home observation, the child is observed in exactly the same context and under the same conditions in which the disordered behavior occurs. However, one is not simply observing the behavioral manifestation of the child's own behavior disorder but is simultaneously observing the combined effect of situational and social interactional variables affecting one's behavior. For disorders that show a good deal of transituational consistency, such as autism or pervasive developmental disorders, it is likely that observational assessments in natural and contrived settings would yield similar information. For disorders that have less transituational stability, and in which social interactional determinants are importantly involved, such as conduct, oppositional, and attention deficit disorders, there is mounting evidence that observations in the two types of settings will lead to different estimates of the amount of disturbance shown by the child (e.g., Dysart, 1973–1974; Martin, Johnson, Johansson, & Wahl, 1976; Mustakas, Siegel, & Schalock, 1956). In a recent study by Zangwill and Kniskern (1982) of families with conduct problem children, the behavior of family members during social interaction was observed in both clinic and home settings, using the same observation system. Whereas the correlations for the family members' behavior across settings was quite high, the correlations for the problem behavior of the referred children was insignificant across settings. In this study, the children were far more oppositional in the clinic than in the home setting. For whatever reason, observations done in the clinic do not relate consistently to behavior in the home, at least for conduct disorders. Because the behavior that has to be dealt with by the parents occurs in the home setting, it is probably safest to conduct observations in that setting, or in the school setting if that is where the problem behavior is reported (Reed & Edelbrock, 1983).

OBSERVATIONAL CODES IN USE: A SELECTIVE REVIEW

Most current observational systems that have clear implications for the clinical assessment of children have been, and are still being, developed by behaviorally oriented clinical researchers whose primary purposes have not typically included general or personality assessment or differential diagnosis. Rather than starting out with the goal of developing measures that would differentiate one sort of child from another, their aim was to measure change in known groups of children (e.g., selected on the basis of referral or psychometric tests) as a function of experimental treatments, or to measure the functional relationships among various target child behaviors and social interactional variables in child's immediate environment.

Most commonly used pencil-and-paper and interview assessment procedures for children have been developed with the goal of contributing to a methodology for personality assessment and classification of children. For most coding systems, it is not possible to match observational variables precisely with specific classifications or symptoms in widely used diagnostic manuals (e.g., DSM-III).

The relevant literature contains scores of simple, highly specific, narrow-bandwidth coding systems that have been used only in one or two investigations. For example, Reid, Hawkins, *et al.* (1967) used simple word counts to measure the effectiveness of a procedure to teach a selectively mute child to speak in a variety of social situations. The procedure was useful for that study but has not been used since. Journals such as the *Journal of Applied Behavior Analysis, Behavioral Assessment, Behavior Therapy, Behavior Modification*, and *Behaviour Research and Therapy* contain hundreds of single-purpose procedures for observing specific behaviors that may be of use in the development of comprehensive observational systems for the assessment of children. In most reports in such journals, some information is provided concerning the reliability, complexity, and costs of the instruments described. Unfortunately, it is still uncommon to see studies comparing similar observational systems, or studies examining the concurrent validity of observational systems with other modes of assessment. Perhaps because of the past tendency of behaviorists to shy away from classification issues and typologies, the psychometric issues studied in observational investigations have tended to center around reliability and observer agreement.

In addition to single-purpose coding systems that have not been used programmatically, there exist a number of observation methods that have been used repeatedly in clinical research. Such systems, also reported in the above-mentioned journals, are accumulating enough validity data to suggest that they hold immediate promise for the study of some sets of childhood problems. Some examples follow.

Social Skill

In the case of social skill in children, the Behavioral Assertiveness Test (Eisler, Hersen, Miller, & Blanchard, 1975; Eisler, Miller, & Hersen, 1973) have been revised by Bornstein, Bellack, and Hersen (1977) for use with children. This system employs an analogue situation requiring children to role-play up to 48 situations (e.g., Michelson, DiLorenzo, Calpin, & Ollendick, 1982), in which assertive or nonassertive responses are evoked. Videotapes are made and are coded by observers using ten highly specific categories and an overall rating of social skill. Its reliability is excellent and it has demonstrated solid construct validity in a number of clinical assessment/outcome studies with both overassertive (read oppositional or conduct disorder) and underassertive (read shy, possibly depressed) children (e.g.,

Bornstein *et al.*, 1977; Bornstein, Bellack, & Hersen, 1980; Michelson & Wood, 1980). Studies designed specifically to evaluate its psychometric characteristics are beginning to appear (e.g., Michelson *et al.*, 1982).

Autism

In the case of autism, systematic and direct observational procedures for assessment and evaluation of treatment outcome have been in existence for more than 20 years (e.g., Lovass *et al.*, 1965; Lovass *et al.*, 1973). As is often the case, the only psychometric measures of data quality reported for observational systems for autism have been interobserver agreement. Freeman and Schroth (1984) conducted a study to evaluate an observation code for discriminating among three groups of children: a group of normals, a group diagnosed as mentally retarded, and a group diagnosed as autistic.

Beginning with 67 categories, derived after a near-exhaustive review of past research (Freeman & Ritvo, 1981), each item was analyzed for its overall mean (modified frequency), difference in rate of occurrence for the groups, the percentage of children who displayed the behavior, and interobserver agreement. Behaviors were then dropped from the code if they did not discriminate groups, if they occurred too rarely for statistical analysis, or if the rater agreement was low. The authors are currently revising this instrument on the basis of the study. The result should be an excellent, usable instrument for use with autistic and mentally retarded children (the observation consisted of only nine 3-minute segments; undergraduates were trained to do the observations).

Obesity

In the case of obesity, some recent research is quite encouraging. Assessment and treatment of obesity is a complex task because, although obesity often results from an imbalance of caloric input and output, the enviromental factors associated with it and the relative roles of overeating versus underactivity vary across patients and can be difficult to identify. As a result, treatments may be inappropriate and less than successful (Foreyt & Goodrick, 1981).

Waxman and Stunkard (1980) observed the caloric intake and expenditure of four obese boys with their nonobese brothers at home and with a nonobese peer at school. Observations centered around physical activity (activity levels and oxygen consumption measured at specific levels yielded caloric output) and eating (food size, portions, and eating rate). They found that the obese boys ate far more than their nonobese brothers (within 2 years of the same age), in contrast to self-reports that obese children eat no more and observational reports that obese adults eat no more in public. Additionally, the obese children ate more rapidly (kilocalories per minute), and were served more food at home. Their physical activity, relative to nonobese controls, depended on setting; obese boys were less active at home but equally active at school. Further, their activity at home appeared to reflect punishment by parents who did not punish their nonobese brothers for the same activities. The authors concluded that the obesity of these children was maintained by excessive caloric intake rather than decreased overall activity. M. Waxman (personal communication, November 1984) is currently engaged in a replication and extension of this study with obese female children, their sisters, and same-height peers. As in the study described, the focus of her research is on the roles of activity and eating in maintaining obesity. Observations are performed in the home before and after dinner, and interviews of the child, her family, and teachers center on perceptions of food- and activity-related behaviors. Measurements in the laboratory provide precise estimates of calories burned by activity type. This work serves as an excellent example of research combining observational measures of behavior with other data to improve the diagnosis and treatment of a physical disorder.

Hyperactivity

For the activity level component in the attention deficit disorders, direct observational systems have been effective in differentiating children diagnosed as hyperactive from normal, oppositional, and conduct-disordered children. Using the Response-Class Matrix, a 14-category code designed to record behavioral interactions between adults and children (Mash *et al.*, 1973), Cunningham and Barkley (1979) successfully differentiated hyperactive from normal control children in classroom settings, free play, and structured laboratory settings.

Using the Family Interaction Coding System described in the next section (Reid, 1978), Carlson and Williams (1984) discriminated among a group of hyperactive, a mixed group of oppositional/conduct-disordered, and a group of normal children. Observational work with hyperactive children may lead to particularly useful applications because of the tendency of such children to be inconsistent in their expression of symptoms across settings.

Aggression

Of all the classes of behavior disorders in children, most observational work has been done with aggression and oppositional behavior. Systems have been developed to observe this class of behaviors in home, playground, classroom, clinic, and laboratory settings. Most of the codes access the immediate reactions of important others to the aggression, and an increasing number of validity studies are being conducted. Studies describing the characteristics of some of the most widely used systems are presented in Table 6-1.

One frequently used code is the Family Interaction Coding System (FICS), initially developed by Patterson, Reid, and their colleagues (Patterson, Ray, Shaw, & Cobb, 1969; Reid, 1967, 1978). It consists of 29 categories that provide for the fine-grained measurement of aversive behaviors in the home setting. Categories for coding the interaction of children with other family members include approval, command, compliance, destructive, play, physical positive, noncompliance, physical negative, whine, and yell. Composite scores, such as contingent punishment or approval, command compliance ratios, total aversive, and total positive behavior can be calculated for any family member observed. As can be seen in Table 6-1, the overall, overt reliability of the FICS is .87 (Weinrott & Jones, 1984), and about 50 to 60 hours are required for observer training. The code reliably discriminates oppositional/conduct-disordered from normal controls. The code has been useful in a large number of treatment outcome studies, and correlates moderately with other assessment instruments (see Patterson, 1982, and Reid, 1978, for reviews).

Wahler et al. (1976) have developed a 24-category code, the System for Ecological Assessment of Child Behavior Problems (EACPB), for use in the home setting, which includes 19 child and 5 parent or sibling categories. It has been used repeatedly in treatment outcome studies of socially disadvantaged, aggressive/oppositional children (e.g., Wahler, 1980), and in studies examining the structural and interpersonal aspects of child oppositional behavior (e.g., Wahler, 1975; Wahler & Dumas, 1983). In comparison to the FICS, the EACPB provides more precise measurement of the positive behaviors displayed by aggressive children. In addition to providing measures of each individual category, composite scores such as child–adult interaction cluster, child–child interaction cluster, negative behavior, opposition, and work can be calculated. In the study by Weinrott and Jones (1984), the average interobserver reliability was .97. Although among the quickest to learn (4–8 hours of observer training), this system can be difficult to use because all behavior categories must be recorded as present or absent in each 10-second interval.

The Social Interaction Scoring System (SISS) was developed by Burgess, Conger, and their colleagues (Burgess & Conger, 1978; Conger, 1982; Conger & McLeod, 1977). The SISS is not an exhaustive code, but classifies child behavior hierarchically, in terms of type of interaction, affect, and a number of content dimensions (e.g., commands and complies). It has been used successfully to differentiate physically abusive from nonabusive mothers (Conger, Lahey, & Smith, 1981), has shown differences in child aggressiveness in abusive and nonabusive homes (Burgess & Conger, 1978), and has been sensitive to outcome effects in a treatment study of abusive mothers (Conger et al., 1981). In the study by Weinrott and Jones (1984), it demonstrated an average reliability of .91. The SISS requires about 60 hours of observer training.

Other coding systems have been designed to assess child behaviors at school (see Table 6-1). Typically, such coding systems have been concerned with measuring disruptive behavioral problems in elementary classroom settings. For example, Reed and Edelbrock (1983) report on a direct observation form of the Child Behavior Checklist (CBC) (Achenbach, 1978; Achenbach & Edelbrock, 1979) for use in the classroom by relatively unsophisticated observers. A wide overlap between the direct observation and parent and teacher versions of the CBC may make it easy to integrate information obtained from different informants. Example "items" include "acts too young, confused, fidgets, impulsive, apathetic, stubborn, and bossy." The 96 "items" can be summarized into a total behavior problem score, school performance, and various aspects of adaptive functioning. In the initial study by Reed and Edelbrock (1983), substantial reliability was demonstrated, as well as validity, when compared to the CBC and to referrals for out-of-control behavior. Though developed only recently, this instrument has tremendous potential because of its low cost and obtrusiveness, the ease with which observers can be trained, and its comparability to parent and teacher report instruments.

Another classroom observation code, designed by Abikoff, Gittelman, and Klein (1980) is specifically devoted to distinguishing between hyperactive and normal children in structured classroom settings. About 50 hours of training are required to use this code reliably. The system distinguished hyperactive and normal children, primarily by categories of interference and off-task behavior, although nine other categories were coded (including solicitation, cross–motor, noncompliance, and aggression). The authors note that their coding system loses reliability during unstructured lessons, when hyperactive and normal children differ less on the two major distinguishing categories.

Viewed only in economic terms, it is generally cheapest to observe family or child problem behaviors in the clinic or laboratory, avoiding the costs of sending trained observers into the home or classroom. Obviously, the main drawback to using structured clinic settings is the fear that behavior observed in the laboratory is not representative of that occurring at home or in school. One means of measuring any important discrepancies between the clinic and home would be to compare clinic observations with parental reports of home behavior. Robinson and Eyberg (1981) observed family interactions in the laboratory under both child-directed and parent-directed play interactions, each 5 minutes long. Families reporting conduct problems in their children and a normative group were compared. The Dyadic Parent–Child Interaction Coding System (see Table 6-1) includes 22 categories applicable to the parent-directed sessions, but only 19 categories applicable to the child-directed observations, since child response to parental command was coded only during parent-directed play. Examples of potential behavior

TABLE 6-1. Selected Child and Family Coding Systems

Study	Code type	Number of categories	Measures	Observers	Focus	Setting	Problem	Uses	Reliability or validity	Comment
Bernal, Gibson, Williams, & Pesses (1971)	Maternal commands	1	Frequency interval	Trained uninvolved	Child	Home	Noncompliance	To measure treatment effects on a mother and her son, baseline and posttreatment	V .89[a]	With audiotape recording (recorder yielding fewer commands) (excluding visual cues)
									R 95%	Agreement between two observers scoring audiotape
									V .86[a]	Between number of commands per 10 minutes, observer versus recorder
									R 80%	Agreement between two observers, either live or scoring audiotape
Greenwood, Todd, Hops, & Walker (1982)	PIC (Preschool Intervention Code)	21	Frequency interval	Trained uninvolved	Child	School	Withdrawn	Gives detailed account of child's interaction behavior	R 91%	Interval agreement (average)
									R 94%[a]	By behavior code (average)
									V .86[a]	Rate measures, PIC and Family Interaction Code
									R .75	Split-half interval consistency
									V .53	Stability across free-play and structured tasks

Study	Instrument	Number of items	Format	Observers	Subject	Setting	Behavior	Purpose	R	Agreement overall / Agreement by category (range)
Michelson & DiLorenzo (1981)		21	Interval rating	Staff	Child	Psychiatric facility for emotionally disturbed/learning-disabled children	Emotionally disturbed/learning disabled	For clinical information regarding social performance during structured games	R 94% R 93%–95%	Agreement overall Agreement by category (range)
Reed & Edelbrock (1983)	CBCL (Child Behavior Checklist Direct Observation Form)	96 items; total behavior problem score and on-task score	Ratings judgments	Graduate student observers	Child	Classrooms	Deviant behaviors	For clinical information regarding disturbed children's behavior in classrooms, and measuring changes in behavior over time	R .85[a] R .77[a]	For behavior problems (per 10-minute session) For on-task (per 10-minute session); presents numerous correlations between instrument and teacher ratings by ratings, for each of two observers and two settings
Weitz (1981)	TBC (Teacher Behavior Code)	9	Interval "teaching trials"	Graduate student observers	Adult (parent)	Clinic, home	Parent, teaching behavior	To measure change in parental teaching behavior following parent training treatment	R 87%	$\bar{X}$ agreement across the categories; range, 66%–98%
Weinrott & Jones (1984)	FICS (Family Interaction Code)	29	Interval (6 seconds)	Experienced	Family	Home	Family interactions	Measures aversive family behavior	R .87 R .69	Overt $\bar{X}$ (60 minutes) Covert $\bar{X}$ (60 minutes)
Weinrott & Jones (1984)	EACPB (Ecological Assessment of Child Problem Behavior)	24	Interval, pencil and paper (10 seconds)	Experienced	Family	Home	Family interactions	Measures aversive family interactive behaviors	R .97 R .67	Overt $\bar{X}$ Covert $\bar{X}$

TABLE 6-1. (cont.)

Study	Code type	Number of categories	Measures	Observers	Focus	Setting	Problem	Uses	Reliability or validity	Comment
Weinrott & Jones (1984)	SISS (Social Interaction Scoring System)	12	Continuous (Datamyte)	Experienced	Family	Home	Family interactions	Classifies behavior on dimensions and general classification	R .91 R .73	Overt $\bar{X}$ Covert $\bar{X}$
Weinrott & Jones (1984)	FOR (Family Observation Record)	16	Interval and continuous (10 seconds)	Experienced	Family	Home	Family interactions	Behavior is scored in relation to family norms (rules), functional and contingent relationships	R .93 R .49	Overt $\bar{X}$ Covert $\bar{X}$
Wahler, House, & Stambaugh (1976)	EACPB (from manual)	26	Interval, pencil and paper	Experienced	Child	Home	Family and school interactions	Clinical aid in child and family interventions	R 54%–97%	Observer agreement; varies by category (see manual)
				Experienced		School			R 52%–96%	Observer agreement; varies by category (see manual)
Robinson & Eyberg (1981)	DPICS (Dyadic Parent–Child Interaction Coding System)	22	Continuous in 5-minute intervals	Experienced	Child	Clinic	Noncompliance	Assessment of young (2–7 years) conduct-disordered children's behavior interacting with their parents	R 91% R 92% V 61%	$\bar{X}$ observer agreement on frequency of parent behaviors $\bar{X}$ observer agreement on frequency of child behaviors Variance in parent reports of child behavior problems at home predicted by DPICS in clinics

Author (year)	System	No.	Observation method/interval	Observers	Subject	Setting	Behavior	Description	Values	Statistics
Weinrott, Jones, & Boler (1981)	OScAR5V STARS, FSIA, CCO, CVC	5	5 comparable categories compared across the 5 systems	All experienced trained by system author or representative	Adult Teacher	Classroom	Teaching behavior	Observation of teacher behavior in classrooms	V .62	Correlation across five systems involving same behavior categories (convergent validity)
Abikoff, Gittelman, & Klein (1980)	SUNY–Stony Brook code (modified)	11	15-second interval	Experienced	Child	Classroom	Hyperactivity	Discrimination of normal and hyperactive children (replication)	R .82 / V 79.2%	θ coefficients, mean across categories; Discrimination of hyperactive from normal child
Abikoff, Gittelman-Klein, & Klein (1977)	SUNY–Stony Brook code (modified)	11	15-second interval	Experienced	Child	Classroom	Hyperactivity	Discrimination of normal and hyperactive children	R .80 / V 79.5%	θ coefficients, mean across categories; Discrimination of hyperactive from normal child
Freeman & Schroth (1984)	BOS (Behavioral Observation System for Autism)	67	3-minute interval; each behavior scored 0-3	Trained undergraduate psychology majors	Child	Clinic	Autistics	Discrimination between behavior of autistic, mentally retarded, and normal children, 2-6 years	R 40%-100% / R 88%	Agreement (range); $\bar{X}$ agreement
Klesges et al. (1984)	FATS (Fargo Activity Time-sampling Survey)	13[b]	10-second interval and intensity rating	Trained psychology students	Child	Home	Overweight	To discriminate the relationship between child activity and parental encouragement with child weight	R 91%-98% / R 85%-95% / R .90 / R .59	Range of agreement on activity; Range of agreement on parent–child interactions; Kappa, overall; Stability of behavior across occasions
Harris & Reid (1981)	BCS (Behavior Coding System)	8	Interval	Good students	Child	Classroom and playground	Continuance of coercive behavior across settings	Originally designed to measure aggression, family interactions; used here to assess situational stability of coercive behaviors	R 93% / R 86% / V .69	Observer agreement in classroom; Observer agreement on playground; Consistency across settings in behavior categories of subjects

[a] Pearson r.

[b] Eight categories of child behavior and five of others' behavior.

categories included direct command, praise, descriptive question, critical statement, and verbal acknowledgement. Child behavior categories focused on deviant behaviors, and included whine, cry, physical negative, yell, and destructiveness. The reliabilities for parent and child behaviors averaged .91 and .92, respectively. When compared with maternal reports of home behavior, 61% of the variance on the Eyberg Child Behavior Inventory (Robinson & Eyberg, 1981) was predicted by observations of parent–child interactions in the clinic (see Table 6-1).

The selected review of coding systems presented here strongly suggests that observational data have a good deal of potential for the assessment of children. It is also clear, however, that most observational procedures available at this time do not match up precisely with other modes of assessment data. One hopes some observational systems will be developed or modified in the future to provide for measures that are directly comparable to those generated by other assessment methods.

CRITERIA USED TO CONSTRUCT OR SELECT AN OBSERVATIONAL SYSTEM

The primary consideration in constructing or selecting an observational system surrounds the precision with which it can measure what the investigator or diagnostician wants to learn. What constitutes an important behavior depends on the specific questions. Sometimes the literature will be helpful in suggesting behaviors, and sometimes one must rely on experience with the subject population. Obviously, one's theoretical orientation will determine not only the kinds of questions asked, but also the specific behaviors deemed important in a given study and the labels given to each behavioral category.

A related question concerns size of behavioral category. Molecular categories are specific, narrowly defined, and more numerous, whereas molar categories clump behavior into relatively large classes requiring some level of inference by observers. Although molecular categories are likely to be found in more complex coding systems, they can be collapsed into larger composites if reliability is a problem.

On methodological grounds, a good argument can be made for constructing an observational coding system in which the categories are mutually exclusive and exhaustive. Systems in which some behaviors cannot be scored suffer from inability to measure those gaps in the behavioral sequences, and systems where a given behavior might be coded in either of two categories will obviously be less reliable than an equivalent mutually exclusive system. Difficulties arise in sequential analysis if more than one behavior appears to occur at a given moment. This section briefly reviews a number of methodological issues likely to arise in the selection or construction of an observational system and its use in behavioral research.

Observer Training

Observers should be able to sustain attention without daydreaming, and take in high levels of stimulation without confusion; compulsivity, insight, and introspective intensity have also been suggested as important observer attributes (Yarrow & Waxler, 1979). Other research suggests that the ideal observer is intelligent, creative, and verbal, but unaware of the specific hypotheses under investigation. Careful training and continued monitoring is necessary to ensure consistently accurate data. Information regarding observer training can be found in Reid (1978, 1986)), Hartmann and Wood (1982), and Van der Molen, Kerkhoff, and Jong (1983). Briefly, once a code has been developed (at least initially), steps in observer training include memorizing code definitions and examples, pairing codes with their numerical or alphabetical abbreviations, and practice on a series of taped examples of graduated difficulty and length before observations are practiced in the field. Reliability is checked repeatedly throughout training and during the actual data collection, and can serve as an indication of ambiguous code discriminations or definitions. Length of observer training depends on code complexity, but can take several weeks.

DeMaster, Reid, and Twentyman (1977) compared the effects of various amounts of feedback during training on observer reliability. They found that feedback regarding both intrapair agreement and criterion reliability was necessary to increase both observer agreement and accuracy (to the standard criterion) during training. Feedback regarding only agreement will tend to increase agreement but may even decrease accuracy (to the standard) and thus replicability by others, as observer pairs drift from standard code definitions.

Finally, it is probably best that observers be unaware of the hypotheses to be tested with their data. Further, feedback given the observers should carefully avoid hinting at what kinds of data would corroborate or contradict the investigator's pet hypotheses. The temptation is too great to look a little harder for deviant behavior or positive changes in the treatment group.

Reliability

Like a test, a scoring system is reliable to the extent that the measures it provides are reproducible. Reliability increases with number of items in a test and with number of data points (i.e., time) in observation studies. Given a marginally significant effect, a more reliable system will be more likely to detect the effect and a less reliable system will be more likely to lose or bury the effect in error variance (noise). Reliability can be measured in various ways. Between-observer agreement refers to the similarity with which two different observers code the same interactions. This corresponds roughly to internal consistency of split-half reliability in testing. Within-observer reliability refers to the similarity with which a given observer codes the same interaction observed on two occasions, several days or months apart. Within-observer reliability measures the stability of the scoring system across time, and the tendency of observers to "drift" in their categorizations of behavior. In testing, a corresponding measure would be test–retest reliability. Note that observer accuracy is a different issue, discussed below in the section on validity.

Overt versus Covert Reliability Assessment

Two important issues to discuss concerning reliability are those of overt versus covert reliability assessment and observer drift. A number of studies have found that when observers know they are being checked for reliability, they are more reliable than when their reliability is covertly assessed. This decline when observing without a partner is most pronounced when highly complex coding systems are used. Apparently it is not the result of fatigue since the decline is measurable within the first few minutes of a 1-hour-long session (Weinrott & Jones, 1984).

Drift

Observer drift is a different problem. It refers to the tendency of an observer to shift category definitions across time, thus losing reliability with earlier observations by the same observer. This tendency can be reduced if observers are carefully selected and thoroughly trained with clear, explicit, and detailed category definitions. In a study of observer drift in four different family observation systems, Weinrott and Jones (1982) found little evidence for drift in experienced observers with three of the systems, when their agreements were compared 2 to 16 months apart. Drift apparently occurs less among specific categories that are narrowly defined and seems to be unaffected by behavior rate. Drift appears to be minimized if observers (1) are hired for a brief period; (2) are trained and periodically compared against a prescored videotaped interaction sample; (3) are initially overtrained to at least .90 observer agreement; and (4) are trained in a single group and meet to discuss problems in this group to reduce the likelihood of splintergroups of varying code interpretations.

Reliability Measures: Kappa

Both within- and between-observer reliability have been described as percent agreement between the observers or across time. This is typically the way reliabilities have been reported in the literature (see Table 6-1). However, precent agreement ignores the possibility of chance agreement, which inflates these reliability estimates above their true levels; this bias is greater for simple coding systems. A preferred method of calculating reliability coefficients, called kappa, takes chance agreement into account (Cohen, 1960; Hollenbeck, 1978).

Another issue concerns the size of the categories to be used in figuring reliability, the length of observation time to select for reporting reliability, and whether the active or quiet stretches of interaction should be used in reliability tests. In general, reliabilities calculated when the scoring system is being developed, or for observer feedback purposes, would be calculated on the raw codes. For publication, reliabilities are most useful if they are presented in the same summary units as analyzed, in observation periods equivalent to the size of observation blocks used in data analysis, and on samples of behavior at least as active as average for the study as a whole.

To summarize, observer bias, reliability, and drift are extremely important considerations. Extreme care must be taken to keep observers from knowing what data are desirable to the researcher. In addition, observers should be admonished about making hypotheses. If possible, observers should also be kept blind as to the group membership of subjects. Although observer bias has proved to be a minimal problem in the case of carefully constructed codes (see Patterson, 1982, chap. 3, for a review), the above precautions should be taken to prevent its occurrence.

Observer reliability and drift must be continuously monitored. Without repeated reliability assessment, observer performance will decay rapidly (Reid, 1970; Taplin & Reid, 1977). Without repeated retraining, observers will drift in their use of the categories over time (DeMaster et al., 1977). In order to prevent these problems, we suggest weekly observer training sessions and that about 10% to 20% of observations be conducted simultaneously and independently by two observers to provide for continuous reliability assessment.

Complexity

In selecting or constructing an observational system, attention should be paid to its complexity. Complexity can be defined as the number of categories in the system divided by the number of category changes coded during a period of time, or as the percentage of nonrepeated entries. (Neither measure is fully satisfactory, however, since neither takes into account the probability of occurrence for each category.) However measured, complexity varies inversely with reliability. That is, reliability decreases as a coding system grows more complex, and also as the rate of observed behavior change increases (Mash & McElwee, 1974; Reid, Skindrud, Taplin, & Jones, 1973). As a general guide, the coding system used should be no more complex than is necessary to categorize the behaviors relevant to the experimenter. It is also important to note the complexity, or rate of behavior change, in the samples used in assessing reliability and training. That is, before actually collecting data, observers should have reached an acceptable level of reliability (e.g., 80%–90% agreement) on a sample of behavior at least as difficult to code as is expected to be observed during data collection.

Generalizability

Another approach to reliability is to estimate the generalizability of data taken by different observers (Cronbach, Gleser, Nanda, & Rajaratnam, 1972; Mitchell, 1979). This approach differs from simply assessing observer agreement because observer disagreement is considered as a source of error variance that may or may not systematically bias the data collected. A portion of the interactions of some subjects are coded by two observers (as in between-observer agreement). The categorical data are then analyzed with observer as an independent (treatment) variable, to see whether disagreements between observers *systematically* biased the behavioral measures. Significant observer effects correspond to areas where observers differ systematically and consistently in their interpretation of the observed behaviors.

The myriad sources of unreliability make the following point particularly important: balancing observers across subject groups or conditions guards against the possibility that unreliability of one or more observers will mask or spuriously reveal treatment differences. This simple precaution can go a long way toward minimizing serious consequences due to observer drift and unreliability.

An additional use of generalizability theory needs mention. A practical benefit of estimating components of variance in the data is to determine the optimal number or length of observations needed to minimize error variance. This procedure is recommended by Cronbach *et al.* (1972), and an example is reported by Klesges *et al.* (1984). Basically, dividing the components of variance by various observation periods yields a predicted generalizability coefficient and standard error at each observation length. The investigator can then select an optimal observation period short of the point at which increased stability does not offset the increased observation costs.

Reactivity

Given that behavior varies across settings (as described above), it probably also varies as a function of the subject's awareness of being observed. This issue is called reactivity, and it poses difficult measurement problems. Investigators thus far have approached the reactivity question in a couple of ways. Alternating periods of overt with covert observation can provide a measure of the subject's behavioral activity with and without knowledge of being observed. A different approach asks individuals (or families) to "fake" good and bad behavior while under observation. Although the theoretical problem of reactivity extends to any behavioral change under observed versus nonobserved conditions, for practical purposes clinicians may be more concerned with a subset of behaviors—such as increased socially desirable behavior or an extended effort at impression management. Recent reviews of research on reactivity (Haynes & Horn, 1982; Kazdin, 1982; Patterson, 1982) have noted that the work to date has not systematically examined the various possible influences of observer, settting, subject, behavior, and hypothesis variables on reactivity. It is not easy to measure the effect our measuring instrument may have on subject behaviors. On the other hand, it is well to note that *any* measure causes some level of reactivity; this problem is not limited to observational measures. Further, reactivity to any measure is likely to vary with individual subjects, settings, and other variables.

Pollack, Vincent, and Williams (1977) conceived of the demand characteristics of observers on subject behavior as a two-dimensional model, including nonspecific reactivity (orienting to the observer, "fiddling," etc.), and impression management (an attempt to present a socially acceptable facade to the observer). The evidence to date suggests that subjects do orient more toward the observer and that adults show some evidence of attempts at impression management. However, there is no clear picture of deviancy suppression in problem families or individuals; instead, setting and sample characteristics seem to determine which adult social behaviors are altered in the observer's presence.

Classroom studies of children offer little support for the impression management factor. For example, Weinrott, Garrett, and Todd (1978) observed the socially appropriate behavior of six aggressive boys (grades K through 3) in a special class. Data were collected by observers hidden behind a one-way mirror, and a nonparticipating observer was sometimes present in the classroom. They concluded that reactivity to the visible observer was not evidenced in these children's behavior throughout the 33 days of observation. (See also Abikoff, Gittelman-Klein, & Klein, 1977, and Abikoff *et al.*, 1980, for a similar finding.) Johnson and Bolstad (1975) compared the behavior of intact families with a single younger child (4–8 years) at home over 6 days as recorded on an audiotape with an observer present or absent. Neither parent nor child behavioral differences were found between conditions, and there was no evidence of adaptation.

If one assumes family members *could* distort their interactions when the observer was present, then it should also be possible to directly manipulate such a set. This, in fact, was the format adopted in a series of classic studies by Johnson and his colleagues. In the first study (Johnson & Lobitz, 1974), 12 parents of normal families were instructed to make their preschool children "look bad or deviant" for three observation sessions, and to "look good" on three alternate sessions. On "bad" days, the rates of deviant child behavior and rates of negative and parent commands were significantly higher than they were during "look good" days. The design made it possible to demonstrate that parents of normal children could definitely alter the behavior of their children. However, it was not clear that parents of distressed families would be equally skilled in controlling child behavior.

A study by Lobitz and Johnson (1975) involved volunteer parents of younger children. One sample of 12 families had "problem children" as labeled by one or both parents. The children in the other sample of 12 families were presumably problem-free. On two consecutive days, the parents in both groups were instructed to make their children "look good"; then on two consecutive days to make them "look bad"; finally, on two consecutive days they were to "look normal." Families were randomly assigned to one of the six possible orderings of these conditions. Parents in both samples produced significant increases in deviant child behaviors when comparing "look normal" to "look bad" conditions. Ten of the 12 deviant families and 9 of the 12 nonproblem families seemed effective in producing this shift. These shifts were accompanied by significant increases in parental commands and punishment, and a significant decrease in parental positive consequences. The data from the combined sample showed no significant shift in child behavior from the normal to the good conditions. Seven of the 12 normal families were effective in producing this shift, whereas only 4 of the 12 in the problem sample were successful. Questionnaires given to the parents showed they generally perceived themselves as more effective in accelerating good behavior than in accelerating bad behavior. However, parent perceptions of behavior change were not in accord with observations of the same behavioral events.

Pending further research in this area, it seems reasonable to assume that both parents and children from out-of-control families find it difficult to "fake good." Habitual modes of interacting provide powerful constraints for familial interaction patterns. Presumably, these constraints are more effective in controlling behavior than is the desire to look good. We remain convinced that the observers do set constraints on the rate and intensity of the expression of familial problems. We are also convinced that the families of antisocial children are sufficiently disrupted that many elements of the basic process are clearly visible: for example, Reid, Taplin and Lorber (1981) found that mothers of abused children were observed to *hit* their children at several times the rates of normal mothers, even though the mothers *knew* that they were being observed *because* they were abusive!

Validity

Validity measures the extent to which the observation system measures what it purports to measure. Validity can be defined in terms of construct, content, and prediction; each will be described briefly. Construct validity refers to the congruence between the categories of behavior that are coded and the psychological concept that these categories are meant to measure: Do differing rates of behavior on these measures differentiate people on the construct of interest, and not on other dimensions? Content validity refers to the completeness of the code categories in describing the behaviors to be assessed. It is particularly important when treatment effects are being measured because it is concerned with the coding system's sensitivity to behavioral changes that may stem from the treatment. Predictive validity is the third principal type. It is concerned with the system's ability to predict behavior in other settings or at other times (e.g., an admission test's ability to predict grades). Validity estimates an observation system's accuracy with respect to some other accepted measure or standard; in contrast, reliability refers to the agreement between observers or of the same observer across time, with the same code. Low reliability may occur for some subtle but important behaviors, though low reliability limits the upper boundary of a code's validity with respect to some other criterion.

An example of validation of an observational system can be found in Bernal, Gibson, Williams, and Pesses (1971). They sent observers into the home to observe the rate of maternal commands to her children. An audiotape recorder was left in the home to record automatically all verbal interactions on a random basis. When observed and recorded command rates were compared, the two measures correlated .86 per 10-minute segment. Observers consistently coded more commands than the recorder because they included both verbal and nonverbal commands. In this experiment, the recorder was found to be a valid means of recording clinically relevant information without the use of home observation. Johnson and Bolstad (1975) replicated and extended this basic design with 12 families, with similar results.

A second example investigated the situational specificity of activity level in behavior-disordered and learning-disabled boys during day hospital school activities, as measured by an actometer and ratings by clinical staff and mothers. Direct behavioral observations were not performed. Stevens, Krupst, Suran, and Schulman (1978) found that maternal ratings correlated most highly with actometer activity in wood shop, gym, and overall, while clinical staff ratings correlated with (lower) actometer activity in the classroom. In this study, the actometer was assumed to be the correct (standard) measure, and the situational specificity of the children's activity provided multiple opportunities to assess the predictive validity of ratings by clinical staff and the children's mothers.

In a similar vein, Abikoff et al. (1977, 1980) reported on the activity of a classroom observation code to discriminate between hyperactive and normal children, replicating this study with a second sample. Each child was observed an average of 1.6 hours over several days. They found that hyperactive children had higher scores and greater variability on all code categories when compared with normal children, and that the pair "interference" and "off-task" codes, when combined, predicted the status of 79.2% and 79.5% of the children in each sample, with a false positive rate of less than 10%. No single code category was able to differentiate hyperactive and normal children, because of overlap between the groups. Although observation alone would not be sufficient for diagnosis, it could provide detailed information about rates of specific behaviors useful in determining and evaluating treatments.

Use of Observation Data in Comparative or Validity Analyses, and for Development of Composite Measures

As stated previously in this chapter, parent, teacher, and self-report data are of critical importance in conducting a comprehensive assessment of most childhood disorders. Such measures are difficult to validate unambiguously because most assessments of children are conducted by involved others. In cases that the observational categories of a given instrument are the same as, or closely parallel to, the items on report instruments, it is possible to use observation data as an independent validity measure for such devices. Two clear examples of this are as follows: In a recent study by Reed and Edelbrock (1983), a direct observation form of the Child Behavior Checklist was developed. The observational device demonstrated solid interobserver reliability and, in a validity study, the behavior problem scores generated by the two modes of assessment were significantly and moderately correlated. In our own work, we have employed the Family Interactional Coding System (FICS) (Reid, 1978) for several years. We also employ a parent daily observation measure that taps the same behavioral dimensions. In a number of studies conducted at our center, we have demonstrated significant correlations between the two measures (in the range .4 to .7) (see Reid, 1978). Typically, the more seriously disturbed the sample, the higher the correlations have been. We are currently conducting analyses to determine whether or not independent observation, parent observation, and parent checklist data account for unique variance in the prediction of official delinquency and teacher/peer-rated problems in school setting.

As a final comment on validity issues, there are assessment problems in which independent assessment information is essential. First, in those cases in which the parents' data cannot be trusted (e.g., alcoholic or neglectful parents), independent observations can be extremely useful. Second, in situations in which the decisions made about the classification of children result in the restriction of their activities or participation in institutions in our society (i.e., in instances where a mistake has dire consequences), independent data should always be collected. For example, in the state of Iowa, the decision to assign any student to a restrictive program or classroom cannot be made without direct observation of the student's behavior in the school setting.

Given that observers have watched and coded the behavior of an individual or a family, it may be possible to increase the yield of information obtained by supplementing observational data with observer impressions. Weinrott, Reid, *et al*. (1981) had observers of families with child management problems complete a rating inventory after each observation session. They found that the combination of observed rates of behavior and subjective impressions yielded a better predictor of child deviance at discharge than either source alone. Thus, the use of observational coding need not prevent the concurrent use of subjective ratings by the same observers. In some applications, a combination of subjective and objective information may improve validity.

DEALING WITH MULTIPLE ASSESSMENT INSTRUMENTS AND BEATING THE BASE RATE PROBLEM

In their recent review of assessment methods for child psychopathology, Achenbach and Edelbrock (1984) acknowledged the potential usefulness of using multiple-method assessment strategies. On the other hand, they expressed pessimism in the ability of clinicians to efficiently aggregate "diverse and often contradictory data into a coherent picture of the child . . . " (p. 232). They went on to state that "studies of clinical judgment show that clinicians (like people in general) are very poor at (a) mentally detecting covariation of attributes across cases (Arkes, 1981), and (b) mentally combining assessment data into judgments of individual cases (Wiggins, 1981)" (p. 232).

We concur that this is a potential stumbling block for the use of multiple measures in the assessment of children. It is particularly difficult because different agents in different settings using different formats will paint different and apparently contradictory pictures of a given child. But this divergence in information provides potential strength to the use of multiple assessment devices. It may well be that children perceived as having a disorder in more than one setting are the most seriously disturbed and at risk for serious long-term outcomes (Loeber & Dishion, 1983).

We also concur with the idea that people are not efficient at detecting covariations across instruments without using a specified format. Further, there is the issue of cost-effectiveness. Assessment is probably most valuable for use in differentiating classes in which the base rate for inclusion in the class is equal to the base rate for exclusion in the class (i.e., a 50–50 split). That is, it is hard for any assessment instrument or battery to beat a base rate prediction when the incidence of the target behavior or syndrome is only 5%: by predicting that everyone is normal, one is right 95% of the time. The problem is that in order to capitalize on the value of multiple assessment, one is, at first glance, left with the prospect of assessing all children with all instruments and still having a prediction problem involving the detection of a very small percentage of children with a disturbance from a very large number of children who do not show the disturbance.

Sequential Assessment

We propose that some developments in observational assessment procedures can be introduced in order to provide relatively unbiased, diagnostically useful information. This additional information is more costly to obtain, but it can serve to increase the reliability and sensitivity of intake procedures to the point that effective classification might be possible. In order to make this feasible, it is necessary to plan how the cost could be kept down. The multiple gating, or sequential assessment, strategy, first introduced by Cronbach and Gleser (1965), nicely serves this purpose. Their idea was to employ the least costly assessment devices first in the series. The initial procedures, such as the diagnostic interview with the child, psychological testing, and interview and report data from the parents, are relatively low cost. As shown in Figure 6-2, all cases referred to the outpatient service would be processed through these filters, or gates. The information available at Gate I should make it possible to make three reliable and important differentiations. The information could be used first to differentiate between (1) no significant child problem, (2) profound problem, and (3) problem exists but further assessment needed.

Let us assume that 30 of 100 cases will be screened out at Gate I (i.e., having no problem, no profound problem, or a clearly less serious problem). The remaining 70 are suspected as having an adjustment problem, but its exact nature and seriousness cannot be pinpointed. These 70 children move to Gate II, where teacher report data might be gathered. Assume that 30 of the remaining 70 can be categorized and referred at this stage. These 30 are culled out of the assessment process and the remaining 40 move to Gate III for a more expensive and intrusive assessment—for example parent daily observations (Chamberlain, 1980). Assume that, at this gate, 20 of the 40 can be classified and referred; the residual 20 are still unclassified (e.g., perhaps the parents are mentally unstable or child abusive, and their data are suspect). These remaining 20 move to the final gate: direct observation in home or school, or both. Such a gating process represents an efficient method for utilizing multiple assessment measures in an efficient and cost-effective way.

Example of a Sequential Gating Model

A recent study conducted at our center by Loeber *et al.* (1984) represents an initial attempt to demonstrate the feasibility of a sequential assessment approach. Because of its importance to the present discussion, that study will be carefully described here. Its purpose was to use a multiple-gating procedure for the assessment of a low-base-rate, but serious problem. A sample of

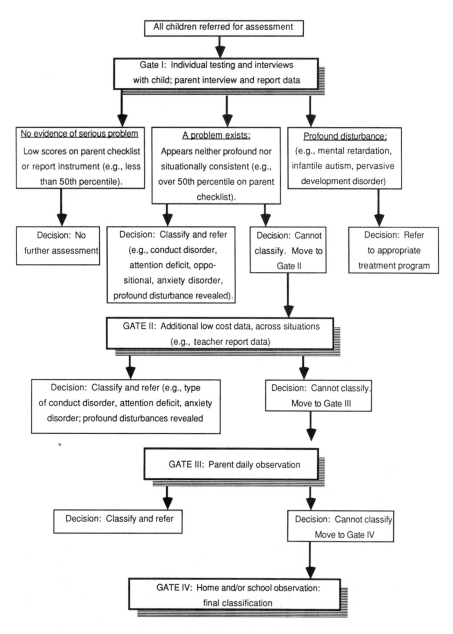

FIGURE 6-2. Multiple gating.

102 boys (ages 12–16) were assessed using a variety of measures related to conduct problems and antisocial behavior. The exercise was to use a sequential combination of inexpensive to expensive assessment measures to predict the 14 boys in the sample who had been arrested prior to or within 6 months following assessment; and further, if possible, to select the seven of those who were recidivists (two or more arrest episodes). This problem is not dissimilar to that faced by clinicians and researchers in this area (i.e., what is the most accurate and cost-effective way to select a small target group from a much larger sample of individuals?).

In this example, the Gate I assessment involved taking teacher ratings on 11 items for each child on his social behavior in school. These items were selected a priori, and were similar in format to the items on the teacher version of the Child Behavior Checklist (Edelbrock & Achenbach, 1984). The goal at Gate I was to set a low cutting score for poor school behavior that the authors hoped would include all of the children who were officially classified as delinquent, and reject a large number of nondelinquent children and as few delinquents as possible from further assessment. Thus, a cutting score was set on a priori grounds as close to the 50th percentile as possible (i.e., the 47th percentile and above). The outcome of Gate I prediction was as follows: of the 14 delinquents, 12 were correctly identified as at risk, along with 43 nondelinquents (false positive errors). Two of the 14 delinquents were misclassified as nondelinquents and 45 were correctly classified as nondelinquents (valid negatives). The 47 youngsters classified as not at risk were then dropped at this gate and not further evaluated. At Gate I, only two of the truly at-risk children were lost (a miss rate of 14%) and the pool of subjects to be further evaluated was cut approximately in half. Reduction in the size of the sample, while retaining all but two of the high-risk children, accomplishes two functions. First, it raised the base rate of the high-risk children from about 13% in the original sample to about 22% in the sample remaining after Gate I, resulting in a much better split for further classification analyses. Second, by the use of an extremely low-cost screening device, nearly 50% of the youngsters required no further assessment.

For the Gate II assessment, only 55 of the original 102 boys were assessed using a moderately expensive evaluation device: parent daily observation data. This procedure involved a set of six telephone interviews with the parent, lasting approximately 10 minutes each. Each day, the parents were asked whether or not each of a list of problems behaviors had occurred during the past 24 hours. A simple total of yes responses comprised the daily score. At this stage, the same strategy was used as at Gate I: to classify as "at risk" those children who were above the 50th percentile on the parent observation assessment. The actual cutting score was the 54th percentile. At Gate II, 10 of the remaining 12 delinquents were correctly classified, 20 were incorrectly classified as false positives, two as false negatives, and 23 as valid negatives. Thus, after two gates of assessment, 10 of the 14 delinquents were classified correctly, 4 were missed, and a total of 68 valid negatives (i.e., children not at risk) were excluded from further analysis. Thirty children were left for further assessment, of whom one-third were truly at risk. Again, the base rate for prediction after Gate II was improved further, and the number of youngsters left to be assessed through more expensive assessment was reduced again by nearly half.

At the final gate used in this example, a rather intensive interview with the parents (approximately $1\frac{1}{2}$ hours) was used for final classification. The interview focused on items having to do with parental supervision of the child and the effectiveness of the parents' discipline practices. The Gate III score consisted of the standardized sum of the supervision and discipline scores. Using a cutoff score at the 47th percentile (for the full sample), the final classification was made. This final classification yielded nine valid positives, seven false positives, one false negative, and 13 valid negatives. Thus, the final sample included more delinquents than nondelinquents, with a total correct classification rate of 73.3%, and a relative improvement over chance prediction of 74.2%. Of perhaps greater interest is the fact that, for the 7 recidivists in the sample of 14 delinquent youngsters, 6 were classified correctly and only 1 was a false negative. Self-reported delinquent life-style scores were available for all children in the total sample. The means for the youngsters in each prediction group are reproduced from Loeber *et al.* (1984) in Table 6-2, in which it can be seen that these scores lend additional and substantial validity to sequential gating procedure.

Looking at the outcome for the three steps of assessment in a slightly different way, the teacher rating procedure at Gate I resulted in an improvement of 37.6% over chance classification, the parent observations at Gate II resulted in a 49.2% improvement over chance, and the predictions at Gate III represented a 74.2% improvement over chance. The savings in costs for using successive gating were marked, as can be seen in Table 6-3.

We conclude by strongly recommending further exploration of multiple gating strategies such as this, using data from different agents in different settings. Such a system holds the possibility for allowing clinicians to use multiple assessments in a sequential manner utilizing preset decision rules for

TABLE 6-2. Distribution of Average Self-Reported Delinquent Life Style Scores by Prediction Outcome Cells

	Actual behavior	
Predicted behavior	Official delinquents	Nondelinquents
Delinquent	Valid positives Mean = 10.6	False positives Mean = 2.6
Nondelinquent	False negatives Mean = 2.22	Valid negatives Mean = 1.24

Note. N = 102. From Loeber, Dishion, and Patterson (1984).

TABLE 6-3. Costs of Screening for the Multiple Gating Procedure Compared to a Single-Stage Approach

Assessment	Professional time per subject (hr)	Single-stage assessment		Multiple gating procedure	
		N	Cost ($)[a]	N	Cost ($)[a]
Teacher ratings	.16	102	212.00	102	212.00
Parent telephone interview (six phone calls)	1.2	102	1,591.00	55	858.00
Structured interview with parent and child	2	102	2,652.00	30	780.00
Total			4,455.00		1,850.00
Mean cost per child			43.68		18.13

Note. From Loeber, Dishion, and Patterson (1984).

[a]Cost of professional time is computed at an hourly wage of $13.00 for a Research Assistant I.

interpreting the data, and shows promise in increasing classification accuracy of childhood disorders.

ACKNOWLEDGMENTS

Preparation of this chapter was supported by a contract from ADAMHA (A. Hussain Tuma, Project Officer). The authors wish to thank Dr. William Mitchell for his help in organizing the content; Dr. Don Hartmann for a critical review of an earlier version of the manuscript; Dr. Lew Bank, Ms. Stella Spyrou, and Mr. Miles Yamamoto for assistance with the statistical analyses; and Mr. Will Mayer and Ms. Mary Perry for editorial assistance.

REFERENCES

Abikoff, H., Gittelman, R., & Klein, D. (1980). Classroom observation code for hyperactive children: A replication of validity. *Journal of Consulting and Clinical Psychology, 48,* 555–565.

Abikoff, H., Gittelman-Klein, R., & Klein, D. (1977). Validation of a classroom observation code for hyperactive children. *Journal of Consulting and Clinical Psychology, 45,* 772–783.

Achenbach, T. M. (1978). The Child Behavior Profile. I. Boys aged 6–11. *Journal of Consulting and Clinical Psychology, 46,* 478–488

Achenbach, T. M., & Edelbrock, C. S. (1979). The Child Behavior Profile. II. Boys aged 12 to 16 and girls aged 6 to 11 and 12 to 16. *Journal of Consulting and Clinical Psychology, 41* 223–233.

Achenbach, T. M., & Edelbrock, C. S. (1984). Psychopathology of childhood. *Annual Review of Psychology, 35,* 227–256.

Altmann, J. (1974). Observational study of behavior: Sampling methods. *Behavior, 49,* 227–267.

American Psychiatric Association (1980). *Diagnostic and statistical manual of mental disorders* (3rd ed.). Washington, DC: Author.

Arkes, H. R. (1981). Impediments to accurate clinical judgment and possible ways to minimize their impact. *Journal of Consulting and Clinical Psychology, 49,* 323–330.

Ary, D. (1984). Mathematical explanation of error in duration recording using partial interval, whole interval, and momentary time sampling. *Behavior Assessment, 6,* 221–228.

Ary, D., & Suen, H. K. (1983). The use of momentary time sampling to assess both frequency and duration behavior. *Journal of Behavior Assessment, 5,* 143–150.

Barkley, R. A. (1981). Hyperactivity. In E. J. Mash & L. Terdal (Eds.), *Behavioral assessment of childhood disorders* (pp. 127–184). New York: Guilford.

Bernal, M. E., Gibson, D. M., Williams, D. E., & Pesses, D. I. (1971). A device for recording automatic audio tape recording. *Journal of Applied Behavior Analysis, 4,* 151–156.

Blau, T. H. (1979). Diagnoses of disturbed children. *American Psychologist, 34,* 969–972.

Bornstein, M. R., Bellack, A. S., & Hersen, M. (1977). Social-skills training for unassertive children: A multiple-baseline analysis. *Journal of Applied Behavior Analysis, 10,* 183–195.

Bornstein, M. R., Bellack, A. S., & Hersen, M. (1980). Social skills training for highly aggressive children in an inpatient psychiatric setting. *Behavior Modification, 4,* 173–186.

Burgess, R. L., & Conger, R. D. (1978). Family interaction in abusive, neglectful, and normal families. *Child Development, 1978, 49,* 1163–1173.

Carlson, W. J., & Williams, W. B. (1984). A factor structure of child home observation data. *Journal of Abnormal Child Psychology, 12,* 245–260.

Chamberlain, P. (1980). *Standardization of a parent report measure.* Unpublished doctoral dissertation, University of Oregon.

Cohen, J. (1960). A coefficient of agreement for nominal scales. *Educational and Psychological Measurement, 20,* 27–46.

Conger, R. D. (1982). *Social Interactional Scoring System: Observer training manual.* Unpublished manuscript. (Available from Rand Conger, Department of Human Development and Family Ecology, University of Illinois, Urbana, IL 61801.)

Conger, R. D., Lahey, B. B., & Smith, S. S. (1981, July). *An intervention program for child abuse: Modifying maternal depression and behavior.* Paper presented at the Family Violence Research Conference, University of New Hampshire.

Conger, R. D., & McLeod, D. (1977). Describing behavior in small groups with the DATAMYTE event recorder. *Behavior Research Methods and Instrumentation, 9,* 418–424.

Cronbach, L. J. (1975). Five decades of public controversy over mental testing. *American Psychologist, 30,* 1–14.

Cronbach, L. J., & Gleser, G. C. (1965). *Psychological tests and personnel decisions.* Urbana: University of Illinois Press.

Cronbach, L. J., Gleser, G., Nanda, H., & Rajaratnam, N. (1972). *The dependability of behavioral measurements.* New York: Wiley.

Cunningham, C. E., & Barkley, R. A. (1979). A comparison of the interactions of hyperactive and normal children with their mothers in free play and structured tasks. *Child Development, 50,* 217–224.

DeMaster, B., Reid, J. B., & Twentyman, C. (1977). The effects of feedback on observer reliability. *Behavior Therapy, 8,* 317–329.

Dysart, R. R. (1973–1974). *A behavioral description of family interactions in the home and clinic* (Unpublished doctoral dissertation, University of Houston). *Dissertation Abstracts International, 34,* 17445.

Edelbrock, C., & Achenbach, T. M. (1984). The teacher version of the Child Behavior Profile: Boys aged 6–11. *Journal of Consulting* and *Clinical Psychology, 52,* 207–217.

Eisler, R. M., Hersen, M., Miller, P. M., & Blanchard, E. B. (1975). Situational determinants of assertive behaviors. *Journal of Consulting and Clinical Psychology, 43,* 330–340.

Eisler, R. M., Miller, P. M., & Hersen, M. (1973). Components of assertive behavior. *Journal of Clinical Psychology, 29*, 295–299.

Eyberg, S. M., & Johnson, S. M. (1974). Multiple assessment of behavior modification and families: Effects of contingency contracting and order of treated problems. *Journal of Consulting and Clinical Psychology, 42*, 594–606.

Forehand, R., & Reed, S. (1979). Training parents to modify noncompliant behavior of their children. In A. J. Finch & P. C. Kendall (Eds.), *Treatment and research in child psychopathology*. New York: Spectrum Publications.

Foreyt, J. P., & Goodrick, G. K., (1981). Childhood obesity. In E. J. Mash & L. G. Terdal (Eds.), *Behavioral assessment of childhood disorders* (pp. 573–599). New York: Guilford.

Freeman, B. J., & Ritvo, E. (1981). The syndrome of autism: A critical review of diagnostic systems and follow-up studies and the theoretical background in Behavior Observation Scale. In J. Gilliam (Ed.), *Autism, diagnosis, instruction, management, and research*. Springfield, IL: Charles C Thomas.

Freeman, B. J., & Schroth, P. (1984), The development of the behavioral observation system (BOS) for autism. *Behavioral Assessment, 6*, 177–187.

Gloglower, F. & Sloop, E. W. (1976). Two strategies of group training parents as effective behavior modifiers. *Behavior Therapy, 7*, 177–184.

Greenwood, C. R., Todd, N. M., Hops, H., & Walker, H. M. (1982). Behavior charge targets in the assessment and treatment of socially withdrawn preschool children. *Behavioral Assessment, 4*, 273–297.

Harris, A. M., & Reid, J. B. (1981). The consistency of a class of coercive child behaviors across school settings for individual subjects. *Journal of Abnormal Child Psychology, 9*, 219–227.

Hartmann, D. P., & Wood, D. D. (1982). Observational methods. In A. S. Bellack, M. Hersen, & A. E. Kazdin (Eds.), *International handbook of behavior modification and therapy* (pp. 109–138). New York: Plenum.

Haynes, S. N., & Horn, W. (1982). Reactivity in behavioral observation: A review. *Behavioral Assessment, 4*, 369–385.

Hetherington, E. M., Cox, M., & Cox, R. (1981). Effects of divorce on parents and children. In M. Lamb (Ed.), *Nontraditional families* (pp. 233–287). Hillsdale, NJ: Erlbaum.

Hollenbeck, A. R. (1978). Problems of reliability in observational research. In G. P. Sackett (Ed.), *Observing behavior. II. Data collection and analysis methods*. Baltimore: University Park Press.

Holm, R. A. (1978). Problems of reliability in observational research. In G. P. Sackett (Ed.), *Observing behavior. II. Data collection and analysis methods*. Baltimore: University Park Press.

Holm, R. A. (1981). Using data-logging equipment. In E. Folsinger & R. Lewis (Eds.), *Assessing marriage: New behavioral approaches* (pp. 171–181). Beverly Hills: Sage Publications.

Johnson, S. M., & Bolstad, O. D. (1975). Reactivity to home observation: A comparison of audio recorded behavior with observers present of absent. *Journal of Applied Behavior Analysis, 8*, 181–185.

Johnson, S. M., & Lobitz, G. A. (1974). Parental manipulations of child behavior in home observations. *Journal of Applied Behavior Analysis, 7*, 23–31.

Kazdin, A. E. (1982). Observer effects: Reactivity of direct observation. In D. P. Hartmann (Ed.), *Using observers to study behavior*. San Francisco; Jossey-Bass.

Klesges, R. C., Coates, T., Moldenhauer-Klesges, L., Holzer, B., Gustavson, J., & Barnes, J. (1984). The FATS: An observational system for assessing physical activity in children and associated parent behavior. *Behavioral Assessment, 6*, 333–345.

Lobitz, W. C., & Johnson, S. M. (1975). Parental manipulation of the behavior of normal and deviant children. *Child Development, 46*, 719–726.

Loeber, R., & Dishion, T. J. (1983). Early predictors of male delinquency: A review. *Psychological Bulletin, 94*, 68–99.

Loeber, R., Dishion, T. J., & Patterson, G. R. (1984). Multiple–gating: A multistage assessment procedure for identifying youths at risk for delinquency. *Journal of Research in Crime and Delinquency, 21*, 7–32.

Loney, J. (1980). Child hyperactivity. In R. H. Woody (Ed.), *Encyclopedia of clinical assessment* (Vol. 1, pp. 265–285). San Francisco: Jossey-Bass.

Lovaas, O. I., Freitag, G., Gold, V. J., & Kassorla, I. C. (1965). Recording apparatus and procedure for observation of children in free settings. *Journal of Experimental Child Psychology, 2*, 108–120.

Lovaas, O. I., Koegel, R., Simmons, J. Q., & Long, J. S. (1973). Some generalization and follow-up measures of autistic children in behavior therapy. *Journal of Applied Behavior Analysis, 6*, 131–166.

Martin, S., Johnson, S. M., Johansson, S., & Wahl, G. (1976). The comparability of behavioral data in laboratory and natural settings. In E. J. Mash, L. A. Hamerlynck, & L. C. Handy (Eds.), *Behavior modification and families*. New York: Brunner/Mazel.

Mash, E. J., & McElwee, J. (1974). Situational effects on observer accuracy: Behavioral predictability, prior experience, and complexity of coding categories. *Child Development, 45*, 367–377.

Mash, E. J., Terdal, L. G., & Anderson, K. (1973). The response class matrix: A procedure for coding parent-child interactions. *Journal of Consulting and Clinical Psychology, 40*, 163–164.

Michelson, L., & DiLorenzo, T. M. (1981). Behavioral assessment of peer interaction and social functioning in institutional and structured settings. *Journal of Clinical Psychology, 37*, 499–504.

Michelson, L., DiLorenzo, T. M., Calpin, J. P., & Ollendick, T. H. (1982). Situational determinants of the Behavioral Assertiveness Role-Play Test for Children. *Behavior Therapy, 13*, 724–734.

Michelson, L., & Wood, R. (1980). Behavioral assessment and training of children's social skills. In M. Hersen, P. Miller, & R. Eisler (Eds.), *Progress in behavior modification* (Vol. 9). New York: Academic Press.

Mitchell, S. K. (1979). Inter-observer agreement, reliability, and generalizability of data collected in observational studies. *Psychological Bulletin, 86*, 376–390.

Mustakas, C. E., Siegel, I. E., & Schalock, H. D. (1956). An objective method for the measurement and analysis of child-adult interaction. *Child Development, 27*, 109–134.

Patterson, G. R. (1964). An empirical approach to the classification of disturbed children. *Journal of Clinical Psychology, 20*, 326–337.

Patterson, G. R. (1974). Retraining of aggressive boys by their parents: Review of recent literature and follow-up evaluation. *Canadian Psychiatric Association Journal, 19*, 142–161.

Patterson, G. R. (1982). *Coercive family process*. Eugene, OR: Castalia.

Patterson, G. R., Ray, R. S., Shaw, D. A., & Cobb, J. A. (1969). *Manual for coding of family interactions*. New York: Microfiche Publications.

Pollack, S., Vincent, J., & Williams, B. (1977). *Demand characteristics in the classroom observation of hyperactive children: Reactivity to naturalistic observation*. Unpublished manuscript.

Powell, J. (1984). On the misrepresentation of behavioral realities by a widely practiced direct observation procedure: Partial interval (on-zero) sampling. *Behavior Assessment, 6*, 209–219.

Reed, M. L., & Edelbrock, C. S. (1983). Reliability and validity of the Direct Observation Form of the Child Behavior Checklist. *Journal of Abnormal Child Psychology, 11*, 521–530.

Reid, J. B. (1967). *Reciprocity in family interaction*. Unpublished doctoral dissertation, University of Oregon.

Reid, J. B. (1970). Reliability assessment of observation data: A possible methodological problem. *Child Development, 41*, 1143–1150.

Reid, J. B. (Ed.) (1978). *A social learning approach to family intervention: II. Observation in home settings.* Eugene, OR: Castalia.

Reid, J. B. (1986). Social interactional patterns in families of abused and nonabused children. In C. Zahn Waxler, M. Cummings, & R. Iannotti (Eds.), *Social and biological origins of altruism and aggression* (pp. 238–255). New York: Cambridge.

Reid, J. B., Hawkins, N., Keutzer, C., McNeal, S. A., Phelps, R. E., Reid, K. M., & Mees, H. L. (1967). A marathon behavior modification of selectively mute child. *Journal of Child Psychology and Psychiatry, 8,* 27–30.

Reid, J. B., Skindrud, K., Taplin, P., & Jones, R. R. (1973, August). *The role of complexity in the collection and evaluation of observation data.* Paper presented at the meeting of the American Psychological Association, Montreal.

Reid, J. B., Taplin, P. S., & Lorber, R. (1981). A social interactional approach to the treatment of abusive families. In R. Stuart (Ed.), *Violent behavior: Social learning approaches to prediction, management, and treatment* (pp. 83–101). New York: Brunner/Mazel.

Rhine, R. J., & Ender, P. (1983). Comparability of methods used in the sampling of primate behavior. *American Journal of Primatology, 5,* 1–15.

Robinson, E. A., & Eyberg, S. (1981). The dyadic parent–child interaction coding system: Standardization and validation. *Journal of Consulting and Clinical Psychology, 49,* 245–250.

Ross, A. O., & Pelham, W. E. (1981). Child psychopathology. *Annual Review of Psychology, 32,* 243–278.

Sackett, G. P., Gluck, J., & Ruppenthal, G. (1978). Introduction: An overview of methodological and statistical problems in observational research. In G. P. Sackett (Ed.), *Observing behavior* (Vol. 2: *Data collection and analysis methods*). Baltimore: University Park Press.

Stevens, T. M., Krupst, M., Suran, B., & Schulman, J. (1978). Activity level: A comparison between actometer scores and observer ratings. *Journal of Abnormal Child Psychology, 6,* 163–173.

Strain, P. S., & Cook, T. P. (1976). An observational investigation of two elementary age autistic children during free play. *Psychology in the Schools, 6,* 317–326.

Taplin, P. S., & Reid, J. B. (1977). Changes in parent consequation as a function of family intervention. *Journal of Consulting and Clinical Psychology, 4,* 973–981.

Tavormina, J. B. (1975). Relative effectiveness of behavioral and reflective group counseling with parents of mentally retarded children. *Journal of Consulting and Clinical Psychology, 43,* 22–31.

Van der Molen, H. H., Kerkhoff, J., & Jong, S. (1983). Training observers to follow children and score their road-crossing behavior. *Ergonomics, 26,* 535–553.

Wahler, R. G. (1975). Some structural aspects of deviant child behavior. *Journal of Applied Behavior Analysis, 8,* 27–42.

Wahler, R. G. (1980). The insular mother: Her problems in parent–child treatment. *Journal of Applied Behavior Analysis, 13,* 207–219.

Wahler, R. G., & Dumas, J. E. (1983). "A chip off the old block": Some interpersonal characteristics of coercive children across generations. In P. Strain (Ed.), *Children's social behavior: Development, assessment, and modification.* New York: Academic Press, 1983.

Wahler, R. G., House, A. E., & Stambaugh, E. E., II. (1976). *Ecological assessment of child problem behaviors: A clinical package for home, school, and institutional settings.* New York: Pergamon.

Waxman, M., & Stunkard, A. (1980). Caloric intake and expenditure of obese boys. *Journal of Pediatrics, 96,* 187–193.

Weinrott, M. R., Garrett, B., & Todd, N. (1978). The influence of observer presence on classroom behavior. *Behavior Therapy, 9,* 900–911.

Weinrott, M. R., & Jones, R. R. (1982). *An unobtrusive study of observer drift.* Unpublished manuscript, Evaluation Research Group, Eugene, OR.

Weinrott, M. R., & Jones, R. R. (1984). Overt versus covert assessment of observer reliability. *Child Development, 55,* 1125–1137.

Weinrott, M. R. Jones R. R., & Boler, G. R. (1981). Convergent and discriminant validity of five classroom observation systems: A secondary analysis. *Journal of Educational Psychology, 73,* 671–680.

Weinrott, M. R., Reid, J. B., Bauske, B. W., & Brummett, B. (1981). Supplementing naturalistic observations with observer impressions. *Behavioral Assessment, 3,* 151–159.

Weitz, S. E. (1981). A code for assessing teaching skills of parents of developmentally disabled children. *Journal of Autism and Developmental Disorders, 12,* 13–24.

Wiggins, J. S. (1981). Clinical and statistical prediction: Where are we and where do we go from here? *Clinical Psychology Review, 1,* 3–18.

Wilcox, J. R., Goocher, B. E., & Grove, D. (1979). *The Family Observation Record.* Unpublished manual, Edgefield Lodge, Troutdale, OR.

Yarrow, M. R., & Waxler, C. (1979). Observing interaction: A confrontation with methodology. In R. B. Cairns (Ed.), *The analysis of social interactions: Methods, issues, and illustrations.* Hillsdale, NJ: Erlbaum.

Zangwill, W. M., & Kniskern, J. R. (1982). Comparison of problems families in the clinic and at home. *Behavior Therapy, 13,* 145–152.

7

FAMILY ASSESSMENT METHODS

THEODORE JACOB
DANIEL L. TENNENBAUM

INTRODUCTION

The purpose of this chapter is to provide an overview of existing and developing family assessment methods relevant to the study of child psychopathology. It is our intention not only to inform the child psychopathologist of the range of valuable family assessment methods that are available, but also to encourage the incorporation of such procedures into future research efforts. In so doing, we believe that our understanding of the etiology, course, treatment, and prevention of childhood disorders will be greatly enriched.

First, a framework for classifying family measurement procedures will be introduced in which three major dimensions are emphasized: unit of analysis, source of data, and construct assessed. Next, brief descriptions of a selected number of methods within each of the major groupings will be presented, together with references to other useful and/or promising procedures that may be of interest to the reader. Finally, we will identify major gaps in this literature; indicate critical issues of methodology—strengths and limitations—that characterize the various types of family measures; and suggest theoretical and methodological studies that future research efforts could profitably address.

CLASSIFYING FAMILY MEASUREMENT PROCEDURES

In the context of describing family assessment procedures relevant to studies of child psychopathology, three organizing dimensions seem to be particularly helpful—the source from which information is obtained; the family unit

Theodore Jacob. Division of Child Development and Family Relations, University of Arizona, Tucson, Arizona.

Daniel L. Tennenbaum. Department of Psychology, Kent State University, Kent, Ohio.

that is the focus of assessment; and the major constructs that the instrument attempts to measure.

Data Source

The major distinction to be made regarding data source involves instruments based upon the reports of family members versus instruments based upon the direct observation of families during some type of actual interaction. Common to all variants of the report approach is the requirement that informants be asked for their perceptions of family events. The advantages of this strategy are many, including the strong face validity that is associated with test items; ease of administration and scoring; test developments based upon large representative samples; and access to family data that cannot be reasonably obtained by other procedures. Observational procedures, on the other hand, provide information regarding actual interactions of family members. Under the best of circumstances, such procedures yield highly detailed descriptions regarding streams of behavior that characterize the family in operation as well as precise information regarding the family's response to solution of, or performance on objective tasks and problems. Given these data, specific coding systems can be applied to these interactions, all allowing for systematic descriptions of family processes and patterns of interaction.

Within each of these major approaches, one can find important subgroups of instruments. Self-report procedures, for example, include objective tests, projective tests, structured interviews, and behavioral reports. Instruments included within the observational grouping can be further subdivided into laboratory analogues and naturalistic observations. Laboratory procedures have included the use of structured tasks or games (which yield some outcome measure based upon the family's performance) as well as the assessment of actual interactions among family members generated from discussions of problems or conflicts. These discussions, often videotaped or audiotaped in order to provide a permanent record, can then be assessed by various coding and rating systems. In contrast with these laboratory-based procedures, naturalistic observations involve the observation and assessment of family interaction in the home setting. These data can also be subjected to detailed coding systems or to more general ratings. In some cases, permanent records (audiotapes or videotapes) are obtained, whereas at other times ratings (assessments, codings) are conducted by "live" observers who remain in the family's home during the period of observation.

The differences between report and observational data—their advantages and liabilities—have been the subject of much discussion in many areas of social science, including the assessment of family behaviors (Hetherington & Martin, 1979). In the last section of this chapter, a more critical discussion of each approach will be presented in which strengths, limitations, and future research needs will be highlighted.

Unit of Assessment

In the measurement of family influences, three assessment levels have received major attention. The first level of analysis (individual assessments) has involved traditional tests of personality or psychopathology, including both objective and projective procedures—instruments that can provide important data regarding the psychiatric and psychosocial status of the individual members. The second level of assessment focuses on dyadic relationships and, most important, includes descriptions of the marital, parent–child and child–sibling dyads. In contrast with the assessment of individuals, relationship assessments provide information about dyadic status and functioning, whether determined from an individual's reports regarding the relationship or from an observer's coding of an ongoing interaction between two family members. Finally, there are assessments of the whole family whereby test scores, ratings, or performance variables are aimed at characterizing the family as a totality. Again, assessments of this unit can be obtained via report procedures (i.e., an individual's perceptions/descriptions of his or her family), laboratory outcome procedures (i.e., the family's performance on a structured task), or process and content codings obtained from laboratory or naturalistic observation of interactions among family members.

Constructs Assessed

How one conceptualizes and examines the relationship between family influences and childhood disorders will vary in relation to one's theoretical model and study objective, as well as the psychopathology under consideration. Although no single family variable or family model can guarantee immediate insights into the domain of child psychopathology, our own survey of the literature reveals several sets of constructs that seem particularly relevant to understanding the family–child psychopathology complex. The four sets of constructs are here referred to as affect, control, communication, and family systems properties.

Affect

The primacy of the affective bond as a determinant of relationship satisfaction has been emphasized across a broad range of disciplines and types of interpersonal relationships. From studies of infant attachment (Ainsworth, Blehar, Waters, & Wall, 1978) and group process (Parsons & Bales, 1955; Steinhauer, 1987) to investigations of marital dissatisfaction (Lewis & Spanier, 1979; Weiss, 1981) and patterns of childhood socialization (Rollins & Thomas, 1979), the importance of a supportive and nurturant affective relationship has been repeatedly underscored.

Control

As with the affective dimension, interpersonal influence has been of major importance in conceptualizations of a wide range of relationships (Foa & Foa, 1974; Leary, 1957). In studies of adult relationships—in particular, the marital dyad—various terms have been used to describe this dimension, the most common descriptors being power, influence, and dominance (Hadley & Jacob, 1976). In studies of relationships involving members of unequal status—namely, the parent–child dyad—the literature has focused on strategies, techniques, and styles of parenting behavior, with an overriding interest in those processes by which parents attempt to control and shape the behavior of their offspring during early childhood and adolescence (Rollins & Thomas, 1979).

Communication

At least two meanings of "communication" can be identified in the family literature of relevance to child psychopathology. First, there has been continued interests in relating certain types of communication distortions to the development and perpetuation of cognitive disorder in children and adolescents. Most importantly, this line of theory and research began during the early 1950s with the appearance of several family theories of schizophrenia (Mishler & Waxler, 1965). During the next 30 years, key concepts from these early efforts—in particular, the notions of double bind, transactional thought disorder, and more recently, communication deviance—guided several research programs aimed at identifying, prospectively, those patterns of family communication which predict severe psychiatric disorder as the offspring enter late adolescence and early adulthood (Lewis, Rodnick, & Goldstein, 1981).

A second focus on family communication has involved studies of family problem solving in dysfunctional family units and the development of treatment programs aimed at enhancing those "communication skills" thought to be most relevant to the effective and satisfactory resolution of conflict (Gottman, Notarius, Gonso, & Markman, 1976; Olson, Russell, & Sprenkle, 1980; Thomas, 1977). In large part, this direction of research and practice has been stimulated by the efforts of family researchers most closely identified with social learning theory (Vincent, 1980).

Systems Properties

This set of constructs derives most directly from the application of systems concepts to the family unit. Most important, Bateson's collaboration with Jackson, Haley, and Weakland during the early 1950s provided the major foundation and stimulus for this clinical–theoretical framework. This framework in turn, generated a variety of provocative and highly influential models of family psychopathology and treatment. In contrast with the other major constructs, attention is here directed toward general properties and principles of family systems that characterize relationships within the family and between the family and extrafamilial systems that influence family functioning. Included in this domain of processes are such characteristics as system flexibility and adaptability and the family's ability to change patterns of control and expression of affect in response to changing needs of members and stresses imposed on the family (Olson, Sprenkle, & Russell, 1979). Other theorists have highlighted the family's use of time and space, as well as the amount of interaction that occurs within different family subsystems, in an effort to understand the nature of functional versus dysfunctional family systems (Kantor & Lehr, 1975; Steinglass, 1979).

A SELECTIVE REVIEW OF METHODS

From the foregoing discussion of major organizing dimensions for classifying family assessment procedures, it is clear that many subgroups of instruments can be defined—many more than it is possible to discuss and evaluate in a single chapter. Within the general domain of report procedures are assessments of individual adults and children based upon structured or unstructured, objective or projective instruments. Given the many measures that can be included in this grouping as well as various reviews that are available (Buros, 1978), we decided not to survey this set of instruments. The one exception to this decision was to discuss the individually based assessment of communication deviance, given the extremely important role that this variable has assumed in family studies of schizophrenia. A second grouping of report instruments focuses on *relationship* assessments (parent–child, child–sibling, whole family) as determined from questionnaires (psychological tests), structured interviews and quasi-observation procedures.

The other major division, observation procedures, can be divided into laboratory-based instruments and naturalistic observational procedures. The former would include structured tasks yielding outcome measures, detailed process and content codings of planned discussions, and global ratings of planned discussions. In contrast, naturalistic observation procedures involve the use of detailed process and content codings of family interaction in the home environment.

In the following presentation, selected procedures within each subgroup of instruments will be briefly described. Instruments were chosen on the basis of several considerations, including psychometric strength, accumulated scientific data, frequency of use, and revelance to key family variables. Since there are many more "worthy" instruments that can be presented in this one chapter, only reference to other important and/or promising methods is included for the interested reader.

Assessment of Individuals

The smallest unit within the family is the individual. Member characteristics relevant to understanding the etiology, course, and treatment of child psychopathology include both hereditary/biological influences and social/personality variables. Notwithstanding uncertainties regarding the relative importance of biological variables, environmental influences, and their complex interactions, it seems clear that the behavior, attitudes, and cognitions of individual members, as well as their perceptions of self and others, can and do influence the expression of childhood disorders. Although a review of the many individual measures of personality, psychopathology, and attitudes is beyond the scope of this chapter, one individual assessment procedure should be noted in view of its continued importance in studies of the family's impact on schizophrenia.

Communication Deviance

The concept and measurement of communication deviance (CD) grew out of Singer and Wynne's (1966) early observations of family interactions of disturbed individuals, typically schizophrenics, and the belief that deficits in "ego development" in the psychotic patient are systematically related to difficulties in parent–child communication. In recent years, CD has been related to severe psychopathology that encompasses schizophrenia and other disorders, such as borderline personality. In their seminal studies, Singer and Wynne (1966) developed a scoring manual for rating 41 communication deficits observed in an individually administered Rorschach, which in turn were subsumed under three main types: closure problems, disruptive behavior, and peculiar verbalizations. During subsequent years, other tasks, coding systems, and revisions of the original procedures have been described in the literature (Doane *et al.*, 1982; Jones, 1977; Sass, Sunderson, Singer, & Wynne, 1984; Singer, 1973; Wild, Shapiro, & Goldenberg, 1975). Recent reliability studies have been reported by Doane *et al.* (1982), as well as Sass *et al.* (1984). Validity studies and applications have included attempts to examine whether CD scores from the individual testing are related to family and spouse interaction data (Herman & Jones 1976); to discriminate diagnostic groups based upon CD score (Wynne, Singer, Bartko, & Toohey, 1977); and to predict the onset of schizophrenia in adolescents from parents' CD scores (Goldstein, 1987; Goldstein, Rodnick, Jones, McPherson, & West, 1978).

Questionnaires for Assessing Parent–Child Relationships

Although the parent–child dyad has been considered critical in understanding the family's role in child psychopathology, recommendable assessment procedures focused on parent–child relationships are far from plentiful. Simply put, most instruments within this domain are characterized by weak psychometric underpinnings, and/or limited use (Olson, 1976; Straus & Brown, 1978). In our own review of this literature, only the following four instruments appeared to be worthy of the researcher's serious consideration.

Structural Analysis of Social Behavior

The Structural Analysis of Social Behavior (SASB) is based on a theory of interpersonal behavior rooted in several interpersonal circle or circumplex models that were first described nearly 30 years ago (Leary, 1957; Schaefer, 1959). Briefly, the full version of the SASB model consists of three diamond-shaped surfaces, each corresponding to a distinct focus: self, other, and intraphysic. For each focus (surface), there are two central dimensions—affiliation, which ranges from friendly to hostile, and interdependence, which extends from domination to emancipation. All the points in between the four poles consist of combinations of varying degrees of affiliation and dominance. Questionnaire items are available for each of the points in the full-scale version of the SASB, which allow the respondent to describe a particular relationship (e.g., a child describing his or her parents). The various item responses are then used to generate a visual profile or map of a respondent's critical ratings. SASB theory holds that the three dimensions of focus, affiliation, and interdependence "are all that are needed to describe a broad range of interpersonal and intrapsychic events." The instrument is typically completed by parents and their children aged 10 and above. The originator, up until now the primary user of this instrument, reports internal consistency as $r = .90$ (Benjamin, 1974) and test–retest reliability as $r = .87$ in normal samples. Additionally, she reports that the SASB clearly discriminates different diagnostic groups. Further information regarding psychometric properties as well as applications can be found in Benjamin (1974, 1977, 1986), Humphrey (1984), and Humphrey, Apple, and Kirschenbaum (1985).

Child Report of Parental Behavior Inventory

Many instruments have been designed to measure children's perceptions of parental behavior, although Schaefer's Child Report of Parental Behavior Inventory (CRPBI) is the most frequently cited and used by researchers. The CRPBI was derived from two sources: (1) the developmental literature, which indicated that the overall quality of the parent–child relationship was an important component in the evolving personality of the child; and (2) an empirical evaluation of previous studies of parental behaviors. Initial development of the instrument involved two major bipolar dimensions of maternal behavior—love versus hostility and autonomy versus control—although subsequent studies (Margolies & Weintraub, 1977; Renson, Schaefer,

& Levy, 1968; Schaefer, 1965b; Teleki, Powell, & Dodder, 1982) revealed three orthogonal dimensions—acceptance versus rejection, psychological autonomy versus psychological control, and firm control versus lax control. During subsequent years, various investigators have revised the original 260-item instrument into shorter versions that retain the original conceptual foundation as well as many of its scales and items. Margolies and Weintraub (1977) published results of the most recent, short version of the CRPBI (56 items), which assesses the three dimensions of acceptance versus rejection (the degree to which children perceive positive involvement vs. hostile detachment in their parents), psychological autonomy versus psychological control (the degree to which children perceive their parents' covert use of control through guilt, intrusiveness, and parental direction), and firm control versus lax control (the degree to which the parents make rules and enforce them). Children complete separate but identical forms for their mother and father. Test–retest reliabilities ranged from .66 to .93, on the 56-item instrument at 1-week and 5-week intervals (Margolies & Weintraub, 1977). Internal consistency (KR-20) of the original 260-item instrument, as reported by Schaefer (1965a), ranged from .60 to .90 (median = .76). Factor analysis of the 56-item version found Factors I and II (acceptance vs. rejection and psychological autonomy vs. psychological control) held up very well. Factor III (lax control vs. firm control) was less stable (Margolies & Weintraub, 1977). The CRPBI has been used in studies of single parent families (Teleki *et al.*, 1982), normal families (Droppleman & Schaefer, 1963), and families with delinquent sons (Schaefer, 1965a, 1965b). Further psychometric properties and applications can be found in Droppleman and Schaefer (1963), Hazzard, Christensen, and Margolin (1983), Margolies and Weintraub (1977), Schaefer (1965a), and Teleki *et al.* (1982).

Parent–Adolescent Communication Scale

The Parent–Adolescent Communication (PAC) scale, developed by Barnes and Olson (1982), assesses adolescents and their parents regarding their perceptions and experiences of communicating with each other. Of particular importance, communication is an important component in the theoretical model of family systems developed by Olson *et al.* (1980). Their circumplex model, which focuses on the dimensions of family cohesion and family adaptability, hypothesizes that effective communication enables families to achieve and maintain a desired balance on these two major dimensions. Further, ineffective communication inhibits attaining such a balance. In attempting to assess parents' and adolescents' views of communication with each other, the PAC scale focuses on the freedom to exchange ideas, intergenerational information and concerns, trust between each other, and the positive or negative emotional tone of the interaction. In its present form, the PAC scale consists of 20 items, with separate forms for adolescents and their parents. Internal consistency estimates (Cronbach's alpha) were .87 (open family communication), .78 (problems in family communication), and .88 (total scale). Test–retest reliabilities ranged from .60 to .78 at 4- to 5-week intervals (Olson et al., 1982). To aid in the interpretation of new applications of this instrument, norms from a large national survey are available. As a cautionary note, the authors reported that the relationship between communication (PAC) and cohesion (FACES) was found to be more linear than predicted by the circumplex model upon which these instruments are based. Further information regarding psychometric properties and applications can be found in Barnes and Olson (1985) and Olson et al. (1982).

Parent–Child Areas of Change Questionnaire

Developed during the early 1970s, the Areas of Change Questionnaire (ACQ) (Weiss, Hops, & Patterson, 1973) attempted to describe marital dissatisfaction in a more behaviorally precise form than extant marital satisfaction measures. Specifically, the instrument evaluates satisfaction in terms of the amount and direction of change that partners would like to see in their marriage across a range of topics and contents. Analogous to the marital ACQ, the Parent–Child Areas of Change Questionnaire (PC-ACQ) was developed for purposes of evaluating parent–child relationships and specifying problem areas (Jacob & Seilhamer, 1985). Although it generally has been assumed that some degree of "conflict" is inherent in relationships between parents and independence-seeking adolescents, there is little empirical data regarding how much global concepts as "conflict" or "satisfaction–dissatisfaction" are behaviorally expressed in these relationships. The PC-ACQ can provide detailed information about parent–child problem areas and about the congruence in perceptions of these relationships. The current PC-ACQ consists of a 34-item parent form on which the mother or father reports on his or her child and a 32-item form on which a child reports on his or her parent. Items on the child form are geared to the preadolescent to adolescent child and are written so that they can be understood by individuals with a fifth-grade reading level. As with the ACQ, respondents are asked to rate items on a seven-point scale ranging from "much less" (-3) to "no change" (0) to "much more" ($+3$). The authors reported that measures of internal consistency (Cronbach's alpha) across all four possible dyadic relationships (mother–child, child–mother, father–child, child–father) ranged from .91 to .94. Concurrent validity was also demonstrated by the significant correlations obtained between parent reports using the Child Behavior Checklist (Achenbach, 1978; Achenbach & Edelbrock, 1979) and the PC-ACQ. More information regarding psychometric properties and applications can be found in Jacob and Seilhamer (1985).

Questionnaires for Assessing Sibling Relationships

Although the study of sibling relationships has received increasing attention during the past decade (Bank & Kahn, 1982; Dunn & Kendrick, 1982; Lamb & Sutton-Smith, 1982), recent empirical efforts have focused primarily on very young children and have employed direct observation methodologies (Dunn & Kendrick, 1981). In contrast, the identification and measurement of core dimensions of sibling relationships for latency age children through adolescents is just beginning to surface in the literature. Only one instrument for the assessment of sibling relationships seemed sufficiently developed to justify serious consideration at the present time.

Sibling Relationship Questionnaire

The Sibling Relationship Questionairre (SRQ) is an extension of its authors' previous work on children's perception of their social networks (Furman, Adler, & Buhrmester, 1984; Furman & Buhrmester, 1985b). Motivated by their interest in a global, multidimensional, cross-situational assessment of sibling relationships, the authors were particularly interested in capturing the child's view of his or her relationships rather than an outsider's judgment. Development of the method began with extensive interviews with children in order to capture the facets they perceived to be most important in sibling relationships, followed by the construction and refinement of questionnaire items thought to include the key qualities of sibling relationships. The final questionnaire, consisting of 51 items, was administered to fifth and sixth graders, followed by a principal components analysis which revealed the four underlying dimensions of warmth/closeness, relative status/power, conflict and rivalry. The mean of all internal consistency coefficients (Cronbach's alpha) for the scales making up the SRQ was .80. For all scales, test–retest reliability at a 10-day interval ranged from .58 to .86 with a mean $r = .71$ (Furman & Buhrmester, 1985a). This recently developed scale has not yet been utilized with distressed samples. Further information regarding psychometric properties and applications can be found in Furman *et al.* (1984) and Furman and Buhrmester (1985a).

Questionnaires for Assessing Whole Families

During the past decade, a considerable number of "whole-family" assessment procedures have emerged within the family field. In contrast with other subsets of measures, a great deal of time and effort has been devoted to development of these instruments, involving relatively careful and systematic attempts to build psychometrically sound and theoretically relevant procedures. Recent reviews of this material can be found in Forman and Hagan (1983, 1984) and Skinner (1987). The three instruments to be described in this chapter approach the family from somewhat different theoretical, clinical, and empirical perspectives, resulting in considerable uniqueness associated with each procedure.

Family Environment Scale

The Family Environment Scale (FES) was one of the first instruments developed specifically for family assessments. Representing one of several social-climate scales developed by Moos during the 1970s, the FES assesses the family in regards to three primary domains, each of which is composed of two or more dimensions: relationship dimensions (cohesion, expressiveness, conflict), personal growth dimensions (independence, achievement orientation, intellectual–cultural orientation, active recreational orientation, moral–religious emphasis), and system maintenance dimensions (organization, control). The current form consists of 90 items, with each of the 10 subscales composed of 9 items. Children 10 years of age and older and parents complete this questionnaire. Internal consistency across the ten subscales ranges from .61 to .78 (Moos & Moos, 1981). Test–retest reliabilities are $r = .78$ (at 8 weeks), $r = .74$ (at 4 months), and $r = .73$ (at 12 months) (Bagarozzi, 1974). Intercorrelations among the subscales average $r = .25$ (Billings & Moos, 1982). Norms are available on large national samples of normal and distressed families as well as smaller groups of single parents, blacks, and Mexican Americans. The FES has been widely used in studies of psychopathology and treatment for differentiating family types and evaluating treatment outcome. Further information regarding the instrument's psychometric properties and applications can be found in Bagarozzi (1984), Billings and Moos (1982), Finney, Moos, Cronkite, and Gamble (1983), Moos, Finney, and Gamble (1982), Moos and Moos (1981, 1984), and Wald, Greenwald, and Jacob (1984).

Family Adaptability and Cohesion Scales

Developed by Olson and colleagues, the Family Adaptability and Cohesion Scales (FACES) operationalize the two primary dimensions of the circumplex model of marital and family systems—cohesion and adaptability (Olson et al., 1979). Family Cohesion is defined as "the emotional bonding members have with one another and the degree of individual autonomy a person experiences in the family system," and ranges from disengagement to separated to connected enmeshed. Family adaptability, "the ability of a marital/family system to change its power structure, role relationship rules in response to situational and developmental stress" (Olson et al., 1979), ranges from rigid to structured to flexible to chaotic. According to the authors, effective family functioning will be found in families with balanced levels of cohesion and adaptability. A third dimension in the circumplex model, family communication, is hypothesized to facilitate movement to and maintenance of the balanced levels of the two major dimensions in the model. In its current form, FACES II consists of 30 items that tap the dimensions of cohesion (16 items) and adaptability (14 items). The response format is a five-point Likert response scale to indicate how applicable the statements are to the respondent's family. Olson indicates that 12-year-olds can comprehend FACES items. The authors report internal consistency (co-efficient alpha) of .87 for cohesion, .78 for adaptability, and .90 for the total scale. Norms from a large national sample for the original FACES are available. Although the scale is easy to administer and is becoming more widely used, a recent report by the authors (Barnes & Olson, 1985) raised questions regarding whether it adequately captures the curvilinear relation-ship predicted by the circumplex model. Further information regarding the instrument's psychometric properties and applications are described in Barnes and Olson (1985), Olson and Portner (1983), and Olson et al. (1982).

Family Assessment Measure

The Family Assessment Measure (FAM) is based on the process model of family functioning, which posits that family members share common goals without which the family would not exist (Skinner, Steinhauer, & Santa-Barbara, 1983; Steinhauer & Tisdall, 1984). It is an extension of the McMaster model of family functioning (i.e., the family categories schema) developed by Epstein and his colleagues (Epstein, Rakoff, & Sigal, 1978). To achieve these family goals, certain tasks must be carried out in the context of important interpersonal processes. The FAM provides an assessment of these critical family characteristics: task accomplishment, values and norms, role performance, communication, affective expression, affective involve-ment, and control. FAM III is a 134-item self-report instrument that mother, father, and all children 10 years of age and older may complete in approxi-mately 45 minutes. Items are organized around three different response for-mats: (1) general scale (50 items focused on the health/pathology of the family as a whole), (2) dyadic relationship scale (42 items, for each dyad assessed, focused on relationships between specific members), and (3) self-rating scale (42 items focused on the individual's perception of his or her functioning in the family). Within each response format, scores are obtained on the FAM's seven primary dimensions and on an overall rating of family functioning; for the general scale, additional scores are obtained regarding measures of social desirability and denial/defensiveness. Although the scales can be used separately, the most complete assessment of family functioning is provided by the combined scales. Internal consistency estimates (co-efficient alpha) were .93 (general scale), .95 (dyadic relationship scale), and .89 (self-rating scale). Intercorrelations among subscales ranged from .25 to .82. Normative data from samples of normal and distressed families are available. Studies in progress are investigating developmentally delayed preschoolers, youths "at risk" for psychiatric disorders (Skinner, 1987), and families with alcoholic, depressed, and normal controls (Jacob, Rushe, & Seilhamer, in press). The instrument's psychometric properties and applications are described in Skinner (1987), Skinner et al. (1983), and Steinhauer (1984, 1987).

Structured Interviews for Assessing Family Relationships

In contrast with questionnaires and objective test procedures, structured interviews involve direct, face-to-face contact between the researcher/ clinician and the subject/patient. As a result, there is increased potential for examining and elaborating the meaning of complex family processes as well as members' beliefs and attributions regarding such phenomena. The one interview method included in the current review is the Expressed Emotion (EE) procedure.

Expressed Emotion

Expressed Emotion (EE) is a measure of critical comments made by a psychiatric patient's relatives about the patient at the time the patient is admitted to the hospital. Evolving from the work of Brown and associates at the Social Psychiatry Unit of the Institute of Psychiatry in London, this area of assessment has directed attention toward the family's influence on the course of schizophrenic disorders—specifically, on the risk of relapse and readmission. A program of research, arising from earlier investigations of the relationship between family life and relapse in psychiatric patients, led to the development of the Camberwell Family Interview Schedule (CFIS). This procedure is a semistructured interview used to elicit material for EE ratings. Several methodological studies evaluating the reliability and validity of the measure (Brown & Rutter, 1966; Quinton, Rutter, & Rowlands, 1976; Rutter & Brown, 1966) encouraged the continued use of this approach. Revised and alternative procedures for assessing EE have been reported by various researchers during the past decade (Valone, Norton, Goldstein, & Doane, 1983; Vaughn & Leff, 1976a, 1976b; Wynne, 1979). As typically used, the interview allows for the assessment of three key variables—the number of critical comments, a rating of hostility, and a rating of emotional overinvolvement of parents. In most studies, ratings on these three scales are used to derive an EE index for a subject. Extensive training is required to learn the interview schedule. The abbreviated interview takes between 1 and 2 hours to complete (Vaughn & Leff, 1976a, 1976b). Reported interrater reliabilities have been high for all three scales, showing a percent agreement $> 90\%$ (Brown, Birley, & Wing, 1972) and a kappa $< .83$ (Valone et al., 1983). The instrument has been found to predict relapse in psychiatric patients and has been used in studies of disturbed adolescents at risk for serious psychopathology (Kuipers, Sturgeon, Berkowitz, & Leff, 1983). Additionally, a strong relationship has been found between marital discord, as assessed with the CFIS, and behavior deviance in children (Quinton, Rutter, & Rowlands, 1976). Further psychometric properties and applications of the original instrument, as well as subsequent revisions, are discussed in Brown, Monck, Carstairs, and Wing (1962), Brown and Rutter (1966), Brown et al. (1972), Doane et al. (1982), Rutter and Brown (1966), Tarrier, Vaughn, Lader, and Leff (1979), Valone et al. (1983), and Vaughn and Leff (1976a, 1976b).

Quasi-Observational Procedures for Assessing Family Relationships

The family unit offers the investigator not only a rich and varied range of assessment targets but also the opportunity for collecting observational data from members themselves. In particular, family members can be asked to observe and record the behavior of other family members, and at the same time important relational data can be gathered that would otherwise be unavailable to outsiders. This strategy has been called "quasi-observational" by Weiss (Weiss & Margolin, 1986) who place this method along a continuum ranging from the highly objective, nonparticipant observation data obtained from "professional" coders to the global, retrospective, self-report data obtained from family members about intrafamilial relationships.

Thus far, quasi-observational approaches have been developed primarily as part of the assessment procedures utilized in behavioral treatment programs (Margolin, 1987)—for example, the Spouse Observation Checklist (SOC) (Wills, Weiss, & Patterson, 1974). Three quasi-observational procedures will be reviewed in this section.

Spouse Observation Checklist

As part of the development of behavioral marital therapy programs during the late 1960s and early 1970s, various assessment procedures were constructed. The behavioral and social exchange theories that guided this work suggested that the daily behaviors of spouses—how they acted and reacted toward one another—would be related to specific and global measures of marital satisfaction. In the development of the SOC, Weiss and his colleagues attempted to compile a "universal" list of pleasing and displeasing behaviors (Weiss & Perry, 1979). Initially, behaviors were drawn from the two major domains of instrumental and affectional events and later expanded to include companionship activities as well. With SOC data, strengths and weaknesses of a couple's relationship, corresponding to the occurrence or nonoccurrence of specific behaviors, can be identified, and the continuing daily use of the SOC by a couple can help document changes that occur in their interactions. In its present form the SOC contains more than 400 "pleasing" and "displeasing" items ranging across 12 content areas. Each SOC item describes a relevant relationship behavior that a spouse may exhibit. For example, "Spouse said something unkind to me" is a displeasing item that falls within the consideration grouping. Spouses complete the SOC independently but at the same time every day. After the SOC is completed, the investigator sums the total number of pleases and displeases within each behavioral category. These subtotals can be used if behavior in specific content areas is of interest or they can all be summed to obtain for each spouse a total daily "pleases" and "displeases" score.

Completion of the SOC takes 20 to 30 minutes. As a method of estimating reliability, interspouse agreement is determined by comparing the SOC completed by one spouse with a self-monitoring version completed by his or her partner with "spouse" items reworded to become "I" (items). Obtained agreement levels have been reported as 48% (Jacobson & Moore, 1981), 46% (Christensen & Nies, 1980), and 62% (Tennenbaum & Jacob, 1985). The instrument has been used to determine the relationship between daily spouse behaviors and ratings of marital satisfaction, and it has been found to discriminate nondistressed couples from distressed couples. Further information regarding the instrument's psychometric properties and applications can be found in Barnett and Nietzel (1979), Christensen and Nies (1980), Jacobson, Follette, and McDonald (1982), Jacobson and Moore (1981), Tennenbaum (1984), and Wills et al. (1974).

Overall, the SOC has proved to be a useful quasi-observational assessment tool, although interpretive issues raised by relatively low levels of interspouse agreement need further exploration. In addition, comparable instruments that assess other family dyads are required. Two such procedures that have recently been developed are the Parent–Child Observation Schedule (Grounds, 1985) and the Sibling Observation Schedule (Seilhamer, 1983).

Parent–Child Observation Schedule

The Parent–Child Observation Schedule (PCOS) affords the same opportunity for assessing parent–adolescent relationships as does the SOC for assessing marital relationships. Building on this common characteristic, the PCOS was developed to describe daily relational behaviors engaged in by parents and their adolescent children. Patterned after the SOC, the PCOS assesses pleasing and displeasing behaviors in parent–adolescent child dyads. Again, behavioral and social exchange theories provide the primary theoretical underpinnings for this approach—in particular, the contention that rates of positive and negative behaviors engaged in by partners in a relationship should affect their perception of the quality of the relationship. The PCOS has two forms—one to be completed by the adolescent (118 items) and the other to be completed by the parent (114 items). Only preliminary reliability and validity data are available, although they follow patterns similar to those shown by the SOC. Further information regarding the instrument's psychometric properties and applications can be found in Grounds (1985).

Sibling Observation Schedule

Of all family subsystems, sibling relationships have been the least studied, and as a consequence, are the most poorly understood. To address this topic, the Sibling Observation Schedule (SOS) (Seilhamer, 1983) was developed (again, patterned after the SOC) to facilitate the description of important, day-to-day interactions within adolescent sibling dyads. Items relevant to all possible gender pairs (i.e., brother–brother, brother–sister, sister–sister) and levels of family distress were included in the SOS. Complimenting the SOC and PCOS, the SOS expands quasi-observational family assessments to include a focus on adolescent children and their siblings. The 165-item SOS is completed daily by relevant sibling pairs. Although intersibling agreements were low, distressed and nondistressed sibling pairs could be differentiated on their SOS responses. Further information regarding the instrument's psychometric properties and applications can be found in Seilhamer (1983).

Laboratory Observational Procedures: Outcome Measures

The assessment of interaction can emphasize the process of interchange as it unfolds over time or its outcome as reflected in some performance or solution variable. Evolving most directly from laboratory studies of small-group behavior, outcome measures involving families have typically engaged members in a laboratory game or structured task. When performed by the participants, this yields measures of the family's success and style in negotiating the task. The common characteristic among the various outcome procedures is that the family's performance is measured in a highly objective and reliable manner, requiring little if any judgment regarding the behavior that is to be described.

Card Sort Procedure

The card sort procedure was devised by Shipstone in 1960, based upon earlier work of Chomsky (1957), Miller (1967), and Reiss (1958). The scoring procedure and its rationale, however, were developed by Reiss, and the current version was first utilized in 1971. As Reiss used the task, he became aware of its utility for studying a family's approach not only to problem-solving situations, but to novel social encounters as well—that is, "how a family searches and explores new experiences and how it interprets what it learns" (Reiss & Klein, 1987). The family members' set of shared assumptions about the nature of the social environment and their place within it are collectively termed the "family paradigm." This paradigm, similar to the concept of a schema, influences the family's approach to its environment, problem solving, and relationships across a variety of contexts. Three major parameters of the paradigm have been proposed—configuration, coordination, and closure. The family's position on the first two dimensions has been used to generate a family typology: environment-sensitive, consensus-sensitive, achievement-sensitive, and distance-sensitive families. Although Reiss originally used these variables to assess differences between pathological and normal families, his recent emphasis has shifted to a more general interest in the social process and the relationship between a family's paradigm and the wider social environment (Reiss, 1981; Reiss & Klein, 1987).

Procedurally, each family member sits in a booth facing a one-way mirror wearing a microphone–earphone apparatus. Each member individually sorts a deck of 15 cards, each containing a sequence of letters or nonsense syllables. Following this, the individual family members sort a second deck of cards, separately but concurrently, and are encouraged to discuss the puzzle with one another (within a closed communication environment) as they go through the deck. After the family task, each member works alone to sort another set of 15 cards (final individual sort). Measures of configuration, coordination, and closure are derived from the various outcomes that result from this set of tasks. This is a most significant instrument, and it has been the methodological core of a long term, programmatic, and highly influential research program exploring the nature of family life and the theoretical linkages between individually defined psychopathology and the complexities of the family matrix.

The scoring of the CSP is very objective and yields highly reliable indices. The temporal stability has been reported to be high over 6- to 9-month interval: $r = .72$ for configuration, $r = .86$ for coordination, and $r = .43$ for closure (Reiss & Klein, 1987). Factor analysis has shown the three key variables to be independent and to account for a large proportion of the test variance. The procedure has differentiated clinical from normal families (Davis, Stern, Jorgenson, & Steier, 1980; Reiss, 1981; Steinglass, 1979), has been predictive of a family's view of other families (Reiss, Costell, Jones, & Berkman, 1980), a family's relationship with its extended family (Oliveri & Reiss, 1981a), and a family's relationship with medical staff when their child is hospitalized (Reiss et al., 1980). Additional applications of the instrument can be found in Oliveri and Reiss (1981b), Reiss and Oliveri (1983), and Reiss and Salzman (1973).

Laboratory Observational Procedures: Coding Systems

Early family studies of psychopathology included families with adolescent-age children since schizophrenia and delinquency were the disorders of major interest at that time. Bales's (1950) coding system, Interaction Process Analysis (IPA), had a major impact on the structure and content of several of these early efforts; in particular, the seminal work of Mishler and Waxler (1968) focused on family interaction and schizophrenia. Subsequently, social learning theory became a dominant influence in the field, highlighted by the development of the Family Interaction Coding System (FICS) (see Patterson, Ray, Shaw, & Cobb, 1969), which in turn led to the development of coding systems for studying marital interactions in laboratory settings (Hops, Wills, Weiss, & Patterson, 1972). A parallel trend involved a developing interest in assessing families of adolescents from a more systems/communications framework (Alexander, 1973), which stimulated the development of additional systems for assessing marital interaction (Hawkins, Weisberg, & Ray, 1977) and family interactions involving adolescent-age children (Hauser *et al.*, 1984).

Marital Interaction Coding System

The Marital Interaction Coding System (MICS) was developed to describe the behavior of couples as they engaged in problem-solving discussions in a laboratory setting as recorded on videotape (Hops, *et al.*, 1972; Weiss & Summers, 1983). Additionally, the applicability of the MICS to family subgroups other than the marital dyad makes it a viable instrument for studying the family context of child psychopathology, particularly for older, adolescent-age children. This general utility has increasingly been exploited by researchers who have used the MICS to describe interactions of parent–child dyads, triads, and tetrads (Baer, Vincent, William, Bourianoff, & Barlett 1980; Blechman & Olson, 1976; Jacob, Ritchey, Cvitkovic, & Blane, 1981). The MICS includes about 30 codes, which are used to describe all behavior observed in the problem-solving discussions of marital or parent–child dyads. Behavior is coded sequentially so that the patterns of interaction can be described. An advance incorporated in MICS-III, building on the work of John Gottman (1979), is that a simultaneous record is maintained of both speaker and listener behavior. The MICS is applied to videotapes of interactions, in which each new behavioral unit is defined as "behavior of homogeneous content, irrespective of duration or formal grammatical accuracy emitted by a single partner" (Weiss & Summers, 1983, p. 89). Codes include positive verbal and nonverbal behavior (e.g., approve, comply, smile/laugh), negative verbal and nonverbal behavior (e.g., complain, put down, turn off), problem-solving behaviors (e.g., (positive solution and compromise), and the two codes—attend and not tracking—that describe the listener state rather than a discrete behavior. Investigators using the MICS usually have grouped MICS codes together into summary categories prior to conducting their analysis—a procedure that greatly simplifies the investigator's task of interpreting obtained outcomes across 30 different behaviors, as well as increasing the power of the analysis and stability of the results. Extensive training and continual supervision is required to maintain raters at 70% agreement level. The MICS has been widely used in substantive studies of marital and family interaction as well as in methodological studies regarding the use of observational procedures. Recently the MICS has been expanded to include parent–child dyads and triads (Baer *et al.*, 1980; Jacob *et al.*, 1981). Further extensive descriptions of the instrument's psychometric properties and applications can be found in Birchler, Weiss, and Vincent (1975), Jacob *et al.* (1981), Jacobson and Anderson (1980), Margolin and Wampold (1981), and Wieder and Weiss (1980).

Constraining and Enabling Coding System

The Constraining and Enabling Coding System (CECS) was designed to assess important family transactions related to adolescent ego development (Hauser, Powers, Weiss, Follansbee, & Bernstein, 1983; Hauser *et al.*, 1984). The theoretical position utilized by these investigators is an extension of the work of Stierlin (1974), who proposed that parents within disturbed families interfere with the development of autonomy in their children. Such behaviors are characterized as "constraining." Additionally, Hauser *et al.* (1984) suggest that certain family interactions can encourage differentiation and autonomy of members. These behaviors are classified as "enabling." Although they derive from a different theoretical source, the constraining and enabling dimensions appear related to the defensive and supportive dimensions suggested by Gibb (1961) and later incorporated into a coding system by Alexander (1973). The CECS also codes for Adolescent Change and Adolescent Response, the former assessing the impact of parental comments on the adolescent's contributions to the discussion and the latter reflecting whether the adolescent responds in an enabling or constraining manner to speeches made by his or her parents. The CECS is applied to transcripts of audiotapes made from family problem-solving discussions. Raters apply the constraining and enabling codes to all speeches and apply the two specific adolescent speech dimensions to the second of each pair of previously unitized adolescent speeches. The enabling dimension is divided into two categories, cognitive codes (explanation, focusing, and problem solving) and affective codes (acceptance and empathy). The constraining dimension is also divided into cognitive codes (distracting, withholding, and judgmental) and affective codes (indifference, affective excess, and devaluing). Parents' speeches only receive the enabling/constraining codes while the unitized adolescents' speeches also receive the change and response dimensions. The adolescent change dimension contains four codes: regression, progression, foreclosure, and topic change. Extensive training is required to rate the audiotapes of adolescents and parents. The authors reported that reliability, using interrater agreement estimates for the individual enabling and constraining codes, varied between 81% and 99%, and kappas ranged from .46 to .82 (Hauser *et al.*, 1984). CECS has identified family behaviors that are correlated with level of adolescent ego development and that are characteristic of families with a diabetic adolescent. Additional information regarding the instrument's psychometric properties and applications can be found in Hauser, Powers, Jacobson, Schwartz, and Noam (1982) and Hauser *et al.* (1984).

Although space limitations do not permit descriptions of other relevant instruments, the interested reader would be encouraged to examine the Family Alliances Coding System (FACS) (Gilbert, Christensen, & Margolin, 1984; Gilbert et al., 1981), which attempts to describe constructs relevant to structural systems theory (Minuchin, 1974); the Adolescent Individuation Coding System (Condon, Cooper, & Grotevant, 1981; Cooper, Grotevant, & Condon, 1983; Grotevant & Cooper, 1985), which focuses on the interface between family interaction and the social development and individuation of adolescents; and the Couple's Interaction Scoring System (CISS) (Gottman, 1979), which incorporates several features of the MICS but emphasizes separate coding of nonverbal, affect-relevant behavior.

Coding Family Interactions with Younger Children

In contrast with studies including adolescents, investigations involving younger children have often been characterized by the development of unique sets of observation codes that are not part of a formal system bearing a distinguishable name. Most frequently, children with conduct disorders or hyperactivity have been the subjects in such studies, with a focus on parental attempts to influence child behavior (i.e., commands) and children's responses to parental commands (i.e., compliance and noncompliance). Additionally, negative child behaviors such as yell, whine, hit, and high rate, have often been included as behaviors of interest (Atkeson & Forehand, 1981; Forehand, King, Peed, & Yoder, 1975; Peed, Roberts, & Forehand, 1977). Although negative behaviors are frequently coded, prosocial behaviors such as "comforts and shares" have not often been well differentiated in studies of clinical populations.

The general format for coding parent–child dyads has been to choose a limited group of parent and child behaviors and to record at least antecedent-consequent relationship. For example, the Response-Class Matrix (RCM) (Mash, Terdal, & Anderson, 1973) requires two observers, one of whom records a tally mark for the appropriate child–mother sequence of behaviors, while the other records a tally mark for the appropriate mother–child sequence. In this way, sequential relationships are captured by the system as well as the more traditional frequency-of-occurrence data. Given the strong influence of learning theory in the development of these assessment strategies, this emphasis on antecedent–consequent relationships is to be expected. However, to evaluate the importance of longer behavioral chains, other coding systems beside the RCM are required (Lobitz & Johnson, 1975). Finally, it should be noted that laboratory interactions have played an important role in attempts to develop comprehensive therapy approaches for difficult children in which codings have served to identify problematic interactions and to measure treatment outcome (e.g., Forehand et al., 1979; Wahler, House, & Stambaugh, 1976). Additionally, such data have successfully differentiated family functioning across groups that varied in terms of type of child disorder. The RCM, for example, has been used to describe mother–child interactions with hyperactive boys (e.g., Mash & Johnson, 1982; Tarver-Behring, Barkley, & Karlsson, 1985) and with retarded children (e.g., Cunningham, Reuler, Blackwell, & Deck, 1981). Another system, the Dyadic Parent–Child Interaction Coding System (DPICS) (Robinson & Eyberg, 1981) has been used to discriminate mother–child interactions with neglected and behavior-problem children (Aragona & Eyberg, 1981).

Naturalistic Observation Procedures

Observations of families in their own homes offer the clearest view of naturally occurring family processes. Work in this area has been most influenced by Patterson and his associates. Both their theory-driven focus on clearly defined, molecular behaviors and the many methodological issues they have addressed have generated a broader interest in naturalistic assessment procedures. In addition to Patterson's procedure, the Home Observation Assessment Measure offers one of the few attempts to assess family systems concepts in the home and, as such, will also be described in this section.

Family Interaction Coding System

The Family Interaction Coding System (FICS) (Patterson *et al.*, 1969; Reid, 1978) was developed as part of a broad attempt on the part of Patterson and his colleagues to develop better treatments for families with aggressive children. Their theoretical approach, social learning theory, suggested that continuous feedback to therapists about how client families were actually interacting would be valuable for guiding treatment, evaluating outcome, and facilitating hypothesis testing about the relationship of family interaction and the expression of aggression in children. The home was chosen as the site of observations to capture as natural a sample of behavior as was possible in the temporal order in which it occurred. Social learning theory's emphasis on the antecedents and consequences of behavior guided the decision to focus on the sequential pattern of behavior.

The FICS is a 29-code system, designed to describe sequentially the interactions of a target subject and any family member with whom the target subject interacts. The actual coding process involves an observer recording a behavioral sequence, including the current target and another family member's behavior, approximately every 6 seconds. An observation session lasts for approximately 45 minutes. The investigators' interest in aggressive children led to the inclusion of 14 codes that made fine discriminations between negative behaviors; for example, noncompliance, destructiveness, and yell. The remaining codes describe positive behaviors (e.g., approval and physical positive); behaviors engaged in so as to influence others (e.g., command); and routine activities (e.g., talk and play). The Patterson group primarily reports the rate per minute of the occurrence of these behaviors. Depending on the question being addressed, data from the 29 codes can be reported for each code or can be lumped together into relatively homogeneous groups. They have found that the most effective group of codes for differentiating families, named total aversive behavior (TAB), is comprised of all 14 negative codes summed together. In addition to assessing group differences using single codes or groups of codes, the Patterson group has also emphasized assessing the sequential patterning of observed behaviors. These temporal descriptions led to the development of their theory concerning coercive family interactions in the homes of aggressive children. The FICS data also allow for testing hypotheses gathered by this theory. Again, either codes or code groups can be used for this purpose.

Observers need thorough training to use this coding system reliably—a process that is described in detail by Maerov, Brummett, and Reid (1978) and Reid (1978). A generalizability study by Jones, Reid, and Patterson (1975) suggested that variance in the data explained by differences due to raters was extremely small. The FICS has been used in studies assessing the differences between groups of normal and deviant children—in suggesting interventions for therapists, in outcome evaluations, and in generating and evaluating hypotheses regarding the etiology and maintenance of problem behaviors in children (Patterson, 1982). The instrument's psychometric properties and applications are described in Jones et al. (1975) and Patterson (1982).

Home Observation Assessment Method

The Home Observation Assessment Method (HOAM), developed by Steinglass (1976, 1979, 1980, 1981) for the purpose of describing family interaction in the home, has unique features that both distinguish it from other coding systems and argue for its broader use. Guided by systems theory, the HOAM focuses on the structure and style of family behavior rather than on the antecedent–consequent relationships emphasized by behavioral theories. With the HOAM, objective events—location within the home, how much people move around, and with whom people interact—are recorded by live observers. In contrast with other systems, the HOAM was developed to observe family behavior over relatively long periods of time. Two observers are required for every observation session, and each observer is assigned to follow and record the behavior of a particular parent. The behavior of children is described as they interact with, or are present in the same room with, a parent. Observations usually take place over a 4-hour time period divided into 40 minutes of observation followed by 15 minutes of rest. During observations family members are unrestricted in their movements about their home. As a result, their use of space and traffic patterns can be described. Each 40-minute observation period is divided into 20 blocks, each 2 minutes long. The observer records certain features of the first "interactional sequence" engaged in by the target parent. First, the observer records the task orientation, which can be one of three types: problem solving, work, or information exchange. Next, the affective level of the interaction is rated on a seven-point scale ranging from anger to warmth. Finally, using the perspective of the target subject, the coder decides whether the outcome of the interaction was positive, unclear, or negative.

Following the coding of the first interactional sequence, observers record the location of their target parent and the path taken by them when they change rooms. They also identify other people who are present in the room with the target, and in what activity the target is engaged (e.g., conversation or physical contact—positive). From the raw HOAM data, 25 indices of family behavior were derived (e.g., location shifts per hour, mean distance between interactors, and mean affect level for verbal exchanges). Approximately half of these codes are activity measures and half are variability measures. To reduce this large number of dependent measures, a principal-components analysis was conducted, resulting in five identified factors: intrafamily engagement, distance regulation, extrafamily engagement, structural variability, and content variability. Steinglass reported that observer reliability varied between 63% and 95%, with kappas greater than .40. The HOAM has only been applied to families with an alcoholic member. Further information on the instrument's psychometric properties and applications, as well as observer training procedures, are described in Steinglass (1976, 1979, 1980, 1981).

CONCLUSIONS AND FUTURE DIRECTIONS

The family measurement domain is characterized by a diversity of instruments, which span a range of constructs, assessment foci, data sources, target populations, and applications. Although most measures in this literature are characterized by significant psychometric limitations, a small set of instruments could be identified and recommended to the interested researcher, given their more-than-adequate reliability and validity and their considerable "promise" as useful measures. On this basis, our evaluation of the field is generally positive and optimistic, yet tempered by the recognition that much work needs to be conducted before the potential contributions of these measures can be realized. In the following discussion, future research needs will be presented with the aim of encouraging rigorous and programmatic research concerned with the development, refinement, and validation of family assessment procedures of relevance to studies of child psychopathology.

General Limitations of Report and Observational Methods

As noted, report procedures not only are convenient and relatively inexpensive, but also allow for the possibility of collecting large-sample, normative data to which individual protocols can be related. Most important, only report procedures can capture members' cognitions and attributions about relationships and events—data that are increasingly viewed as essential to understanding and predicting family processes and outcomes (Robinson & Jacobson, 1987). On the other hand, report procedures are, in the end, an individual's perceptions of self and others—perceptions that can be inaccurate, biased, and at times seriously distorted views of what other observers might conclude about the same events. Furthermore, the researcher must reconcile the inevitable inconsistencies that are seen in the reports from different family members. Finally, most report data provide little in the way of the fine-grained details of moment-to-moment, day-to-day interaction between family members—data that are of great importance to researchers interested in the analysis of actual family processes.

In contrast, observational procedures inform us most directly about actual interchanges among family members and, at their best, can yield data that are critical for the development of empirically based theories of family interaction and psychopathology. At the same time, direct-observation strategies involving the use of complex coding procedures are costly and labor intensive, requiring a significant commitment of time and resources in order to collect, collate, and analyze the "prized" interaction data. Furthermore, there are methodological issues of continuing concern involving this approach, including subject reactivity and the meaningfulness of highly specific behavioral codes as indices of the larger dimensions and constructs of relevance to family theory and therapy.

In our view, it would be a mistake to conclude that one class of methods is generally more valuable, useful, or defensible than the other in family studies of psychopathology. Instead, we would suggest that both strategies are necessary for a full understanding of so complex a process as family interaction and psychopathology. It does not seem very useful to ask the question: Which approach is better? Instead, determining what understanding of what problems can be achieved with what methodologies seems to be a more frutiful strategy.

Within-Method Assessments

Within each major assessment approach there remains a need to examine basic issues of instrument reliability and validity. For many of the reviewed instruments such data were adequate but certainly not compelling; for the procedures identified as promising, such support had only began to appear. Beyond obvious psychometric weaknesses, each major approach is associated with certain characteristics that raise important questions bearing on an instrument's interpretability and, as a result, its usefulness.

First, family assessment instruments often include a variety of subscales (codes, rating scales, outcome measures) purporting to assess particular concepts of general or specific relevance to the theoretical model on which the instrument is based. In many instances, however, a convincing case has not been made for the statistical independence of these component scales (Fowler, 1981; 1982; Skinner *et al.*, 1983); hence one is required to question the conceptual differentiations initially proposed by the model. A parallel issue is relevant to various observational procedures, including multicode coding systems (Weiss & Summers, 1983) and sets of rating scales along which observed interactions are assessed (Thomas, 1977). Evaluating the dimensionality of any instrument, be it a report procedure or observational technique, would certainly be of importance to the goals of both theory and instrument development.

A second issue, of particular relevance to report procedures, concerns the investigator's interpretation and use of test data obtained from different members—specifically, differences in the responses of two or more members completing the same questionnaire. With observational methods, the researcher usually provides raters (coders) with a great deal of training in the assessment of relatively specific behaviors or behavioral dimensions. Assuming that high interrater agreement can be achieved, the investigator can be reasonably confident that different observers will generally "see things" in the same way and that one set of observations can be interchanged with another. With questionnaires, tests, quasi-observational procedures, or structured interviews, however, it is not only possible, but almost a certainty, that the correspondence among different members' reports and perceptions will be far from perfect and most often will be only moderate.

Potentially fruitful approaches for clarifying this issue would include (1) the careful assessment of the reports of different family members plus other appropriate measures, such as a Social Desirability Scale (Crowne & Marlowe, 1967), in order to identify sources of variance accounting for intermember discrepancies—for example, differential sensitivity to interpersonal meanings; and differences in motivation to report carefully and accurately; differences in "person" variables, such as defensiveness and denial, which may influence and distort responses; and differences in how items/ questions are interpreted; (2) the development of composite or complex scores from individual reports (e.g., mean scores, difference scores, extreme scores), followed by the systematic comparison of individual and complex scores regarding their relationship with key methodological and theoretical variables; and (3) the application of multivariate analytic procedures whereby all individual records can be retained within a "family profile," which in turn, can be the basis on which families are grouped and subsequently analyzed; for example, families reflecting high agreement among all members versus families reflecting high agreement between parents and low agreement between parents and children versus families reflecting low agreement among all members (Fisher, Kokes, Ransom, Phillips, & Rudd, 1985).

Correspondence between Methods

Discrepancies that occur when different members' reports are compared on the same instrument actually represents one, and probably the least complex, example of correspondence. That is, for such comparisons, there is but one instrument (e.g., scores on the FAM) and one method (report procedure). As one begins to introduce other "differences," however, comparisons become increasingly complicated—for example, when comparisons are made within methods but across instruments (e.g., mothers' responses on the FACES vs. the FAM) or between two instruments based on different methods (e.g., mothers' reports on the FAM vs. laboratory observations coded with the MICS). Stated otherwise, comparisons involving family assessment procedures can reflect differences between data sources, between instruments, between methods, between concepts, or any combination of these conditions. Given such complexity, it seems clear that cross-method comparisons can involve much more than differences in general method and that interpretation of low correspondence becomes increasingly difficult as the number of differences between the two assessment procedures increases.

In light of these considerations, it seems necessary to begin rigorous and programmatic efforts aimed at determining the degree of correspondence within and across important subsets of family measurement procedures. Most important, a series of precise comparisons, which systematically vary the number and kind of differences between assessment procedures, should be initiated. Throughout this enterprise, theoretical considerations, as much as possible, should help guide the investigator to choose the best questions and to sift through the various explanations that will be available upon completion of data collection and analyses. Reiss's recent analyses of report versus observational methodologies—in terms of the type of relationship the subject attempts to create with the experimenter and the impact of instrument ambiguity on the subject's ability to communicate a particular relationship—represents an unusually insightful conceptualization of a most complicated issue (Oliveri & Reiss, 1984; Sigafoos, Reiss, Rich, & Douglas, 1985).

Underdeveloped Assessment Targets and Concepts

In our review of family assessment procedures relevant to studies of child psychopathology, several subsets of measures appeared to be largely underdeveloped. First, the assessment of sibling relationships—especially among preadolescent- and adolescent-age children—is an area of both great concern and relative neglect (Bank & Kahn, 1982; Lamb & Sutton-Smith, 1982). Within the domain of report procedures, only one, Furman's SRQ, was sufficiently developed to warrant a detailed review in this chapter (Furman

& Buhrmester, 1985). Based upon a very different methodology, a quasi-observational procedure, Seilhamer's (1983) SOS shows considerable promise as a relatively objective, behaviorally specific cataloguing procedure whereby important day-to-day events transpiring in sibling relationships can be collected. Both the SRQ and the SOS have only negotiated the early stages of test development, and their ultimate value as useful instruments will obviously depend upon the considerable amount of psychometric and application experiences that lie ahead. In addition to the need for new sibling assessment procedures, it is possible that various instruments, though not developed specifically to assess child–sibling relationships, can be modified to provide such data should investigators find this procedure to be of particular interest to their research objectives—for example, the relative amount of EE transmitted between index case and sibling (vs. index case and parent), the inclusion of the index child and one sibling in laboratory interactions so that the child–sibling dyad (as well as the marital and parent-child dyads) can be subjected to careful scrutiny, and the modification of outcome measures such as the CSP to include different combinations of family members (e.g., two siblings) in order to assess for differences in performance outcomes.

A second area in which there is a surprising scarcity of psychometrically sound, well-researched instruments involves reports of parent–child relationships. The report measures selected for detailed review represent an interesting but rather small set of procedures, varying considerably in terms of established psychometric foundations, range of applications, and concepts assessed. On the other hand, it must be recognized that a plethora of laboratory and naturalistic observation coding systems for describing family and, more particularly, parent–child interaction have been carefully developed and widely applied during the past two decades. Furthermore, other sets of procedures do allow for assessment of parent–child relationships as part of a more general family assessment goal (e.g., the dyadic format section of the FAM), whereas several newly developed instruments within other domains (e.g., the PCOS, as a quasi-observational procedure) offer considerable promise for the future.

Finally, instruments specifically designed for the assessment of family systems properties, though sometimes found within the literature, are relatively few in number, are still at an early stage of development, and do not include various key constructs and relationships relevant to this focus. An important exception is the recent effort by Steinglass (1979, 1980, 1981) in the development of the HOAM coding system which is relevant to the family's regulation of its internal environment. Additionally, from our perspective, family researchers have not given sustained attention to the assessment of systems properties that link the family with extrafamilial systems, notwithstanding the obvious need to put such potentially key processes into operation. A recent effort worth noting, however, is Wahler's attempt to understand the "insular" family—interests that have motivated efforts to describe and assess relationships between community institutions (systems) and the parent–child relationships (Wahler, 1980; Wahler & Dumas, 1987). Other efforts such as this one would certainly be encouraged.

Need for Additional Assessment Methods

Despite the considerable range of available family assessment procedures, each major grouping is nevertheless characterized by significant limitations. Our earlier discussion of the two major methods—report and observational approaches—indicated various threats to internal and external validity that characterize such techniques. In turn, we encouraged the development of strategies that reflected greater promise in these areas than could be expected of the "parent" instruments themselves. A relatively new and particularly promising method—viewed as an addition rather than replacement—can be noted.

As described, there is a developing set of quasi-observational techniques—the prototype being Weiss's SOC. Although these techniques represent family members' reports or perceptions of self, other, and associated interactions, their strength resides in the potential for collecting information on objective, contemporary patterns of interchange among family members. Weiss's term "quasi-observational" was intended to capture a point along the continuum ranging from global self-reports of a retrospective nature to detailed codings (observations) of current family interactions as rated by highly trained ("stranger") observers. In contrast with the former, quasi-observational procedures emphasize more molecular and contemporary behaviors of specific relevance to relationship processes. Moreover, they differ from detailed codings in terms of utilizing a participant observer format that allows access to events and interactions that "outsiders" would not be able to "see." Beyond these characteristics, quasi-observational data methods are still relatively inexpensive to obtain, allowing for the collection of large data sets to which powerful multivariate data analytic procedures can be applied. Although they certainly do not lack methodological difficulties of their own, their uniqueness and potential significance would encourage continued examination, refinement, and validation of these procedures.

The Interplay between Theory and Instrument Development

Although referred to throughout this chapter, it seems necessary to make explicit our belief that theory and instrument development must proceed simultaneously and in an integrated fashion. Although by now it must certainly sound like an old saw, research cannot take place in a theoretical vacuum; in like manner, the development, refinement, and validation of any family assessment instrument must ultimately arise from and be relatable to some theoretical matrix, whether loosely construed as a conceptual model or tightly and systematically organized around a set of testable propositions and axioms. To conclude that the field is "theory barren" is certainly not our intention. Quite to the contrary, the influences of sociological, systems/communications, developmental, and learning theories are clearly evident in many of the family models and concepts found within the literature. Although "formal" theories of the family's role in pschopathology are not easily identified, the past several decades have witnessed the development and refinement of several "mini theories" focused on a limited sector of the family–child psychopathology matrix. Furthermore, several of these research programs have been characterized by a clear and continued commitment to integrate theoretical and instrument development efforts. Most notably, through their influential work, such investigators as Patterson, Weiss, Wahler and Jacobson—beginning with a rather unadorned social learning theory and gradually incorporating constructs from other theoretical perspectives—not only have made significant contributions to family theory but also have clearly demonstrated the intimate and necessary interplay among concepts, assessment techniques, and theory development.

The development and validation of family assessment procedures relevant to child psychopathology is an admittedly complex process. To pursue and achieve a reliable, valid, and useful set of procedures will require an understanding of various materials in the fields of epistemology and test theory and development. Inadequate appreciation of the need for both theory and methodology, and their interdependencies, will attenuate progress in validity studies, lessen the potential usefulness of the various methods in general, and compromise efforts to measure family influences in psychopathology.

REFERENCES

Achenbach, T. M. (1978). The Child Behavior Profile: I. Boys aged 6–11. *Journal of Consulting and Clinical Psychology, 46,* 478–488.

Achenbach, T. M. & Edelbrock, C. (1979). The Child Behavior Profile: II. Boys aged 12–16 and girls aged 6–11 and 12–16. *Journal of Consulting and Clinical Psychology, 47,* 223–233.

Ainsworth, M. D. S., Blehar, M. C., Waters, E., & Wall, S. (1978). *Patterns of attachment: A psychological study of the strange situation.* Hillsdale, NJ: Erlbaum.

Alexander, J. F. (1973). Defensive and supportive communications in normal and deviant families. *Journal of Consulting and Clinical Psychology, 40,* 223–231.

Aragona, J. A., & Eyberg, S. M. (1981). Neglected children: Mothers' report of child behavior problems and observed verbal behavior. *Child Development, 52,* 596–602.

Atkeson, B. M., & Forehand, R. (1981). Conduct disorders. In E. J. Mash & L. G. Terdal (Eds.), *Behavioral assessment of childhood disorders.* New York: Guilford.

Baer, P., Vincent, J., William, B., Bourianoff, G., & Bartlett, P. (1980). Behavioral response to induced conflict in families with a hypertensive father. *Hypertension, 2,* 170–177.

Bagarozzi, D. A. (1984). Family measurement techniques. *American Journal of Family Therapy, 12,* 59–62.

Bales, R. F. (1950). *Interaction process analysis.* Cambridge, MA: Addison-Wesley.

Bank, S., & Kahn, M. D. (1982). *The sibling bond.* New York: Basic Books.

Barnes, H. L., & Olson, D. H. (1982). Parent–adolescent communication. In D. H. Olson, H. I. McCubbin, H. Barnes, A. Larsen, M. Muxen, & M. Wilson (Eds.), *Family inventories: Inventories used in a national survey of families across the family life cycle.* St. Paul, MN: Family Social Science.

Barnes, H. L., & Olson D. H. (1985). Parent–adolescent communication and the circumplex model. *Child Development, 56,* 438–447.

Barnett, L. R., & Nietzel, M. T. (1979). Relationship of instrumental and affectional behaviors and self-esteem to marital satisfaction in distressed and nondistressed couples. *Journal of Consulting and Clinical Psychology, 44,* 946–957.

Benjamin, L. S., (1974). Structural analysis of social behavior. *Psychological Review, 81,* 392–425.

Benjamin, L. S., (1977). Structural analysis of a family in therapy. *Journal of Consulting and Clinical Psychology, 45,* 391–406.

Benjamin, L. S., (1986). Adding social and intrapsychic descriptors to axis I of DSM-III. In T. Millon & G. L., Klerman (Eds.), *Contemporary directions in psychopathology: Toward the DSM-IV.* New York: Guilford.

Billings, A. G., & Moos, R. H. (1982). Family environments and adaptation; A clinically-applicable typology. *American Journal of Family Therapy, 10,* 26–38.

Birchler, G. R., Weiss, R. L., & Vincent, J. P. (1975). Multimethod analysis of social reinforcement exchange between maritally distressed spouse and nondistressed spouse and stranger dyads. *Journal of Personality and Social Psychology, 31,* 349–360.

Blechman, E. A., & Olson, D. H. L. (1976). The family contract game: Description and effectiveness. In D. H. L. Olson (Ed.), *Treating relationships.* Lake Mills, IA: Graphic Publishing.

Brown, G. W., Birley, J. L. T., & Wing, J. F. (1972). Influence of family life on the course of schizophrenic disorders: A replication. *British Journal of Psychiatry, 121,* 241–258.

Brown, G. W., Monck, E. M., Carstairs, G. M., & Wing, J. K. (1962). The influence of family life on the course of schizophrenic illness. *British Journal of Preventive Social Medicine, 16,* 355–368.

Brown, G. W., & Rutter, M. (1966). The measurement of family activities and relationships: A methodological study. *Human Relations, 19,* 241–263.

Buros, O. K. (Ed.) (1978). *Eighth mental measurements yearbook.* Highland Park, NJ: Gryphon.

Chomsky, N. (1957). *Syntactic structures.* The Hague: Mouton.

Christensen, A., & Niles, D. C. (1980). The spouse observation checklist: Empirical analysis and critique. *American Journal of Family Therapy, 8,* 69–79.

Condon, S. M., Cooper, C. R., & Grotevant, H. D. (1981). *Manual for the analysis of family discourse.* Austin: University of Texas.

Cooper, C. R., Grotevant, H. D., & Condon, S. M. (1983). Individuality and connectedness in the family as a context for adolescent identity formation and role-taking skill. In H. D. Grotevant & C. R. Cooper (Eds.), *Adolescent development in the family: New directions for child development.* San Francisco: Jossey-Bass.

Crowne, D. P., & Marlowe, D. (1967). *The approval motive.* New York: Wiley.

Cunningham, C. E., Reuler, E., Blackwell, J., & Deck, J. (1981). Behavioral and linguistic developments in the interactions of normal and retarded children with their mothers. *Child Development, 52,* 62–70.

Davis, P., Stern, D., Jorgenson, J., & Steier, F. (1980). *Typologies of the alcoholic family: An integrated systems approach.* Unpublished manuscript, University of Pennsylvania, Wharton Applied Research Center.

Doane, J., Jones, J. E., Fisher, L., Ritzler, B., Singer, M. T., & Wynne, L. C. (1982). Parental communication deviance as a predictor of competence in children at risk for adult psychiatric disorder. *Family Process, 21,* 211–223.

Droppleman, L. F., & Schaefer, E. S. (1963) Boys' and girls' report of maternal and paternal behavior. *Journal of Abnormal and Social Psychology, 67,* 648–654.

Dunn, J., & Kendrick, C. (1981). Social behavior of young siblings in the family context: Differences between same-sex and different-sex dyads. *Child Development, 52,* 1265–1273.

Dunn, J., & Kendrick, C. (1982). *Siblings: Love, envy, and understanding.* Cambridge, MA: Harvard University Press.

Epstein, N. B., Rakoff, V., & Sigal, J. J. (1978). The McMaster model of family functioning. *Journal of Marriage and Family Counselling, 4,* 19–31.

Finney, J. W., Moos, R. H., Cronkite, R. C., & Gamble W. (1983). A conceptual model of the functioning of married persons with impaired partners: Spouses of alcoholic patients. *Journal of Marriage and the Family, 45,* 23–34.

Fisher, L., Kokes, R. F., Ransom, D. C., Phillips, S. L., & Rudd, P. (1985). Alternative strategies for creating "relational" data. *Family Process, 24,* 213–224.

Foa, V., & Foa, E. (1974). *Societal structures of the mind.* Springfield, IL: Charles C Thomas.

Forehand, R., King, H. E., Peed, S., & Yoder, P. (1975). Mother–child interactions: Comparison of a noncompliant clinic group and a nonclinic group. *Behaviour Research and Therapy, 13,* 79–84.

Forehand, R., Sturgis, E. T., McMahon, R., Aguar, D., Green, K., Wells, K. C., & Breiner, J. (1979). Parent behavioral training to modify child noncompliance: Treatment generalization across time and from home to school. *Behavior Modification, 3,* 3–25.

Forman, B. D., & Hagan, B. J. (1983). A comparative review of total family functioning measures. *American Journal of Family Therapy, 11,* 25–40.

Forman, B. D., & Hagan, B. J. (1984). Measures for evaluating total family functioning. *Family Therapy, 11,* 1–36.

Fowler, P. C. (1981). Maximum likelihood factor structure of the Family Environment Scale. *Journal of Clinical Psychology, 37,* 160–164.

Fowler, P. C. (1982). Factor structure of the Family Environment Scale: Effects of social desirability. *Journal of Clinical Psychology, 38,* 285–292.

Furman, W., Adler, T., & Buhrmester, D. (1984, July). *Structural aspects of relationships: A search for a common framework.* Paper presented at the Second International Conference of Personal Relationships, Madison, WI.

Furman, W., & Buhrmester, D. (1985a). Children's perceptions of the qualities of sibling relationships. *Child Development, 56,* 448–461.

Furman, W., & Buhrmester, D. (1985b). Children's perceptions of the personal relationships in their social networks. *Developmental Psychology, 21,* 1016–1024.

Gibb, J. R. (1961). Defensive communications. *Journal of Communication, 3,* 141–148.

Gilbert, R., Christensen, A., & Margolin, C. (1984). Patterns of alliances in nondistressed and multiproblem families. *Family Process, 23,* 75–87.

Gilbert, R., Saltar, K., Deskin, T., Karagozian, A., Severance, G., & Christensen, A. (1981). *The Family Alliances Coding System (FACS) manual.* Unpublished manuscript, University of California, Los Angeles.

Goldstein, M. J. (1987). The family and schizophrenia. In T. Jacob (Ed.), *Family interaction and psychopathology: Theory, methods and findings.* New York: Plenum.

Goldstein, M. J., Rodnick, E. H., Jones, J. E., McPherson, S. R., & West, K. (1978). Familial precursors of schizophrenia spectrum disorders. In L. C. Wynne, R. L. Cromwell, & S. Matthysse (Eds.), *The nature of schizophrenia: New approaches to research and treatment* (pp. 487–498). New York: Wiley.

Gottman, J. M. (1979). *Marital interaction: Experimental investigations.* New York: Academic Press.

Gottman, J., Notarius, C., Gonso, J., & Markman, H. (1976). *A couple's guide to communication.* Champaign, IL: Research Press.

Grotevent, H. D., & Cooper, C. R. (1985). Patterns of interaction in family relationships and the development of identity exploration in adolescence. *Child Development, 56,* 415–428.

Grounds, L. M. (1985). *The Parent Child Observation Schedule: An instrument for the assessment of parent–adolescent relationships.* Unpublished doctoral dissertation, University of Pittsburgh.

Hadley, T. R., & Jacob, T. (1976). The measurement of family power: A methodological study. *Sociometry, 39,* 384–395.

Hauser, S., Powers, S., Jacobson, A. M., Schwartz, J., & Noam, G. (1982). Family interactions and ego development in diabetic adolescents. *Pediatric adolescent endocrinology* (Vol. 10, pp. 69–76). Basel: Karger.

Hauser, S., Powers, S., Weiss, B., Follansbee, D., & Bernstein, E. (1983). *Family Constraining and Enabling Coding System (CECS) manual.* Unpublished manuscript, Boston.

Hauser, S. T., Powers, S. I., Noam, G. G., Jacobson, A. M., Weiss, B., & Follansbee, D. J. (1984). Familial contexts of adolescents ego development. *Child Development, 55,* 195–213.

Hawkins, J. L., Weisberg, C., & Ray, D. L. (1977). Marital communication and social class. *Journal of Marriage and the Family, 39,* 479–490.

Hazzard, A., Christensen, A., & Margolin, C. (1983). Children's perceptions of parental behaviors. *Journal of Abnormal Child Psychology, 11,* 49–59.

Herman, B. F., & Jones, J. E. (1976). Lack of acknowledgement in the family Rorschachs of families with a child at risk for schizophrenia. *Family Process, 15,* 289–302.

Hetherington, E. M., & Martin, B. (1979). Family interaction. In H. C. Quay & J. S. Werry (Eds.), *Psychopathological disorders of childhood* (2nd ed.). New York: Wiley.

Hops, H., Wills, T. A., Weiss, R. L., & Patterson, G. R. (1972). *Marital Interaction Coding System.* Eugene: University of Oregon and Oregon Research Institute.

Humphrey, L. L. (1984). A sequential analysis of family processes in anorexia and bulimia. In *New directions in anorexia nervosa: Proceedings of the Fourth Ross Conference on Medical Research.* Columbus, OH: Ross Laboratories.

Humphrey, L. L., Apple, R., & Kirschenbaum, D. S. (1985). *Differentiating bulimic–anorexic from normal families using an interpersonal and a behavioral observation system.* Unpublished manuscript, University of Wisconsin.

Jacob, T., Ritchey, D., Cvitkovic, J., & Blane, H. (1981). Communication styles of alcoholic and nonalcoholic families when drinking and not drinking. *Journal of Studies on Alcohol, 42,* 466–482.

Jacob, T., Rushe, R., & Seilhamer, R. A. (in press). Alcoholism and family interaction: A research paradigm. *American Journal of Drug and Alcohol Abuse.*

Jacob, T., & Seilhamer, R. A. (1985). Adaptation of the Areas of Change Questionnaire for parent–child relationship assessment. *American Journal of Family Therapy, 13,* 28–38.

Jacobson, N. S., & Anderson, E. A. (1980). The effects of behavior rehearsal and feedback on the acquisition of problem-solving skills in distressed and nondistressed couples. *Behaviour Research and Therapy, 18,* 25–36.

Jacobson, N. S., Follette, W. C., & McDonald, D. W. (1982). Reactivity to positive and negative behavior in distressed and nondistressed married couples. *Journal of Consulting and Clinical Psychology, 50,* 706–714.

Jacobson, N. S., & Moore, D. (1981). Spouses as observers of the events in their relationship. *Journal of Consulting and Clinical Psychology, 49,* 269–277.

Jones, J. E. (1977). Patterns of transactional style deviance in the TAT's of parents of schizophrenics. *Family Process, 16,* 327–337.

Jones, R. R., Reid, J. B., & Patterson, G. R. (1975). Naturalistic observation in clinical assessment. In P. McReynolds (Ed.), *Advances in psychological assessment* (Vol. 3). San Francisco: Jossey-Bass.

Kantor, D., & Lehr, W. (1985). *Inside the family.* San Francisco: Jossey-Bass.

Kuipers, L., Sturgeon, D., Berkowitz, R., & Leff, T P. (1983). Characteristics of expressed emotion: Its relationship to speech and looking in schizophrenic patients and their relatives. *British Journal of Clinical Psychology, 22,* 257–264.

Lamb, M. E., & Sutton-Smith, B. (1982). *Sibling relationships: Their nature and significance across the life span.* Hillsdale, NJ: Erlbaum.

Leary, T. (1957). *Interpersonal diagnosis of personality.* New York: Ronald.

Lewis, J. M., Rodnick, E. H., & Goldstein, M. J. (1981). Intrafamilial interactive behavior, parental communication deviance and risk for schizophrenics. *Journal of Abnormal Behavior, 90,* 448–457.

Lewis, R. A., & Spanier, G. B. (1979). Theorizing about the quality and stability of marriage. In W. R. Burr, R. Hill, F. I. Nye, & I. L. Reiss (Eds.), *Contemporary theories about the family* (Vol. 1). New York: Free Press.

Lobitz, W. C., & Johnson, S. M. (1975). Parental manipulation of the behavior of normal and deviant children. *Child Development, 46,* 719–726.

Maerov, S. L., Brummett, B., & Reid, J. B. (1978). Observer training. In J. B. Reid (Ed.), *A social learning approach to family intervention* Vol. 2: *Observation in home settings.* Eugene, OR: Castalia.

Margolies, P. J., & Weintraub, S. (1977). The revised 56-item CRPBI as a research instrument: Reliability and factor structure. *Journal of Clinical Psychology, 33,* 472–476.

Margolin, G. (1987). Participant observation procedures in marital and family assessment. In T. Jacob (Ed.), *Family interaction and psychopathology: Theory, methods and findings.* New York: Plenum.

Margolin, G., & Wampold, B. E. (1981). Sequential analysis of conflict and accord in distressed and nondistressed marital partners. *Journal of Consulting and Clinical Psychology, 49,* 554–567.

Mash, E. J., & Johnston, C. (1982). A comparison of the mother–child interactions of younger and older hyperactive and normal children. *Child Development, 53,* 1371–1381.

Mash, E. J., Terdal, L. G., & Anderson, K. (1973). The response-class matrix: A procedure for recording parent–child interactions. *Journal of Consulting and Clinical Psychology, 40,* 163–164.

Miller, G. A. (1967). Project grammarama. In *The psychology of communication.* New York: Basic Books.

Minuchin, S. (1974). *Families and family therapy.* Cambridge, MA: Harvard University Press.

Mishler, E. G., & Waxler, N. E. (1965). Family interaction processes and schizophrenia: A review of current theories. *Merrill-Palmer Quarterly of Behavior and Development, 11,* 269–315.

Mishler, E. G., & Waxler, N. E. (1968). *Interaction in families: An experimental study of family process in schizophrenia.* New York: Wiley.

Moos, R., Finney, J. & Gamble, W. (1982). The process of recovery from alcoholism: II. Comparing spouses of alcoholic patients and matched community controls. *Journal of Studies on Alcohol, 43,* 888–909.

Moos, R. & Moos, B. S. (1981). *Family Environment Scale: Manual.* Palo Alto: Consulting Psychologists Press.

Moos, R. & Moos, B. S. (1984). The process of recovery from alcoholism: III. Comparing functioning in families of alcoholics and matched control families. *Journal of Studies on Alcohol, 45,* 111–118.

Oliveri, M. W., & Reiss, D. (1981a). The structure of families' ties to their kin: The shaping role of social constructions. *Journal of Marriage and the Family, 43,* 391–407.

Oliveri, M. W., & Reiss, D. (1981b). A theory-based empirical classification of family problem-solving behavior. *Family Process, 20,* 409–418.

Oliveri, M. W., & Reiss, D. (1984). Family concepts and their measurement: Things are seldom what they seem. *Family Process, 23,* 33–48.

Olson, D. H. L. (1976). Treating relationships: Trends and overview. In D. H. L. Olson (Ed.), *Treating relationships.* Lake Mills, IA: Graphic.

Olson, D. H., McCubbin, H. I., Barnes, H. Larsen, A. Muxen, M., & Wilson, M. (1982). *Family inventories: Inventories used in a national survey of families across the family life cycle.* St. Paul, MN: Family Social Science.

Olson, D. H., & Portner, J. (1983). Family adaptability and cohesion evaluation scales. In E. E. Filsinger (Ed.), *Marriage and family assessment.* Beverly Hills: Sage Publications.

Olson, D. H., Russell, C. S., & Sprenkle, D. H. (1980). Circumplex model of marital and family systems. II: Empirical studies and clinical intervention. In J. Vincent (Ed.), *Advances in family intervention assessment and theory* (Vol. 1). Greenwich, CT: JAI Press.

Olson, D. H., Sprenkle, D. H., & Russell, C. S. (1979). Circumplex model of marital and family systems: I. Cohension and adaptability dimensions, family types, and clinical applications. *Family Process, 18*, 3–28.

Parsons, T., & Bales, R. E. (1955). *Family, socialization and interaction process.* New York: Free Press.

Patterson, G. R. (1982). *A social learning approach* (Vol. 3: *Coercive family process*). Eugene, OR: Castalia.

Patterson, G. R., Ray, R. S., Shaw, D. A., & Cobb, J. A. (1969). *Manual for coding of family interaction.* New York: Microfiche Publications (revised).

Peed, S., Roberts, M., & Forehand, R. (1977). Evaluation of the effectiveness of a standardized parent training program in altering the interaction of mothers and their noncompliant children. *Behavior Modification, 1*, 323–350.

Quinton, D., Rutter, M., & Rowlands, O. (1976). An evaluation of an interview assessment of marriage. *Psychological Medicine, 6*, 557–586.

Reid, J. B. (Ed.). (1978). *A social learning approach to family intervention* (Vol. II: *Observation in home settings*). Eugene, OR: Castalia.

Reiss, D. (1958). *Subjective models of finite state grammars.* Honors thesis, Harvard College.

Reiss, D. (1981). *The family's construction of reality.* Cambridge, MA: Harvard University Press.

Reiss, D., Costell, R., Jones, C., & Berkman, H. (1980). The family meets the hospital: A laboratory forecast of the encounter. *Archives of General Psychiatry, 37*, 141–154.

Reiss, D., & Klein, D. (1987). Paradigm and pathogenesis: A family-centered approach to problems of etiology and treatment of psychiatric disorders. In T. Jacob (Ed.), *Family interaction and psychopathology: Theory, methods and findings.* New York: Plenum.

Reiss, D., & Oliveri, M. E. (1983). Sensory experience and family process. Perceptual styles tend to run in but not necessarily run families. *Family Process, 22*, 289–308.

Reiss, D., & Salzman, C. (1973). Resilience of family process: Effect of secobarbital. *Archives of General Psychiatry, 28*, 425–433.

Renson, G. J., Schaefer, E. S., & Levy, B. I. (1968). Cross-national validity of a spherical conceptual model for parent behavior. *Child Development, 39*, 1229–1235.

Robinson, E. A., & Eyberg, S. M. (1981). The Dyadic Parent–Child Coding System: Standardization and validation. *Journal of Consulting and Clinical Psychology, 49*, 245–250.

Robinson, E. A., & Jacobson, N. S. (1987). Social learning theory and family psychopathology: A Kantian model in behaviorism? In T. Jacob (Ed.), *Family interaction and psychopathology: Theory, methods and findings.* New York: Plenum.

Rollins, B. C., & Thomas, D. L. (1979). Parental support, power, and control techniques in the socialization of children. In W. R. Burr, R. Hill, F. I. Nye, & I. L. Reiss (Eds.), *Contemporary theories about the family* (pp. 317–364). New York: Free Press.

Rutter, M., & Brown, G. W. (1966). The reliability and validity of measures of family life and relationships in families containing a psychiatric patient. *Social Psychiatry, 1*, 38–53.

Sass, L. A., Sunderson, J. L., Singer, M. T., & Wynne, L. L. (1984). Parental communication deviance and forms of thinking in male schizophrenic offspring. *Journal of Nervous and Mental Disease, 172*, 513–520.

Schaefer, E. S. (1959). The circumplex model for maternal behavior. *Journal of Abnormal and Social Psychology, 59*, 226–235.

Schaefer, E. S. (1965a). Children's reports of parental behavior: An inventory. *Child Development, 36*, 413–424.

Schaefer, E. S. (1965b). A configurational analysis of children's reports of parent behavior. *Journal of Consulting Psychology, 29*, 552–557.

Seilhamer, R. (1983). *The Sibling Observation Schedule: An instrument for the assessment of sibling relationships.* Unpublished master's thesis, University of Pittsburgh.

Sigafoos, A., Reiss, D., Rich, J., & Douglas, E. (1985). Pragmatics in the measurement of family functioning. *Family Process, 24,* 189–203.

Singer, M. T. (1973). *Scoring manual for communication deviances seen in individually adminis-tered Rorschach.* Unpublished manuscript, University of California, Berkeley.

Singer, M. T., & Wynne, L. (1966). Principles for scoring communication defects and deviances in parents of schizophrenics: Rorschach and TAT scoring manuals. *Psychiatry, 25,* 260–288.

Skinner, H. A., (1987). Self-report instruments for family assessment. In T. Jacob (Ed.), *Family interaction and psychopathology: Theories, methods and findings.* New York: Plenum.

Skinner, H. A., Steinhauer, P. S., & Santa-Barbara, J. (1983). The family assessment measure. *Canadian Journal of Community Mental Health, 2,* 91–105.

Steinglass, P. (1976). *Family interaction coding instrument.* Unpublished manuscript.

Steinglass, P. (1979). The Home Observation Assessment Method (HOAM): Real-time natural-istic observation of families in their homes. *Family Process, 18,* 337–354.

Steinglass, P. (1980). Assessing families in their own homes. *American Journal of Psychiatry, 137,* 1523–1529.

Steinglass, P. (1981). The alcoholic family at home: Patterns of interaction in dry, wet, and transitional stages of alcoholism. *Archives of General Psychiatry, 38,* 578–584.

Steinhauer, P. D. (1984). Clinical applications of the process model of family functioning. *Canadian Journal of Psychiatry, 29,* 98–111.

Steinhauer, P. D. (1987). the family as a small group: The process model of family functioning. In T. Jacob (Ed.), *Family interaction and psychopathology: Theories, methods and find-ings.* New York: Plenum.

Steinhauer, P. D., & Tisdall, G. W. (1984). The integrated use of individual and family psy-chotherapy. *Canadian Journal of Psychiatry, 29,* 89–97.

Stierlin, H. (1974). *Separating, parents and adolescents.* New York: Quadrangle.

Straus, M. A., & Brown, B. W. (1978). *Family measurement techniques: Abstracts of published instruments, 1935–1974.* Minneapolis: University of Minnesota Press.

Tarrier, N., Vaughn, C. E., Lader, M. H., & Leff, J. P. (1979). Bodily reactions to people and events in schizophrenia. *Archives of General Psychiatry, 36,* 311–318.

Tarver-Behring, S., Barkley, R. A., & Karlsson, J. (1985). The mother–child interactions of hyperactive boys and their normal siblings. *American Journal of Orthopsychiatry, 55,* 202–209.

Teleki, J. K., Powell, J. A., & Dodder, R. (1982). Factor analysis of reports of parental behavior by children living in divorced and married families. *Journal of Psychology, 112,* 295–302.

Tennenbaum, D. L. (1984). *Spouse observation: An investigation of reactivity effects.* Unpub-lished doctoral dissertation, University of Pittsburgh.

Tennebaum, D., & Jacob, T. (1985, November). *An investigation of reactivity effects in spouse observation.* Poster session presented at the meeting of the Association for Advancement of Behavior Therapy, Houston.

Thomas, E. J. (1977). *Marital communication and decision making: Analysis, assessment, and change.* New York: Free Press.

Valone, K., Norton, J. P., Goldstein, M. J., & Doane, J. A. (1983). Parental expressed emotion and affective style in an adolescent sample at risk for schizophrenia spectrum disorder. *Journal of Abnormal Psychiatry, 92,* 399–407.

Vaughn, C. E., & Leff, J. P. (1976a). The influence of family and social factors on the course of psychiatric patients. *British Journal of Psychiatry, 129,* 125–137.

Vaughn, C. E., & Leff, J. P. (1976b). The measurement of expressed emotion in the families of psychiatric patients. *British Journal of Social and Clinical Psychology, 15,* 157–165.

Vincent, J. (1980). The empirical–clinical study of families: Social learning theory as a point of departure. In J. Vincent (Ed.), *Advances in family intervention, assessment and theory* (Vol. I). Greenwich, CT: JAI Press.

Wahler, R. G. (1980). The insular mother: Her problem in parent–child treatment. *Journal of Applied Behavior Analysis, 13,* 207–219.

Wahler, R. G., & Dumas, J. E. (1987). Family factors in childhood psychopathology: Towards a coercion-neglect model. In T. Jacob (Ed.), *Family interaction and psychopathology: Theory, methods and findings*. New York: Plenum.

Wahler, R. G., House, A. E., & Stambaugh, E. E. (1976). *Ecological assessment of child problem behavior: A clinical package for home, school and institutional settings*. New York: Pergamon.

Wald, H., Greenwald, M., & Jacob, T. (1984, August). *Perceived family environments among children of alcoholics, depressed and normal fathers*. Paper presented at the meeting of the American Psychological Association, Toronto.

Weiss, R. L. (1981). Strategic behavioral marital therapy: Toward a model for assessment and intervention. In J. P. Vincent (Ed.), *Advances in family intervention, assessment and theory* (Vol. 1). Greenwich, CT: JAI Press.

Weiss, R. L., Hops, H., & Patterson, G. R. (1973). A framework for conceptualizing marital conflict: A technology for altering it, some data for evaluating it. In R. W. Clark & L. A. Hamerlynck (Eds.), *Critical issues in research and practice: Proceedings of the Fourth Banff International Conference*. Champaign, IL: Research Press.

Weiss, R. L., & Margolin, G. (1986). Assessment of conflict and accord: A second look. In A. Ciminero (Ed.), *Handbook of behavioral assessment* (Vol. 2). New York: Wiley.

Weiss, R. L., & Perry, B. A. (1979). *Assessment and treatment of marital dysfunction*. Eugene: Oregon Marital Studies Program.

Weiss, R. L., & Summers, K. J. (1983). Marital Interaction Coding System-III. In E. Filsinger (Ed.), *Marriage and family assessment*. Beverly Hills: Sage Publications.

Wieder, G. B., & Weiss, R. .L. (1980). Generalizability theory and the coding of marital interactions. *Journal of Consulting and Clinical Psychology, 48,* 469–477.

Wild, C. Shapiro, L., & Goldenberg, L. (1975). Transitional communication disturbances in families of male schizophrenics. *Family process, 14,* 131–160.

Wills, T. A., Weiss, R. L., & Patterson, G. R. (1974). A behavioral analysis of the determinants of marital satisfaction. *Journal of Consulting and Clinical Psychology, 42,* 808–811.

Wynne, L. (1979). *Five-minute speech sample and expressed emotion*. Personal communication.

Wynne, L., Singer, M. T., Bartko, J., & Toohey, M. (1977). Schizophrenics and their families: Recent research on parental communication. In J. M. Tanner (Ed.), *Developments in psychiatric research*. London: Hodder & Stoughton.

8

PSYCHOBIOLOGICAL MEASURES

H. BRUCE FERGUSON
HARRY N. BAWDEN

INTRODUCTION

The attraction of biological measures for researchers interested in psychopathology has been evident since Freud's time. As the various technologies have developed (e.g., electronic and chemical), an increasing amount of research has incorporated biological variables. In the past two decades, this biological perspective has become an influential presence in research on childhood psychopathology. The attractions of a biological approach are the same for both child and adult research: (1) defining biological differences between normals and psychopathological groups may help us understand etiology and mechanisms, and allow development of effective treatments; and (2) in fields plagued with vague diagnostic criteria, biological measures hold out the promise of improving the reliability and validity of diagnosis.

The growing influence of the biological approach is based on several important advances in related fields. First, our knowledge of neurotransmitter systems and their relation to behavior has grown rapidly. In parallel, our ability to intervene pharmacologically in these systems becomes gradually more precise and specific. Second, psychopharmacological research has resulted in the development of a large number of drugs that are efficacious in treating a variety of psychopathological disorders. While the initial model of specific, single drug-to-disorder relationships has not been supported, it is clear that particular classes of drugs are generally useful with groups of related disorders. Nevertheless, the widespread success of pharmacotherapy has heightened the view of psychopathology as biologically mediated if not biologically caused. A third factor promoting a biological perspective has

H. Bruce Ferguson. Departments of Psychology, Carleton University and Royal Ottawa Hospital, Ottawa, Ontario, Canada.

Harry N. Bawden. Department of Psychology, Izaak Walton Killam Hospital for Children, Halifax, Nova Scotia, Canada.

been the elegant research in human genetics in the past decade. Extensive follow-up studies of children adopted away as infants have established that genetic variables play an important role in the manifestation of schizophrenia and alcoholism. Although this type of research has been very difficult, it is now widely accepted as demonstrating unequivocally the influence of heredity independent of social environment in the manifestation of these disorders.

Research examining biological variables and behavior has often incorporated the most recent developments in psychology's analysis of behavior. So we have seen electrophysiological techniques combined with recently developed measures of aspects of cognitive functioning, as well as new behavioral rating scales (see Barkley, Chapter 5, this volume) used to help standardize diagnostic groups as well as to measure biological change in response to drug therapy. Thus, a set of variables exists that can be legitimately termed "psychobiological variables." In this review we are concerned with the use of psychobiological measures in research on child and adolescent psychopathology. We will review and comment on electrophysiological techniques, biochemical measures, physical and motor variables, and perceptual/cognitive measures.

The disorders covered are autism, psychoses, affective disorders, attention deficit disorders (minimal brain dysfunction, hyperactivity), and conduct disorders (delinquency, aggression), and children at risk for schizophrenia. Autism and attention deficit disorder have received the most research attention. These two disorders have been subjected to the most scrutiny with regard to diagnosis. For attention deficit disorder with hyperactivity, there has emerged a set of criteria widely used for diagnosis in research studies (Barkley, 1982). For recent studies of this disorder we can be reasonably confident that all the subjects included did, in fact, have attention deficit disorder with hyperactivity; however, we are often unsure as to how many of them also met the criteria for conduct disorder. Such information is critical since children with attention deficit disorder with and without conduct disorder may constitute two quite different groups.

In autism, the important confounding factor is retardation. Most studies provide no way of controlling for the role of accompanying retardation, and therefore researchers will have to try to control for this variable in future psychobiological research; that is, contrasts of autistics and normals are in most cases not valid. For other diagnostic groups, the picture is less clear. Even if the Research Diagnostic Criteria (RDC) or the criteria described in the third edition of the *Diagnostic and Statistical Manual of Mental Disorders* (DSM-III) of the American Psychiatric Association (1980) were used to determine depression in adolescents or children, there is as yet no consensus on what constitutes the core symptoms or how the criteria for adult symptoms (e.g., vegetative symptoms) should be applied. Thus, it is our belief that all psychobiological research findings should be interpreted cautiously until the limits of their generalizability can be established.

ELECTROPHYSIOLOGICAL MEASURES

Electrophysiological measures have been used in research in psychopathology since soon after the electroencephalograph (EEG) was developed. From the outset, the EEG was recorded in an attempt to screen for organicity (i.e., brain damage), which might explain the observed behavioral abnormalities. As EEG-related computer technology has progressed, we have gained the ability to use sophisticated analyses of EEG in research. Typically, investigators have extolled the potential value of using computerized EEG analysis, which permits examination of a myriad of measures (e.g., wave bands, relative amplitude, power spectral analysis, auto-correlation techniques) and their interrelations. Despite the fact that the virtues of this approach have been sung for over a decade, a search of the literature reveals that very little actual research has been done. This probably underlines the fact that, although the technology exists, it is expensive and difficult to master. Thus, there are few centers capable of conducting research effectively. The latest promising technique, brain electrical activity mapping (BEAM), appears to be encountering exactly the same problems. Nevertheless, there have been some interesting and encouraging findings and we will review them.

Peripheral electrophysiological measures of autonomic nervous system variables (e.g., heart rate, blood pressure, and skin resistance/conductance) have been used primarily to test hypotheses relating to arousal levels. These measures appear to have been most popular in the mid-1970s, and interest in them has declined markedly since that time. During this period there has been increasing interest in cognitive differences across disorders. The focus on cognitive processes has shifted the emphasis in psychophysiological research to averaged cortical-evoked potentials as the measures most likely to shed light on underlying brain mechanisms. Although we are not concerned here with evoked potentials (see Courchesne & Yeung-Courchesne, Chapter 9, this volume), we will review the status of the autonomic measures.

Autism and Other Childhood Psychoses

Visually Scored EEG Measures

Studies of EEG activity in autistic children have reported incidences of abnormalities ranging from 10% to 83% (see Small, 1975). Types of abnormalities have included generalized low-voltage activity without rhythms (Hutt, Hutt, Lee, & Ounsted, 1965); generalized dysrhythmia, slow waves, and spike discharges (Hinton, 1963); unusually persistent alpha rhythms (Stevens & Milstein, 1970); and spikes, paroxysmal spike and wave activity, and severe slowing (De Myer et al., 1973). Several reviews of EEG studies in autism (Andriola, 1983; James & Barry, 1980; Small, 1975) arrive at similar conclusions: (1) the evidence to date suggests that autism is an organic CNS disorder producing a high incidence of EEG abnormalities, which unfortunately are not unique to this disorder; (2) some but not all abnormal EEG findings can be interpreted as resulting from abnormalities in central nervous system (CNS) "arousal" systems; and (3) many of the collected data are suspect in their specificity to autism since most studies used normal age-matched controls rather than the more appropriate mental age and chronological age matches (i.e., retarded controls).

Although the diagnostic distinction between autism and childhood psychosis or schizophrenia is difficult clinically, there have been a number of EEG investigations of such children. Again, a variety of EEG abnormalities have been reported; sharp spike or spike-wave paroxysms (Small, 1968); paroxysmal slow activity (Colbert, Koegler, & Markham, 1959); and dysrhythmia and instability (Kennard, 1959). Thus, once again, there was a high incidence of both diffuse and focal abnormalities with no uniformity of abnormality nor suggestion of specificity.

Computer-Analyzed EEG Measures

Itil, Simeon, and Coffin (1976) provided an interesting comparison of visual and computer analyses of the spontaneous waking EEG of schizophrenic, autistic, and age-matched normal boys. Visual evaluation revealed that psychotic boys had beta activity and fewer alpha bursts than normals. Computer period analysis revealed more slow waves and over-fast activity in the psychotic boys as well as a greater average frequency and frequency deviation in both the primary wave and first derivative measures. This initial evaluation at least suggests that more information is available from computer analysis than from the more usual visual analysis.

Sleep EEG Measures

In general, studies have failed to find differences between psychotic/autistic and normal children on measures of patterning of sleep stages and tonic and phasic aspects of rapid-eye-movement (REM) sleep (Onheiber, White, DeMyer, & Ottinger, 1965; Caldwell, Brané, & Beckett, 1970; Ornitz et al., 1969). Some differences have been found between autistic and normal children. In REM sleep, autistic children showed more spindlelike EEG activity and fewer single eye movements and bursts of eye movements than normals. This finding, along with other results from Ornitz et al. (1969) was interpreted as indicating CNS immaturity in the autistics.

Cardiovascular Measures

Studies of adults have reported consistently higher heart rate (HR) for schizophrenics than normals. Although two studies have reported elevated HR in autistic children (Cohen & Johnson, 1977; Lake, Ziegler, & Murphy, 1977), a number of other studies have found no difference in HR between autistic and normal children (Miller & Bernal, 1971; Hutt *et al.* 1965; Mac-Culloch & Williams, 1971), and schizophrenic children and normals (Pigott, Ax, Bamford, & Fetzner, 1973). The studies reporting no difference in HR level did find evidence for increased HR variability or arrhythmias which has most often been interpreted as indicating a labile and sympathetically dominated autonomic nervous system (ANS).

Bernal and Miller (1970) compared the HR responses of 20 "autistic schizophrenic" and 20 age-matched normal children to repeated auditory and visual stimuli. They found no significant differences between groups. In contrast, Bagshaw, Schwartzkroin, and Burk (1974) reported that the HR deceleration of autistic boys to pure tones was of abnormally high amplitude with short latencies and durations. Finally, Palkovitz and Wiesenfeld (1980) found that autistic boys tended to show accelerative or reduced decelerative heart rate responses to tones, nonsense words, or meaningful verbalizations. Age-matched normal controls showed significant decelerations to all three types of stimuli.

Electrodermal Measures

Early research with psychotic children suggested no differences between psychotic children and normals in resting skin conductance (Bernal & Miller, 1970). However, a recent study reported that autistic boys had higher mean skin conductance levels than age-matched normals. In fact, there was very little overlap in scores between the groups.

Bernal and Miller (1970) found no differences between their autistic schizophrenic group and normals on spontaneous conductance responses or skin conductance responsivity to auditory and visual stimuli. Their failure to differentiate groups on the basis of evoked responses was corroborated by Palkovitz and Wiesenfeld (1980) but in the latter study, the autistic boys showed markedly more spontaneous skin conductance responses than the normals.

Attention Deficit Disorder, Conduct Disorders, and Specific Learning Disabilities

Visually Scored EEG Measures

We have grouped these disorders since many early reports do not allow us to distinguish between them, referring to their subjects as "behavior problems." Once again, studies report a higher than normal incidence of abnormalities, primarily excessively slow EEG activity with poor background organization and frequent occurrence of paroxysmal or epileptiform acitvity (e.g., Grunewald-Zuberbier, Grunewald, & Rosche, 1975; Hughes & Myklebust, 1971; Knights & Hinton, 1969; Stevens, Kuldip, & Milstein, 1968). Although the proportion of children showing excessive slowing varied from study to study, such results have been interpreted as indicating low CNS arousal. However, it is not clear that EEG slowing is associated with a specific subgroup of children in these heterogeneous subject samples. Here again, we have the recurring pattern of diffuse and nonspecific abnormalities.

Computer-Analyzed EEG Measures

Currently the best-known application of computer-analyzed EEG with children from these groups is the "neurometrics" work of John and his colleagues (Ahn *et al.*, 1980; John *et al.*, 1977, 1983). The neurometric analysis uses a multivariate approach, combining the results of a large number of computer-derived "neurometric EEG features." Thus far, it has been shown (Ahn *et al.*, 1980) that the neurometric approach does discriminate between normals and pediatric neurology patients and between normals and learning-disabled children. However, neurometric analysis is complex and expensive, and its limited group of users have yet to demonstrate that it can discriminate among various subgroups of children experiencing learning problems. As far as we can determine, neurometric analysis has not as yet been applied to groups of children showing psychopathology. Dykman, Holcomb, Oglesby, and Ackerman (1982) provided yet another demonstration of the potential utility of computer-analyzed EEG. They submitted the EEG recordings of hyperactive, learning disabled, mixed, and normal children to a fast-Fourier transform analysis. Subsequent principal components analysis produced one component that discriminated between the learning-disabled hyperactive and control groups. While such distinction would be of little diagnostic utility, the fact that such a discrimination was possible with small groups suggests promise in computer-based analysis of EEG.

Sleep EEG Measures

A number of studies comparing "hyperactive" children to normal controls have shown no evidence of differences in sleep EEG measures. This result is surprising in view of the many electrophysiological differences in other areas reported for hyperactive children over the years.

A recent report on EEG sleep abnormalities in conduct-disordered boys is intriguing. Coble *et al.* (1984) compared standard visual analysis and automated computer analysis of sleep EEG in boys with conduct disorder and age-matched controls. They found that standard EEG sleep summary measures revealed a longer second REM/non-REM cycle for the conduct disorder group. On the other hand, the automated analysis showed whole-night delta wave counts that were markedly different for the two groups. In fact, there appeared to be a subgroup of the conduct-disordered boys for whom this difference was particularly striking. Although these findings obviously need to be replicated, they are suggestive of the utility of careful, systematic application of computer-based analysis of EEG measures. If such findings prove to be specific to conduct-disordered children, then we would have the best evidence to date for a biological/organic correlate in this diagnostic group.

Cardiovascular Measures

Measures of resting or tonic heart rate have repeatedly failed to discriminate between hyperactives and controls (e.g., Barkley & Jackson, 1977; Zahn, Abate, Little, & Wender, 1975). On the other hand, conflicting findings have been reported for phasic heart rate response both to nonsignal—smaller responses for hyperactives than normals (Zahn *et al.*, 1975) and no difference between hyperactives and hyperactive clinic controls (Ferguson, Simpson, & Trites, 1976)—and signal stimuli—reduced deceleration for hyperactives (Sroufe, Sonies, West, & Wright, 1973) and no difference (Zahn *et al.*, 1975).

Electrodermal Measures

One study reported that hyperkinetic children had lower basal skin conductance levels than matched normal controls (Satterfield & Dawson, 1971). However, a number of subsequent studies, including one from the same laboratory, have found no differences between groups (Ferguson *et al.*, 1976; Satterfield, Cantwell, Lesser, & Podosin, 1972; Zahn *et al.*, 1975).

The findings on electrodermal responses to nonsignal stimuli are conflicting with the majority of studies reporting no differences between hyperactive and control groups. During performance of reaction time tasks, controls have been reported to show increased frequencies of specific electrodermal responses to reaction stimuli (Firestone & Douglas, 1975; Zahn *et al.*, 1975) and larger-amplitude specific responses (Cohen & Douglas, 1972; Zahn *et al.*, 1975).

Major Depressive Disorder

Sleep EEG Measures

Investigations of adults have revealed a number of characteristic differences in sleep parameters between depressed and normal subjects; increased total sleep time, decreased delta sleep, shortened REM latency, decreased sleep efficiency, increased sleep latency, and early-morning awakenings (see review by Kupfer & Foster, 1979). Two studies of child and adolescent patient groups have failed to find any significant differences in sleep architecture, continuity, or REM latency (Kupfer, Coble, Kane, Petti, & Conners, 1979; Puig-Antich *et al.*, 1982). In a subsequent study, Puig-Antich *et al.* (1983) compared 28 fully recovered prepubertal major depressives with nondepressed neurotics and age-matched normal controls. The recovered depressives showed significantly shorter latency to first REM sleep period and significantly more such periods than the other two groups and than themselves when depressed. Also, measures of sleep continuity in the depressed group were improved during recovery. These results are encouraging but at this time indicate only that the shortened latency to the first REM sleep period is either a marker for major depressive disorder or a sequela of having had the disorder.

Children at Risk for Alcoholism

Computer-Analyzed EEG Measures

In a study of 11- to 13-year-old Danish children, Gabrielli *et al.* (1982) found that the sons of alcoholic fathers had significantly faster EEG activity (> 18 Hz) than sons of nonalcoholic fathers. This relationship did not hold for girls of alcoholic fathers but the authors argue that it is only the sons who are in the high-risk group.

Children at Risk for Schizophrenia

Electrodermal Measures

Mednick and Schulsinger (1973) reported relatively labile skin conductance responsiveness, more rapid skin conductance recovery, and greater conditioning of skin conductance response among the high-risk offspring of schizophrenics. However, subsequent studies have generally failed to replicate these findings. For example, Janes and Stern (1976) and Janes, Hesselbrock, and Stern (1978) found essentially no difference in electrodermal activity between offspring of schizophrenics and normals. In addition, Prentky, Salzman, and Klein (1981) compared skin conductance responses of 7- and 10-year-old children of schizophrenics, of patients with an affective or personality disorder and a mixed group of nonpsychotic patients. They found no evidence for differences in rate of habituation or recovery time, and evidence for better conditioning in only the 10-year-old children of schizophrenics.

Summary of Electrophysiological Measures

Considered in total, the electrophysiological findings to date are not encouraging. It could be argued that, on the whole, the evidence suggests autistic/psychotic children have overaroused CNS, and hyperactive children have underaroused CNS. Unfortunately, the data thus far have revealed no measure on which differences are specific to a disorder—that is, no measure useful in diagnosis. Thus, electrophysiological measures are not currently useful as diagnostic criteria. Nor has any of these measures been used to subgroup children within disorders to examine outcome or treatment efficacy. It is possible that the poor reliability of findings may be increased by use of more homogeneous subgroups which would then permit an accurate evaluation of the validity of subgrouping disorders. In this regard attempts to integrate the varied physiological findings (e.g., Ornitz, 1985) may produce speculative models of underlying neural dysfunction that suggest measures on which research might attempt to subgroup children within disorders.

These electrophysiological measures may be useful in selecting subgroups of children for research. In particular, the computer-analyzed EEG appears to hold special promise in this regard. Used in conjunction with careful DSM-IV diagnostic criteria, computer-derived EEG measures may provide variables to differentiate between groups. Also, Itil (1981) has provided a model for pharmaco-EEG analysis, using single-dose computer-analyzed EEG responses to determine choice of medication. The capacity and flexibility of computer analysis also permits examination of medication induced changes in the relations between behavior and EEG. Studies of these relationships may improve our knowledge of the mechanisms underlying both the disorders themselves and their responsiveness to various drugs. Carrying out useful work in this area will require systematic EEG assessments over time of a large number of children with a variety of diagnoses and receiving a variety of medications. Supporting such a project represents a considerable research investment and, therefore, the potential payoffs will have to be carefully weighed against the costs.

BIOCHEMICAL MEASURES

The recent rapid advances in neurochemistry have provided a wealth of biological strategies for investigating childhood disorders and the mechanisms of action underlying the effectiveness of commonly used psychoactive drugs. A historical marker in this field of endeavor is the widely cited article, "Neurochemistry and Child Psychiatry," by Cohen and Young (1977). This seminal review article initiated an upsurge of interest in the application of neurochemical research to childhood psychopathological disorders.

Thus far, investigators have used two broad groups of biochemical measures. The first group consists of measures of neurotransmitters, their metabolites, and certain of the enzymes performing a regulatory function in neurotransmitter synthesis. These measures are meant to provide indices of levels and turnover (synthesis and degradation) rates in transmitter systems. The catecholamines norepinephrine (NE) and dopamine (DA), and the indoleamine serotonin (5-HT), have all been implicated in psychopathological disorders (e.g., dopamine in autism, schizophrenia, and depression; serotonin in depression; and all three transmitters in attention deficit disorder with hyperactivity).

The second group of measures are neuroendocrine (hormonal) responses to a variety of provocative tests. As with the neurotransmitter measures, most of these neuroendocrine tests have been borrowed directly from research with adults. In particular, in research on childhood and adolescent depression, neuroendocrine measures have been used in attempts to establish the similarity of adult and childhood disorders. Since the diagnosis of major depressive disorder is more problematic in children and adolescents than in adults, any reliable and valid biological marker for the disorder would be especially welcome.

Other than in the case of childhood and adolescent depression, most biochemical research has been conducted in the context of attempts to define underlying mechanisms. For this reason, there has usually been a small number of studies examining a given hypothesis (e.g., serotonin and hyperactivity). Typically, such studies are expensive and difficult to carry out. Children dislike giving blood samples, and even urine samples, and the routine taking of samples of cerebrospinal fluid (CSF) for mechanism-oriented research is not ethically defensible. In addition, as in all clinical research, patients are enrolled at uneven rates. When subject accumulation is slow, or studies long, the blood or urine samples have to be analyzed in multiple runs, a procedure that adds yet another source of unwanted variance. Also, much of this research has been conducted in the absence of a proper context; that is, age and sex norms for the various biochemical levels were properly established before small groups of patients and normals were contrasted.

Finally, there has been a continuing controversy regarding the validity of measuring peripheral biochemical levels and inferring the activity of CNS neurotransmitter systems on the basis of those samples. Cohen and coworkers at Yale have argued that CSF determinations are most useful, and they have made the most use of such measures. We do not intend to enter this controversy. However, until the issue of validity can be properly established, it seems to us most reasonable to regard as meaningful any consistent biochemical–behavioral associations that are defined. It is from this perspective that we carried out this selective review.

Autism

A number of studies have compared catecholamine metabolites in CSF for autistics and various comparison groups. Cohen, Caparulo, Shaywitz, and Bowers (1977) compared homovanillic acid (HVA, a dopamine metabolite) and 5-hydroxyindoleacetic acid (5-HIAA, a serotonin metabolite) in severe autistics with four groups of children. Their only significant between-group finding was that 5-HIAA was decreased in autistics relative to children with other psychoses. In contrast, Gillberg, Svinnerholm, and Hamilton-Hellberg (1983) compared autistic children and other psychotic children with age-matched normal comparison groups and found that whereas the two groups of psychotic patients showed similar levels, autistic children showed higher HVA than their comparison group and the children with other psychoses had raised levels of both HVA and 5-HIAA. Contrasts with groups of mentally retarded children revealed that the increased levels of monoamine metabolites was not due to retardation per se.

Studies of peripheral measures have also yielded differences. Lake et al. (1977) reported that autistics had increased plasma levels of norepinephrine relative to age controls. A number of studies have reported elevated blood serotonin levels in autistic children (Goldstein, 1976; Ritvo et al., 1970) but similar elevations in blood serotonin have been reported for nonautistic retarded children (Campbell, Friedman, DeVito, Greenspan, & Collins, 1974).

Plasma dopamine beta-hydroxylase (DBH) levels have been measured in autistic children to index peripheral sympathetic nervous system function. Early reports indicated elevated DBH levels for autistic children (Freedman, Rottman, & Goldstein, 1973), no difference (Coleman et al., 1974), and decreased DBH in autistics relative to age controls (Lake et al., 1977). This picture is further clouded by the findings of Belmaker, Hattab, and Ebstein (1978) that DBH levels were elevated in children with a functional psychosis (including autism) compared to children with organic psychosis.

Depression

Since norepinephrine had been implicated in adult depression, an early series of studies examined the NE system via assay of urinary 3-methoxy-4-hydroxy-phenyleneglycol (MHPG) (Cytryn, Logue, & Desai, 1974; McKnew & Cytryn, 1979). These studies failed to replicate consistently the findings of decreased excretion of MHPG reported earlier in adult depressed patients.

The number of studies examining neuroendocrine responses in depressed children and adolescents has multiplied rapidly. The dexamethasone suppression test (DST) was developed by Carroll and his associates (1981). This test was based on the extensive evidence of disinhibited limbic–hypothalamic–pituitary–adrenal (LHPA) axis activity in adult endogenous depression. Carroll (1982a, 1982b) and coworkers demonstrated that patients with endogenous depression were resistant to the LHPA-suppressant action of dexamethasone, a synthetic glucocorticoid. Thus, these patients did not show the normal reductions in plasma cortisol subsequent to ingestion of dexamethasone. Carroll and coworkers developed standardized procedures, established norms (across age and sex), and determined the reliability of the procedures. Subsequent research has shown that the sensitivity of the procedure is approximately 60% and the specificity over 90% (Carroll et al., 1981). While not all studies have been able to replicate these encouraging results, the initial data indicate the DST in adults may be a powerful research tool. Current research is examining the utility of the DST in diagnostic confirmation of endogenous depression, in monitoring response to treatment, and in predicting response to tricyclic antidepressants.

Up to 1985, there had been three studies of the DST in depressed children. Puig-Antich, Chambers, Halpern, Hanlon, and Sachar (1979) reported that two of four depressed children showed abnormally high plasma levels of cortisol. Subsequently, Poznanski, Carroll, Banegas, Cook, and Grossman (1982) found that five of nine depressed children showed abnormal DST results while only one of nine controls failed to suppress cortisol release. A year later, Geller, Rogol, and Knitter (1983) reported that only 2 of 14 depressed children were nonsuppressors. More recently, Puig-Antich (1987) reported that only approximately 10% of depressed children hypersecreted cortisol. In all the above studies, most of the children met RDC criteria for endogenous subtype of depression. Even from these limited data it is apparent that cortisol levels and the DST may not be as useful measures with prepubertal children as with adults. However, Weller, Weller, Fristad, Preskorn, and Teare (1985) reported a sensitivity of 82% for the DST with 50 prepubertal depressed children. The specificity in this study was 72% for psychiatric patients and 89% for normal controls. These results are more encouraging and are important theoretically, since they suggest a similar pathophysiology for the disorder in children and adults.

We found seven recent reports examining the DST with depressed adolescents. Robbins, Alessi, Yanchyshyn, and Colfer (1982) reported that two of four depressed adolescents had abnormal DST results, whereas none of the five inpatient psychiatric controls had abnormal results. Crumley, Clevenger, Sheinfink, and Oldham (1982) and Extein, Rosenberg, Pottash, and Gold (1982) reported similar results. In a more extensive sample Robbins, Alessi, Yanchyshyn, and Colfer (1983) reported 4 of 9 adolescents with endogenous depression showed abnormal DST results, whereas 19 other adolescent psychiatric inpatients had normal DST results, including 10 endogenous depressed patients. Another report presented DST results on 101 adolescent inpatients (Hsu et al., 1983). Nine of 14 (64%) patients with major depressive disorder failed to suppress cortisol secretion while 4 of 26 (15%) of conduct disordered adolescents showed abnormal DST results. Strober (1983) reported DST results for 38 adolescent patients. Twelve of these (32%) were nonsuppressors. The breakdown by diagnosis was as follows: 9 of 18 (50%) endogenous depression; 2 of 11 (18%) nonendogenous depression; and 1 of 9 (11%) secondary depression. Finally, Targum and Capodanno (1983) used the DST with a series of 120 adolescent psychiatric inpatients. Nonsuppression of cortisol was noted in 7 of 17 (41%) with major depressive disorder; 7 of 38 (18%) with dysthymic disorder; 7 of 45 (15%) with conduct disorder; and 4 of 15 (27%) with schizophreniform disorder.

The DST findings with adolescents look much more similar to those of adults than do those for prepubertal children. However, although the sensitivities are similar (40%–64%), the specificity for adolescents looks much lower than those for adults. This reduced specificity is underlined by the finding (Jensen, Realmuto, & Garfinkel, 1985) that all but 2 of 13 autistic children and adolescents were nonsupressors. The reasons for the differences are not readily apparent. The DST procedures, norms, and reliability are not well defined for children or adolescents. Even a method for standardizing the dose of dexamethasone is lacking. Also, diagnostic criteria and core symptoms are not well established for children or adolescents. Thus, the possibility always exists that the groups are not comparable across studies. Finally, as Leckman (1983) pointed out, the role of extraneous factors such as eating abnormalities and weight loss need to be carefully established. However, the development of new techniques for measuring cortisol from saliva (Woolston, Gianfredi, Gertner, Paugas, & Mason, 1983) should facilitate use of the DST with children and adolescents. Certainly the results with adolescents are encouraging enough to deserve more detailed investigation. Diagnostically this is a particularly difficult group, and a biological marker would aid in both diagnosis and assessment of treatment efficacy.

The secretion of growth hormone (GH) also has been studied in children in an attempt to further examine the similarities between adult and childhood depressive disorders. The secretion of GH is influenced by both catecholamines and indoleamines, both of which have been implicated in the pathophysiology of depression. It appears that about one-half of severe adult depressives show GH hyporesponsivity to insulin-induced hypoglycemia. Similar decreases in GH response have been reported for some drugs (desmethylimipramine) and not others (apomorphine). Puig-Antich, Tabrizi, et al. (1981) found that in prepubertal children with endogenous major depression, GH secretion in response to an insulin tolerance test was lower than either nonendogenous depressed patients or those diagnosed as nondepressed neurotic. Using an arbitrary cutoff for plasma GH levels 60 minutes after insulin infusion correctly identified 90% of the endogenous depressives and 50% of the nonendogenous depressives, while none of the neurotics were identified as hyposecreters. These data have been interpreted by the authors as validating the diagnosis of endogenous major depressive disorder in prepubertal children. These findings were confirmed at the end of the study with a larger sample (Puig-Antich, Novacenko, Davies, Chambers, et al., 1984). A follow-up to this study (Puig-Antich, Novacenko, Davies, Tabrizi, et al., 1984) showed that even after recovery, the endogenous depressive group continued to have significant hyposecretion of GH. These data suggest that GH hyporesponse to insulin tolerance testing is a sensitive and specific marker for endogenous prepubertal depression or an index of a past episode of the disorder. In parallel studies (Puig-Antich, Goetz, Davies, Fein, et al., 1984; Puig-Antich, Goetz, Davies, Tabrizi, et al., 1984) GH secretion was monitored during sleep in endogenous and nonendogenous depressed children, nondepressed neurotics, and normal controls. Depressed children secreted more GH than either group of control children. The fact that this hypersecretion continued after the depressed children were fully recovered holds out the possibility that GH may be a trait marker for depressive disorder in children. However, both these findings need to be replicated, and acceptable normative data for children and adolescents on GH levels during sleep and following insulin-induced hypoglycemia will have to be obtained before this measure can be used either diagnostically or to indicate risk.

Attention Deficit Disorder with Hyperactivity and Conduct Disorders

There have been several catecholamine hypotheses put forward as models to explain attention deficit disorder with hyperactivity (ADD-H) (e.g., Shaywitz, Cohen, & Bowers, 1977; Wender, 1974; Shaywitz, Cohen, & Shaywitz, 1978; Shekim, Dekirmenjian, & Chapel, 1979). Past research measuring levels of NE, DA, or 5-HT and their metabolites in CSF, plasma, and urine have failed to provide consistent support for a deficit in any single neurotransmitter system (Ferguson & Pappas, 1979; Hunt, Cohen, Shaywitz, & Shaywitz, 1982). Since those reviews were done, Shekim and coworkers have produced a series of studies indicating that boys with ADD-H have lower urinary MHPG than normals, and that treatment with d-amphetamine produces decreased MHPG and increased HVA in good clinical responders (Shekim, Gavaid, Davis, & Bylund, 1983). While some past studies reported no MHPG differences (Rapoport et al., 1978; Wender, Epstein, Kopin, & Gordon, 1971), Shekim has suggested that this conflict is due to urinary sampling procedures. Reanalyses of some of his most recent data have supported this viewpoint. Moreover, these MHPG findings have recently been replicated in a large sample of children with minimal brain dyfunction (MBD) in the People's Republic of China (Shen & Wang, 1984). Indeed, these Chinese investigators reported lower MHPG levels in MBD children with a history of MBD in first-degree relatives than MBD children without such a genetic factor. Thus, these studies together indicate that ADD-H may result from hypoactive central NE systems so that stimulant medications may achieve their clinical effects by inhibiting NE and potentiating DA activity. As has so often been the case, just when a handful of studies were beginning to paint a coherent picture, recent findings indicate that the effects of methylphenidate and d-amphetamine on urinary norepinephrine metabolites (MHPG) are distinctly different. These data underline the risk involved in basing hypotheses about central functioning on information derived from peripheral measures and make it clear that more research will be necessary to define the neurochemical nechanisms underlying ADD-H and conduct disorders.

Of interest, and providing nonspecific support for the above NE hypothesis, Shekim et al. (1982) reorted that ADD-H children had lower levels of platelet monoamine oxidase (MAO) in blood than controls. After 2 weeks of d-amphetamine therapy, there was no difference between groups. Rapoport,

Quinn, and Lamprecht (1974) also reported higher DBH levels in plasma in hyperactive children with high physical-anomalies scores. Finally, Zametkin and colleagues reported that ADD-H boys had lower phenylethylamine in urine than age-matched controls (Zametkin, Karoum, Rapoport, Brown, & Wyatt, 1984). This finding is perhaps confounded by volume of urine excretion since when expressed per gram of creatinine, the phenylethylamine difference was no longer significant.

Coleman (1971) has proposed a relationship between hyperactivity and serotonin on the basis of her findings that total blood 5-hydroxyindole values in a heterogeneous sample of hyperactive children were below the normal values established from an unspecified group of outpatients. Subsequent findings (Ferguson, Pappas, Trites, Peters, & Taub, 1981; Rapoport & Quinn, 1975; Shaywitz et al., 1977) have failed to support this early work and there has been no evidence that stimulant drugs alter serotonin activity in these children. However, a recent report (Zametkin, Linnoila, Karoum, & Sallee, 1985) indicated that pemoline produced clinical improvements in 11 ADD-H boys who showed no changes in urinary excretion of catecholamines or metabolites but did show a significant decrease in 5-HIAA.

Hunt et al. (1982) argue that the clinical heterogeneity of ADD-H and the varying activity levels of children make it unlikely that static (state) measures of neurotransmitters will reflect the functional significance of these systems. They suggest the alternative strategy of using discrete pharmacological probes having well-established neurochemical and behavioral responses.

In conduct disorders, an initial report (Rogeness, Hernandez, Macedo, & Mitchell, 1982) found that boys with undersocialized conduct disorder had lower plasma DBH activity than those with socialized conduct disorder or controls, while boys with socialized conduct disorder had higher red-blood-cell catechol-O-methyltransferase activity. A more recent report (Rogeness, Hernandez, Macedo, Amrung, & Hoppe, 1985) indicated that the socialized/undersocialized distinction did not hold but that there was a relationship between near-zero plasma DBH and conduct-disorder symptomatology in boys. Unfortunately, these researchers did not discriminate between ADD-H and other disorders. The meaning of these findings is as yet unclear, although there is evidence that levels of both substances appear to be genetically determined. The relation of peripheral levels of these rate-limiting enzymes to central levels is not known; therefore, inferences about neurotransmitter availability are purely speculative.

Summary of Biochemical Measures

Widely accepted, established biochemical differences have not yet been found between diagnostic groups in childhood psychopathology. Given the difficulties of differential diagnosis, and the resulting heterogeneity of research samples, as well as the rapidly developing technology of biochemical assays, this is not surprising. However, more research is warranted before the neurochemical models and research strategies are abandoned. There are initial encouraging results in relation to autism (NE, DBH), depression (DST, GH), attention deficit disorder (MHPG, HVA), and conduct disorder (DBH).

This research area would benefit from the collection of normative data using standardized measurement procedures. For instance, the work of Young, Kyprie, Ross, and Cohen (1980) reporting sex and age distribution and reliability data for plasma DBH is almost unique in the field. Much more of this type of normative work must be done if we are to use these measures to their potential. Together with increasing refinement of diagnostic processes, the provision of such standardization and reliability data may lead to the clarification of some of the conflicting findings in the literature. In addition, we need to capitalize on new research strategies such as the pharmacological provocation approach suggested by Hunt *et al.* (1982). Combining the best neurochemical, EEG, and behavioral technologies appears to offer the only real hope of determining the potential of such biological variables in contributing to differential diagnosis, and measurement of change over time and as a result of treatment.

PHYSICAL AND MOTOR MEASURES

In general, physical and motor psychobiological assessment procedures have received little attention in the literature on childhood psychopathology. Potentially useful tests such as computerized tomography (CT) scans, positron emission tomography (PET) scans, magnetic resonance imaging (MRI), analyses of cerebral blood flow (CBF), and smooth-pursuit eye-tracking tasks have, to our knowledge, been used to a very limited extent. The exceptions are measures of neurological soft signs and minor physical anomalies (MPA). Both of these measures have been studied in various populations of children with behavior disorders largely with the hope of delineating organic etiological factors.

Autism

Minor Physical Anomalies

Autistic children have more MPA than normal controls (Campbell, Geller, Small, Petti, & Ferris, 1978; Steg & Rapoport, 1975; Walker, 1977). Maternal age as well as frequency of prenatal and perinatal complications were related to number of MPA in autistic children (Links, 1980; Links, Stockwell, Abichanandi, & Simeon, 1980). However, there was not an excess of first trimester complications (Campbell *et al.*, 1978; Links *et al.*, 1980). Given the nonspecificity of MPA, it is unlikely that elucidation of the causes of

MPA will appreciably add to diagnostic accuracy or our understanding of the etiology of autism.

Attention Deficit Disorder

Neurological Soft Signs

Although several authors have developed examination procedures for detecting neurological soft signs (e.g., Hart, Rennick, Klinge, & Schwartz, 1974; Peters, Romine, & Dykman, 1975; Shapiro, Burkes, Petti, & Ranz, 1978), none of these methods appears to be as promising as the Physical and Neurological Examination for Soft Signs (PANESS) developed at the National Institute of Mental Health (Close, 1973; Guy, 1976). Using the PANESS, Werry and Aman (1976) did not find any differences in number of signs between small groups of normal controls, hyperactive/aggressive children, and neurological impaired children. Camp, Bialer, Sverd, and Winsberg (1978) grouped hyperactive and normal children into age levels and found no differences in PANESS scores. On the other hand, Mikkelsen, Brown, Minichiello, Millican, and Rapoport (1982) statistically controlled for the effects of age and found that the mean PANESS score for the hyperactives was significantly higher than that for normal controls and enuretics. Thus, at the present time it is not clear whether hyperactives and normals differ in PANESS scores, but the consistent finding of substantial overlap among groups suggests that this instrument will not be useful in the diagnosis of attention deficit disorder.

A revised version of the PANESS (Denckla, 1985) contains a number of items reported to be very reliable and sensitive to neurodevelopmental differences and deviations in populations of interest in child psychiatry. Although this examination clearly is a useful tool in assessing the child's current state of neurodevelopmental maturity, it remains to be seen whether the revised PANESS will be useful in diagnosis of childhood psychopathology.

Minor Physical Anomalies

Hyperactive children have more MPA than normal controls (Firestone, Lewy, & Douglas, 1976; Firestone, Peters, Rivier, & Knights, 1978; Firestone & Prabhu, 1983). MPA scores are associated with an early age of onset of hyperactivity, teachers' ratings of hyperactivity, obstetrical complications, and a paternal history of hyperactivity (Quinn & Rapoport, 1974; Rapoport & Quinn, 1975). In addition, MPA are associated with excessive activity, short attention span, impulsivity, and peer aggression in normal preschool males (Waldrop, Bell, McLaughlin, & Halverson, 1978; Waldrop & Goering, 1971; Waldrop, Pedersen, & Bell, 1968). However, MPA are not specifically associated with hyperactivity because no differences in the number of MPA between hyperactives and either neurotic or conduct disordered children have been reported (Firestone & Prabhu, 1983; Quinn & Rapoport, 1974). No differences in MPA were found between hyperactive boys and their apparently normal parents and siblings (Firestone et al., 1978). Furthermore, no differences in MPA between hyperactives and mentally retarded (Firestone et al., 1978) or learning-disabled children (Steg & Rapoport, 1975) have been reported. Thus, it is not yet clear whether high-anomaly hyperactive children constitute a valid biologically defined subgroup (Rapoport, Quinn, Burg, & Bartley, 1979).

Summary of Physical and Motor Measures

The presence of neurological soft signs is characteristic of several diagnostic groups, and they probably should be regarded as indicators of a nonspecific etiologic influence that increases the risk for a variety of disorders (Shaffer, O'Conner, Shafer, & Prupis, 1983). Their high base rate in the normal population also makes it unlikely that they will be useful in screening or prediction (Shaffer et al., 1983). An unresolved issue in this area is the extent to which attentional problems and the motivational state of the child influences test results. This issue could be approached profitably by comparing the variability of performance of normals and children with various types of psychopathology such as hyperactivity. In addition, relationships between PANESS scores and objective measures of attention such as Continuous Performance Test scores should be determined.

MPA occur in several groups of children who exhibit psychopathology and in the normal population. Thus, the relationship between MPA and deviant behavior is weak. By themselves, MPA will be of limited use in screening for hyperactivity, or for problem behavior in general, because of the expected high rate of false positives. The notion of a single biological variable that can be used to predict behavior problems may be rather simplistic. It is more likely that multivariate approaches in which high MPA scores are combined with other biological and psychosocial risk factors will turn out to be more profitable (Burg, Rapoport, Bartley, Quinn, & Timmins, 1980; Loney, Kramer, & Milich, 1981). Kinsbourne's (1979) suggested approach of focusing on specific anomalies and their correlates deserves consideration. It is of interest that a recent study (Paulhus & Martin, 1986) found associations between MPA total scores and temperament and life-style variables for males, but not females, in an unselected sample of university undergraduates. To follow up this work, the researchers are examining specific clusters of MPA with the aim of predicting more specific behaviors.

PERCEPTUAL AND COGNITIVE MEASURES

Perceptual and cognitive measures could be used profitably in conjunction with psychobiological measures as aids in differential diagnosis, selecting patients for research, and the assessment of treatment effects. Only a few measures of attention, memory, and learning will be described for illustrative purposes. The measures chosen all have been used in research on childhood psychopathology and appear to be promising. Throughout this discussion, the reader should keep in mind that although some of these measures have produced findings of interest, the tests involved are largely unstandardized across institutions, and normative data do not exist for many of them.

Attention Deficit Disorder

Sustained Attention

The Continuous Performance Test (CPT) is the most commonly used measure of ability to sustain attention. Hyperactive children make more errors of omission and commission on vigilance tests such as the CPT than normal controls (Barkley, 1977; Douglas, 1983). Several investigators have shown that stimulants improve the ability of hyperactive children to sustain attention as reflected by stimulant-induced reductions in the number of errors of omission and commission (e.g., Sostek, Buchsbaum, & Rapoport, 1980; Sykes, Douglas, & Morgenstern, 1972). Furthermore, improvements in CPT performance produced by administration of methylphenidate often were accompanied by increases in attentive behavior and academic productivity in a classroom setting (Rapport, DuPaul, Stoner, & Jones, 1986). These findings suggest that ability to sustain attention as measured by the CPT is an ecologically valid measure. Klee and Garfinkel (1983) found that CPT performance correlated with ratings on the inattention factor and hyperactivity index but not with ratings on the conduct problems factor of the Conners Teacher Rating Scale (CTRS). Poor performers on the CPT were characterized by behaviors typically exhibited by hyperactive children. Thus, performance on objective measures of attention such as the CPT combined with rating scale data and anamnestic information could be useful in making the differential diagnosis between attention deficit disorder with hyperactivity and conduct disorder. The CPT also could be used in conjunction with the CTRS as screening instruments for the selection of subjects for research projects and in the evaluation of therapies such as cognitive behavior modification programs designed to alter the impulsive and inattentive behavior of hyperactive children.

Memory

Rapid advances in information processing models of human memory have led to the development of sophisticated strategies for study of the nature of stored and remembered information. These techniques have been applied to only a limited extent in the study of stimulant medication effects on the cognitive processes of hyperactive children. For example, Weingartner *et al.*

(1980) found that hyperactive children remembered fewer words under free-recall conditions than normal children, but there was not a difference between the groups in the amount of information that they remembered under cued-recall conditions. They found a tendency for d-amphetamine to enhance the encoding strategy ordinarily used by each group to process words. Hyperactive children relied more on acoustic processing than on semantic processing, and d-amphetamine had a greater effect on the recall of semantically processed words in this group. Normals tended to rely more on semantic processing, and d-amphetamine enhanced the recall of semantically processed words to a greater extent in this group. These stimulant-induced changes in cognition were independent of the improvements in vigilance performance.

Paired-Associate Learning

Paired-associate learning tests have been used by some investigators as an aid in the diagnosis of hyperactivity. Swanson, Kinsbourne, and coworkers have argued that a favorable cognitive response to an acute administration of a stimulant drug provides supplementary evidence for the diagnosis of hyperactivity, and that an adverse cognitive response should be taken as evidence against the diagnosis of hyperactivity (Dalby, Kinsbourne, Swanson, & Sobol, 1977; Swanson, Barlow & Kinsbourne, 1979; Swanson & Kinsbourne, 1976, 1979; Swanson, Kinsbourne, Roberts, & Zucker, 1978). The basis for the diagnostic drug trial is that stimulant therapy corrects a presumed brain dysfunction that causes hyperactive behavior. Hyperactive children exhibit deficits on paired-associate learning (Benezra, 1980), and most investigators have found that stimulants improve their performance on paired-associate tasks (e.g., Douglas, Barr, O'Neill, & Britton, 1986; Gan & Cantwell, 1982; Swanson & Kinsbourne, 1976) although negative results also have been reported (e.g., Stephens, Pelham, & Skinner, 1984). The unspecified brain dysfunction is presumed not to exist in normal children and adults, and they are not expected to exhibit a favorable response to stimulant medication. In fact, normal adults exhibit a stimulant-induced impairment on paired-associate learning tests (Burns, House, Fensch, & Miller, 1967; Smith, 1967). This controversial position has not been widely accepted because recent research has shown that hyperactive children, normal children and adults, and children with learning disabilities including dyslexia exhibit similar responses to stimulants on several behavioral, psychophysiological, and cognitive measures (Ackerman, Dykman, Holcomb, & McCray, 1982; Gittelman-Klein & Klein, 1975; Rapoport et al., 1980). In addition, some hyperactive children may have brain dysfunctions, but the evidence for a specific relationship between any biological factor and hyperactivity is not compelling (Ferguson & Rapoport, 1983; Rutter, 1982). Swanson and Kinsbourne (1979) suggested that the critical feature of the paired-associate learning test is that it requires the acquisition of new associations through repeated practice. A crucial question that needs to be answered before the diagnostic drug trial procedure can be accepted as valid is whether normal children exhibit stimulant-induced improvements on paired-associate learning tests in particular and on learning tests in general.

Thus at the present time there is insufficient evidence to determine whether the diagnostic drug trial procedure advocated by Swanson and Kinsbourne is valid. Nevertheless, their work has been extremely useful in elucidating the cognitive effects of stimulant drugs and in stimulating other research. For example, improvements in paired-associate performance typically are accompanied by increases in attentiveness in the classroom as well as improvements in short-term academic productivity, accuracy, and efficiency (Douglas, Barr, O'Neill, & Britton, 1986; Rapport, Stoner, DuPaul, Birmingham, & Tucker, 1985), and psychiatrists' and teachers' ratings of improvement (Gittelman-Klein & Klein, 1975). Although false negative classifications can occur if one relies solely on paired-associate performance in determining responsiveness to stimulant medication (Bawden, Knights, & Firestone, 1987; Rapport *et al.*, 1985), these findings point to the usefulness of the paired-associate test in a clinic-based testing battery designed to determine stimulant medication responsivity.

Children at Risk for Schizophrenia

Sustained Attention

Information processing deficits in individuals who are at risk for the development of schizophrenia recently have received increased attention. Studies in this area attempt to identify genetically influenced markers of vulnerability to schizophrenia that are present in schizophrenics and their nonaffected siblings, but not in normal control children or the children of nonschizophrenic psychiatric patients. Performance deficits on vigilance tasks may reflect the operation of a vulnerability factor for schizophrenia (Nuechterlein & Dawson, 1984). Deficits in vigilance performance among subjects at risk for the development of schizophrenia appear to be related to the information processing load of the particular CPT that was used (Nuechterlein & Dawson, 1984). Thus, no differences in vigilance performance between offspring of schizophrenic mothers and normal adolescents were reported when subjects were required to respond to a single target stimulus (e.g., Asarnow, Steffy, MacCrimmon & Cleghorn, 1977, 1978; Nuechterlein, 1984a). Poor hit rates and lower sensitivity on vigilance tasks with high information processing loads have been found to characterize the performance of children of schizophrenics (e.g., Erlenmeyer-Kimling & Cornblatt, 1978; Nuechterlein, 1984b). It is not clear whether their performance deficits reflect an impaired ability to sustain attention, inasmuch as Nuechterlein (1983) found a nonsignificant trend for hit rate to decrease at a faster than normal rate over time. A lower overall level of sensitivity was found throughout the task. A crucial question is whether these vigilance performance deficits can be used to predict which of the high-risk children will develop schizophrenia. Preliminary data on this issue have been collected by Erlenmeyer-Kimling, Kestenbaum, Bird, and Hilldoff (1984), who followed 80 children of schizophrenic parents and found that 15 had psychiatric disorders, including 5 hospitalized subjects who had schizophrenia or schizo-affective disorders. All five of the hospitalized subjects and seven out of ten of the remaining clinically deviant offspring exhibited performance below the fifth percentile of the normal controls. These data support the clinical predictive utility of measures of CPT performance for this high-risk group.

Perceptual sensitivity deficits do occur in some hyperactive children (O'Dougherty, Nuechterlein, & Drew, 1984), but they differ from children of schizophrenics in that they exhibit a more impulsive style of responding than normal children (Nuechterlein, 1983). The response criterion of the offspring of schizophrenics does not differ from that of normal children. In addition, preliminary findings suggest that children of parents with an affective disorder or nonpsychotic disorders do not exhibit the vigilance performance deficit, that characterizes some of the children of schizophrenics (Erlenmeyer-Kimling, Marcuse, et al., 1984; Nuechterlein, 1983). These data provide further support for the predictive validity of CPT performance for children of schizophrenics.

Summary of Perceptual and Cognitive Measures

Properly standardized and normed, objective measures of attention could prove to be extremely valuable in the diagnosis of hyperactivity and in the selection of hyperactive children for research projects. Recently, normative data have been collected on a computerized version of the CPT (Ferguson, 1983). Vigilance performance, especially on versions of the CPT that have a relatively high information processing load also may serve as a genetically influenced indicator of vulnerability for the deveopment of schizophrenia.

Memory tests mainly have been used to measure changes in mnemonic processing resulting from the administration of psychoactive agents. Information processing approaches not only could be used profitably to study medication effects, but also may be useful in characterizing children with various types of psychopathology.

It is not clear that subdividing children who exhibit symptoms of hyperactivity into favorable and adverse responders to stimulants on the basis of their paired-associate learning-test performance is a valid way of biologically categorizing these behaviorally disordered children. Nevertheless, paired-associate performance is useful in helping to determine stimulant medication responsivity.

CONCLUSIONS

We have carried out a selective review of the use of a group of "psychobiologic assessment procedures" in research on child and adolescent psychopathology. Most of the findings are conflicting. With the advantage of hindsight, this is not surprising. All the research in this area over the past 25 years has been done in the context of changing diagnostic criteria for the psychopathologic groups. Therefore, not only were many research samples heterogeneous in themselves, but it is virtually impossible to know how comparable samples were from study to study. Even at present, with DSM-III criteria used predominantly in North America and DSM-IV in development, there is an acknowledged absence of consensus about how to interpret these diagnostic criteria; that is, we still cannot be certain of having comparable groups across studies.

In addition, the measures themselves are rarely standardized. In the case of the psychological tests, their psychometric properties have not been established. For the psychophysiological and biochemical measures, standardized procedures and controls are needed, as are data on reliability. Since such psychometric issues are attended to routinely for psychological tests, this situation may seem unusual. However, in context this situation too is understandable. Most psychobiological measures have been used to test hypotheses regarding mechanisms underlying disorders (e.g., attention—children at risk for schizophrenia, children with ADD; electrophysiology—arousal in autism, ADD; biochemistry—monoamine deficiency in autism, ADD), or to indicate organic biological involvement in the disorder (e.g., MPA in autism, ADD; soft signs in ADD). Thus, researchers did not start out with the plan of using these measures routinely in assessing children. Moreover, many past studies represent instances where techniques or technologies were "borrowed" to test hypotheses in another field. Although this strategy seems to represent a frequently profitable one in science, it is obvious that scientific progress depends upon properly mastering and applying the various techniques. Finally, the research application of many of these techniques is very expensive. This fact makes systematic, long-term studies difficult to conduct, especially under current conditions of research funding.

It is clear that there are areas where psychobiological measures appear to hold real promise (e.g., urinary metabolites of monoamines in ADD and conduct disorder; the DST and measures of growth hormone in depression; the application of computer-analyzed EEG in conduct disorder as well as in sleep and learning disorders). Particularly, it appears to us that rapid gains might be made by applying several of these procedures together (e.g., by examining measures of monoamine metabolites or DBH in combination with computerized EEG analysis) in a number of patient groups (e.g., ADD, conduct disorder, normal controls). And, furthermore, to compare baseline measures with those obtained after single doses of drugs whose pharmacologic, EEG, and behavioral effects are known.

There is a final caveat to be dealt with. Our review has indicated that research efforts with these psychobiologic variables have produced weak (to moderate) associations and a lack of specificity for particular psychopathologic disorders. A somewhat similar situation in adult psychopathology has been interpreted as suggesting that the diagnostic categories do not represent unitary syndromes and need further subdivision (Buchsbaum & Rieder, 1979). If this hypothesis represents a reasonable possibility then appropriate strategies for further research are clear; that is, we need to define our groups on the basis of the results of selected psychobiological measures and then look for distinguishing features with respect to history, symptomatology, course, and treatment responsiveness. Certainly, there is no shortage of hypotheses to test. Our job will be to select the most likely ones and test them adequately.

REFERENCES

Ackerman, P. T., Dykman, R. A., Holcomb, P. J., & McCray, D. S. (1982). Methylphenidate effects on cognitive style and reaction time in four groups of children. *Psychiatry Research, 7,* 199–213.

Ahn, H., Prichep, L., John, E. R., Baird, H., Trepeten., M, & Kaye, H. (1980). Developmental equations reflect brain dysfunctions. *Science, 210,* 1259.

American Psychiatric Association. (1980). *Diagnostic and statistical manual of mental disorders* (3rd ed.). Washington, DC: Author.

Andriola, M. (1983). EEG in childhood psychiatric disorders. In J. R. Hughes & W. R. Wilson (Eds.), *EEG and evoked potentials in psychiatry and behavioral neurology.* Woburn, MA: Butterworth.

Asarnow, R. F., Steffy, R. A., MacCrimmon, D. J., & Cleghorn, J. M. (1977). An attentional assessment of foster children at risk for schizophrenia. *Journal of Abnormal Psychology, 86,* 267–275.

Asarnow, R. F., Steffy, R. A., MacCrimmon, D. J. & Cleghorn, J. M. (1978). An attentional assessment of foster children at risk for schizophrenia. In L. C. Wyne, R. L. Cromwell, & S. Matthysse (Eds.), *The nature of schizophrenia: New approaches to research and treatment.* New York: Wiley.

Bagshaw, M. H., Schwartzkroin, P., & Burk, E. D. (1974). Dissociation of motor and cardiac orienting reactions in autistic children. *Psychophysiology, 11,* 220–221.

Barkley, R. A. (1977). The effects of methylphenidate on various measures of activity level and distractibility in hyperactive and nonhyperactive children. *Journal of Abnormal Child Psychology, 5,* 351–369.

Barkley, R. A. (1982). Guidelines for defining hyperactivity in children. In B. Lahey & A. Kazdin (Eds.), *Advances in clinical child psychology,* (Vol. 5.). New York: Plenum.

Barkley, R. A., & Jackson, T. L. (1977). Hyperkinesis, autonomic nervous system activity, and stimulant drug effects. *Journal of Child Psychology and Psychiatry, 18,* 347–357.

Bawden, H. N., Knights, R. M., & Firestone, P. (1987). *The cognitive effects of methylphenidate on conduct-disordered boys.* Manuscript submitted for publication.

Belmaker, R. H., Hattab, G, & Ebstein, R. P. (1978). Plasma dopamine-beta-hydroxylase in childhood disorders. *Journal of Autism and Childhood Schizophrenia, 8,* 293–298.

Benezra, E. (1980). *Verbal and nonverbal memory in hyperactive, reading-disabled, and normal children.* Unpublished doctoral dissertation, McGill University.

Bernal, M.E., & Miller, W. H. (1970). Electrodermal and cardiac responses of schizophrenic children to sensory stimuli. *Psychophysiology, 7,* 155–168.

Buchsbaum, M., & Rieder, R. (1979). Biological heterogeneity and psychiatric research. *Archives of General Psychiatry, 36*; 1163–1169.

Burg, C., Rapoport, J. L., Bartley, L. S., Quinn, P. O., & Timmins, P. (1980). Newborn minor physical anomalies and problem behavior at age three. *American Journal of Psychiatry, 137*, 791–796.

Burns, J. T., House, R. F., Fensch, F. C., & Miller, J. G. (1967). Effects of magnesium pemoline and dextroamphetamine on human learning. *Science, 155*, 849–851.

Caldwell, D. F., Brané, H. J., & Beckett, P. G. S. (1970). Sleep patterns in normal and psychotic children. *Archives of General Psychiatry, 22*, 500–503.

Camp, J., Bialer, I., Sverd, J., & Winsberg, B. (1978). Clinical usefulness of the NIMH Physical and Neurological Examination for Soft Signs. *American Journal of Psychiatry, 135*, 362–364.

Campbell, M., Friedman, E., DeVito, E., Greenspan, L., & Collins, P. J. (1974). Blood serotonin in psychotic and brain-damaged children. *Journal of Autism and Childhood Schizophrenia, 4*, 33–41.

Campbell, M., Geller, B., Small, A. M., Petti, T. A., & Ferris, S. H. (1978). Minor physical anomalies in young psychotic children. *American Journal of Psychiatry, 135*, 573–575.

Carroll, B. J. (1982a). Clinical applications of the dexamethasone suppression test for endogenous depression. *Pharmacopsychiatry, 15*, 19–25.

Carroll, B. J. (1982b). The dexamethasone suppression test for melancholia. *British Journal of Psychiatry, 140*, 292–304.

Carroll, B. J., Feinberg, M., Greden, J. F., Tarika, J., Albala, A. A., *et al.* (1981). A specific laboratory test for the diagnosis of melancholia: Standardization, validation and clinical utility. *Archives of General Psychiatry, 38*, 15–22.

Close, J. (1973). Scored neurological examination in pharmacotherapy of children. *Psychopharmacology Bulletin, 9*, 142–148.

Coble, P. A., Taska, L. S., Kupfer, D. J., Kazdin, A. E., Unis, A., & French, N. (1984). EEG sleep abnormalities in preadolescent boys with a diagnosis of conduct disorder, *Journal of the American Academy of Child Psychiatry, 23*, 438–447.

Cohen, N., & Douglas, V. I. (1972). Characteristics of the orienting, response in hyperactive and normal children. *Psychophysiology, 9*, 238–245.

Cohen, D. J., & Johnson, W. T. (1977). Cardiovascular correlates of attention in normal and psychiatrically disturbed children. *Archives of General Psychiatry, 34*, 561–657.

Cohen, D. J., & Young, J. G. (1977). Neurochemistry and child psychiatry. *Journal of the American Academy of Child Psychiatry, 16*, 353–411.

Cohen, S. G., Caparulo, B. K., Shaywitz, B. A., & Bowers, M. B. (1977). Dopamine and serotonin metabolism in neuropsychiatrically disturbed children. *Archives of General Psychiatry, 34*, 545–550.

Colbert, E. G., Koegler, R. R., & Markham, C. H. (1959). Vestibular dysfunction in childhood schizophrenia. *Archives of General Psychiatry, 1*, 600–617.

Coleman, M. (1971). Serotonin concentration in whole blood of hyperactive children. *Journal of Pediatrics, 78*, 985–990.

Coleman, M., Campbell, M., Freedman, L. S., Roffman, M., Epstein, R. B., & Goldstein, M. (1974). Serum dopamine-beta-hydroxylase levels in Down's syndrome. *Clinical Genetics, 5*, 312–315.

Crumley, F. E., Clevenger, J., Sheinfink, D., & Oldham, D. (1982). Preliminary report on the dexamethasone suppression test for psychiatrically disturbed adolescents. *American Journal of Psychiatry, 139*, 1062–1064.

Cytryn, L., Logue, M., & Desai, R. B. (1974). Biochemical correlates of affective disorders in children. *Archives of General Psychiatry, 31*, 659–661.

Dalby, J. T., Kinsbourne, M., Swanson, J. M., & Sobol, M. P. (1977). Hyperactive children's underuse of learning time: Correction by stimulant treatment. *Child Development, 48*, 1448–1453.

De Myer, M. K., Barton, S., De Myer, W. E., Norton, J. A., Allen, J., & Steele, R. (1973). Prognosis in autism: A follow-up study. *Journal of Autism and Childhood Schizophrenia, 3,* 199–246.

Denckla, M. B. (1985). Revised neurological examination for subtle signs. *Psychopharmacology Bulletin, 21,* 773–789.

Douglas, V. I. (1983). Attentional and cognitive problems. In M. Rutter (Ed.), *Developmental neuropsychiatry.* New York: Guilford.

Douglas, V. I., Barr, E., O'Neill, M. E., & Britton, B. G. (1986). Short term effects of methylphenidate on the cognitive, learning and academic performance of children with Attention Deficit Disorder in the laboratory and the classroom. *Journal of Child Psychology and Psychiatry, 27,* 191–211.

Dykman, R. A., Holcomb, P. J., Oglesby, D. M., & Ackerman, P. T. (1982). Electrocortical frequencies in hyperactive learning disabled, mixed, and normal children. *Biological Psychiatry, 17,* 675–685.

Erlenmeyer-Kimling, L., & Cornblatt, B. (1978). Attentional measures in a study of children at high risk for schizophrenia. In L. C. Wynne, R. Cromwell, & S. Matthysse (Eds.), *The nature of schizophrenia: New approaches to research and treatment.* New York: Wiley.

Erlenmeyer-Kimling, L., Kestenbaum, C., Bird, H., & Hilldoff, U. (1984). Assessment of the New York High-Risk Project subjects in Sample A who are now clinically deviant. In N. F. Watt, E. J. Anthony, L. C. Wynne, & J. E. Rolf (Eds.), *Children at risk for schizophrenia: A longitudinal perspective.* New York: Cambridge.

Erlenmeyer-Kimling, L., Marcuse, Y., Cornblatt, B., Friedman, D., Rainer, J. D., & Rutschmann, J. (1984). The New York High-Risk Project. In N. F. Watt, E. J. Anthony, L. C. Wynne, & J. E. Rolf (Eds.), *Children at risk for schizophrenia: A longitudinal perspective.* New York: Cambridge.

Extein, I., Rosenberg, G., Pottash, A. L., & Gold, M. S. (1982). The dexamethasone suppression test in depressed adolescents. *American Journal of Psychiatry, 139,* 1617–1619.

Ferguson, H. B. (1983). *Normative data for the continuous performance task.* Unpublished manuscript, Carleton University.

Ferguson, H. B., & Pappas, B. A. (1979). Evaluation of psychophysiological, neurochemical, and animal models of hyperactivity. In R. L. Trites (Ed.), *Hyperactivity in children: Etiology, measurement and treatment implications.* Baltimore: University Park Press.

Ferguson, H. B., Pappas, B. A., Trites, R. L., Peters, D. A. V. & Taub, H. (1981). Plasma free and total tryptophan, blood serotonin, and the hyperactivity syndrome: No evidence for the serotonin deficiency hypothesis. *Biological Psychiatry, 16,* 231–238.

Ferguson, H. B., & Rapoport, J. L. (1983). Nosological issues and biological validation. In M. Rutter (Ed.), *Developmental neuropsychiatry.* New York: Guilford.

Ferguson, H. B., Simpson, S., & Trites, R. L. (1976). Psychophysiological study of methylphenidate responders and nonresponders. In R. Knights & D. Bakker (Eds.), *The neuropsychology of learning disorders.* Baltimore: University Park Press.

Firestone, P., & Douglas, V. I. (1975). the effects of reward and punishment on reaction times and autonomic activity in hyperacitve and normal children. *Journal of Abnormal Child Psychology, 3,* 201–216.

Firestone, P., Lewy, F., & Douglas, V. I. (1976). Hyperactivity and physical anomalies. *Canadian Psychiatric Association Journal, 21,* 23–26.

Firestone, P., Peters, S., Rivier, M., & Knights, R. M. (1978). Minor physical anomalies in hyperactive, retarded and normal children and their families. *Journal of Child Psychology and Psychiatry, 19,* 155–160.

Firestone, P., & Prabhu, A. (1983). Minor physical anomalies and obstetrical complications: Their relationship to hyperactive, psychoneurotic and normal children and their families. *Journal of Abnormal Child Psychology, 11,* 207–216.

Freedman, L. S., Rottman, R. H., & Goldstein, M. (1973). Changes in human serum dopamine-beta-hydroxylase activity in various physiological and pathological states. In E. Usdin & S. Snyder (Eds.), *Frontiers of catecholamine research.* New York: Pergamon.

Gabrielli, W. F., Mednick, S. A., Volanka, J., Pollock, V. E., Schulsinger, F., & Itil, T. (1982). Electroencephalograms in children of alcoholic fathers. *Psychophysiology*, *19*, 404–407.

Gan, J., & Cantwell, D. P. (1982). Dosage effect of methylphenidate on paired associate learning: Positive/negative placebo responders. *Journal of Abnormal Child Psychology*, *6*, 237–242.

Geller, B., Rogol, A. D., & Knitter, E. F. (1983). Preliminary data on the dexamethasone suppression test in children with major depression. *American Journal of Psychiatry*, *140*, 620–624.

Gillberg, C., Svinnerholm, L., & Hamilton-Hellberg, C. (1983). Childhood psychosis and monamine metabolites in spinal fluid. *Journal of Autism and Development Disorders*, *13*, 383–396.

Gittelman-Klein, R., & Klein, D. (1975). Are behavioral and psychometric changes related in methylphenidate-treated children? *International Journal of Mental Health*, *4*, 182–198.

Goldstein, M.(1976). Dopamine-beta-hydroxylase and endogenous total 5-hydroxindole levels in autistic patients and controls. In M. Coleman (Ed.), *The autistic syndrome*. New York: North-Holland.

Grunewald-Zuberbier, E., Grunewald, G., & Rosche, A. (1975). Hyperactive behavior and EEG arousal reactions in children. *Electroencephalography and Clinical Neurophysiology*, *38*, 149–159.

Guy, H. (1976). Physical and neurological assessment for soft signs. In *ECDEU assessment manual for psychopharmacology*. Rockville, MD: National Institute of Mental Health.

Hart, Z., Rennick, P. M., Klinge, V., & Schwartz, M. L. (1974). A pediatric neurologist's contribution to evaluations of school underachievers. *American Journal of Diseases of Children*, *128*, 319–323.

Hinton, G. G. (1963). Childhood psychosis or mental retardation: A diagnostic dilemma. II. Pediatric and neurological aspects. *Canadian Medical Association Journal*, *89*, 1020–1024.

Hsu, L. K. G., Malcan, K., Cashman, M. A., Lee, S., Lonr, G., & Hindmarsh, D. (1983). The dexamethasone suppression test in adolescent depression. *Journal of the American Academy of Child Psychiatry*, *22*, 470–473.

Hughes, J. R., & Myklebust, H. R. (1971). The EEG in a controlled study of measured brain dysfunction. *Electroencephalography and Clinical Neurophysiology*, *31*, 292.

Hunt, R. D., Cohen, D. G., Shaywitz, S. E., & Shaywitz, B. A. (1982). Strategies for the study of the neurochemistry of attention deficit disorder in children. *Schizophrenia Bulletin*, *8*, 236–252.

Hutt, S. J., Hutt, C., Lee, D., & Ounsted, C. (1965). A behavioral and electrographic study of autistic children. *Journal of Psychiatric Research*, *3*, 181–197.

Itil, T. M. (1981). Clinical psychopharmacology of aggression. In I. Valzelli & I. Morghese (Eds.), *Aggression and violence: A Psychobiological and clinical approach*. Edizioni: St. Vincent.

Itil, T. M., Simeon, J. G., & Coffin, C. (1976). Qualitative and quantitative EEG in psychotic children. *Diseases of the Nervous System*, *37*, 247–252.

James, A. L., & Barry, R. J. (1980). A review of psychophysiology in early onset psychosis. *Schizophrenia Bulletin*, *6*, 506–527.

Janes, C. L., Hesselbrock, U., & Stern, J. A. (1978). Parental psychopathology, age, and race as related to electrodermal activity of children. *Psychophysiology*, *15*, 24–34.

Janes, C. L., & Stern, J. A. (1976). Electrodermal response configuration as a function of rated psychopathology in children. *Journal of Nervous and Mental Disease*, *162*, 184–194.

Jensen, J. B., Realmuto, G., & Garfinkel, B. D. (1985). The dexamethasone suppression test in infantile autism. *Journal of the American Academy of Child Psychiatry*, *24*, 263–265.

John, E. R., Prichep, L., Ahn, H., Easton, P., Fridman, J., & Kaye, H. (1983). Neurometric evaluation of cognitive dysfunctions and neurological disorders in children. *Progress in Neurobiology*.

John, E. R., Karmel, B. Z., Corning, W. C., Easton, P., Brown, D., Ahn, H., John, M., Harmony, T., Prichep, L., Toro, A., Gerson, I., Barlett, F., Thatcher, F., Kaye, H., Valdes, P., & Schwartz, E. (1977). Neurometrics numerical taxonomy identifies different profiles of brain dysfunction within groups of similar people. *Science, 196,* 1393–1410.

Kennard, M. A. (1959). The characteristics of thought disturbances as related to electroencephalographic findings in children and adolescents. *American Journal of Psychiatry, 115,* 911–921.

Kinsbourne, M. (1979). Discussion of "Can hyperactives be identified in infancy?" In R. L. Trites (Ed.), *Hyperactivity in children: Etiology, measurement and treatment implications.* Baltimore: University Park Press.

Klee, S. H., & Garfinkel, B. D. (1983). The Computerized Continuous Performance Task: A new measure of inattention. *Journal of Abnormal Child Psychology, 11,* 487–486.

Knights, R. M., & Hinton, C. G. (1969). The effects of methylphenidate on the motor skills and behavior of children with learning problems. *Journal of Nervous and Mental Disease, 148,* 643–654.

Kupfer, D., Coble, P., Kane, J., Petti, T., & Conners, C. K. (1979). Imipramine and EEG sleep in children with depressive symptoms. *Psychopharmacology, 60,* 117–123.

Kupfer, D., & Foster, F. G. (1979). EEG sleep and depression. In R. L. Williams & I. Karacan (Eds.) *Sleep disorders: Diagnosis and treatment.* New York: Wiley.

Lake, C. R., Ziegler, M. G., & Murphy, D. L. (1977). Increase norepinephrine levels and decreased dopamine-beta-hydroxylase activity in primary autism. *Archives of General Psychiatry, 34,* 553–556.

Leckman, J. F. (1983). Editorial: The dexamethasone suppression test. *Journal of the American Academy of Child Psychiatry, 22,* 477–479.

Links, P. S. (1980). Minor physical anomalies in childhood autism. II. Their relationship to maternal age. *Journal of Autism and Developmental Disorders, 10,* 287–292.

Links, P. S., Stockwell, M., Abichanandi, F., & Simeon, J. (1980). Minor physical anomalies in childhood autism. I. Their relationship to pre- and perinatal complications. *Journal of Autism and Developmental Disorders, 10,* 273–285.

Loney, J., Kramer, J., & Milich, R. S. (1981). The hyperactive child grows up: Predictors of symptoms, delinquency and achievement at follow-up. In K. D. Gadow & J. Loney (Eds.), *Psychosocial aspects of drug treatment for hyperactivity.* Boulder, CO: Westview.

MacCulloch, M. J., & Williams, C. (1971). On the nature of infantile autism. *Acta Psychiatrica Scandinavica, 47,* 295–314.

McKnew, D. H., & Cytryn, L. (1979). Urinary metabolites in chronically depressed children. *Journal of the American Academy of Child Psychiatry, 18,* 608–615.

Mednick, S. A., & Schulsinger, F. (1973). Some premorbid characteristics related to breakdown in children with schizophrenic mothers. In D. Rosenthal & S. S. Kety (Eds.), *The transmission of schizophrenia.* New York: Pergamon.

Mikkelsen, E. J., Brown, G. L., Minichiello, M. D., Millican, F. K., & Rapoport, J. L. (1982). Neurologic status in hyperactive, enuretic encopretic and normal boys. *Journal of the American Academy of Child Psychiatry, 21,* 75–81.

Miller, W. H., & Bernal, M. E. (1971). Measurement of the cardiac response in schizophrenic and normal children. *Psychophysiology, 8,* 533–537.

Nuechterlein, K. H. (1983). Signal detection in vigilance tasks and behavioral attributes among offspring of schizophrenic mothers and among hyperactive children. *Journal of Abnormal Psychology, 92,* 4–28.

Nuechterlein, K. H. (1984a). Discussion (Cromwell, Magaro, & Venables). In W. D. Spaulding & J. K. Cole (Eds.), *Nebraska Symposium on Motivation, 1983* (Vol. 31: *Theories of schizophrenia and psychosis*). Lincoln: University of Nebraska Press.

Nuechterlein, K. H. (1984b). Perspectives on future studies of attentional functioning in children at risk for schizophrenia. In N. F. Watt, E. J. Anthony, L. C. Wynne, & J. E. Rolf (Eds.), *Children at risk for schizophrenia: A longitudinal perspective.* New York: Cambridge.

Nuechterlein, K. H., & Dawson, M. E. (1984). Information processing and attentional functioning in the developmental course of schizophrenic disorders. *Schizophrenia Bulletin, 10,* 160–203.

O'Dougherty, M., Nuechterlein, K. H., & Drew, B. (1984). Hyperactive and hypoxic children: Signal detection, sustained attention, and behavior. *Journal of Abnormal Psychology, 93,* 178–191.

Onheiber, P., White, P. T., DeMyer, M. K., & Ottinger, D. R. (1965). Sleep and dream patterns of child schizophrenics. *Archives of General Psychiatry, 12,* 568–571.

Ornitz, E. M. (1985). Neurophysiology of infantile autism. *Journal of the American Academy of Child Psychiatry, 24,* 251–262.

Ornitz, E. M., Ritvo, E. R., Brown, W. B., La Franchi, S., Parmelle, T., & Walter, R. D. (1969). The EEG and rapid eye movements during REM sleep in normal and autistic children. *Electroencephalography and Clinical Neurophysiology, 26,* 167–175.

Palkovitz, R. J., & Wiesenfeld, A. R. (1980). Differential autonomic responses of autistic and normal children. *Journal of Autism and Developmental Disorders, 10,* 347–360.

Paulhus, D. L., & Martin, C. L. (1986). Predicting adult temperament from minor physical anomalies. *Journal of Personality and Social Psychology, 50,* 1235–1239.

Peters, J. E., Romine, J. S., & Dykman, R. A. (1975). A special neurological examination of children with learning disabilities. *Developmental Medicine and Child Neurology, 17,* 63–78.

Piggott, R., Ax, A. F., Bamford, J. L., & Fetzner, J. M. (1973). Respiration sinus arrhythmia in psychotic children. *Psychophysiology, 10,* 401–414.

Poznanski, E. O., Carroll, B. J., Banegas, M. C., Cook, S. C., & Grossman, G. A. (1982). The dexamethasone suppression test in prepubertal depressed children. *American Journal of Psychiatry, 193,* 321–324.

Prentky, R. A., Salzman, L. F., & Klein, R. H. (1981). Habituation and conditioning of skin conductance responses in children at risk. *Schizophrenia Bulletin, 7,* 281–291.

Puig-Antich, J. (1987). Affective disorders in children and adolescents: Diagnostic validity and psychobiology. In *Psychopharmacology: A generation of progress.* New York: Raven Press.

Puig-Antich, J., Chambers, W., Halpern, F., Hanlon, C., & Sacher, E. J. (1979). Cortisol hypersecretion in prepubertal depressive illness: A preliminary report. *Psychoendocrinology, 4,* 191–197.

Puig-Antich, J., Goetz, R., Davies, M., Fein, M., Hanlon, C., Chambers, W. J., Tabrizi, M. A., Sachar, E. J., & Weitzman, E. D. (1984). Growth hormone secretion in prepubertal children with major depression. II. Sleep-related plasma concentrations during a depressive episode. *Archives of General Psychiatry, 41,* 463–466.

Puig-Antich, J., Goetz, R., Davies, M., Tabrizi, M. A., Novacenko, H., Hanlon, C., Sachar, E. J. & Weitzman, E. D. (1984). Growth hormone secretion in prepubertal children with major depression. IV. Sleep-related plasma concentrations in a drug-free, fully recovered clinical state. *Archives of General Psychiatry, 41,* 479–483.

Puig-Antich, J., Goetz, R., Hanlon, C., Davies, M., Thompson, J., Chambers, W. J., Tabrizi, M. A., & Weitzman, E. D. (1982). Sleep architecture and REM sleep measures in prepubertal children with major depression: A controlled study. *Archives of General Psychiatry, 39,* 932–939.

Puig-Antich, J., Goetz, R., Hanlon, C., Tabrizi, M. A., Davies M., & Weitzman, E. D. (1983). Sleep architecture and REM sleep measures in prepubertal major depressives: Studies during recovery from the depressive episode in a drug-free state. *Archives of General Psychiatry, 40,* 187–192.

Puig-Antich, J., Novacenko, H., Davies, M., Chambers, W. J., Tabrizi, M. A., Krawiec, V., Ambrosini, P. J., & Sachar, E. J. (1984). Growth hormone secretion in prepubertal children with major depression. I. Final report on response to insulin-induced hypoglycemia during a depressive episode. *Archives of General Psychiatry, 41,* 455–460.

Puig-Antich, J., Novacenko, M. S., Davies, M., Tabrizi, M. A., Ambrosini, P., Goetz, R., Bianca, J., Goetz, R., & Sachar, E. J. (1984). Growth hormone secretion in prepubertal children with major depression. III. Response to insulin-induced hypoglycemia after recovery from a depressive episode and in a drug-free state. *Archives of General Psychiatry*, *41*, 471–475.

Puig-Antich, J., Tabrizi, M. A., Davies, M., Goetz, R., Chambers, W. J., Halpern, F., & Sachar, E. J. (1981). Prepubertal endogenous major depressives hyposecrete growth hormone in response to insulin-induced hypoglycemia. *Biological Psychiatry*, *16*, 801–819.

Quinn, P. O., & Rapoport, J. L. (1974). Minor physical anomalies and neurologic status in hyperactive boys. *Pediatrics*, *53*, 742–747.

Rapoport, J. L., Buchsbaum, M. S., Weingartner, H., Zahn, T. P., Ludlow, C., & Mikkelsen, E. J. (1980). Dextroamphetamine: Its cognitive and behavioral effects in normal and hyperactive boys and normal men. *Archives of General Psychiatry*, *37*, 933–943.

Rapoport, J. L., Mikkelsen, E. J., Ebert, M. H., Lavonne Brown, G., Weise, V. K., & Kopin, I. J. (1978). Urinary catecholamines and amphetamine excretion in hyperactive and normal boys. *Journal of Nervous and Mental Disease*, *166*, 731–737.

Rapoport, J. L., & Quinn, P. O. (1975). Minor physical anomalies (stigmata) and early developmental deviation: A major biologic subgroup of "hyperactive children." *International Journal of Mental Health*, *4*, 29–44.

Rapoport, J. L., Quinn, P. O., Burg, C., & Bartley, L. (1979). Can hyperactives be identified in infancy? In R. L. Trites (Ed.), *Hyperactivity in children: Etiology, measurement and treatment implications*. Baltimore: University Park Press.

Rapoport, J. L., Quinn, P. O., & Lamprecht, F. (1974). Minor physical anomalies and plasma dopamine-beta-hydroxylase activity in hyperactive boys. *American Journal of Psychiatry*, *131*, 386–390.

Rapport, M. D., DuPaul, G. J., Stoner, G., & Jones, J. T. (1986). Comparing classroom and clinic measures of Attention Deficit Disorder: Differential, idiosyncratic, and dose–response effects of methylphenidate. *Journal of Consulting and Clinical Psychology*, *54*, 334–341.

Rapport, M. D., Stoner, G., DuPaul, G. J., Birmingham, B. K., & Tucker, S. (1985). Methylphenidate in hyperactive children: Differential effects of dose on academic, learning, and social behavior. *Journal of Abnormal Child Psychology*, *13*, 227–224.

Ritvo, E. R., Yuwiler, A., Geller, E., Ornitz, E. M., Saeger, K., & Plotkin, S. (1970). Increased blood serotonin and platelets in early infantile autism. *Archives of General Psychiatry*, *23*, 566–572.

Robbins, D. R., Alessi, N. E., Yanchyshyn, G. W., & Colfer, M. V. (1982). Preliminary report on the dexamethasone suppression test in adolescents. *American Journal of Psychiatry*, *139*, 942–943.

Robbins, D. R., Alessi, N. E., Yanchyshyn, G. W., & Colfer, M. V. (1983). The dexamethasone suppression test in psychiatrically hosptialized adolescents. *Journal of the American Academy of Child Psychiatry*, *22*, 467–469.

Rogeness, G. A., Hernandez, J. M., Macedo, C. A., Amrung, S. A., & Hoppe, S. K. (1985, October). *Near-zero dopamine-B-hydroxylase and conduct disorder in emotionally disturbed boys*. Poster presented at the American Academy of Child Psychiatry Meeting.

Rogeness, G. A., Hernandez, J. M., Macedo, C. A., & Mitchell, E. L. (1982). Biochemical differences in children with conduct disorder socialized and undersocialized. *American Journal of Psychiatry*, *139*, 307–311.

Rutter, M. (1982). Syndromes attributed to "minimal brain dysfunction" in children. *American Journal of Psychiatry*, *139*, 21–33.

Satterfield, J. H., Cantwell, D. P., Lesser, L., & Podosin, R. L. (1972). Physiological studies of the hyperkinetic child. *American Journal of Psychiatry*, *128*, 1418–1424.

Satterfield, J. H., & Dawson, M. E. (1971). Electrodermal correlates of hyperactivity in children. *Psychophysiology*, *8*, 191–197.

Shaffer, D., O'Connor, P. A., Shafer, S. Q., & Prupis, S. (1983). Neurological "soft signs": Their origins and significance for behavior. In M. Rutter (Ed.), *Developmental neuropsychiatry.* New York: Guilford.

Shapiro, T., Burkes, L., Petti, T. A., & Ranz, J. (1978). Consistency of "nonfocal" neurological signs. *Journal of the American Academy of Child Psychiatry, 17,* 76–79.

Shaywitz, B. A., Cohen, D. J., & Bowers, M. B. (1977). CSF monoamine metabolites in children with minimal brain dysfunction: Evidence for alteration of brain dopamine. *Journal of Pediatrics, 90,* 67–71.

Shaywitz, S. E., Cohen, D. J., & Shaywitz, B. A. (1978). The biochemical basis of minimal brain dysfunction. *Journal of Pediatrics, 92,* 179–187.

Shekim, W. O., Davis, L. G., Bylund, D. B., Brunngraber, E., Fikes, L., & Lanham, J. (1982). Platelet MAO in children with attention deficit disorder and hyperactivity: A pilot study. *American Journal of Psychiatry, 139,* 936–938.

Shekim, W. O., Dekirmenjian, H., & Chapel, J. (1979). Urinary MHPG excretion in minimal brain dysfunction and its modification by *d*-amphetamine. *American Journal of Psychiatry, 136,* 667–671.

Shekim, W. O., Gavaid, J., Davis, J. M., & Bylund, D. B. (1983). Urinary MHPG and HVA excretion in boys with attention deficit disorder and hyperactivity treated with *d*-amphetamine. *Biological Psychiatry, 18,* 705–715.

Shen, Y., & Wang, Y. (1984). Urinary 3-methoxy-4-hydroxphenylglycol sulfate excretion in seventy-three school children with minimal brain dysfunction syndrome. *Biological Psychiatry, 19,* 861–877.

Small, J. G. (1968). Epileptiform electroencephalographic abnormalities in mentally ill children. *Journal of Nervous and Mental Disorders, 147,* 341–348.

Small, J. G. (1975). EEG and neurophysiological studies of early infantile autism. *Biological Psychiatry, 10,* 385–397.

Smith, R. G. (1967). Magnesium pemoline: Lack of facilitation in human learning, memory and performance tests. *Science, 155,* 603–605.

Sostek, A. J., Buchsbaum, M. S., & Rapoport, J. L. (1980). Effects of amphetamine on vigilance performance in normal and hyperactive children. *Journal of Abnormal Child Psychology, 8,* 491–500.

Sroufe, L. A., Sonies, B. C., West, W. D., & Wright, F. S. (1973). Anticipatory heart rate deceleration and reaction time in children with and without referral for learning disability. *Child Development, 44,* 267–273

Steg, J. P., & Rapoport, J. L. (1975). Minor physical anomalies in normal, neurotic, learning disabled, and severely disturbed children. *Journal of Autism and Childhood Schizophrenia, 5,* 299–307.

Stephens, R. S., Pelham, W. E., & Skinner, R. (1984). State-dependent and main effects of methylphenidate and pemoline on paired-associate learning and spelling in hyperactive children. *Journal of Consulting and Clinical Psychology, 52,* 104–113.

Stevens, J. R., Kuldip, S., & Milstein, V. (1968). Behavior disorders of childhood and the electroencephalogram. *Archives of Neurology, 18,* 160–177.

Stevens, J. R., & Milstein, V. (1970). Severe psychiatric disorders of childhood. Electroencephalogram and clinical correlates. *American Journal of Diseases of Children, 120,* 182–192.

Strober, M. (1983). Clinical and biological perspectives on depressive disorders in adolescence. In D. Cantwell & G. A. Carlson (Eds.), *Affective disorders in childhood and adolescence.* New York: Spectrum Publications.

Swanson, J. M., Barlow, A., & Kinsbourne, M. (1979). Task specificity of responses to stimulant drugs in laboratory tests. *International Journal of Mental Health, 8,* 67–82.

Swanson, J. M., & Kinsbourne, M. (1976). Stimulant-related state-dependent learning in hyperactive children. *Science, 192,* 1354–1357.

Swanson, J. M., & Kinsbourne, M. (1979). The cognitive effects of stimulant drugs on hyperactive children. In G. A. Hale & M. Lewis (Eds.), *Attention and cognitive development.* New York: Plenum.

Swanson, J. M., Kinsbourne, M., Roberts, W., & Zucker, K. (1978). Time-response analysis of the effect of stimulant medication on the learning ability of children referred for hyperactivity. *Pediatrics, 61,* 21–29.

Sykes, D. H., Douglas, V. I., & Morgenstern, G. (1972). The effect of methylphenidate (Ritalin) on sustained attention in hyperactive children. *Psychopharmacologia, 25,* 262–274.

Targum, S. D., & Capodanno, A. E. (1983). The dexamethasone suppression test in adolescent psychiatric inpatients. *American Journal of Psychiatry, 140,* 589–591.

Waldrop, M. F., Bell, R. Q., McLaughlin, B., & Halverson, C. F. (1978). Newborn minor physical anomalies predict short attention span, peer aggression and impulsivity at age 3. *Science, 199,* 563–565.

Waldrop, M. F., & Goering, J. D. (1971). Hyperactivity and minor physical anomalies in elementary school children. *American Journal of Orthopsychiatry, 41,* 602–607.

Waldrop, M. F., Pedersen, F. A., & Bell, R. Q. (1968). Minor physical anomalies and behavior in preschool children. *Child Development, 39,* 391–400.

Walker, H. A. (1977). Incidence of minor physical anomalies in autism. *Journal of Autism and Childhood Schizophrenia, 7,* 165–176.

Weingartner, H., Rapoport, J. L., Buchsbaum, M. S., Bunney, W. E., Ebert, M. H., Mikkelsen, E. J., & Caine, E. D. (1980). Cognitive processes in normal and hyperactive children and their response to amphetamine treatment. *Journal of Abnormal Psychology, 89,* 25–37.

Weller, E. B., Weller, R. A., Fristad, M. A., Preskorn, S. H., & Teare, M. (1985). The dexamethasone suppression test in prepubertal depressed children. *Journal of Clinical Psychiatry, 46,* 511–513.

Wender, P. H. (1974). Some possible speculations regarding a possible biochemical basis of minimal brain dysfunction. *Life Sciences, 14,* 1605–1621.

Wender, P. H., Epstein, R. S., Kopin, I. J., & Gordon, E. K. (1971). Urinary monoamine metabolites in children with minimal brain dysfunction. *American Journal of Psychiatry, 127,* 1411–1415.

Werry, J. S., & Aman, M. G. (1976). The reliability and diagnostic validity of the Physical and Neurological Examination for Soft Signs (PANESS). *Journal of Autism and Childhood Schizophrenia, 6,* 253–262.

Woolston, J. L., Gianfredi, S., Gertner, J. M., Paugas, J. A., & Mason, J. W. (1983). Salivary cortisol: A nontraumatic sampling technique for assaying cortisol dynamics. *Journal of the American Academy of Child Psychiatry, 22,* 474–476.

Young, J. G., Kyprie, R. M., Ross, N. T., & Cohen, D. J. (1980). Serum dopamine-beta-hydroxylase activity: Clinical applications in child psychiatry. *Journal of Autism and Development Disorders, 10,* 1–4.

Zahn, T. P., Abate, F., Little, B. C., & Wender, P. H. (1975). Minimal brain dysfunction, stimulant drugs and autonomic nervous system activity. *Archives of General Psychiatry, 32,* 381–387.

Zametkin, A. J., Karoum, F., Rapoport, J. L., Brown, G. L., & Wyatt, R. J. (1984). Phenylethylamine excretion in attention deficit disorder. *Journal of the American Academy of Child Psychiatry, 23,* 310–314.

Zametkin, A. J., Linnoila, M., Karoum, F., & Sallee, R. (1985, October). *Pemoline and the urinary excretion of catecholamines and indoleamines in ADDH.* Poster presented at the American Academy of Child Psychiatry Annual Meeting.

9

EVENT-RELATED BRAIN POTENTIALS

ERIC COURCHESNE
RACHEL YEUNG-COURCHESNE

INTRODUCTION

One of several techniques available for the neurobiological classification and diagnosis of developmental disorders of the nervous system is the event-related brain potential (ERP) technique, which records a person's neural responses elicited by specific auditory, visual, or somatosensory information. ERP responses represent the "real-time" neural activity in sensory, cognitive, and motor systems that occurs in response to information specifically presented by the clinician or experimenter (Figure 9-1).

There is active research directed at elucidating the possible neural systems that generate ERP responses or "components." For some components the neural generators have been ascertained (e.g., the contingent negative variation [CNV] is probably generated by neural responses to acetylcholine input to cortex from nucleus basalis; see Pirch, Corbus, Rigdon, & Lyness, 1986), and for many components the number of possibilities has been considerably narrowed (e.g., the A/Pcz/300 and possibly the P3b may, in part, be dependent upon noradrenergic input to cortex from locus ceruleus; see Pineda, Foote, & Neville, in press). Thus, ERP technology offers the possibility of measuring the functioning of numerous neural systems. This can be done in a completely noninvasive fashion in newborns, infants, children, and adolescents. ERP technology, then, provides a special opportunity to study the physiological development of the human brain from the first day of life onward in normal as well as in disordered individuals.

By testing these responses under a variety of conditions, it is possible to characterize the normal and the pathophysiological responses at the sensory,

Eric Courchesne. Neuropsychology Research Laboratory, Children's Hospital Research Center, San Diego, California, and Neurosciences Department, University of California at San Diego, La Jolla, California.

Rachel Yeung-Courchesne. Neuropsychology Research Laboratory, Children's Hospital Research Center, San Diego, California.

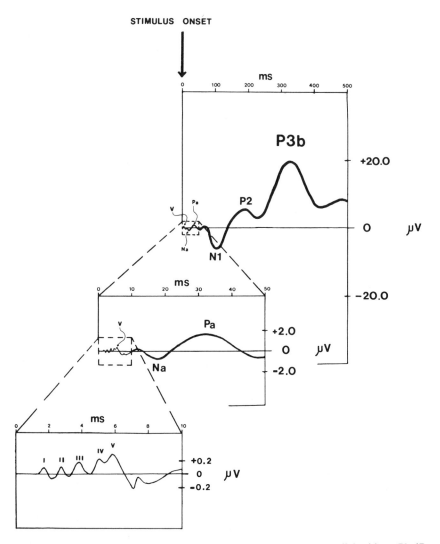

FIGURE 9-1. Idealized illustration of a single-trial ERP response elicited by a 70-dB normal-hearing-level sound—a click. The ERP is a continuous series of components occurring at various latencies after stimulus onset and having various amplitudes and durations. Shorter latency components—Waves I, II, III, IV, and Na and Pa—are classic examples of exogenous (or sensory) components. The longer latency component P3b is a classic example of an endogenous (or cognitive) component. From Courchesne (1987).

cognitive, and motor levels of the nervous system. By comparing pathophysiological responses of various developmental disorders, it is possible to determine the patterns of pathophysiology that are distinctive of each disorder and differentiate them from other developmental disorders. By comparing pathophysiological responses to developmental norms, it is possible to determine whether they are delayed or deviant.

We will consider below the evidence for diagnostically distinctive pathophysiologies at sensory and cognitive stages of information processing in infantile autism, receptive developmental dysphasia (or "receptive developmental language disorder"), Down's syndrome, dyslexia, and attention deficit disorder. In order to discern distinctive patterns of pathophysiology, we will compare the same neurophysiological responses recorded under comparable conditions in each disorder. These neurophysiological responses will be sensory and cognitive ERP components for which substantial information exists on their normal course of development; they are the auditory brainstem ERPs, A/Pcz/300, P3b, and Nc. In order to appreciate the full implications of ERP findings in these five developmental psychopathologies, we will present basic and developmental research evidence about each component.

SENSORY ERP COMPONENTS

Sutton, Braren, Zubin, and John (1965) pointed out that ERP components may be divided into two classes: "One of these is largely *exogenous* or related to the character of the stimulus. The other is largely *endogenous* and related to the reaction or attitude of the subject to the stimulus." Sensory, or exogenous, ERP components are typified by the auditory brainstem-evoked response.

Functioning of the Auditory Brainstem Sensory Pathways
Normal: Basic and Developmental Evidence

The functioning of auditory brainstem sensory pathways is studied by recording five ERP components generated by neural activity in them (Achor & Starr, 1980a, 1980b; Picton, Stapells, & Campbell, 1981; Robinson & Rudge, 1982). The components are called Waves I, II, III, IV, and V and are triggered by click stimuli (Figure 9-1). They reflect some of the neural activity that takes place during the first 8 milliseconds following the onset of the click; each component represents a different step in auditory sensory processing. The latency (time of occurrence after stimulus onset) and amplitude of each component is affected by stimulus intensity, rate of stimulus delivery, and ear of stimulus delivery. These ERP responses are also affected by gender and body temperature (Stockard, Stockard, & Sharbrough, 1978).

Except for Wave I, which is generated by the auditory nerve, the neural generators are not known with absolute certainty, but they are likely to include neural activity in or near the cochlear nucleus, superior olive, lateral lemniscus, inferior colliculus, and acoustic radiations (Legatt, Arezzo, & Vaughan, 1986a, 1986b; Scherg & Von Cramon, 1985). The recording of these components provides neurologists with a reliable metric for assessing the functioning of auditory brainstem sensory systems. The auditory brainstem response appears at birth and matures quite rapidly; it is nearly fully mature before the end of the second year of life (Galambos, 1982).

Infantile Autism

These components have been studied in several developmental psychopathologies. Research on autism has been most intense (Courchesne, Courchesne, Hicks, & Lincoln, 1985; Gillberg, Rosenhall, & Johansson, 1983; Novick, Vaughan, Kurtzberg, & Simson, 1980; Rumsey, Grimes, Pikus, Duara, & Ismond, 1984; Skoff, Mirsky, & Turner, 1980; Tanguay, Edwards, Buchwald, Schwafel, & Allen, 1982; Taylor, Rosenblatt, & Linschoten, 1982). Several of these reports indicate that some individuals with autism have clinically identifiable audiological problems. However, audiological problems exist in many clinical populations.

The critical issue is whether autism involves a distinctive form of pathophysiology in auditory brainstem sensory pathways, or, for that matter, any pathophysiology when one eliminates from study autistic subjects who have complicating neurological diseases in addition to autism.

Rumsey et al. (1984) and Tanguay et al. (1982) tested autistic subjects under a variety of stimulus conditions and controlled for gender. They found a low incidence of abnormal responses among their autistic subjects. We (Courchesne, Courchesne, et al., 1985) tested autistic subjects under a variety of stimulus conditions, controlled for gender and accounted for body temperature, and only tested autistic subjects who did not have complicating neurological diseases. We found that *every* autistic subject had *normal* auditory brainstem components. Figure 9-2 shows the auditory brainstem ERPs from our autistic and normal control subjects elicited under a variety of sensory stimulation conditions. This figure shows how very similar the ERP components were in autistic and normal subjects.

It would appear, therefore, that, although audiological abnormalities may be found in some autistic individuals, there is no evidence that autism involves a distinctive form of pathophysiology in the auditory sensory pathways generating these ERP components.

Receptive Developmental Dysphasia

Auditory brainstem ERPs reflect responses to high-frequency rather than low-frequency acoustical stimulation in humans. Since a leading hypothesis explains developmental dysphasia as the result of difficulties in processing rapidly changing acoustical events (Tallal, 1980, 1985; Tallal & Piercy,

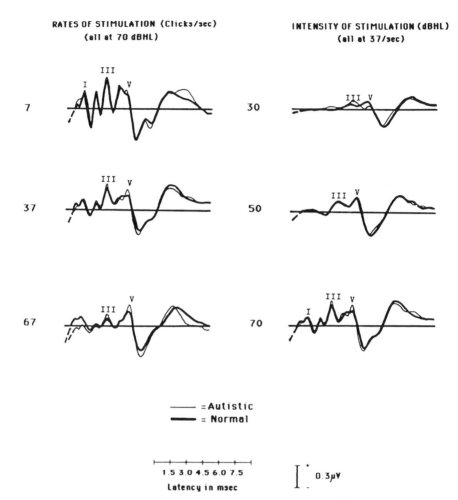

FIGURE 9-2. Similarity of auditory brainstem ERPs between normal and autistic subjects. ERPs were evoked by different stimulation rates and intensities. The thick tracings are the averages of ERP responses from right and left ears from 14 normals. Superimposed onto these are thin tracings representing the averages of ERPs from right and left ears from 14 autistic subjects. From Courchesne, Courchesne, Hicks, and Lincoln (1985).

1975), it is important to know whether initial stages of auditory sensory processing are abnormal in receptive developmental dysphasia. It is surprising, therefore, that there is so little known about the auditory brainstem ERPs in receptive developmental dysphasia. In fact, there is more brainstem ERP evidence on children who have *expressive* language impairment (e.g., Mason & Mellor, 1984) than on those who have receptive language impairment. Of the few available brainstem ERP studies, some have not provided adequate psycholinguistic and historical descriptions of their "language-impaired" subjects; others have made a large number of post hoc comparisons of the ERP data without employing the necessary statistical corrections.

We have recently obtained preliminary evidence on the auditory brain-stem ERP response of 10 people with receptive developmental dysphasia. These individuals met the full DSM-III criteria (American Psychiatric Association, 1980) for "Developmental Language Disorder, Receptive Type." In addition, each had a documented history of early onset of abnormal language development (by 4 years of age); normal oral–motor functioning; and more than a decade of receptive language inpairment, and treatment thereof, up to the present time (mean age at the time of ERP testing was 15.3 years). These adolescents had severe language and verbal deficits (mean "language quotient" of 67; mean Wechsler Verbal IQ of 74), but normal nonverbal abilities (mean Wechsler Performance IQ of 101). Although our preliminary results hint at the possibility of very slightly unusual ERP responses to monaural stimulation of the right ear, we have found no statistically significant differences between our small group of receptive developmental dysphasics and normal controls. Clinically significant abnormalities included one dysphasic with a conductive hearing loss, and another with a sensorineural loss.

Down's Syndrome

Squires (1984) found that there is a distinctive pathology in the auditory brainstem response in Down's syndrome and suggested that this may create a distorted acoustic perception. First, a shortened time interval was reported between the latencies of Waves I and II and between Waves III and IV (Figure 9-3). Second, the latency of Wave V did not increase normally in response to increases in the rate of auditory stimulus delivery. It is this second effect that seems most unusual; it raises the question of how faithfully the initial stages of auditory sensory processing in Down's syndrome temporally encode or mark successive pieces of information.

These patterns of abnormal auditory brainstem ERP responses in Down's syndrome are deviations from the normal ERP patterns found during development; they are not developmental delays.

COGNITIVE ERP COMPONENTS

Among the large number of cognitive, or endogenous, ERP components, three which represent different physiological systems triggered by attention-getting information are A/Pcz/300, P3b, and Nc (Courchesne, 1983, 1987; Courchesne, Elmasian, & Yeung-Courchesne, 1987). Considerable evidence shows that each of these components emerges early during development, and their maturational time course has been charted in experiments analogous to

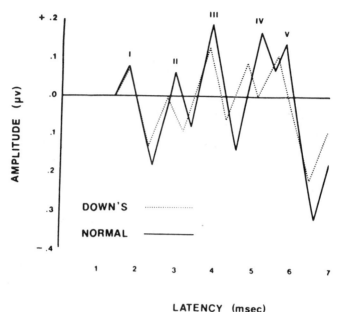

FIGURE 9-3. Differences in latency of certain auditory brainstem ERP peaks between normal and Down's syndrome people. From Squires, Aine, Buchwald, Norman, and Galbraith (1980).

those that have been used to study various developmental psychopathologies.

To be valid, studies of these components require the experimenter to include in the experimental design controls for performance, general attentiveness, and cooperativeness. Subjects must be able to understand simple instructions, to remain still and attentive for relatively long periods of time (about half an hour at a time), and to perform behavioral tasks reliably during ERP recording.

The A/Pcz/300 Component

Normal: Basic and Developmental Evidence

The A/Pcz/300 component is one of several elicited by the detection of novel, surprising sounds; although it may be akin to the P3a component, its location over cortex differs from earlier reports about P3a (Courchesne, 1983; Holcomb, Ackerman, & Dykman, 1986; Knight, 1984; Roth, 1973; Squires, Squires, & Hillyard, 1975). It is possible that this component is specific to the auditory modality (Courchesne, 1983, in press). As seen in Figure 9-4, it is large in amplitude at scalp electrode sites over superior parietal, central and frontal cortex, and has a peak latency of about 300 milliseconds following

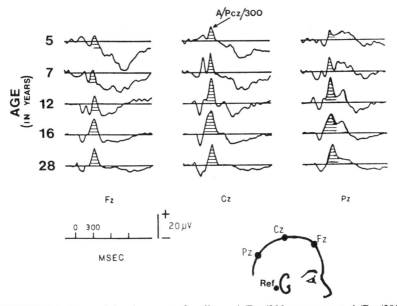

FIGURE 9-4. Normal development of auditory A/Pcz/300 component. A/Pcz/300 is elicited by novel sounds (complex, unrecognizable patchworks of vocalizations, mechanical noises, and digitally synthesized nonsense sounds) in people of various ages (age range: 4–44 years). Novel sounds occur occasionally ($p = .10$) in a series of monotonously presented sounds. Each trace is the average of five or more subjects per age group. Shaded component at each electrode site is A/Pcz/300. Adapted from Courchesne (1983).

stimulation. Recent research raises the possibility that it could be generated in the cortex and may be dependent, in part, upon noradrenergic input to the cortex from locus ceruleus (Pineda *et al.*, in press).

In our data, we have found that it is present at all ages between 4 and 44 years (Figure 9-4) (Courchesne, 1983). It is not known when it emerges during development, but ERP data from work in progress by Kurtzberg and Vaughan suggest to us that it may emerge very early indeed.

Since detecting, paying attention to, and learning about new events are essential requirements for normal development, a deficit in orienting to novelty could have considerable consequences. Such a deficit could be reflected in the A/Pcz/300 response to novelty. The A/Pcz/300 component has been studied in very similar experimental designs in autism, Down's syndrome, dyslexia, and attention deficit disorder (Courchesne, Kilman, Galambos, & Lincoln, 1984; Courchesne, Lincoln, Kilman, & Galambos, 1985; Holcomb *et al.*, 1986; Lincoln, Courchesne, Kilman, & Galambos, 1985). In each of these studies, a monotonous, repetitive series of stimuli was presented to subjects; occasionally, a surprising, novel sound (e.g., a patchwork of pieces of human vocalizations and mechanical noises), was inserted into this series. Subjects were not told that a novel sound would be presented. These designs were analogous to Sokolov-type research designs (Berlyne, 1960; Bernstein, 1979; Luria & Homskaya, 1970; Sokolov, 1958, 1960, 1963). To control for attention, general arousal, and cooperation, subjects were required to press a button whenever they detected a specific "target" sound (e.g., the word "you").

Infantile Autism

It has long been noted that autistic individuals do not orient normally to novel information. Our ERP evidence shows that pathophysiology in autism involves the A/Pcz/300 response to novelty (Courchesne *et al.*, 1984). The auditory A/Pcz/300 component was much smaller in autistic subjects than in normals (see Figure 9-5); however, it was still larger to the novel sounds than it was to the monotonous, insignificant sounds. This indicates that, although autistic subjects do detect and perceive novelty when it occurs, they nonetheless have a limited or diminished capacity to react to novelty relative to normals of all ages, even 4-year-olds—this despite the high level of functioning of these autistic subjects. The abnormality in the A/Pcz/300 response amplitude in autism is a developmental deficit or deviation rather than a developmental delay.

The smaller A/Pcz/300 in our autistic subjects may be a sign of defective mechanism(s) for the automatic detection of auditory novelty. Such a defec-

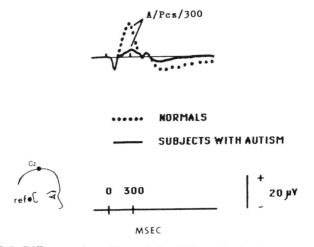

FIGURE 9-5. Differences in auditory A/Pcz/300 amplitudes between normal and autistic subjects. ERPs elicited by novel stimuli show the A/Pcz/300 component at the Cz electrode site in an experiment identical to that used to acquire the normative A/Pcz/300 data in Figure 9-4. The thick tracings are the averages of ERP responses form ten autistic subjects. Superimposed onto these are dotted tracings representing the averages of ERP responses from ten normal subjects. Adapted from Courchesne, Kilman, Galambos, and Lincoln (1984).

tive mechanism would involve the reticular formation, limbic structures, and prefrontal cortex (Groves & Lynch, 1972; Luria & Homskaya, 1970; O'Keefe, 1976; Ranck, 1973; Sokolov, 1963; Vinogradova, 1970). Adults who have sustained lesions of the prefrontal cortex also have smaller A/Pcz/300 responses to auditory novelty (Knight, 1984). This coincidence of results may be a useful clue about the neural disorder in autism.

Because autistic and normal subjects were almost equally accurate in giving a behavioral response to the targets (which were randomly mixed into the presentation of the novels and standards), the smaller A/Pcz/300 response cannot easily be accounted for by subject group differences in general arousal, cooperation, or task difficulty.

Down's Syndrome

In contrast to autism, the A/Pcz/300 is normal in *amplitude* in 12-year-olds with Down's syndrome when recorded in a design identical to that used in the above autism study (Figure 9-6) (Lincoln *et al.*, 1985). Although the A/Pcz/300 response amplitude is normal in 12-year-olds with Down's syndrome, this component is not completely normal in these children. Lincoln *et al.* (1985) found that the A/Pcz/300 *latency* in Down's syndrome was *later* than in mental-age-matched normal children (6-year-olds) as well as chronological-age-matched normal children (12-year-olds). Indeed, their latency

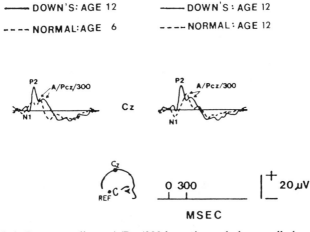

FIGURE 9-6. Longer auditory A/Pcz/300 latencies and abnormally large P2 amplitude in Down's syndrome compared to normal. ERPs elicited by novel stimuli in 12-year-old Down's syndrome children and normal 6- and 12-year-old children. A/Pcz/300 responses are shown at the Cz electrode site in an experiment identical to that used to acquire the normative A/Pcz/300 data in Figure 9-4 and A/Pcz/300 responses from autistic subjects shown in Figure 9-5. Adapted from Lincoln, Courchesne, Kilman, and Galambos (1985).

was even later than normal 4-year-olds (compare Figures 9-4 and 9-6). When A/Pcz/300 latency in this study is compared with that in comparable studies, it appears that it is later in Down's syndrome than in autistic, dyslexic, attention deficit disorder, as well as normal mental- and chronological-age-matched groups. Thus, the neural reaction to auditory novelty in Down's syndrome is much slower than in normals or in other developmental psychopathologies; but, when it does finally occur, the neural reaction that generates A/Pcz/300 has a magnitude similar to normal. So, once again (see above subsection on auditory brainstem responses), pathophysiology in Down's syndrome involves a latency abnormality; we shall see this type of abnormality again in the ERP data of Down's syndrome (see P3b and Nc subsections below).

Figure 9-6 shows another prominent feature of the Down's ERPs: a much larger than normal P2 amplitude. This has been found in response to monotonously presented stimuli as well as to novel stimuli (Callner, Dustman, Madsen, Schenkenberg, & Beck, 1978; Dustman & Callner, 1979; Lincoln *et al.*, 1985; Schafer & Peeke, 1982).

Dyslexia and Attention Deficit Disorder

Unlike the data on autism and Down's syndrome, A/Pcz/300 is normal in dyslexia and attention deficit disorder (Figure 9-7) (Holcomb *et al.*, 1986). It

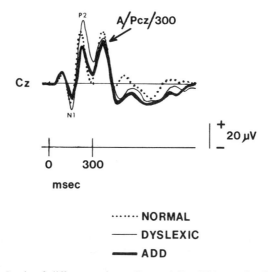

FIGURE 9-7. Lack of differences in auditory A/Pcz/300 amplitudes between normal, dyslexic, and attention deficit disorder (ADD) children (all subjects 8 to 11 years of age). Paradigm is similar to that used to acquire A/Pcz/300 data in Figures 9-4, 9-5, and 9-6. ERP data from ADD with and without hyperactivity are combined in this figure. It is our conclusion that the waveforms in this figure are A/Pcz/300 components and are so labeled by us; our conclusion is based on the fact that these waveforms are comparable to the A/Pcz/300 in Figure 9-4 in terms of latency, scalp topography, waveshape, amplitude, and the stimulus conditions that elicit them. Adapted from Holcomb, Ackerman, and Dykman (1986).

has normal amplitude and latency in these disorders. Thus, there is no ERP evidence of deficit in alerting to auditory novelty in these latter disorders.

In conclusion, present evidence shows that the abnormally small A/Pcz/ 300 amplitude (but normal latency) elicited by auditory novelty in autism may differentiate this disorder from Down's syndrome, dyslexia, and attention deficit disorder with and without hyperactivity.

The P3b Component

Normal: Basic and Developmental Evidence

P3b is one of the most thoroughly studied of all human ERP components (Pritchard, 1981; Sutton & Ruchkin, 1984). When recorded with scalp electrodes it appears largest in amplitude over the parietal cortex, and has a peak latency ranging from 280 to 1,000 milliseconds following stimulation (Figures 9-8 and 9-9).

Donchin has proposed that P3b is elicited when attention-getting or important information requires memory modification or updating of cognitive schemata (Donchin, 1981; Donchin et al., 1984). In experiments that require adults to make two or more rapid (e.g., in fractions of a second) conscious decisions about such information, we have shown that the P3b amplitude elicited by each decision is large even when each decision is separated by only 300–500 milliseconds (Figure 9-10) (Woods & Courchesne, 1986; Woods, Courchesne, Hillyard, & Galambos, 1980a, 1980b; Woods, Hillyard, Courchesne, & Galambos, 1980). Thus, the "recovery cycle" of P3b is very short (less than 300–500 milliseconds). The "recovery cycle" of a response is the minimum time interval that must exist between any two stimuli in order for the response to the second stimulus to be similar to the first. For instance, humans can make two or more conscious decisions in a row, provided that each is separated by at least 300–500 milliseconds. This may be referred to as the "psychological" recovery cycle.

A great deal of current research is focused on the question of the neural generators of P3b (Halgren et al., 1980; Harrison, Buchwald, & Kaga, 1986; Johnson & Fedio, in press; Knight, 1984; Pineda et al., in press; Smith, Stapleton, & Halgren, 1986; Wood & McCarthy, in press; Wood et al., 1984; Yingling & Hosobuchi, 1984). Although initial attention was focused on a possible generator in the medial temporal lobe, most especially the hippocampus, current hypotheses (Courchesne, Elmasian, et al., 1987) and animal research (Pineda et al., in press) seem to be pointing at cortical synaptic potentials triggered by noradrenergic input from locus ceruleus; the most recent depth electrode studies with humans have provided evidence also supporting the possibility of a cortical generator of P3b (Wood & McCarthy, in press).

Traditionally, it has been held that there is only one neural generator of P3b which serves all modalities (Pritchard, 1981). However, evidence from our studies on autism and dysphasia (see below) suggests a significant degree of independence of auditory P3b from visual P3b. In recent experiments on

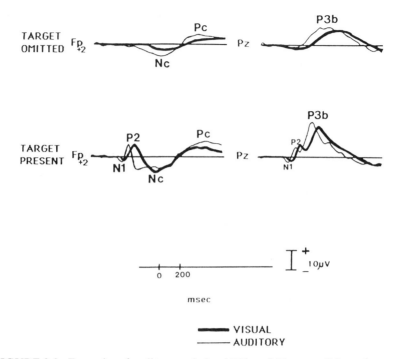

FIGURE 9-8. Examples of auditory and visual P3b and Nc, two of the endogenous components examined in this chapter, elicited in normal adult subjects. P3b and Nc are elicited by the correct detection of "target" events. Target events are of two types: (a) "target omitted" events are occasional stimulus omissions in sequences of non-target tones (or flashes); and (b) "target present" events are occasional tones or flashes that are different from the frequently presented nontarget tones (or flashes). P3b is elicited at an electrode site located over parietal cortex (Pz) at about the same time as Nc is elicited at an electrode site located over frontal cortex (Fp + 2, which is halfway between electrode locations Fp2 and F8 of the international 10–20 system). Exogenous components N1 and P2 are evoked only when the target event is actually a sensory stimulus (i.e., "target present" stimuli; bottom row). Exogenous components are evoked only by sensory stimuli, and cannot be evoked by stimulus omissions. So the ERPs to "target omitted" events are purely endogenous.

the recovery cycle of P3b in normal adults, we have shown that auditory P3b characteristics are not predictive of visual P3b characteristics within the same subject (Woods & Courchesne, in press). Also, in reevaluating the auditory P3b and visual P3b in children, we found these P3b responses to be also uncorrelated within the same subject (Courchesne, in press). Moreover, a review of cross-sectional studies of ERP development raises the possibility that auditory P3b and visual P3b have radically different developmental origins (Courchesne, in press). Resolution of this issue is of great importance to research on developmental psychopathologies

•

Grand Averages

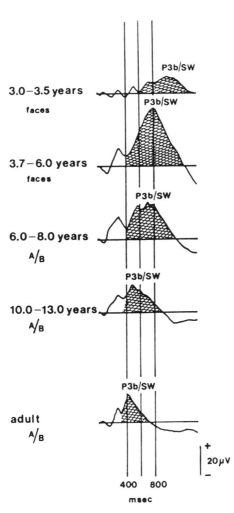

FIGURE 9-9. Normal development of P3b (P3b/SW complex) from early childhood to adulthood. P3b (P3b/SW complex) evoked by target stimuli ("target present" events) in subjects of different ages. These stimuli occurred infrequently in sequences of nontarget stimuli. P3b (P3b/SW complex) is shaded. Waveforms for 3- to 3.5-year-olds and 3.7- to 6.0-year-olds are from Courchesne, Ganz, and Norcia (1986) in which the target stimuli were human faces. Waveforms for 6- to 8-year-olds, 10- to 13-year-olds, and 24- to 36-year-olds are from Courchesne (1978) in which the target stimulus was the letter A and the nontarget stimulus was the letter B. Adapted from Courchesne, Ganz, and Norcia (1986).

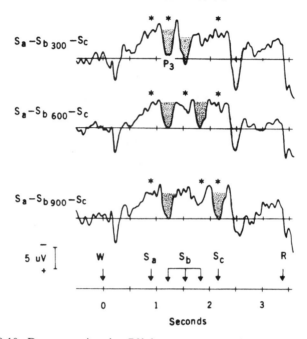

FIGURE 9-10. Demonstration that P3b has a recovery cycle that parallels the speed with which accurate decisions can be made in a signal detection task. On each trace, stimulus onsets are marked by an asterisk (*). The shaded downward deflections occurring about 300 milliseconds after stimulus onsets are P3b responses. Note that the P3b elicited by the second stimulus (Sb) is nearly as large as the P3b elicited by the first stimulus (Sa), even though stimulus Sb onsets as rapidly as 300 milliseconds (top trace), 600 milliseconds (middle trace), or 900 milliseconds (bottom trace) after stimulus Sa. *Note*: In contrast to other figures in this chapter, positivity (and hence P3b) is drawn *downward* here. From Woods, Hillyard, Courchesne, and Galambos (1980).

because P3b, particularly the auditory P3b, is abnormal in a number of these disorders.

Figure 9-9 shows the normal developmental sequence of the visual P3b. The visual P3b may begin to emerge before 2, and is quite distinct by 3 years of age (Courchesne, Ganz, & Norcia, 1986). Thereafter, the visual P3b is found in normal people of all ages (Courchesne, 1977, 1978, 1983; Mullis, Holcomb, Diner, & Dykman, 1985). Visual P3b latency in early childhood is about 600–800 milliseconds and decreases gradually until puberty, when its latency is about 400 milliseconds (Figure 9-9).

Data on the normal development of the auditory P3b may be interpreted in two ways (Courchesne, in press). First, its development exactly parallels that of the visual P3b, consistent with the traditional idea that there is only one P3b neural generator. Alternatively, the auditory P3b is a positivity with a latency of about 350 milliseconds at all ages. It grows in amplitude until preadolescence.

Auditory and visual P3b responses have been studied in a wide variety of developmental psychopathologies, including autism, receptive developmental dysphasia, Down's syndrome, mental retardation, attention deficit disorder, dyslexia, and childhood schizophrenia.

Infantile Autism

The pathophysiology in autism involves the auditory P3b; it is consistently smaller than normal (Courchesne *et al.*, 1984; Courchesne, Lincoln, *et al.*, 1985; Courchesne, Lincoln, Yeung-Courchesne, Elmasian, & Grillon, 1986; Dawson, Finley, Phillips, & Galpert, 1986; Martineau, Garreau, Barthelemy, & Lelord, 1984; Novick, Kurtzberg, & Vaughan, 1979; Novick *et al.*, 1980). Abnormally small auditory P3b amplitudes have been elicited by verbal, phonemic, nonverbal, and nonsenory (i.e., stimulus omissions) information in several laboratories in autistic children, adolescents, and adults whose nonverbal IQs range from 45 to 112. There is no doubt that an abnormally small auditory P3b is a ubiquitous characteristic in autism. For example, Novick *et al.* (1979, 1980) and Courchesne, Lincoln *et al.* (1986) asked autistic subjects to pay attention to sequences of tones (e.g., a 1,000-Hz tone) or colored flashes (e.g., red) and to press a button each time they detected an occasional stimulus change (e.g., a 2,000-Hz tone or a blue flash) or an *omission* of a stimulus. Figure 9-11 shows that the aberrantly small auditory P3b response in autism occurs whether the detected target event is the stimulus change or a stimulus omission. (Note that there is no sensory stimulus triggering the P3b elicited by a stimulus omission; the triggering is internally intiated by the subject's decision.)

In a recently completed experiment, we considered the possibility that the small auditory P3b amplitude in autism might be due to an abnormal P3b recovery cycle or to abnormal perception of a priori target probabilities. For instance, it might be the case that autistic people need longer intervals between successive pieces of information; otherwise they become overloaded. In our experiment we found that auditory P3b was abnormally small regardless of the rate of information delivery—that is, whether stimuli occurred in rapid succession with 0.4-second intervals or occurred very slowly with intervals of 5.0 seconds (Figure 9-12). Another possible explanation for the small P3b might be that autistic people do not keep a general notion of the overall ongoing stimulus context—for example, the global probability of certain important events (such as "target" stimuli to be responded to) that are taking place. In fact, the auditory P3b of the autistic people was abnormally small in response to important target information regardless of whether the information was very probable or highly improbable.

Therefore, evidence seems to be accumulating that the small auditory P3b is intrinsic to the physioanatomy of autism: it is present regardless of the

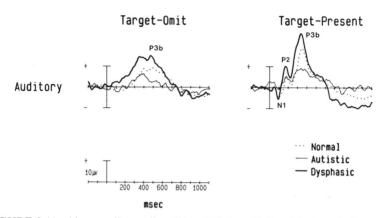

FIGURE 9-11. Abnormally small auditory P3b in autistic subjects and abnormally large auditory P3b in dysphasic subjects. These abnormalities were found no matter whether auditory P3b was elicited by a stimulus omission ("target omitted" event) or a target stimulus ("target present" event). The experimental design was identical to that described in Figure 9-8. Scalp electrode site showing P3b is Pz, located over parietal cortex. In addition to P3b, "target present" events elicited N1 ("N100") and P2 ("P200") components; they are exogenous components that must be elicited by a physical stimulus and cannot be elicited by an omitted event.

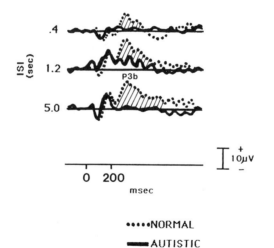

FIGURE 9-12. Demonstration that auditory P3b amplitudes in autism are small whether information is presented rapidly or slowly. Comparison of "recovery cycle" of P3b in normal and autistic subjects. P3b was elicited by auditory targets (tones) presented either 0.4, 1.2, or 5.0 seconds following another stimulus. In the results depicted, auditory targets ("target present" events) occurred on 50% of the total stimulus trials. Electrode site is Pz.

type of information eliciting it (verbal, nonverbal, even stimulus omissions), the rate of information delivery, or the a priori probability of important information. Moreover, the smaller auditory P3b cannot be due to poor understanding of the required task, poor task performance, or lack of cooperation because it occurs when autistic subjects perform as accurately and rapidly as normals (Courchesne et al., 1984; Courchesne, Lincoln, et al., 1985; Dawson et al., 1986; Novick et al., 1980). Nonetheless, if it is found that, for instance, special contextual factors, attentional demands, or incentive manipulations can produce normal amplitude auditory P3b responses, we would learn a great deal about autism.

Receptive Developmental Dysphasia

In our current research, subjects with receptive developmental dysphasia (whose severe language impairment and normal nonverbal abilities were stated earlier) had a P3b abnormality opposite to that in autism: they had abnormally enlarged auditory P3b (Figure 9-11 and 9-13) (Courchesne, Lincoln, et al., 1986). We found this enlarged auditory P3b under two

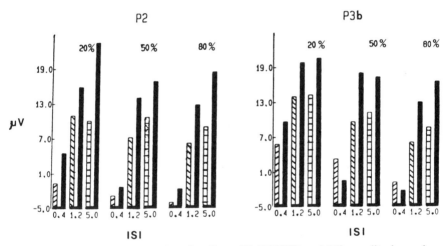

FIGURE 9-13. Recovery cycles of auditory P2 ("P200") and P3b amplitudes under different target a priori probability levels in dysphasic and normal subjects. It can be seen that auditory P2 amplitudes elicited by target stimuli (tones) in dysphasia are larger than P2 in normal subjects at 0.4-, 1.2-, and 5.0-second interstimulus intervals (ISIs) and at 20%, 50%, and 80% a priori probability levels. The figure also shows that auditory P3b amplitudes elicited by targets (tones) in dysphasia are larger than P3b in normal subjects except in two situations: at 0.4-second ISI when target a priori probabilities are 50% and 80%. Vertical axis: amplitude in microvolts; horizontal axis: ISI in seconds. (Black bars = dysphasics; shaded bars = normals.) Preliminary data are from research now in progress by Adams, Courchesne, Elmasian, and Lincoln.

information processing conditions; it was elicited by *omitted* target events as well as by targets that were stimulus changes. The enlarged auditory P3b in these dysphasic subjects is the first ERP evidence of aberrance in endogenous components in this developmental disorder.

However, in a recovery cycle experiment in progress, we have found an important exception to this overall finding of enlarged P3b in our dysphasic subjects. When we increased the rate of target information delivery by increasing the number of target detections they had to make in a short span of time, dysphasics had a smaller P3b than normals (in Figure 9-13 see conditions with 50% and 80% target probabilities when interstimulus intervals were 0.4 second). But as long as acoustical information was presented slowly and spread out across long intervals of 1 second or more, the P3b responses in dysphasics were abnormally large. These ERP effects were reflected in the behavioral performance of dysphasics in this high-speed decision-making task.

We have compared the auditory and visual P3b responses between autistic and dysphasic subjects (Courchesne, Lincoln, *et al.*, 1986). Although auditory P3b is abnormally small in autism and enlarged in dysphasia under most conditions, the visual P3b in each disorder is not statistically significantly different from normal, but does show trends that parallel the auditory P3b evidence.

The P2 component is an exogenous component preceding P3b. In research that characterized the recovery cycles of auditory P3b in autistic, dysphasic, and normal subject, we (Adams, Courchesne, Elmasian, & Lincoln, in press) also characterized the recovery cycle of the auditory vertex P2 (or P200) component in each group. The interesting finding was that at all interstimulus intervals (0.4, 1.2, and 5.0 seconds) and all a priori probabilities (20%, 50%, 80%), P2 in dysphasics was significantly enlarged compared to that of the normal and autistic groups (Figure 9-13). Thus, in addition to the enlarged auditory P3b, dysphasics have another enlarged auditory ERP component—that is, P2.

Down's Syndrome

Auditory P3b latency is longer in Down's syndrome than in age-matched normal people, but not as long as in normal children matched to them in mental age (Figure 9-14) (Lincoln *et al.*, 1985). Thus, in addition to abnormal latencies in the auditory brainstem ERPs and the A/Pcz/300 component in Down's syndrome, the P3b component is yet another one with abnormal latencies in this disorder. In fact, other ERP components—P2, SW, and Nc—are abnormally late as well (Figure 9-14). In addition to being abnormally late, P3b has an abnormal amplitude at central and frontal scalp electrode sites; at these locations it is much larger in amplitude than in chronological-age-matched and mental-age-matched normals (Figure 9-14). This was also true of P2; once again P2 in Down's is larger than normal (see

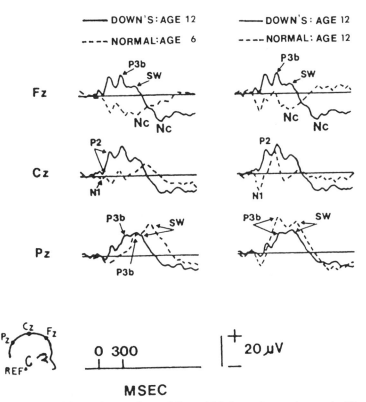

FIGURE 9-14. Evidence that auditory P3b and Nc latencies are longer in 12-year-old Down's syndrome children than in age-matched normal children. It can also be seen that P3b amplitude is larger at central and frontal sites in Down's syndrome children than in normal children. Adapted from Lincoln, Courchesne, Kilman, and Galambos (1985).

Figure 9-6) (Callner *et al.*, 1978; Dustman & Callner, 1979; Schafer & Peeke, 1982). Indeed, the waveshape involving P2, P3b, and SW at central and frontal electrode sites is strikingly different from any normal developmental pattern (Courchesne, 1983) and from any pattern in other developmental disorders.

Dyslexia and Attention Deficit Disorder

In contrast to autism and dysphasia in which only the auditory P3b seems particularly abnormal, children with dyslexia and attention deficit disorder (with and without hyperactivity) have abnormal P3b responses in both auditory and visual modalities. In studies of these disorders, auditory and visual P3b have been found to be smaller than normal in information processing conditions that require subjects to sustain attention for long periods of time while performing relatively monotonous signal detection tasks (Holcomb, Ackerman, & Dykman, 1985; Holcomb *et al.*, 1986; Loiselle, Stamm, Maitinsky, & Whipple, 1980; Lovrich & Stamm 1983). However, P3b was not abnormal in a study that required hyperactive subjects to pay attention for only very brief moments to important information (Prichep, Sutton, & Hakerem, 1976). In Prichep *et al.* (1976), subjects were asked to play a guessing game; they were given money for every correct guess, but no punishment for incorrect guesses. Under these conditions, hyperactive boys and normal boys had statistically similar auditory P3b responses to "target present" events and to "omitted" events.

The Nc Component

Normal: Basic and Developmental Evidence

Nc is elicited by any attention-getting information, be it novel, surprising, or significant. In fact, Nc is elicited by attention-getting, orienting stimuli just as is the RAS (reticular–thalamic–cortical activating system). When recorded with scalp electrodes, Nc appears largest in amplitude over frontal and central cortex, and has a peak latency ranging from 350 to 1,000 milliseconds following stimulation (Figures 9-15 and 9-16). We have suggested elsewhere that Nc is generated by depolarizing potentials in cortical synapses, which are triggered by input from the intralaminar thalamic nuclei as one phase of the action of the RAS (Courchesne, 1987; Courchesne, Elmasian, *et al.*, 1987).

In the process of investigating Nc in autism and dysphasia, we have just completed studies that have established two basic facts about Nc. First, we established that Nc is a purely endogenous component by showing that it is elicited by the omission (or absence) of a stimulus when it was the subject's task to detect this omission (Figure 9-8). Thus Nc meets one of the central criteria for being an endogenous component (Donchin, Ritter, & McCallum, 1978), defined as neurophysiological responses initiated by internal attentional and cognitive mechanisms. Since Nc may be present at birth (Kurtzberg, 1985; Kurtzberg & Vaughan, 1985), establishing that Nc is an endogenous component could significantly influence theories of the development of human cognition and consciousness.

In addition to proving that Nc is an endogenous component, we have also shown for the first time the normal recovery cycle of Nc (Figure 9-17). Its recovery cycle is between 400 and 1,200 milliseconds (Figure 9-17), which is similar to recovery cycle data on two other endogenous components, P3b and Nd (Woods & Courchesne, 1986). These short recovery cycles of endogenous components distinguish them from the recovery cycles of exogenous, stimulus-dependent components, which can be up to 10 seconds or more.

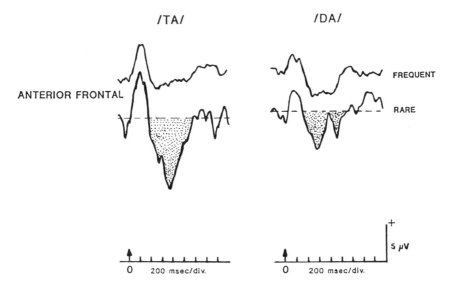

FIGURE 9-15. Nc component at frontal electrode sites in normal neonates (high-lighted by stippled area). It is our conclusion that the stippled waveforms in this figure are Nc components, as discussed in the text; our conclusion is based on the comparability of the conditions triggering these waveforms and on the comparability of their latencies, scalp topography, waveshape, and amplitudes to those Nc components found by and predicted from the research of Courchesne (1977, 1978, 1983), Courchesne, Ganz, and Norcia (1981), Holcomb, Ackerman, and Dykman (1985, 1986), and Karrer and Ackles (in press). Nc in neonates is largest at electrode sites over frontal cortex (but the Nc waveform is evident at all electrode sites shown), and larger in amplitude when elicited by an infrequently presented novel ("rare") stimulus randomly occurring in a series of frequently presented ("frequent") stimuli. In some sequences, the "rare" stimulus was the sound /da/ and the "frequent" stimulus was the sound /ta/, and in others, the reverse was true. ERPs are grand-average responses from 14 full-term normal neonates. Note that Nc latency is about 600 to 800 milliseconds, and amplitudes at frontal sites are about 5 to 9 microvolts. Adapted from Kurtzberg, (1985).

Our report that Nc could be found in infants (Courchesne, Ganz, & Norcia, 1981) has been confirmed by sophisticated studies conducted in other laboratories (Karrer & Ackles, in press; Kurtzberg, 1985; Kurtzberg & Vaughan, 1985). They show that Nc may be elicited in the newborn by auditory information (Figure 9-15) (Kurtzberg, 1985) and, in the 2-month-old, by visual information (Karrer & Ackles, in press). Nc is found in normal people from birth through adulthood (Figures 9-15 and 9-16) (Courchesne, 1977, 1978, 1983; Courchesne et al., 1981; Holcomb et al., 1985; Karrer & Ackles, in press; Kurtzberg, 1985).

Developmental changes in Nc amplitude and latency parallel developmental changes in the number of cortical synapses and in myelination of the

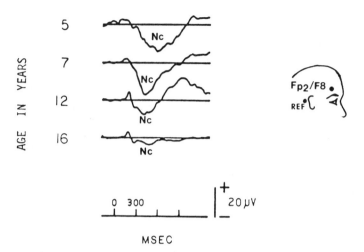

FIGURE 9-16. Normal development of Nc from childhood to adulthood in response to novel sounds. Nc is elicited in the same experiment, in the same subjects, and by the same novel sounds as A/Pcz/300 in Figure 9-4. As shown, Nc latency and amplitude change with development. Nc is elicited at an electrode site located over frontal cortex (midway between electrode locations Fp2 and F8 of the international 10–20 system). Adapted from Courchesne (1983).

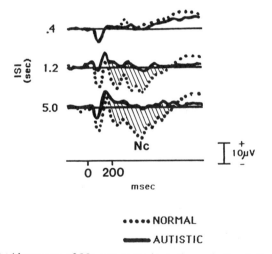

FIGURE 9-17. Aberrance of Nc responses in autism whether information is presented rapidly or slowly. Comparison of "recovery cycle" of Nc in normal and autistic subjects. Nc was elicited by auditory targets (tones) presented 0.4, 1.2, and 5.0 seconds following another stimulus. In the results depicted, auditory targets ("target present" events) occurred on 50% of the total stimulus trials. In autism, Nc is negligible at all ISIs, even at very long ISIs of 5 seconds. In normals, Nc is negligible at ISIs of 0.4 second, but is fully recovered in amplitude at ISIs of 1.2 and 5 seconds. Scalp electrode site showing Nc is located over frontal cortex midway between Fp2 and F8.

nonspecific thalamic radiations, which include fibers from the intralaminar thalamic nuclei (Courchesne, in press; Courchesne, Elmasian, *et al.*, 1987). First, in the human and nonhuman primate, the number of cortical synapses in frontal cortex increases greatly during infancy and early childhood, and thereafter decreases gradually until puberty (Huttenlocher, 1979; Rakic, Bourgeois, Eckenhoff, Zecevic, & Goldman-Rakic, 1986). Nc amplitude increases and decreases in parallel with these changes (Courchesne, in press). Second, Nc latency decreases from about 800–1,000 milliseconds in infants to about 350–500 milliseconds by 7 years of age. This parallels the time course of myelination of the nonspecific thalamic radiations (increases in myelin increase neural transmission speed and thereby decrease response latencies) (Courchesne, in press).

Infantile Autism

We have found solid evidence that pathophysiology in autism involves the Nc response (Figures 9-17 and 9-18) (Courchesne, 1987; Courchesne, Lincoln, *et al.*, 1985). Nc is aberrant under a variety of experimental conditions in both auditory and visual modalities. It is usually abnormally small and, under some conditions, a positive potential is present instead of the normal negative Nc potential.

We have recorded the Nc response elicited by (1) auditory and visual stimuli; (2) auditory and visual targets of various sorts, such as spoken

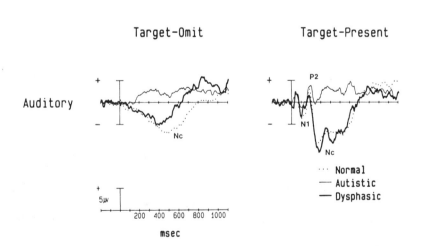

FIGURE 9-18. Aberrant Nc in autistic subjects contrasted with normal Nc in dysphasic and normal subjects. These abnormalities were found no matter whether Nc was elicited by a stimulus omission ("target omitted" event) or a target stimulus ("target present" event). The experimental design was identical to that described in Figure 9-8. Scalp electrode site showing Nc is located over frontal cortex midway between Fp2 and F8.

words, tones, omitted auditory stimuli, letters, flashes of a colored slide, and omitted visual stimuli; and (3) auditory and visual targets presented at various a priori probabilities (20%, 50%, 80%), and at various inter-stimulus intervals (0.4, 1.0, 1.2, and 5.0 seconds) (Courchesne, 1987; Courchesne, Lincoln, et al., 1985; and research in progress). In these experiments, autistic subjects performed required tasks as accurately as normal—and often as rapidly. Yet their ERPs show that they did so with abnormal neurophysiology.

In nearly all experiments, Nc responses were either aberrantly small or were "replaced" by a *positive* potential at the latency range normally occupied by the negative Nc potential (Figures 9-17 and 9-18). This Nc pathophysiology was present in even the simplest and least demanding information processing conditions (such as the detection of nonverbal stimulus changes or stimulus omission: Figure 9-18), as well as in more complex and demanding tasks (Figure 9-17). We have found that, in order to get near-normal Nc amplitudes, the most extremely deviant auditory stimuli (e.g., clanging, ringing, novel sounds) must be presented; with anything less, Nc becomes very small or is replaced by the aberrant positive potential. This positive potential does not appear to be simply the absence of Nc, because target stimuli actually elicited significantly more positivity than did nontarget stimuli. This pattern is opposite to that of normals, in whom target stimuli elicited more negative Nc amplitudes than did nontargets. Thus, this pathophysiology may reflect abnormal neural physiology, not just an absence or diminution of normal physiology.

The concept of an "endogenous" neurophysiological response, and proof that Nc is such a response, is especially important in autism. The aberrant "Nc" response elicited by stimulus omissions in autism is indicative of an impairment of the *internal initiation* of attentional mechanisms; but the presence of Nc (albeit small) in response to stimuli that are extreme in some way may indicate that, in autism, special external events may be required to engage the attentional mechanisms underlying Nc.

As we mentioned above, one candidate neural generator of Nc is the initial depolarization in superficial layers of cortex, which occurs as one phase of the action of the RAS. It is interesting that aberrant RAS functioning was the first neurobiological hypothesis proposed to explain autism (Rimland, 1964). This system is crucial to the activation, adjustment, and maintenance of attention and consciousness (Castaigne, Buge, Escourolle, & Masson, 1962; Facon, Steriade, & Wertheim, 1958; Hobson & Steriade, 1985; Steriade & Glenn, 1982). Faulty function of this system from the earliest days of development could explain autism (Courchesne, 1987; Rimland, 1964). If we could determine whether Nc is aberrant in autistic infants and young children, and whether Nc is indeed generated by the physiological activity of the RAS, a major advance in our understanding of autism would be achieved.

Receptive Developmental Dysphasia

On the other hand, in these same series of experiments, we have found Nc to be within normal limits in dysphasics (Figure 9-18) (Courchesne, Lincoln, *et al.*, 1986).

Down's Syndrome

Karrer and Ackles (in press) have recorded Nc in 6-, 12-, and 24-month-old Down's syndrome babies. The latency and amplitude of Nc was comparable to normal infants. However, whereas normal babies have Nc amplitudes that are larger in response to surprising stimuli than to repetitively presented stimuli, Down's babies have *similar* Nc amplitudes in response to surprising and repetitively presented stimuli. Thus, the Down's baby is nonselectively responsive to any stimulus change.

Lincoln *et al.* (1985) found that 12-year-old Down's syndrome children had abnormally prolonged Nc latencies in response to "target present" events (Figure 9-14). In fact, Nc latencies were as late as those in normal infants and very young children. The fact that Nc latency in preadolescent Down's children is no earlier than in Down's babies may reflect the failure of pathways involved in the generation of Nc to myelinate properly. The Nc latency abnormalities in Down's syndrome preadolescents and the nonselective responsiveness in even 24-month-old Down's babies differentiate Down's pathophysiology from autism, receptive developmental dysphasia, dyslexia, and attention deficit disorder. Whether these abnormalities differentiate Down's from other forms of mental retardation remain to be established.

Dyslexia and Attention Deficit Disorder

Holcomb *et al.* (1985, 1986) recently reported that, when elicited by "target present" auditory or visual events comparable to those we have used to study autism and dysphasia, Nc is normal in dyslexic and attention deficit disorder children (Figure 9-19).

PATTERNS OF PATHOPHYSIOLOGY

Infantile autism, receptive developmental dysphasia, Down's syndrome, and dyslexia and attention deficit disorder exhibit different patterns of pathophysiology.

Infantile Autism

The ERP data suggest that, in autism, attentional mechanisms function aberrantly, and do so in a fashion unlike any other developmental psychopathology. We suggest that pathophysiology in attentional mechanisms is

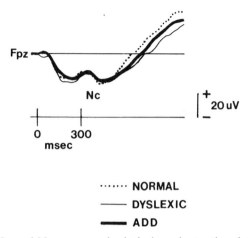

······· **NORMAL**

——— **DYSLEXIC**

━━━ **ADD**

FIGURE 9-19. Normal Nc responses in dyslexia and attention deficit disorder. Nc elicited by "target present" events in an experimental design analogous to that used to acquire the Nc data on autism in Figure 9-18. Scalp electrode site at Fpz, over frontal cortex. ADD = attention deficit disorder (with and without hyperactivity combined in this figure). Adapted from Holcomb, Ackerman, and Dykman (1986).

fundamental to autism. It impedes the proper selective enhancement or alteration of attention in response to important or new information.

The ERP data on Nc point to either a malfunctioning of the reticular activating system or an abnormal modulation of its functioning by other neural systems (such as cerebellum, hippocampus, frontal cortex, or nucleus reticularis) (Courchesne, 1987). The precise points and nature of the malfunctioning now need to be determined (see Courchesne, Hesselink, Jernigan, & Yeung-Courchesne, 1987; Courchesne, Yeung-Courchesne, Press, Hesselink, & Jernigan, 1987). This can be done by systematically assessing the functioning of several ERP components. A/Pcz/300 is very likely to be generated by noradrenergic input to cortex from locus ceruleus, and this may also be the case for auditory P3b. The CNV is generated by acetylcholine input to cortex from nucleus basalis (a system implicated in Alzheimer's dementia), and is triggered by important, attention-getting events. Nc is generated by a physiological system apparently functional at birth, and is probably dependent upon either the reticular activating system or the nucleus basalis–acetylcholine system.

The nucleus reticularis of the thalamus modulates sensory transmission through the thalamus as well as the functioning of the reticular activating system at the thalamic level. Although modulation of sensory transmission—as distinct from attentional modulation—has been suggested to be abnormal in autism, there is no single methodologically valid ERP study that supports this contention. Even so, ERPs might be able to provide evidence regarding modulation of sensory transmission at this level if the necessary state-of-the-art designs were attempted.

Auditory sensory functioning from the periphery up through the thalamic sensory relay station (as indexed by auditory brainstem ERPs) is intact. Behavioral performance on tasks that revealed aberrant attentional neurophysiology indicates that autistic people are capable of normal sensory perception, recognition, categorization, and motor response selection. The speed of information processing is also normal at all levels of neurophysiological functioning as indicated by ERP latencies from the earliest sensory responses to the latest cognitive ones.

Receptive Developmental Dysphasia

There are vanishingly few studies of this disorder. The available data, including research in progress in our laboratory, suggests that there may be an unusual pattern of pathophysiology in people who have severe receptive language problems but normal nonverbal IQ. We have found that two auditory components have unusually enlarged amplitudes; the components are a sensory one, P2, and a cognitive one, P3b. Visual ERP responses have not yet been found to differ from normal controls. No other developmental psychopathology has such a pattern.

This pattern raises the question of whether the pathophysiology in these dysphasic subjects is due to an auditory-specific deficit in inhibitory or neuromodulatory mechanisms at several levels of the brain. Perhaps a neurochemical explanation of this deficit would seem to be an appropriate initial working hypothesis. Nonetheless, an important question now is whether this abnormal pattern of ERP responses in receptive dysphasia occurs only in the auditory modality. Detailed studies of sensory and cognitive (exogenous and endogenous) components in the visual and somatosensory modalities are needed. Also, the functional consequences of the enlarged ERP responses remain to be ascertained.

The P3b recovery cycle in dysphasia seems to suggest that when a great deal of auditory target information is packed into a very short period of time, dysphasics are unable to make rapid, accurate, and conscious decisions about that information. These neurophysiological data predict, for example, that if dysphasics were spoken to rapidly, they would have a great deal of trouble comprehending the information. In fact, these neurophysiological results are compatible with Tallal's (1985) theory that dysphasia is due to impairments in the processing of rapid acoustical information and that one must slow down acoustic information if dysphasics are to sucessfully comprehend it.

Tallal (1985) argues that the impairment in dysphasia is fundamentally one of acoustic temporal processing, rather than of linguistic processing. That is, the linguistic impairment in dysphasia is due to this more basic level of processing sound. An analogous position in autism, is Rutter's (1979, 1983) contention that the social deficits in autism result from more basic cognitive processes. Research shows that the pathophysiologies in autism and dysphasia appeared even in the absence of sensory and linguistic stimulation and were independent of whether sensory stimulation was present or completely absent (Figures 9-11 and 9-18). Thus, ERP data concur with the position of these theorists that abnormality in autism and receptive dysphasia are not easily explained in terms of linguistic dysfunction per se.

Aside from the research on receptive developmental dysphasia discussed herein, we are not aware of any other ERP studies of cognitive, "endogenous" ERPs in this disorder. Clearly, a great deal remains to be learned. For instance, since receptive developmental dysphasia is likely to be composed of neurobiologically distinct subgroups, another important question is whether the findings on the severely impaired dysphasics mark them as one such subgroup.

Down's Syndrome

Down's syndrome involves substantial neuropathology throughout the nervous system, including maldevelopment of dendrites, dendritic spines, synapses, myelin, and cortical gyri (Malamud & Hirano, 1974; Takashima, Becker, Armstrong, & Chan, 1981). This disorder also involves equally substantial pathophysiology at many stages from the earliest auditory brainstem ones to later cognitive ones. The most common finding is that component latencies are abnormally prolonged (P2, P3b, Nc, A/Pcz/300), and probably reflect both a failure of normal myelinogenesis and reduced processing capacity. The earlier-than-normal latencies of their auditory brainstem responses remain unexplained by experimentation, but they could reflect reduced inhibitory or integrative mechanisms in these brainstem neural systems.

The tremendously enlarged P2 in Down's syndrome (Figures 9-6 and 9-14) (Callner et al., 1978; Dustman & Callner, 1979; Lincoln et al., 1985; Schafer & Peeke, 1982) is reminiscent of the enlarged P2 in receptive developmental dysphasia. Reduced inhibition has been considered to be the explanation for the enlarged P2 responses in Down's syndrome (Schafer & Peeke, 1982).

The observation that P3b is large at frontal and central scalp electrode sites is not surprising when we consider that cortical gyri are malformed and the anterior–posterior span of cortex is abnormal. In addition, the unusual scalp location of P3b results not only from the position of its neural generators, but also from the way other components, such as Nc, overlap P3b in time. Normally, Nc occurs at about the same time as P3b at frontal sites; thus, P3b may be "sitting" in the negative trough of Nc at those sites. In Down's syndrome, Nc latency is apparently very late and occurs *after* the auditory P3b; in this way the P3b may appear to be more positive because it is not "sitting" in the negative trough of Nc as is the case with normals. The complete pattern of pathophysiology in Down's is unlike that of any other developmental disorder or any stage in normal development.

Dyslexia and Attention Deficit Disorder

Given sufficiently attention-getting or interesting information or monetary rewards, children with these disorders have normal-appearing attention-related A/Pcz/300, Nc, and auditory P3b responses, and, in behavioral studies, they may perform as well as normals when given monetary incentives (Douglas, 1983). Given sufficiently long and boring tasks with no rewards, P3b responses elicited by "task-relevant" target stimuli in these children are smaller than normal children (Holcomb et al., 1985, 1986).

The P3b component, in particular, may be a sensitive index of the degree to which dyslexic and attention deficit disorder children are actively engaged in a task. Further, within a task, ERPs may be a sensitive index of what specific type of information they attend to in a normal fashion. For instance, in a long and boring task, they produce large ERP responses to novel sounds similar to normals, but concurrently produce smaller-than-normal P3b responses to ordinary 2,000-Hz target tones (Holcomb et al., 1986).

Systematic ERP studies of dyslexia and attention deficit disorder are needed to establish precisely which conditions and types of stimuli engage and sustain active attention and which do not. Also needed are ERP studies that chart the time course of attentional changes across seconds and minutes during task performance. For example, in boring vigilance tasks the average P3b response is smaller than normal; but what about the first trial or first few trials versus later trials? How quickly does attention wane and what controls the rate of waning? ERPs are very sensitive indices of moment-to-moment fluctuations in information processing, but this sensitivity has yet to be translated into studies of different facets of attention capability in dyslexia and attention deficit disorder. If such systematic studies are focused on factors that have ecological validity, they might be especially helpful to parents and teachers for improving behavior at school and at home.

Studies of dyslexia have yet to take advantage of research during the past 6 years that shows that the N400 component in adults is an index of semantic expectancies during natural reading as well as during semantic priming tasks (Kutas & Hillyard, 1980, 1984). To do so, however, researchers will first have to determine the normal development of this ERP component.

CONCLUDING REMARKS

Each of the developmental disorders we have examined has its own distinctive pattern of pathophysiology. It is these *patterns* that characterize a disorder. A single abnormality of an ERP component, when seen in isolation, is insufficient to diagnose or understand a disorder. For example, P2 is abnormally large in both receptive developmental dysphasia and Down's syndrome. However, receptive developmental dysphasia is distinguished by a pattern of abnormally large positive peaks, whereas Down's syndrome shows a pattern of increased latency of virtually all ERP peaks that occur beyond the brainstem level. Likewise, a single test condition is insufficient to determine the functioning of a particular component. For example, at slow stimulation rates, P3b amplitude was enlarged in our dysphasic subjects, but at very fast rates when many targets had to be detected, it was not enlarged. Thus, it is not an abnormality in a single component by itself, but rather the overall pattern of normal and abnormal sensory and cognitive physiology in auditory, visual, and somatosensory modalities that differentiates one disorder from another.

ACKNOWLEDGMENTS

This work was supported by NIMH grant 1-R01-MH36840 and by NINCDS grant 5-R01-NS19855 awarded to Eric Courchesne. Special thanks to Robert Elmasian for his valuable comments on the manuscript.

REFERENCES

Achor, L. J., & Starr, A. (1980a). Auditory brain stem responses in the cat. I. Intracranial and extracranial recordings. *Electroencephalography and Clinical Neurophysiology, 48*, 154–173.

Achor, L. J., & Starr, A. (1980b). Auditory brain stem responses in the cat. II. Effects of lesions. *Electroencephalography and Clinical Neurophysiology, 48,* 174–190.

Adams, J., Courchesne, E., Elmasian, R. O., & Lincoln, A. J. (in press). Increased amplitude of the auditory P2 and P3b components in adolescents with developmental dysphasia. *Electroencephalography and Clinical Neurophysiology, Supplement.*

American Psychiatric Association. (1980). *Diagnostic and statistical manual of mental disorders* (3rd ed.). Washington, DC: Author.

Berlyne, D. D. (1960). *Conflict, arousal and curiosity.* New York: McGraw-Hill.

Bernstein, A. S. (1979). The orienting response as novelty and significance detector: Reply to O'Gorman. *Psychophysiology, 16*, 263–273.

Callner, D. A., Dustman, R. E., Madsen, J. A., Schenkenberg, T., & Beck, E. C. (1978). Life span changes in the average evoked responses of Down's syndrome and non-retarded persons. *American Journal of Mental Deficiency, 82*, 398–405.

Castaigne, P., Buge, A., Escourolle, R., & Masson, M. (1962). Ramollissement pédonculaire médian, tegmento-thalamique avec ophtalmoplégie et hypersomnie. *Revue Neurologique, 106*, 357–367.

Courchesne, E. (1977). Event-related brain potentials: A comparison between children and adults. *Science, 197*, 589–592.

Courchesne, E. (1978). Neurophysiological correlates of cognitive development: Changes in long-latency event-related potentials from childhood to adulthood. *Electroencephalography and Clinical Neurophysiology, 45*, 468–482.

Courchesne, E. (1983). Cognitive components of the event-related brain potential: Changes associated with development. In A. W. K. Gaillard & W. Ritter (Eds.). *Tutorials in ERP research: Endogenous components* (pp. 329–344). Amsterdam: North-Holland.

Courchesne, E. (1987). A neurophysiological view of autism. In E. Schopler & G. B. Mesibov (Eds.), *Neurobiological issues in autism* (pp. 285–234). New York: Plenum.

Courchesne, E. (in press). Chronology of postnatal human brain development: ERP, PET, myelinogenesis, and synaptogenesis studies. In J. W. Rohrbaugh, R. Parasuraman, & R. Johnson (Eds.), *Event-related brain potentials: Issues and interdisciplinary vantages*. New York: Oxford.

Courchesne, E., Courchesne, R. Y., Hicks, G., & Lincoln, A. J. (1985). Functioning of the brainstem auditory pathway in non-retarded autistic individuals. *Electroencephalography and Clinical Neurophysiology, 61*, 491–501.

Courchesne, E., Elmasian, R. O., & Yeung-Courchesne, R. (1987). Electrophysiological correlates of cognitive processing: P3b and Nc, basic, clinical and developmental research. In A. M. Halliday, S. R. Butler, & R. Paul (Eds.), *A textbook of clinical neurophysiology* (pp. 645–676). New York: Wiley.

Courchesne, E., Ganz, L., & Norcia, A. (1981). Event-related brain potentials to human faces in infants. *Child Development, 52*, 804–811.

Courchesne, E., Ganz, L., & Norcia, A. (1986). *The P3b/SW complex in young children in a face discrimination task*. Manuscript submitted for publication.

Courchesne, E., Hesselink, J. R., Jernigan, T. L., & Yeung-Courchesne, R. (1987). Abnormal neuroanatomy in a non-retarded person with autism. *Archives of Neurology, 44*, 335–341.

Courchesne, E., Kilman, B. A., Galambos, R., and Lincoln, A. J. (1984). Autism: Processing of novel auditory information assessed by event-related brain potentials. *Electroencephalography and Clinical Neurophysiology: Evoked Potentials, 59*, 238-248.

Courchesne, E., Lincoln, A. J., Kilman, B. A., & Galambos, R. (1985). Event-related brain potential correlates of the processing of novel visual and auditory information in autism. *Journal of Autism and Developmental Disorders, 15*, 55–76.

Courchesne, E., Lincoln, A. J., Yeung-Courchesne, R., Elmasian, R., & Grillon, C. (1986). *Pathophysiologic findings in social and language disorders: Autism and receptive developmental dysphasia*. Manuscript submitted for publication.

Courchesne, E., Yeung-Courchesne, R., Press, G., Hesselink, J. R., & Jernigan, T. L. (1987). *Hypoplasia of cerebellar vermal lobules VI and VII in infantile autism*. Manuscript submitted for publication.

Dawson, G., Finley, C., Phillips, P., & Galpert, L. (1986). *P300 of the auditory evoked potential and the language abilities of autistic children*. Unpublished manuscript.

Donchin, E. (1981). Surprise! ... Surprise? *Psychophysiology, 18*, 493–513.

Donchin, E., Heffly, E., Hillyard, S. A., Loveless, N., Maltzman, I., Ohman, A., Rosler, F., Ruchkin, D., & Siddle, D. (1984). Cognition and event-related potentials: II. The orienting reflex and P300. In R. Karrer, J. Cohen, & P. Tueting (Eds.), *Brain and information: Event-related potentials* (pp. 39–57). New York: New York Academy of Sciences.

Donchin, E., Ritter, W., & McCallum, W. C. (1978). Cognitive psychophysiology: The endogenous components of the ERP. In E. Callaway, P. Tueting, & S. H. Koslow (Eds.), *Event-related brain potentials in man* (pp. 349–411). New York: Academic Press.

Douglas, V. I. (1983). Attentional and cognitive problems. In M. Rutter (Ed.), *Developmental neuropsychiatry* (pp. 280–329). New York: Guilford.

Dustman, R. E., & Callner, D. A. (1979). Cortical evoked responses and response decrement in non-retarded and Down's syndrome individuals. *American Journal of Mental Deficiency, 83*, 391–397.

Facon, E., Steriade, M., & Wertheim, N. (1958). Hypersomie prolongée engendrée par des lésions bilatérales du système activateur médial. Le syndrôme thrombotique de la bifurcation du tronc basilaire. *Revue Neurologique, 106*, 357–367.

Galambos, R. (1982). Maturation of auditory evoked potentials. In G. A. Chiarenza & D. Papakostopoulos (Eds.), *Clinical application of cerebral evoked potentials in pediatric medicine* (pp. 323–343). Amsterdam: Excerpta Media.

Gillberg, C., Rosenhall, U., & Johansson, E. (1983). Auditory brainstem responses in childhood psychosis. *Journal of Autism and Developmental Disorders, 13*, 181–195.

Groves, P. M., & Lynch, G. S. (1972). Mechanisms of habituation in the brain stem *Psychological Review*, *79*, 237–244.

Halgren, E., Squires, N. K., Wilson, C. L., Rohrbaugh, J. W., Babb, T. L., & Crandall, P. H. (1980). Endogenous potentials generated in the human hippocampal-formation and amygdala by infrequent events. *Science*, *210*, 803–805.

Harrison, J., Buchwald, J., & Kaga, K. (1986). Cat P300 present after primary auditory cortex ablation. *Electroencephalography and Clinical Neurophysiology*, *63*, 180–187.

Hobson, J. A., & Steriade, M. (1985). The neuronal basis of behavioral state control: Internal systems of the brain. In F. E. Bloom (Ed.), *Handbook of physiology: Intrinsic regulatory systems of the brain*. Bethesda, MD: American Physiology Society Press.

Holcomb, P. J., Ackerman, P. T., & Dykman, R. A. (1985). Cognitive event-related brain potentials in children with attention and reading deficits. *Psychophysiology*, *22*, 656–667.

Holcomb, P. J., Ackerman, P. T., & Dykman, R. A. (1986). Auditory event-related potentials in attention and reading disabled boys. *International Journal of Psychophysiology*, *3*, 263–273.

Huttenlocher, P. R. (1979). Synaptic density in human frontal cortex—Developmental changes and effects of aging. *Brain Research*, *163*, 195–205.

Johnson, R., Jr., & Fedio, P. (in press). Task-related changes in P300 scalp distribution in temporal lobectomy patients. *Electroencephalography and Clinical Neurophysiology*, *Supplement*.

Karrer, R. & Ackles, P. K. (in press). Visual event-related potentials of infants during a modified oddball procedure. *Electroencephalography and Clinical Neurophysiology*, *Supplement*.

Knight, R. (1984). Decreased response to novel stimuli after prefrontal lesions in man. *Electroencephalography and Clinical Neurophysiology, Evoked Potentials*, *59*, 9–20.

Kurtzberg, D. (1985). *Late auditory evoked potentials and speech sound discrimination in newborns*. Paper presented at the meeting of the Society for Research in Child Development, Toronto.

Kurtzberg, D., & Vaughan, H. G., Jr. (1985). Electrophysiologic assessment of auditory and visual function in the newborn. *Clinics in Perinatology*, *12*, 277–299.

Kutas, M., & Hillyard, S. A. (1980). Reading between the lines: Event-related brain potentials during natural sentence processing. *Brain and Language*, *11*, 354–373.

Kutas, M., & Hillyard, S. A. (1984). Brain potentials during reading reflect word expectancy and semantic association. *Nature*, *307*, 161–163.

Legatt, A. D., Arezzo, J. C., & Vaughan, H. G., Jr. (1986a). Short latency auditory evoked potentials in the monkey. I. Wave shape and surface topography. *Electroencephalography and Clinical Neurophysiology*, *64*, 41–52.

Legatt, A. D., Arezzo, J. C., & Vaughan, H. G., Jr., (1986b). Short latency auditory evoked potentials in the monkey. II. Intracranial generators. *Electroencephalography and Clinical Neurophysiology*, *64*, 53-73.

Lincoln, A. J., Courchesne, E., Kilman, B. A., & Galambos, R. (1985). Neurophysiological correlates of information processing in children with Down's syndrome. *American Journal of Mental Deficiency*. *89*, 403–414.

Loiselle, D. L., Stamm, J. S., Maitinsky, S., & Whipple, S. C. (1980). Evoked potential and behavioral signs of attentive dysfunctions in hyperactive boys. *Psychophysiology*, *17*, 193–201.

Lovrich, D., & Stamm, J. S. (1983). Event-related potential and behavior correlates of attention in reading retardation. *Journal of Clinical Neuropsychology*, *5*, 13–37.

Luria, A. R., & Homskaya, E. D. (1970). Frontal lobes and the regulation of arousal process. In D. I. Mostofsky (Ed.), *Attention: Contemporary theory and analysis* (pp. 303–330). New York: Appleton-Century-Crofts.

Malamud, N., & Hirano, A. (1974). *Atlas of neuropathology* (pp. 436–437). Berkeley: University of California Press.

Martineau, J., Garreau, B., Barthelemy, C., & Lelord, G. (1984). Evoked potentials and P300 during sensory conditioning in autistic children. In R. Karrer, J. Cohen, & P. Tueting (Eds.), *Brain and information: Event-related potentials* (pp. 362–369). New York: New York Academy of Sciences.

Mason, S. N., & Mellor, D. H. (1984). Brainstem, middle latency and late cortical evoked potentials in children with speech and language disorders. *Electroencephalography and Clinical Neurophysiology: Evoked Potentials, 59*, 297–309.

Mullis, R. J., Holcomb, P. J., Diner, B. C., & Dykman, R. A. (1985). The effects of aging on the P3 component of the visual event-related potential. *Electroencephalography Clinical Neurophysiology, 62*, 141–149.

Novick, B., Kurtzberg, D., and Vaughan, H. G., Jr. (1979). An electrophysiologic indication of defective information storage in childhood autism. *Psychiatry Research, 1*, 101–108.

Novick, B., Vaughan, H. G., Jr., Kurtzberg, D., & Simson, R. (1980). An electrophysiologic indication of auditory processing defects in autism. *Psychiatry Research, 3*, 107–114.

O'Keefe, J. (1976). Place units in the hippocampus of the freely moving rat. *Experimental Neurology, 51*, 78–109.

Picton, T. W., Stapells, D. R., & Campbell, K. B. (1981). Auditory evoked potentials from the human cochlea and brainstem. *Journal of Otolaryngology, 10*, 1–41.

Pineda, J. A., Foote, S. L., & Neville, H. J. (in press). Effects of noradrenergic locus coeruleus lesions on squirrel monkey event-related potentials. *Electroencephalography and Clinical Neurophysiology, Supplement.*

Pirch, J. H., Corbus, M. J., Rigdon, G. C., & Lyness, W. H. (1986). Generation of cortical event-related slow potentials in the rat involves nucleus basalis cholinergic innervation. *Electroencephalography and Clinical Neurophysiology; Evoked Potentials, 63*, 464–475.

Prichep, L. S., Sutton, S., & Hakerem, G. (1976). Evoked potentials in hyperkinetic and normal children under certainty and uncertainty: A placebo and methylphenidate study. *Psychophysiology. 13*, 419–428.

Pritchard, W. S. (1981). Psychophysiology of P300. *Psychological Bulletin, 89*, 506–540.

Rakic, P., Bourgeois, J. P., Eckenhoff, M. F., Zecevic, N., & Goldman-Rakic, P. S. (1986). Concurrent overproduction of synapses in diverse regions of the primate cerebral cortex. *Science, 232*, 232–235.

Ranck, J. B. (1973). Studies on single neurons in dorsal hippocampal formation and septum in unrestrained rats. I. Behavioral correlates and firing repertories. *Experimental Neurology, 4*, 185–200.

Rimland, B. (1964). *Infantile autism.* New York: Appleton-Century-Crofts.

Robinson, K., & Rudge, P. (1982). The use of auditory potentials in neurology. In A. M. Halliday (Ed.), *Evoked potentials in clinical testing* (pp. 373–392). New York: Churchill Livingstone.

Roth, W. T. (1973). Auditory evoked responses to unpredictable stimuli. *Psychophysiology, 10*, 125–138.

Rumsey, J. M., Grimes, A. M., Pikus, A. M., Duara, R., & Ismond, D. R. (1984). Auditory brainstem responses in pervasive developmental disorders. *Biological Psychiatry, 19*, 1403–1418.

Rutter, M. (1979). Language, cognition, and autism. In R. Katzman (Ed.), *Congenital and acquired cognitive disorders* (pp. 247–264). New York: Raven Press.

Rutter, M. (1983). Cognitive deficits in the pathogenesis of autism. *Journal of Child Psychology and Psychiatry, 24*, 513–531.

Schafer, E. W. P., & Peeke, H. V. S. (1982). Down syndrome individuals fail to habituate cortical evoked potentials. *American Journal of Mental Deficiency, 87*, 332–337.

Scherg, M., & Von Cramon, D. (1985). A new interpretation of the generators of BAEP waves I–V: Results of a spatio-temporal dipole model. *Electroencephalography and Clinical Neuropysiology: Evoked Potentials, 62*, 290–299.

Skoff, B. F., Mirsky, A. F., & Turner, D. (1980). Prolonged brainstem transmission time in autism. *Psychiatry Research*, *2*, 157–166.

Smith, M. E., Stapleton, J. M., & Halgren, E. (1986). Human medial temporal lobe potentials evoked in memory and language tasks. *Electroencephalography and Clinical Neurophysiology*, *63*, 145–159.

Sokolov, E. N. (1958). The orienting reflex, its structure and mechanisms. In L. G. Voronin, A. N. Leontiev, A. R. Luria, E. N. Sokolov, & O. S. Vinogradova (Eds.), *Orienting reflex and exploratory behavior* (pp. 141–151). Moscow: Academy of Pedagogical Sciences of RSFSR.

Sokolov, E. N. (1960). Neuronal models and the orienting reflex. In M. A. B. Brazier (Ed.), *The central nervous system and behavior* (pp. 187–276). New York: Macy Foundation.

Sokolov, E. N. (1963). Higher nervous functions: The orienting reflex. In V. E. Hall, R. R. Sonnenschein, & A. C. Giese (Eds.), *Annual review of physiology* (pp. 545–580). Palo Alto: Anual Reviews.

Squires, N. K. (1984). Auditory brainstem responses in aberrant development: The case for a different approach to ERP research. (In D. Otto, R. Karrer, R. Halliday, L. Horst, R. Klorman, N. Squires, W. Thatcher, B. Fenelon, & G. Lelord. Developmental aspects of event-related potentials: Aberrant development.) In R. Karrer, J. Cohen, & P. Tueting (Eds.), *Brain and information: Event-related potentials* (pp. 319–328). New York: New York Academy of Sciences.

Squires, N. K., Squires, K. C., & Hillyard, S. A. (1975). Two varieties of long-latency positive waves evoked by unpredictable auditory stimuli in man. *Electroencephalography and Clinical neurophysiology*, *38*, 387–401.

Squires, N. K. Aine, C., Buchwald, J., Norman, R., & Galbraith, G. (1980). Auditory brainstem response abnormalities in severely and profoundly retarded adults. *Electroencephalography and Clinical Neurophysiology*, *50*, 172–185.

Steriade, M., & Glenn, L. (1982). Neocortical and caudate projections of intralaminar thalamic neurons and their synaptic excitation from midbrain reticular core. *Journal of Neurophysiology*, *48*, 352–371.

Stockard, J. J., Stockard, J. E., & Sharbrough, F. W. (1978). Nonpathologic factors influencing brainstem auditory evoked potentials. *American Journal of EEG Technology*, *18*, 177–209.

Sutton, S., Braren, M., Zubin, J., & John, E. R. (1965). Evoked potential correlates of stimulus uncertainty. Science, *150*, 1187–1188.

Sutton, S., & Ruchkin, D. S. (1984). The late positive complex: Advances and new problems. In R. Karrer, J. Cohen, & P. Tueting (Eds.), *Brain and information: Event-related potentials* (pp. 1–23). New York: New York Academy of Sciences.

Takashima, S., Becker, L. E., Armstrong, D. L., & Chan, F. (1981). Abnormal neuronal development in the visual cortex of the human fetus and infant with Down's syndrome: A quantitative and qualitative Golgi study. *Brain Research*, *225*, 1–21.

Tallal, P. (1980). Language disabilities in children: A perceptual or linguistic deficit. *Journal of Pediatric Psychology*. *4*, 127–140.

Tallal, P. (1985). Neuropsychological foundations of specific developmental disorders of speech and language: Implications for theories of hemispheric specialization. In J. O. Cavenar (Ed.), *Psychiatry: Psychobiological foundations of clinical psychiatry* (Vol. 3, pp. 1–15). Philladelphia: Lippincott.

Tallal, P., & Piercy, M. (1975). Developmental aphasia: The perception of brief vowels and extended stop consonants. *Neuropsychologica*, *13*, 69–74.

Tanguay, P., Edwards, R. M., Buchwald, J., Schwafel, J., & Allen, V. (1982). Auditory brainstem evoked responses in autistic children. *Archives of General Psychiatry*, *39*, 174–180.

Taylor, M. J., Rosenblatt, B., & Linschoten, L. (1982). Electreophysiological study of the auditory system in autistic children. In A. Rothenberger (Ed.), *Event-related potentials in children* (pp. 379–386). New York: Elsevier.

Vinogradova, O. S. (1970). Registration of information and the limbic system. In G. Horn & R. A. Hinde (Eds.), *Short-term changes in neural activity and behavior* (pp. 95–140). New York: Cambridge.

Wood, C C., & McCarthy, G. (in press). A possible frontal lobe contribution to scalp P300. *Electroencephalography and Clinical Neurophysiology, Supplement.*

Wood, C. C., McCarthy, G., Squires, N. K., Vaughan, H. G., Jr., Woods, D. L., & McCallum, W. C. (1984). Anatomical and physiological substrates of event-related potentials. In R. Karrer, J. Cohen, & P. Tueting (Eds.), *Brain and information: Event-related potentials* (pp. 681–721). New York: New York Academy of Sciences.

Woods, D. L., & Courchesne, E. (1986). The recovery functions of auditory event-related potentials during split-second discriminations. *Electroencephalography and Clinical Neurophysiology. 65,* 304–315.

Woods, D. L., & Courchesne, E. (in press). Intersubject variability elucidates the cerebral generators and psychological correlates of ERPs. *Electroencephalography and Clinical Neurophysiology, Supplement.*

Woods, D. L., Courchesne, E., Hillyard, S. A., & Galambos, R. (1980a). Recovery cycles of event-related potentials in multiple detection tasks, *Electroencephalography and Clinical Neurophysiology, 50,* 335–347.

Woods, D. L., Courchesne, E., Hillyard, S. A., & Galambos, R. (1980b). Split-second recovery of the P3 component in multiple decision tasks. In H. H. Kornhuber & L. Deeke (Eds.) *Motivation, motor and sensory processes of the brain: Electrical potentials, behavior, and clinical use (Progress in brain research,* Vol. 54, pp. 322–330). Amsterdam: Elsevier/ North-Holland.

Woods, D. L., Hillyard, S. A., Courchesne, E., & Galambos, R. (1980). Electrophysiological signs of split-second decision-making, *Science, 207,* 655–657.

Yingling, C. D., & Hosobuchi, Y. (1984). A subcortical correlate of P300 in man. *Electroencephalography and Clinical Neurophysiology: Evoked Potentials, 59,* 72-76.

10

INTEGRATING ASSESSMENT AND TAXONOMY

THOMAS M. ACHENBACH

INTRODUCTION

This chapter deals with the overarching issues of assessment, taxonomy, and the relations between them. The relations between them are especially crucial since assessment and taxonomy should constitute two phases of a single process. *Assessment* identifies the distinguishing features of each case, whereas *taxonomy* groups cases according to their distinguishing features. Because it involves grouping cases according to their own distinguishing features, the concept of taxonomy is narrower than the concept of classification, which includes groupings based on extrinsic criteria as well as those based on features of the cases themselves. Children referred to a clinic, for example, can be classified according to referral source or according to the therapist assigned to them, but these classifications do not reflect characteristics of the children or their disorders. Not all classifications are taxonomies, but all taxonomies involve classification.

Despite the complementary roles of assessment and taxonomy, they have tended to develop independently of each other. In considering the relations between them, I will first provide a summary overview of the assessment approaches critiqued elsewhere in this book. The detailed presentations of assessment in other chapters make it unnecessary to do more than highlight the differences between approaches to assessment. With regard to taxonomic issues, however, we need a close look at various alternatives before addressing the integration of assessment with taxonomy.

It should be noted that no one approach to assessment or taxonomy of childhood disorders is intrinsically superior to all others and that multiple approaches will continue to be needed. Yet, to advance our understanding we need to clarify the challenges to be met and the possibilities for improving existing approaches. In addressing these issues, I focus on generic problems

Thomas M. Achenbach. Department of Psychiatry, College of Medicine, University of Vermont, Burlington, Vermont.

and possible future solutions more than on exhaustive comparisons of the strengths and limitations of specific methods. The emphasis is on possibilities for better integration between assessment and taxonomic procedures rather than on integrating each of the existing approaches with the others. It is a tribute to the progress made within several specific approaches that we are now able to address the more generic problems and look ahead to possible solutions, provisional though they be.

OVERVIEW OF ASSESSMENT METHODS

For the foreseeable future, assessment of child psychopathology is likely to require multiple methods, for the following reasons:

1. Where specific etiologies are unknown, as in most childhood disorders, no single method is uniquely capable of identifying the disorder a child has.
2. If specific etiologies are discovered that can be uniquely identified by particular methods, it will still be necessary to assess multiple aspects of children's functioning for purposes of treatment, educational planning, and so on.
3. Because children's functioning must be judged in relation to their developmental levels and prospects, assessment should take account of progress along multiple dimensions, such as biological, cognitive, social–emotional, and educational development.
4. Because most children's functioning varies from one situation and interaction partner to another, their functioning should be assessed in multiple contexts—such as home, school, and clinic—which require different assessment methods.
5. Children are often more reactive to assessment procedures and less able to provide accurate accounts of their functioning across situations than adults. This raises measurement problems that must be addressed through multiple methods, no one of which is apt to be totally accurate or comprehensive.

As shown by the chapters on direct observations, rating scales, psychobiological methods, family assessment, and clinical interviews, each approach focuses on one part of the proverbial elephant that evokes different reactions from blind men touching its different parts. Each approach captures one aspect of phenomena whose overall shape cannot be grasped through any one approach. Although it is tempting to reject one approach when it fails to agree with another, discrepant approaches may ultimately be more informative than a single approach that captures only one aspect of the target phenomena. It is therefore preferable to view different approaches as potential collaborators, rather than as competitors from which only one winner can emerge. In this spirit, Table 10-1 summarizes the five main

TABLE 10-1. Summary of Assessment Methods for Childhood Disorders

Method	Source of data	Data collection site	Strengths	Limitations	Current status
Direct observations	Trained observers	Natural settings	1. High reliability when two observers are used 2. Detailed record of actual behavior 3. Identification of environmental contingencies 4. Direct assessment of behavioral change points	1. Limited practicality 2. Limited generalizability 3. Observer drift 4. Lack of aggregation 5. Lack of normative reference	1. Large body of research 2. Many specific techniques 3. Provides model for behavioral assessment
Rating scales	Parents; teachers; children; clinicians	Anywhere	1. Easy to use 2. Inexpensive 3. Cover many problems 4. Can be norm-based 5. Can be psychometrically sound 6. High test–retest reliability 7. Can tap low-frequency behaviors	1. Limited to the informant's perspective 2. Limited agreement between informants 3. Limited to structured scores for standardized items	1. Large body of research 2. Many specific instruments 3. Widely used for many purposes

Method	Assessors/Tools	Setting	Advantages	Limitations	Status/Comments
Biomedical and psychobiological	Physicians; lab tests	Clinical setting	May indicate organic abnormalities	1. Lack of normative/developmental reference points 2. Lack of evidence for validity in assessment of psychopathology	Many well-established biomedical tests for physical disorders, but further work is needed to determine value for child psychopathology
Family assessment	Family members; clinicians; trained observers	Home; clinical setting	1. Focus on family context of child's problems 2. Potential for tapping dynamics of family system 3. Potential for coordinating assessment of multiple family members	1. Difficulty of operationalizing theoretical variables 2. Reactivity of measures 3. Problems in application to individual child 4. Lack of normative and developmental reference	1. Much theory 2. Many possible techniques and foci 3. Few well-validated measures
Clinical interviews	Trained interviewers of parents and children	Clinical setting	1. Two-way interchange between clinician and client 2. Opportunity to probe client's response	1. Low reliability for child interviews 2. Low agreement between parent and child interviews	Unstandardized interviews are widely used for clinical assessment; standardized interviews are increasingly used for research

Note. Methods are those surveyed in other chapters of this book. Additional methods include standardized tests of personality, ability, and achievement; projective tests; developmental measures; anxiety hierarchies; simulated problem situations; role playing; tests of perceptual–motor functioning; social competence measures; social cognition; sociometrics; and ecological assessment. Achenbach (1985) compares these approaches.

approaches considered in the book, along with strengths and limitations characterizing their present stage of development. Table 10-1 also lists other approaches not detailed in this book but compared elsewhere (Achenbach, 1985).

Direct Observations

The blossoming of behavior modification in the 1960s and 1970s fostered a model of behavioral assessment stressing observable relations between environmental contingencies and behavioral responses (Mash & Terdal, 1981). The behavioral model promoted a host of new techniques for identifying problem behaviors and their supporting contingencies under diverse environmental conditions, as well as better documentation of relations between assessment and treatment.

One of behavioral assessment's most valuable contributions is a large body of research on children's disorders observed in various naturalistic settings. This research has yielded sophisticated techniques for obtaining high interobserver reliability in the recording of molecular behavioral events. These techniques, in turn, have made it possible to compare children's functioning under various conditions, to assess sequential contingencies between environmental events and behavior, to target interventions on specific behaviors, and to evaluate the effects of the interventions on the target behaviors.

As behavioral assessment has spread and matured, it has become clear that psychometric questions of reliability, standardization, aggregation of data, norm-referencing, and relations to other variables cannot be avoided. Although high reliability is often achieved in studies where observers simultaneously record the same behavior, reliability is considerably lower under the more typical conditions where observers work alone, believing that they will not be checked (Weinrott & Jones, 1984). Besides the costs and practical problems of placing multiple trained observers in the naturalistic situations where problem behavior occurs, observational techniques may be limited by the reactivity of the child to the observer's presence, the lack of generalizability from observed behavior to behavior occurring elsewhere or covertly, and the difficulty of aggregating molecular behavioral events for comparison with normative samples. Limitations of this sort call for meshing observational assessment with assessment methods that do not suffer from these particular limitations, recognizing that the other methods may, however, lack the particular strengths of observational assessment.

Rating Scales

Whereas direct observations are designed to record samples of behavioral events as they occur, rating scales are designed to obtain judgments of a child's functioning by a particular kind of informant. Most rating scales are designed for informants—such as parents, teachers, and peers—who interact with the subjects over a substantial period of time under a variety of conditions. Scales are also available for self-ratings and ratings by observers who see the subjects for briefer periods under more limited conditions, such as clinical interviews and time samples of the school day. Even when based on specific observational samples, however, such scales are designed to obtain the rater's judgment of the child's functioning rather than a count of specific behavioral events.

Most rating scales yield quantitative indices of the raters' judgments, either by computing scores across items judged as absent-versus-present (scored 0 vs. 1) or by having raters quantify their own judgments on multi-step scales. The scores are usually aggregated for groups of items intended to tap a particular variable or set of variables. The level of quantification for rating scales is likely to be more precise than rank-ordering (ordinal scale), but less precise than quantification in terms of equal intervals (interval scale). "Quasi-interval" scales of this sort permit a wide variety of score distributions and statistical manipulations.

Because rating scales are readily standardized, are quantifiable, can be completed by many kinds of informants without special training, and can include diverse attributes over a variety of time periods, they lend themselves well to psychometric models of assessment. Norms can be obtained for large representative samples of particular classes of informants, such as parents and teachers. The scales can also be tested for interinformant agreement, internal consistency, test–retest reliability, and various types of validity. The fact that all this is feasible does not mean that it is always done, however. As Barkley (Chapter 5, this volume) points out, most scales have neither been adequately normed nor shown to be psychometrically sound. Yet there is a large body of research on scales for judgments of children's disorders. This research shows high test–retest reliability and good concurrent and discriminative validity for several instruments. General population norms for children of each sex at different ages, analyzed for socioeconomic and ethnic differences, make it possible to link findings from diverse clinical samples with each other and with findings for nonreferred children, a strength not yet shared by the other approaches reviewed in this book.

Because rating scales obtain informants' judgments of children's functioning, the role of the informant must always be considered. Parents, teachers, and peers may have idiosyncratic biases, but their perceptions of a child are often important in their own right. If they see a child as significantly deviant from what is typically reported of that child's age-mates, this suggests the presence of a problem, although in some cases it may be the informant, family, or environment rather than the child that requires change. The modest correlations typically found between different informants' ratings of the same children demonstrate the need for multiple sources and types of assessment data (Achenbach, McConaughy, & Howell, 1987).

Furthermore, standardization may limit the sensitivity of rating scales to the idiosyncratic aspects of individual cases. This, too, argues for the use of multiple assessment procedures that can jointly contribute to taxonomic decisions.

Biomedical and Psychobiological Methods

Beside rating scales and observational assessment of behavior, medical and neurological exams are widely used in the assessment of children referred for mental health services. When no specific organic abnormalities are found, borderline or equivocal signs ("soft signs") of neurological dysfunction are often interpreted as evidence that minimal brain dysfunction contributes to a child's problems. The Physical and Neurological Examination for Soft Signs (PANESS) (Guy, 1976) has been developed to provide standardized assessment and scoring procedures for subtle neurological abnormalities of childhood. This is a necessary step in improving neurological assessment of children. Where no blatant abnormality is evident, however, the main determinant of PANESS scores appears to be the child's general developmental level, as indexed by chronological age and cognitive ability (Mikkelsen, Brown, Minichiello, Millican, & Rapoport, 1982).

Numerous psychobiological measures have been developed to test hypothesized dysfunctions of the nervous system. Although some of these measures are widely used for clinical assessment of adult disorders, the reviews by Ferguson and Bawden and Courchesne and Yeung-Courchesne (Chapters 8 and 9, this volume) show that better normative data and standardization from study to study are needed to determine their value for the assessment of child and adolescent disorders. Because most of the measures are costly and are targeted on very specific hypothesized dysfunctions, they are likely to be used mainly in cases where such dysfunctions are suspected, rather than being routinely applied to every case. Examples include the dexamethasone suppression test, measures of serotonin level, and specialized EEG assessment.

Family Assessment

Most children live in families and are highly dependent on them. Clinical assessment routinely includes information on the family history and constellation. Family systems theorists, however, view the family itself as the primary focus of assessment, rather than the family member or "identified patient" for whom help happens to be sought. Their efforts have therefore been directed largely toward assessing the dynamics of interactions among family members in order to characterize the family as a whole. As detailed by Jacob and Tennenbaum (Chapter 7, this volume), this orientation has generated a variety of assessment techniques, including home observations, observations of family interactions during experimental tasks, assessment of dyadic relationships (e.g., husband–wife, parent–child), and ratings by family members of each other and of the family as a whole. These assessment techniques have focused on a variety of constructs, including affective bonds between family members, interpersonal control, communication, and properties of family systems, such as adaptibility and ability to change patterns of control.

Although family theories of specific disorders, such as schizophrenia, and family therapy for many kinds of problems have spawned a rich literature over the past 30 years, efforts to translate family concepts into assessment procedures relevant to child psychopathology are more recent. Jacob and Tennenbaum's review of specific procedures shows a wide range of constructs, assessment foci, data sources, target populations, and applications. A few measures have shown adequate reliability and validity, and family assessment unquestionably represents a crucial dimension in understanding children that is lacking in other approaches. It is not yet clear, however, how family assessment can be meshed with other approaches or with common research questions. Furthermore, as Jacob and Tennenbaum point out, family assessment, like the other approaches, must face the inconsistencies that occur in data from multiple sources. In this case, the inconsistencies involve the multiple family members who are both the subjects and the sources of assessment data, as well as inconsistencies in family functioning under different conditions. When efforts are made to obtain veridical records of family interactions by using trained observers, family assessment—like direct behavioral assessment of individual children—must deal with subject reactivity, the potential unrepresentativeness of the observational conditions, and the aggregation of molecular data points. Jacob and Tennenbaum also point out that the existing measures do not yet empirically discriminate among the many variables hypothesized to be involved in family functioning. In common with other assessment approaches, this problem raises questions of how to relate assessment to taxonomy.

Clinical Interviews

The most widely used assessment procedure is the clinical interview. When a child is the identified patient, clinical interviews with parents are typically used to obtain descriptions of the referring complaints, course of the problems, developmental history, and family background. Beside information of this sort, parent interviews provide an opportunity to get acquainted, make practical arrangements, form clinical hypotheses about the parents' role in the child's problems, and explore parents' attitudes toward various treatment options. Structured interviews with parents can yield assessment data like those from rating scales completed by parents, with similar levels of reliability (Edelbrock & Costello, Chapter 4, this volume). Clinical interviews with children, however, are oriented less toward obtaining specific information than toward forming impressions of the child, making clinical inferences about the child's functioning, and establishing a therapeutic relationship. Because clinicians differ greatly in their approach and their impact on parents and children, the data obtained from clinical interviews vary from one interview to another and one clinician to another.

Efforts to increase the yield of clinical interviews with children have taken several approaches. As reviewed by Edelbrock & Costello (Chapter 4, this volume), one approach is the highly structured interview consisting of questions about specific symptoms, which are then scored as present or absent to make particular diagnoses—for example, the Diagnostic Interview Schedule for Children (DISC) (Costello, Edelbrock, Dulcan, Kalas, & Klaric, 1984). At the other extreme, minimally structured interviews are used to make more global judgments about the child's overall functioning (e.g., Kestenbaum & Bird, 1978). Intermediate between these extremes are semistructured interviews designed to cover particular content areas in a flexible manner (e.g., friends, school, family), but for which structured scoring procedures are provided (e.g., Achenbach & McConaughy, 1985; Hodges, McKnew, Cytryn, Stern, & Kline, 1982; Kovacs, 1982; Rutter & Graham, 1968).

The salience of impressions derived from interviews makes it especially important to determine what can be reliably obtained from them that cannot be more readily obtained in other ways. Children's cognitive levels and communication abilities often limit the information they can convey in interviews. Young children may be especially unable to interpret structured questions about their problems, consider all the relevant aspects of their experience, and formulate accurate answers.

The test–retest reliability of children's responses varies greatly with age, as shown by intraclass correlations averaging .43 for DISC responses by 6- to 9-year-old children, .60 for 10- to 13-year-olds, and .71 for 14- to 18-year-olds (Edelbrock & Costello, Chapter 4, this volume; Edelbrock, Costello, Dulcan, Kalas, & Conover, 1985). The DISC research also showed a marked tendency for young children to reverse their responses from "yes" to "no," as shown by a 33% decline in DISC symptom scores from the first interview to the second among 6- to 9-year-olds, a 24% decline among 10- to 13-year-olds, and a 16% decline among 14- to 18-year-olds. This suggests that yeasaying response sets at the first interview change to naysaying response sets at the second. Pearson correlations between symptom scores from the parent and child DISC interviews averaged only .27, whereas diagnoses[1] made from child interviews did not agree with those made from parent interviews or from complete clinical work-ups (Costello *et al.*, 1984). Despite

1. According to the criteria of the third edition of the *Diagnostic and Statistical Manual of Mental Disorders* (DSM-III) of the American Psychiatric Association (1980).

the evident limitations on child interviews, they will undoubtedly remain widely used to provide practitioners with first-hand impressions of their child clients. It is therefore important to understand how their potential contributions might mesh with those of other assessment procedures. To do so, we first need to consider the overarching taxonomic aims of assessment.

TAXONOMIC PARADIGMS

Assessment techniques vary widely with respect to the questions they address, the source and nature of their data, the conclusions they yield, and their current stage of development. Since it is clear that no single assessment technique can answer all questions, a taxonomic structure is needed for integrating diverse techniques and data. This is especially important where we lack a litmus test for making positive diagnoses of disorders, as is the case for most child and adolescent psychopathology. Many approaches to taxonomy are feasible; no one approach is intrinsically more correct than the others for all situations. Their strengths and weaknesses vary according to the phenomena in question, the stage of our knowledge, and the taxonomic needs to be met. We will first summarize the leading taxonomic paradigms and then evaluate them in light of current taxonomic needs.

Kraepelinian Paradigm

The progress of 19th-century medical research fostered the assumption that mental disorders are brain diseases (Griesinger, 1845). Accordingly, the task of assessment was to identify signs and symptoms of organic abnormalities. The task of taxonomy was to construct syndromes of signs and symptoms for distinguishing between disorders expected to have distinctive organic etiologies. It was expected that mental disorders would eventually join physical disorders in a general medical nosology.

The prototype for the nosology of mental disorders was general paralysis (*paresis*) of the insane (GPI), which received progressively better clinical descriptions during the first half of the 19th century. The discovery of inflammation in the brains of people who died of GPI and Krafft-Ebing's confirmation of syphilis as the cause helped entrench the nosological model for mental disorders. The nosological model was also supported by the identification of organic syndromes among the mentally retarded, such as Down's syndrome by Langdon Down in 1866.

Although clinical descriptions were successful in identifying organic abnormalities, a general taxonomy was needed to organize the welter of descriptions, especially for cases lacking clear-cut physical symptoms. Amid a variety of taxonomic efforts, the most influential was published by Emil Kraepelin in 1883 and continually revised until he died in 1926. In his 1915 revision Kraepelin added disorders that he regarded as psychogenic rather than organic plus personality disorders that he viewed as bordering between illness and common eccentricity.

Kraepelinian principles and categories have continued to mold psychiatric nosologies through the present day, as exemplified by systems such as the three versions of the DSM, World Health Organization (WHO) multiaxial classification (Rutter, Shaffer, & Shepherd, 1975), GAP (Group for the Advancement of Psychiatry, 1966), and the ninth edition of the World Health Organization's *International Classification of Diseases* (ICD-9) (WHO, 1978). Current Kraepelinian taxonomies of childhood disorders are based on clinical constructs for which descriptions were formulated by a process of discussion and negotiation (see Spitzer & Cantwell, 1980, p. 369). In the WHO, GAP, ICD-9, and the first two editions of the DSM, the descriptions are largely in narrative form. Some of the behavior disorders of childhood listed in DSM-II were suggested by the case-history research of Richard Jenkins (e.g., Jenkins & Glickman, 1946), but the descriptions were based on the DSM-II committee's concepts of these disorders, rather than being operationalized from Jenkins's actual findings.

The DSM-III departed from the other systems in providing explicit criteria and fixed rules for each diagnostic category. For most DSM-III childhood disorders, there are four types of criteria:

1. A list of descriptive features from which a specified number must be judged present.
2. A minimum period during which the behaviors specified in item 1 above must be present (e.g., 2 weeks).
3. An age criterion (e.g., age at least 3 years).
4. Criteria for excluding a particular disorder if it is "due to" certain other disorders.

The DSM-III criteria for some adult disorders were based on experience with several versions of research diagnostic criteria. The lack of any prior research criteria for the DSM-III child and adolescent disorders, however, made their criteria rather arbitrary, as pointed out by Cantwell (Chapter 1, this volume).

Psychodynamic Paradigm

Although there is no general psychodynamic taxonomy analogous to Kraepelinian nosologies, psychoanalytic theory suggested the DSM-I and GAP definitions of neurotic disorders. In both systems, these disorders were defined in terms of unconscious conflicts that produced anxiety, which in turn triggered a variety of Freudian defense mechanisms. From the 1930s through the 1960s, there was also a dominant psychoanalytic assumption that major depressions could occur only after the superego was fully internalized during adolescence (see Kashani *et al.* 1981). This left anaclitic depression of infancy and depressive neuroses as the only depressive disorders considered possible for children (GAP, 1966).

Beside the influence of psychoanalysis on nosology, Anna Freud (1965) proposed a Developmental Profile as a model for psychodynamic taxonomy of children's disorders. Her basic principle was to judge children according to psychoanalytic concepts of *developmental lines*—that is, sequences of libidinal phases, ego and superego development, advances from id-dominated primary process thinking to ego-dominated secondary process thinking, and progress from the pleasure principle to the reality principle. The Developmental Profile is basically a list of psychodynamic inferences about libidinal and aggressive drive development; ego and superego development; conflicts; regressions; and fixations. The taxonomic objective is to classify children in terms of categories such as those shown in Table 10-2.

Anna Freud's approach to taxonomy differs from the Kraepelinian paradigm in focusing on theoretical inferences about psychological functioning and in categorizing disorders according to the depth of inferred psychopathology. The Developmental Profile assumes an intimate knowledge of the child, but it prescribes no specific assessment procedures. A simplified version of the profile, called the Metapsychological Assessment Profile, employs four-step ratings for 11 inferential categories, such as ego flexibility, superego functioning, affects, and defenses (Greenspan, Hatleberg, & Cullander, 1980). Published reports of both this version and Anna Freud's version provide single-case illustrations, but no reliability or validity data (e.g., Yorke, 1980).

TABLE 10-2. Taxonomic Categories Derived from Anna Freud's Developmental Profile

---

A. In spite of current behavior disturbance, personality growth is within the wide range of "normality."

B. Symptoms are of a transitory nature and can be classed as by-products of developmental strain.

C. There is a permanent drive regression to fixation points that leads to neurotic conflicts.

D. There is drive regression plus ego and superego regressions that lead to infantilisms, borderline psychotic, delinquent, or psychotic disturbances.

E. There are primary organic deficiencies or early deprivations that distort development and produce retarded, defective, and nontypical personalities.

F. There are destructive processes at work of organic, toxic, or psychic origin that have caused or are about to cause a disruption of mental growth.

Note. Adapted from Freud (1965, p. 147).

Multivariate Paradigm

The lack of a satisfactory taxonomy of childhood disorders has stimulated numerous efforts to identify syndromes through statistical analyses of children's behavior problems. These efforts began with the computation of correlations between pairs of problems scored from case histories and the formation of syndromes from the most highly correlated sets of items (Hewitt & Jenkins, 1946; Jenkins & Glickman, 1946). Since the advent of electronic computers, factor analysis has been used to derive syndromes from ratings by a variety of informants, including parents, teachers, and mental health workers.

Despite differences in the raters, subject samples, rating instruments, and analytic methods, considerable similarity has been found among syndromes derived from different multivariate analyses. In a review of 27 multivariate studies, Achenbach and Edelbrock (1978) concluded that 18 syndromes had clear counterparts in two or more of the studies. Fourteen syndromes, designated "narrow band," involved a level of specificity analogous to that of most syndromes in Kraepelinian taxonomies. Four of the syndromes were designated as "broad band" because they included items spanning two or more narrow-band syndromes. In a review of broad-band syndromes, Quay (1979) also concluded that there were major consistencies in findings from the different studies. When narrow-band syndromes are viewed hierarchically as subtypes of the broad-band syndromes, Quay (personal communication) agrees that there is consistency among findings of narrow-band syndromes as well.

Because the syndromes are by no means identical from one study to another, Lessing, Williams, and Revelle (1981) have questioned whether the multivariate findings actually show much consistency. However, after Achenbach and Edelbrock (1978) had grouped the syndromes from 27 studies into 14 narrow-band and 4 broad-band categories, other psychologists independently classified 90% of the 124 obtained syndromes into the same categories. As further evidence for consistency between syndromes obtained with different instruments, significant correlations have been found between nearly all the analogous syndrome scales derived from separate factor analyses of the Achenbach (1978), Connors (1973), and Quay and Peterson (1983) checklists (see Achenbach & Edelbrock, 1983, 1986).

Relations to Nosological Syndromes

Syndromes derived from multivariate analyses are analogous to nosological syndromes in the following ways:

1. Both kinds of syndromes consist of subsets of features that individuals might display rather than representing "types" of individuals.
2. An individual can manifest features of more than one syndrome

derived from multivariate analyses, just as an individual can manifest symptoms of diabetes, influenza, and otitis media at the same time ("comorbidity").

3. Some features may characterize more than one multivariate syndrome, just as some symptoms—such as headache, fever, and vomiting—characterize more than one physical syndrome.

4. The features of a particular multivariate or nosological syndrome do not always occur together.

Besides the formal similarities between nosological and multivariate syndromes, there are similarities between the descriptive features of some of them. The descriptive features used to define DSM-III disorders offer the clearest basis for comparison with the multivariate findings. As summarized in Table 10-3, the descriptive features of many DSM-III syndromes have counterparts in the statistically derived syndromes. Furthermore, when the descriptive features of the DSM-III syndromes are scored quantitatively, they correlate significantly with scores for the corresponding statistically derived syndromes (Costello et al., 1984; Edelbrock, 1984). There is thus considerable overlap between the content of the DSM-III and multivariate syndromes.

There are also differences between the multivariate syndromes and those of the DSM type. Minor differences include the wording of descriptive features, the number of features, and the cutoff points for identifying deviance. A more important difference is the contrast between the quantitative nature of the multivariate syndromes and the DSM's requirement that disorders be judged as either present or absent, based on fixed rules for the number of descriptive features, duration of the problems, age of onset, and exclusion of a disorder when it is "due to" certain other disorders.

As Rutter and Schopler (Chapter 13, this volume) point out, the discovery of underlying abnormalities is a goal that usually leads to redefinition of a disorder in terms of the abnormalities, rather than relying on descriptive features that may have different causes in different cases. Rutter and Schopler indicate, however, that the search for underlying abnormalities must usually start with the grouping of cases according to descriptive features. Where neither underlying abnormalities nor physical symptoms have been confirmed, it is difficult to draw precise boundaries between disorders. DSM-III draws boundaries by providing differential diagnostic criteria for some disorders and by preempting some disorders that are assumed to be due to others. Yet, there is no empirical basis for the exclusionary criteria, and considerable overlap has been found between diagnoses of certain disorders, such as oppositional disorder, conduct disorder, and attention deficit disorder (Costello et al., 1984; Taylor, Chapter 12, this volume). The DSM-III-R (American Psychiatric Association, 1987) reduces the number of child categories and the use of exclusionary criteria, but these changes do not solve the general problem of boundaries between descriptive categories.

TABLE 10-3. Approximate Relations between DSM-III and Empirically Derived Syndromes of Childhood Behavior Disorders

DSM-III		Empirically derived narrow-band syndromes
Attention deficit disorders		
314.01	With hyperactivity	Hyperactive
314.00	Without hyperactivity (omitted from DSM-III-R)	Inattentive (teacher ratings only)
Conduct disorders		
312.00	Undersocialized, aggressive (aggressive in DSM-III-R)	Aggressive
312.10	Undersocialized, nonaggressive (omitted from DSM-III-R)	—
312.23	Socialized, aggressive ⎫ Group delinquent	Delinquent (boys)
312.21	Socialized, nonaggressive ⎭ in DSM-III-R	Delinquent (girls)
Anxiety disorders of childhood or adolescence		
309.21	Separation anxiety disorder	—
313.21	Avoidant disorder	—
313.00	Overanxious disorder	Anxious
Other disorders of childhood or adolescence		
313.22	Schizoid disorder (omitted from DSM-III-R)	Social withdrawal (?)
313.23	Elective mutism	Uncommunicative
313.81	Oppositional disorder	—
313.82	Identity disorder	—
Pervasive developmental disorders		
299.8	Childhood onset pervasive developmental	—
299.9	Atypical	—
302.60	Gender identity disorder of childhood	Sex problems (boys 4–5)
V62.30	Academic problem	Academic disability
Disorders not specific to childhood or adolescence		
300.30	Obsessive–compulsive disorder	Obsessive–compulsive
300.81	Somatization disorder	Somatic complaints
296.20	Major depressive episode; 300.4 Dysthymic disorder, 309.0 Adjustment disorder with depressed mood	Depressed
301.22	Schizotypal personality disorder (?)	Schizoid
	—	Immature
	—	Sexual problems
	—	Sleep problems
	—	Cruel (girls)

The multivariate approach can avoid rigid boundaries between syndromes by scoring the *degree* to which a child manifests the features of each syndrome. This is usually done by summing the scores obtained by the child on all the features of each syndrome. Scores of all the syndromes can be transformed to a common scale by the use of standard scores based on normative data. By displaying all the syndromes appropriate for a child's age and sex in a profile format, the areas of greatest and least deviance can be seen. A profile encompassing multiple syndromes provides a more comprehensive basis for taxonomy than individual syndromes do.

From Syndromes to Typologies

To group disorders according to similarities in profile patterns, profiles have been cluster analyzed to create typologies of the patterns formed by scores on the descriptive syndromes. Some of the resulting profile types have been distinguished by a peak on a single syndrome scale, such as hyperactivity (Achenbach & Edelbrock, 1983). This suggests that certain disorders are effectively described in terms of a single kind of deviance. However, we have also found profile types that are distinguished by peaks on two or more syndrome scales. Among 6- to 11-year-old boys, for example, cluster analyses have identified a profile pattern showing exceptional deviance in depression, social withdrawal, and aggression.

Using the DSM-III approach of classifying cases in terms of yes-or-no assignments to each diagnostic category, such patterns would be difficult to detect and categorize. If the co-occurrence of deviance in three DSM-III categories were recognized, however, the boys showing this pattern would be viewed as having three distinct DSM disorders, referred to as "comorbidity." Furthermore, if we classified boys solely on the basis of DSM-III categories such as aggressive conduct disorder, their apparent homogeneity with respect to that disorder would mask their heterogeneity with respect to other syndromes that could easily be detected in profile patterns. Whereas some boys who are deviant in aggression are not deviant in other areas, certain boys who are deviant in aggression are equally or more deviant in other areas, such as social withdrawal and depression.

CURRENT STATUS OF TAXONOMIC PARADIGMS

Considering the relatively short history of interest in the taxonomy of child and adolescent disorders, it is not surprising that all approaches are in rudimentary stages of development. Any approach adopted now is likely to remain provisional for the foreseeable future, subject to change as research progresses. Furthermore, the Kraepelinian and multivariate approaches need not be mutually exclusive. As enumerated earlier and shown in Table 10-3, there are important parallels between these approaches. Yet, we need to be aware of the strengths and limitations of each approach, as discussed next.

Reliability

A basic question asked of any taxonomy is whether the target phenomena can be reliably classified. Although this question pertains to all approaches, the focus differs from one approach to another.

Kraepelinian Paradigm

The DSM, WHO, GAP, and ICD-9 do not specify particular assessment operations for making taxonomic distinctions. Although the DSM-III attention deficit category requires assessment data from parents and teachers, it does not specify standard procedures for obtaining these data or for using them to classify cases. The failure of the DSM, WHO, GAP, and ICD-9 to specify assessment procedures leaves them largely to the discretion of the diagnostician, although, as discussed later, efforts have been made to standardize assessment of these criteria.

Most research on the reliability of these systems focuses on the final categorization of cases by diagnosticians who have been exposed to a variety of data. Several studies have provided diagnosticians with written case histories from which they then made DSM, WHO, GAP, or ICD-9 diagnoses (Beitchman, Dielman, Landis, Benson, & Kemp, 1978; Freeman, 1971; Gould, Shaffer, Rutter, & Sturge, Chapter 2, this volume; Mattison, Cantwell, Russell, & Will, 1979; Mezzich & Mezzich, 1979; Mezzich, Mezzich, & Coffman, 1985; Remschmidt, Chapter 3, this volume; Rutter, Shaffer, & Shepherd, 1975). The findings for interjudge reliability can be summarized as follows (Achenbach, 1985, provides a more detailed analysis):

1. Interjudge reliability was mediocre for most specific categories of disorders (e.g., specific ADD, conduct disorders, anxiety disorders), although the degree of agreement varied from category to category within each study.
2. When diagnoses were counted as agreeing if they fell within a particular broad category (e.g., personality disorders, neurotic disorders, psychotic disorders, "other" disorders), the highest interjudge reliability across categories was 67% in a study that did not correct for chance agreements (Rutter *et al.*, 1975) and kappa = .38 in a study that did correct for chance (Gould *et al.*, Chapter 2, this volume).

Use of written case histories to test interjudge reliability has the advantages of ensuring that each judge receives exactly the same data on each case, judges do not influence each other, and the data are documented in hard copy for repeated review. Case histories have the disadvantage, however, of vulnerability to biases in what is presented. Such biases can either inflate or reduce agreement, depending on whether there is selectivity with respect to data that conform to or violate taxonomic categories. Case histories also may omit data that could be obtained through more direct involvement with a case, such as direct observations of facial expression, voice, and posture.

Beside the case history studies, there have been two studies of DSM-III in which pairs of diagnosticians were involved in interviewing each case (American Psychiatric Association, 1980; Strober, Green, & Carlson, 1981), and one in which the diagnosticians heard each case presented at a case conference (Werry, Methven, Fitzpatrick, & Dixon, 1983). Cantwell (Chapter 1, this volume) provides further details of these studies. Data from the first study were obtained in the DSM-III field trials, where clinicians were given general instructions for making diagnoses, but where the procedures varied from case to case and were vulnerable to diverse biases (see Rutter & Shaffer, 1980.) Although the specific reliability estimates should therefore not be taken literally, they suggest three conclusions:

1. For all four axes that were assessed (Axis III was not), reliability improved from the first version of DSM-III to the final one for adults, but declined for children and adolescents.
2. Despite the joint involvement of each diagnostician with each child, reliability was not much better than in the case history studies. In the final field trial, the overall kappa for child and adolescent disorders was .52, despite the crediting of agreement for discrepant judgments that fell within broad categories. For Axis II, the kappa was .55, even though the 18 specific categories were collapsed into two categories, *developmental disorders* and *personality disorders*.
3. In the final field trial, reliability was better for adults than children on all four axes assessed: Axis I kappa = .72 for adults versus .52 for children; Axis II kappa = .64 versus .55; Axis IV (severity of psychosocial stressors) intraclass correlation = .66 versus .59; Axis V (highest level of attained functioning) intraclass correlation = .80 versus .52.

The remaining two studies were distinguished from the others by employing only inpatients. In the Strober *et al.* (1981) study, two clinicians jointly interviewed adolescent inpatients and a family member using a highly structured interview. They also reviewed all other available information, including school records, referral notes, and nursing observations. In the Werry *et al.* (1983) study, the number of diagnosticians ranged from two to four, depending on the "punctiliousness of the raters in completing their sheets" (p. 343) after the cases were presented. Strober *et al.* used an early draft of DSM-III for all cases; Werry *et al.* used it for most of theirs. For broad categories, the overall kappas of .74 (Strober) and .71 (Werry) were slightly higher than the kappa of .68 obtained with the early draft of the

DSM used in the first field trial and considerably higher than the kappa of .52 obtained with the later draft of DSM-III used in the last field trial. The relatively high reliabilities in the Strober and Werry studies may reflect a possible superiority of the earlier draft, as well as more extensive data, greater severity, or more distinctiveness associated with inpatient disorders.

In the only study reporting test–retest reliability, Freeman (1971) found 72% agreement (uncorrected for chance) between GAP diagnoses by psychiatrists who reread the same case histories after a 3-month interval. The fact that information about each case stayed the same suggests that inconsistencies in the diagnosticians' judgments of the same material limit the reliability of the GAP system, and perhaps the others as well.

Although current Kraepelinian categories are not operationally defined via particular assessment procedures, the DISC was developed to assess specific DSM-III taxonomic criteria via structured interviews with children, while the DISC-P was designed to get similar data from their parents (Edelbrock & Costello, Chapter 4, this volume). Computer algorithms were also developed to avoid inconsistencies in translating DISC data into DSM-III diagnoses. It is therefore worth considering what was found when an assessment method was designed specifically to make DSM diagnoses in this fashion. The findings can be summarized as follows (Costello *et al.*, 1984):

1. Because many DSM-III criteria could not be reliably scored dichotomously as present or absent, they were converted to 0–1–2 scoring scales anchored by never/sometimes/often.
2. The DSM-III criteria for excluding certain disorders on the grounds of being "due to" others create logical contradictions that necessitated dropping these criteria.
3. Both lay and clinical interviewers could be trained to administer the DISC and score child and parent responses with high reliability.
4. As reported earlier in this chapter, repeat interviews by both types of interviewers revealed a marked tendency for children to change their reponses from "yes" to "no," severely limiting test–retest reliability until the adolescent years, when it became more adequate.
5. DSM-III diagnoses derived from DISC interviews with children showed little agreement with diagnoses derived from DISC-P interviews with their parents or with diagnoses made from complete clinical workups.
6. For some diagnoses, DSM-III criteria produced such high base rates and so many overlaps with other diagnoses as to severely limit their utility. The DISC-P, for example, diagnosed 79% of clinic children as having oppositional disorder, 52% as having one or more conduct disorders, and 46% as having attention deficit disorders, with many children meeting the criteria for all three types of disorders.

The DISC effort to derive a specific assessment procedure from current Kraepelinian nosology thus suggests that changes are required in the nosology and that structured interviews with children are unlikely to provide definitive assessment data.

Psychodynamic Paradigm

In the psychodynamic approach, the lack of any prescribed assessment procedures or explicit classification rules leaves the entire assessment and classification process to the discretion of the diagnostician. The psychodynamic categories shown in Table 10-2 are based on inferences about personality functioning rather than phenotypic disorders. Each category encompasses diverse possibilities for which no descriptive criteria are provided. This makes it hard to apply specific assessment procedures that can be evaluated for reliability in their own right, separately from the final taxonomic judgments. The four-step ratings employed for the 11 categories of the Greenspan et al. (1980) Metapsychological Assessment Profile could be tested for reliability, but reliability data have not been published for either these ratings or the categorical judgments of Anna Freud's Developmental Profile. Psychoanalysts' ratings of similar variables in adult patients have not yielded high reliability, however (Auerbach & Luborsky, 1968; Garduk & Haggard, 1972).

Multivariate Paradigm

Unlike the Kraepelinian and psychodynamic paradigms, the multivariate paradigm does not require us to match diverse data to verbally specified taxonomic categories. Instead, standardized assessment data are aggregated mathematically. When multivariate findings are used to make taxonomic distinctions, it is by computing the scores of individual cases on the standardized measures and determining whether they exceed cutoff points previously established for discriminating between particular criterion groups. For classification based on entire profile patterns, quantitative indices of similarity to profile types—such as the intraclass correlation—can be used; Achenbach and Edelbrock (1983) present detailed illustrations. Although subjective decisions are involved in constructing such procedures, once the procedures are finalized, a particular set of assessment data should always produce the same taxonomic results. Because the process of assigning cases to classes is thus not a source of unreliability, questions of reliability can focus entirely on the assessment data that serve as input.

Table 10-4 summarizes findings for the reliability and stability of multivariate syndromes scored from ratings by parents, teachers, and mental health workers. The findings are summarized in terms of the mean Pearson correlations between the scores obtained from pairs of raters or the same rater on two occasions.

The correlations in Table 10-4 primarily reflect similarities in the *rank-ordering* of scores obtained from two raters or the same rater on two occasions. In those studies that provided sufficient data for comparison of the

TABLE 10-4. Reliability and Stability of Ratings in Multivariate Studies

Type of measure	Type of rater	Types of syndromes[a]	
		Narrow-band	Broad-band
Test–retest reliability (1 week to 1 month)	Parents	.88	.90
	Teachers	.85	.88
Short-term stability ($1\frac{1}{2}$ to 6 months)	Parents	.77	.83
	Teachers	.71	.77
	Mental health workers	.65	.69
Long-term stability (15 months to 5 years)	Parents	.52	.60
Interrater correlations	Parents	.69	.69
	Teachers		.79
	Mental health workers	.72	
Different raters seeing children in different contexts		.19	.37

[a]Averages computed for z-transformed Pearson correlations in studies reported by Achenbach and Edelbrock (1978, 1983), Edelbrock and Achenbach (1984), and Edelbrock, Greenbaum, and Conover (1985).

magnitude of scores, there were no consistent differences between two types of informants (e.g., mothers vs. fathers) who rated children at the same time. In test–retest ratings of nonreferred children by the parents and teachers on two occasions over short periods (1 week to 1 month), behavior problem scores tended to decline from the first to the second occasion (Achenbach & Edelbrock 1983, 1986; Evans, 1975; Milich, Roberts, Loney, & Caputo, 1980). Because these findings pertain to nonreferred children, they are probably due not to regression effects but to "practice" effects on ratings repeated over a short period. Similar small declines were found in DISC-P test–retest data obtained from parents of referred children, but much larger declines were found in DISC data obtained from the children themselves (Edelbrock & Costello, Chapter 4, this volume). The small declines in problems reported by parents and teachers over brief intervals are less likely to affect diagnostic classification than are the major declines found in DISC interviews with children.

Because they were not exposed to identical data about the children, ratings by pairs of parents and pairs of mental health workers might reflect real differences between the children's actions in the presence of each rater. The lowest correlations in Table 10-4 occurred where there were major differences between both the situation and the type of rater (e.g., parent vs.

teacher vs. clinician). This may reflect differences in the judgmental standards of different types of informants, as well as differences in the child's behavior in their presence. Integration of differing assessment data is a key taxonomic challenge to be addressed later in the chapter.

The findings summarized in Table 10-4 concern syndrome scores, but not classification according to profile patterns. Although children can be classified by computing the similarity (e.g., intraclass correlation) of their profiles to profile types, data from different informants might produce profiles differing enough to result in assignment to different profile types. To test this possibility, Edelbrock and Achenbach (1980) scored profiles from Child Behavior Checklists completed by mothers of outpatient children and by a psychologist who interviewed the child and parents and examined checklist ratings by the parents, teachers, and—for those more than 10 years old—the children themselves. Because the psychologist obtained data from the mothers, her judgments were not completely independent of the mothers' ratings. However, the psychologist's ratings were also based on interviews with the child, ratings by fathers, teachers, and older children, and her judgment of the accuracy of each of the other informants. When profiles were classified according to objective quantitative criteria (detailed by Edelbrock & Achenbach, 1980), classifications derived from the psychologist's and mothers' ratings averaged 74% agreement for differentiated profile types and 83% for more global groupings of these differentiated profiles. The mean kappas were .64 for the differentiated profile types and .62 for the global types.

Validity

In our present stage of knowledge it is hard to select validity criteria for a taxonomy of child and adolescent disorders, because we lack independent operational definitions against which to test taxonomies. Spitzer and Cantwell (1980) emphasized "face validity" as a basis for the choice of DSM-III categories and their defining criteria. This refers to a judgment by the authors of the categories that their criteria accurately reflect the constructs they have in mind, but it is merely a starting point for constructing a taxonomy, rather than a test of its adequacy.

The lack of preexisting validity criteria means that taxonomies must be validated largely in terms of their relations to a variety of imperfect external criteria. Both the taxonomies and the external criteria may need to be progressively revised in order to improve the constructs as well as their defining criteria. In the process we modify the theoretical constructs, their operational definitions, and the validity criteria in response to new data. Because there has been little formal research on psychodynamic taxonomies of childhood disorders we will focus on Kraepelinian and multivariate taxonomies.

Kraepelinian Paradigm

Kraepelinian categories of childhood disorders have originated largely with constructs based on clinical observations, whereas multivariate analyses yield operational definitions of syndromes and profile types that can then be a source of theoretical constructs. As Table 10-3 indicated, there are similarities between the descriptive features of several DSM-III and multivariate syndromes. Furthermore, when the DSM-III descriptive features were quantified from DISC-P interviews, several of the syndromes correlated significantly with corresponding multivariate syndromes scored from standardized checklists filled out by the parents (Costello *et al.*, 1984; Edelbrock, 1984). When children were grouped according to whether they exceeded, met, or failed to meet DSM-III criteria for each disorder, these groupings showed a clear association with clinical cutoff points on the scores of corresponding multivariate syndromes, as illustrated in Figure 10-1. It can thus be seen that when the descriptive features of certain DSM-III syndromes are quantified, they agree with the findings of certain multivariate syndromes scored from reports by the same informants (i.e., the parents).

Beside the construct validity implied for both the DISC-P and multivariate syndromes by their mutual association, the construct validity of some Kraepelinian syndromes has been supported by research on a variety of correlates. Although underlying abnormalities have not been identified to account for the phenotypic features, autism seems to be the best validated childhood syndrome (Rutter & Schopler, Chapter 13, this volume). Autism is distinctive not only with respect to the co-occurrence of particular behaviors, but with respect to the rarity of many of the behaviors, early evidence of extreme abnormalities, unusual cognitive and social deficits, and long-term debilitation. It fits the nosological model better than any other childhood disorder yet delineated and is quite different from most of those to which multivariate approaches have been addressed. Even with this disorder, however,

> It is all too apparent that there is no readily recognizable separation point between "true" autism and other disorders that share some behavioral features but do not fulfill the complete set of accepted diagnostic criteria. Of course, in reality, such a differentiation could only be based on some unequivocal indication of some specifically and uniquely autistic feature. Such a feature has yet to be identified. Moreover, many behavioral disorders are best conceptualized in dimensional rather than categorical terms; accordingly, it should not be assumed that there will prove to be any pathognomonic defining feature for autism. (Rutter & Schopler, Chapter 13, this volume)

Aside from autism, research has identified correlates of conduct disorders, attention deficit disorders, and childhood depression. As the chapters by Taylor (12) and Rutter (11) persuasively show, however, specific nosological conceptions of these heavily researched and relatively common disorders

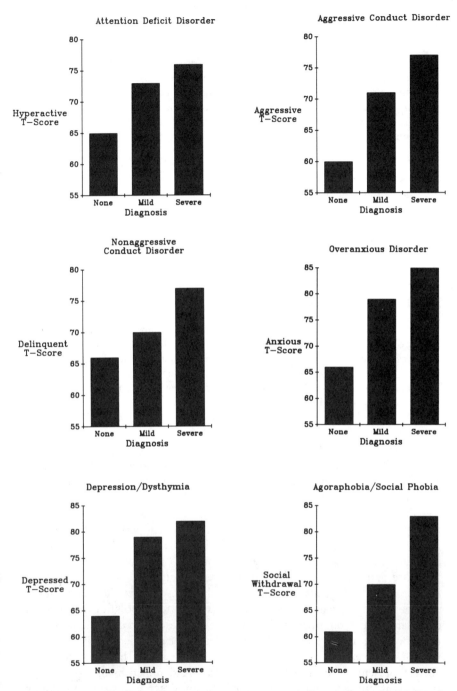

FIGURE 10-1. Relations between DSM-III syndrome scores from the DISC-P and *T* scores on corresponding scales of the Child Behavior Profile. A *T* score of 70 is the upper limit of the normal range on scales of the Child Behavior Profile. From Edelbrock (1984). Reprinted by permission.

have not been well validated. With respect to attention deficit disorders and their separation from conduct disorders, Taylor maintains that

> The lesson from these very different comparisons of diagnostic groups is not that the nosological questions are near solution. Rather, there are quite strong indications that existing diagnostic schemes are unsatisfactory and that many approaches to describing a hyperactive subgroup of the externalizing behavior disorders have failed. (Taylor, Chapter 12, this volume)

In critiquing the nosology of adult depression as a model for child depression research, Rutter cites substantial progress in understanding and treatment, but concludes that

> ... it is sometimes assumed that all is well with respect to the nosology of depressive disorders as they occur in adults. It is evident that this is far from the case, although it is equally true that a good deal is known. (Rutter, Chapter 11, this volume)

Over and above problems with the specific categories of specific taxonomies, Gould, Shaffer, Rutter, and Sturge observe that

> Problems in the reliability and validity of diagnoses appear to stem from problems of measurement or psychiatric conceptualization rather than from difficulties in a particular classification system. Both ICD-9 and DSM-III include a much more detailed subcategorization of disorders than could be justified on the basis of findings regarding either reliability or validity. (Gould *et al.*, Chapter 2, this volume)

Multivariate Paradigm

Like nosological categories, multivariate syndromes and profile types must be tested against external criteria. Ready-made validity criteria are no more available for multivariate taxonomic efforts than for Kraepelinian efforts. Yet the conceptual frameworks of the multivariate and Kraepelinian approaches differ enough to warrant somewhat different perspectives on validity. As it is currently applied to childhood disorders, the Kraepelinian approach can be viewed as proceeding from the "top down." That is, decisions are first reached about what disorders exist; criteria are then formulated to identify these disorders in actual children. The decisions and criteria may be based on clinical observations, theory, extrapolation from adult disorders, and so on; once made, however, they establish a strong presumption about the nature and types of disorders to be considered. The DSM-III version of Kraepelinian disorders generally implies that they exist in a categorical, present-versus-absent form that can be identified by fixed-rule criteria. This is not an essential feature of the top down approach to defining disorders, but it has yielded more explicit criteria than most other Kraepelinian efforts.

The multivariate approach, by contrast, moves more from the "bottom up." That is, it starts with data on actual cases and analyzes the data to determine what syndromes exist on the basis of what features tend to co-occur. Decisions are obviously required about the data to obtain, whom to obtain the data from, subject samples, methods of analysis, and so forth. However, the aim is to build up taxonomic constructs from findings on sample of cases. Questions of validity therefore start with methodological issues, such as whether findings are replicated across samples, instruments, and procedures. In fact, research on multivariate syndromes has shown significant correlations between syndromes scored from different instruments (see Achenbach & Edelbrock, 1978, 1983, 1986; Edelbrock et al., 1985). When a single instrument was factor analyzed for several different populations, similar syndromes were also found (see Achenbach & Edelbrock, 1978; Quay, 1979). Furthermore, by factor analyzing an instrument designed to test syndromes hypothesized on the basis of previous multivariate findings, Achenbach, Conners, and Quay (1985) confirmed nearly all of the hypothesized syndromes. Evidence is thus accumulating for the replicability of a group of syndromes that can be assessed by means of several different instruments for quantitatively scoring descriptive features.

Beyond the replicability of syndromes, there is a growing body of findings on the correlates of quantitatively scored syndromes. The power of a common set of multivariate syndromes to discriminate between clinically referred and "normal" children has been demonstrated in several countries, including the United States (Achenbach & Edelbrock, 1983), Chile (Montenegro, 1983), and Holland (Verhulst, 1985). Several studies show that children manifesting broad-band syndromes of externalizing problems have less adequate families, are less socially competent, have worse outcomes, and are less appropriate candidates for traditional mental health services than children manifesting broad-band syndromes of internalizing problems (see Achenbach & Edelbrock, 1978). Research also shows associations between narrow-band multivariate syndromes and variables such as attention deficits, impulsivity, gender disturbance, depression, firesetting, epilepsy, conduct problems, child abuse, and ego functioning (see Achenbach & Edelbrock, 1983, Appendix F). Classification of children according to profile types derived by cluster analysis has shown significant discrimination with respect to other variables, such as social competencies and demographic characteristics (Achenbach & Edelbrock, 1983; Langner, Gersten, & Eisenberg, 1974).

The identification of correlates is necessary to build confidence in any taxonomy, but the correlates identified to date for the multivariate findings are no more decisive as validity criteria than are the correlates identified for Kraepelinian categories of childhood disorders. Instead, to advance taxonomy through either approach we need to examine the cognitive underpinnings of the taxonomic process, to which we now turn. Thereafter, we will consider some possibilities for a more complete integration of assessment with taxonomy, as geared to our present stage of knowledge and the tasks that face us.

PROTOTYPES AS A BASIS FOR TAXONOMY

The process of categorization is traditionally viewed as governed by criteria that are "singly necessary and jointly sufficient" for defining a case as a member of a category (Cantor, Smith, French, & Mezzich, 1980, p. 182). Cognitive research indicates, however, that human thought processes do not conform to this model. Studies of common categories such as furniture, for example, show that the items people categorize together do not all share any particular defining features (Rosch & Mervis, 1975). Instead, the concept of a particular category seems to be based largely on clear-cut exemplars of the category, called *prototypes*. The features of these cases tend to define the category, but not all cases assigned to a category share all the same features. In the category of furniture, for example, tables and chairs are prototypic exemplars that share few features with less prototypic exemplars, such as lamps and rugs. Items with relatively few prototypic features are less reliably classified than those with many prototypic features (Smith, 1978).

According to the prototype view, conceptual categories consist of sets of imperfectly correlated features that encompass cases ranging from clear-cut prototypes having many of the category's features, to borderline cases having few of the category's features. This implies that category membership is a matter of degree, rather than being all or none; it can therefore be computed in terms of the overlap between the features of a case and the list of features that define a category.

Applications to Psychopathology

Prototype concepts have been applied to psychopathology in several ways. Cantor *et al.* (1980), for example, asked 13 clinicians to list the features of nine diagnostic categories. In all nine categories, many features were listed by only one clinician, a smaller number were listed by two to four clinicians, and very few were listed by most of the clinicians. The different degrees of agreement for different features suggested that the diagnostic categories consisted of imperfectly correlated features rather than necessary and sufficient defining criteria that are shared by all clinicians. When the clinicians were asked to make diagnoses from case histories, the interclinician reliability was found to be significantly worse for patients having only four features than for those having more. Another study showed that a major reason for low diagnostic reliability when few features are present is that some clinicians infer a complete diagnostic prototype from a few features, whereas others do not (Horowitz, Post, French, Wallis, & Siegelman, 1981).

In an application of prototype analysis to concepts of childhood disorders, experienced staff members of a residential treatment program were asked to list the features of three types of disturbed children, designated as the *aggressive–impulsive* child, the *depressed–withdrawn* child, and the *borderline–disorganized* child (Horowitz, Wright, Lowenstein, & Parad, 1981). Prototypes were formed from features that were listed with a probability of at least .29 for a type of child. Several features met the criteria for more than one type of child, with the disorganized-borderline prototype showing the most overlap with the others (9 unique features vs. 12 features shared with the other two prototypes).

Prototypes were similarly derived from features listed by college student staff members who were returning after one previous summer of experience ("returnees") and a second group with no previous experience ("novices"). The prototypes generated by returnees shared somewhat more features with those of the regular staff than did the prototypes generated by the novices. Some features listed by a large proportion of novices were not included in the prototypes generated by the more experienced staff. This suggests a progressive convergence toward particular sets of prototypic features as experience increased.

To apply prototype analyses to covariation among features in actual patients, cases receiving DSM-III Axis II diagnoses of borderline personality disorder were studied by Clarkin, Widiger, Frances, Hurt, and Gilmore (1983). DSM-III specifies eight descriptive criteria for borderline personality disorder, of which at least five must be present to make the diagnosis. Clarkin *et al.* tested the relations between each of the features and diagnoses of borderline personality versus other personality disorders by scoring each feature from standardized interviews with the patients.

Patients were diagnosed as having borderline personality when a majority of raters scored them as having at least five of the eight features specified by DSM-III. Three of the features were present in at least 90% of the patients diagnosed as borderline, while one feature was present in only 25%. There was also variation in the proportion of features present, as 10% of the patients had all eight, 25% had seven, 40% had five. This meant that patients receiving the diagnosis varied not only in the degree of prototypicality but in the combination of features displayed.

Clarkin *et al.* computed conditional probabilities for the presence of criterial features in borderline versus other personality disorders (conditional probability = the percent of all cases manifesting the feature who also met the criterion for borderline personality). They found that one criterial feature was present in *fewer* cases diagnosed as borderline than receiving other diagnoses (conditional probability = .38). Five other features had conditional probabilities ranging from .50 to .59, while the remaining two were in the .60s. The diagnostic efficiency of individual criterial features was thus low. The findings demonstrated a generally poor match between the DSM-III's a priori criteria and the "empirical prevalence and covariation of diagnostic features" for this particular diagnostic category (Clarkin *et al.*, 1983, p. 294). Similar findings have been obtained for a priori classifications of behavior assessed by direct observations, indicating that the problems are not confined to the DSM's diagnostic categories (Stouthamer-Loeber & Peters, 1984).

Empirically Derived Prototypes

The foregoing section concerned *conceptual prototypes*, comprised of features that people *think of* as occurring together. As suggested by the studies of borderline personality and behavioral classifications, however, conceptual prototypes may not accurately reflect covariation among the features of the phenomena to be categorized. There is no way of knowing what features really occur together without recording the actual covariation among the features.

Multivariate techniques, such as factor analysis, can be used to derive syndromes that reflect the actual covariation among features scored in a sample of cases. If the sample is large enough to be statistically reliable and is representative of a particular population, the results constitute *empirically derived prototypes*. Because human attributes are seldom perfectly correlated with each other, few members of the population will manifest every feature of a prototype. However, the number of prototypic features manifested by an individual can be used as a quantitative index of the degree to which he or she matches the prototype.

Although each feature of a conceptual prototype is typically judged as either present or absent, this binary categorization is apt to mask quantitative variations in the features and our perception of them. Features are most likely to be judged present when they are especially salient, intense, or otherwise evident in high degree. Even behaviors that are theoretically either present or absent are subject to quantitative variations in people's awareness of them. If a child tells minor lies at intervals of several months, for example, the probability of detection is lower and the judgment that the problem behavior exists is less likely than if the child often tells major lies. In categorizing behavior problems, quantitative considerations thus affect our judgment of each criterial feature, which in turn affects the number of features judged present, and hence the degree to which a case matches a prototype.

If quantitative variations underlie our judgments of criterial features and our categorization of cases, why not tap these quantitative variations directly in the derivation and use of taxonomic prototypes? Although neither the criterial features nor the prototypes are quantifiable with perfect precision, even crude metrification can link our taxonomic constructs more closely to the target phenomena than a priori categorical constructs currently do.

Implications of Prototype Views

The implications of prototype views can be summarized as follows:

1. Cognitive categories are based largely on conceptual prototypes comprising groups of features thought to correlate with each other.
2. Categorization of cases involves judgments of the degree to which the features of each case correspond to a set of prototypic features.
3. The judgment of correspondence between an individual case and a category is implicitly quantitative, based on the number of prototypic features judged to be present in the case.
4. Judgments of each prototypic feature are also implicitly quantitative, in that judgments of the feature's presence are based on its salience, intensity, and rate of occurrence.
5. Prototypes can be derived empirically through multivariate analyses of features scored in samples of individuals.
6. The similarity between individual cases and empirically derived prototypes can be computed from scores based on the degree to which prototypic features are present.

A TAXOMETRIC APPROACH TO ASSESSMENT AND TAXONOMY

By chunking information, categorical thinking helps us cope with multiple variables and the multiple values that each variable can assume. Yet, recognition of the quantitative underpinnings of categorical judgments shows that there is no intrinsic contradiction between categorical and quantitative approaches to assessment and taxonomy. Instead, it suggests that more explicit quantification can sharpen assessment and taxonomy, as well as strengthening the links between them. To appreciate the possibilities, let us view the overall structure of taxonomy from a metrical perspective.

The term *taxometry* emphasizes quantitative aspects of attributes and syndromes, in contrast to viewing individuals as all-or-none exemplars of mutually exclusive categories. The term "taxometrics" has previously been applied to the use of cluster analysis for classifying biological species (Sneath & Sokal, 1973) and to psychometric procedures for identifying people hypothesized to have genotypes for schizophrenia (Meehl & Golden, 1982). In both instances, however, metrical methods are intended to categorize cases in an ultimately yes-or-no fashion, corresponding to classical, nonquantitative taxonomies.

Even if a disorder truly exists in categorical form, incomplete knowledge of its specific etiology or a lack of definitive diagnostic techniques argue for assessing quantitative variations in its features. (Note that using quantitative variations to help define disorders is a separate task from using quantitative variations to judge the severity of disorders that are already well defined.) If categories are imposed when the true boundaries of disorders are unknown, some individuals who do not have the disorders will be treated in the same way as those who do, and vice versa. A metrical approach, on the other hand, can reflect both quantitative variations in phenotypic features and the probabilistic nature of features that do not inevitably signify the presence of the disorder. Where multiple features are scored in degrees and their scores are aggregated into a total score, individuals with the highest scores are the most likely to have the disorder, whereas those with the lowest scores are least likely to have it.

Research on prototypic concepts shows that the ease with which a case is recognized as a member of a category depends on the degree to which it manifests prototypic features of the category (Horowitz, Post, *et al.*, 1981; Rosch, Mervis, Gray, Johnson, & Boyes-Graem, 1976; Smith, 1978). Using a quantitative index of prototypic features, we can regard cases having the highest scores as the most likely true positive and those with the lowest scores as the most likely true negative instances of a disorder. Decisions about cases with intermediate scores can be based on the relative disadvantages of false-positive and false-negative misclassifications. If incorrectly classifying cases as positive is most undesirable, the cutoff can be set high on the distribution of scores for prototypic features, thereby minimizing false positives. If, on the other hand, incorrectly classifying cases as negative is most undesirable, the cutoff point can be set low to minimize false negatives.

A further benefit of quantifying prototypic features is that an intermediate range of scores can be identified for which no classification decisions are justified without further data. Even with additional data, some cases might be better left unclassified rather than risk incorrect decisions. Any choice of cutoff points for distinguishing between negative, unclassifiable, and positive cases should be validated against external criteria. However, distributions of quantitative scores typically provide a better basis for validation than do categorical classifications, which fail to reflect differences between weak, moderate, and strong evidence for a disorder.

Although metrification may be helpful even with categorical disorders, there is little reason to assume that most childhood disorders actually exist in categorical form, such that all children can be definitively divided into those who do versus those who do not have each disorder. Instead, etiologic factors are likely to operate in varying combinations and degrees, and their effects are likely to depend on multiple variables, such as a child's constitutional strengths and vulnerabilities, temperament, developmental level, competencies, family dynamics, and life stress. Considering the range of influences and variations in childhood disorders, a taxometric approach is especially helpful where there are no a priori categorical commitments.

By viewing disorders in terms of quantifiable prototypic syndromes, we can avoid dilemmas arising when children display more than one kind of maladaptive behavior. Nonquantitative categorical systems, such as DSM-III, handle this through multiple diagnoses of the same child, although DSM-III excludes certain diagnoses when the criteria for other diagnoses met. Costello *et al.* (1984) found, however, that the DSM-III exclusion rules contain too many mutual contradictions to be applied consistently. (DSM-III-R uses fewer exclusion rules.) Furthermore, the use of multiple diagnoses to reflect different kinds of problem behavior in the same child implies that the child is suffering from several distinct disorders (termed comorbidity), whereas the different kinds of behavior may be closely interrelated. When different kinds of problems are present, it has been found that people tend to ignore those that are inconsistent with the category uppermost in their mind (Horrowitz, Post, *et al.*, 1981). By scoring syndromes quantitiatively and displaying scores for all relevant syndromes in a profile format, the need for forced choices between categories is eliminated and there is less risk of neglecting features that do not conform to the most salient category. The transformation of syndrome scores into norm-based standard scores makes it possible to compare the child's degree of deviance on each syndrome relative to the others.

Taxometric Typologies

Many current technological advances involve innovative ways of reducing large masses of data to more comprehensible form. In medical diagnosis, for example, computed tomography (CT scanning) integrates many low-grade data points into higher-grade images of inner structures. Similar procedures are applied to EEG data, as detailed by Ferguson and Bawden (Chapter 8, this volume) and Courchesne and Yeung-Courchesne (Chapter 9, this volume). Assessment of psychopathology might also benefit from the use of information processing technology to integrate multiple low-grade data points into higher-grade findings.

Our data points may include reports by parents and teachers, self-reports, structured observations of behavior, test responses, and medical findings. A fundamental challenge is to integrate diverse assessment data of differing reliability and relevance into a picture of the individual case that enables us to accumulate and draw on knowledge regarding similar cases. In other words, we need to form a conceptual construct of each case that can be linked with taxonomic constructs capable of highlighting the most informative similarities and differences between cases. How might we approach this?

There are numerous possible criteria for linking the individual case to other cases, but the child's age, sex, and cognitive level should always be considered in seeking comparable cases. Within groups of a particular age, sex, and cognitive level, typologies of features can be constructed from profiles of syndrome scores, using cluster analysis and other multivariate methods. The same children can be simultaneously classified by several typologies, such as those derived from standardized ratings by parents, teachers, clinicians, or the children themselves. Because important aspects of functioning are detectable only under certain conditions, it may be desirable to have taxometric typologies derived separately from different assessment techniques, such as ratings by different informants and psychometric measures. It may also be important to compare the patterns identified by different techniques in a single cluster analysis.

If a pattern derived from one technique is consistently associated with a pattern derived from another technique, the two patterns can be joined in a single type. There are often reasons, however, for maintaining the separation between different types of data in the assessment of individual children because particular assessment data—parent, teacher, or clinician ratings, direct observations, psychometrics, etc.—are not uniformly credible or available in all cases.

Clinical judgment is crucial in deciding what to do about individual cases, but the ability of assessment data to link cases with previously accumulated knowledge can be greatly enhanced through taxometric procedures. The process of linkage itself can be objectified by computing quantitative indices of similarity, such as the intraclass correlation between individual profiles and profile types. By using a quantitative index of similarity between a child's profile and previously established profile types we can avoid information processing biases that affect our subjective assignment of cases to categories (Achenbach, 1985, provides illustrations). The use of a quantitative index operationalizes the process of categorization. It also provides an objective basis for choosing among categories and for deciding against categorization when cases do not fit existing categories.

Summary of Taxometry

The main points of a taxometric approach can be summarized as follows:

1. Recognition of the quantitative underpinnings of categorical judgments shows that there is no intrinsic contradiction between categorical and quantitative approaches to assessment and taxonomy.
2. The term *taxometry* emphasizes quantitative aspects of attributes and syndromes, in contrast to viewing individuals as all-or-none exemplars of mutually exclusive categories.
3. Quantification of prototypes facilitates the selection and validation of cutoff points for discriminating between the most likely true-positive, true-negative, and unclassifiable cases.
4. Metrification can be helpful even for categorical disorders, but it is especially useful for childhood disorders where varying combinations of etiological factors and other variables are apt to affect phenotypic features.

5. By scoring syndromes quantitatively and displaying scores for all relevant syndromes in a profile format we avoid the need for forced choices between syndromes and reduce the risk of neglecting features that differ from the category uppermost in our mind.

6. A taxometric approach can integrate masses of low grade data into a conceptual construct of the individual case that can be operationally linked with taxonomic constructs.

7. Separate taxometic typologies can be constructed from different assessment techniques and sources of data.

8. Cases can be assigned to types on the basis of quantitative indices that enable us to choose the degree of prototypicality required for categorization.

9. A taxometric approach can take advantage of the increasing availability of computers to convert large quantities of data on each case to norm-based standard scores for syndromes, profiles, and quantitative indices of similarity to profile types.

MULTIAXIAL FACETS OF TAXONIC INTEGRATION

In taxometric approaches, taxa are derived directly from a particular set of assessment data. The data should be obtained, scored, and analyzed in a standardized fashion for all cases. This differs from most taxonomies of psychopathology, which leave the diagnostician to decide what data to obtain and how to use it in categorizing disorders. Because no single set of taxonomic constructs—such as psychiatric syndromes—can provide a comprehensive picture, multiaxial systems have been devised to highlight multiple facets of functioning. The use of multiple axes is an important advance likely to be useful in all approaches. The WHO system proposed by Rutter *et al.* (1975), for example, has four axes, while the ICD-9 and DSM-III have five.

Whatever taxonomic approach we favour, it is helpful to base axes on methods of assessment that can be translated directly into taxonomic constructs for different aspects of functioning. As illustrated in Table 10-5, one axis can reflect functioning as reported by parents or parent surrogates via standardized ratings. Once children reach school age, teachers' judgments contribute a second important axis, also assessed via standardized ratings. Because nonreactive observational assessment is usually more feasible in the school than home, observational procedures can supplement teacher reports, although teachers' ratings provide a more uniform basis for norm-based typologies.

Beside standardized data obtained from parents and teachers, standardized assessment of cognitive functioning can constitute a third axis, which is already included in the WHO and ICD-9 systems. DSM-III takes account of

TABLE 10-5. Examples of Multiaxial Assessment and Taxonomy

Age range (yr)	Axis I Parents' judgments	Axis II Teachers' judgments	Axis III Cognitive assessment	Axis IV Physical conditions	Axis V Clinician's assessment[b]
0–2	Developmental history; Minnesota Child Development Inventory[a] (Ireton & Thwing, 1974)	—	Bayley (1969) Infant Scales[a]	Height, weight, neurological and medical exam	Observations during developmental testing
2–5	Developmental history; Child Behavior Checklist[a] (Achenbach & Edelbrock, 1983); Lousiville Behavior Checklist[a] (Miller, 1981)	Kohn (1977) Symptom Checklist[a]; Preschool Behavior Checklist[a] (Behar & Stringfield, 1974)	McCarthy (1972) Scales[a]	Height, weight, neurological and medical exam	Observations during play interview
6–11	Developmental history; Child Behavior Checklist[a] (Achenbach & Edelbrock, 1983); Lousiville Behavior Checklist[a] (Miller, 1981)	CBCL—Teacher's Report Form[a] (Edelbrock & Achenbach, 1984); School Behavior Checklist[a] (Miller, 1972)	Achievement tests[a]; Kaufman Assessment Battery[a] (Kaufman & Kaufman, 1983); Koppitz (1975) Bender Gestalt; WISC-R[a] (Wechsler, 1974)	Height, weight, neurological and medical exam	Child Assessment Schedule (Hodges et al., 1982); Semistructured Clinical Interview for Children[a] (Achenbach & McConaughy, 1985)
12–18	Developmental history; Child Behavior Checklist[a] (Achenbach & Edelbrock, 1983); Lousiville Behavior Checklist[a] (Miller, 1981)	CBCL—Teacher's Report Form[a] (Edelbrock & Achenbach, 1984); School Behavior Checklist[a] (Miller, 1972)	Achievement tests[a]; WISC-R[a]; WAIS-R[a] (Wechsler, 1981)	Height, weight, neurological and medical exam	DISC[a] (Costello et al., 1984); Youth Self-Report[a] (Achenbach & Edelbrock, 1983)

Note. Where multiple instruments are available, those with the most promising reliability, validity, and normative data are listed. From Achenbach (1985). Reprinted by permission.

[a]Taxometric approach feasible.

[b]This axis can include many other procedures, such as home and school observations; family assessment; reports from other clinicians; and behavioral tests, such as role playing and measures of avoidance and physiological reactions to fear stimuli.

cognitive level only by means of diagnoses of mental retardation, with sub-types defined in terms of IQ and listed on the same axis as psychiatric syndromes. As pointed out by Rutter and Shaffer (1980), it makes more sense to view cognitive ability as a continuous dimension on which all levels are important, rather than in terms of arbitrary cutoffs for defining retardation as a disorder. Beside IQ scores, other important measures of cognitive functioning, such as achievement tests and standardized measures of perceptual–motor functioning, can be listed on this axis.

The importance of physical abnormalities deserves recognition on a separate axis, as included in the WHO, ICD-9, and DSM-III systems. The listing of medical disorders can follow prevailing medical taxonomies, but age-based percentiles for height and weight should also be listed to highlight deviations relevant to the overall case formulation. If adequate normative data are obtained for measures of neurological functioning, such as the PANESS (Guy, 1976), these could be included, too.

Since practitioners need to form personal mental constructs of their cases, it is important to maximize the reliability, validity, and utility of such constructs. The clinical interview with the child is the most universal assessment procedure and the one we would be most loathe to omit before making a case formulation. Yet, it is one of the least validated procedures, and its reliability is limited by vast differences in interviewers' effects on children, their interview techniques, and the way in which they draw conclusions from interviews. If taxometric principles are applied to practitioners' personal assessments of the child and family, they could potentially yield a set of operationally defined taxonomic constructs analogous to the syndromes and profile types derived empirically from parents' and teachers' ratings.

Although parent and teacher ratings span a variety of occasions and situations, practitioners' contacts with children may be limited to interview situations that are unrepresentative of the child's usual environment. How can these brief opportunities provide reliable, valid, and clinically useful data that could not be more easily obtained in other ways?

As discussed earlier, children below the age of about 11 may not be able to provide reliable and valid answers to such highly structured questions as those in the DISC. On the other hand, unstructured interviews do not provide standardized coverage of a uniform set of questions. As a compromise, semistructured interviews can be used to obtain elementary school children's responses to open-ended questions about important issues, such as family, school, peer relations, feelings about the self, anxieties, aspirations, and fantasies. Having children draw pictures of their family can also encourage the expression of feelings that are difficult to reach through direct questions. School-related tasks, such as individual achievement tests, can be included to sample children's ways of coping with academic demands.

Although the precise course of such interviews will vary from child to child, it is possible to apply taxometric procedures to the scoring and aggregation of interview data. This is being done by Achenbach and McConaughy

(1985), who have developed separate instruments for rating what 6- to 11-year-old children say and what they do during semistructured clinical interviews. From this research, it is evident that what some children do is more informative than what they say, whereas other children show the opposite pattern. There is a developmental trend in these patterns, with verbal self-reports typically becoming more informative after the age of about 8. However, some younger children convey more by talk than action, whereas some older children convey more by action than talk. Direct clinical assessment must therefore be flexible enough to encompass the variations from child to child. Accordingly, the taxometric use of interviews requires recognition that their yield varies and that they must always be evaluated in relation to the other facets of multiaxial assessment and taxonomy.

Adolescents' ability to grasp structured-interview questions can yield higher test–retest reliability than obtained for younger children in interviews such as the DISC (Edelbrock et al., 1985). This does not necessarily mean, however, that it is easy to gain adolescents' confidence or candor, or that highly structured questioning is the best use of interview time with adolescents. Instead, adolescents can complete self-report checklists paralleling those used to obtain taxometric data from parents and teachers (see Achenbach & Edelbrock, 1983, 1986, 1987). Not only do these provide standardized data for taxometric purposes, but they elicit adolescents' responses to a large variety of questions without requiring the clinician's time. Because it is often awkward to ask about topics such as suicidal ideation, hallucinations, and anxieties in an initial interview with adolescents, the value of interviews can be increased by using them to follow up on adolescents' responses to a problem list that includes these items.

The salience of impressions produced by interviews makes it necessary to guard against the information processing biases to which they are vulnerable. If we apply taxometric principles to direct clinical assessment, we can increase the rigor of the fifth axis shown in Table 10-5. The profile patterns derived from adolescents' checklist responses and elementary school children's semistructured interviews may be especially useful as guides to the selection of therapies. For example, a child's tendency to acknowledge and verbalize problems or to deny and act out problems may indicate the degree to which talking therapies versus other approaches are appropriate. It is important to note, however, that the potential of a taxometric approach for standardizing, quantifying, and integrating large quantities of data does not reduce the clinician's role in the case formulation. On the contrary, taxometric approaches should strengthen the clinician's ability to make precise case formulations by reducing the effects of information overload, subjective biases, and arbitrary categorization.

IMPLICATIONS FOR CLINICAL SERVICES AND RESEARCH

The implications of the views presented in this chapter can be summarized as follows:

1. The multiple facets of children's functioning require multiple assessment procedures which fulfill different taxonic functions, as outlined in Table 10-5.
2. Certain axes will tell us less in some cases than in others, such as Axis II (teacher judgments) if the child is not attending school; Axis III (cognitive assessment) if the child's abilities and achievement are all in the average range; and Axis IV (physical conditions) if there are no organic abnormalities. Nevertheless, multiaxial perspectives highlight each facet in its own right, rather than collapsing all facets into a single diagnostic construct. Similarities and differences in the way children are seen by their parents, teachers, and clinicians can thus be preserved rather than obscured.
3. Within Axes I, II, and V (parent, teacher, and clinician assessments), taxometric methods can objectively classify children according to profile types that are scored from standardized assessment procedures. The assessment data are not limited to reports of overt behavior, because all the relevant informants can also rate children's emotions and social relations. IQ, achievement, and perceptual–motor tests provide an analogous basis for Axis III classification.
4. By using the same standardized assessment procedures for clinical and research taxometry, we can reduce existing gaps between clinical practice and research.
5. The same standardized taxometric procedures can be used in epidemiological studies of specific problems, syndromes, and profile patterns, thereby linking epidemiology more directly with research and clinical practice.
6. The definition of disorders for purposes of third-party payment is an increasing problem. DSM-III's diagnoses are intended to conform to the medical model for reimbursement, but their modest reliability for childhood disorders and vulnerability to manipulation raise questions about proper reimbursement. A stronger empirical basis is therefore needed for defining and treating disorders.
7. If the rationale for the taxometric approach is accepted, the following types of research should receive high priority.
   a. Further development of standardized taxometric procedures for clinicians' assessment of children and adolescents.
   b. Testing of relations between taxometric classification made on different axes to determine whether multiaxial patterns are useful (e.g., apply cluster analysis to profiles comprised of scales scored from parent, teacher, and interview instruments).

  c. Testing of correlates of profile types, including biological and other
     etiologies, typical course and outcome, and responsiveness to differ-
     ent treatments.

SUMMARY

This chapter addressed issues of assessment, taxonomy, and the integration
of assessment with taxonomy. *Assessment* aims to identify the distinguishing
features of each case, while *taxonomy* groups cases according to their distinguishing features. As indicated by detailed reviews in other chapters, the
differing strengths and limitations of major assessment approaches call for
multimethod assessment, rather than reliance on any one approach.

In taxonomy, the Kraepelinian paradigm has long shaped concepts of
adult disorders, and there is evidence for the validity of its major adult
categories. Its application to childhood disorders is more recent, however,
and, as indicated by several chapters of this book, is likely to require modification. Anna Freud proposed a psychodynamic taxonomy of inferred psychopathology, but it has not been adequately tested for reliability or validity.

Multivariate analyses of ratings by parents, teachers, and mental health
workers have yielded numerous narrow-band syndromes and a few broad-
band syndromes that show considerable consistency across studies. Some of
these syndromes are similar to those of DSM-III and correlate significantly
with the descriptive features of DSM-III syndromes. There are thus important parallels between the descriptive aspects of the multivariate and DSM-
III approach.

The multivariate approach can avoid forced choices between syndromes
by scoring the degree to which a child manifests the features of each syndrome, displaying standard scores in a profile format, and grouping children
according to their profile patterns. Because syndrome and profile scores are
derived quantitatively from standardized assessment procedures, this approach avoids taxonomic errors arising from unreliability in combining data.
The assessment data for multivariate taxonomic scores generally show good
test–retest reliability, moderate agreement between informants seeing children under fairly similar conditions (e.g., mothers vs. fathers), but lower
agreement between different types of informants seeing children under different conditions (e.g., parents vs. teachers vs. clinicians). This underlines the
need to obtain multiple perspectives on children's behavior.

Cognitive research indicates that conceptual categories have quantitative underpinnings, in that people categorize according to the degree to
which a particular case is perceived to have a category's prototypic features.
Conceptual prototypes of psychopathology, however, may not accurately
reflect the covariation among features occurring in actual cases. Multivariate
analyses of large, representative samples can provide empirically derived
prototypes that do reflect the actual covariation among features.

A *taxometric* approach explicitly quantifies attributes, syndromes, and profiles, rather than classifying individuals as all-or-none exemplars of categories. By quantifying prototypic features, we can discriminate between the most likely true-positive, true-negative, and unclassifiable cases. Cutoff points can be based on empirical criteria for minimizing false positives or false negatives, as desired.

Taxometric typologies can integrate multiple low-grade data points into comprehensive taxonomic constructs defined in terms of profile patterns. Separate taxometric typologies can be constructed from different assessment techniques and sources of data.

It was proposed that multiple axes be used to reflect different aspects of children's functioning assessed in different ways as follows: Axis I—parents' judgments; Axis II—teachers' judgments; Axis III—cognitive assessment; Axis IV—physical conditions; and Axis V—clinician's assessment. Axes I, II, and V include judgments of emotions and social relations, as well as specific behavioral problems and competencies. By using the same taxometric procedures for epidemiology, research, and clinical services, we can reduce existing gaps between these areas. According to this view, research is needed on taxometric procedures for clinicians' assessments, relations between taxometric classification on different axes, and correlates of taxometric typologies.

ACKNOWLEDGMENTS

This work was facilitated by support from the W. T. Grant and Spencer Foundations.

REFERENCES

Achenbach, T. M. (1978). The Child Behavior Profile. I. Boys aged 6–11. *Journal of Consulting and Clinical Psychology, 46,* 478–488.

Achenbach, T. M. (1985). *Assessment and taxonomy of child and adolescent psychopathology.* Beverly Hills: Sage Publications.

Achenbach, T. M., Conners, C. K., & Quay, H. C. (1985). *The ACQ Behavior Checklist.* Burlington: University of Vermont Department of Psychiatry.

Achenbach, T. M., & Edelbrock, C. (1978). The classification of child psychopathology: A review and analysis of empirical efforts. *Psychological Bulletin, 85,* 1275–1301.

Achenbach, T. M., & Edelbrock, C. (1983). *Manual for the Child Behavior Checklist and Revised Child Behavior Profile.* Burlington: University of Vermont Department of Psychiatry.

Achenbach, T. M., & Edelbrock, C. (1986). *Manual for the Teacher's Report Form and Teacher Version of the Child Behavior Profile.* Burlington: University of Vermont Department of Psychiatry.

Achenbach, T. M., & Edelbrock, C. (1987). *Manual for the Youth Self-Report and Profile.* Burlington: University of Vermont Department of Psychiatry.

Achenbach, T. M., & McConaughy, S. H. (1985). *Child Interview Checklist—Self Report Form; Child Interview Checklist—Observation Form.* Burlington: University of Vermont Department of Psychiatry.

Achenbach, T. M., McConaughy, S. H., & Howell, C. T. (1987). Child/adolescent behavioral and emotional problems: Implications of cross-informant correlations for situational specificity. *Psychological Bulletin, 101,* 213–232.

American Psychiatric Association. (1980). *Diagnostic and statistical manual of mental disorders* (3rd ed.). Washington DC: Author.

American Psychiatric Association. (1987). *Diagnostic and statistical manual of mental disorders* (3rd ed.—revised). Washington, DC: Author.

Auerbach, A. H., & Luborsky, L. (1968). Accuracy of judgments and the nature of the "good hour." In J. M. Shlien (Ed.), *Research in psychotherapy* (Vol. III). Washington, DC: American Psychological Association.

Bayley, N. (1969). *Bayley Scales of Infant Development.* New York: Psychological Corporation.

Behar, L. B., & Stringfield, S. (1974). A behavior rating scale for the preschool child. *Developmental Psychology, 10,* 601–610.

Beitchman, J. H., Dielman, T. E., Landis, J. R., Benson, R. M., & Kemp, P. L. (1978). Reliability of the Group for the Advancement of Psychiatry diagnostic categories in child psychiatry. *Archives of General Psychiatry, 35,* 1461–1466.

Cantor, N., Smith, E. E., French, R. deS., & Mezzich, J. (1980). Psychiatric diagnoses as prototype categorization. *Journal of Abnormal Psychology, 89,* 181–193.

Clarkin, J. F., Widiger, T. A., Frances, A., Hurt, S. W., & Gilmore, M. (1983). Prototypic typology and the borderline personality disorder. *Journal of Abnormal Psychology, 92,* 263–275.

Conners, C. K. (1973). Rating scales for use in drug studies with children. *Psychopharmacology bulletin: Pharmacotherapy with children.* Washington, DC: U.S. Government Printing Office.

Costello, A. J., Edelbrock, C., Dulcan, M. K., Kalas, R., & Klaric, S. H. (1984). *Report on the Diagnostic Interview Schedule for Children (DISC).* Pittsburgh: University of Pittsburgh Department of Psychiatry.

Edelbrock, C. (1984, October). *Relations between the NIMH Diagnostic Interview Schedule for Children (DISC) and the Child Behavior Checklist and Profile.* Paper presented at the meeting of the American Academy of Child Psychiatry, Toronto.

Edelbrock, C., & Achenbach, T. (1980). A typology of Child Behavior Profile patterns: Distribution and correlates for disturbed children aged 6–16. *Journal of Abnormal Child Psychology, 8,* 441–470.

Edelbrock, C., & Achenbach, T. M. (1984). The Teacher Version of the Child Behavior Profile. I. Boys aged 6–11. *Journal of Consulting and Clinical Psychology, 52,* 207–217.

Edelbrock, C., Costello, A. J., Dulcan, M. K., Kalas, R., & Conover, N. C. (1985). Age differences in the reliability of the psychiatric interview of the child. *Child Development, 56,* 265–275.

Evans, W. R. (1975). The Behavior Problem Checklist; Data from an inner city population. *Psychology in the Schools, 35,* 427–431.

Freeman, M. (1971). A reliability study of psychiatric diagnosis in childhood and adolescence. *Journal of Child Psychology and Psychiatry, 12,* 43–54.

Freud, A. (1965). *Normality and pathology in childhood.* New York: International Universities Press.

Garduk, E. L., & Haggard, E. A. (1972). Immediate effects on patients of psychoanalytic interpretations. *Psychological Issues, 7,* Monograph 28.

Greenspan, S. I., Hatleberg, J. L., & Cullander, C. C. H. (1980). A developmental approach to systematic personality assessment: Illustrated with the case of a 6-year-old child. In S. I. Greenspan & G. Pollock (Eds.), *The course of life: Psychoanalytic contributions toward understanding personality development* (Vol. II: *Latency, adolescence, and youth*). Washington, DC: U.S. Department of Health, Education, and Welfare.

Griesinger, W. (1845). *Die Pathologie und Therapie der psychischen Krankheiten*. [*Mental pathology and therapeutics*, C. L. Robertson & J. Rutherford (trans.).] London: New Sydenham Society, 1867.

Group for the Advancement of Psychiatry. (1966). *Psychopathological disorders in childhood: Theoretical considerations and a proposed classification* (GAP Report No. 62), New York: Author.

Guy, W. (Ed.). (1976). Physical and neurological assessment for soft signs. In *ECDEU assessment manual for psychopharmacology* (pp. 383–393): Rockville, MD: National Institute of Mental Health.

Hewitt, L. E., & Jenkins, R. L. (1946). *Fundamental patterns of maladjustment: The dynamics of their origin*. Springfield: State of Illinois.

Hodges, K., McKnew, D., Cytryn, L., Stern, L., & Kline, J. (1982). The Child Assessment Schedule (CAS) diagnostic interview: A report on reliability and validity. *Journal of the American Academy of Child Psychiatry, 21*, 468–473.

Horowitz, L. M., Post, D. L., French, R. deS., Wallis, K. D., & Siegelman, E. Y. (1981). The prototype as a construct in abnormal psychology. 2. Clarifying disagreement in psychiatric judgments. *Journal of Abnormal Psychology, 90*, 575–585.

Horowitz, L. M., Wright, J. C., Lowenstein, E., & Parad, H. W. (1981). The prototype as a construct in abnormal psychology: I. A method for deriving prototypes, *Journal of Abnormal Psychology, 90*, 568–574.

Ireton, H., & Thwing, E. J. (1974). *Minnesota Child Development Inventory*. Minneapolis: Behavior Science Systems.

Jenkins, R. L., & Glickman, S. (1946) Common syndromes in child psychiatry. I. Deviant behavior traits. II. The schizoid child. *American Journal of Orthopsychiatry, 16*, 244–261.

Kashani, J. M., Husain, A., Shekim, W. O., Hodges, K. K., Cytryn, L., & McKnew, D. H. (1981). Current perspectives on childhood depression: An overview. *American Journal of Psychiatry, 138*, 143–153.

Kaufman, A. S., & Kaufman, N. L. (1983). *Kaufman Assessment Battery for Children*. Circle Pines, MN: American Guidance Service.

Kestenbaum, C. J., & Bird, H. R. (1978). A reliability study of the Mental Health Assessment Form for school-age children. *Journal of the American Academy of Child Psychiatry, 17*, 338–347.

Kohn, M. (1977). *Social competence, symptoms, and underachievement in childhood: A longitudinal perspective*. New York: Wiley.

Koppitz, E. M. (1975). *The Bender Gestalt Test for young children* (Vol. II). New York: Grune & Stratton.

Kovacs, M. (1982). *The Interview Schedule for Children (ISC)*. Pittsburgh: University of Pittsburgh Department of Psychiatry.

Kraepelin, E. (1883). *Psychiatrie* (1st ed.). Leipzig: Abel; (1915). 8th ed. Leipzig: Barth.

Langner, T. S., Gersten, J. C., & Eisenberg, J. G. (1974). Approaches to measurement and definition in the epidemiology of behavioral disorders: Ethnic background and child behavior. *International Journal of Health Services, 4*, 483–501.

Lessing, E. E., Williams, V., & Revelle, W. (1981). Parallel forms of the IJR Behavior Checklist for parents, teachers, and clinicians. *Journal of Consulting and Clinical Psychology, 49*, 34–50.

Mash, E. J., & Terdal, L. G. (Eds.). (1981). *Behavioral assessment of childhood disorders*. New York: Guilford.

Mattison, R., Cantwell, D. P., Russell, A. T., & Will, L. (1979). A comparison of DSM-II and DSM-III in the diagnosis of childhood psychiatric disorders. *Archives of General Psychiatry, 36*, 1217–1222.

McCarthy, D. (1972). *McCarthy Scales of Children's Abilities*. New York: Psychological Corporation.

Meehl, P. E., & Golden, R. R. (1982). Taxometric methods. In P. C. Kendall & J. N. Butcher (Eds.), *Handbook of research methods in clinical psychology*. New York: Wiley.

Mezzich, A. C., & Mezzich, J. E. (1979, September). *Diagnostic reliability of childhood and adolescent behavior disorders*. Paper presented at the meeting of the American Psychological Association, New York.

Mezzich, A. C., Mezzich, J. E., & Coffman, G. A. (1985). Reliability of DSM-III vs. DSM-II in child psychopathology. *Journal of the American Academy of Child Psychiatry, 24,* 273–280.

Mikkelsen, E. J., Brown, G. L., Minichiello, M. D., Millican, F. K., & Rapoport, J. L. (1982). Neurologic status in hyperactive, enuretic, encopretic, and normal boys. *Journal of the American Academy of Child Psychiatry, 21,* 75–81.

Milich, R., Roberts, M., Loney, J., & Caputo, J. (1980). Differentiating practice effects and statistical regression on the Conners Hyperkinesis Index. *Journal of Abnormal Child Psychology, 8,* 549–552.

Miller, L. C. (1972). School Behavior Checklist: An inventory of deviant behavior for elementary school children. *Journal of Consulting and Clinical Psychology, 38,* 134–144.

Miller, L. C. (1981). *Louisville Behavior Checklist manual*. Los Angeles: Western Psychological Services.

Montenegro, H. (1983). *Salud mental del escolar: Estandarización del inventario de problemas conductuales y destrezas sociales de T. Achenbach en niños de 6 a 11 años*. Santiago, Chile: Centro de Estudios de Desarollo y Estimulación Psicosocial.

Quay, H. C. (1979). Classification. In H. C. Quay & J. S. Werry (Eds.), *Psychopathological disorders of childhood* (2nd ed.). New York: Wiley.

Quay, H. C., & Peterson, D. R. (1983). *Interim manual for the Revised Behavior Problem Checklist*. Coral Gables, FL: Applied Social Sciences, University of Miami.

Rosch, E., & Mervis, C. B. (1975). Family resemblances: Studies in the internal structure of categories. *Cognitive Psychology, 7,* 573–605.

Rosch, E., Mervis, C. B., Gray, W. E., Johnson, D. M., & Boyes-Graem, P. (1976). Basic objects in natural categories. *Cognitive Psychology, 8,* 382–439.

Rutter, M., & Graham, P. (1968). The reliability and validity of the psychiatric assessment of the child. I. Interview with the child. *British Journal of Psychiatry, 114,* 563–579.

Rutter, M., & Shaffer, D. (1980). DSM-III: A step forward or back in terms of the classification of child psychiatric disorders? *Journal of the American Academy of Child Psychiatry, 19,* 371–394.

Rutter, M., Shaffer, D., & Shepherd, M. (1975). *A multiaxial classification of child psychiatric disorders: An evaluation of a proposal*. Geneva: World Health Organization.

Smith, E. E. (1978). Theories of semantic memory. In W. K. Estes (Ed.), *Handbook of learning and cognitive processes* (Vol. 5). Hillsdale, NJ: Erlbaum.

Sneath, P. H. A., & Sokal, R. R. (1973). *Numerical taxonomy: The principles and practice of numerical classification*. San Francisco: Freeman.

Spitzer, R. L., & Cantwell, D. P. (1980). The DSM-III classification of the psychiatric disorders of infancy, childhood, and adolescence. *Journal of the American Academy of Child Psychiatry, 19,* 356–370.

Stouthamer-Loeber, M., & Peters, R. DeV. (1984). A priori classification systems of observation data: The eye of the beholder. *Behavioral Assessment, 6,* 275–282.

Strober, M., Green, J., & Carlson, G. (1981). The reliability of psychiatric diagnosis in hospitalized adolescents: Interrater agreement using the DSM-III. *Archives of General Psychiatry, 38,* 141–145.

Verhulst, F. (1985). *A Dutch epidemiologic study using the Achenbach Child Behavior Checklist*. Rotterdam: University of Rotterdam, Department of Child Psychiatry.

Wechsler, D. (1974). *Wechsler Intelligence Scale for Children—Revised*. New York: Psychological Corporation.

Wechsler, D. (1981). *Wechsler Adult Intelligence Scale—Revised*. New York: Psychological Corporation.

Weinrott, M. R., & Jones, R. R. (1984). Overt versus covert assessment of observer reliability. *Child Development, 55*, 1125–1137.

Werry, J. S., Methven, R. J., Fitzpatrick, J., & Dixon, H. (1983). The interrater reliability of DSM-III in children. *Journal of Abnormal Child Psychology, 11*, 341–354.

World Health Organization. (1978). *Mental disorders: Glossary and guide to their classification in accordance with the ninth revision of the international classification of diseases.* Geneva: Author.

Yorke, C. (1980). The contributions of the Diagnostic Profile and the assessment of development lines to child psychiatry. *Psychiatric Clinics of North America, 3*, 593–603.

III

PROBLEMS OF SYNDROME DEFINITION AND VALIDATION

11

DEPRESSIVE DISORDERS

MICHAEL RUTTER

INTRODUCTION

Until relatively recently there was a prevailing assumption that depressive disorders rarely occurred in children (Puig-Antich & Gittelman, 1982). In part this view stemmed from theoretical considerations that supposed that children lacked the necessary intrapsychic maturity for depression to occur (Rie, 1966), and in part from the observation that overt manic–depressive psychoses were infrequently seen before puberty (Anthony & Scott, 1960). Then during the late 1960s and early 1970s, there were arguments that depressive conditions *did* arise in childhood but that they took a "masked" form in which somatic symptoms, enuresis, or conduct disturbances constituted depressive "equivalents" (Cytryn & McKnew, 1972; Frommer, 1968; 1972; Glaser, 1967). During the last decade, however, there has been an increasing recognition that depressive conditions meeting adult criteria can and do appear in childhood (Cantwell, 1983; Puig-Antich & Gittelman, 1982). Indeed, it has become fashionable to think that a high proportion of child psychiatric referrals, perhaps even a majority, exhibit depressive disorders. In that these estimates derive from the use of operational diagnostic criteria, it might be supposed that the matter is now settled. Nevertheless, it is clear that this is far from the case (Shaffer, 1985). Cantwell (1983) pointed out that many of the criteria rely heavily on inferences and that the inferences vary from one set of criteria to the next. The purpose of this chapter is to review the issues that are involved in the diagnosis and classification of depressive disorders arising during childhood and adolescence, to consider the means available to resolve the key controversies, and to suggest some of the research implications.

Michael Rutter. Department of Child and Adolescent Psychiatry, University of London Institute of Psychiatry, London, England.

CONCEPTS OF DEPRESSIVE CONDITIONS

Depression as a Symptom

It is necessary to begin, by considering just what is involved in psychiatric concepts of depressive disorders. The first point that requires emphasis is that the concept of depression (as a symptom or a syndrome) is not synonymous with sadness or unhappiness. Moreover, even when present to a severe degree, sadness does not necessarily constitute depression (Hamilton, 1982). It is true that dysphoria is universally regarded as a *necessary* element in depression but it is not a *sufficient* criterion. Also, although sadness is a very common component of the dysphoric mood associated with depression, it is by no means a universal feature. Thus, the negative mood of depression may be represented more by a loss of interest or pleasure, by an emotional emptiness, a lack of responsiveness to ongoing activities, or by a feeling of "flatness" (Hamilton, 1982). It remains uncertain whether these nonverbal components of depression are the same in childhood as in adult life (Kazdin, Sherick, Esveldt-Dawson, & Pancurello, 1985). Although some pediatric specialists have laid emphasis on the clinician's empathic response to depression (Emde, Harmon, & Good, 1986), probably this emphasis confuses sadness and depression. It is true that another person's misery evokes empathy, but the hostile withdrawal and lack of response to comfort so often found with depression is as likely to be felt as rebuffing. Adults with a major depressive disorder frequently draw a sharp distinction between the "black cloud" of depression and the sadness or unhappiness they feel at times when they are not ill, maintaining that the two emotions do not feel the same (Hamilton, 1982).

More important, the concept of depression includes certain key cognitive features, as well as mood components (Bebbington, 1985; Beck, 1976). Thus emphasis tends to be laid on feelings of self-blame, self-reproach, and guilt; on thoughts of self-depreciation and worthlessness; on helplessness in the face of a life situation felt to be oppressive; and on hopelessness about the future. In other words, depressed people's thoughts include three key elements: (1) a concept of themselves as in some way unworthy or to blame for their own or other people's plight; (2) a belief that there is nothing that they can do to change the situation; and (3) a view that things will not get better in the future. Beck (1976) put these notions in terms of a cognitive triad comprising a negative view of one's self, a negative view of the world, and a negative view of the future.

It will be appreciated that these cognitive ideations may be present in depressive mood disturbances that are not part of any overt depressive disorder, that the cognitions do not necessarily amount to psychopathological symptoms of guilt, that there is individual variation in the extent to which these cognitive components dominate depressive thinking, and that these thoughts are not a necessary part of even very severe sadness. Thus, when a much-loved pet dies, a person may be very sad and greatly distressed, may well be tearful and may even lie awake thinking about the pet's death. Nevertheless, probably the person will not regard himself or herself as unworthy, feelings of helplessness will be restricted to the loss-of-pet situation, and the future will not seem black or hopeless. On the other hand, it would not be correct to see grief as qualitatively distinct from depression; bereavement commonly gives rise to a depressive state (Clayton, 1982). Most bereaved persons accept their depression as a normal response to death—emphasising that the *phenomenon* of depressive feelings is part of the normal range of human emotions and reactions.

Depression as a Psychiatric Condition

The second point with respect to concepts of depression is that the phenomenon (or symptom) and the syndrome or condition are not synonymous. Many people feel depressed (in terms of both dysthymia and depressive cognitions) when they experience task failure, a personal rebuff, or some other life stress. Indeed, depressive feelings may also occur in the absence of any obvious environmental precipitant. Autochthonous mood swings are relatively common and may be a prominent feature in individuals with a cyclothymic or depressive personality.

In adult psychiatry, three main criteria tend to be used to determine when there is a depressive *condition*, as distinct from a depressive symptom—associated phenomena, social impairment, and persistence. Hamilton (1982) argued that loss of interest and anxiety (shown not only by apprehension but also by irritability, forgetfulness, inability to concentrate, and tension) are almost universal and that difficulty falling asleep or early morning waking, loss of appetite, lack of energy and fatigability, psychomotor retardation (or agitation), and suicidal thoughts are very common. Loss of libido and hypochondriacal preoccupations, too, are relatively frequent. The third edition of the *Diagnostic and Statistical Manual of Mental Disorders* (DSM-III) (American Psychiatric Association, 1980) provides much the same list of depressive symptoms but specifies that only four out of eight need be present. Studies of the covariance over time of depressive symptoms confirm the close association between sadness, retardation, and an inability to feel (i.e., a lack of interest in hitherto pleasurable activities), as well as the links with pessimism, tension, and poor concentration (Hibbert, Teasdale, & Spencer, 1984). Impairments in appetite and sleep disturbance are less closely associated with changes in other features of depression. Similarly, it has been found that the cognitive features of unworthiness, helplessness, and hopelessness are prominent features of clinically significant depression and that these cognitions change strikingly as the depression remits or responds to treatment (Blackburn & Bishop, 1983; Hamilton & Abramson, 1983; Norman, Miller, & Klee, 1983; Raps, Peterson, Reinhard, Abramson, & Seligman, 1982).

Curiously, DSM-III does not demand any assessment of degree of social impairment—presumably on the grounds that people with the required number of symptoms are likely to be significantly affected in their day-to-day activities. However, most investigators studying nonpatient populations have required the presence of social impairment of a degree easily recognized by others (e.g., Gershon, et al., 1982; Weissman, Gershon, et al., 1984).

DSM-III has rather minimal criteria for persistence in requiring only that the symptoms have been present "nearly every day for a period of at least two weeks" (p. 213) but, again, many researchers have demanded a duration of at least 4 weeks (Weissman, Gershon, et. al., 1984).

Differentiation from Normality

It might be thought that the criteria of multiple depressive phenomena, persisting over time and associated with substantial social impairment, should be sufficient to differentiate depressive disorders from normality, but this has been disputed. The controversies center around three main issues: (1) depression versus "demoralization," (2) depression versus normal grief (or other stress) reactions, and (3) depression versus "distress" reactions to physical illness.

The criteria for a depressive condition outlined above apply to major depressive disorders, but DSM-III and other schemes of classification, such as the ninth edition of the *International Classification of Diseases* (ICD-9) (World Health Organization, 1978), also recognize the existence of lesser, but chronic, depressive disorders—termed "dysthymic disorders" or "depressive neuroses." The phenomena are regarded as generally similar to those found with major depressive disorders, but they are less severe and less pervasive. However, to be included the disorder must have been present chronically or recurrently for at least 2 years, according to DSM-III. A category of "atypical depression" is provided for those disorders that fall between the categories of major depression and dysthymic disorders.

The dispute has focused on the depressive disorders very commonly found in women in community surveys. For example, Brown and Harris (1978) found that 17% of women in their London surveys were definite "cases" and a further 19% were "borderline." Rates of depression among working-class women were even higher (22% definite cases). It has been argued that those highly prevalent depressive disorders found in the general population are not the same as those seen in psychiatric clinics or hospitals (Tennant & Bebbington, 1978) and that it is better to conceptualize them as "demoralization" rather than a psychiatric condition of depression (Link & Dohrenwend, 1980). However, community survey diagnoses of depression (Finlay-Jones et al., 1980), when obtained through systematic interview methods, *do* accord with the operational criteria applied to patients using either the Feighner, Robins, Guze, Woodroff, and Winokur (1972), the

Wing, Cooper, and Sartorius (1974), or the Bedford College (Brown, Craig, & Harris, 1985) criteria. Not surprisingly, however, the most severe cases of depression are more likely to be found in hospital samples (Sireling, Freeling, Paykel, & Rao, 1985; Sireling, Paykel, Freeling, Rao, & Patel, 1985). Accordingly, the issue is better considered in terms of the links or lack of links between major depressive disorders and mild dysthymic disorders (see below).

The differentiation between depression and "normal" grief or stress reactions raises rather different issues. It is accepted that many grief reactions fulfill the diagnostic criteria for major depressive disorders, but it is argued that they should be regarded as "normal" phenomena rather than illnesses because they are both common and understandable (Clayton, 1982). Although at first sight this argument is apparently persuasive, it is clear that such a position serves, by edict, to rule out psychosocial features as common causes of psychiatric conditions. We do not follow this convention with physical causes for physical illness (to a substantial extent we understand how the influenza virus causes influenza and influenza is exceedingly common, but we do not thereby regard influenza as "normality"). So why should we do so for psychosocial causes of psychiatric disorders? That does not seem a logical approach. Instead, the matter is better approached by asking whether depressive disorders that follow bereavement or some other acute stress differ from other depressive conditions in their correlates, course, or response to treatment. The evidence on these points, however, is so far contradictory and inconclusive (Brown & Harris, 1978; Parker, 1983; Paykel, 1982). Tennant, Bebbington, and Hurry (1981) found that neurotic disorders in the community were more likely to remit if precipitated by an acute stress, but remission was also a function of recent onset and recent peaks of disorder; it is not clear whether outcome was influenced by the presence of stress precipitation after taking account of the existence of the disorder. Brugha and Conroy (1985) found that severe depressive disorders with so-called "endogenous" symptoms were often preceded by significant social precipitants (differing significantly from controls in that respect). It appears that life events may trigger the onset of all manner of depressive conditions—and may also precipitate mania. If there are differences in the type of depression according to psychosocial causation, they are likely to be matters of degree or frequency rather than of kind. That conclusion, however, applies to conditions that meet the full criteria for a depressive disorder. Stress or adjustment reactions that do *not* meet such criteria may have a substantially better prognosis (Kovacs, Feinberg, Crouse-Novak, Paulauskas, & Finkelstein, 1984; Kovacs, Feinberg, Crouse-Novak, Paulauskas, Pollack, & Finkelstein, 1984), but this may be a function of their mildness and acuteness rather than their mode of causation.

Broadly comparable issues arise with respect to the diagnosis of affective disturbance that occurs in the context of a physical illness. Lloyd and Cawley (1983) found that a third of adult patients suffering their first acute myocardial infarction showed psychiatric morbidity 1 week after admission; in half of those the psychiatric problems had been precipitated by the infarction. Of that half ($n = 19$), only a quarter showed psychiatric morbidity 4 months later. It was concluded that most acute psychiatric symptoms precipitated by a severe physical illness are better viewed as a "normal" stress response than as a psychiatric disorder. Once again, it is clear that acute stress reactions, whether precipitated by psychosocial or physical stresses, tend to have a good prognosis. There appear to be grounds for differentiating them from depressive disorders, but it is not clear whether the stress constitutes a significant independent differentiating feature, once acuteness and symptom features have been taken into account.

"Primary" and "Secondary" Depression

It is widely recognized that symptoms of depression can arise in many different forms of psychiatric illness. Thus, depressive symptoms occur in about half of schizophrenic disorders (Johnson, 1981). However, because schizophrenia and affective disorders have been shown to differ with respect to both family history findings and long-term prognosis (see, e.g., Tsuang, Winokur, & Crowe, 1980; Tsuang, Woolsam, & Simpson, 1981), the presence of depression does not give rise to an additional diagnosis if there is a clear-cut clinical picture of schizophrenia. Rather, it is assumed that the depressive symptoms are part of the schizophrenia. Thus, DSM-III specifies that major depressive disorder should *not* be diagnosed if the depressive syndrome is superimposed on schizophrenia.

However, the same issues also arise with respect to other clinical conditions as it is relatively common for depressive syndromes to accompany alcoholism, anxiety states, hysteria, anorexia nervosa, and personality disorders. The usual convention here has been different from that employed with schizophrenia; that is, with these other psychiatric conditions *both* tend to be diagnosed (i.e., depression and the other disorder). But, it has been argued by some researchers that these cases of "secondary" depression should be differentiated from "primary" cases in which there is no antecedent nondepressive psychiatric disorder (Guze, Woodruff, & Clayton, 1971). Although it seems reasonable to suppose that primary and secondary depression might well differ in many important respects, so far it has not been well validated (Andreasen, 1982; Stancer, Persad, Jorna, Flood, & Wagener, 1984). On the whole, the two groups have differed only slightly in terms of course, response to treatment, or familial clustering.

In summary, although great progress has been made in the differentiation and diagnosis of depressive disorders as they occur in adult life, it is evident that many issues still await resolution.

SUBCLASSIFICATION OF DEPRESSIVE DISORDERS

As already noted, DSM-III draws a distinction between major depressive episodes and minor dysthymic disorders. In addition, however, a differentiation is made between bipolar and unipolar affective disorders (i.e., those in which there have and those in which there have not been manic episodes). A further subclassification is provided to note the presence of psychotic features and "melancholic" characteristics. The latter approximate to what others have termed "endogenous" features (Spitzer, Endicott, & Robins, 1978)—namely, lack of reactivity to usually pleasurable stimuli, a depressive mood that differs in quality from that normally experienced, early morning wakening and intensification of depression, marked psychomotor retardation or agitation, significant anorexia or weight loss, and excessive or inappropriate guilt. Schizo-affective disorders (i.e., those with an admixture of major depressive symptomatology and mood-incongruent psychotic features) are not included with affective conditions in DSM-III; anxiety disorders, too, are classified separately.

ICD-9 has a rather more complex approach to the subclassification of affective disorders. Since the respects in which it differs from DSM-III are not empirically validated, they will not be considered further here.

Several rather different research strategies have been employed in order to test the validity of these nosological distinctions. Firstly, genetic family studies have been used to determine whether or not the familial loading differs in pattern between the hypothesized different varieties of depressive disorder. Most attention has been paid to the unipolar–bipolar distinction (Perris, 1982)—sometimes with the further differentiation of bipolar into types I and II according to whether or not the manic pole involved a history of frank mania (I) or just hypomania (II). Although some studies have found no differences in familial loading between unipolar and bipolar cases (Tsuang, Faraone, & Fleming, 1985), most have found that bipolar illness in the probands is associated with an increased rate of both bipolar and unipolar disorders in the relatives; whereas unipolar illness in the probands is associated with a high rate of unipolar, but not bipolar, disorders in first degree relatives (see, e.g., Gershon *et al.*, 1982; Weissman, Gershon, *et al.*, 1984). However, there is continuing uncertainty on whether the findings are better interpreted in terms of a continuum of underlying multifactorial vulnerability (with bipolar disorder the most severe variant), or in terms of two genetically distinct (but overlapping) types of affective disorder.

The same family studies suggest that at least some forms of schizoaffective disorder (a condition over which there is considerable disagreement on definition; see Brockington & Leff, 1979), minor depressive conditions, and anxiety states (especially panic disorders) are genetically associated with major depression. However, the findings are by no means conclusive, and Torgersen's (1985) twin data suggested that anxiety states and neurotic depression are genetically distinct; it is clear that further research using the genetic family study strategy is required. In that connection, three major requirements are evident. First, comparisons between possibly overlapping conditions (such as depression and anxiety, or depression and personality disorder) are needed. Secondly, family risk must be determined systematically for both depressive and supposedly nondepressive conditions. Thirdly, a *nonhierarchical* approach to diagnosis must be followed (Leckman, Weissman, Merikangas, Pauls, & Prusoff, 1983). Until recently, most investigators have imposed hierarchic schemes in order to aid clarity, but it seems that the procedure may have obscured genetic relationships between supposedly different conditions.

A variety of biological measures have been used to test the validity of the bipolar–unipolar distinction; on the whole these have tended to show differences (with the bipolar more "abnormal"). However, the results have shown substantial overlap between the groups, with some inconsistency in findings between studies (Andreasen, 1982; Perris, 1982). Nonsuppression on the dexamethasone test (DST) has been proposed as an important feature differentiating depressive from nondepressive disorders and, within depression, melancholic from nonmelancholic conditions (Carroll, 1982). However, as data have accumulated, it has become clear that the DST provides only a moderate depression versus nondepression differentiation and very little differentiation within the range of depressive disorders (see, e.g., Coppen *et al.*, 1983; Mendlewicz, Charles, & Franckson, 1982; Stokes *et al.*, 1984).

Response to treatment and long-term course have, however, tended to provide a better separation of subgroups of depressive disorders. Endogenous, or "melancholic," features have been found to predict a good response to both antidepressant medication and to electroconvulsive therapy (ECT), as well as a better long-term outcome (Andreasen, 1982). However, it seems that the presence of delusions suggests resistance to tricyclic antidepressants but responsiveness to ECT (Clinical Research Centre, 1984). Bipolar disorders differ to some extent from unipolar disorders in terms of an early age of onset, more frequent episodes of illness, and greater social impairment.

Symptom clustering, too, has been used to subdivide depressive disorders. On the whole the results have separated a group with severe psychotic or endogenous depression, but the findings have not been at all consistent in delineating other groupings (Andreasen, 1982). It should be noted, incidentally, that although bipolar disorders differ from unipolar disorders in several respects, the clinical picture of the depressed phase in the two types seems much the same (Brockington, Altman, Hillier, Meltzer, & Nand, 1982). In other words, the bipolar-group cases are differentiated by the history of manic episodes rather than by the features of the depressive state.

In summary, it has proved clinically useful to make various distinctions within the broad group of depressive disorders. That between unipolar and bipolar disorder is the best established, but also there is support for a differentiation according to the presence of endogenous or melancholic features (although it may be that this is better done in dimensional than categorical terms). Delusional depression, too, warrants separation. However, it remains quite uncertain whether these types refer to different conditions or, rather, variations within the same condition. Also, there is continuing doubt on where to draw the boundaries of depression—especially with respect to schizoaffective disorders, conditions with predominant anxiety, and minor but chronic mood disturbances.

DEPRESSION IN CHILDHOOD AND ADOLESCENCE

It may be assumed that the problems already discussed in relation to the diagnosis and classification of depressive disorders in adults are likely also to apply to those arising in childhood. However, there are a variety of other issues that need consideration with respect to childhood depression.

Age Differences in Depressive Phenomena

To begin with, it is clear that there are important and large age differences in the occurrence of depressive and depression-related conditions. The data on such age differences are limited and inadequate in many respects; indeed, they cannot be really satisfactory until the methodological issues outlined below are resolved. Nevertheless, the available findings are sufficiently striking to raise a host of crucial questions:

1. General population surveys suggest that depressive feelings are more prevalent in adolescence than in earlier childhood (Kaplan, Hong, & Weinhold, 1984; Rutter, Graham, Chadwick, & Yule, 1976) and that the rise may be more a function of puberty than chronological age (Rutter, 1979).
2. Clinic data suggest that overt depressive disorders also become more frequent during adolescence with a possible parallel shift in the sex ratio from a male preponderance before puberty to a female preponderance after puberty (Rutter, 1986).
3. Mania also becomes more frequent during the teenage years, although (less commonly) it can occur before puberty (Anthony & Scott, 1960; Hassanyeh & Davison 1980; Loranger & Levine, 1978; Lowe & Cohen, 1980).
4. Immediate grief reactions following bereavement (of the form seen in adults) tend to be both milder and of shorter duration in young children than in adolescents or adults (Bowlby, 1980; Kliman, 1968; Rutter, 1966; van Eerdewegh, Bieri, Parilla, & Clayton, 1982). However, the overall risk of psychopathology during the year following

parental death does not vary markedly according to the age of the children (Black & Urbanowicz, 1985; van Eerdewegh, Clayton, & van Eerdewegh, 1985).

5. Suicide is excessively rare before puberty but shows a massive rise over the adolescent years; moreover, the rate continues to rise through adult life into old age (Eisenberg, 1980; Kosky, 1982; McClure, 1984; Shaffer, 1974; Shaffer & Fisher, 1981).

6. Attempted suicide, or parasuicide, also exhibits a huge increase in frequency during adolescence (Hawton & Boldacre, 1982)— although it differs from suicide in reaching a peak in early adult life rather than old age.

7. Within psychiatric clinic samples, suicidal ideation increases in frequency during adolescence (Carlson & Cantwell, 1982).

These findings raise a multitude of rather varied questions. To begin with, of course, there is the problem that the data are not as systematic and standardized as one would wish. It is possible that some of the age effects may be a consequence of referral artifacts or of different modes of assessment at different ages. On the other hand, that explanation carries little weight with regard to the findings on suicide and attempted suicide. But it should not necessarily be assumed that all the age trends for the different phenomena are due to the same causes. Perhaps, some of the age effects for suicide derive from variations in readiness of access to suicidal means or variations in the determination or ability to carry through a suicidal act.

A second issue concerns the measurement of depression. Insofar as the diagnosis of a major depressive disorder requires the reporting of complex emotions and cognitive ideations, it might be that young children are not able to report, or to experience, these in the form usual in adults (see below). If that is the case, does that mean that major depressive disorders cannot be diagnosed so readily in early childhood, or should one expect that depression will be manifest in somewhat different ways in younger age groups? If the latter applies, how is one to know that it is "truly" equivalent to adult depression (see below); indeed, what is the aspect of adult depression to which equivalence should be required? It will be appreciated that recourse to the widely adopted strategy of requiring the use in childhood of adult criteria provides no solution to this problem. Of course, it is important that it has been demonstrated that adult-type depressive conditions do occur in childhood but still the issue of age trends requires consideration of the possibility of age-related variations in the manifestations of depression.

In that connection it would be unduly restricting to focus exclusively on the apparent increase in depression during adolescence. There is the additional feature of infant's protest–despair–detachment responses to institutional admission to consider. These reactions are seen in many toddlers admitted to a hospital or to a residential nursery (Bowlby, 1969, 1980) but are most likely to occur during the 6- month to 4-year age period (Rutter, 1981). Naturally, in children as young as that it would be extremely difficult to elicit verbal reports of adult-type depressive ideations. Nevertheless, Bowlby (1980) has argued that they represent depressive equivalents. That claim is arguable (Rutter, 1986), but it cannot be denied that they constitute some form of dysthymic affective state. If protest–despair–detachment responses are not depressive, a rather different explanation may be required for these early age trends in affective reaction than that applicable to the adolescent increase in major depressive disorders. But, if these early dysthymic responses are depressive, there is the question of why depressive phenomena should fall in frequency during the early school years, only to rise again at puberty.

If further research should confirm the reality of age differences in depressive conditions and in the expression of depressive phenomena, as well it might, it will be necessary to determine the reasons for the age trend. A variety of quite different types of explanations could be proffered (Rutter, 1986). Perhaps, to a large extent, major depressive disorders are genetically determined and perhaps the genes do not usually "switch on" until later childhood or adolescence (in the way that Huntington's chorea, though due to a dominant gene, does not become manifest until adult life). Or, perhaps, sex hormones play a role in the vulnerability to depression in that the increase in sex hormones at puberty increases susceptibility to depression.

Alternatively, it could be suggested that depression becomes more frequent during the teenage years because the stressors or loss events that predispose to depression become more prevalent at that time (we lack good data on age-related changes in the experience of stressors). Similarly, it could be argued that depression rises in frequency during adolescence because family supports and other protective factors become less operative or less available at that time. Different types of explanations stem from considerations of cognitive sets. It could be that experiences during later childhood and adolescence increase the likelihood of a set of "learned helplessness" (Dweck, Davidson, Nelson, & Enns, 1978). Or it might be that there are developmental changes in children's ability to make depressive-type cognitive attributions (Rholes, Blackwell, Jordan, & Walters, 1980), so younger children may be less susceptible to feelings of helplessness because they tend not to view failure as implying a stable and lasting limitation on their performance. Perhaps, too, the age-related changes in depression reflect developmentally mediated alterations in children's concepts of emotions, in their awareness of emotions in others, and in their appreciation of the emotional connotations of social situations.

It is all too obvious that the relevant data to test these hypotheses are lacking. It is also apparent that their testing is likely to raise difficult methodological issues.

Age Trends in Depression-Related Cognitive Ideations

Insofar as depression involves thoughts of guilt, helplessness in the face of task failure, and hopelessness about the future, it is important to consider how far children possess the ability to experience such cognitions. There is a surprising lack of knowledge on these matters, but some limited evidence is available.

Many theorists place great weight on the effects of loss of a love relationship as a precipitant of depression (Bowlby, 1980; Brown & Harris, 1978). Hence, the age at which children are able to experience selective attachments to particular people would seem relevant. There are good data indicating that this capacity usually becomes manifest during the second half of the first year of life (Rutter, 1980, 1981). If children are to experience guilt, feelings of unworthiness, and a sense of failure, presumably it is necessary that they appreciate the meaning of "standards," that they are able to compare themselves with others, and that they can understand the concept of failure to achieve particular standards of performance. Kagan's (1981, 1982) data suggest that these self concepts related to the capacity to feel guilt arise at about the age of 2 years. However, depressive cognitions involve more than a sense of specific task failure, they require that the sense of failure be experienced as generalized and that it be projected into the future.

Less is known on the developmental changes in these aspects of social cognition as they apply specifically to depressive ideation, but something is known on the broader aspects of such thought processes. Thus, for example, at about the age of 5 or 6 years there is an increase in children's ability to differentiate accidental and intentional behavior shown by others (Shantz, 1983). At first there is some tendency to assume that bad outcomes are unintended, but this bias begins to wane during the early elementary school years. Also, at about the age of 7 years children begin to shift from a view of task performance and skills as specific to a conception of general abilities that are global, stable, and persistent (Dweck & Elliott, 1983). Probably too, this is accompanied by an increasing tendency for children to use social comparisons to evaluate their own competence. Young children tend to have an overoptimistic view of their own competence and it is only during the early years of schooling that they begin to adjust their self-perceptions as a consequence of task failure. Perhaps this tendency accounts for the finding by Rholes *et al.* (1980) that young children are less likely to have learned helplessness in response to repeated (experimentally induced) task failure. Children as young as age 4 or 5 years are aware that *other* people may feel proud or ashamed of them, but it is not until 8 years or so that most children talk about being proud or ashamed of *themselves* (Harter, 1983). Self-awareness in the form of marked self-consciousness probably increases during adolescence (Rosenberg, 1979). Also, it seems that anxieties about the future may increase during the teenage period (Coleman, 1974; Coleman, Herzberg, & Morris, 1977). Young children do not think much about the long-term future, nor do they conceptualize actions in terms of distant consequences. Probably it is only during later childhood and early adolescence that future perspectives come to the fore. It would seem that such perspectives may be important in the development of feelings of hopelessness about the rest of life.

It is clear that there is much more to be learned about the development of children's social cognitions and self-perceptions, and we are only just beginning to study the possible links between that development and the emergence of depressive phenomena.

Children's Reporting of Depressive Feelings

In addition to the question of children's abilities to *experience* depressive affects and cognitions there is the further issue of their ability to *report* them—a crucial matter with respect to the clinical assessment of depressive states. The limited available data on developmental competencies relevant to children's reporting of depression have been well summarized by Kovacs (1986). She, like other researchers, concluded that much can be gained by direct interviewing of the child with specific questions about mood and functioning. However, she also noted young children's limitations with regard to reporting on certain key features required for DSM-III diagnosis of major depressive disorder. Specifically, she drew attention to the difficulties experienced by children up to the age of 8 years or so in considering their own affect separate from particular environmental contexts, and in differentiating normal sadness from authochthonous dysphoria. Probably the ability to locate the antecedents of emotional states within themselves is not achieved until adolescence. Concepts of guilt, too, show important developmental trends with young children normally feeling responsible for many events outside their control.

The gradual development of metacognition—that is, children's ability to reflect on their own cognitive processes—will constrain their capacity to report (as well as to experience) depressive cognitions. It seems that a conceptual integration of the dimensions of the self, the use of stable personality characterizations, and true self-reflection emerge only in adolescence (Damon & Hart, 1982; Selman, Jaquette, & Redman, 1977). Accordingly, it is unlikely that children as young as 6 or 7 years old could provide valid reports on features of their own thinking (such as "slowness" or "emptiness"). Moreover, it is probable that during the middle years of childhood it will be difficult to get meaningful reports regarding feelings of worthlessness, helplessness, and hopelessness.

A further consideration concerns children's abilities to report either depressive feelings in the past or the duration of present feelings. The evidence indicates that although young children have some sense of time, their capacity to give accurate accounts of the past and to provide estimates of absolute duration are severely limited. Accounts of these features will need to be obtained from parents when the children are below the age of 10 to 12 years. However, it is likely that children will vary greatly in these (and other) cognitive skills; also, it may be that the presence of psychiatric disorder will itself alter the children's abilities to conceptualize time dimensions (Kovacs, 1986).

Measures of Depression in Childhood

During the past decade or so there has been the development of quite a range of questionnaire and interview methods for the assessment of depression in childhood (Carlson & Cantwell, 1980a; Chambers et. al., 1985; Costello, Edelbrock, & Costello, 1985; Costello, Edelbrock, Dulcan, Kales, & Klavic, 1984; Edelbrock, Costello, Dulcan, Kales, & Conover, 1985; Kazdin, 1981; Kazdin & Petti, 1982; Kazdin, French, Unis, & Esveldt-Dawson, 1983; Rotundo & Hensley, 1985; Weissman, Orvaschel, & Padian, 1980). They provide a set of usable instruments that can be employed to diagnose depressive phenomena and syndromes in children and adolescents. However, important problems remain. First, the test–retest reliability is least satisfactory for the crucial cognitive components of depression and for the differentiation between normal sadness and authochthonous dysthymia. This is especially so with the younger children. Second, there is generally only low to moderate agreement between parent and child on depressive features. The finding that the agreement is lower in adolescence than in childhood suggests that, at least in part, this may be a function of parents' lack of appreciation of their teenager's feelings—a feature noted also in earlier epidemiological studies (Rutter et al., 1976). One study found that, at least as far as self-report questionnaires are concerned, parental measures provide a better differentiation of clinically diagnosed depressed and nondepressed groups than do child measures (Kazdin et al., 1983). However, Moretti, Fine, Haley, and Marriage (1985) found the reverse. Third, little is known on the degree to which different measures tap the same features or give rise to the designation of comparable syndromes. However, it is clear that there is only moderate agreement between different sets of operational criteria (Cantwell, 1983). Fourth, the available structured interviews for children do not give rise to reliable measures of depression; the clinical-type interviews seem to be more satisfactory for this purpose. Fifth, in trying to make assessments more applicable for use with children, there is a danger that the meaning of items is changed. For example, Chambers et al. (1985), using the Kiddie-SADS-P, reported that the quality of depressive mood could be assessed more reliably if children were asked about missing someone or feeling lonely. It seems dubious, to say the least, that loneliness and depression are synonymous. Similarly, the Weinberg criteria for depressive disorder treat "negative and difficult to please" as indicative of dysphoric mood, and "desire to run away or leave home" as evidence of self-deprecatory ideation (Cantwell, 1983). But are they?

Lastly, there is the vexed question of the validity of these measures. Some studies have shown poor and some good differentiation between patients diagnosed as depressed and nondepressed. But what is the validity of the clinical diagnoses (see below)? Also, when it is found that many patients with other psychiatric disorders or with learning disabilities meet the operational criteria for major depressive disorder, as has often been the case (see, e.g., Frommer, 1968; Hendren, 1983; Puig-Antich, 1982; Puig-Antich & Gittelman, 1982; Weinberg & Rehmet, 1983), does this imply that the measure of depression has poor validity or rather does it mean that depression frequently coexists with other disorders?

Variations in the Manifestations of Depression

It is now accepted that children and adolescents can show major depressive disorders that fully meet the diagnostic criteria used with adults. So far as those disorders are concerned, the main issues are the same as those that apply to depressive conditions arising in adult life (see above). However, there is an additional interest in whether the very early age of onset carries with it any specific implications. For example, Weissman, Wickramaratne, et al. (1984) found that the familial loading for major depression was highest when the depressive disorder had an onset before 30 years of age; Puig-Antich et al. (in press) found that the familial aggregation of depressive disorders was particularly high in children with a major depressive disorder. Perhaps, depressive disorders with an onset in childhood represent those with the strongest genetic loading. In adults various sleep EEG abnormalities have been found to be present during episodes of depression but Puig-Antich et al. (1982) failed to find them in a controlled study of severely depressed children. Does this mean that the type of depression seen in childhood differs from that in adult life or rather does it mean that there are developmentally mediated effects on sleep that alter the sleep phenomena in depression? In adults there is a fair amount of evidence (though not without its problems; Mindham, 1982) that depression showing endogenous or melancholic features usually responds to tricyclic antidepressants. The limited evidence on the drug treatment of depressive disorders in childhood shows little difference between active drug and placebo, although there is some indication of drug effect (Kashani, Shekim, & Reid, 1984; Kramer & Feiguine, 1981; Puig-Antich et al., 1987). The apparently weaker drug effect in childhood requires confirmation (or refutation); if confirmed, however, it could reflect either a greater placebo effect in early life or a weaker drug effect. The latter possibility might be a consequence of age-related differences in drug response rather than any difference in depressive disorder. Thus, prepubertal children seem to lack the euphoriant response to dextroamphetamine seen in adults (Rapoport *et al.*, 1980). For all these reasons, and others of a similar kind, it is necessary for there to be further research into "classical" major depressive disorders arising in childhood.

However, in addition, there is a particular need to study further those depressive disorders in childhood that fail fully to meet the adult criteria for major depressive disorder, or that meet the criteria in circumstances that give rise to doubts about their comparability. These fall into six main groups.

1. It is common for depression to be associated with other psychiatric conditions. Thus, Puig-Antich (1982) found that one-third of boys fitting research diagnostic criteria for major depressive disorder also fit DSM-III criteria for conduct disorder; the majority showed pathological levels of separation anxiety (Puig-Antich & Gittelman, 1982) and most exhibited major difficulties in interpersonal relationships (Puig-Antich *et al.*, 1985). Weinberg and Rehmet (1983) reported that over half the children admitted to a school for children with specific learning disabilities had a depressive disorder; Hendren (1983) found that among patients meeting DSM-III criteria for anorexia nervosa, more than half also met the criteria for a major depressive disorder and a third met the criteria for an endogenous depression. Do depressive syndromes have the same meaning when they occur in conjunction with other psychiatric disorders?

2. In some cases the criteria are met only by making inferences about the meaning of particular child behaviors that are not isomorphic with those in adult depressive disorders (see above). Are these inferences valid?

3. What is the meaning of the dysthymic states seen in middle childhood and adolescence that fall short of the criteria for a major depressive disorder? Many of these are quite long-standing, without the clear onset more typical of acute depressive conditions. The one study with good data on the long-term outcome of these dysthymic states (Kovacs, Feinberg, Crouse-Novak, Paulauskas, & Finkelstein, 1984; Kovacs, Feinberg, Crouse-Novak, Paulauskas, Pollack, & Finkelstein, 1984) showed that two-thirds developed a major depressive disorder over the next 5 years. The findings provides a strong pointer to the likely link between chronic dysthymia and major depressive disorder, but the interpretation of the finding is not free from ambiguity (see below).

4. What is the meaning of the protest–despair–detachment syndromes seen in some preschool children following institutional admission, and of the rarer "anaclitic depression" of infancy (Spitz, 1946; Harmon, Wagonfeld, & Emde, 1982)? Is this the form that major depression takes in early childhood or does it constitute a response to institutional care and separation from family that has little in common with the major depressive disorders of adult life?

5. Is there any validity to the notion of "masked depression" or "depressive equivalents," in which such features as enuresis, somatic complaints or conduct disturbance are thought to stem from depression even though overt depressive manifestations are absent? Interest in this concept has

greatly diminished since it has been shown that many of the children with these clinical pictures in fact *do* show overt depression (Carlson & Cantwell, 1980b). Nevertheless, it is possible that the manifestations of depression might be greatly modified in early childhood (McConville, Boag, & Purchit, 1973).

6. What are the consequences of the DSM-III practice of not including social impairment in the criteria for depressive disorders? The available evidence suggests that depressive disorders are diagnosed surprisingly frequently in supposedly normal populations. Does this mean that such disorders are indeed very common in the community or, rather, does depression in the absence of social impairment have a different meaning?

7. Does major depression have the same significance when it occurs in the context of severe environmental stress or adversity and when it remits rapidly following removal from the stress environment? This applies to most of the cases of anaclitic depression described by Spitz (1946) and to many of the cases of masked depression described by Cytryn and McKnew (1972). However, it also applies to many acute syndromes of major depression.

Doubts about the comparability of these various depressive syndromes with the major endogenous-type depressive conditions of adult life have led to some skepticism about the true frequency of depressive conditions in prepubertal children (Graham, 1981). The issues remain unresolved, and in the remainder of this chapter I consider how they might be tackled.

RESEARCH APPROACHES TO CHILDHOOD DEPRESSION

Developmental/Epidemiologic Studies

In many respects, perhaps the most basic need of all is to determine how the manifestations of depression vary with age. In frustrating fashion the satisfactory investigation of developmental trends awaits the availability of reliable and valid measures of depressive affect and cognition, while in parallel the methodological problems inherent in the creation of measures applicable to all age groups awaits knowledge on the developmental features that influence the manifestations of depression. The dilemma cannot be circumvented; it is necessary to take the bull by the horns and seek to deal with the substantive and methodological issues in tandem. For that to work effectively it is clearly essential to separate children's reports, parental accounts, observations of the child, and inferences based upon each. This means, for example, that the inference that loneliness is the equivalent of depression must be tested rather than assumed. Also, it requires that information be sought from the child independently from that obtained from the parent, rather than with that foreknowledge as has been the pattern in most clinical studies so far. Questions need to be raised, too, regarding the consequences of using different types of instrument. For example, the highly structured questionnaire-type interview epitomized by the DISC (Costello *et al.*, 1985) differs from the more clinically oriented semi-structured interview such as the Kiddie-SADS (Chambers *et al.*, 1985; Puig-Antich, Chambers, & Tabrizi, 1983) in at least two rather different respects. First, the latter allows the use of observations as well as verbal reports. Second, it relies on detailed personalized cross-questioning and the obtaining of examples in order for the interviewer (rather than the interviewee) to be confident that a rating can be made. A systematic comparison of the two types of interview method, as measures of depression, is needed. This should also aim to determine how far the differences stem from the type of questioning (i.e., a comparison using ratings based on typescripts) and how far from the observations of the child.

Crucial to the developmental/epidemiologic study of depression, of course, is the use of instruments that discriminate within the different elements of depressive mood (such as sadness, emptiness, and loss of pleasurable response), within the different elements of depressive cognition (such as feelings of guilt or unworthiness, helplessness about the life situation, and hopelessness about the future), and between the affective and cognitive domains. For the reasons already given it will be necessary *both* to use measures across age groups that are directly comparable *and* to seek to make adaptations that reflect developmental variations in children's cognitive capacity. (The latter should also be used in adolescents and adults in order to provide a part check on their comparability with the traditional adult measures).

Clinic Populations

Probably it is best to apply these developmental approaches in the first instance to clinic populations. This seems desirable because this is the only way to ensure an adequate sample of major depressive disorders and because there is the continuing uncertainty (with adults as well as with children) regarding the parallels between the more severe depressive disorders seen in hospital practice and the less severe disorders found in community surveys (although clearly the two overlap). The necessary assumption underlying the suggested clinical studies is that, insofar as there are any age-related psychiatric referral biases, they will not differ between depressive and nondepressive psychiatric conditions. That seems to be a fairly reasonable assumption, but still the need to test it makes it essential to go on to apply comparable methods in general population surveys.

The prime question to be asked in such clinical studies is whether the different manifestations of depression, together with their patterning and correlates, vary with age. Of course, it would be desirable in such studies to relate the findings to some specific biological "marker" of depression. Unfortunately, such markers have not as yet been found. Nevertheless, it may be desirable to use the nearest approaches that are available—such as a familial loading of depressive disorders (with the data obtained blind to the child's age and diagnosis) and, possibly, nonsuppression on the dexamethasone suppression test (Carroll, 1982; Leckman, 1983), using salivary estimations of cortisol level (Woolston, Gianfredi, Gertner, Pangas, & Mason, 1983). The point of such measures would be to determine whether or not indices of depression that are separate from the child's symptomatology vary with age. If they do, this would suggest that depressive disorders truly vary in frequency with age. If they do not, but if the frequency of operationally defined depressive syndromes do vary, this would suggest that depression changes with age in its clinical manifestations.

General Population Studies

The clinic studies are required in order to derive and test valid measures of depressive affect and cognition. General population studies are required to test the assumptions required in the clinic studies (see above). More important, however, they are needed to obtain valid measures of possible age trends in depressive phenomena in children without, as well as those with, overt socially handicapping psychiatric disorders. Obviously, it would be important at the same time to obtain data on age changes in the various features that might possibly explain age differences in depression (see above), such as frequency of stressors or availability of social supports. Ideally, such epidemiologic strategies should be combined with a longitudinal follow-up in order to examine age changes in the same individuals.

One specific issue requiring investigation is the apparent change in sex ratio from approximately equal before puberty to a female excess in adult life (see Rutter, 1986). First, it is necessary to confirm or refute the finding that the sex ratio does in fact change over the years of adolescence. Second, if confirmed, the reasons for the change should be identified. This will be no straightforward matter, inasmuch as the reasons for female preponderance in adult life remain obscure. The sex difference seems real and not an artifact of reporting (Weissman & Klerman, 1977); however, family data indicate that the female excess cannot be attributed to any increased genetic loading for depression in women (Merikangas, Weissman, & Pauls, 1985). Rather, it appears that the female susceptibility may be associated with either hormonal differences or social factors. Thus, men and women seem to vary in their response to marital dissolution (Reissman & Gerstel, 1985). It would be fruitful to examine whether age changes in depression are associated with either puberty or variations in stress events or sources of support. The differentiation of the two types of variables is greatly facilitated by the fact that whereas boys and girls differ by some 2 years in the age at which they reach puberty, they do not differ in the timing of their course through schooling and leaving school.

Natural History Studies

A second, rather different, research approach is provided by the "natural history" or follow-up strategy applied to clinically diagnosed depressive conditions in childhood. The rationale here is that major depressive disorders tend to be recurrent conditions (Coryell & Winokur, 1982). This is particularly the case with bipolar disorders, both in adulthood and in adolescence (Strober & Carlson, 1982). Thus the validation (or rather part validation) of depressive syndromes in childhood relies on the demonstration that depressed children are more likely than children with other forms of psychiatric disorder to develop major depressive disorders in adult life. There is no published study that does just that, but there are some that provide important pointers. Kovacs and colleagues undertook a 5-year follow-up of child patients with a major depressive disorder, a dysthymic disorder, an adjustment disorder with depressed mood, and some other psychiatric condition (Kovacs, Feinberg, Crouse-Novak, Paulauskas, & Finkelstein, 1984; Kovacs, Feinberg, Crouse-Novak, Paulauskas, Pollack, & Finkelstein, 1984). The findings are striking in showing that recovery was fastest in the case of major depressive disorders and adjustment reactions, but that the development of *subsequent* episodes of major depression was virtually confined to children with major depressive disorders and dysthymic disorders (about two-thirds after 5 years of follow-up in both groups). There are four main limitations to this important well-planned study. First, it seems that the follow-up assessments were not made blind to the original diagnosis. Second, the nondepressive comparison group was not closely matched on symptomatology (it was defined solely in terms of absence of dysthymic mood as such). Third, the follow-up did not extend into adult life. Fourth, the published findings do not as yet provide data on the outcome with respect to nondepressive disorders.

The relevance of this last limitation is shown by the evidence that depressed children often also show other forms of psychiatric disturbance (see above) and that this may persist after recovery from the initial depressive episode (e.g., Eastgate & Gilmour, 1984; Puig-Antich, 1982; Poznanski, 1981). Moreover, in a systematic study of Maudsley Hospital patients seen both as children and as adults, Zeitlin (1986) found substantial continuity in the phenomena of depression as operationally defined, but considerable variations over time in the other psychiatric phenomena with which it was associated. A systematic follow-up study from childhood to adult life of matched depressed and nondepressed psychiatric patients—one that deals with the limitations of the research to date—would be most informative.

Genetic Family Studies

As already noted, research with adult patients has shown that those with major depressive disorders differ from those with other psychiatric conditions in the rate of depression in first-degree relatives. The possible relevance of this to the study of depression in childhood is shown both by the high familial loading for depression (Puig-Antich *et al.*, in press) and by the high rate of psychiatric disorders in the offspring of adults with major depressive disorder; the evidence is contradictory on the extent to which the main risk in the offspring is for affective disorders (Beardslee, Bemporad, Keller, & Klerman, 1983; Gershon et al., 1985; Weissman, Leckman, et al., 1984; Weissman, Prusoff, et al., 1984). However, in planning research strategies it is necessary to appreciate that parental depression constitutes an environmental as well as a genetic risk factor for the children, and that the risk is for nondepressive as well as depressive disorders in the offspring (Rutter & Quinton, 1985; Rutter, 1986). Moreover, parental mental illness is a common occurrence with a wide range of child psychiatric problems (Rutter, 1966) and also it appears that there may be familial loading for nondepressive as well as depressive conditions in children with depressive states (Puig-Antich et al., in press). This may arise as a result of the overlap with other psychiatric disorders but, whatever the explanation, it needs to be taken into account.

What is required is a genetic family study of depressive and nondepressive disorders in childhood (matched on nondepressive symptomatology), in which there is systematic direct assessment of psychiatric conditions in relatives undertaken blind to the child's diagnosis (Leckman, Sholomskas, Thompson, Belanger, & Weissman, 1982; Orvaschel, Thompson, Belanger, Prusoff, & Kidd, 1982; Thompson, Kidd, & Weissman, 1980; Thompson, Orvaschel, Prusoff, & Kidd, 1982). In such a study it would be essential to determine the familial risk for both depressive and nondepressive conditions in relatives. If such a study could be combined with a follow-up from childhood to adult life (see above), it would be advantageous to assess the familial risk separately for depressive disorders arising in childhood, those recurring in adult life, and for those present in both age periods.

Biological Correlates

There is a substantial body of research into the biological correlates of depression in adult life (see Åsberg, Martensson, & Wägner, in press; McKinney & Moran, 1982; Sachar, 1982; Zis & Goodwin, 1982), and equivalent data for children are accumulating (Puig-Antich, 1986). Unfortunately, so far the biological correlates of depression have but moderate sensitivity and specificity. Moreover, most represent markers of state rather than trait (that is to say, they are abnormal during the depressive episode but return to normal after recovery). However, there are some promising leads from research in adults that warrant following up, and these should be accompanied by comparable research in childhood. As already noted, it will certainly be necessary in such research to take account of possible age-related changes in biological functioning.

Drug Response

Potentially, a specific drug response to antidepressant medication might prove to be useful in the study of depressive conditions in childhood. However, up to now it has been of very limited utility in the study of the classification of depressive and nondepressive conditions. This is because of three main limitations. First, there is no drug as yet available that has a certain, or even near-certain, effect in major depressive disorders in adults. Hence, a lack of drug response is no indication that the disorder is not depressive in origin. Second, the antidepressant drugs in general use have an astonishingly wide range of pharmacological effects. Thus, for example, the tricyclics have been shown to relieve enuresis and to be of benefit in the treatment of attention deficit disorders (see Taylor, 1985). Accordingly, any beneficial effect may stem from the drugs' nonantidepressant as well as antidepressant properties. Third, there may be age-related differences in the way in which individuals respond to drugs (see above). In addition, there are the practical problems in the assessment of drug response that stem from children's noncompliance in taking drugs.

Stress Correlates

In adults, there is a good deal of evidence that depressive disorders are commonly precipitated by stress events, perhaps especially those involving "loss" or the breaking of important (love) relationships (Brown & Harris, 1978; Paykel, 1982). There is also some preliminary evidence that the type of life events associated with depression may differ from those associated with anxiety states (Finlay-Jones & Brown, 1981). Thus, it might be supposed that one useful approach to the study of childhood depression would be the determination of possible associations with stress events of different kinds—once more making systematic comparisons with nondepressive disorders. Indeed, that would be a useful strategy. However, certain constraints need to be borne in mind. First, there is uncertainty over the extent to which there is specificity in the kinds of stressors associated with depression (Paykel, 1982). Second, loss events have been shown to lead to quite a range of disorders, both somatic and psychic (Craig, in press; Weiner, in press). Third, the study of stress in childhood is in its infancy (Garmezy, 1986; Garmezy & Rutter 1983, 1985; Goodyer, Kolvin, & Gatzanis, 1985; Johnson, 1982; Monck & Dobbs, 1985), adequately tested instruments are not yet available and it remains uncertain how far the life events that constitute stressors to adults pose a similar risk to children. In particular, it remains to be determined how far the risks impinge *directly* on the child and how far they operate through effects on the parents and the family. Nevertheless, in spite of these limitations there is no doubt that this is a research strategy well worth pursuing.

CONCLUSIONS

In discussions concerning the difficulties involved in the diagnosis and classification of depression in childhood it is sometimes assumed that all is well with respect to the nosology of depressive disorders as they occur in adults. It is evident that this is far from the case, although it is equally true that a good deal is known. This chapter has sought to provide a brief overview of the diagnostic and classification issues that apply to all age groups as well as those that apply specifically to children. An outline has been provided of some of the research strategies that might be employed in attempts to resolve the remaining issues.

ACKNOWLEDGMENTS

This chapter is based in part on "Depressive Feelings, Cognitions, and Disorders: A Research Postscript" by M. Rutter (1986). In M. Rutter, C. Izard, and P. Read (Eds.), *Depression in Young People: Developmental and Clinical Perspectives*, New York: Guilford Press. Reprinted by permission.

REFERENCES

American Psychiatric Association (1980). *Diagnostic and statistical manual of mental disorders* (3rd ed.). Washington, DC: Author.

Andreasen, N. C. (1982). Concepts, diagnosis and classification. In E. S. Paykel (Ed.), *Handbook of affective disorders* (pp. 24–44). Edinburgh: Churchill Livingstone.

Anthony, J., & Scott, P. D. (1960). Manic-depressive psychosis in childhood. *Journal of Child Psychology and Psychiatry, 1*, 53–72.

Åsberg, M., Mårtensson, B., & Wägner, A. (in press). On the psychobiology of depression and suicidal behaviour. In D. Magnusson & A. Öhman (Eds.), *Psychopathology in the perspective of person–environment interaction*. New York: Academic Press.

Beardslee, W. R., Bemporad, J., Keller, M. B., & Klerman, G. L. (1983). Children of parents with major affective disorder: A review. *American Journal of Psychiatry, 140*, 825–832.

Bebbington, P. (1985). Three cognitive theories of depression. *Psychological Medicine, 15*, 759–769.

Beck, A. T. (1976). *Cognitive therapy and the emotional disorders*. New York: International Universities Press.

Black, D., & Urbanowicz, M. A. (1985). Bereaved children—family intervention. In J. E. Stevenson (Ed.), *Recent research in developmental psychopathology*. Supplement to *Journal of Child Psychology and Psychiatry, 4*, 179–187.

Blackburn, I. M., & Bishop, S. (1983). Changes in cognition with pharmacotherapy and cognitive therapy. *British Journal of Psychiatry, 143*, 609–617.

Bowlby, J. (1969). *Attachment and loss. I. Attachment*. London: Hogarth.

Bowlby, J. (1980). *Attachment and loss. III. Loss, sadness and depression*. New York: Basic Books.

Brockington, I. F., Altman, E., Hillier, V., Meltzer, H. Y., & Nand, S. (1982). The clinical picture of bipolar affective disorder in its depressed phase: A report from London and Chicago. *British Journal of Psychiatry, 141*, 558–562.

Brockington, I. F., & Leff, J. P. (1979). Schizoaffective psychosis: Definition and incidence. *Psychological Medicine, 9*, 91–99.

Brown, G. W., Craig, T. K. J., & Harris, T. O. (1985). Depression, distress or disease? Some epidemiological considerations. *British Journal of Psychiatry, 147,* 612–622.

Brown, G. W., & Harris, T. (1978). *Social origins of depression.* London: Tavistock Press.

Brugha, T. S., & Conroy, R. (1985). Categories of depression: Reported life events in a controlled design. *British Journal of Psychiatry, 147,* 641–646.

Cantwell, D. P. (1983). Depression in childhood: Clinical picture and diagnostic criteria. In D. P. Cantwell & G. A. Carlson (Eds.), *Affective disorders in childhood and adolescence : An update* (pp. 3–18). Lancaster, England: MTP Press.

Carlson, G. A., & Cantwell, D. P. (1980a). A survey of depressive symptoms, syndrome and disorder in a child psychiatric population. *Journal of Child Psychology and Psychiatry, 21,* 19–25.

Carlson, G. A., & Cantwell, D. P. (1980b). Unmasking masked depression in children and adolescents. *American Journal of Psychiatry, 137,* 445–449.

Carlson, G. A., & Cantwell, D. P. (1982). Suicidal behavior and depression in children and adolescents. *Journal of the American Academy of Child Psychiatry, 21,* 361–368.

Carroll, B. J. (1982). The dexamethasone suppression test for melancholia. *British Journal of Psychiatry, 140,* 292–304.

Chambers, W. J., Puig-Antich, J., Hirsch, M., Paez, P., Ambrosini, P. J., Tabrizi, M. A., & Davies, M. (1985). The assessment of affective disorders in children and adolescents by semistructured interview: Test–retest reliability of the Schedule for Affective Disorders and Schizophrenia for School-Age Children, present episode version. *Archives of General Psychiatry, 42,* 696–702.

Clayton, P. J. (1982). Bereavement. In E. S. Paykel (Ed.), *Handbook of affective disorders* (pp. 403–415). Edinburgh: Churchill Livingstone.

Clinical Research Centre, Division of Psychiatry. (1984). The Northwick Park ECT trial: Predictors of response to real and simulated ECT. *British Journal of Psychiatry, 144,* 227–237.

Coleman, J. C. (1974). *Relationships in adolescence.* London: Routledge and Kegan Paul.

Coleman, J. C., Herzberg, J., & Morris, M. (1977). Identity in adolescence: Present and future self-concepts. *Journal of Youth and Adolescence, 6,* 63–75.

Coppen, A., Abou-Saleh, M., Miller, P., Metcalfe, M., Harwood, J., & Bailey, J. (1983). Dexamethasone suppression test in depressive and other psychiatric illness. *British Journal of Psychiatry, 142,* 498–504.

Costello, A. J., Edelbrock, C. S., Dulcan, M. H., Kales, R., & Klavic, S. H. (1984). *Report on the NIMH Diagnostic Interview Schedule for Children (DISC).* Bethesda, MD: National Institute of Mental Health.

Costello, E. J., Edelbrock, C. S., & Costello, A. J. (1985). Validity of the NIMH Diagnostic Interview Schedule for Children: A comparison between pediatric and psychiatric referrals. *Journal of Abnormal Child Psychiatry, 13,* 579–596.

Coryell, W., & Winokur, G. (1982). Course and outcome. In E. S. Paykel (Ed.), *Handbook of affective disorders* (pp. 93–106). Edinburgh: Churchill Livingstone.

Craig, T. K. J. (in press). Stress and contextual meaning: Specific causal effects in psychiatric and physical disorders. In D. Magnusson & A. Öhman (Eds.), *Psychopathology in the perspective of person–environment interaction.* New York: Academic Press.

Cytryn, L., & McKnew, D. H. (1972). Proposed classification of childhood depression. *American Journal of Psychiatry, 129,* 149–155.

Damon, W., & Hart, D. (1982). The development of self-understanding from infancy through adolescence. *Child Development, 53,* 841–864.

Dweck, C. S., & Elliott, E. S. (1983). Achievement motivation. In E. M. Hetherington (Ed.), *Socialization, personality, and social development* (Vol. 4, *Mussen's handbook of child psychology,* 4th ed., pp. 643–691). New York: Wiley.

Dweck, C. S., Davidson, W., Nelson S., & Enns, B. (1978). Sex differences in learned helplessness. II. The contingencies of evaluative feedback in the classroom. III. An experimental analysis. *Developmental Psychology, 14,* 268–276.

Eastgate, J., & Gilmour, L. (1984). Long-term outcome of depressed children: A follow-up study. *Developmental Medicine and Child Neurology*, *26*, 68–72.

Edelbrock, C., Costello, A. J., Dulcan, M. K., Kales, R., & Conover, N. C. (1985). Age differences in the reliability of the psychiatric interview of the child. *Child Development*, *56*, 265–275.

Eisenberg, L. (1980). Adolescent suicide: On taking arms against a sea of troubles. *Pediatrics*, *66*, 315–320.

Emde, R., Harmon, R., & Good, W. (1986). Depressive feelings in children: A transactional model for research. In M. Rutter, C. Izard, & P. Read (Eds.), *Depression in young people: Developmental and clinical perspectives*. New York: Guilford.

Feighner, J. P., Robins, E., Guze, S. B., Woodruff, R. A., & Winokur, G. (1972). Diagnostic criteria for use in psychiatric research. *Archives of General Psychiatry*, *26*, 57–63.

Finlay-Jones, R. A., & Brown, G. W. (1981). Types of stressful life events and the onset of anxiety and depressive disorders. *Psychological Medicine*, *11*, 803–815.

Finlay-Jones, R. A., Brown, G. W., Duncan-Jones, P., Harris, T., Murphy, E., & Prudo, R. (1980). Depression and anxiety in the community: Replicating the diagnosis of a case. *Psychological Medicine*, *10*, 445–454.

Frommer, E. A. (1968). Depressive illness in childhood. In A. J. Coppen & A. Walk (Eds.), *Recent developments in affective disorders* (*British Journal of Psychiatry* Special Publication No. 2). England: Headley, Ashford.

Frommer, E. A. (1972). Indication for antidepressant treatment with special reference to depressed pre-school children. In A. L. Annell (Ed.), *Depressive states in childhood and adolescence* (pp. 449–454). New York: Wiley.

Garmezy, N., (1986). Developmental aspects of children's responses to the stress of separation and loss. In M. Rutter, C. Izard, & P. Read (Eds.) *Depression in young people: Developmental and clinical perspectives*. New York: Guilford.

Garmezy, N., & Rutter, M. (Eds.) (1983). *Stress, coping, and development in children*. New York: McGraw-Hill.

Garmezy, N., & Rutter, M. (1985). Acute reactions to stress. In M. Rutter & L. Hersov (Eds.), *Child and adolescent psychiatry: Modern approaches* (2nd ed.). Oxford: Blackwell.

Gershon, E. S., Hamovit, J., Guroff, J., Dibble, E., Leckman, J. F., Sceery, W., Targum, S. D., Nurnberger, J. P., Jr., Golden, L. R., & Bunney, W. C. S., Jr. (1982). A family study of schizoaffective, bipolar I, bipolar II, unipolar, and normal controls. *Archives of General Psychiatry*, *39*, 1157–1167.

Gershon, E. S., McKnew, D., Cytryn, L. Hamovit, J., Schreiber, J., Hibbs, E., & Pellegrini, D. (1985). Diagnoses in school-age children of bipolar affective disorder patients and normal controls. *Journal of Affective Disorders*, *8*, 283–291.

Glaser, K. (1967). Masked depression in children and adolescents. *American Journal of Psychotherapy*, *19*, 228–240.

Goodyer, I., Kolvin, I., & Gatzanis, S. (1985). Recent undesirable life events and psychiatric disorder in children and adolescence. *British Journal of Psychiatry*, *147*, 517–523.

Graham, P. J. (1981). Depressive disorders—A reconsideration. *Acta Pedopsychiatrica*, *46*, 285–296.

Guze, S. B., Woodruff, R. A., & Clayton, P. J. (1971). "Secondary" affective disorder: A study of 95 cases. *Psychological Medicine*, *1*, 426–428.

Hamilton, E. W., & Abramson, L. Y. (1983). Cognitive patterns and major depressive disorder: A longitudinal study in a hospital setting. *Journal of Abnormal Psychology*, *92*, 173–184.

Hamilton, M. (1982). Symptoms and assessment of depression. In E. S. Paykel (Ed.), *Handbook of affective disorders* (pp. 3–11). Edinburgh: Churchill Livingstone.

Harmon, R. J., Wagonfeld, S., & Emde, R. N. (1982). Anaclitic depression: A follow-up from infancy to puberty. *Psychoanalytic Study of the Child*, *37*, 67–94.

Harter, S. (1983). Developmental perspectives on the self-system. In E. M. Hetherington (Ed.), *Socialization, personality, and social development* (Vol. 4, *Mussen's handbook of child psychology*, 4th ed., pp. 275–385). New York: Wiley.

Hassanyeh, F., & Davison, K. (1980). Bipolar affective psychosis with onset before age 16 years: Report of 10 cases. *British Journal of Psychiatry, 137*, 530–539.

Hawton, K., & Boldacre, M. (1982). Hospital admissions for adverse effects of medicinal agents (mainly self-poisoning) among adolescents in the Oxford region. *British Journal of Psychiatry, 141*, 166–170.

Hendren, R. L. (1983). Depression in anorexia nervosa. *Journal of the American Academy of Child Psychiatry, 22*, 59–62.

Hibbert, G. A., Teasdale, J. D., & Spencer, P. (1984). Covariation of depressive symptoms over time. *Psychological Medicine, 14*, 451–456.

Johnson, D. A. W. (1981). Studies of depressive symptoms in schizophrenia. *British Journal of Psychiatry, 139*, 89–101.

Johnson, J. H. (1982). Life events as stressors in childhood and adolescence. In B. B. Lahey & A. E. Kazdin (Eds.), *Advances in clinical child psychology* (Vol. 5, pp. 219–253). New York: Plenum.

Kagan, J. (1981). *The second year*. Cambridge, MA: Harvard University Press.

Kagan, J. (1982). The emergence of self. *Journal of Child Psychology and Psychiatry, 23*, 363–382.

Kaplan, S. L., Hong, G. K., & Weinhold, C. (1984). Epidemiology of depressive symptomatology in adolescents. *Journal of the American Academy of Child Psychiatry, 23*, 91–98.

Kashani, J. H., Shekim, W. D., & Reid, J. C. (1984). Amitriptyline in children with major depressive disorder: A double-blind crossover pilot study. *Journal of the American Academy of Child Psychiatry, 23*, 348–351.

Kazdin, A. E. (1981). Assessment techniques for childhood depression: A critical appraisal. *Journal of the American Academy of Child Psychiatry, 20*, 358–375.

Kazdin, A. E., & Petti, J. A. (1982). Self-report and interview measures of childhood and adolescent depression. *Journal of Child Psychology and Psychiatry, 23*, 437–458.

Kazdin, A. E., French, N. M., Unis, A. S., & Esveldt-Dawson, K. (1983). Assessment of childhood depression: Correspondence of child and parent ratings. *Journal of the American Academy of Child Psychiatry, 22*, 157–164.

Kazdin, A. E., Sherick, R. B., Esveldt-Dawson, K., & Pancurello, M. D. (1985). Nonverbal behavior and childhood depression. *Journal of the American Academy of Child Psychiatry, 24*, 303–309.

Kliman, G. W. (1968). *Psychological emergencies of childhood*. New York: Grune & Stratton.

Kosky, R. (1982). Suicide and attempted suicide among Australian children. *Medical Journal of Australia, 1*, 121–126.

Kovacs, M. (1986). A developmental perspective on methods and measures in the assessment of depressive disorders: The clinical interview. In M. Rutter, C. Izard, & P. Read (Eds.), *Depression in young people: Developmental and clinical perspectives*. New York: Guilford.

Kovacs, M., Feinberg, T. L., Crouse-Novak, H. A., Paulauskas, S. L., & Finkelstein, R. (1984). Depressive disorders in childhood. I. A longitudinal prospective study of characteristics and recovery. *Archives of General Psychiatry, 41*, 229–237.

Kovacs, M., Feinberg, T. L., Crouse-Novak, H. A., Paulauskas, S. L., Pollack, M., & Finkelstein, R. (1984). Depressive disorders in childhood. II. A longitudinal study of the risk for a subsequent major depression. *Archives of General Psychiatry, 41*, 643–649.

Kramer, A. D., and Feiguine, R. J. (1981). Clinical effects of amitriptyline in adolescent depression. *Journal of the American Academy of Child Psychiatry, 20*, 636–644.

Leckman, J. F. (1983). The dexamethasone suppression test. *Journal of the American Academy of Child Psychiatry, 22*, 477–479.

Leckman, J. F., Sholomskas, D., Thompson, W. D., Belanger, A., & Weissman, M. M. (1982). Best estimate of lifetime psychiatric diagnosis: A methodological study. *Archives of General Psychiatry 39*, 879–883.

Leckman, J. F., Weissman, M. M., Merikangas, K. R., Pauls, D. L., & Prusoff, B. A. (1983). Panic disorder and major depression: Increased rate of major depression, alcoholism, panic and phobic disorders in families of depressed probands with panic disorder. *Archives of General Psychiatry*, *40*, 1055–1060.

Link, B., & Dohrenwend, B. P. (1980). Formulation of hypotheses about the true prevalence of demoralization in the United States, In B. P. Dohrenwend, B. S. Dohrenwend, M. S. Gould, B. Link, R. Neugebauer, & R. Wunst-Hilzig, (Eds.), *Mental illness in the United States: Epidemiological estimates* (pp. 114–132). New York: Praeger.

Lloyd, G. G., & Cawley, R. H. (1983). Distress or illness? A study of psychological symptoms after myocardial infarction. *British Journal of Psychiatry*, *142*, 120–125.

Loranger, A. W., & Levine, P. M. (1978). Age at onset of bipolar affective illness. *Archives of General Psychiatry 35*, 1345–1348.

Lowe, T. L., & Cohen, D. J. (1980). Mania in childhood and adolescence. In R. H. Belmaker & H. M. van Praag (Eds.), *Mania : An evolving concept*. New York: Spectrum Publications.

McClure, G. M. C. (1984). Recent trends in suicide amongst the young. *British Journal of Psychiatry*, *144*, 134-138.

McConville, B. J., Boag, L. C., & Purchit, A. P. (1973). Three types of childhood depression. *Canadian Psychiatric Association Journal*, *18*, 133–138.

McKinney, W. T., & Moran, E. C. (1982). Animal models. In E. S. Paykel (Ed.), *Handbook of affective disorders* (pp. 202–211). New York: Churchill Livingstone.

Mendlewicz, J., Charles, G., & Franckson, J. M. (1982). The dexamethasone suppression test in affective disorder: Relationship to clinical and genetic subgroups. *British Journal of Psychiatry*, *141*, 464–470.

Merikangas, K. R., Weissman, M. M., & Pauls, D. L. (1985). Genetic factors in the sex ratio of major depression. *Psychological Medicine*, *15*, 63–69.

Mindham, R. H. S. (1982). Tricyclic antidepressants and amine precursors. In E. S. Paykel (Ed.), *Handbook of affective disorders* (pp. 231–245). Edinburgh: Churchill Livingstone.

Monck, E., & Dobbs, R. (1985). Measuring life events in an adolescent population: Methological issues and related findings. *Psychological Medicine*, *15*, 841–850.

Moretti, M. M., Fine, S., Haley, G., & Marriage, K. (1985). Childhood and adolescent depression: Child-report versus parent-report information. *Journal of the American Academy of Child Psychiatry*, *24*, 298–302.

Norman, W. H., Miller, I. W., & Klee, S. H. (1983). Assessment of cognitive distortion in a clinically depressed population. *Cognitive Therapy and Research*, *7*, 133–140.

Orvaschel, H., Thompson, W. D., Belanger, A., Prusoff, B. A., & Kidd, K. K. (1982). Comparison of the family history method to direct interviews: Factors affecting the diagnosis of depression. *Journal of Affective Disorders*, *4*, 49–59.

Parker, G. (1983). *Parental overprotection: A risk factor in psychosocial development*. New York: Grune & Stratton.

Paykel, E. S. (1982). Life events and early environment. In E. S. Paykel (Ed.), *Handbook of affective disorders* (pp. 146–161). Edinburgh: Churchill Livingstone.

Perris, C. (1982). The distinction between bipolar and unipolar affective disorders. In E. S. Paykel (Ed.), *Handbook of affective disorders* (pp. 45–58). Edinburgh: Churchill Livingstone.

Poznanski, E. (1981). Childhood depression: The outcome. *Acta Pedopsychiatrica*, *46*, 297–304.

Puig-Antich, J. (1982). Major depression and conduct disorder in prepuberty. *Journal of the American Academy of Child Psychiatry*, *21*, 118–128.

Puig-Antich, J. (1986). Psychobiological markers: Effects of age and puberty. In M. Rutter, C. Izard, & P. Read (Eds.), *Depression in young people: Developmental and clinical perspectives*. New York: Guilford.

Puig-Antich, J., Chambers, W. J., & Tabrizi, M. A. (1983). The clinical assessment of current depressive episodes in children and adolescents: Interviews with parents and children. In

D. P. Cantwell & G. A. Carlson (Eds.), *Affective disorders in childhood and adolescence*: *An update.* (pp. 157–179). Lancaster, England: MTP Press.

Puig-Antich, J., & Gittelman, R. (1982). Depression in childhood and adolescence. In E. S. Paykel (Ed.), *Handbook of affective disorders* (pp. 379–392). Edinburgh: Churchill Livingstone.

Puig-Antich, J., Goetz, R., Davies, M., Kaplan, T., Davies, S., Ostrow, L., & Asmis, L. (in press). A controlled family history study of prepubertal major depressive disorder. *Archives of General Psychiatry.*

Puig-Antich, J., Goetz, R., Hanlon, C., Davies, M., Thompson, J., Chambers, W. J., Tabrizi, M. A., & Weitzman, E. D. (1982). Sleep architecture and REM sleep measures in prepubertal children with major depression: A controlled study. *Archives of General Psychiatry, 39,* 932–939.

Puig-Antich, J., Lukens, E., Davies, M., Goetz, D., Brennan-Quattrack, J., & Todak, G. (1985). Psychosocial functioning in prepubertal major depressive disorders. *Archives of General Psychiatry, 42,* 500–507, 511–517.

Puig-Antich, J., Perels, J. M., Luputkin, W., Chambers, W. J., Tabrizi, M. A., King, J., Goetz, R., Davies, M., & Stiller, R. L. (1987). Imipramine in prepubertal major depressive disorders. *Archives of General Psychiatry, 44,* 81–89.

Rapoport, J., Buchsbaum, M., Weingartner, H., Zahn, T., Ludlow, C., Bartko, J., & Mikkelsen, E. J. (1980). Dextroamphetamine: Cognitive and behavioral effects in normal and hyperactive boys and normal adult males. *Archives of General Psychiatry, 37,* 933–943.

Raps, C. S., Peterson, C., Reinhard, K. E., Abramson, L. Y., & Seligman, M. E. P. (1982). Attributional style among depressed patients. *Journal of Abnormal Psychology, 91,* 102–108.

Reissman, C. K., & Gerstel, N. (1985). Marital dissolution and health: Do males or females have greater risk? *Social Science Medicine, 20,* 627–635.

Rholes, W. S., Blackwell, J., Jordan, C., & Walters, C. (1980). A developmental study of learned helplessness. *Developmental Psychology, 16,* 616–624.

Rie, H. E. (1966). Depression in childhood: A survey of some pertinent contributions. *Journal of the American Academy of Child Psychiatry, 5,* 653–683.

Rosenberg, M. (1979). *Conceiving the Self.* New York: Basic Books.

Rotundo, N., & Hensley, V. R. (1985). The Children's Depression Scales: A study of its validity. *Journal of Child Psychology and Psychiatry, 26,* 917–927.

Rutter, M. (1966). *Children of sick parents: An environmental and psychiatric study.* Institute of Psychiatry, Maudsley Monographs No. 16. New York: Oxford.

Rutter, M. (1979). *Changing youth in a changing society: Patterns of adolescent development and disorder.* London: Nuffield Provincial Trust. (U.S. edition, 1980. Cambridge, MA: Harvard University Press.)

Rutter, M. (1980). Attachment and the development of social relationships. In M. Rutter (Ed.), *Scientific foundations of developmental psychiatry* (pp. 267–279). London: Heinemann.

Rutter, M. (1981). *Maternal deprivation reassessed* (2nd ed.). Harmondsworth, England: Penguin Books.

Rutter, M. (1986). The developmental psychopathology of depression: Issues and perspectives. In M. Rutter, C. Izard, & P. Read (Eds.), *Depression in young people: Developmental and clinical perspectives.* New York: Guilford.

Rutter, M., Graham, P., Chadwick, O., & Yule, W. (1976). Adolescent turmoil: Fact or fiction? *Journal of Child Psychology and Psychiatry, 17,* 35–56.

Rutter, M., & Quinton, D. (1985). Family pathology and child psychiatric disorder: A four year prospective study. In A. R. Nicol (Ed.), *Longitudinal studies in child psychology and psychiatry: Practical lessons from research experience.* New York: Wiley.

Sachar, E. J. (1982). Endocrine abnormalities in depression. In E. S. Paykel (Ed.), *Handbook of affective disorders* (pp. 191–201). Edinburgh: Churchill Livingstone.

Selman, R. L., Jaquette, D., & Redman, L. D. (1977). Interpersonal awareness in children.

Toward an integration of developmental and clinical child psychology. *American Journal of Orthopsychiatry*, *47*, 264–274.

Shaffer, D. (1974). Suicide in childhood and early adolescence. *Journal of Child Psychology and Psychiatry*. *15*, 275–292.

Shaffer, D. (1985). Depression, mania and suicidal acts. In M. Rutter & L. Hersov (Eds.), *Child and adolescent psychiatry: Modern approaches* (2nd ed.). Oxford: Blackwell.

Shaffer, D., & Fisher, P. (1981). The epidemiology of suicide in children and young adolescents. *Journal of the American Academy of Child Psychiatry*, *20*, 545–565.

Shantz, C. (1983). Social cognition. In J. H. Flavell & E. M. Markman (Eds.), *Cognitive development* (Vol. 3, *Mussen's handbook of child psychology*, 4th ed., pp. 495–555). New York: Wiley.

Sireling, L. I., Freeling, P., Paykel, E. S., & Rao, B. M. (1985). Depression in general practice: Clinical features and comparison with outpatients. *British Journal of Psychiatry*, *147*, 119–126.

Sireling, L. I., Paykel, E. S., Freeling, P., Rao, B. M., & Patel, S. P. (1985). Depression in general practice: Case thresholds and diagnosis. *British Journal of Psychiatry*, *147*, 113–119.

Spitz, R. (1946). Anaclitic depression. *Psychoanalytic Study of the Child*, *2*, 313-342.

Spitzer, R. L., Endicott, J., & Robins, E. (1978). Research diagnostic criteria: Rationale and reliability. *Archives of General Psychiatry*, *35*, 773–782.

Stancer, H. C., Persad, E., Jorna, T., Flood, C., & Wagener, D. (1984). The occurrence of secondary affective disorder in an in-patient population and severe and recurrent affective disorder. *British Journal of Psychiatry*, *144*, 630–635.

Stokes, P. E., Stoll, P. M., Koslow, S. A., Maas, J. W., David, J. M., Swann, A. C., & Robins, E. (1984). Pretreatment DST and hypothalamic–pituitary–adrenocortical function in depressed patients and comparison groups. *Archives of General Psychiatry*, *41*, 257–267.

Strober, M., & Carlson, G. (1982). Bipolar illness in adolescents with major depression: Clinical, genetic, and psychopharmacologic predictors in a three- to four-year prospective follow-up investigation. *Archives of General Psychiatry*, *39*, 549–555.

Taylor, E. (1985). Drug treatment. In M. Rutter & L. Hersov (Eds.), *Child and adolescent psychiatry: Modern approaches* (2nd ed.). Oxford: Blackwell.

Tennant, C., & Bebbington, P. (1978). The social causation of depression: A critique of the work of Brown and his colleagues. *Psychological Medicine*, *8*, 556–576.

Tennant, C., Bebbington, P., & Hurry, J. (1981). The short-term outcome of neurotic disorders in the community: The relation of remission to clinical factors and to "neutralizing" life events. *British Journal of Psychiatry*, *139*, 213–220.

Thompson, W. D., Kidd, J. R., & Weissman, M. M. (1980). A procedure for the efficient collection and processing of pedigree data suitable for genetic analysis. *Journal of Psychiatric Research*, *15*, 291–303.

Thompson, W. D., Orvaschel, H., Prusoff, B. A., & Kidd, K. K. (1982). An evaluation of the family history method for ascertaining psychiatric disorders. *Archives of General Psychiatry*, *39*, 53-58.

Torgersen, S. (1985). Hereditary differentiation of anxiety and affective neuroses. *British Journal of Psychiatry*, *146*, 530–534.

Tsuang, M. T., Faraone, S. W., & Fleming, J. A. (1985). Familial transmission of major affective disorders. Is there evidence supporting the distinction between unipolar and bipolar disorders? *British Journal of Psychiatry*, *146*, 268–271.

Tsuang, M. T., Winokur, G., & Crowe, R. R. (1980). Morbidity risks of schizophrenia and affective disorders among first-degree relatives of patients with schizophrenia, mania, depression and surgical conditions. *British Journal of Psychiatry*, *133*, 497–504.

Tsuang, M. T., Woolsam, R. F., & Simpson, J. C. (1981). An evaluation of the Feighner criteria for schizophrenia and affective disorders using long-term outome data. *Psychological Medicine*, *11*, 281–288.

van Eerdewegh, M. M., Bieri, M. D., Parilla, R. H., & Clayton, P. (1982). The bereaved child. *British Journal of Psychiatry*, *140*, 23–29.

van Eerdewegh, M. M., Clayton, P. J., & van Eerdewegh, P. (1985). The bereaved child: Variables influencing early psychopathology. *British Journal of Psychiatry, 147,* 188–194.

Weinberg, W., & Rehmet, A. (1983). Childhood affective disorder and school problems. In D. P. Cantwell & G. A. Carlson (Eds.), *Affective disorders in childhood and adolescence: An update* (pp. 109–128). Lancaster, England: MTP Press.

Weiner, H. (in press). Human relationships in health, illness and disease. In D. Magnusson & A. Öhman (Eds.), *Psychopathology in the perspective of person–environment interaction.* New York: Academic Press.

Weissman, M. M., Gershon, E. S., Kidd, K. K., Prusoff, B. A., Leckman, J. F., Dibble, E., Hamovit, J., Thompson, N. D., Pauls, D. L., & Guroff, J. J. (1984). Psychiatric disorders in the relatives of probands with affective disorders: The Yale University–National Institute of Mental Health collaborative study. *Archives of General Psychiatry, 41,* 13–21.

Weissman, M. M., & Klerman, G. L. (1977). Sex differences and the epidemiology of depression. *Archives of General Psychiatry, 34,* 98–111.

Weissman, M. M., Leckman, J. F., Merikangas, K. R., & Gammon, G. D. (1984). Depression and anxiety disorders in children (ages 6–18) of parents with depression and anxiety disorders. *Archives of General Psychiatry, 41,* 845–852.

Weissman, M. M., Orvaschel, H., & Padian, H. (1980). Children's symptoms and social functioning self-report scales: Comparison of mothers' and children's reports. *Journal of Nervous and Mental Diseases, 168,* 736–740.

Weissman, M. M., Prusoff, B. A., Gammon, P. D., Merikangas, K. R., Leckman, J. F., & Kidd, K. K. (1984). Psychopathology in the children (ages 6–18) of depressed and normal parents. *Journal of the American Academy of Child Psychiatry, 23,* 78–84.

Weissman, M. M., Wickramaratne, P., Merikangas, K. R., Leckman, J. F., Prusoff, B. A., Caruso, K. A., Kidd, K. K., & Gammon, G. D. (1984). Onset of major depression in early adulthood: Increased familial loading and specificity. *Archives of General Psychiatry, 41,* 1135–1143.

Wing, J. K., Cooper, J. E., & Sartorius, N. (1974). *The measurement and classification of psychiatric symptoms.* New York: Cambridge.

Woolston, J. L., Gianfredi, S., Gertner, J. H., Pangas, J. A., & Mason, J. W. (1983). Salivary cortisol: A nontraumatic sampling technique for assaying cortisol dynamics. *Journal of the American Academy of Child Psychiatry, 22,* 474–476.

World Health Organization. (1978). *International classification of diseases* (9th ed.). Geneva: Author.

Zeitlin, H. (1986). *The natural history of psychiatric disorder in children.* Unpublished MD thesis, University of London.

Zis, A. P., & Goodwin, F. K. (1982). The amine hypothesis. In E. S. Paykel (Ed.), *Handbook of affective disorders* (pp. 175–190). Edinburgh: Churchill Livingstone.

12

ATTENTION DEFICIT AND
CONDUCT DISORDER SYNDROMES

ERIC TAYLOR

INTRODUCTION

The main scientific purpose of a syndromic classification is to enable sharp conclusions to be drawn about the causes, pathogenesis, and course of a disorder that distinguish it from other disorders.

Epidemiologic and longitudinal studies have gone a long way to establish the value of a concept of conduct disorder (Rutter, 1978). There is a general agreement that children with this disorder are properly to be differentiated from those whose disorder takes the form of emotional upsets. The various kinds of antisocial conduct can be identified replicably, and they tend to associate together and to segregate from anxiety symptoms. Issues about the distribution of cases have not been thoroughly addressed (see below), but they have been rather preempted by the strong ability of conduct disorder to predict concurrent associations and future adjustment. In other words, the concept of conduct disorder has fulfilled several of the usual requirements of a psychiatric class: clarity and reliability of definition of symptoms, replicable association of symptoms, coherent distribution of cases, and predictive and discriminative validity.

So far, so good. Nevertheless, the diagnostic concept of conduct disorder has some major weaknesses that make it difficult to manage. It is a large and (in clinical and prognostic terms) a heterogeneous group; yet it has not been subdivided in any way that commands general confidence (Rutter & Garmezy, 1983). Indeed, some authorities doubt whether there are any coherent subgroups to be found, reject the separation of hyperactivity from conduct disorder, and prefer to recognize a broad group of externalized problems of behavior (Lahey, Green, & Forehand, 1980; O'Leary, 1980; Sandberg, 1981; Wolff 1985). The diagnostic uncertainty generated is great,

Eric Taylor. Department of Child and Adolescent Psychiatry, University of London Institute of Psychiatry. London. England.

and accounts for much of the enormous twentyfold discrepancy between rates of hyperactivity in the United States and the United Kingdom. It has been argued elsewhere that much of the difference stems from differences in diagnostic preference for the categories of hyperactivity and conduct disorder (Taylor & Sandberg, 1984). Although U.S. and U.K. children may not be very different, they are dealt with using different diagnostic approaches.

This review will focus upon one question in the subclassification of the externalizing behavior problems. *Is a hyperkinetic disorder properly to be distinguished from the broad group of those behaviors that are in conflict with society?* The issue is a good example of the other questions in nosology. It raises general problems of interpreting research findings, as well as issues that can be applied to other nosological considerations such as the value of affective, reactive, and unsocialized types of conduct disorder.

PROBLEMS FOR CLASSIFICATION

The classifier's problems are of several different kinds. The first of these is the ambiguity that has crept into some definitions of terms such as "impulsiveness" and "attention deficit." Next comes the uncertainty about just what level of symptomatology needs to exist before a subject can be classified as a case. This problem will be more severe if it turns out that problems such as attention deficit are continuously distributed as a dimension in the population, so that no obvious cutoff point exists. It will then be necessary to assess the predictive value of different grades of severity in different populations.

A third obstacle to a successful nosology is the frequent coexistence of attention deficit disorder and conduct disorder with each other and with other psychiatric conditions. Clinical experience seems to argue that mixtures of problems are the rule, but it is necessary to test this idea and to inquire about the meaning and implications of overlap. Indeed, the meaning of various kinds of overlap may well be somewhat different; hence the issues will be in rather different form for the overlaps between, for example, attention deficit order on the one hand and conduct disorder, depression, learning disorders, autism, and multiple tics on the other.

Fourth, there is still considerable uncertainty about the relationships of several of the symptom patterns in this area. What is the relationship of "attention deficit disorder with hyperactivity" (ADD-H) to the severe hyperkinetic syndrome encountered in some intellectually retarded children? What is the relationship between attention deficit disorder and the probable deficiency of attention in those at high risk for schizophrenia? Several of the apparent divisions of conduct disorder have proved to be best seen as aspects of a single condition, at least as far as longitudinal course is concerned. This may or may not be the case for different aspects of hyperactivity: it needs a systematic examination.

The fifth problem lies in the uncertainty about the relative status of several competing definitions. What, for example, are the implications of including impulsiveness in the definition of ADD-H given in the third edition of the *Diagnostic and Statistical Manual of Mental Disorders* (DSM-III) of the American Psychiatric Association (1980)? What should be the relative importance of the purity of attention deficit, of its pervasiveness, and of its severity in the criteria for a hyperkinetic disorder?

Sixth, there is still some uncertainty concerning the meaning of changes of symptom picture with time. If a young child with clear hyperactivity develops into an older child with conduct disorder and then into a young adult with an immature personality disorder, how are these concepts to be related? Are the earlier conditions embryonic forms of the later, or age-appropriate manifestations of the same thing, or diffuse risk factors whose outcome is determined by later events?

Finally, the conceptual nature of a good nosological scheme is not at all clear. Should it be based upon dimensions, upon mutually exclusive categories, or upon hierarchies of categories? More meaningfully, for what different purposes are these different styles of classification best fitted? On what grounds should one differentiate between them?

These uncertainties exist in spite of a substantial amount of well-planned empirical research. This chapter will discuss the issues in relation to the distinctions between attention deficit and defiant or antisocial conduct.

STATUS OF A HYPERKINETIC SYNDROME

For a hyperkinetic disorder to earn its place in classification, it must survive the successive hurdles sketched above for conduct disorder: clear, reliable and unbiased definition of symptoms; coherence of symptoms; appropriate distribution of cases; and predictive validity by comparison with other conditions as well as with normal controls.

Definition of Symptoms and Classes

Restlessness, inattentiveness, and impulsiveness sound like hard and reliable symptoms, but in practice their ascertainment leaves much to be desired. Other chapters consider questionnaires, interviews, ratings and observations as tools of assessment. A severe judge might simply conclude at this point that the technology of recording symptoms is too primitive to allow any useful classification and end the account here. There are three reasons, however, to discourage such pessimism and carry the discussion further.

First, the main disagreements stem from diagnostic weighting of symptoms rather than from doubt concerning the presence of symptoms (Taylor & Sandberg, 1984). Two observers can agree tolerably about whether a child behaves inattentively and restlessly in a classroom (Sandberg, 1986) or in a home or laboratory setting (Taylor, 1986a). Their agreement is far from perfect, but it is enough for a beginning.

Second, the technology of assessment is under continuing improvement. It is therefore worth taking stock of the various achievements made to date. Further refinements are likely to be increasingly expensive in investigator time. Are they necessary?

Third, the existing clinical assessments are good enough to give modest predictions of objective assessments of the same phenomena. For example, children diagnosed as hyperactive do tend to make more movements than normal controls when their activity is physically measured (Barkley & Ullman, 1975; Cunningham & Barkley 1979; Firestone & Martin, 1979; Juliano, 1974; Montagu, 1975; Pope, 1970; Porrino et al., 1983; Worland, North-Jones, & Stern, 1973). An often-cited study that found "hyperactives" to move no more than anybody else was in fact based upon the diagnoses of private pediatricians and was intended to caution against casual and overfrequent diagnosis, not the enterprise of diagnosis itself (Plomin & Foch, 1981).

Accordingly, it is worthwhile to continue with considerations of how far the symptoms of overactivity, inattentiveness, and impulsiveness are associated with one another rather than with the antisocial behaviors that define conduct disorder. Nevertheless (and even at the risk of repeating previous reviewers) some cautions must be entered. Words such as "inattention" and "impulsiveness" have many meanings. Impulsiveness can mean the cognitive style of making rapid and inaccurate decisions under conditions of uncertainty; or risk-taking behavior that can lead to accidents; or an unwillingness to put off immediate pleasures for the sake of pleasure deferred; or even a lack of rule-governed behavior, which is indistinguishable from rule-breaking and antisocial acts. These meanings stem from common language, or from specific cognitive theories, or from 19th-century theories about the reasons for antisocial conduct. There is a disastrous uncertainty of meaning when the word is used out of context (as in a questionnaire).

Rather similarly, "inattention" can mean *behaviors* such as being distractible or failing to persist at tasks; or it can mean *deficiencies in processing information* of a rather specific kind. Use of the word often implies a theory in which the behavior and the information processing are closely linked. This is likely to be a very interesting theory since it offers a bridge between the neuropsychological and psychiatric domains. However, the testing of the theory should not be avoided by the use of a single construct that reifies the idea of an attention deficit.

The general point is, of course, that the symptoms involved in a hyperkinetic syndrome do indeed require substantially better definition; and this involves conceptual advances in what is to be measured.

Not only the symptoms need clarification; the process of diagnostic inference is at present somewhat chaotic. Comparisons of how diagnoses are made should illuminate the road to improving them. In particular, the international differences in diagnostic rates of hyperactivity have been a crux for the replicability of classification. It seems probable on the face of it that much of the difference in diagnostic rates stems from the weighting of symptoms into categories rather than from variations in the recognition of symptoms. Understanding of the reasons for differences is therefore important in itself and also a likely avenue for refining on diagnostic schemes.

Accordingly, Judith Rapoport's team at the National Institute of Mental Health (NIMH) and the team at the Institute of Psychiatry in London have been trying to tackle some of the problems raised by collaborations across nations and across diagnostic schemes. We began by establishing a bank of 40 case histories in a readable but standardized format and, for half of them, videotapes of psychiatric interviews with the children. Half the children came from the Washington clinic, half from London. We then obtained DSM-III and ICD-9 (World Health Organization, 1978) ratings on all of them, made by the research teams and also by a panel of American clinicians and a panel of British.

All the cases came from the controversial area of conduct disorder and attention deficit disorder; they were normally intelligent boys between 6 and 10. We have therefore consciously chosen a group in whom diagnostic distinctions are likely to be uncertain and vexatious. It is therefore encouraging to find a solid agreement between us, comparable with or better than that found in studies of more securely differentiated conditions. On Axis I of DSM-III the research teams have a kappa of .69 (for three-digit agreement). For Axis I of ICD-9 the equivalent figure is .60; even this corresponds to a perfect agreement on better than 80% of cases.

The nature of the disagreements between schemes is suggestive. They nearly all seem to come in the arena of deciding where to place a mixed case. Thus, there were three cases for whom the British research team diagnosed ICD-9 conduct disorder and the American research team diagnosed hyperkinetic syndrome. In every one of them the British team had diagnosed ADD-H as one of their DSM-III diagnoses and the U.S. team had included a DSM-III diagnosis of conduct disorder. In another three cases, the British diagnosed emotional disorder in ICD-9 whereas the Americans diagnosed hyperkinesis; again, in all of those the British also recognized ADD-H in their DSM-III list and in two of the three the Americans had recognized an emotional disorder. The difference arises from the difficulty that any single-diagnosis scheme will have in coping with mixed cases. Its development needs to be in the direction of more explicit rules for handling them.

The two schemes generate slightly different numbers of cases of hyperactivity. For the U.S. team, ICD-9 gave 27 cases and DSM-III gave 33; for the U.K. team, ICD-9 gave 23 cases and DSM-III gave 35.

The panels of clinicians were much less reliable. The U.S. panel obtained a kappa of .25 for overall DSM-III diagnosis, .26 for ICD-9; the U.K. team had .28 for DSM-III and .29 for ICD-9. Diagnostic rates were also more at variance. The U.S. panel generated a total of 398 diagnoses of ADD-H in DSM-III and 335 of hyperkinetic syndrome in ICD-9; for the U.K. panel the corresponding figures were 425 and 251. In other words. there is an interaction between the scheme used and the nationality of the diagnostician using it. When multiple diagnoses are in use, clinicians in both countries recognize the presence of hyperactivity with similar frequency. When a single diagnosis is required, hyperactivity is given less weight by U.K. than by U.S. clinicians.

Disagreements between clinicians are severe enough to be a major limitation on the possibility of advancing knowledge and treatment. Nevertheless, it is clear that special training of diagnosticians can result in useful agreement even in the subdivision of this difficult group.

Association of Symptoms

Do the behaviors used to define hyperactivity in fact occur together, and do they segregate from aggressive and antisocial behavior? The questions have invited investigation by numerical taxonomy; the ratings made by teachers or parents of their children's behavior have frequently been subjected to factor analysis. This procedure aims to describe the intercorrelations between items in terms of a limited number of dimensions common to all subjects. Partial, but not conclusive, support has been given to the notion that hyperactive behaviors make up a dimension of behavior problems independent of antisocial conduct disorder.

The clearest support comes from some studies of rating scales for teachers—especially the scale developed by Conners (1969). Hyperactivity emerges as a factor distinct from defiance when this scale is applied to adequate samples from the general population of schoolchildren in the United States (Goyette, Conners, & Ulrich, 1978; Trites & Laprade, 1983; Werry, Sprague, & Cohen, 1975), New Zealand (Werry & Hawthorne, 1976), Australia (Glow, 1981), and England (Taylor & Sandberg, 1984). There is less agreement on whether hyperactivity and inattentiveness constitute one factor (Glow, 1981; Taylor & Sandberg, 1984; Werry et al., 1975) or two (Goyette et al., 1978; Werry & Hawthorne, 1976), and the method is unlikely to be strong enough to decide this further point. Table 12-1 summarizes the factorial findings in different investigations.

Some other rating scales yield an equally clear and distinct factor of hyperactivity–inattentiveness in American populations (Achenbach & Edelbrock, 1978; Dreger et al., 1964; Patterson, 1964) and among English schoolchildren (Schachar, Rutter, & Smith, 1981) and children in New Zealand (McGee et al., 1985). Other scales do not show this (Langner et al., 1976; Quay, 1964, 1977; Spivack & Spotts, 1965). Indeed, Quay (1979) reviewed the field and argued that the vast majority of deviant behaviors could be subsumed under the four major patterns of conduct disorder, anxiety-

TABLE 12-1. Comparison of Factor Analyses in Different Studies.

Item	Conners (1969)	Taylor & Sandberg (1984)	Werry, Sprague, & Cohen (1975)	Werry & Hawthorne (1975)	Goyette, Conners, & Ulrich (1978)[a]	Glow (1981)	Trites, Blouin, & Laprade (1982)
12. Sullen or sulky	CP	CP	CP	CP	CP	CP	E
15. Quarrelsome	CP	CP	CP	CP	CP	CP	CP
17. Acts "smart"	CP	CP	CP	HA	CP	CP	HA
21. Temper outbursts	CP	CP	CP	CP	CP	CP	CP+E
25. No sense of fair play	CP	—[b]	CP	CP	—[c]	CP	—[b]
31. Defiant	CP	CP	CP	CP	—[c]	CP	CP
32. Impudent	CP	CP	CP	CP	—[c]	CP	CP
36. Stubborn	CP	CP	CP	CP	CP	CP	CP+E
38. Uncooperative	CP	CP	CP	CP	—[c]	CP	CP
18. Destructive	CP	AS	AS	CP	—[c]	AS	CP
19. Steals	CP	AS	AS	CP	—[c]	AS	CP
20. Lies	CP	AS	AS	CP	—[c]	AS	CP
1. Constantly fidgeting	HA	HA-IA	HA-IA	HA	HA	HA-IA	HA-IA
2. Odd noises	HA	HA-IA	HA-IA	HA	HA	HA-IA	HA-IA
5. Restless, overactive	HA	HA-IA	HA-IA	HA	HA	HA-IA	HA-IA
6. Excitable, impulsive	HA	CP	CP	HA	HA	HA-IA	HA-IA
14. Disturbs others	HA	HA-IA	CP	HA	HA	HA-IA	HA-IA
29. Teases others	HA	CP	CP	CP+HA	—[c]	CP	HA-IA
4. Coordination poor	IA	HA-IA	HA-IA	—[b]	—[c]	—[b]	HA-IA
7. Easily distracted	IA	HA-IA	HA-IA	HA	IA	HA-IA	HA-IA
8. Short attention span	IA	HA-IA	HA-IA	IA	IA	HA-IA	HA-IA
11. Daydreams	IA	—[b]	HA-IA	IA	IA	—[b]	—[b]
24. Easily led	IA	—[b]	HA-IA	IA	IA	—[b]	—[b]
26. Leadership lacking	IA	—[b]	—[b]	—[b]	IA	—[b]	—[b]

Note. Letters indicate factor on which item *chiefly* loads in each study: CP = conduct problem; HA = hyperactivity; IA = inattentive–passive; AS = antisocial conduct; HA–IA = combined factor of hyperactivity and inattentiveness; E = emotional overindulgence.

[a] Wording and numbering of items slightly varied from original questionnaire; presented here in the original number system.

[b] Item loads on a factor relating to poor social interactions; details of factor differ in different studies.

[c] Item not present in this version of the questionnaire.

withdrawal, immaturity and socialized aggression; overactivity and inattentiveness would then be parts of "conduct disorder" and "immaturity." Nevertheless, "immaturity" can well be seen as akin to an "attention deficit" dimension. Furthermore, much of the discrepancy can be traced to disparities of just what items are included in a particular scale. Accordingly, a partial statistical separation between inattentive and aggressive behaviors seems clear. It is only partial. Items loading on a "hyperactivity" factor typically load on other factors as well. "Factor scores" based on summing items with unit weight are therefore highly intercorrelated in all studies. One must note that the blind reliance upon principal component analysis and varimax rotation assumes that orthogonal (noncorrelated) dimensions are present; yet the finding of correlation emphasizes that the assumption of the analysis is violated.

The results from mathematical attempts to classify *ratings* are therefore suggestive, but not yet conclusive, that hyperactivity is a separate dimension of perceived behavioral deviance in the classroom. However, the relationship between hyperactivity in school settings and at home is rather weak (Sandberg, Rutter, & Taylor, 1978; Sandberg, Wieselberg, & Shaffer, 1980). This should make one cautious about a classification based on so variable a property. Glow (1981) has reported on the use of Multimethod Multitrait Analysis, which is explicitly designed to counteract the usual tendency of factor analysis to produce factors derived from just one measure. This produced separate factors of hyperactivity and conduct disturbance, with loadings from both parent and teacher ratings. Obviously, however, this does not show that hyperactivity is a constant trait transcending situations.

There is a further caveat about the studies of rating scales: all findings could stem from the perceptions of raters rather than the behavior of children. The operation of halo effects is often invoked to account for the awkwardly high correlation of "hyperactivity" and "conduct disorder" factors (e.g., by Milich, Loney, & Landau, 1982). In all logic, therefore, one must entertain the possibility that halo effects account for the very emergence of the factors.

It is therefore important to note the smaller number of attempts to separate different dimensions from different kinds of source material. Loney and colleagues have repeatedly used trained raters to extract information from clinicians' assessments, and have found hyperactivity to be factorially distinct from a dimension of defiant aggression (Loney, Langhorne, & Paternite, 1978; Milich *et al.*, 1982) in a mixed population of children referred for treatment of hyperactivity. Thorley (1984a, 1984b) has cited an unpublished factor analysis of the systematic ratings made by clinicians at the Bethlem Royal and Maudsley Hospitals: this too found a distinction between factors of aggressive conduct disorder and of hyperactivity with developmental immaturity. However, neither of these kinds of source is free from rater bias. They are both based upon the assessments of clinicians, whose training may well lead them more readily to detect symptom A when they have already noted the presence of a symptom, B, that they believe to be associated with symptom A. The same halo effect could be at work as with teachers' ratings.

Taylor, Schachar, Thorley, and Wieselberg (1986) have described ratings of known reliability made by trained researchers on the basis of a detailed and standardized interview with the parents of children referred for psychiatric treatment. In this method too, inattentive and restless behaviors emerged as a factor distinct from other dimensions of disordered conduct. The sample was small, but the results were consistent with those from less intensive measures in larger samples.

In short, the question of taxonomy is not solved; but there is fair support for using the construct of hyperactivity in the description of psychopathology.

Distribution of Individuals

The above exercises in the statistical classification of symptoms are conceptually distinct from the several issues about the distribution of cases. These should give powerful clues about what sort of classification is likely to prove most useful; but they can also lead to fallacious reasoning.

As one example of the pitfalls that can be involved in interpreting the distribution of individuals, consider the investigation reported by Trites and Laprade (1983). This study was based upon a large sample of unselected schoolchildren; the Conners Teacher Rating Scale yielded separate factors of hyperactivity and defiance in a principal component analysis. The investigators then went on to report, in effect, that those individuals who scored high on hyperactivity obtained lower scores on defiance than children selected by virtue of their high scores on the defiance scale. Such a finding should not be regarded as evidential. It is inevitable, given that the dimension of hyperactivity is less than perfectly correlated with that of defiance. Yet the finding was used to argue that hyperactivity and defiant conduct disorder should be seen as separate categories, or poles, of disturbance.

It would have been somewhat more informative to consider the bivariate distribution of those "cases" who had high scores on one or the other scale or both. If their hyperactivity scores were plotted against defiance, then a two-condition theory might predict a different distribution from a single class.

Analyses like this are essentially seeking points of rarity in the distribution of cases. They are comparable with those studies in adult psychiatry that have sought to establish whether, for example, endogenous and reactive depression are related as two poles of one spectrum or as two separate categories (Kendell, 1976). Those adult studies have usually collapsed the variables into one discriminant function distinguishing between clinical diagnoses and examined whether the distribution of cases on that one variable is unimodal or bimodal.

For the present example, considering only two dimensions, the distribution can readily be examined on a single variable, (defiance score–hyperactivity score). Figure 12-1 presents data on this, based upon the teacher ratings of 3,107 boys aged 6 to 7 years. These children were the subjects for an epidemiological survey in East London, carried out by my colleagues Sandberg, Thorley, and Giles as well as myself, and funded by the Medical Research Council. The children received teacher and parent ratings on Rutter A(2) and B(2) scales as the screening stage of a two-part investigation (which will be separately reported). The teacher rating scale yields separate factors of conduct disorder (range 0–12) and hyperactivity (range 0–6). A cutoff at 2 *SD* above the mean is equivalent to a score of 6 or more on the conduct disorder scale, and 5 or more on the hyperactivity scale. These are higher cutoffs than those used by Schachar *et al.* (1981) in a report about 9-year-olds, but identical to those used by McGee, Williams, and Silva (1984a, 1984b) for 7-year-olds. From the original sample of 3,107 we identified 385 "cases" who scored above two *SD* on either conduct disorder or hyperactivity or both. For each case, a discriminant score was calculated by subtracting the hyperactivity score from the defiance. A score of zero then means that the child obtained equal scores on both scales; a high negative score means a case of hyperactivity without conduct disorder; a high positive score implies a case of conduct disorder without hyperactivity. Figure 12-1 shows the distribution of scores.

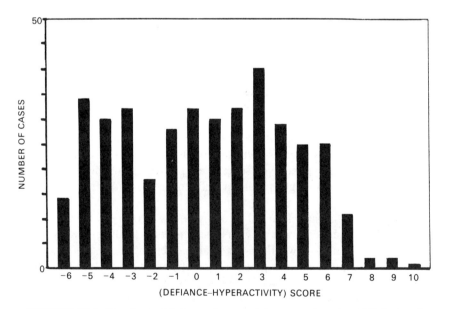

FIGURE 12-1. Bar chart of defiance–hyperactivity scores based on 385 deviant boys taken from a sample of 3,107 boys aged 6 to 7 years.

On the whole, the evidence for separate conditions is not conclusive. Most cases seem to be mixed in form. One can argue for a bimodal distribution with a point of rarity at -2, and a rather small group with pure hyperactivity (27.8% of all cases). Indeed, Kolmogorov–Smirnov testing shows a significant deviation from a single normal distribution. The case looks rather different if one considers the relative numbers of "pure" and "mixed" cases. For this purpose, a "mixed" case is defined as one with scores above 2 SD above the mean on both factors; a "purely hyperactive" scores more than 2 SD above the mean for hyperactivity but less than 1 SD above the mean for conduct disorder; while, conversely, one with "pure conduct disorder" scores above 2 SD for that scale and less than 1 SD for hyperactivity. On this basis, 29.9% of all cases ($N = 385$) are mixed, 15.3% show pure hyperactivity, and 6.0% show pure conduct disorder. (The remainder, with scores between 1 and 2 SD above the mean on one scale and more than 2 SD on the other, are left in obscurity.) On balance, this sort of questionnaire information only weakly supports the idea of a separate but less common group of hyperactive children.

However, this example is not presented to argue for two conditions but to illustrate the methodological and logical issues of classification. Before rushing to collect very large amounts of questionnaire data, one should examine the possible pitfalls.

This particular example, like other studies in the literature, is based upon unsuitable data. The use of a single source (teachers' ratings) is likely to reduce the chances of finding a real distinction between conditions because of the operation of halo effects as already considered. The choice of only two dimensions would be a very serious limitation if others ought to enter into case definition. (Thus, one reason for a poor performance by the DSM-III diagnosis in predicting drug responsiveness in a recent trial was its failure to take into account the important factor of emotional disturbance; see below.) Indeed, the low correlations between measures of hyperactivity from different sources imply that they should be considered as separate dimensions. The correlations between teacher-rated hyperactivity and parent-rated hyperactivity are usually found to be lower than the correlations between hyperactivity and conduct disorder from a single questionnaire.

Even if the data had been more adequate, there would still be three major limitations in all such approaches to making inferences from distributions of cases. In the first place, the units chosen for the comparison are arbitrary yet may determine the findings (Eysenck, 1970). A point of rarity may be obscured by a choice of units that combines the point of rarity with other points. On the other hand, an excessively fine-grained choice of units will lead to a small number of cases in each category, with the consequent opportunity for spurious points of rarity to appear by random fluctuation. A second objection is the lack of power in the statistical tests with which one examines the distributional hypotheses. Frequently one can conclude only that one cannot tell—and that very large numbers of cases indeed would be required to distinguish securely between the different possibilities.

The third limitation of the conclusions to be drawn is logical and fundamental. The distinction between unimodal and bimodal distributions does not correspond to that between one condition and two but to that between a dimensional and a categorical ordering. It would be quite possible for two unrelated dimensions, each one distributed normally, to yield a single and unimodal distribution when plotted on one ordinate. There are several theories, not two, in this area: hyperactivity and defiant antisociality could be two aspects of one categorical syndrome; or of one dimension that affects most children to some degree; or two separate categories; or two separate dimensions; or peripheral to some more complex arrangement of categories or dimensions. Different kinds of evidence are appropriate to the separate questions of the number of conditions and their dimensional or categorical nature.

Studies of the Clustering of Cases

I have already referred to the likelihood that multiple measures of behavior will have to be drawn on if a robust nosology is to be created. To do so, multivariate statistics are of course necessary. The techniques of cluster analysis seek to order individual cases into groups on the basis of their similarities to one another. This is intuitively close to the spirit of the diagnostic enterprise. However, they are not based on any single theoretical approach, the different techniques are diverse, spurious groupings can be created, and there is no accepted way of deciding how many clusters should be chosen to describe a given set of cases. These difficulties have meant that rather few investigators have chosen to use the techniques. Those who have employed them to generate typologies have obtained rather conflicting results. Thus, Lessing, Williams, and Revelle (1981) reported a hierarchical cluster analytic method applied to a parents' behavior checklist. One of the 15 clusters identified comprised overactive, distractible, clumsy children with low tolerance for frustration. This could well be taken as a separate "hyperactivity" group. On the other hand, Lessing, Williams, and Gil (1982) went on from this to choose only clusters that replicated across different kinds of samples. This time they reported seven groups with different behavioral profiles. The most relevant of these comprised children with both hyperactive and aggressive symptomatology into a rather nonspecific "aggressive, overactive" group.

Other clustering studies of children's psychological disorders are divided between those that find a hyperactive group distinct from the run of antisocial disorders (Edelbrock & Achenbach, 1980; Patterson, 1964) and those that combine the two kinds of problem into one cluster of acting-out children (Langner, Gersten, & Eisenberg, 1974; Lorion, Cowen, & Caldwell, 1974).

These contradictory results are not encouraging. Nevertheless, some of the weaknesses relate to details of studies rather than to the whole approach. They are certainly arguments against its blind, mechanical application to error-laden and single-source data in the hope that a good classification will somehow emerge from the machine. However, the approach may be more valid when used with reliable data to address a specific question. Indeed, my colleagues and I have recently completed a study in which we applied cluster analysis to the particular question of the presence of a natural subgroup of the hyperactive among the general run of children with antisocial, disruptive, or troublesome behavior (Taylor, 1986b). The subjects were 60 6- to 10-year-old schoolboys referred for psychiatric help because of antisocial or disruptive behavior. The group included children exhibiting hyperactivity as one kind of behavior problem but was not confined to those children.

Nine key measures were taken of the current psychological state of the children. From the domain of home behavior, indexed by the Parental Account of Children's Symptoms (PACS), we chose the scales of hyperactivity, defiance, and emotional disorder. From the Conners Teacher Rating Scale we took the subscales of hyperactivity, defiance and anxiety. From the Rutter–Graham psychiatric interview with the child, we took a scale of hyperactivity and one of depression. From the neuropsychological tests, we took a composite scale of "attention performance." The four different sources of information were independent and blind to other assessments; all scales were acceptably reliable. Two different kinds of cluster analysis were performed: Ward's method and the method of complete linkage. The reason for doing it in two different ways was so that we could detect spurious groupings resulting from quirks of an analysis rather than the structure of the data.

In fact, both kinds of analysis gave very similar results. When the division into four clusters was taken, 90% of the cases were identically classified by both procedures.

The differences between these four clusters (from Ward's method) are illustrated in Figure 12-2. This gives the profile of each cluster—that is, its mean scores on each of the nine variables that defined it. The relevant group is the second largest cluster. We have labeled it H. It is characterized by pervasive hyperactivity and poor performances on attentional tests; and comprises 15 cases—a quarter of the whole group. It is not simply a severely affected group, for it is characterized also by low scores on measures of affective disturbance.

The choice of a four-cluster solution was, admittedly, arbitrary. However, the separate emergence of cluster H did not depend upon this choice. No matter whether we chose a grouping into two, three, four or five clusters, the same 15 cases appeared as a distinct group.

This subgrouping did not give total support either to the ICD-9 or the DSM-III clinical diagnosis; but it gave partial support to both. The ICD-9 diagnosis of "hyperkinetic syndrome" was made on only seven children, all of whom emerged in group H (the "pervasively hyperactive" cluster). The

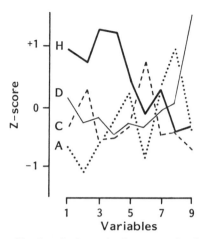

FIGURE 12-2. The profile of each cluster is shown on nine baseline variables, each transformed to a z-score, for comparability. In each case a positive score indicates a higher degree of pathology than the group average. Variable 1 = parent—hyperactivity; 2 = teacher—hyperactivity; 3 = psychiatrist—hyperactivity; 4 = attention performance; 5 = parent—defiance; 6 = teacher—defiance; 7 = parent—emotional disorder; 8 = teacher—anxiety; 9 = psychiatrist—depression. H = hyperkinetic; D = depressed; C = classroom problems of conduct; A = anxious. From Taylor (1986b). Reprinted by permission of MacKeith Press.

other eight in the cluster were similar in their test scores, but had all been diagnosed as "conduct disorder" in the ICD-9 scheme. By contrast, the DSM-III diagnosis of "attention deficit disorder with hyperactivity" was much commoner (40 children). Of the 15 children in cluster H, 13 had been identified by clinical diagnosis as ADD-H. The remaining ADD-H children were scattered evenly over the other clusters.

The numbers involved are evidently too small to provide any faith in the robustness of the classification generally, although the division into hyperkinetic, depressive, and anxiety-based groups and a larger group with situational problems at school has some clinical plausibility. (Situation-specific problems at home would probably not be referred to clinics.) Nevertheless, it suggests the classificatory value of a subgroup of children with pervasive hyperkinesis and poor test performance. It does not support the distinction of "pure ADD-H," "pure conduct disorder," and "mixed ADDH-CD" subtypes. We should therefore avoid perseveration upon this one way of carving up the cake.

In summary, numerical taxonomy has so far contributed only rather weakly to this nosological question. It has in general been limited by the rather unsuitable data to which it has been applied, and it deserves a better chance to show its power. It seems clear that a construct of hyperactivity should be used in describing children with conduct problems, and this is a step forward. It is not at all so clear how that construct should be used in defining syndromes.

If statistical considerations had led to a clearly demarcated syndrome, it would still have been necessary to consider its validation in terms of clinical features other than those used to define it. It would, however, have been likely to command some clinical consensus. As it is, the external validation of any hyperkinetic syndrome is made more difficult by the obstacles in replicating diagnoses across groups of investigators. Members of each group, very properly, will wish to stay with the definitions closest to their clinical experience. The best strategy will probably be to accept and institutionalize the presence of multiple diagnostic schemes. It would be a mistake to put all one's research eggs into the evaluation of any one scheme (whether that be DSM-III-R, ICD-10, or anyone's pet set of research diagnostic criteria). Rather, the priority should be on agreeing schemes of assessment across research groups that are rich enough to allow for several different ways of classifying. The most successful classification scheme will then be the one that most usefully predicts; it may be necessary to use different schemes for different purposes. The virtue of collaboration is that the present state of knowledge calls for detailed and time-consuming measures, applied to defined cases, in sufficient numbers to allow for replicable multivariate analyses. Both clinically and epidemiologically defined samples will be needed. This will require either different investigators to pool resources or massive investment in a single group.

Predictive and Discriminative Validity

Children with attention deficit disorder may well be different from normal controls in many ways (Taylor, 1985). Those differences will not be rehearsed in this review. Rather, the nosological question at issue requires that such children be shown to differ from psychiatric controls with other sorts of disorder—especially conduct disorder. Either a category of hyperkinesis should be distinguished from conduct disorder or a dimension of hyperactivity should be validated within a group of children with externalizing disorders of conduct. These issues are now beginning to receive attention, and they need immediate study.

Symptoms

The least demanding way of making such a study is to compare hyperkinetic and conduct disordered cases by their levels of behavioral symptoms as rated by the diagnostician. This is virtually tautologous, for of course the diagnosis is supposed to be founded upon the symptoms. Nevertheless, it does at least clarify what diagnosticians are doing and suggest ways of standardizing whatever it is. Thorley (1984a) showed that children with the diagnosis of hyperkinetic syndrome (in the rather rare form defined by ICD-9 and applied at the Maudsley Hospital) are distinguishable from matched controls with conduct disorder. They have more motor disturbance, inattention, and impairment of articulation and less aggressive, antisocial, and emotional disturbance. It would, of course, have been exceptionally damaging to the concept of hyperkinesis if it had not survived this challenge; and nobody will be surprised that it did.

Putative syndromes or dimensions can also be distinguished on the basis of independent measures of behavior. For example, Milich *et al*, (1982) extended their distinction of hyperactive and aggressive dimensions from ratings of case histories by showing that they could differentially predict playroom observations of off-task and otherwise distractible behaviors. I hope that we shall not see too many studies demonstrating that different clinical diagnostic groups get different scores on questionnaires. They have methodological value in establishing coherence of measures, but they can easily become tautologous. Parental or teacher ratings of symptoms may be formally independent of clinical diagnosis, but they are usually just a more systematic way of recording the information that led to the diagnosis in the first place.

On the other hand, patterns of rated symptoms may be useful in pointing to internal consistency, or its lack, in existing diagnoses. This is especially useful in the very earliest stage of a suggested diagnosis—such as that of ADD without hyperactivity. Thus Edelbrock, Costello, and Kessler (1984) found children with ADD to be more inattentive than controls, whereas ADD-H children were more overactive than children with ADD alone. Lahey, Schaughency, Strauss, and Frame (1984) reported a comparison of ADD-H with ADD alone that found them to be so different as to raise a doubt as to whether they should truly be classified together. Those with ADD-H were aggressive, guiltless, and unpopular, whereas those with ADD only were anxious, shy, and withdrawn. This echoes the doubt of many clinicians about their comparability. However, whether they do indeed belong together is unlikely to be settled in those terms only but will require external knowledge—for example, about their similarity in the fundamental processing of information.

Comparisons between hyperactive and conduct-disordered children become more evidential as the assessment of symptoms becomes more independent of the original diagnosis. Stewart, Cummings, Singer, and deBlois (1981) compared hyperactive and unsocialized–aggressive clinic attenders on behavioral scales, which were still derived from a diagnostic interview with parents and therefore *not* completely independent. They found that three-quarters of conduct-disordered children were hyperactive, and two-thirds of hyperactive children also had a conduct disorder. Those with both problems were similar to those with conduct disorder only (not to those with hyperactivity only) on scales of antisocial behavior, egocentricity, and reactivity. It seems to follow that the majority of referred children fall into a mixed group, which is essentially part of conduct disorder, and that there is a separate and smaller hyperactive group. The conclusion is weakened by the data limitations, but is in line with their evidence above and below. August and Stewart

(1982) extended their analysis of this series so as to include pervasiveness as one part of their definition of hyperactivity. Unfortunately, although multiple measures were used, most of them were derived one way or another from the parental account. On this basis, hyperactives with aggressive problems were similar to those without. (A small group of "pure pervasives with low IQ" did turn out to be dissimilar from other cases; not surprisingly, they had more evidence of developmental delay.) This seemed to suggest that the purity of the hyperactivity was not necessarily an important diagnostic feature. Once again, however, data limitations prevent strong conclusions.

Direct observation and mechanical recording of activity offer much more interesting contrasts. Loney (1983) has described how they are significantly predicted by *dimensional* ratings of case histories, and accordingly offers research diagnostic criteria based upon the observations. Similarly, Taylor (1986a) reported that a *dimension* of hyperactivity from structured interview correlates with direct observations in a way that dimensions of defiant conduct disorder do not. Teacher questionnaire dimensions, by contrast seem to be much less related to direct observations (Lahey *et al.*, 1980; Sandberg *et al.*, 1978). Perhaps the dimensions are too highly intercorrelated to make unique contributions to any dependent variable; or perhaps classroom behavior is often determined by the situation. Dimensions seem to perform quite well in predicting direct observations of behavior; however, categories have mostly been less effective. It is not enough to know that hyperactive children move more than normal controls in most situations. We also need information on whether they are different from children with other kinds of psychiatric problems, particularly conduct disorder. The evidence here is much more scanty. Children with broadly defined hyperactivity move only slightly more than children with conduct disorder (Barkley & Ullman, 1975; Firestone & Martin, 1979; Sandberg *et al.*, 1978). On the other hand, children with gross hyperactivity move much more than matched clinic controls (Hutt & Hutt, 1964; Luk, 1984). The implication is again that a narrowly defined class may be more valid than a broad, common one.

Discriminative Prediction of Possible Etiologic Factors

The most important sign of success of a diagnosis would be its pointing to etiologic processes, distinct from other diagnoses. This is the main hope of the medical model. In general, the hope has not yet been fulfilled. For instance, Thorley's (1984a) comparison of hyperkinetic syndrome with matched cases of conduct disorder found no difference in the rates of clinically diagnosed brain disease. However, the comparison has seldom been made in quite such sharp terms. Rather, reviewers have sought to integrate separate studies of hyperactive and conduct-disordered children. Ferguson and Rapoport (1983) have made a thorough review of the biological validation of syndrome. I cannot better their conclusion that findings are highly nonspecific. If anything is validated, it is only a broad-band description of "impulsive conduct disorder." Any possible biological marker (such as minor congenital anomalies, neurological soft signs or pre- and perinatal risk) seems to be associated with conduct disorder as closely as with hyperactivity—or else has been examined only in a contrast between the hyperactive and normal controls. Nevertheless, the strong overlap between hyperactivity and conduct disorder leaves it possible that abnormalities in the conduct disordered are due simply to the presence of hyperactivity. The rare group of children who are conduct disordered, but have *no* symptoms of attention deficit disorder (which is much more stringent than just falling short of diagnostic criteria for ADD) therefore becomes particularly important from the nosological point of view. They need to be identified and studied with high priority.

Aman (1984) has argued that the link between hyperactivity and poor performance on cognitive tests of attention is so strong that it validates a diagnosis of attention deficit. The difficulty, however, is that poor attention is a very nonspecific symptom. Rated inattention is extremely common in most psychiatric disorders (Shaffer, 1980); and impaired performance on attention tests is a feature of the conduct disordered generally (Sandberg *et al.*, 1978; Shaffer, McNamara, & Pincus, 1974). Only when hyperactive behavior is more narrowly defined has it been shown to have a specific correlation with tests of information processing—such as the continuous performance test of vigilance—and even then the cognitive deficit seems to be diffuse (Taylor, 1986a).

Sandberg, Rutter, and I (1978) have argued for some time that even direct comparisons of broadly defined hyperactive and conduct-disordered children have so far failed to show very much in the way of differential associations with biological or psychosocial adversity. The argument has been based simply upon negative findings when the conditions are defined on the basis of questionnaire scores (Sandberg *et al.*, 1978, 1980). Counterarguments have stressed that things could be very different when properly made diagnoses are used (e.g., Aman, 1984); and I certainly hope that this will be so. Others too have found scant distinction between the hyperactive and the conduct disordered (Firestone & Martin, 1979). McGee *et al.* (1984a, 1984b) carried out an epidemiologic study in which the hyperactive (H) were compared with the conduct disordered (C) and those with both problems (HC) (as defined by questionnaire). They found no differences in background factors such as socioeconomic status, perinatal history, and family relationships. Performance IQ was somewhat lower in the two hyperactive groups (H and HC), verbal IQ in all three groups (H, C, and HC) by contrast with normals, and specific reading retardation was high only in the mixed group. The full results are hard to interpret because of small numbers and a large proportion of missing data. Indeed, a rather different story emerged from a different analysis of the same study, separately published by the same authors (McGee *et al.*, 1985). A correlational analysis of scales from the Rutter teacher questionnaire suggested that hyperactivity was weakly but significantly associated with lower IQ scores; but that the correlation was not significant for conduct disorder or emotional disorder.

Questionnaire studies are not very powerful. Several lines of argument now suggest that a more narrowly defined group of hyperkinetic children has different patterns of associations. Taylor (1980) found that Maudsley patients with the rare diagnosis of hyperkinetic syndrome (1.5%) or the rare symptom of gross overactivity (5%) were characterized by early onset, high rates of specific developmental delays and intellectual retardation (IQ < 70), and relatively normal patterns of family interaction. Sandberg et al. (1978) found the pervasively hyperactive—at home, at school, and at clinic—to have an early onset, clumsiness in neurodevelopmental assessment, and a tendency to make errors on the Matching Familiar Figures test. Schleifer et al. (1975), Campbell, Endman, and Bernfeld (1977), and Schachar et al. (1981) found a prognostic distinction between situationally and pervasively hyperactive children, and in the last study the pervasively hyperactive could be distinguished even from the conduct disordered (see below). The cluster of pervasively hyperactive and inattentive children, identified earlier, also proved to differ from other clusters of conduct-disordered children in several aspects independent of the initial definition; that is, their problems had an earlier onset, the children had more incoordination on a scored neurological examination, they were more likely to show a specific delay of motor or language development, they were more likely to be isolated and unpopular among their peers, and they had suffered more accidents serious enough to need hospital treatment (Taylor, 1986b).

There are several possible reasons why the pervasively hyperactive should be distinctive. It could be that two or three poor measures work much better than one; that a single rating is more likely to be affected by the child's relationship with the rater; that a pervasive problem is a pointer to a persisting trait, not just to an adverse situation; or that the pervasively hyperactive are simply the more severely affected. These possibilities should be investigated. However, it is noteworthy that dimensional ratings can also work well when the "rater variance" is reduced by using the judgment of trained researchers on the presence of symptoms. Loney et al. (1978) have found hyperactivity to be distinguished from defiance in a group of hyperkinetic/MBD clinic referrals by a relative lack of psychosocial correlates and the presence of developmental delays. Taylor et al. (1986) have found hyperactivity to be distinguished from defiance in a group of conduct-disordered clinic referrals; by a lack of significant correlations with reliable measures of adverse family interactions (which were present for defiance) and by the presence of significant correlations with clumsiness, lower IQ, and poorer attention.

Epidemiologic studies are now required, not only to confirm or reject the suggestions from clinically based investigations. In addition, they offer an avenue to understanding what is primary and what is peripheral to the condition. There appear to be populations with very different rates of hyperactivity (e.g., girls compared with boys, and possibly Chinese compared with

Americans, have low rates). If so, the comparison of these populations is likely to shed light on what factors must be present if the disorder is to appear in a protected group—and how its presentation can be altered.

Genetic Studies

There is only suggestive evidence for a genetic component in the transmission of attention deficit with hyperactivity, but nothing contradicts it (Cantwell, 1975; Morrison & Stewart, 1973; Willerman, 1973). Any future study must reckon with the nosological difficulties and should prove a powerful means of distinguishing between possibilities. There is certainly overlap of conditions to be expected. Stewart, deBlois, and Cummings (1980) made blind diagnoses of the psychiatric status of parents of children at a psychiatric clinic, and the association with parental disorder was as strong for the conduct disordered as for the hyperactive. However, the overlap may not be complete. Cunningham, Cadoret, Loftus, and Edwards (1975) compared the adopted-away offspring of psychiatrically normal and disturbed parents. Not only was disorder generally more common in the biological offspring of disordered parents, but the tendency was also particularly strong (and significant) for the children diagnosed as hyperkinetic syndrome.

It will be particularly important to know the risks for hyperkinesis and for conduct disorder in the relatives of probands with hyperkinesis (or ADD-H) but without conduct disorder as contrasted with the relatives of probands who show both problems. Even if both disorders are more common in the relatives, the method should allow for determining whether they behave as one entity or two. For this analysis nothing short of direct ascertainment of relatives during their childhood will do since retrospective diagnosis in adults and family history data are both very unlikely to be able to discriminate between the two disorders.

Prognostic Studies

The course of a disorder is likely to be affected by many extraneous factors such as the type of treatment. The course should therefore not have overwhelming weight in validation, but is just one aspect to be considered.

Several follow-up studies of children with hyperactivity have now been described, and they are reviewed by Weiss (1983). It is clear that schoolchildren with hyperactivity are vulnerable to later antisocial problems as well as to continued impulsiveness and educational failure. The point has recently been emphasized by the Gittelman, Manuzza, Shenker, and Bonagura (1985) report of the psychiatric outcome, in late adolescence and early adulthood, of children seen at a research clinic. By comparison with "normal" controls (boys from medical clinics who did not have behavior problems in childhood), the boys who had previously shown ADD-H were ten times more likely to show diagnostic features of ADD-H at the follow-up.

Furthermore, the persistence of ADD-H was a good predictor of whether conduct problems would develop; and both conduct disorder and substance abuse were disproportionately common in those with ADD-H.

Findings such as these have been used to argue for a single, broad condition that evolves from ADD-H in childhood to conduct disorder in later adolescence. The argument is not at all airtight. It could be, for example, that attention deficit is a consequence of conduct disorder developing rather than the cause: this possibility is supported by the overlap of attention deficit and conduct disorder symptomatology even in Gittelman's controls, who by definition did not show ADD in childhood. It could also be that a true separation of attention deficit from conduct disorder is obscured by inadequacy of the DSM-III diagnoses. Something of the kind is suggested by the extremely high rate of ADD in the control group (13% had met criteria at some point during the follow-up). It is also possible that the vulnerability of children with ADD-H to conduct disorder should be described as a vulnerability to avoidable complications rather than the evolution of a disease entity.

Accordingly, research on prognosis will have to shift to designs that allow for children with ADD-H to be contrasted with other psychiatrically disturbed groups. The few such studies available suggest that hyperactivity and defiance have rather different implications for later development, even when both are present together. The multivariate studies of Loney et al. (1978) and the long-term follow-up by Weiss and her colleagues (Hechtman, Weiss, Perlman, & Amsel, 1984) both indicate that the course of "North American hyperactives" is not determined by any single factor but by multiple interacting agents. Aggressive behavior in children, and family factors, predict later antisociality more strongly than does hyperactivity. On the other hand, the children were all hyperactive, and hence the lack of predictive power of hyperactivity might reflect its initially low variance.

Schachar et al.'s (1981) study of epidemiologically ascertained "English" conduct disorder indicated that *pervasive* hyperactivity strongly predicted the persistence of psychiatric disorder from 9 to 14. Thorley's recent, unpublished follow-up of *severely* hyperkinetic cases and matched psychiatric controls into adult life showed that their initial diagnosis predicted a poor outcome in adolescence (more psychiatric referrals, more special school placements, more accidental injuries, more fits) but that by adult life their global outcome was similar to that of other ex-patients. Aggressive behavior and low IQ in childhood were stronger predictors of adult outcome than was hyperactivity. McGee et al. (1984a, 1984b) found, in line with the above, that those with both hyperactivity and conduct disorder were more prone to later behavior disturbance, reading retardation, and psychiatric referral than those with one problem. The suggestion that comes out of these studies is that both problems have different implications, and both need recognizing even when they are present together. Two problems are worse than one, but the two things do not simply add together; they have rather different implications. It may be that hyperactivity is a risk factor for anti-sociality, and that antisociality (however caused) tends to perpetuate itself.

The response to treatment is not just a confounder of prognosis but an important aspect of predictive validity as well. Historically and practically it is perhaps the most important—even though scientifically it is limited by the multiplicity of actions of most therapies. Several studies have suggested that poor concentration predicts a good response to amphetamine-type drugs (Taylor, 1983). A recent systematic study suggested that behavioral measures could indeed predict the outcome but that their combinations into the existing diagnostic categories of DSM-III and ICD-9 did not predict at all well. A better prediction was achieved by the clustering scheme already described, with the pervasively hyperactive and inattentive group responding (Taylor, 1986b). High levels of emotional symptomatology predicted a poor response; and since the DSM-III category of ADD-H is independent of emotional symptoms, its predictive power was weakened. It may also have been weakened by its explicit reliance on teacher reports. Ratings by teachers of inattentive and restless behavior (which predicted response) were probably diluted by being based partly on defiant and noncompliant behavior (which was not predictive).

The lesson from these very different comparisons of diagnostic groups is not that the nosological questions are near solution. Rather, there are fairly strong indications that existing diagnostic schemes are unsatisfactory and that many approaches to describing a hyperactive subgroup of the externalizing behavior disorders have failed. Equally, it seems that hyperactivity is a useful construct and that a relatively small and carefully defined group needs much more investigation. One must remark that studies intended to be about the causes and course have probably given more helpful leads to classification than those intended purely for classification purposes. They would have given even more useful information if the subjects had been described in sufficient detail that diagnostic schemes alternative to the authors' own could have been applied to them. A lesson for other areas of investigation is the crucial need for replicability of diagnoses. This is more important than the general adoption of a uniform scheme.

SUBDIVISION OF SYNDROMES

Subgroupings of Hyperactivity

I have argued that a smaller group of hyperkinetic children should be separated from the larger group of children with more or less severe degrees of inattentive and restless behavior. Provisionally, the major grounds could be pervasiveness of hyperactivity and its accompaniment by tested impairment of attentional performance (rather than being defined by a lack of conduct-disorder symptoms); but more research will be necessary to determine how the diagnostic cake should be divided up.

If a smaller group such as this is delimited, where does that leave the remainder? Some will be showing the symptoms of overactivity and inattention as a nonspecific part of other psychopathologies (and should therefore be classified with them). A depressed and agitated group may be particularly important to recognize. Some individuals will show inattention without locomotor excess, or locomotor excess without inattention; and some will have both those problems. These groups (or dimensions) will need to be disentangled in the same way that conduct disorder and hyperactivity have been distinguished. Only then will there be solid grounds for considering—as both DSM-III and ICD-9 consider—that the essential psychopathology of hyperactivity is an impairment of attention. Until then the hypothesis deserves only the respect owed to a good idea based on clinical intuition.

One important group of hyperactive children has been expressly omitted from the vast majority of studies so far. The intellectually retarded, those with pervasive developmental disorders, and those with overt neurological disease have usually been excluded, both by American and European investigators—for good reasons. The status of hyperkinesis is different in the moderately or severely intellectually retarded.

To begin with, hyperkinesis in retarded children is often associated with stereotyped and repetitive behaviors (Thorley, 1984a). This is also the case for many of the animal models of hyperactivity (Robbins & Sahakian, 1979). By contrast, stereotyped and repetitive movements have not been seen in any of the pervasively hyperactive children of normal intelligence assessed in any of our clinical or epidemiologic studies.

Autism and atypical childhood psychosis are both quite common diagnoses in hyperkinetic retarded children; but they do not figure in series of normally intelligent hyperactives (Thorley, 1984a).

Another distinguishing feature is the immediate response to treatment. Stimulant drugs are usually effective in reducing the hyperactivity of the normally intelligent. By contrast, they do not improve the severe hyperkinesis seen in retarded people (Aman & Singh, 1982). Indeed, stereotypies are often worsened (Campbell, 1975).

The longer-term outcome is also different. In retarded people, hyperkinesis is often succeeded in later adolescence by an apathetic lack of activity. This has been documented for autistic individuals (Lotter, 1974). Yet followup studies of normally intelligent hyperactive children have not shown this outcome. To the contrary, they have made it quite clear that the likely outcome is that of a continued (though lessening) impulsiveness and restlessness (Weiss, 1983).

Accordingly, the question of hyperkinesis in the mentally handicapped is not solved. Some may show the kind of pervasive hyperactivity that this review has emphasised. Others show hyperkinetic behavior as one part of autism or other infantile psychoses. Taylor (1986b) has presented a discriminant function analysis arguing for the separation of hyperkinesis from atypical psychosis. Perhaps, in addition, there is a separate category of hyperkinesis-with-stereotypies. This will need the same kind of examination of predictive validity. Like pervasive hyperactivity, it will need to be distinguished from other conditions: in this case, from pervasive developmental disorder on the one hand and the conduct disorders of handicapped people on the other. Aman (1984) has argued that the difference is based upon altered patterns of attention. The excessive breadth of attention in the hyperactive is then supposed to be helped by stimulants, while the unduly narrow range of attention that has been linked to stereotypies (Robbins & Sahakian, 1979) would then require other strategies of intervention.

Subgroupings of Conduct Disorder

Most of the conduct disordered will not be included in a narrow diagnosis of hyperkinetic syndrome. How should they be subdivided further? The question has received a number of reviews (e.g., Rutter & Garmezy, 1983). I will summarize only by stating the impression that the traditional divisions of unsocialized versus socialized or of aggressive versus nonaggressive have failed to prove themselves by predicting important factors other than those that defined them.

The further development of such distinctions would need to begin with the improvement of assessment methods. Socialization, especially interaction with other children, ought to be a major developmental variable, of prognostic importance. It is also predictive in normal populations (e.g., Roff, Sells, & Golden, 1972), and so it remains uncertain whether its significance is for psychopathology or for the "normal" course of development.

Another promising line of nosological distinction is that of those conduct disorders that arise after a defined stress. One value of a categorical rather than a dimensional approach is that it allows for information such as the style of onset to be included. Nevertheless, it remains a matter of empirical inquiry whether such "adjustment" reactions are indeed separate or whether they represent one particular point in the evolution of a single disorder.

COPING WITH MIXED CASES: DIMENSIONS, CATEGORIES, AND HIERARCHIES

Methods of numerical taxonomy or simple contrasts between diagnostic groups are not going to determine the dimensional or categorical nature of a clinical entity. Factor analysis will produce dimensions or cluster analysis categories: that is all that it will do. For some purposes, the distinction is not very important. Many investigators who order their researches in terms of dimensional strategies are still quite content to speak of "hyperactive children": a category can be simply composed of those who score above a cutoff on a dimension. DSM-III itself is cast in rather similar terms. Disorders such as ADD-H are defined essentially by a rating scale with an unvalidated cutoff point. The conduct disorders consist essentially of the four categories derived from the two dimensions of aggressiveness and socialization. ICD-9 is different in philosophy, and individuals are expected to fit a single pattern: it has corresponding problems in dealing with mixed cases.

Nevertheless, the concept of a dimensional ordering entails a number of testable predictions. First, a dimension is present to a greater or lesser degree in most children; that is, the severely affected are different only in degree from the mildly affected. Examination of the external associations of mildly and severely affected groups should show a different pattern if the latter are qualitatively distinct. Second, dimensions are conceptually independent. Although they may interact, for a useful diagnostic model the interactions need to be similar in different ranges of the dimensions. In such a model, hyperactive behavior carries the same significance (and therefore the same pattern of external associations) whether it occurs in those with conduct disorder, those with emotional disorder, those with multiple tics, or those with no other symptoms. Furthermore, mixed cases of conduct and attention deficit disorder will have the associations of both disorders; while in a categorical model they should fit more clearly with one or the other. Third, the potential value of a categorical scheme is its ability to synthesize information of different kinds and from different sources (a synthesis that at present is made essentially by the unguided acumen of the diagnostician). It is therefore possible to assess any increase in predictive value that it brings over dimensional descriptions. Fourth, as considered above, the distribution of cases will be different in a dimensional than in a categorical ordering.

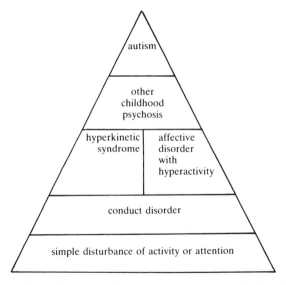

FIGURE 12-3. Hierarchical classification of overactive behavior. From Taylor (1986b). Reprinted by permission of MacKeith Press.

Hierarchies of diagnosis are an implicit feature of most diagnostic schemes, and are discussed explicitly by Foulds (1976). Successively higher categories in the hierarchy include the symptoms of lower-level diagnoses but are not included in them. Figure 12-3 sets out such an arrangement for the classification of overactivity and related symptoms. It is, needless to add, not a proposal, but rather a clarification of how such a model might operate. The position of "affective" category is particularly hard to determine. It could, for instance, be treated as an exclusive alternative to "pervasive hyperactivity with inattention" at the same level if both proved empirically to include "lower" diagnoses but not each other. However, if the predictions of such a model are fulfilled, then it offers a more rational approach to the determination of inclusion and exclusion criteria of diagnostic definitions.

In summary, the large quantity of research on hyperactivity and attention deficit has not succeeded in establishing a clear nosology; but it has allowed clarification of the issues of what obstacles need to be overcome. Hyperactivity is clearly worth defining, but its definition is still diffuse.

FUTURE LINES OF RESEARCH

Several of the research avenues that seem to be called for have already been touched on. In conclusion I shall try to draw together some of those threads.

The most immediately pressing of the issues with which this chapter began is the strong need to disentangle the overlaps between categories. Concepts and methods have reached a point where this becomes a useful exercise. The question is going to need a combination of epidemiologic and clinical approaches. Representative samples of defined populations need to be taken because of the several kinds of bias that can appear in clinically referred samples—such as the likelihood that the extent of overlap will be exaggerated. Clinical studies are still likely to be necessary because of the need to identify some quite uncommon but informative groups.

I have stressed the example of attention deficit and conduct disorder, but of course this is only an example. To take another example, the overlap between both of those and emotional disorder—especially depression—needs just as much attention. This is not only because the subject is important in itself but because it could, if neglected, confound the comparisons on which a distinction between ADD and conduct disorder is to be based. The design is to contrast pure cases of each condition and the several groups of mixed cases.

The combination of clinical and epidemiologic studies, unified by a similarity of method, is also a good approach to the issues of distribution of cases. It can allow for a systematic examination of the similarity—or lack of it—between identified cases and more minor community morbidity.

These studies will make it necessary to advance methodology in the assessment of behavior in different kinds of settings. Combinations of measures seem particularly likely to be useful, with emphasis on the refinement of interview and direct observational techniques. The need is to compare different ways of ascertaining symptoms—and also sets of diagnostic criteria. This can usefully begin with investigations of how diagnostic inferences are in fact made. There also needs to be systematic comparison of different sets of diagnostic criteria so that we may learn which are most sharply predictive for different purposes.

Studies of possible etiology are deeply relevant to classification. There is a two-way traffic between them. We need to know about etiology to decide on our categories, but only when we have good categories can we powerfully address the questions of cause. There are several promising leads in fields such as electrophysiology and neurochemistry that deserve to be followed up. The time seems particularly ripe for addressing the question of whether an attention deficit is truly fundamental to hyperactivity. This will need comparisons of those with overactivity but normal attention, those with poor attention and normal activity, and those with both problems. It would also be well served by the advance of cognitive analyses of the impairment of the hyperactive and by the establishment of norms. Useful lessons could also be expected from the comparison of high-rate and low-rate populations with regard to whether neurodevelopmental differences account for their differences in rate of hyperactivity. The question would most fundamentally be addressed by long-term controlled comparisons of the effects of treatment.

These are all relatively expensive forms of study, but they need to be undertaken. Nor do they by any means exhaust the studies that seem to be immediately feasible and desirable. The systematic examination of hyperkinesis in retarded children is overdue; the comparison of the hyperactive with those at high risk for schizophrenia is only beginning. New generations of longitudinal studies need to extend the questions from those of good and bad outcome in the hyperactive to the significance of changes in form of the condition, the nature of mediating factors rather than predictive ones, and the continuities and discontinuities with adult disorders. I have tried to indicate how we might compare dimensional and categorical accounts.

For the moment, the existing uncertainties are enough that we are probably going to have to tolerate the coexistence of several different kinds of diagnostic concept of hyperactivity. The natural selection of ideas will in the long run ensure that the most sharply predictive concepts also survive. Meanwhile, an explicit goal for investigators ought to be the development and use of assessment schemes that are sufficiently explicit to be replicable and sufficiently rich to allow for the translation of their ideas into those of other systems. The solution to Babel is not necessarily a world language but the ability to translate.

ACKNOWLEDGMENTS

The assistance of the MacArthur Foundation is acknowledged with gratitude. Research cited here was supported by several bodies, including the Medical Research Council, the Bethlem and Maudsley Hospital Research Fund, and CIBA.

REFERENCES

Achenbach, T. M., & Edelbrock, C. S. (1978). The classification of child psychopathology: A review and analysis of empirical efforts. *Psychological Bulletin, 85,* 1275–1301.

Aman, M. G. (1984). Hyperactivity: Nature of the syndrome and its natural history. *Journal of Autism and Developmental Disabilities, 14,* 39–56.

Aman, M. G., & Singh, N. N. (1982). Methylphenidate in severely retarded residents and the clinical significance of stereotypic behavior. *Applied Research in Mental Retardation, 3,* 345–358.

American Psychiatric Association. (1980). *Diagnostic and statistical manual of mental disorders* (3rd ed.). Washington, DC: Author.

August, G. J., & Stewart, M. A. (1982). Is there a syndrome of pure hyperactivity? *British Journal of Psychiatry, 140,* 305–311.

Barkley, R., & Ullman, D. (1975). A comparison of objective measures of activity and distractibility in hyperkinetic and nonhyperkinetic children. *Journal of Abnormal Child Psychology, 3,* 231–244.

Campbell, M. (1975). Pharmacotherapy in early infantile autism. *Biological Psychiatry, 10,* 394–423.

Campbell, S. B., Endman, M. W., & Bernfeld, G. (1977). A 3-year follow-up of hyperactive preschoolers into elementary school. *Journal of Child Psychology and Psychiatry, 18,* 239–249.

Cantwell, D. (1975). Genetic studies of hyperactive children: psychiatric illness in biologic and adopting parents. In R. Fieve, D. Rosenthal, & H. Brill (Eds.), *Genetic research in psychiatry.* Baltimore: Johns Hopkins University Press.

Conners, C. K. (1969). A teacher rating scale for use in drug studies with children. *American Journal of Psychiatry, 126,* 884–888.

Cunningham, C. E., & Barkley, R. A. (1979). The interactions of normal and hyperactive children with their mothers in free play and structured tasks. *Child Development, 50,* 217–224.

Cunningham, L., Cadoret, R., Loftus, R., & Edwards, J. E. (1975). Studies of adoptees from psychiatrically disturbed biological parents. *British Journal of Psychiatry, 126,* 534–539.

Dreger, R. M., Reid, M. P., Lewis, P. D., Overlade, D. C., Rich, T. A., Miller, K. J., & Flemming, E. L. (1964). Behavioral classification project. *Journal of Consulting Psychology, 28,* 1–13.

Edelbrock, C. S., & Achenbach, C. S. (1980). A typology of child behavior profile patterns: Distribution and correlates for disturbed children aged 6–16. *Journal of Abnormal Child Psychology, 8,* 441–470.

Edelbrock, C., Costello, A. J., & Kessler, M. D. (1984). Empirical corroboration of attention deficit disorder. *Journal of the American Academy of Child Psychiatry, 23,* 285–290.

Eysenck, H. J. (1970). The classification of depressive illnesses. *British Journal of Psychiatry, 117,* 241–250.

Ferguson, H. B., & Rapoport, J. L. (1983). Nosological issues and biological validation. In M. Rutter (Ed.), *Developmental neuropsychiatry.* New York: Guilford.

Firestone, P., & Martin, J. E. (1979). An analysis of the hyperactive syndrome: A comparison of hyperactive, behavior problem, asthmatic and normal children. *Journal of Abnormal Child Psychology, 7,* 261–273.

Foulds, G. A. (1976). *Hierarchical nature of personal illness.* London: Academic Press.

Gittelman, R., Manuzza, S., Shenker, R., & Bonagura, N. (1985). Hyperactive boys almost grown up. I. Psychiatric status. *Archives of General Psychiatry, 42,* 937–947.

Glow, R. A. (1981). Cross-validity and normative data on the Conners' Parent and Teacher Rating Scales. In K. D. Gadow & J. Loney (Eds.), *The psychosocial aspects of drug treatment for hyperactivity.* Boulder, CO: Westview Press.

Goyette, C. H., Conners, C. K., & Ulrich, R. F. (1978). Normative data on revised Conners' Parent and Teacher Rating Scales. *Journal of Abnormal Child Psychology, 6,* 221–236.

Hechtman, L., Weiss, G., Perlman, T., & Amsel, R. (1984). Hyperactives as young adults: Initial predictors of adult outcome. *Journal of the American Academy of Child Psychiatry, 23,* 250–260.

Hutt, S. J., & Hutt, C. (1964). Hyperactivity in a group of epileptic (and some non-epileptic) brain damaged children. *Epilepsia, 5,* 334–351.

Juliano, D. B. (1974). Conceptual tempo, activity and concept learning in hyperactive and normal children. *Journal of Abnormal Psychology, 83,* 629–634.

Kendell, R. E. (1976). The classification of depressions: A review of contemporary confusion. *British Journal of Psychiatry, 129,* 15–28.

Lahey, B., Green, K., & Forehand, R. (1980). On the independence of ratings of hyperactivity, conduct problems, and attention deficits in children: A multiple regression analysis. *Journal of Consulting and Clinical Psychology, 48,* 566–574.

Lahey, B. B., Schaughency, E. A., Strauss, C. C., & Frame, C. L. (1984). Are attention deficit disorders with and without hyperactivity similar or dissimilar disorders? *Journal of the American Academy of Child Psychiatry, 23,* 302–309.

Langner, T. S., Gersten, J. G., & Eisenberg, J. G. (1974). Approaches to measurement and definition in the epidemiology of behavior disorders: Ethnic background and child behavior. *International Journal of Health Services, 4,* 483–501.

Langner, T. S., Gersten, J. C., McCarthy, E. D., Eisenberg, J. G., Greene, E. L., Herson, J. H., & Jameson, J. D. (1976). A screening inventory for assessing psychiatric impairment in children 6 to 18. *Journal of Consulting and Clinical Psychology, 44,* 286–296.

Lessing, E. E., Williams, V. & Gil, E. (1982). A cluster-analytically derived typology: Feasible alternative to clinical diagnostic classification of children? *Journal of Abnormal Child Psychology, 10,* 451–482.

Lessing, E. R., Williams, V., & Revelle, W. (1981). Parallel forms of the IJR Behavior Checklist for parents, teachers and clinicians. *Journal of Consulting and Clinical Psychology, 49,* 34–50.

Loney, J., Langhorne, J., & Paternite, C. (1978). An empirical basis for subgrouping the hyperkinetic/minimal brain dysfunction syndrome. *Journal of Abnormal Psychology, 87,* 431–441.

Loney, J. (1983). Research diagnostic criteria for childhood hyperactivity. In S. B. Guze, F. J. Earls, & J. E. Barrett (Eds.), *Childhood psychopathology and development.* New York: Raven Press.

Lorion, R. P., Cowen, E. L., & Caldwell, R. A. (1974). Problem types of children referred to a school-based mental health program: Identification and outcome. *Journal of Consulting and Clinical Psychology, 42,* 491–496.

Lotter, V. (1974). Social adjustment and placement of autistic children in Middlesex: A follow-up study. *Journal of Autism and Childhood Schizophrenia, 4,* 11–32.

Luk, S. L. (1984). *Direct observation of grossly overactive child psychiatric patients.* MD thesis, University of Hong Kong.

McGee, R., Williams, S., Bradshaw, J., Chapel, J. L., Robins, A., & Silva, P. A. (1985). The Rutter scale for completion by teachers: Factor structure and relationships with cognitive abilities and family adversity for a sample of New Zealand children. *Journal of Child Psychology and Psychiatry, 26,* 727–740.

McGee, R., Williams, S., & Silva, P. A. (1984a). Background characteristics of aggressive, hyperactive and aggressive–hyperactive boys. *Journal of the American Academy of Child Psychiatry, 23,* 280–284.

McGee R., Williams, S., & Silva, P. A. (1984b). Behavioral and developmental characteristics of aggressive, hyperactive and aggressive–hyperactive boys. *Journal of the American Academy of Child Psychiatry, 23,* 270–279.

Milich, R., Loney, J., & Landau, S. (1982). Independent dimensions of hyperactivity and aggression: A validation with playroom observation data. *Journal of Abnormal Psychology, 91,* 183–198.

Montagu, J. D. (1975). The hyperkinetic child: A behavioural, electrodermal and EEG investigation. *Developmental Medicine and Child Neurology, 17,* 299–305.

Morrison, J., & Stewart, M. (1973). The psychiatric status of the legal families of adopted hyperactive children. *Archives of General Psychiatry, 28,* 888–891.

O'Leary, K. (1980). Pills or skills for hyperactive children. *Journal of Applied Behavior Analysis, 13,* 191–204.

Patterson, G. R. (1964). An empirical approach to the classification of disturbed children. *Journal of Clinical Psychology, 20,* 326–337.

Plomin, R., & Foch, T. (1981). Hyperactivity and pediatrician diagnoses: Parental ratings, specific cognitive abilities, and laboratory measures. *Journal of Abnormal Child Psychology, 9,* 55–64.

Pope, L. (1970). Motor activity in brain-injured children. *American Journal of Orthopsychiatry, 40,* 783–794.

Porrino, L. J., Rapoport, J. L., Behar, D., Sceery, W., Ismond, D. R., & Bunney, W. E., Jr. (1983). A naturalistic assessment of the motor activity of hyperactive boys. I. Comparison with normal controls. *Archives of General Psychiatry, 40,* 681–687.

Quay, H. C. (1964). Personality dimensions in delinquent males as inferred from the factor analysis of behavior ratings. *Journal of Research on Crime and Delinquency, 1,* 33-37.

Quay, H. C. (1977). Measuring dimensions of deviant behavior: The behavior problem checklist. *Journal of Abnormal Child Psychology, 5,* 277–289.

Quay, H. C. (1979). Classification: Patterns of aggression, anxiety-withdrawal and immaturity. In H. C. Quay & J. S. Werry (Eds.), *Psychopathological disorders of childhood* (2nd ed.). New York: Wiley.

Robbins, T. W. & Sahakian, B. J. (1979). "Paradoxical" effects of psychomotor stimulant drugs in hyperactive children from the standpoint of behavioural pharmacology. *Neuropharmacology, 18,* 931–950.

Roff, M., Sells, S. B, & Golden, M. M. (1972) *Social adjustment and personality development in children.* Minneapolis: University of Minnesota.

Rutter, M. (1978). Diagnostic validity in child psychiatry. *Advances in Biological Psychiatry, 2,* 2–22.

Rutter, M., & Garmezy, N. (1983). Developmental psychopathology. In P. H. Mussen (Ed.), *Handbook of child psychology* (Vol. IV: *Socialization, personality and social development*). New York: Wiley.

Sandberg, S. T. (1981). The overinclusiveness of the diagnosis of hyperkinetic syndrome. In R. Gittelman (Ed.), *Strategic interventions for hyperactive children.* New York: M. E. Sharpe.

Sandberg, S. (1986). Overactivity: Behaviour or syndrome? In E. Taylor (Ed.), *The overactive child.* Oxford: SIMP/Blackwell.

Sandberg, S., Rutter, M., & Taylor, E. (1978). Hyperkinetic disorder in psychiatric clinic attenders. *Developmental Medicine and Child Neurology, 20,* 279–299.

Sandberg, S., Wieselberg, M., & Shaffer, D. (1980). Hyperkinetic and conduct problem children in a primary school population: Some epidemiological considerations. *Journal of Child Psychology and Psychiatry, 21,* 293–311.

Schachar, R., Rutter, M., & Smith, A. (1981). The characteristics of situationally and pervasively hyperactive children: Implications for syndrome definition. *Journal of Child Psychology and Psychiatry, 22,* 375–392.

Schleifer, M., Weiss, G., Cohen, N., Elman, M., Cvejic, H., & Kruger, E. (1975). Hyperactivity in preschoolers and the effect of methylphenidate. *American Journal of Orthopsychiatry, 45,* 38–50.

Shaffer, D. (1980). An approach to the validation of clinical syndromes in childhood. In S. Salzinger, J. Antrobus, & J. Glick (Eds.), *The ecosystem of the "sick" child*. London: Academic Press.

Shaffer, D., McNamara, N., & Pincus, J. H. (1974). Controlled observations on patterns of activity, attention and impulsivity in brain damaged and psychiatrically disturbed boys. *Psychological Medicine, 4*, 4–18.

Spivack, G., & Spotts, J. (1965). The Devereux Child Behavior Scale: Symptom behaviors in latency age children. *American Journal of Mental Deficiency, 69*, 839–853.

Stewart, M. A., Cummings, C., Singer, S., & deBlois, C. S. (1981). The overlap between hyperactive and unsocialized aggressive children. *Journal of Child Psychology and Psychiatry, 22*, 35–46.

Stewart, M. A., deBlois, C. S. & Cummings, C. (1980). Psychiatric disorder in the parents of hyperactive boys and those with conduct disorder. *Journal of Child Psychology and Psychiatry, 21*, 283–292.

Taylor, E. (1980). Brain damage: Evidence from measures of neurological function in children with psychiatric disorder. In E. F. Purcell (Ed.), *Psychopathology of child and youth: A cross-cultural perspective*. New York: Macy Foundation.

Taylor, E. (1983). Drug response and diagnostic validation. In M. Rutter (Ed.), *Developmental neuropsychiatry*. New York: Guilford.

Taylor, E. (1985). Syndromes of overactivity and attention deficit. In M. Rutter & L. Hersov (Eds.), *Child and adolescent psychiatry: Modern approaches* (2nd ed.). Oxford: Blackwell.

Taylor, E. (1986a). Attention deficit. In E. Taylor (Ed.), *The overactive child*. Oxford: SIMP/ Blackwell.

Taylor, E. (1986b). Subclassification and diagnosis. In E. Taylor (Ed.), *The overactive child*. Oxford: SIMP/Blackwell.

Taylor, E., & Sandberg, S. (1984). Hyperactive behavior in English schoolchildren: A questionnaire survey. *Journal of Abnormal Child Psychology, 12*, 143–156.

Taylor, E., Schachar, R., Thorley, G., & Wieselberg, M. (1986). Conduct disorder and hyperactivity. *British Journal of Psychiatry, 149*, 760–777.

Thorley, G. (1984a). *A fourteen-year follow-up study of severely hyperactive children and psychiatric controls*. Thesis submitted in partial fulfillment of PhD degree, University of London.

Thorley, G. (1984b). Hyperkinetic syndrome of childhood: Clinical characteristics. *British Journal of Psychiatry, 144*, 16–24.

Trites, R. L., Blouin, A. G. A., & Laprade, K. (1982). Factor analysis of the Conners' Teacher Rating Scale based on a large normative sample. *Journal of Consulting and Clinical Psychology, 50*, 615–623.

Trites, R. L., & Laprade, K. (1983). Evidence for an independent syndrome of hyperactivity. *Journal of Child Psychology and Psychiatry, 24*, 573–586.

Weiss, G. (1983). Long-term outcome: Findings, concepts, and practical implications. In M. Rutter (Ed.), *Developmental neuropsychiatry*. New York: Guilford.

Werry, J. S. & Hawthorne, D. (1976). Conners' Teacher Questionnaire—Norms and validity. *Australian and New Zealand Journal of Psychiatry, 10*, 257–262.

Werry, J. S., Sprague, R. L. & Cohen, M. N. (1975). Conners' Teacher Rating Scale for use in drug studies with children—An empirical study. *Journal of Abnormal Child Psychology, 3*, 217–229.

Willerman, L. (1973). Activity level and hyperactivity in twins. *Child Development, 44*, 288–293.

Wolff, S. (1985). Nondelinquent disturbances of conduct. In M. Rutter & L. Hersov (Eds.), *Child and adolescent psychiatry: Modern approaches* (2nd ed.). Oxford: Blackwell.

Worland, J., North-Jones, M., & Stern, J. (1973). Performance and activity of hyperactive and normal boys as a function of distraction and reward. *Journal of Abnormal Child Psychology, 1*, 363–377.

World Health Organization. (1978). *International classification of diseases* (9th ed.). Geneva: Author.

13

AUTISM AND PERVASIVE DEVELOPMENTAL DISORDERS

MICHAEL RUTTER
ERIC SCHOPLER

INTRODUCTION

For more than 100 years there have been isolated case reports of very young children with severe mental disorders that have involved a marked distortion of the developmental process (Maudsley, 1867). Nevertheless, the general recognition of these conditions is a much more recent phenomenon. During the first half of this century there were a variety of descriptions of syndromes of this type; these included dementia precocissima (De Sanctis, 1906), childhood schizophrenia (Bender, 1947), and dementia infantilis (Heller, 1930). The terminology used reflected the general assumption that these represented the very early onset of adult-type psychoses. Kanner's (1943) incisive description of the syndrome of infantile autism was somewhat of an exception in that he set forth the diagnostic criteria in terms of specific child behaviors as he observed them rather than in terms of modifications of adult criteria. Nevertheless, the overall climate of psychiatric thinking led to an acceptance that autism, too, was an unusual form of schizphrenia that happened to begin very early in life (see Schopler, 1983, for a fuller account of the ways in which diagnostic concepts of autism have varied over time in relation to changing theories, therapeutic approaches, and empirical knowledge).

For some years there was a confusing proliferation of diagnostic terms and subclassification under the broad umbrella of "childhood schizophrenia" (Eisenberg, 1972; Kolvin, 1974; Makita, 1974; Rutter, 1972, 1978). Then, during the 1970s there came a growing recognition that it was necessary to differentiate between severe mental disorders arising during the

Michael Rutter. Department of Child and Adolescent Psychiatry, University of London Institute of Psychiatry, London, England.

Eric Schopler. Department of Psychiatry, University of North Carolina Memorial Hospital, Chapel Hill, North Carolina.

infancy period, of which autism is the prototype, and the psychoses arising in later childhood or adolescence, of which schizophrenia is the prototype (Rutter, 1985a). The latter group of conditions involve a *loss* of reality sense in individuals who have previously functioned normally or near normally and hence may properly be termed psychoses (insofar as that word has any precise meaning). However, the former are more usefully considered as a serious abnormality in the developmental process itself—an abnormality present from early in life. It is for that reason that the term *pervasive developmental disorders* was used in the third edition of the *Diagnostic and Statistical Manual of Mental Disorders* (DSM-III) of the American Psychiatric Association (1980).

The adoption of the term "pervasive developmental disorder" was important in its emphasis on the developmental origins of the abnormalities and in its highlighting of the differentiation from mental illnesses as they occur in adult life. The adjective "pervasive" was meant to draw attention to the widespread distortion of the developmental process (involving communication, socialization, and thought processes)—a breadth of abnormality that makes autism different from the specific developmental disorders of speech or language, in which the problems are much more restricted in scope (even though associated socioemotional difficulties are relatively common; see Cantwell & Baker, 1985). Nevertheless, not everyone has been satisfied with the term because, although the disorders affect a wide range of developmental processes, some are unimpaired. The disorders are pervasive but they are not all-pervasive. Indeed, it is the very fact that general intelligence may be relatively spared (perhaps a fifth of the autistic children have performance IQs within the normal range) that underlines the need to separate autism from global mental handicap.

DISTINCTIVENESS AND VALIDITY OF THE AUTISTIC SYNDROME

There is continuing dispute over both the boundaries and the subdivision of pervasive developmental disorders (see below), but questions on diagnosis and classification are best considered by first examining the narrower issue of whether autism constitutes a syndrome that is meaningfully different from acute psychiatric conditions (such as emotional and conduct disorders), from the psychoses of later childhood (such as schizophrenia), from general mental retardation, and from the specific developmental disorders of speech and language. As the evidence has been fully discussed previously (Rutter, 1978; Rutter & Gould, 1985) the findings may be summarized quite briefly.

The likely discontinuity between autism and schizophrenia is strongly indicated by the sharply bimodal distribution of age of onset (Rutter, 1974). Severe mental disorders of a kind that might possibly be linked with either autism or schizophrenia rarely begin in middle childhood. There is a peak in infancy made up of autistic-like disorders and a peak in adolescence made up of schizophrenia-like disorders, but a marked trough in between. This finding in itself makes it improbable that autism and schizophrenia constitute subvarieties of the same basic condition. However, in addition, autism and schizophrenia differ sharply in family history (a familial loading of schizophrenia is rare with autism); in phenomenology (delusions and hallucinations are rare in autism): in course (often episodic with periods of normality or near-normality in schizophrenia, but persistent in autism); and in the association with epileptic seizures (rare in schizophrenia but present in about a quarter of cases of autism).

Initially, Kanner (1943) asserted that autistic children all had a normal cognitive potential. That is now known not to be the case; to the contrary, over three-quarters of autistic children are also mentally retarded (Rutter, 1979). Nevertheless, autistic children have been found to differ sharply from nonautistic mentally handicapped children of comparable mental age. Thus, although seizures occur in about a quarter of children in both the groups, there are marked differences with respect to the following:

1. Age of onset (usually in early childhood in mental retardation but in adolescence in autism; see Deykin & MacMahon, 1979; Richardson, Koller, Katz, & McLaren, 1980).
2. Medical correlates (e.g., Down's syndrome is the most common cause of mental handicap, but it is very rarely associated with autism; see Wing & Gould, 1979).
3. Sex distribution (a slight male preponderance in mental retardation—see Birch, Richardson, Baird, Horobin, & Illsley, 1970—but a 4 to 1 sex ratio in autism—see Rutter, 1985a).
4. Patterns of cognitive disability (autistic children are more likely to fail on tasks that require skills in abstraction, language, and the use of meaning; see Hermelin & O'Connor, 1970; Rutter, 1983).
5. Their discrimination of socioemotional cues (markedly impaired in autism but not in mental handicap; see Hobson, 1986).

On the face of it, autism might seem to be very similar to the most severe developmental disorders of receptive language. Indeed, there are similarities and there is some overlap (Paul, Cohen, & Caparulo, 1983; Paul & Cohen, 1984). However, there also are marked differences (Rutter, 1979). Thus, autism is distinctive in terms of its sex distribution (specific developmental disorders of expressive language show a male preponderance but the disorders of *receptive* language, which are closest to autism, do not—although autism does); its worse prognosis (Cantwell, Baker, Rutter, & Mawhood, 1987); its pattern of cognitive disabilities (both wider and more severe in autism, even after equating for level of language handicap; see Bartak, Rutter, & Cox, 1975); and in its persisting pattern of socioemotional–behavioral abnormalities (Cantwell *et al.*, 1987).

Although there have been claims that autism arises on the basis of fear over social contacts (Tinbergen & Tinbergen, 1983) or of parental rejection (Bettelheim, 1967), the available evidence does not support either concept. It is true, of course, that abnormalities in rearing can lead to serious social problems, but the nature of the social abnormalities differs markedly from that found in autism. Thus, institution-reared children tend to be clinging and excessively friendly in an indiscriminate fashion (see Rutter, 1981), and abused children show marked insecurities in their personal attachments (see Mrazek & Mrazek, 1985). Neither feature is characteristic of autism.

Autism differs in so many ways from the ordinary run of emotional and behavioral disorders of childhood that its distinctiveness is beyond dispute. Thus, it stands out in terms of its strong association with mental retardation and with organic brain dysfunction, as well as in its worse prognosis, and its persisting differences in symptomatology (Rutter, 1979).

We may conclude that there is no doubt that autism constitutes a valid and meaningfully different psychiatric syndrome; indeed the evidence on its validity is stronger than for any other psychiatric condition in childhood. Nevertheless, as we shall see, that does not mean that there are no crucial diagnostic and classification issues that await resolution. We consider these issues in some detail below.

DIAGNOSTIC CRITERIA FOR AUTISM

Before proceeding further it is necessary to pause to outline the diagnostic criteria for autism. Not suprisingly, these have varied in emphasis over the years as concepts have varied in their focus and preoccupations. When autism was viewed as an infantile psychosis, most attention tended to be paid to bizarre behaviors. As clinicians and researchers began to appreciate the importance of the cognitive deficits, the spotlight shifted to impairments in language and in social development. Most recently, it has come to be realized that what differentiates autism from other disorders of development is the *deviance*, rather than the delay, in the developmental process. It is essential to understand that these shifts in concept have *not* meant that the term "autism" has come to be applied to different conditions. Autistic children usually show an admixture of bizarre behaviors, developmental delay, and developmental deviance. What has happened is that research findings have led people to recognize that although the first two groups of features are indeed common in autism, it is the third group that most sharply sets it apart from other conditions. Thus, schizophrenic children also show an assortment of bizarre behaviors but generally they do not exhibit the same deviance of language and social development characteristic of autism. Similarly, impaired language and socialization is found in many developmental disorders (especially general mental retardation) but the particular pattern of deviance found in autism is distinctive to that syndrome.

For these reasons, both the major systems of classification, the ninth edition of the World Health Organization's *International Classification of Diseases* (ICD-9) (1978) and the American Psychiatric Association's DSM-III, tended to concentrate on four main sets of diagnostic criteria (see Rutter, 1984; Schopler, 1983). First, there is the requirement that the disorder be manifest before 30 months of age. This stipulation has led to some confusion because of the ambiguity as to whether this means that there must be evidence of developmental impairment or distortion before 30 months, or rather that the specifically autistic features must be apparent before 30 months. As the latter vary appreciably in the age at which they are detectable (i.e., the disorder may have an onset in early infancy but yet not be recognized until some time later), it is clear that the first approach is the most appropriate one. Two main diagnostic issues arise with respect to age of manifestation. The first query is how to classify disorders that appear indistinguishable from autism but which differ in terms of development, the children having been apparently normal until after the age of 30 months. This problem most often applies to children for whom the information on early development is inadequate for certainty on the timing of onset of abnormality. A lifting of the cutoff from 30 months to 3 years removes most of these difficulties without altering the basic concept of the syndrome. Occasional cases of autistic-like disorders do occur after the age of 3 but they are rare and usually due to acquired brain disease (or genetic disorders of later manifestation—such as the cerebral lipoidoses). For the moment, at least, it seems useful to separate those late-onset conditions off from "classic" autism.[1]

The second query is whether autism that seems to have been preceded by a period of definitely normal development differs in any fundamental way from autism in which development has been abnormal from the outset. General principles suggest that the two are likely to differ in etiology; nevertheless research so far has failed to demonstrate any such differences. Indeed, one pair of MZ twins were concordant for autism but markedly discordant for age of onset (Folstein & Rutter, 1977). This remains one of many areas requiring further investigation.

The second set of diagnostic criteria concern various aspects of deviance in the development of social relationships. The accurate delineation of the social abnormalities characteristic of autism were impeded for many years by two tendencies. First, for many years investigators tended to ignore the need to take account of the mental retardation that so often accompanies autism. Some delay or impairment in social development is likely to occur as a result

---

1. We have used the adjective "classic" in quotes to make clear that there is no assumption that Kanner's original diagnostic criteria should have precedence. The whole burden of our argument is that the choice of criteria should be based on empirical evidence regarding validity of diagnostic distinctions. Nevertheless, because the term "autism" has come to be used in rather varied ways, it has been necessary to have some way of indicating when we are using it in Kanner's original sense.

of the mental handicap quite independently of the autism. It is now appreciated that it is crucial to define the social abnormalities in terms of *deviance* in relation to the child's mental age; this means, of course, that diagnostic assessment must include a careful and systematic cognitive evaluation (Rutter, 1984). Second, until recently there was a lack of an adequate conceptualization or vocabulary of social features. Accordingly, the social abnormalities of autism tended to be defined in terms of vague descriptors such as "aloofness" or "social withdrawal," or in terms of nonspecific features such as "lack of eye-to-eye gaze" that may arise from a variety of causes (e.g., very anxious or very shy children are likely to avoid visual contact).

Gains in knowledge of normal social development, as well as an improved understanding of autism, have recently led to a better specification of the particular social abnormalities that characterize autism. These are thought to reflect a basic deficit in the capacity to form relationships. This is evident in the autistic child's inadequate appreciation of socioemotional cues and in the lack of response to other people's emotions and a lack of modulation of behavior according to social context; in his or her poor use of social signals and weak integration of social, emotional, and communicative behaviors; and especially in the lack of socioemotional reciprocity. These deficits are shown in features such as (1) a failure to use eye-to-eye gaze, facial expression, body posture, and gesture to regulate social interaction; (2) rarely seeking others for comfort or affection; (3) rarely initiating interactive play with others; (4) rarely offering comfort to others or responding to other people's distress or happiness; (5) rarely greeting others; and (6) a failure to develop peer friendships in terms of a mutual sharing of interests, activities, and emotions—despite ample opportunities. In each case these behaviors should be assessed in terms of difference from those appropriate for the child's *mental* age.

The third set of diagnostic criteria comprise abnormalities in communication. At one time these tended to be framed in terms of speech or language impairment, but it is clear that the characteristic features involve deviance rather than delay (although delay in development is also usual), and the abnormalities extend beyond speech to many aspects of the communicative process. Indeed, the strictly linguistic features (i.e., the use of grammar) are least affected. Rather there appears to be a basic deficit in the capacity to use language for social communication. This is evident in the autistic child's relative lack of *social* usage of such language skills he possesses and in the poor synchrony and lack of reciprocity in conversational interchange; a poor flexibility in language expression and a relative lack of creativity and fantasy in thought processes; an inadequate response to other people's verbal and nonverbal overtures; and an impaired use of variations in cadence or emphasis to reflect communicative modulation. These features may be shown by (1) a delay in, or total lack of, the development of spoken language that is not compensated for by use of gesture or mime as alternative modes of communication (often preceded by a lack of communicative babbling); (2) a failure to respond to the communications of others such as (when young) not responding when called by name; (3) a relative failure to initiate or sustain conversational interchange in which there is a to-and-fro aspect and responsivity to the communications of the other person; (4) stereotyped and repetitive use of language; (5) use of "you" when "I" is meant; (6) idiosyncratic use of words; and (7) abnormalities in pitch, stress, rate, rhythm, and intonation of speech. The lack of creativity and spontaneity in autistic children's use of social language is paralleled by a similar deficit in preverbal skills. Thus, a lack of varied spontaneous "make-believe" play is especially characteristic.

It is evident that, because these features concern abnormalities in the communicative process and not just speech, they can be manifest both before the child can talk and after language competence has reached normal levels. Thus, the normal infant uses sounds to communicate well before he can talk, and these vocalizations exhibit conversational synchrony and reciprocity; this is not so with the autistic infant. Moreover, the deaf child who lacks speech nevertheless succeeds in communicating by other means; the autistic child does not. Also the autistic adult who is able to speak fluently is likely still to show abnormalities in the flow of conversational interchanges, a formality of language, a lack of emotional expression in speech, and a lack of fantasy and imagination.

The fourth set of diagnostic criteria concern restricted, repetitive, and stereotyped patterns of behavior. The meaning of this tendency to impose rigidity and routine on a wide range of aspects of day-to-day functioning remains obscure. However, it does appear to be a general tendency as it applies to novel activities and not just to familiar habits and play patterns (Frith, 1971). In part probably, the stereotypy reflects the lack of creativity associated with autism, but it seems to represent more in that it applies so widely even in the least intellectually handicapped individuals. The ways in which the stereotyped patterns may be shown include (1) an encompassing preoccupation with stereotyped and restricted patterns of interest; (2) attachments to unusual objects; (3) compulsive rituals; (4) stereotyped and repetitive motor mannerisms; (5) preoccupations with part-objects or nonfunctional elements of play materials; and (6) distress over changes in small details of the environment.

NATURE OF THE BASIC DEFICIT

It is clear from this account of the diagnostic criteria for autism that over the past two decades there have been progressive attempts to move from abnormal behaviors expressed in general terms, to *qualitatively* distinct features that are syndrome-specific, to the reformulation of those features in terms of the particular psychological processes thought to be affected. Such attempts, of course, are essential if the nature of the basic deficit is to identified. Once this is accomplished, the usual procedure in medicine is to redefine the condition in terms of the underlying abnormality rather than the signs and symptoms that first identified the syndrome. Thus, thyrotoxicosis is defined in terms of the abnormality in thyroxin production and not the palpitations, loss of weight, and exophthalmos that the abnormality tends to produce. Patients with such symptoms who do not show abnormalities in thyroxin production are not diagnosed as suffering from the thyrotoxicosis. It should be emphasized that this identification of the basic abnormality is *not* synonymous with discovery of the cause. Not only may the cause not be known, but also, there may be more than one cause for a single abnormality. That would be the case, for example, with many blood dyscrasias and also with immune disorders.

It should be added that there need not necessarily be any unitary basic deficit. For example, that applies to cerebral palsy. There is a general sort of unity in terms of abnormalities in motor functioning, but such abnormalities take several rather different forms. Athetosis, spasticity, and apraxia reflect rather different neurophysiological abnormalities. The particular pattern of motor deficit depends on the distribution of brain damage and on the type of abnormal brain functioning with which that damage happens to be associated. There is no one basic deficit because the disorder reflects varying patterns of organic brain dysfunction rather than any single disease state. Inevitably, when that is the state of affairs there is an essential ambiguity over the boundaries of the disorder in question.

A further point that needs to be made is that this delineation of the basic deficit need not be an all or none affair. Thus, for example, mental retardation is comparable to cerebral palsy insofar as it constitutes a general syndrome (characterized by a deficit in intellectual development) rather than by a specific unitary abnormality of one underlying process. Nevertheless, this general syndrome is gradually being broken down as specific disease entities become identified. Thus, Down's syndrome is defined by particular chromosome anomalies. In this instance the delineation is not made in terms of a particular type of cognitive deficit; nevertheless the cognitive pattern associated with Down's syndrome tends to have some distinctive features (Anwar, 1983).

The key question is what sort of disorder does autism constitute? At one level, of course, it must be a general syndrome like cerebral palsy or mental retardation. This is because it is known that many children with severe mental handicap show some autistic features, because the autistic pattern is rather variable, and because it may be found with a variety of medical conditions (Wing & Gould, 1979). Thus, conditions that give rise to widespread organic brain dysfunction may sometimes cause patterns of brain pathology that affect the systems that underlie the autistic abnormalities. However, that does not seem to be a satisfactory general answer for several different reasons. In the first place, there are very marked differences in the rate of autism between medical conditions that commonly give rise to mental handicap (Rutter, 1979). For example, autism is quite rare in children with Down's syndrome or with cerebral palsy; in contrast, it is relatively common in those with infantile spasms or congential rubella. It appears that there must be something particular about the pathological processes that give rise to autism, although what that is remains obscure.

Second, most autistic individuals do not show any gross structural abnormalities of the brain—at least not on the basis of the data available from the techniques used so far. Thus computerized axial tomography (CAT scans) have not revealed any consistent abnormality (Caparulo et al., 1981; Creasey et al., 1986; Damasio, Maurer, Damasio, & Chui, 1980; Gillberg & Svendsen, 1983; Prior, Tress, Hoffman, & Boldt, 1984; Rosenbloom et al., 1984), nor apparently is there any diagnostically distinctive metabolic pattern as reflected in positron emission tomography findings (Herold, Frackowiak, Rutter, & Howlin, 1986; Rumsey et al., 1985). There have been very few neuropathological studies but these, too, have either shown quite subtle histological changes or no detectable abnormalities (Bauman & Kemper, 1985; Coleman, Romano, Lapham, & Simon, 1985; Darby, 1976; Williams, Hauser, Purpura, Delong, & Swisher, 1980). Moreover, although autistic children show a modest increase in perinatal complications (Deykin & MacMahon, 1980; Finegan & Quadrington 1979; Gillberg & Gillberg, 1983; Torrey, Hersh, & McCabe, 1975), the increase is *not* mainly in the more severe complications commonly associated with brain damage (such as very low birth weight or extreme prematurity). Third, so far, the identified medical causes account for a tiny proportion of cases of autism. The one possible exception to that statement is provided by the fragile X phenomenon which may account for as many as 5% to 17% of cases (Blomquist et al., 1985), although several investigations have found very few cases of fragile X in substantial series of cases of autism (see below for a fuller description of the fragile X disorder).

We must conclude that it appears that the majority of autistic cases do not fall into the nonspecific organic brain syndrome pattern, in spite of the strong evidence that autism has an organic basis. That is to say, unlike the case with severe mental retardation or cerebral palsy, autism is *not* usually associated with gross abnormalities of brain structure or histology. Moreover, it is *unusual* for generalized brain damage to give rise to autism. The organic basis of autism must be of some more subtle, less easy to detect, variety. Most autistic individuals are physically normal, do not exhibit any evidence of overt structural brain pathology, and have not experienced hazards known to be likely to cause brain damage. That is particularly so with respect to autistic individuals without general mental retardation. Whereas certainly we do not know that there *is* any unitary basic deficit in autism (whether defined in neuropsychological, neurophysiological, or neuropathological terms), it is possible that there may be one. Accordingly, it is most important that research continue to be directed toward its possible identification.

A good deal of progress has been made in this connection. Thus it is now clear that in most cases there is a basic cognitive deficit that involves impaired language, sequencing, abstraction, and coding functions (Dawson, 1983; Rutter, 1983). Moreover, it has also been shown that autism is *not* particularly associated with abnormalities in perceptual discrimination, in the appreciation of visuospatial perspectives, or in self-recognition (Ferrari & Matthews, 1983; Spiker & Ricks, 1984). These findings constitute highly worthwhile progress. Not only have they been crucial in demonstrating the basic importance of cognitive deficits as usual (if not essential) parts of the syndrome, but also they have gone a long way toward demonstrations of just what sort of cognitive deficit is particularly associated with autism.

Nevertheless, it is equally apparent that much remains unexplained. Most especially, it is far from clear *how* these cognitive deficits give rise to the abnormalities in social functioning or even *whether* they do so. In recent years experimental approaches have been directed to the elucidation of which psychological processes relevant to socialization might be impaired. So far, three possibilities appear to be leading contenders: (1) discrimination of emotional cues; (2) differentiations of age and gender; and (3) ability to appreciate what other people are thinking. Hobson (1983, 1986) in a series of well-planned experiments (mainly using the paradigm of matching videos with labeled pictures) has shown that autistic children differ markedly from both normal and mentally retarded children of comparable mental age in their ability to discriminate either emotional cues or differentiations based on age and gender. It would seem plausible that if autistic individuals cannot perceive when other people are happy, angry, or sad, they are likely to be handicapped in their social relationships. Hobson (1986) postulated that this lack of emotional discrimination may reflect a deficit in empathy. It is not clear what is involved in autistic children's poor discrimination of adults and children, males and females—is it that such differentiations lack salience for them or are they unable to appreciate the significance of the behavioral differences associated with age and gender? Also is this the same deficit that underlies the failure in emotional discrimination or is it different?

The third possibility stems from an experiment by Baron-Cohen, Leslie, and Frith (1985) in which the task involved a doll play setup in which a hidden object was moved while a doll figure was "out of the room." The experiment tested whether the subject reported that the doll figure would look for the hidden object where she had last seen it or rather in the place where it now was (a place known to the subject but not to the doll figure). Autistic children differed from controls in being more likely to report that the object would be looked for in its present location—a finding interpreted as meaning that autistic individuals are impaired in their capacity to appreciate what another person is thinking. Again, this raises the question of whether this deficit (if confirmed by further research) is part of the already demonstrated impaired ability to appreciate emotional and gender cues.

These studies have moved us an important step toward a better under-standing of autistic individual's socioemotional disabilities, but it is by no means self-evident just what neuropsychological functions underlie the skills being tapped. Nor is it clear whether the findings reflect one deficit that encompasses these various skills, or rather that we are dealing with a constel-lation of associated deficits. In view of the crucial importance of the cogni-tive deficits associated with language and the abstraction of meaning, it may be supposed that these socioemotional deficits are in some way part of, linked with, the other cognitive problems, but how and in what way do they interlink?

A further query is whether the autistic children's impaired ability to discriminate socioemotional cues or appreciate how another person is think-ing are *necessary* features of autism. In other words, are these deficits so basic that if they are not found the diagnosis of autism should not be made. Or, alternatively, does their presence or absence serve to differentiate mean-ingful subcategories of autism? As we have argued above, that is an essential question to put.

Nevertheless, it is obvious that we are far from ready to provide an answer. The *degree* of difference between autistic and mentally retarded groups of comparable mental age suggests the probable importance of the function being examined. But the deficits were least apparent in the intellec-tually normal individuals. At present it remains uncertain how far that ob-servation was a reflection of a ceiling effect in the test used and how far a real difference in pattern of handicaps in the intellectually most able autistic individuals (an issue that also has been apparent with the study of other functions, such as the use of meaning in memory processes; see Fyffe & Prior, 1978).

A further query concerns the *specificity* of these deficits to autism. So far, the direct comparisons have been between autism and mental handicap, but do the deficits also differentiate autism from, say, schizophrenia or other psychiatric disorders associated with social impairment? The question is pertinent and important both because the deficits might constitute a nonspe-cific accompaniment of any form of severe social disability and because somewhat comparable (although apparently lesser) deficits have been re-ported in schizophrenia (Novic, Luchins, & Perline, 1984; Walker, Bettes, & McGuire, 1984). This area of research is a most promising one, and it carries with it the tantalizing possibility of defining the basic psychological deficit in autism—but that definition remains as yet some distance away.

An alternative approach to the possible identification of the basic deficit in autism has been through the use of neurophysiological rather than psy-chological techniques. Thus, there have been investigations using EEG measures, contingent and noncontingent sensory-evoked responses, auto-nomic reactivity and vestibular responses (James & Barry, 1980; Ornitz, 1978). The findings have been quite inconsistent and inconclusive; also, in many cases inadequate or inappropriate control groups have been used

(Yule, 1978). Nevertheless, various abnormalities have been reported (see James & Barry; 1980; Rutter, 1985a). Perhaps those most likely to be associated with autism are the indicators of increased brainstem transmission times (Fein, Skoff, & Mirsky, 1981; Rosenblum et al., 1980; Skoff, Mirsky, & Turner, 1980); of defective information storage (Novick, Kurtzberg, & Vaughn, 1979); and of impaired development of hemispheric dominance (James & Barry, 1983). Further research on these functions, together with investigations of attentional processes (see Taylor, Chapter 12, this volume) should prove rewarding. However, so far the meaning of the neurophysiological findings in autism remain obscure, and it is not at all clear how they might be linked to the findings on psychological deficits.

RATING INSTRUMENTS

The major problems inherent in research based on varying approaches to diagnosis has led to a variety of attempts to devise standardized rating instruments from which individual diagnoses can be derived (see Parks, 1983). Broadly speaking, these fall into three main groups: (1) those based on questionnaires completed by parents or teachers—such as the checklists devised by Rimland (1984) and by Krug, Arick, and Almond (1980); (2) those based on structured observations of the child—such as Behavior Rating Instrument for Autistic and Other Atypical Children (BRIAAC) (Ruttenberg, Dratman, Fraknoi, & Wener, 1966), Behavior Observation Scale (BOS) (Freeman, Ritvo, Guthrie, Schroth, & Ball, 1978; Freeman, Ritvo, & Schroth, 1984), and Child Autism Rating Scale (CARS) (Schopler, Reichler, DeVellis, & Daly, 1980; Schlopler, Reichler, & Renner, 1985); and (3) those based on a standardized interview of the parents (Wing & Gould, 1978).

Most of these instruments have been shown to have satisfactory reliability and to discriminate between autistic, mentally retarded, and normal samples. Moreover, they provide a useful way of recording various items of behavior needed both for diagnosis and for the planning of treatment and provision of services (see Schopler & Rutter, 1978, and Schopler, 1983, for an account of how different approaches to classification may be needed for different purposes). Nevertheless, it is doubtful whether they provide a satisfactory solution to problems of individual diagnosis. In the first place, most are devised for severely handicapped children and appear likely to be less applicable to the more intellectually able individuals. Also, many of the items reflect a *lack* of particular skills rather than the deviance characteristic of autism. Not surprisingly, therefore, many of the items reflect intellectual handicap as much as autism. Also, the parental questionnaires cannot satisfactorily tap the distinctions on the *quality* of behaviors needed for diagnosis.

The instruments based on observation are potentially more satisfactory but necessarily they are limited to the behaviors likely to be manifest during a relatively brief period in a single setting; the consequence is that they most readily detect the gross abnormalities seen in the most handicapped children. The detailed interview schedules should be able to tap a wider range of behaviors, but the items tend not to reflect some of the key distinctions contained in the diagnostic criteria; moreover, they fail to utilize the professional observational skills necessary for some of these distinctions. The rating instruments comprise a valuable set of tools for behavioral assessment, but as yet they fall short of a comprehensively satisfactory approach to diagnosis.

We suggest that what is needed for specific diagnostic purposes is a combination of a detailed standarized parental interview designed to elicit the key diagnostic features, together with a standardized observation system. The main limitation regarding the latter is that it is unlikely that a single structured interaction could be equally appropriate for a mute mentally handicapped autistic child and a verbal autistic individual within the normal range of general intelligence. Nevertheless, such an observation could be devised to tap a predetermined set of social, conversational, and behavioral qualities—using a standard set of ratings that reflect the key diagnostic features. The CARS approach provides a well-tested route toward that end.

BOUNDARIES OF AUTISM

Five main areas of controversy remain with respect to the boundaries of autism as a valid diagnostic entity: (1) autistic-like syndromes in children with severe mental handicap; (2) autistic-like disorders in individuals of normal intelligence without gross developmental delay, general or specific; (3) later-onset autistic-like disorders following a prolonged period of normal development; (4) severe disorders arising in early or middle childhood characterized by grossly bizarre behavior; and (5) the overlap between autism and severe developmental disorders of receptive language.

It is all too apparent that there is no readily recognizable separation point between "true" autism and other disorders that share some behavioral features but do not fulfill the complete set of accepted diagnostic criteria. Of course, in reality, such a differentiation could only be based on some unequivocal indication of some specifically and uniquely autistic feature. Such a feature has yet to be identified. Moreover, many behavioral disorders are best conceptualized in dimensional rather than categorical terms; accordingly, it should not be assumed that there will prove to be any pathognomonic defining feature for autism. For the present the nearest approach to validation or invalidation of the distinctions must rely on those features that have been shown most clearly to differentiate autistic children from nonautistic children of comparable mental age. These features include (1) abnormalities in the appreciation of socioemotional cues (as identified through the experimental studies of Hobson); (2) cognitive deficits in the abstraction of meaning (as derived originally from the studies of Hermelin and O'Connor); (3) the differential association with particular medical syndromes (e.g., strong with congenital rubella and weak with Down's syndrome); (4) the association with seizures that develop in adolescence rather than in early childhood; (5) concordance in monozygotic pairs of twins; and (6) familial loading on language and language-related cognitive impairments. Such "tests" have not yet been systematically applied to any of the "boundary" conditions mentioned.

The differentiation from autism is most problematical of all in the case of children who are very seriously retarded (say those with a mental age below about 2 years). In their general population survey, Wing and Gould (Wing, 1981; Wing & Gould 1979) found that about half of all children with severe mental handicap (IQ < 50) showed the autistic-type triad of social and language impairments and repetitive behaviors. It is clear that this triad parallels the diagnostic criteria for autism as described earlier in the chapter; the difference lies in the emphasis on *impairment* rather than on a specific type of deviance. The consequences of this difference is most evident in the group of children with an IQ below 20; of these, 82% showed the triad but only 2% showed typical autism. The comparable figures for children in the IQ range of 35–49 was 40% and 14%. Overall, the triad children showed similar medical condition associations to those characteristic of autism (e.g., infantile spasms common but Down's syndrome rare), but no data are available on the other possibly discriminatory features.

The second area of difficulty concerns the differentiation between autism and autistic-like disorders in individuals of normal intelligence. These include both the disorders termed Asperger's syndrome (Wing, 1981) and those sometimes classified as schizoid disorder of childhood (Chick, Waterhouse, & Wolff, 1979; Wolff & Barlow, 1979; Wolff & Chick, 1980). As ordinarily diagnosed, Asperger's syndrome requires the presence of lack of empathy, deviant styles of communication, and constricted intellectual interests and (often) idiosyncratic attachments to objects. The features all suggest that the condition represents mild autism without associated mental handicap, as do the findings on recognition and production of emotions (Scott, 1985). However, it seems that sometimes this clinical picture can occur without the language delay and impairment usually found with autism; the observation raises the interesting possibility that although such language deficits are usual in autism, perhaps they may not constitute a necessary feature (Rutter & Garmezy, 1983). The possibility warrants further study. As used by Wolff and her colleagues, the diagnosis of schizoid disorder clearly includes cases that would be diagnosed by others as Asperger's syndrome. On the other hand, the frequency of schizoid disorders in the Wolff clinic sample (3% to 4% of psychiatric clinic referrals) suggests that it must extend more broadly than that. It remains quite unknown whether such cases represent subclinical varieties of autism or some quite different condition. Again, the possibility demands systematic investigation.

The third type of clinical picture that gives rise to difficulties in diagnostic differentiation is that in which there is a profound regression and behavioral disintegration following some 3 to 4 years of apparently normal development—a syndrome that roughly follows Heller's (1930) account of dementia infantilis, but which now tends to be termed "disintegrative psychosis" (Rutter, 1985a). Often there is a premonitory period of vague illness during or following which the child becomes restive, irritable, anxious, and overactive. Over the course of a few months there is an impoverishment and then a loss of speech and language. Comprehension of language deteriorates and intelligence often declines, although an intelligent facial expression is usually retained. There is a loss of social skills, impairment of interpersonal relationships, a general loss of interest in objects, and the development of stereotypies and mannerisms (Rutter, 1985a).

Clearly there is a substantial overlap in symptomatology with autism, and it seems likely that some cases represent atypical forms of autism. Nevertheless, the gradual and severe loss of cognitive skills (often with loss of bowel and bladder control as well) after some years of normal development is not the picture usually seen in autism even when the onset seems to have followed initially normal early development. The apparently good cognitive potential implied by the normality of the first 3 years in these disintegrative disorders is unfortunately misleading. In most cases the prognosis is very poor, with the children usually remaining without speech and severely mentally handicapped. The importance of these late-onset cases lies in the frequency with which they are associated with progressive neurological disorders either congenital or acquired—such as the lipoidoses or leukodystrophies (e.g., Corbett, Harris, Taylor, & Trimble, 1977; Malamud, 1959). In girls, there is also the special need to identify Rett's syndrome (a progressive dementing disorder associated with loss of facial expression and of interpersonal contact, stereotyped movements, ataxia, and loss of purposeful hand use) that can be mistaken for autism in its early stages (Hagberg, Aicardi, Dias, & Ramos, 1983). Nevertheless, it is clear that in some cases the cause is unknown, without any unambiguous evidence of brain disease or damage; this is probably especially the case when the regression occurs at about $2\frac{1}{2}$ to 3 years following the pattern seen in some cases of autism at a slightly earlier age (Evan-Jones & Rosenbloom, 1978).[2] Occasionally, the deterioration seems to follow some life event (such as hospital admission) but such events are in any case very common during the preschool years and it is dubious whether they play any essential part in etiology. These later-onset disintegrative disorders are much less common than autism and less is known about their characteristics. Nevertheless, it is our very ignorance regarding their meaning that makes it important to recognize their existence and to accept

2. In autism it is relatively common for parents to report a regression in language after initial acquisition of some speech. In most cases, however, it is clear that the early development was never fully normal (although, occasionally, it seems to have been so).

that as yet we do not know how far they overlap with the more usual early-onset autistic disorders.

The fourth major area of diagnostic controversy and uncertainty concerns conditions arising in early or middle childhood in which there is the onset of grossly disturbed behavior together with abnormalities in language and thought processes. There is no doubt that some of these conditions represent schizophrenic disorders of particularly early onset. This is best demonstrated for those beginning in the years leading up to adolescence but there are undoubted cases with an onset as early as age 6 (Eggers, 1978; Green *et al.*, 1984; Kolvin, 1971; Kydd & Werry, 1982). Such children show many of the features associated with schizophrenia occurring in adult life, and both the course and family history are also similar. However, there are three main problem issues. First, Cantor, Evans, Pearce, and Pezzot-Pearce (1982) have argued that schizophrenia can begin in infancy; the disorders differing from autism in terms of (1) relatively good social relationships, (2) thought disorder, (3) sometimes the presence of delusions and hallucinations, (4) marked hypotonicity, and (5) often a family history of schizophrenia. For obvious reasons there are major difficulties in the recognition of thought disorder and delusions in infants or very young children, and the nosological validity of schizophrenia beginning in infancy has not been established. Nevertheless, it may be accepted that there are serious nonautistic disorders of development manifest at that age.

Second, there are severe disorders that arise in middle childhood in which there is a loss of reality sense and severe distortions in behavior and in thinking, but in which the specific diagnostic features of schizophrenia are lacking. At present, there is a lack of evidence on the nature of these serious psychiatric disturbances and it is quite likely that they constitute a heterogeneous group. In most cases the diagnostic uncertainty concerns the question of schizophrenia rather than autism, but occasionally the picture can be somewhat autistic-like. For example, this was so with two published cases of children subjected to gross abuse and/or neglect (Curtiss, 1977; Skuse, 1984). In both instances it remains unclear whether the disorder stemmed from the severe environmental distortions, from some constitutional deficit, or a combination of the two.

Third, there are isolated reports of young children who were diagnosed autistic who later appear to manifest schizophrenic symptomatology (Petty, Ornitz, Michelman, & Zimmerman, 1984; Howells & Guirguis, 1984). It is difficult to know what weight to attach to these reports in that the systematic studies of children diagnosed as autistic according to traditional criteria have *not* found this transition (Eisenberg, 1956; Kanner, 1973; Rutter, 1970). It may be that the supposed autism to schizophrenia change reflects a broader concept of autism or of schizophrenia or a difference in the interpretation of the odd thinking that is quite common in older autistic individuals. Alternatively, these unusual cases may represent a small subgroup that requires separate categorization. So far the data needed for a choice between these alternatives are lacking. Nevertheless, Tanguay (1984) has used these cases together with a potpourri of other reports of varying quality to argue for the invalidity of the diagnosis of autism. His argument ignores contrary evidence and relies on a misinterpretation of the findings that are quoted. For example, it is wrongly asserted that the medical conditions associated with autism are the "very same" as those linked with nonautistic forms of mental retardation—an incorrect statement, as we have already noted. What is needed is a systematic testing of alternative explanations rather than a moving back to nondiscriminating models of developmental failure.

The final area of uncertainty over the boundaries of autism concerns the overlap with severe developmental disorders of receptive language. The systematic comparative studies of autistic and dysphasic children by Bartak, Rutter, and Cox (1975) showed that most children with specific developmental receptive language disorders differed sharply from autistic children in linguistic, cognitive, and behavioral features. On the other hand, the same study also demonstrated that there was a small group with mixed features. A further follow-up by Cantwell et al. (1987) was informative in showing that as they got older, some dysphasic children showed severe behavioral and social difficulties, even though the two groups tended to remain distinctive. Paul et al.'s (1983) follow-up of 28 children with severe developmental language disorders also showed that many exhibited autistic-like features; however, progress in social relationships was as much a function of the severity of the deficit in language comprehension as of initial autistic-like features. Both twin (Folstein & Rutter, 1977) and family (August, Stewart, & Tsai, 1981) studies have also shown that some cases of autism are associated with a familial loading of language and intellectual retardation. The three diagnostic/classification issues are: (1) How do the cases of autism associated with language problems in the family differ from those without this familial component? (2) What is the nosological status of the cases with mixed autistic and developmental language disorder features? (3) Since presumably only some types of developmental language disorder are linked with autism, what are the features that distinguish those that are associated with autism?

ETIOLOGIC HETEROGENEITY WITHIN AUTISTIC SYNDROMES

The last issue concerns the question of etiologic heterogeneity within the field of autistic syndromes. We have noted already that there *is* undoubted heterogeneity. The very fact that the clinical picture of autism can arise from diseases as diverse as congenital rubella (Chess, Fernandez, & Korn, 1978; Chess, Korn, & Fernandez, 1971), tuberous sclerosis (Creak, 1963; Lotter, 1974), encephalopathy (Wing & Gould, 1979), infantile spasms with hypsarrhythmia (Riikonen & Amnell, 1981; Taft & Cohen, 1971), cerebral lipoidosis (Creak, 1963), and neurofibromatosis (Gillberg & Forsell, 1984) makes that clear. However, even when all these conditions are combined, they account for a tiny minority of cases of autism. In the vast majority of instances there is *no* identifiable medical cause. Accordingly, it remains quite uncertain whether the minority of cases with a known pathological cause represent phenocopies of some other unitary disorder with (an as yet undiscovered) single etiology; or rather whether the behavioral syndrome of autism represents just the final common pathway for a diverse range of organic brain conditions that happen to impinge on similar brain systems. In order to decide between these two contrasting alternatives, it is essential to have systematic research that focuses on the question of heterogeneity within autistic syndromes.

It will be appreciated that such research must go well beyond the mere noting of heterogeneity. It is crucial that it be designed to determine the ways (if any) in which the diversity on one parameter coincides with diversity on other dimensions. The investigation of heterogeneity should include studies based on several different starting points.

Firstly, the research may start with some identified medical condition. For example, the Swedish multicenter study of infantile autism (Blomquist *et al.*, 1985) found the fragile X phenomenon in 16% of the 83 boys studied (but in none of the 19 girls). As the Yale group (Watson *et al.*, 1984) found the fragile X in only 5% of 75 autistic males, and as there were no instances of fragile X in the 57 cases studied by Venter, Hof, Coetzee, Van der Walt, and Retief (1984), in the 18 cases with either dysmorphic features or a family history of mental retardation studied by Pueschel, Herman, and Groden (1985), or in the 37 cases studied by Goldfine *et al.* (1985), the evidence is contradictory on whether or not the incidence of fragile X in autism exceeds that in mental retardation (4% to 7%; Blomquist *et al.*, 1982, 1983). Nevertheless, either way there is a need to compare cases of autism with and without the fragile X. Do they differ, for instance, in phenomenology, course, or cognitive characteristics? Similarly, within a mentally retarded population does the phenomenon relate to behavioral features? (For example, Largo & Schinzel, 1985, and Levitas *et al.*, 1983, suggested an association with autistic features even in individuals without classical autism.)

Comparable questions arise with respect to other genetic factors (Folstein & Rutter, 1987). Folstein and Rutter (1977) found an MZ–DZ difference in concordance that pointed to an important genetic factor in etiology.[3] August *et al.*'s (1981) finding that some 15% of the siblings of autistic children compared with only 3% of the siblings of Down's syndrome

3. Ritvo and his colleagues (1985) have used their twin and family study data to argue for autosomal recessive inheritance. However their data are based on biased samples (e.g., a marked excess of MZ over same-sex DZ pairs) and inappropriate analyses (e.g., the inclusion of opposite-sex DZ pairs; see Ritvo, Freeman, *et al.*, 1985; Ritvo, Spence, *et al.*, 1985). Accordingly, little weight can be attached to their findings; moreover, their own data include some that are inconsistent with their hypothesis (Spence *et al.*, 1985). It is quite premature to postulate specific models of inheritance before the necessary data for such models are available.

individuals had language disorders, learning disabilities, or mental retardation also suggested the likely role of an inherited predisposition to language and cognitive abnormalities of which autism constitutes one important part. Several rather different issues arise with respect to this possibility. In the first instance it is necessary to check whether or not the twin concordance and familial loading are a function of the fragile X phenomenon. Isolated case reports suggest that it may be in some instances (August & Lockhart, 1984; Gillberg, 1983). However, if it does prove to be a general explanation of the familial findings it is crucial to go on to use genetic family studies to examine heterogeneity within autism. For example, does the familial loading apply preponderantly to autistic children who are also mentally handicapped (August *et al.*'s findings suggested that it might)? Does it vary according to the sex of the autistic child, to the development of seizures in adolescence, or to pattern of phenomenology?

The same "search for heterogeneity" strategy may be applied to other biological features associated with autism. Thus, for example, how do the autistic children who develop seizures during adolescence differ from those who do not? It seems that the risk of seizures is substantially higher in those with associated mental handicap (Bartak & Rutter, 1976) but does the risk vary according to medical correlates, sex, phenomenology, or course? Research is needed in order to find out.

Second, the research may begin with some behavioral feature, or some phenomenological constellation. Rimland (1971, 1984) has repeatedly argued that scores on his E2 scale serve to differentiate a distinctive biochemically different syndrome of autism. However, the study on which he bases his claim (Boullin, Coleman, O'Brien, & Rimland, 1971) could not be replicated by the same biochemical investigator when using a different sample (Boullin *et al.*, 1982). Although the claim is premature, the research strategy is pertinent. We need to know, for example, whether there are meaningful differences (on some external criterion) according to age of onset, typical versus atypical clinical pictures, deterioration in adolescence (Gillberg & Schauman, 1981), and so forth?

Third, it is important also to consider the ways in which male and female autistic individuals differ. It is well established that autism is much more common in boys than girls, in a ratio of 3 or 4 to 1. Furthermore, it seems that autistic girls may be more likely to show severe mental retardation and possibly more likely to have a family history of cognitive problems (Lord & Schopler, 1985; Lord, Schopler, & Revick, 1982; Tsai, Stewart, & August, 1981; Wing, 1981). These findings need replication, but also extension in order to determine whether there are any other differences in pattern between autism in boys and that in girls.

Fourth, response to treatment may be used as a differentiating factor. It appears that, on the whole, behavioral and educational methods of treatment are most effective (Bartak, 1978; Hemsley *et al.*, 1978; Howlin & Rutter, in press; Rutter, 1985b; Schopler, Mesibov, & Baker, 1982). The marked individual differences in treatment response mainly relate to the severity of intellectual and language impairment. That finding, of course, raises the possibility that autism in children of normal general intelligence may differ from autism associated with severe mental handicap. On the whole, the weight of findings suggest that the differences reflect variations on a continuum of degree of severity of disorder. However, the matter is far from resolved. Drug response constitutes, perhaps, a potentially better candidate for the investigation of diagnostic heterogeneity. Unfortunately, to date, although the major tranquilizers may serve to reduce agitation, tension and overactivity (Campbell, 1978; Corbett, 1976) there is no evidence of any autism-specific drug effect. Rather premature excitement was generated by a case study of just three children (Geller, Ritvo, Freeman, & Yuwiler, 1982) in which it was suggested that fenfluramine, a drug that lowers serotonin levels, may be of benefit in autism. The excitement arose over the possibility that the improvements in autism might be a consequence of a specific biochemical change—namely, a reduction in serotonin. That did not seem a likely possibility in that although serotonin levels are indeed raised in about a third of autistic children, so also are they in severe mental handicap and a host of other neurological conditions. In the event, further studies (August et al., 1984; Ritvo, Freeman, Geller, & Yuwiler, 1983) suggest that whatever benefits there may be from fenfluramine administration, they do not result from normalization of pathologically high serotonin levels. Nevertheless, though unrewarding so far, the use of differences in therapeutic response to specific treatments remains a worthwhile research strategy.

CONCLUSIONS

Of all the psychiatric syndromes arising in childhood, autism is much the best validated by empirical research. It stands out from the bulk of common psychiatric conditions in terms of its strong association with both cognitive deficits and evidence of organic brain dysfunction. Also it is differentiated from both general and specific developmental disorders of cognition in terms of psychological features (including the pattern of language-related cognitive deficits and also the serious impairment in the discrimination of socioemotional cues) and medical correlates (including the age of onset of seizures and the types of medical disorder with which it is associated). Nevertheless, uncertainties remain on the boundaries of this behaviorally defined syndrome, on its links with other disorders, on the extent to which within undoubted pathological heterogeneity there is a single etiologically homogeneous core condition, and on the ways (if any) in which the concept of autism should either be broadened or subdivided. In this essay we have sought to indicate the possible avenues of research that might serve to resolve these issues. Ultimately, the answers must rely on identification of the nature of the brain deficit that defines autism—whether this be in neuropsychological, neurophysiological, or neuropathological terms. Even though that identification is not yet in sight, there are several quite promising leads available.

REFERENCES

American Psychiatric Association. (1980). *Diagnostic and statistical manual of mental disorders* (3rd ed.). Washington, DC: Author.

Anwar, F. (1983). The role of sensory modality for the reproduction of shape by the severely retarded. *British Journal of Developmental Psychology, 1,* 317–328.

August, G. J., & Lockhart, L. H. (1984). Familial autism and the fragile-X chromosome. *Journal of Autism and Developmental Disorders, 14,* 197–204.

August, G. J., Raz, N., Papanicolaon, A. C., Baird, T. D., Hirsch, S. L., & Hsu, L. L. (1984). Fenfluramine treatment in infantile autism: neurochemical, electrophysiological, and behavioural effects. *Journal of Nervous and Mental Disease, 172,* 604–612.

August, G. J., Stewart, M. A., & Tsai, L. (1981). The incidence of cognitive disabilities in the siblings of autistic children. *British Journal of Psychiatry, 138,* 416–422.

Baron-Cohen, S., Leslie, A. M., and Frith, U. (1985). Does the autistic child have a "theory of mind"? *Cognition, 21,* 37–46.

Bartak, L. (1978) Educational approaches. In M. Rutter & E. Schopler (Eds.), *Autism: A reappraisal of concepts and treatment.* New York: Plenum.

Bartak, L., & Rutter, M. (1976). Differences between mentally retarded and normally intelligent autistic children. *Journal of Autism and Childhood Schizophrenia, 6,* 109–120.

Bartak, L., Rutter, M., & Cox, A. (1975). A comparative study of infantile autism and specific developmental receptive language disorder. I. The children. *British Journal of Psychiatry, 126,* 127–145.

Bauman, M., & Kemper, T. L. (1985). Histoanatomic observations of the brain in early infantile autism. *Neurology, 35,* 866–874.

Bender, L. (1947). Childhood schizophrenia. Clinical study of one hundred schizophrenic children. *American Journal of Orthopsychiatry, 17,* 40–56.

Bettelheim, B. (1967). *The empty fortress: Infantile autism and the birth of the self.* New York: Free Press.

Birch, H. G., Richardson, S. A., Baird, D., Horobin, G., & Illsley, R. (1970). *Mental subnormality in the community: A clinical and epidemiological study.* Baltimore: Williams & Wilkins.

Blomquist, H. K., Bohman, M., Edvinsson, S. O., Gillberg, C., Gustavson, K. H., Holmgren, G., & Wahlstorm, J. (1985). Frequency of the fragile X syndrome in infantile autism: A Swedish multicenter study. *Clinical Genetics, 27,* 113–117.

Blomquist, H. K., Gustavson, K. H., Holmgren, G., Nordenson, I., & Palsson-Strae, U. (1983). Fragile X syndrome in mildly mentally retarded children in a northern Swedish county: A prevalence study. *Clinical Genetics, 24,* 393–399.

Blomquist, H. K., Gustavson, K. H., Holmgren, G., Nordenson, I., & Sweins, A. (1982). Fragile site X-chromosomes and X-linked mental retardation in severely retarded boys in a northern Swedish county: A prevalence study. *Clinical Genetics, 21,* 209–214.

Boullin, D. J., Coleman, M., O'Brien, R. A., & Rimland, B. (1971). Laboratory predictions of infantile autism, based on 5-hydroxytryptamine efflux from blood platelets and their correlation with the Rimland E2 scores. *Journal of Autism and Childhood Schizophrenia, 1,* 63–71.

Boullin, D. J., Freeman, B. J., Geller, E., Ritvo, E., Rutter, M., & Yuwiler, A. (1982). Toward the resolution of conflicting findings (Letter to the editor). *Journal of Autism and Developmental Disorders, 12,* 97–98.

Campbell, M. (1978). Pharmacotherapy. In M. Rutter & E. Schopler (Eds.), *Autism: A reappraisal of concepts and treatment.* New York: Plenum.

Cantor, S., Evans, J., Pearce, J., & Pezzot-Pearce, T. (1982). Childhood schizophrenia: Present but not accounted for. *American Journal of Psychiatry, 139*, 758–762.

Cantwell, D., & Baker, L. (1985). Speech and language: Development and disorders. In M. Rutter & L. Hersov (Eds.), *Child and adolescent psychiatry: Modern approaches* (2nd ed., pp. 526–544). Oxford: Blackwell.

Cantwell, D., Baker, L., Rutter, M., & Mawhood, L (1987). *A comparative follow-up study of infantile autism and developmental receptive dysphasia.* Submitted for publication.

Caparulo, B. K., Cohen, D. J., Young, G., Katz, J. D., Shaywitz, S. E., Shaywitz, B. A., & Rothman, S. L. (1981). Computed tomographic brain scanning in children with developmental neuropsychiatric disorders. *Journal of the American Academy of Child Psychiatry, 20*, 338–357.

Chess, S., Fernandez, P., & Korn, S. (1978). Behavioural consequences of congenital rubella. *Journal of Paediatrics, 93*, 699–703.

Chess S., Korn, S. J., & Fernandez, P. E. (1971). *Psychiatric disorders of children with congenital rubella.* New York: Brunner/Mazel.

Chick, J., Waterhouse, L., & Wolff, S. (1979). Psychological construing in schizoid children grown up. *British Journal of Psychiatry, 135*, 425–430.

Coleman, P. D., Romano, J., Lapham, L., & Simon, W. (1985). Cell counts in cerebral cortex of an autistic patient. *Journal of Autism and Developmental Disorders, 15*, 245–256.

Corbett, J. A. (1976). Medical management. In L. Wing (Ed.), *Early childhood autism: Clinical, educational and social aspects* (2nd ed.). New York: Pergamon.

Corbett, J., Harris, R., Taylor, E., & Trimble, M. (1977). Progressive disintegrative psychosis of childhood. *Journal of Child Psychology and Psychiatry, 18*, 211–219.

Creak, M. (1963). Childhood psychosis: A review of 100 cases. *British Journal of Psychiatry, 109*, 84–89.

Creasey, H., Rumsey, J. M., Schwartz, M., Duara, R., Rapoport, J. L., & Rapoport, S. I. (1986). Brain morphometry in autistic men as measured by volumetric computed tomography. *Archives of Neurology, 43*, 669–672.

Curtiss, S. (1977). *Genie: A psycholinguistic study of a modern-day "Wild Child."* London: Academic Press.

Damasio, H., Maurer, R. G., Damasio, A. R., & Chui, H. C. (1980). Computerized tomographic scan findings in patients with autistic behaviour. *Archives of Neurology, 37*, 504–510.

Darby, J. K. (1976). Neuropathologic aspects of psychosis in childhood. *Journal of Autism and Childhood Schizophrenia, 6*, 339–352.

Dawson, G. (1983). Lateralized brain function in autism: Evidence from the Halstead–Reitan neuropsychological battery. *Journal of Autism and Developmental Disorders, 13*, 369–386.

De Sanctis, S. (1906). On some varieties of dementia praecox. *Rivista Sperimentale di Freniatria, 32*, 141–165. Translated and reprinted in J. G. Howells (Ed.), *Modern perspectives in international child psychiatry.* Edinburgh: Oliver & Boyd.

Deykin, E. Y., & MacMahon, B. (1979). The incidence of seizures among children with autistic symptoms. *American Journal of Psychiatry, 136*, 1310–1312.

Deykin, E. Y., & MacMahon, B. (1980). Pregnancy, delivery and neonatal complications among autistic children. *American Journal of Diseases of Children, 134*, 860–864.

Eggers, C. (1978). Course and prognosis of childhood schizophrenia. *Journal of Autism and Childhood Schizophrenia, 8*, 21–36

Eisenberg, L. (1956). The autistic child in adolescence. *American Journal of Psychiatry, 112*, 607–612.

Eisenberg, L. (1972). The classification of childhood psychosis reconsidered. *Journal of Autism and Childhood Schizophrenia, 2*, 338–342.

Evans-Jones, L. G., & Rosenbloom, L. (1978). Disintegrative psychosis in childhood. *Developmental Medicine and Child Neurology, 20*, 462–470.

Fein, D., Skoff, B., & Mirsky, A. F. (1981). Clinical correlates of brain-stem dysfunction in autistic children. *Journal of Autism and Developmental Disorders, 11,* 303–316.

Ferrari, M., & Matthews, W.S. (1983). Self-recognition deficits in autism: Syndrome specific or general developmental delay? *Journal of Autism and Developmental Disorders, 13,* 317–324.

Finegan, J., & Quadrington, B. (1979). Pre-, peri- and neonatal factors and infantile autism. *Journal of Child Psychology and Psychiatry, 20,* 119–128.

Folstein, S., & Rutter, M. (1977). Infantile autism: A genetic study of 21 twin pairs. *Journal of Child Psychology and Psychiatry, 18,* 297–321.

Folstein, S., & Rutter, M. (1987). Autism: Familial aggregation and genetic implications. In E. Schopler & G. B. Mesibov (Eds.), *Neurobiological issues in autism.* New York and London: Plenum.

Freeman, B. J., Ritvo, E. R., Guthrie, D., Schroth, P., & Ball, J. (1978). The Behavior Observation Scale for Autism: Initial methodology, data analysis, and preliminary findings on 89 children. *Journal of the American Academy of Child Psychiatry, 17,* 576–588.

Freeman, B. J., Ritvo, E. R., & Schroth, P. C. (1984). Behaviour assessment of the syndrome of autism: Behavior Observation System. *Journal of the American Academy of Child Psychiatry, 23,* 588–594.

Frith, U. (1971). Spontaneous patterns produced by autistic, normal and subnormal children. In M. Rutter (Ed.), *Infantile autism: Concepts, characteristic and treatment.* London: Churchill Livingstone.

Fyffe, C., & Prior, M. R. (1978). Evidence of language recoding in autistic children: A re-examination. *British Journal of Psychiatry, 69,* 393–403.

Geller, E., Ritvo, E. R., Freeman, B. J., & Yuwiler, A. (1982). Preliminary observations of the effect of fenfluramine on blood serotonin and symptoms in three autistic boys. *New England Journal of Medicine, 307,* 165–169.

Gillberg, C. (1983). Identical triplets with infantile autism and the fragile-X syndrome. *British Journal of Psychiatry, 143,* 256–260.

Gillberg, C. & Forsell, C. (1984). Childhood psychosis and neurofibromatosis—More than a coincidence? *Journal of Autism and Developmental Disorders, 14,* 1–8.

Gillberg, C., & Gillberg, I. C. (1983). Infantile autism: A total population study of non-optimal, pre-, peri- and neonatal conditions. *Journal of Autism and Developmental Disorders, 13,* 153–166.

Gillberg, C., & Schaumann, H. (1981). Infantile autism and puberty. *Journal of Autism and Developmental Disorders, 11,* 356–371.

Gillberg, C., & Svendsen, P. (1983). Childhood psychosis and computed tomographic brain scan findings. *Journal of Autism and Developmental Disorders, 13,* 19–32.

Goldfine, P. E., McPherson, P. M., Heath, G. A., Hardesty, V. A., Beauregard, L. J., & Gordon, S. (1985). Association of fragile X syndrome with autism. *American Journal of Psychiatry, 142,* 108–110.

Green, W. H., Campbell, M., Hardesty, A. S., Grega, D. M., Padron-Gayol, M., Shell, J., & Erlenmeyer-Kimling, L. (1984). A comparison of schizophrenic and autistic children. *Journal of the American Academy of Child Psychiatry, 23,* 399–409.

Hagberg, B., Aicardi, J., Dias, K., & Ramos, O. (1983). A progressive syndrome of autism, dementia, ataxia, and loss of purposeful hand use in girls: Rett's syndrome: Report of 35 cases. *Annals of Neurology, 14,* 471–479.

Heller, T. (1930). About dementia infantilis. Reprinted in J. G. Howells (Ed.) (1969), *Modern perspectives in international child psychiatry.* Edinburgh: Oliver & Boyd.

Hemsley, R., Howlin, P., Berger, M., Hersov, L., Holbrook, D., Rutter, M., & Yule, W. (1978). Training autistic children in a family context. In M. Rutter & E. Schopler (Eds.), *Autism: A reappraisal of concepts and treatment.* New York: Plenum.

Hermelin, B., & O'Connor, N. (1970). *Psychological experiments with autistic children.* New York: Pergamon.

Herold, S., Frackowiak, R. S. J., Rutter M., & Howlin, P. (1986). Regional cerebral blood flow, oxygen and glucose metabolism in young autistic adults. *Journal of Cerebral Blood Flow and Metabolism, 5* (Suppl. 1), S189–S190.

Hobson, R. P. (1983). The autistic child's recognition of age-related features of people, animals and things. *British Journal of Developmental Psychology, 4*, 343–352.

Hobson, R. P. (1986). The autistic child's appraisal of expressions of emotion: An experimental investigation. *Journal of Child Psychology and Psychiatry, 27*, 321–342.

Howells, J. G., & Guirguis, W. R. (1984). Childhood schizophrenia 20 years later. *Archives of General Psychiatry, 41*, 123–128.

Howlin, P., & Rutter, M., with Hemsley, R., Berger, M., Hersov, L., & Yule, W. (in press). *Treatment of autistic children.* New York: Wiley.

James, A. L. & Barry, R. J. (1980). A review of psychophysiology in early onset psychosis. *Schizophrenia Bulletin, 6*, 506–525.

James, A. L., & Barry, R. J. (1983). Developmental effects in the cerebral lateralization of autistic, retarded and normal children. *Journal of Autism and Developmental Disorders, 13*, 43–56.

Kanner, L. (1943). Autistic disturbances of affective contact. *Nervous Child, 2*, 217–230.

Kanner, L. (1973). *Childhood psychosis: Initial studies and new insights.* Washington, DC: Winston.

Kolvin, I. (1971). Psychoses in childhood—A comparative study. In M. Rutter (Ed.), *Infantile autism: Concepts, characteristics and treatment.* London: Churchill Livingstone.

Kolvin, I. (1974). Research into childhood psychoses: A crosscultural comparison and commentary. *International Journal of Mental Health, 2*, 192–212.

Krug, D. A., Arick, J. R., & Almond, P. J. (1980). Behaviour checklist for identifying severely handicapped individuals with high levels of autistic behaviour. *Journal of Child Psychology and Psychiatry, 21*, 221–229.

Kydd, R. R., & Werry, J. S. (1982). Schizophrenia in children under 16 years. *Journal of Autism and Developmental Disorders, 12*, 343–358.

Largo, R. H., & Schinzel, A. (1985). Developmental and behavioural disturbances in 13 boys with fragile X syndrome. *European Journal of Paediatrics, 143*, 269–275.

Levitas, A., Hagerman, R. J., Braden, M., Rimland, B., McBog, P., & Matteus, I. (1983). Autism and fragile X syndrome. *Journal of Developmental and Behavioural Pediatrics, 3*, 151–158.

Lord, C., & Schopler, E. (1985). Differences in sex ratios in autism as a function of measured intelligence. *Journal of Autism and Developmental Disorders, 15*, 185–194.

Lord, C., Schopler, E., & Revick, D. (1982). Sex differences in autism. *Journal of Autism and Developmental Disorders, 12*, 317–330.

Lotter, V. (1974). Factors related to outcome in autistic children. *Journal of Autism and Childhood Schizophrenia, 4*, 263–277.

Makita, K. (1974). What is this thing called childhood schizophrenia? *International Journal of Mental Health, 2*, 179–193.

Malamud, N. (1959). Heller's disease and childhood schizophrenia. *American Journal of Psychiatry, 116*, 215–218.

Maudsley, H. (1867). *The physiology and pathology of the mind.* London: Macmillan.

Mrazek, D., & Mrazek, P. (1985). Child maltreatment. In M. Rutter & L. Hersov (Eds.), *Child and adolescent psychiatry: Modern approaches* (2nd ed.). Oxford: Blackwell.

Novic, J., Luchins, D. J., & Perline, R. (1984). Facial affect recognition in schizophrenia: Is there a differential deficit? *British Journal of Psychiatry, 144*, 533–537.

Novick, B., Kurtzberg, D., & Vaughn, H. G. (1979). An electrophysiologic indication of defective informate storage in childhood autism. *Psychiatric Research, 1*, 101–198.

Ornitz, E. M. (1978). Neurophysiologic studies. In M. Rutter & E. Schopler (Eds.), *Autism: A reappraisal of concepts and treatment.* New York: Plenum.

Parks, S. L. (1983). The assessment of autistic children: A selective review of available instruments. *Journal of Autism and Developmental Disorders, 13*, 255–267.

Paul, R., & Cohen, D. J. (1984). Outcomes of severe disorders of language acquisition. *Journal of Autism and Developmental Disorders, 14,* 405–422.

Paul, R., Cohen, D. J., & Caparulo, B. K. (1983). A longitudinal study of patients with severe developmental disorders of language learning. *Journal of the American Academy of Child Psychiatry, 22,* 525–534.

Petty, L., Ornitz, E. M., Michelman, J. D., & Zimmerman, E. G. (1984). Autistic children who become schizophrenic. *Archives of General Psychiatry, 41,* 129–135.

Prior, M. R., Tress, B., Hoffman, W. L., & Boldt, D. (1984). Computed tomographic study of children with classic autism. *Archives of Neurology, 41,* 482–484.

Peuschel, S. M., Herman, R., & Groden, G. (1985). Brief report: Screening children with autism for fragile-X syndrome and phenylketonuria. *Journal of Autism and Developmental Disorders, 15,* 335–338.

Richardson, S. A., Koller, H., Katz, M., & McLaren, J. (1980). Seizures and epilepsy in a mentally retarded population over the first 22 years of life. *Applied Research in Mental Retardation, 1,* 123–138.

Riikonen, R., & Amnell, G. (1981). Psychiatric disorders in children with earlier infantile spasms. *Developmental Medicine and Child Neurology, 23,* 747–760.

Rimland, B. (1971). The differentiation of childhood psychoses: An analysis of checklists for 2,218 psychotic children. *Journal of Autism and Childhood Schizophrenia, 1,* 161–174.

Rimland, B. (1984). Diagnostic checklist form E2: A reply to Parks. *Journal of Autism and Developmental Disorders, 14,* 343–345.

Ritvo, E. R., Freeman, B. J., Geller, E., & Yuwiler, A. (1983). Effects of fenfluramine on 14 outpatients with the syndrome of autism. *Journal of the American Academy of Child Psychiatry, 22,* 549–558.

Ritvo, E. R., Freeman, B. J., Mason-Brothers, A., Mo, A., & Ritvo, A. M. (1985). Concordance for the syndrome of autism in 40 pairs of afflicted twins. *American Journal of Psychiatry, 142,* 74–77.

Ritvo, E. R., Spence, M. A., Freeman, B. J., Mason-Brothers, A., Mo, A., & Marazita, M. L. (1985). Evidence for autosomal recessive inheritance in 46 families with multiple incidences of autism. *American Journal of Psychiatry, 142,* 187–191.

Rosenbloom, S., Campbell, M. George, A. E., Kricheff, I., Taleporos, E., Anderson, L., Reuben, R. N., & Korein, J. (1984). High resolution CT scanning in infantile autism: A quantitative appraoch. *Journal of the American Academy of Child Psychiatry, 23,* 72–77.

Rosenblum, S. M., Arick, J. R., Krug, D. A., Stubbs, E. G., Young, N. B., & Pelson, R. O. (1980). Auditory brain-stem-evoked responses in autistic children. *Journal of Autism and Developmental Disorders, 10,* 215–226.

Rumsey, J. M., Duara, R., Grady, C., Rapoport, J. L., Margolin, R. A., Rapoport, S. I., & Cutler, N. R. (1985). Brain metabolism in autism: Resting cerebral glucose utilization as measured with positron emission tomography (PET). *Archives of General Psychiatry, 15,* 448–457.

Ruttenberg, B. A., Dratman, M. L., Fraknoi, J., & Wenar, C. (1966). An instrument for evaluating autistic children. *Journal of the American Academy of Child Psychiatry, 5,* 453–478.

Rutter, M. (1970). Autistic children: Infancy to adulthood. *Seminars in Psychiatry, 2,* 435–450.

Rutter, M. (1972). Childhood schizophrenia reconsidered. *Journal of Autism and Childhood Schizophrenia, 2,* 315–337.

Rutter, M. (1974). The development of infantile autism. *Psychological Medicine, 4,* 147–163.

Rutter, M. (1978). Diagnosis and definition. In M. Rutter & E. Schopler (Eds.), *Autism: A reappraisal of concepts and treatment.* New York: Plenum.

Rutter, M. (1979). Language, cognition and autism. In R. Katzman (Ed.), *Congenital and acquired cognitive disorders.* New York: Raven Press.

Rutter, M. (1981). *Maternal deprivation reassessed* (2nd ed.). Harmondsworth, England: Penguin.

Rutter, M. (1983). Cognitive deficits in the pathogenesis of autism. *Journal of Child Psychology and Psychiatry, 24*, 513–531.

Rutter, M. (1984). Infantile autism. In D. Shaffer, A. Erhardt, & L. Greenhill (Eds.), *A clinician's guide to child psychiatry*. New York: Free Press.

Rutter, M. (1985a). Infantile autism and other pervasive developmental disorders. In M. Rutter & L. Hersov (Eds.), *Child and adolescent psychiatry: Modern approaches* (2nd ed.). Oxford: Blackwell.

Rutter, M. (1985b). The treatment of autistic children. *Journal of Child Psychology and Psychiatry, 26*, 193–214.

Rutter, M., & Garmezy, N. (1983). Developmental psychopathology. In E. M. Hetherington (Ed.), *Socialization, personality, and social development* (Vol. 4, *Mussen's handbook of child psychology*, 4th ed., pp. 775–911). New York: Wiley.

Rutter, M., & Gould, M. (1985). Classification. In M. Rutter & L. Hersov (Eds.), *Child and adolescent psychiatry: Modern approaches* (2nd ed.). Oxford: Blackwell.

Schopler, E. (1983). New developments in the definition and disgnosis of autism. In B. B. Lahey & A. E. Kazdin (Eds.), *Advances in clinical child psychology*. (Vol. 6). New York: Plenum.

Schopler, E., Mesibov, G., & Baker, A. (1982). Evaluation of treatment for autistic children and their parents. *Journal of the American Academy of Child Psychiatry, 21*, 262–267.

Schopler, E., Reichler, R. J., DeVellis, R. F., & Daly, K. (1980). Toward objective classification of childhood autism: Childhood Autism Rating Scale (CARS). *Journal of Autism and Developmental Disorders, 10*, 91–103.

Schopler, E., Reichler, R. J., & Renner, B. R. (1985). *Childhood Autism Rating Scale (CARS)*. New York: Irvington Publishers.

Schopler, E., & Rutter, M. (1978). Subgroups vary with selection purpose. In M. Rutter & E. Schopler (Eds.), *Autism: A reappraisal of concepts and treatment*. New York: Plenum.

Scott, D. W. (1985). Asperger's syndrome and non-verbal connunications: A pilot study. *Psychological Medicine, 15*, 683–687.

Skoff, B. F., Mirsky, A. F., & Turner, D. (1980). Prolonged brain-stem transmission time in autism. *Psychiatric Research, 2*, 157–166.

Skuse, D. (1984). Extreme deprivation in early childhood: I. Diverse outcomes for three siblings from an extraordinary family. *Journal of Child Psychology and Psychiatry, 26*, 523–541.

Spence, M. A., Ritvo, E. R., Marazita, M. L., Funderburk, S. J., Sparkes, R. S., & Freeman, B. J. (1985). Gene mapping studies with the syndrome of autism. *Behaviour Genetics, 15*, 1–13.

Spiker, D., & Ricks, M. (1984). Developmental relationships in self-recognition: A study of 52 autistic children. *Child Development, 1984, 55*, 214–225.

Taft, L. T., & Cohen, H. J. (1971). Hypsarrhythmia and infantile autism: A clinical report. *Journal of Autism and Childhood Schizophrenia, 1*, 327–336.

Tanguay, P. E. (1984). Toward a new classification of serious psychopathology in children. *Journal of the American Academy of Child Psychiatry, 23*, 373–384.

Tinbergen, N., & Tinbergen, E. A. (1983). *"Autistic children": New hope for a cure*. London: G. Allen & Unwin.

Torrey, E. F., Hersh, S. P., & McCabe, K. D. (1975). Early childhood psychosis and bleeding during pregnancy. *Journal of Autism and Childhood Schizophrenia, 5*, 287–297.

Tsai, L., Stewart, M. A., & August, G. (1981). Implication of sex differences in the familial transmission of infantile autism. *Journal of Autism and Developmental Disorders, 11*, 165–173.

Venter, P. A., Hof, J. O., Coetzee, D. J., Van der Walt, C., & Retief, A. E. (1984). No marker (X) syndrome in autistic children. *Human Genetics, 67*, 107.

Walker, E., Bettes, B., & McGuire, M. (1984). Recognition and identification of facial stimuli by schizophrenics and patients with affective disorder. *British Journal of Clinical Psychology, 23*, 37–44.

Watson, M. S., Leckman, J. F., Annex, B., Breg, W. R., Boles, D., Volkmar, F. R., Cohen, D. J., & Carter, C. (1984). Fragile X in a survey of 75 autistic males. *New England Journal of Medicine, 310*, 1462.

Williams, R. S., Hauser, S. L., Purpura, D., Delong, R., & Swisher, C. N. (1980). Autism and mental retardation: neuropathological studies performed in four retarded persons with autistic behavior. *Archives of Neurology, 37*, 749–753.

Wing, L. (1981). Language, social, and cognitive impairments in autism and severe mental retardation. *Journal of Autism and Developmental Disorders, 11*, 31–44.

Wing, L., & Gould, J. (1978). Systematic recording of behaviors and skills of retarded and psychotic children. *Journal of Autism and Childhood Schizophrenia, 8*, 79–97.

Wing, L., & Gould, J. (1979). Severe impairments of social interaction and associated abnormalities in children: Epidemiology and classification. *Journal of Autism and Developmental Disorders, 9*, 11–30.

Wolff, S., & Barlow, A. (1979). Schizoid personality in childhood: A comparative study of schizoid, autistic and normal children. *Journal of Child Psychology and Psychiatry, 20*, 19–46.

Wolff. S., & Chick, J. (1980). Schizoid personality in childhood: A controlled follow-up study. *Psychological Medicine, 10*, 85–100.

World Health Organization. (1978). *International classification of diseases* (9th ed.). Geneva: Author.

Yule, W. (1978). Research methodology: What are the "correct controls"? In M. Rutter & E. Schopler (Eds.), *Autism: A reappraisal of concepts and treatment*. New York: Plenum.

IV

EPILOGUE

14

DIAGNOSIS AND CLASSIFICATION: SOME OUTSTANDING ISSUES

MICHAEL RUTTER
A. HUSSAIN TUMA

INTRODUCTION

Earlier chapters in this volume document the substantial progress that has been made in the fields of measurement, diagnosis, and classification of psychopathology in childhood and adolescence. This is evident in advances in theoretical models of psychopathology, in the major systems of diagnosis and classification, in the measurement of children's behavior in different settings, and in the assessment of people's attitudes and expectations. In this epilogue we highlight only a few of these developments in order to discuss some of the major unresolved problems that require further research

Moderate interrater reliability has been found for most of the major diagnostic groupings in current classification systems when this has been studied by means of case history exercises. However, the reliabilities have been substantially lower than those usually obtained by clinical researchers. The higher reliabilities generally found in the research setting probably stem from several rather different considerations. First, researchers usually carry out standardized diagnostic interviews and/or observations. Reliability is as much a function of the diagnostic tools used as the classification system that is employed. Second, reliability can be much improved by systematic training in the use of classification systems (as shown, for example, by studies of attention deficit disorders; see Prendergast et al., 1987). Both considerations have implications for clinical training and practice. But, in addition, it may well be that reliability is lowered as a result of the limitations that are inherent in the use of written case summaries. Inevitably they contain far less

Michael Rutter. Department of Child and Adolescent Psychiatry, University of London Institute of Psychiatry, London, England.

A. Hussain Tuma. Western Psychiatric Institute and Clinic, University of Pittsburgh, Pittsburgh, Pennsylvania.

information than that obtained in a regular clinical assessment. This possibility suggests the need to explore the use of videotaped interviews and observations in future reliability studies.

The several chapters in the middle section of this volume amply document the advances that have been made in the measurement of behavior (using interviews, questionnaires, and direct observations), as well as in laboratory techniques for assessing psychobiological processes, and in procedures for the study of family functioning. These methods still have limitations, and require further development but they are sufficiently powerful for efficient use in many situations. Nevertheless, there is a need for continuing methodological development. The pressure to produce reliable diagnostic instruments has led to an increasing reliance on highly structured questionnaire-style interviews. There can be no doubt that they have provided important advances in large scale general population studies. Yet, questions remain on the extent to which they entail a loss of clinical penetration; a loss that derives both from the necessary reliance on the subject's (rather than the clinician's) ability to differentiate between various facets of behavior and from the lack of use of observational data. Perhaps that is particularly the case with interviews with young children. Further work is needed to assess the merits and demerits of different styles of interviewing different subject groups for different purposes.

An additional problem stems from the fact that many of the available standard interview schedules are tied to particular diagnostic classification systems. This is shown in the content of the areas covered, in the formulation of screening questions, and in the diagnostic hierarchies employed. For example, little attention is paid to the pervasiveness or situation specificity of deviant behaviors, to their developmental appropriateness, or to factors that influence their expression—variables that may well be of some clinical importance (Rutter & Garmezy, 1983). Systems of classification inevitably will change as knowledge advances. Even the diagnoses that seem most satisfactory now are unlikely to prove wholly correct in their definitions once satisfactory validating data are available. It is crucial that our diagnostic tools have sufficient flexibility to adapt to these changes in classification criteria and rules. Of course, often, it will be just a matter of altering the relevant algorithm but still it is crucial to ensure that the component "bits" of any diagnostic interview or observation protocol are based on discrete behaviors rather than on currently fashionable diagnostic concepts or composites.

COMORBIDITY OR MIXED DISORDERS

It is also important that the measures are such that they can be used to test the advantages and disadvantages of particular approaches to classification. For example, DSM-III and ICD-9 differ in their approach to multiple diagnoses (Rutter & Gould, 1985). ICD-9 is based on the medically traditional assumption that in most cases there is just *one* syndrome, in spite of the fact that it is common for each to include quite diverse manifestations. Thus, psychiatrists are expected to use the overall pattern of clinical findings to decide whether the preponderant picture is that of an anxiety state, major depression, autism or schizophrenia. In any individual case, the differential diagnosis may be difficult, but the expectation is that ordinarily there will be just one disorder. As in internal medicine, it is entirely possible to have two or more conditions concurrently but the assumption is that multiple diagnosis will be the exception rather than the rule. DSM-III makes no such assumption. Instead, each diagnosis has a particular set of rules requiring the presence of certain specified behaviors. The consequence is that with mixed clinical pictures (a very frequent occurrence in child psychiatry), it will be common for children to have several different, but concurrent, diagnoses. The effect is that the same children included in one study as depressed may well be included in another investigation as having a conduct disorder or an attention deficit syndrome. That follows from the consistent finding that many children show quite heterogeneous clinical pictures that fulfill several different sets of diagnostic criteria.

It is by no means self-evident which approach is to be preferred. Intuitively, there seems good sense to the ICD-9 assumption that a mixed clinical picture is more likely to mean a single disorder with varied manifestations than that the child coincidentally happens to have three or four separate disorders at the same time. However, in most cases we lack the evidence to decide which behavioral constellation should have priority. Moreover, in practice the need to place most weight on the clinical features that are most prominent at the moment means that the diagnosis for any one individual with a chronic or recurrent condition tend to change over time—even though, almost certainly, the disorder does not (Zeitlin, 1986).

The DSM-III solution of allowing multiple diagnoses seems attractive in its avoidance of the need to make arbitrary decisions on which symptoms should have precedence. However, the consequence is an inevitable blurring of diagnostic distinctions, a blurring that arises because the *same* children will appear in several supposedly quite different diagnostic groupings.

At least three very different solutions may be considered. First, there could be a marked cut in the number of diagnostic categories, so reducing the problem of overlap. Almost certainly both ICD-9 and DSM-III have more categories than can be justified on the basis of either reliability or validity data. Nevertheless, the degree of reduction required to obviate the problem of diagnostic overlap would be so great as to involve an unacceptable loss of diagnostic precision. Second, there could be a move away from a categorical classification to a dimensional system. That may well be desirable for some purposes but, at least in some circumstances, syndromic patterns or behavioral composites may have a meaning that is different from that deriving from the linear combinations of dimensional measures (Hinde & Dennis, 1986; Magnusson, 1987). Third, mixed diagnostic categories could be retained both in order to maintain the "purity" of diagnostic distinctions and as a reminder that we lack the data to decide how to deal with them. Much of the difficulty stems from the fact that our diagnoses are based on the presenting clinical symptoms and not on any validated unifying psychopathological concept. Clearly, the matter of how to deal with mixed clinical pictures in classification schemes is one that warrants serious research investment in the future.

DIMENSIONS OR CATEGORIES

Already we have considerable research data to validate many of the diagnostic distinctions in the prevailing psychiatric classification schemes (Rutter & Gould, 1985). Some of these findings are mentioned in the chapters reviewing depressive disorders, autism, and attention deficit syndromes. However, much more evidence is available. For example, the traditional distinctions between mild and severe mental retardation (made originally on IQ levels) is supported by the major differences between the two categories on organic brain damage, fertility, mortality, social class, family history, psychiatric correlates, scholastic attainment, employment, and adult adjustment (Rutter & Gould, 1985). Similarly, the differentiation between the global diagnostic grouping of emotional disturbances and conduct disorders is validated by the findings on sex distribution, family characteristics, educational correlates, and adult outcome. However, the validating evidence mainly applies to broadly defined diagnostic grouping and not to the finer subdivisions found in both the third edition of the *Diagnostic and Statistical Manual of Mental Disorders* (DSM-III) of the American Psychiatric Association (1980) and the ninth edition of the *International Classification of Diseases* (ICD-9) of the World Health Organization (1978). Thus, we lack data on the value of the differentiation between emotional disorders with an onset specific to childhood and adult-type neurotic conditions, and on the value of subcategorization of different types of emotional disorder.

Too many challenges remain for it to be helpful to review them comprehensively, or even to list them all. But some of the main issues may be highlighted. To begin with, there is the basic question of whether the most appropriate classification scheme is categorical or dimensional. Psychologists have long pointed out both the loss of information in categorical approaches and the arbitrariness of many of the cut offs. Dimensional schemes would avoid the difficulty inherent in deciding how severe a depression (or fear or conduct disturbance) must be to count as a "case"—a prevailing problem in psychiatry but one that occurs in internal medicine as well (Rutter & Sandberg, 1985). As already noted, in addition they would circumvent the problem of how to deal with mixed clinical pictures. On the other hand, they assume that variables have the same meaning throughout the distribution, a consistency that may not be present. We have already noted the extensive evidence that there is a discontinuity in intelligence—where severe mental handicap differs in kind, and not just degree, from normal intelligence. The same probably applies to severe developmental language disorders (which tend to be associated with a range of persisting psychological problems; see Yule & Rutter, 1987), to nocturnal enuresis (where the spontaneous remission rate reaches a plateau after age 5 years or so; see Oppel, Harper, & Rider, 1968), and to the conditions such as schizophrenia or autism that probably involve qualitative rather than quantitative departures from normality. A further limitation of dimensional schemes is that classification is necessarily cumbersome to apply to individuals (thus, instead of a single main category there would be scores on some dozen or so different dimensions).

The dichotomy between dimensional and categorical approaches is not as clear-cut as it seems at first sight, however. Usually dimensions are translatable into categories, and vice versa. Intelligence and mental handicap constitute a good illustration. Moreover, that example emphasizes that often it may be useful to retain both approaches for different purposes. The categorical distinctions between severe and mild mental retardation and between both of these and normality are powerful and useful for etiological and service planning purposes. Nevertheless, within the normal range, IQ is best treated as a dimensional variable. Even in the abnormal range, the IQ level is a useful indicator in designing educational, care, and rehabilitation programs. Similarly, in respiratory medicine the dimensional variable of respiratory air flow is a better predictor for some purposes than the disease categorization of asthma, emphysema, or chronic bronchitis (Fletcher, Peto, Tinker & Speizer, 1976). We are beginning to see formal efforts at this type of integration in psychiatry as illustrated in DSM-III-R, which provides a global scale for evaluating psychological, social, and occupational functioning along a continuum of mental health–illness. The best mix of categorical and dimensional approaches has yet to be determined but the answer is likely to be a mix rather than an exclusive preference for one over the other.

MULTICATEGORY OR MULTIAXIAL CLASSIFICATION

A further choice is required between the traditional multicategory classification scheme and the multiaxial approaches that have become popular in recent years. It may be expected that the latter are here to stay because they are easy to apply and correspond to the usual clinical style. However, more importantly, they recognize that diagnosis commonly involves several distinct aspects (or axes) that are not alternatives to one another. Thus, autism refers to a pattern of behavioral *deviance*, whereas mental handicap refers to a *level* of functioning. A child may be diagnosed as having either, both, or neither. The two aspects reflect quite different qualities, information on which is cruical for clinical purposes. Accordingly, it is desirable to have separate axes for psychiatric disorder and for mental handicap (or intellectual level).

Most multiaxial schemes have an axis for medical syndromes. It might be thought that this should supercede the psychiatric axis when it is known that the mental disorder has a specific medical etiology, on the grounds that etiology is the crucial differentiating feature. However, although etiology is crucial, it is not a sufficient differentiating feature. For example, the fragile X anomaly may give rise to mental handicap without autism, autism without mental handicap, autism plus mental retardation, or occasionally, even normality. A failure to record and classify the resulting disorder would mean a major loss of clinically important information. By the same token, of course, it would be a serious failure not to note the chromosomal basis of the mental disorder. Similarly, a severe brain injury may give rise to an acute reversible confusional state, a permanent dementia, or a frontal-lobe syndrome of socioemotional disinhibition. The clinical implications are quite different according to which it is.

There is a general wish to see an axis for abnormal psychosocial situations because of the importance of psychosocial factors in etiology, in prognosis, and in the planning of therapeutic interventions. However, an adequate classification of psychosocial factors has yet to be devised. The axis in DSM-III had been little researched until fairly recently (Williams, 1985), but it seems unsound in concept (see Cantwell, Chapter 1, this volume). The stipulation that stressors should be coded only if they are judged to be etiologically important introduces value judgments that make the axis inappropriate for research purposes (Schrader, Gordon, & Harcourt, 1986). Moreover, the guidelines on rating severity lack empirical support and assume a uniform mode of operation for all stressors. Clearly, major revisions are required. The approach in the ICD-9 scheme is somewhat more in keeping with the research findings on psychosocial influences, but it has an unacceptably low reliability and an uncertain validity. A radical revision with an improved conceptualizaion and guidelines on usage has been prepared by van Goor-Lambo, Orley, Poustka, and Rutter (1986), but its systematic testing is still in the planning stage. It seeks to deal with some of the major issues that have bedeviled psychosocial classifications up to now. These include a clear specification of the time period to which it applies, the level of abnormality/severity required for coding, the concept reflected in each category, and the operational criteria to be applied. The revised scheme also allows for separate codings on each and every one of the psychosocial categories rather than forcing a choice of the most important features; this seems desirable in view of the frequency with which abnormal psychosocial situations involve several different types of abnormality.

A further need that has been recognized is an adequate data base for making any classification of psychosocial features. It was demonstrated some years ago that research instruments could produce reliable and valid assessments even of features as subtle as warmth, hostility and the quality of the marital relationships (Brown & Rutter, 1966; Quinton, Rutter, & Rowlands, 1976; Rutter & Brown, 1966; see Jacob & Tennenbaum, Chapter 7, this volume, for a review of currently available measures). However, these rely heavily on training (together with specially designed measures), and usually they require an investment of time greater than that available in routine clinical evaluations. Van Goor-Lambo *et al.* (1986) have set themselves the task of specifying the information demands of the revised psychosocial classification and of devising a clinically applicable interview schedule to produce such information. How far these modifications will improve the classification remains to be seen, but there can be no doubt that major improvements are needed in order for it to be serviceable.

The value of other axes of classification remains uncertain. DSM-III has an axis for previous level of adaptive functioning. This seems potentially valuable as a measure of premorbid state, but at present its construction is not optimal for this purpose (Rutter & Shaffer, 1980). Nevertheless, further development of this axis seems likely to be worthwhile.

DIAGNOSTIC MEASURES

As the chapters in Part II of this volume indicate, there is now a wide range of available diagnostic measures, and for most purposes these measures will suffice. There are substantial disadvantages to the unnecessary proliferation of measures, with each clinical or research group using a set that differs from those employed by others. There is a great need for comparability across studies and this can be accomplished by standard use of existing methods and procedures. Nevertheless, it is clear that in some areas new or improved instruments are needed.

Thus the highly structured diagnostic interviews seem least satisfactory for the detection of depressive disorders in young children. The pioneering studies using the DISC and the Kiddie-SADS (see Edelbrock & Costello, Chapter 4, this volume) have blazed the trail; however, now that the way ahead has been shown, it is necessary for refinements to be introduced so as to remedy the demonstrated limitations of the available interviews. It is clear from what has been done already that an enormous amount can be gained from talking with children and from asking them directly about possible symptoms. There need no longer be a reluctance to use this direct approach, and indeed it is evident that a total reliance on information from parents is no longer acceptable in most circumstances. However, the cognitive and emotional immaturities of young children mean that the approach cannot be the same as with adults (Kovacs, 1986). This is especially the case with preschool children, to whom none of the standard interviews is readily applicable. Further research is needed to determine the most appropriate interview style for preschoolers and to develop interview protocols.

DSM-III introduced a new category of reactive attachment disorder. There were criticisms of the specific criteria for this hypothesized syndrome (Rutter & Shaffer, 1980) and there was a paucity of data on how it should be conceptualized and defined. Nevertheless, the category constituted a necessary addition. It had become apparent that many children who suffer gross abuse or neglect develop a socioemotional disorder (Mrazek & Mrazek, 1985) that does not fit the criteria for any of the other psychiatric conditions arising in childhood. Since DSM-III was published, better evidence has become available on this behavioral pattern (Crittenden, 1985; Main & George, 1985). It appears that the abnormality in selective attachment is rather different from the relatively common insecure attachment as assessed from Ainsworth's strange situation (Campos, Barrett, Lamb, Goldsmith, & Stenberg, 1983), but also it seems to arise in response to severe parental depression as well as physical abuse (Radke-Yarrow, Cummings, Kuczynski, & Chapman, 1985). Not surprisingly, therefore, the draft of the World Health Organization's ICD-10 has also added a category for this group of social disorders (Rutter, 1986). Clearly, further investigations are required so that the syndrome can be more accurately pinpointed. Particularly as it arises in very young children, there is a need to develop new measures of assessment. Whether these should be primarily based on interviews, observations, or experimental situations remains uncertain.

Attention deficit disorders raise a rather different issue. They are defined in behavioral terms, but the prevailing concept is that they arise on the basis of an abnormality in information processing. As Taylor (1986; Chapter 12, this volume) discusses, there is an essential ambiguity in the way in which disordered attention is used both as a psychological description and as a supposed indicator of an hypothesized underlying physiological deficit. To what extent the elucidation of psychological–physiological links in the field of attention requires improved methods of measurement is not apparent. However, it is clear that a degree of standardization of measurement would help comparability across studies, that we need to know how different measures relate to one another, and that it is crucial to determine whether the attentional problems found in so many psychiatric disorders are similar in kind or whether there are important diagnostic specificities in the types of attentional problems associated with different psychiatric syndromes.

Autistic disorders raise yet another set of measurements issues. As Rutter and Schopler (Chapter 13, this volume) indicate, a variety of interview and observation measures are available. These have proved reasonably satisfactory for the differentiation of autism from other disorders. However, most were developed for prime use in the planning of psychoeducational interventions with mentally retarded groups and they may have limitations when applied to older, more intelligent subjects. Moreover, they may lack the discriminative power required for the effective subcategorization of autistic disorders. We need to know, for example, whether the behavioral pattern seen in autism associated with the fragile X anomaly is the same as or different from that found in idiopathic autism. Also, genetic studies of both twins and families indicate that autism is associated with a wider range of cognitive and social disorders in cotwins and other family members (Folstein & Rutter, 1987). So far it is not apparent what is distinctive about these associated disorders. There is a need to move from global concepts of social or language impairment to a more specific delineation of the particular types of social or linguistic deviance that are diagnostic of autism, and to determination of the pathognomonic features of the process abnormality (if they exist). Some progress has been made in the development of measures that might go some way toward that goal (see Rutter *et al.*, in press) but it remains to be seen how far they achieve their purpose.

DIAGNOSTIC DIFFERENTIATION

It is apparent throughout the book that although much has been achieved in the validation of diagnostic categories in child psychopathology, even more remains to be accomplished. Autism constitutes a valid category, but major questions concerning its boundaries and its heterogeneity remain. Hyperactivity/attention deficit disorders probably include a valid syndrome but, at least as judged from the currently available evidence, it is unlikely to coinicide exactly with the definitions employed by either DSM-III or ICD-9. The concept of depressive disorder in adult life has received substantial validation, and it seems likely that valid distinctive syndromes also occur in childhood. However, numerous questions remain unresolved and there are major uncertainties on the definition of affective disturbances in young children. These are the areas discussed in some detail in Part III of this volume; however, as the studies of classification that were reviewed in earlier chapters showed, they are by no means the most problematic diagnostic categories.

Epidemiologic studies show that the two overall categories of emotional disturbances and conduct disorder account for the bulk of psychiatirc disorders occurring in childhood (Graham, 1979; Yule, 1981). The validity of the differentiation between them is well demonstrated, but we lack knowledge on how to subdivide these two large groupings. Traditionally, a distinction is drawn between those emotional disorders that are specific to childhood and adult-type neurotic disorders. The reason for the differentiation is clear to see; most children with emotional disorders grow up to be normal adults, and many neurotic conditions do not have an onset until adult life (Rutter, 1984). But how do you tell in advance which emotional disturbances in childhood constitute the precursors of adult neurotic conditions? We do not know. The draft guidelines for ICD-10 (Rutter, 1986) suggest that age-appropriate exaggerations of normal developmental trends (such as extreme separation anxiety in preschoolers but not in adolescents) may constitute the childhood-specific varieties. There is limited evidence in support (such as the better prognosis for school refusal in young children compared with adolescents; see Rodriguez, Rodriguez, & Eisenberg, 1959), but that method of differentiation remains untested. Obviously, too, there are difficulties yet to be resolved in the criteria for what are and are not exaggerations of normal age trends. Perhaps, too, a distinction needs to be drawn between states of generalized anxiety and situation-specific or object-focus phobias. However, with the possible exception of obsessional disorders, there is little evidence in support of the subcategorization of emotional disorders. The form often changes over time with substantial interchangeability between the supposedly different types of emotional disorder. Much remains to be done in the study of this group of conditions.

A related issue, applicable to both childhood and adult life, concerns the validity of differentiations between anxiety and depression (Stavrakaki & Vargo, 1986). There is no doubt that patients often show a mixture of two. Yet twin studies suggest that genetically they may not be the same (Torgersen, 1985); the temporal continuities differ (Rutter, 1984); and anxiety states seem not to show the rise in frequency during adolescence that is found with depression (Rutter & Garmezy, 1983). Anxiety disorders in childhood have been subjected to very little study up to now (Gittelman, 1986). They tend to be thought of as psychic disorders without an organic component; however, there is good evidence of a neurobiological substrate (Gray, 1982), anxiety states in adolescence have been linked with neurological "soft" signs in childhood (Shaffer et al., 1985), and there are associations with temperamental and physiological variables (Reznick et al., 1986). How these findings should be used to define diagnostic categories remains uncertain, and further research is required.

The situation with conduct disorder remains equally unsatisfactory. It seems that there is considerable heterogeneity within this very broad grouping (see Rutter & Giller, 1983), but there is little agreement on how it should be subdivided because of a lack of information on the sources or meaning of the heterogeneity. Several possible distinctions need to be considered. First, there is a need to differentiate between those conduct disorders that constitute transient problems during childhood and/or adolescence and those that represent the precursors of sociopathic or personality disorders in adult life. The latter tend to have an onset earlier in childhood, to involve a more varied and wider range of disruptive and delinquent behaviors, to extend across a multiplicity of situations, and to be associated with poor interpersonal relationships (Loeber, 1982; Rutter, 1984). The last feature has tended to provide the defining criteria for the subcategory of "unsocialized" conduct disorders (Henn, Bardwell, & Jenkins, 1980), but the reliability of this category leaves something to be desired and it is evident that an improved conceptualization, including a more satisfactory definition, is needed. Second, it seems that some conduct disorders represent a more focused representation of hostility or resentment rather than delinquency or personality disturbance. Moore, Chamberlain, and Mukai (1979) found that aggression (by implication in the family) unassociated with stealing did not predict later delinquency. However, maybe it is not the absence of stealing that is critical but the confinement of the disorder to the home. Thus, children sometimes steal only from a resented stepparent as a way of expressing their anger (Rich, 1956). Perhaps it would be useful separately to categorize conduct disorders that are restricted to the family setting or are specifically targeted on a particular person or persons. It is generally accepted that there is a need to subdivide the broad group of conduct disorders, but we lack knowledge on how best to do so. Research to test and compare different approaches should be rewarding. However, as judged by past research, the solution is *not* likely to be found in the particular constellation of socially disapproved or delinquent behaviors. Rather, it will be necessary to assess such items as age of onset, problems in interpersonal relationships, situation specificity or pervasiveness, and focus or target of the conduct disturbance. In addition, it may be worthwhile to consider the presence or absence of hyperactivity, inattention, aggressiveness, and physiological unresponsiveness. Such considerations would extend into the domain of attention deficit disorders—a reminder that their differentiation from conduct disorders remains a crucial item on the research agenda.

The field of specific developmental disorders is another where numerous diagnostic and classificatory issues remain to be resolved. There are two key dilemmas: the differentiation from normal variation and subclassification. It is well documented that there is a wide range of normal variation in the ages at which children pass any particular developmental milestones (such as walking without support or first use of meaningful words). Yet marked delays are associated with a high rate of persistent socioemotional and educational difficulties (see Yule & Rutter, 1987). The validity of the concept of pathological varieties of specific developmental delay is well established (Smith, 1986). Nevertheless, the problem remains of how to differentiate these from normal variation. The severity of the specific delay or impairment helps in that the further the departure from the mean of the normal range, the more likely it is that the problem represents some form of pathology. Nevertheless, that is unsatisfactory as a sole criterion for two different reasons. First, in the absence of adequate psychometric standardization data, it is impossible to produce a clinically usable cutoff that applies in the same way across all age groups. Second, severity in itself is not an adequate criterion, as reference to the parallel situation with height indicates. Not all individuals with the XYY chromosome anomaly are clearly beyond the normal range of height; conversely, some extremely tall individuals are genetically normal. The same applies with dwarfism. Severity is an excellent screening indicator, but it cannot be a diagnostic criterion in itself. The draft guidelines for ICD-10 (Rutter, 1986) suggest several other criteria that may be taken into account. These include whether the pattern of development is deviant as well as delayed, whether there are associated abnormalities in other psychological functions (socioemotional or cognitive), and historical course. However, the adequacy of these guidelines has yet to be put to the test.

Finally, the topic of disorders in the infancy and preschool age periods should be mentioned (Emde, 1985; Richman, 1985). At one time many people supposed that psychopathological problems in early life were of little moment in terms of later development. It is now clear that that was a mistaken assumption. Richman, Stevenson, and Graham's (1982) epidemiologic follow-up study from 3 to 8 years showed a relatively high level of persistence. The degree of persistence varied with the pattern of symptomatology (e.g., overactivity was prognostic of a poor outcome in boys), but we lack an adequate scheme for diagnosing disorders in very young children (outside the realm of autistic conditions). The new social categories of attachment disorder help, but they do not encompass the bulk of problems in this age period. Once more, further research is indicated.

MULTIPLE APPROACHES TO DIAGNOSIS

For the most part, current systems of classification pay little attention to the sources and types of data used in diagnosis. Although this may represent the current state of the art, it is unlikely to remain so. Many disorders in young people show substantial situation specificity. What implications does this have for the psychological mechanisms that are involved? An increased understanding of person–environment interactions will depend on more discriminating measures of both situations and children's behavior. It was for this reason that chapters on observational methods and on family assessments (Chapters 6 and 7, respectively) were included, in addition to those on interviews (Chapter 4) and rating scales (Chapter 5). However, a more effective triangulation on diagnosis may be obtained by combining behavioral data with neurobiological, physiological, and psychometric measures; hence the appraisals of some aspects of these approaches in Chapters 8 and 9. At present, there have been few attempts to bring together these different aspects of measurement for diagnostic purposes, and it remains to be seen what could be achieved in this regard. However, it is evident that this should be attempted.

BIOLOGICAL VALIDATION

Up to now it has been necessary to define diagnostic categories in child psychiatry in behavioral terms, with validation largely based on features such as clinical course and family correlates. This has worked well enough as a rough-and-ready means of sorting out broad diagnostic groupings, but it is likely that research advances in the future will require different approaches. Thus, in internal medicine, diseases have been redefined once knowledge on the underlying processes has become available. Thyrotoxicosis is no longer defined on the basis of tremulousness, loss of weight, and staring eyes; rather the key criterion is abnormal circulating thyroxin levels. Will the same apply with child and adolescent psychopathology? It is not likely that all, or even most disorders, could be reconceptualized in disease state terms. Some problems represent exaggerations of normal developmental trends and others are closely connected to ongoing disturbed family interactions, without any necessary implication of disordered individual pathology in the sense implied by disease concepts.

Of course, that is not to say that individual characteristics do not play a role in etiology. But such individual features may be better considered in multidimensional terms rather than as single disease states. However, it is quite possible that neuropsychological or neurobiological advances will allow some syndromes to be reconceptualized in process terms. For example, this might happen with autism if the disordered processes underlying the abnormalities in communication and socioemotional functioning could be identified. Similarly, it is possible that some varieties of hyperkinetic disorder could be redefined in terms of some abnormality in central information processing. Alternatively, advances in genetic research, in brain sciences or in imaging techniques may bring us sufficiently close to the etiological mechanisms to allow some psychiatric disorders to be redefined. These possibilities lie well into the future but they are inherent in the advances in neurobiology that are taking place.

CONCLUSIONS

In this chapter we have made no attempt to provide a full agenda of the research tasks that remain, nor are all the examples we have chosen necessarily the most important. What we have sought to do is to outline some of the rather different issues that need to be tackled. Very great progress has been made during recent years in the diagnosis and classification of child psychopathology. It is obvious that the problems that bedevil ICD-9 and DSM-III are closely comparable and stem from lack of relevant data. There is no mileage to be gained in arguing which system is better. Moreover, the main need is not for theoretical dispute but rather for empirical study. Such investigations, often internationally collaborative in nature, are already taking place, and it is realistic to be optimistic that the next decade will see substantial progress. Perhaps, too, it is reasonable to hope that such international collaboration will result in a pooling of knowledge and experience, a willingness to bury doctrinal disputes, and that in their next revisions the World Health Organization and American Psychiatric Association's classifications can come together in an agreed format.

ACKNOWLEDGMENTS

The work by Michael Rutter relevant to Chapters 2, 11, and 13 was supported in part by the John D. and Catherine R. MacArthur Foundation Mental Health Network on Risk and Protective Factors in the Major Mental Disorders. A. Hussain Tuma's contributions to this volume were made principally while he was on the staff of the National Institute of Mental Health, Alcohol, Drug Abuse and Mental Health Administration, U.S. Public Health Service.

REFERENCES

American Psychiatric Association. (1980). *Diagnostic and statistical manual of mental disorders* (3rd ed.). Washington, DC: Author.

Brown, G. W., & Rutter, M. (1966). The measurement of family activities and relationships: A methodological study. *Human Relations, 19,* 241–263

Campos, J. J., Barrett, K. C., Lamb, M. E., Goldsmith, H. H., & Stenberg, C. (1983). Socioemotional development. In M. M. Haith & J. J. Campos (Eds.), *Infancy and developmental psychobiology* (Vol. 2, *Mussen's handbook of child psychology,* 4th ed.). New York: Wiley.

Crittenden, P. M. (1985). Maltreated infants: Vulnerability and resilience. *Journal of Child Psychology and Psychiatry, 26,* 85–96.

Emde, R. N. (1985). Assessment of infancy disorders. In M. Rutter & L. Hersov (Eds.), *Child and adolescent psychiatry: Modern approaches* (2nd ed.). Oxford: Blackwell.

Fletcher, C., Peto, R., Tinker, C., & Speizer, F. E. (1976). *The natural history of chronic bronchitis and emphysema.* New York: Oxford.

Folstein, S., & Rutter, M. (1987). Autism: Familial aggregation and genetic implications. In E. Schopler & G. B. Mesibov (Eds.), *Neurobiological issues in autism.* New York and London: Plenum.

Gittelman, R. (Ed.). (1986). *Anxiety disorders of childhood.* New York: Guilford.

Graham, P. (1979). Epidemiology of psychopathological disorders of childhood. In H. C. Quay & J. S. Werry (Eds.), *Pathological disorders of childhood* (2nd ed.). New York: Wiley.

Gray, J. A. (1982). *The neuropsychology of anxiety: An enquiry into the function of the septohippocampal system.* New York: Oxford.

Henn, F. A., Bardwell, R., & Jenkins, R. L. (1980). Juvenile delinquents revisited: Adult criminal activity. *Archives of General Psychiatry, 37,* 505–513.

Hinde, R. A., & Dennis, A. (1986). Categorizing individuals: An alternative to linear analysis. *International Journal of Behavioral Development, 9,* 105–119.

Kovacs, M. (1986). A developmental perspective on methods and measures in the assessment of depressive disorders: The clinical interview. In M. Rutter, C. E. Izard, & P. B. Read (Eds.), *Depression in young people: Clinical and developmental perspectives.* New York: Guilford.

Loeber, R. (1982). The stability of antisocial and delinquent child behavior: A review. *Child Development, 53,* 1431–1446.

Magnusson, D. (1987). *Individual development in an interactional perspective* (*Paths through life,* Vol. 1). Hillsdale, NJ: Erlbaum.

Main, M., & George, C. (1985). Responses of abused and disadvantaged toddlers to distress in age mates: A study in the day care setting. *Developmental Psychology, 21,* 407–412.

Moore, D. R., Chamberlain, P., & Mulkai, P. (1979). Children at risk for delinquency: A follow-up of aggressive children and children who steal. *Journal of Abnormal Child Psychology, 7,* 345–355.

Mrazek, D., & Mrazek, P. (1985). Child maltreatment. In M. Rutter & L. Hersov (Eds.), *Child and adolescent psychiatry: Modern approaches* (2nd ed.). Oxford: Blackwell.

Oppel, W. C., Harper, P. A. & Rider, R. V. (1968). The age of attaining bladder control. *Pediatrics, 42,* 614–626.

Prendergast, M., Taylor, E., Rapoport, J., Bartko, J., Donnelly, M., Zametkin, A., Ahearn, M. B., Dunn, G., & Wieselberg, H. M. (1987). *The diagnosis of childhood hyperactivity: A US–UK cross-national study of DSM-III and ICD-9.* Submitted for publication.

Quinton, D., Rutter, M., & Rowlands, O. (1976). An evaluation of an interview assessment of marriage. *Psychological Medicine, 6,* 577–586.

Radke-Yarrow, M., Cummings, E. M., Kuczynski, L., & Chapman, M. (1985). Patterns of attachment in two and three year old normal families and families with parental depression. *Child Development, 56,* 884–893.

Reznick, J. A., Kagan, J., Snidman, N., Gersten, M., Baak, K., & Rosenberg, A. (1986). Inhibited and uninhibited children: A follow-up study. *Child Development, 55,* 660–680.

Rich, J. (1956). Types of stealing. *Lancet, 1,* 496–498.

Richman, N. (1985). Disorders in pre-school children. In M. Rutter & L. Hersov (Eds.), *Child and adolescent psychiatry: Modern approaches* (2nd ed.). Oxford: Blackwell.

Richman, N., Stevenson, J., & Graham, P. (1982). *Preschool to school: A behavioural study.* London: Academic Press.

Rodriguez A., Rodriguez., M., & Eisenberg, L. (1959). The outcome of school phobia: A follow-up study based on 41 cases, *American Journal of Psychiatry, 116,* 540–544.

Rutter, M. (1984). Psychopathology and development. I. Childhood antecedents of adult psychiatric disorder. *Australian and New Zealand Journal of Psychiatry, 18,* 225–234.

Rutter, M. (1986, July). *Child psychiatric disorders in ICD-10.* Paper presented at the 11th International Congress on Child and Adolescent Psychiatry and Allied Professions, Paris.

Rutter, M., & Brown, G. W. (1966). The reliability and validity of measures of family life and relationships in families containing a psychiatric patient. *Social Psychiatry, 1,* 38–53.

Rutter, M., & Garmezy, N. (1983). Developmental psychopathology. In E. M. Hetherington (Ed.), *Socialization, personality and social development* (Vol. 4, *Mussen's handbook of child psychology,* 4th ed.). New York: Wiley.

Rutter, M., & Giller, H. (1983). *Juvenile delinquency: Trends and perspectives.* Harmondsworth, England: Penguin Books.

Rutter, M., & Gould, M. (1985). Classification. In M. Rutter & L. Hersov (Eds.), *Child and adolescent psychiatry: Modern approaches* (2nd ed.). Oxford: Blackwell.

Rutter, M., & Sandberg, S. (1985). Epidemiology of child psychiatric disorder: Methodological issues and some substantive findings. *Child Psychology and Human Development, 15,* 209–233.

Rutter, M., & Shaffer, D. (1980). DSM-III: A step forward or back in terms of classification of child psychiatric disorders? *Journal of the American Academy of Child Psychiatry, 19,* 371–394.

Rutter, M., LeCouteur, A., Lord, C., MacDonald, H., Rios, P., & Folstein, S. (in press). Diagnosis and subclassification of autism: Concepts and instrument development. In E. Schopler & G. Mesibov (Eds.), *Diagnosis and assessment of autism.* New York: Plenum.

Schrader, G., Gordon, M., & Harcourt, R. (1986) The usefulness of DSM-III axis IV and axis V assessments. *American Journal of Psychiatry, 143,* 904–907.

Shaffer, D., Schonfeld, I., O'Connor, P. A., Stockman, C., Trautman, P., Shafer, S., & Ng, S. (1985). Neurological soft signs: Their relationship to psychiatric disorder and intelligence in childhood and adolescence. *Archives of General Psychiatry, 42,* 342–351.

Smith, S. D. (Ed.). (1986). *Genetics and learning disabilities.* London: Taylor and Francis.

Stavrakaki, C., & Vargo, B. (1986). The relationship of anxiety and depression: A review of the literature. *British Journal of Psychiatry, 149,* 7–16.

Taylor, E. A. (Ed) (1986). *The overactive child.* London: MacKeith/Blackwell; Philadelphia: Lippincott.

Torgersen, S. (1985). Hereditary differentiation of anxiety and affective neuroses, *British Journal of Psychiatry, 146*, 530–534.

van Goor-Lambo, G., Orley, J., Poustka, F., & Rutter, M. (1986, July). *New developments on the psychosocial axis of classification.* Paper presented at the 11th International Congress on Child and Adolescent Psychiatry and Allied Professions, Paris.

Williams, J. B. W. (1985). The multiaxial system of DSM-III: Where did it come from and where should it go? *Archives of General Psychiatry, 42*, 175–186.

World Health Organization (1978). *International classification of diseases* (9th ed.). Geneva: Author.

Yule, W. (1981). The epidemiology of child psychopathology. In B. B. Lahey & A. E. Kazdin (Eds.), *Advances in clinical child psychology* (Vol. 4). New York: Plenum.

Yule, W., & Rutter, M. (Eds.). (1987). *Language development and disorders: Clinics in developmental medicine, Nos. 101/102.* London: MacKeith/Blackwell.

Zeitlin, H. (1986). *The natural history of psychiatric disorder in childhood.* Institute of Psychiatry/Maudsley Monograph No 29. New York: Oxford.

15

DSM-III-R: A POSTSCRIPT

MICHAEL RUTTER

Well after this volume was typeset, the American Psychiatric Association (1987) published a revision of the third edition of the *Diagnostic and Statistical Manual of Mental Disorders* (DSM-III). As the introduction to the new edition, DSM-III-R, notes, a revision was needed because in some cases diagnostic criteria were inconsistent with new empirical research findings and because there were "many instances in which the criteria were not entirely clear, were inconsistent across categories, or were even contradictory" (American Psychiatric Association, 1987, p. xvii). An additional impetus came from the need to provide input to the tenth revision of the *International Classification of Diseases* (ICD-10). This is not expected to go into full operation until the early 1990s, but a draft version for use in field trials was published by the World Health Organization (1987) at about the same time as DSM-III-R. As the chapters in this book have been addressed to the various ways in which both DSM-III and ICD-9 might be improved, this postscript considers how far the principal issues raised have been dealt with successfully. The prime focus of the discussion is on DSM-III-R, as ICD-10 is still only in draft form, but brief note is taken of some of the main ways in which ICD-10 differs from ICD-9 and in which it has adopted solutions that contrast with those in DSM-III-R.

OVERALL ORGANIZATION OF DSM-III-R

The main structural change in DSM-III-R that has implications for the classification of child psychiatric disorders concerns Axis II. In DSM-III, Axis II comprised only personality disorders and specific developmental disorders. These remain in DSM-III-R, but mental retardation and pervasive developmental disorders have been added. The placement of mental retardation on Axis II should be generally welcomed, as both clinical experience and research findings suggest that this should be helpful (see Cantwell, Chapter 1, this

Michael Rutter. Department of Child and Adolescent Psychiatry, University of London Institute of Psychiatry, London, England.

volume). The inclusion of pervasive developmental disorders (PDD) is perhaps somewhat more controversial (if only because it is defined in terms of deviance rather than retardation of function), but it is entirely consistent with the extensive data indicating that autism both involves a distortion of development from infancy onward and also probably is genetically associated with some forms of specific developmental disorder and mental retardation (Folstein & Rutter, 1987). The reorganization of categories in ICD-10 similarly brings pervasive and specific developmental disorders under the same broad grouping. The main worry about having PDD and mental retardation on the same axis in both DSM-III-R and ICD-10 is that clinicians may fail to code one or the other when both are present. This would be serious, because associated mental handicap is a strong prognostic factor in autism (Lotter, 1978) and its presence has important implications for service provision.

The other axis change in DSM-III-R is that Axis IV (severity of psychosocial stressors) suggests a further specification as to whether the stressor is predominantly acute (duration less than 6 months) or predominantly enduring. Potentially this distinction might be helpful but, as detailed in DSM-III-R, it is likely to be of very limited value. Thus, parental divorce and death are both listed as "acute" events even though they bring about lasting changes in the life of the child. There is a good deal of evidence that these lasting changes are of considerable importance with respect to psychiatric risk both in childhood (Hetherington, Cox, & Cox, 1982; Rutter, 1981) and in adult life (Harris, Brown, & Bifulco, 1986; Parker, 1983). Moreover, the list of events still includes those brought about as a result of the person's own actions (e.g., arrest). It is clear that this axis requires much more thought and, probably, radical revision. The research evidence suggests that it is not appropriate to view all stressors as operating via the same mechanisms or on the same dimension of severity.

One useful change stemming from empirical research (e.g., Leckman, Weissman, Merikangas, Pauls, & Prusoff, 1983) is the elimination of the previous DSM-III hierarchic rule that an anxiety disorder is preempted by a diagnosis of another major mental disorder such as depression. Unfortunately, however, this change has not been extended to the section on children's disorders. Thus "generalized anxiety disorder" (which, according to DSM-III-R, may occur in children) *can* be diagnosed together with major depression, but "overanxious disorder" *cannot*. The situation is further complicated by the fact that "separation anxiety disorder" follows the adult nonhierarchical pattern in spite of the fact that "overanxious disorder" does not. The logic of this difference in rule remains quite obscure. It is evident that the useful advances in the conceptualization of the effects of hierarchies in adult psychiatry have not yet been extended to child psychiatry.

There is an equal need for further thought on the differentiation between "anxiety disorders of childhood and adolescence" and "anxiety disorders." DSM-III-R is clear that *both* sets of diagnoses apply to children, but the former provides no guidance on the features that are considered to separate this group from the anxiety disorders that arise in later life. Curiously, "anxiety disorder" is not even mentioned in the differential diagnosis of "overanxious disorder" in spite of the fact that the symptom criteria given for the two diagnoses are quite similar. There does not seem to be any point in having these two supposedly different groups of anxiety disorders when they have much the same symptoms, when they both apply to children, and when no guidance is given on their differential diagnosis. The draft of ICD-10 grasps this nettle by outlining the reasons why traditionally the distinction has been made and by giving "developmental appropriateness" as the key feature distinguishing the childhood group. This leads to the two systems dealing with "separation anxiety disorder" in a broadly comparable fashion but to a lack in ICD-10 of any equivalent of DSM-III-R's "overanxious disorder." ICD-10 makes clear that "the validity of this distinction [on "developmental appropriateness"] is uncertain," but it seems preferable to make the criteria explicit so that the validity can be tested in the future, rather than to leave the differentiation totally obscure as in DSM-III-R.

ATTENTION DEFICIT AND CONDUCT DISORDERS

One of the biggest changes in the children's section of DSM-III-R is the bringing together of attention deficit, conduct, and oppositional disorders under the general heading of "disruptive behavior disorders." This reflects the growing recognition that these three syndromes share many features and that their differentiation poses many problems (see Taylor, Chapter 12, this volume). The regrouping has been accompanied by a substantial sharpening of the diagnostic concepts and criteria, strongly influenced by empirical research findings. There can be little doubt that this section constitutes a major advance over DSM-III, and for this reason it is worthwhile noting some of the most significant changes. DSM-III listed only inattention and impulsivity as essential features, removed hyperactivity from the diagnostic title, and split the disorder into two subgroups, with and without hyperactivity. DSM-III-R has put hyperactivity back into the title ("attention-deficit hyperactivity disorder"; ADHD), has reintroduced hyperactivity as an essential feature, and has eliminated the "attention deficit disorder without hyperactivity" category. DSM-III-R, unlike DSM-III, also specifies that the symptoms are manifest "in most situations." These changes (closely mirrored in ICD-10) definitely constitute an improvement and go some way to meeting the problems in both ICD-9 and DSM-III (see Taylor, Chapter 12, this volume; Rutter, in press). There has been a growing appreciation that hyperactivity (for all its many problems in measurement) is a crucial part of the disorder; that inattention is a complex multifaceted concept that has not resolved the diagnostic issue; and that the specific hypothesis that a defect in selective attention is basic to the disorder has *not* been supported by empirical evidence. Moreover, it seems that attention deficit disorders without hyperactivity differ in many respects from those with hyperactivity (Carlson, 1986). Time will tell whether the decision to eliminate the former syndrome altogether was correct (on the grounds that it is little used). Field trials were used to derive the list of symptoms required for the diagnosis of ADHD (the splitting of symptoms into three groups, all of which must be present, has also been eliminated). Certainly it is good that research findings were employed so directly in formulating diagnostic criteria, but it is most unfortunate that DSM-III-R gives no details of either the strategy or results of the field trials so that readers can make their own judgments about the validity of the decisions taken.

The title of "oppositional disorder" has been altered to "oppositional defiant disorder" in order to bring out the distinctive features, and the threshold for diagnosis has been raised substantially to avoid the use of this category in essentially normal children. Thus, five symptoms rather than two are required, and it is firmly stated that each symptom criterion requires that the behavior be "considerably more frequent than that of most people of the same mental age." The evolution into, and overlap with, conduct disorder is also made explicit. The changes may not be sufficient to satisfy those who worry about the validity of using tempers and arguments as indications of a psychiatric diagnosis, but clearly the changes are in the right direction.

The diagnostic criteria for conduct disorder in DSM-III-R follow much the same set of general concepts as those employed in DSM-III but they are better organized and appear to be easier to apply than those in the earlier version. The revised subcategorization of conduct disorders into "group type" and "solitary aggressive type" seems a less happy choice in that it lacks an adequate empirical basis. As DSM-III-R suggests, it may be that the "undifferentiated type" will prove in practice to be the most used category. If so, that would be a pity as there is a great need to provide a good differentiation within this rather broad diagnostic grouping. In particular, it would be valuable to be able to differentiate the majority of conduct disorders that do not persist into adult life from the minority (albeit a large minority) that go on to become personality disorders in adult life (Robins, 1978; Rutter, 1984, 1987). The change was made on the grounds that the previous unsocialized–socialized distinction had not worked well, as indeed it had not, but whether the new subdivision is any better seems doubtful. ICD-10 has stuck with the unsocialized–socialized subdivision but has sought to deal with the very real problems in this split by improving the criteria (among other things, by making explicit that the quality of interpersonal relationships has precedence over all other differentiations). Whether or not these new guidelines will work in practice remains to be seen; it is clear that the subdivision of conduct disorders greatly needs further empirical data. ICD-10 has also introduced a new subdivision of "conduct disorder confined to the family context," indicating that "the nosological validity of this category remains uncertain." In spite of the difference in title, the description and criteria show that it has much in common with DSM-III-R's "oppositional defiant disorder."

In spite of the differences in detail noted, it is evident that in most respects ICD-10 and DSM-III-R are much closer together in their classification of "disruptive behavior disorders" than were ICD-9 and DSM-III. Both have moved in relation to the influence from empirical research findings. This is as it should be, and it provides considerable encouragement for the future, even though both manuals are forthright in their indication that many problems remain to be solved.

AUTISM AND PERVASIVE DEVELOPMENTAL DISORDERS

Although the overall concept of pervasive developmental disorders in DSM-III-R closely parallels that in DSM-III, it is much better described in the revised version, and the diagnostic criteria for autism are much better expressed in DSM-III-R. The same applies to the difference between ICD-10 and ICD-9. In most respects, too, ICD-10 and DSM-III-R have come closer together than their predecessors. Both require that the behavior must be abnormal for the person's developmental level, and that *all three* of the key diagnostic criteria must be met—namely, "qualitative impairment in reciprocal social interaction," "qualitative impairment in verbal and nonverbal communication and in imaginative activity," and "markedly restricted repertoire of activities and interests." It is a minor point, but it seems unfortunate that headbanging, a relatively common behavior in otherwise normal children and a symptom that is not particularly associated with autism, should be sufficient to meet the third criterion. The ways in which these three criteria may be manifest are carefully and fully outlined. In all these respects, DSM-III-R and ICD-10 constitute marked improvements over DSM-III and ICD-9.

There are, however, important differences between the two classifications in some other respects. DSM-III-R has eliminated the category of "childhood onset pervasive developmental disorder" and has removed the criterion that autism must have an onset before 30 months of age. Unlike ICD-10, it also does not have a category of "childhood disintegrative disorder." The elimination of the childhood onset category will not please everyone, but it has to be admitted that the criteria in DSM-III were not particularly satisfactory and the syndrome has not given rise to any appreciable research literature. Possibly it was right to drop it. The loss of the criterion of an onset before 30 months of age reflects both the difficulty of determining (particularly in late-referred individuals) whether development was abnormal in the first $2\frac{1}{2}$ years and also the lack of evidence that children with a slightly later onset differ from those in whom development has been abnormal from infancy. It may be accepted that evidence for keeping the onset criterion is decidedly weak. However, the consequence of recognizing only one pervasive developmental disorder (i.e., autism) has been to create considerable difficulties in the classification of three groups of disorders.

First, there are the atypical varieties of autism in which some, but not all, of the criteria for autism are met. This atypicality arises most often in profoundly retarded children whose very low level of functioning provides little scope for exhibition of the specific deviant behaviors required for the diagnosis of autism. As DSM-III-R notes, probably this group is more common than autism (Wing & Gould, 1979). The instructions are to classify the disorder as "pervasive developmental disorder not otherwise specified" (PDDNOS). That might well be satisfactory, but as no description and no diagnostic criteria are given in the manual, there is a considerable danger that in practice this disorder will be slipped into the main autism group. If that happens, the waters will be muddied in ways that will make it difficult to test whether or not basically this group forms part of the same disorder as autism. However, this is by no means the only atypical variety of autism. In addition, there are the social disorders associated with some cases of severe specific developmental disorders of receptive language (Pauls, Cohen, & Caparulo, 1983). They are not mentioned in the manual but presumably they should also be coded PDDNOS. Then there are the cases of autism that arise after a period of several years' normal development, which are now to be included in autism (although there should be specification if the onset is after 3 years of age). There seems to be an important difference between DSM-III-R and ICD-10 in the way that "onset" is conceptualized. ICD-10 is explicit that the issue is whether or not development has been abnormal in some way before 3 years and not whether the syndrome, as specified, has been manifest at that age. When considered in that fashion, onsets after 3 years are quite rare. The shift (in both DSM-III-R and ICD-10) from 30 months to 3 years has certainly helped in making it easier to determine whether early development was abnormal, without altering the concept in any important fashion. In contrast, DSM-III-R discusses "onset" in terms of parental recognition of the disorder; when considered in that fashion, later "onsets" are somewhat more frequent, although still quite uncommon (Volkmar, Stier, & Cohen, 1985).

The second group of disorders that pose problems in classification are those in which, after a period of normal development, there is a definite phase of pervasive loss of previously acquired skills together with behavioral disintegration. DSM-III instructed that such disorder be coded with "dementia," thereby contravening its diagnostic criterion for dementia that specified a "uniformly progressive deteriorating course" (many disintegrative disorders in childhood plateau and do not progress; Evans-Jones & Rosenbloom, 1978; Hill & Rosenbloom, 1986). Also, the instruction ran counter to the expectation that the diagnosis of dementia requires evidence of organic brain disease—evidence that is often lacking in disintegrative disorders, although like autism, such a basis is thought by most clinicians to be present. DSM-III-R has deleted this instruction and has replaced it with the advice to code either autism or PDDNOS. This might be appropriate with the cases that plateau, as certainly their clinical picture mirrors that in autism in many ways (although evidence is lacking on whether or not they in fact constitute the same disorder). However, it does not seem appropriate for the progressive cases that follow some form of acquired brain disease (Corbett, Harris, Taylor, & Trimble, 1977). It seems even more inappropriate for diagnosable neurological disorders that are known to differ from autism in crucial respects. Thus, Rett's syndrome (Hagberg, Aicardi, Dias, & Ramos, 1983), which in its early stages may be confused with autism, is found only in girls (whereas autism shows a marked male preponderance) and follows a quite different course. In girls, its prevalence is about a third that of autism (Kerr & Stephenson, 1985)—scarcely "extremely rare" as stated by DSM-III-R. As developmental neuropsychiatry advances with the identification of specific syndromes, it seems most unfortunate that DSM-III-R steps backward in removing potentially important clinical distinctions that may aid in the delineation of etiologically different conditions.

The third group of disorders posing a classification problem are those variously termed "schizoid disorder of childhood" (Chick, Waterhouse, & Wolff, 1979; Wolff & Barlow, 1979; Wolff & Chick, 1980) or Asperger's syndrome (Wing, 1981). DSM-III included a "schizoid disorder of childhood" category, but this has been eliminated in DSM-III-R on the grounds that it "has been observed only in the presence of other signs of psychopathology that suggest a Pervasive Developmental Disorder" (American Psychiatric Association, 1987, p. 412). The probable link with PDD is recognized in ICD-10 by including the category as a subvariety of PDD (but separate from autism). There has been a tendency by some investigators to include Asperger's syndrome cases that also meet the criteria for autism (see Wing, 1981); these, of course, are properly classified with autism. Nevertheless, it is equally clear that most of Wolff's series did not fit the criteria for autism; moreover, the prevalence she reported (3%–4% of referrals to an outpatient clinic) makes it unlikely that these all exhibited autism. Once again, it seems unfortunate to prejudge the issue in the absence of relevant empirical findings; another diagnostic distinction has been lost. Both ICD-9 and DSM-III have been criticized on the grounds of having too many ill-validated and unreliable diagnostic distinctions (Rutter & Shaffer, 1980; see also Gould, Shaffer, Rutter, & Sturge, Chapter 2, this volume), but, in this instance, perhaps a little less lumping and a little more splitting might have been advisable. It is not, of course, that we know that these various groups are truly different diagnostic entities, but putting them all in the same diagnostic category will make it more difficult to conduct the studies needed to test the validity of the distinctions.

SPECIFIC DEVELOPMENTAL DISORDERS

The section on specific developmental disorders in DSM-III-R seems better than that in DSM-III in both its definition and its coverage. This group of disorders suffers from the inherent difficulty of having to create a category out of a dimension. A decision has to be made on how severely a developmental function must be impaired for a disorder to be diagnosed. DSM-III-R does not solve the problem in that it specifies only that scores on a standardized measure must be "substantially below" the level expected on the basis of the child's age and IQ. It seems a pity that this was not specified more precisely in statistical terms. However, what is a help is the additional requirement that the impairment "significantly interferes with academic achievement or activities of daily living." That should make it less likely for transient minor developmental delays to be included, but it still leaves a degree of ambiguity on how to decide what is "substantially below" and what is required for "significantly interferes." No entirely adequate solution is available in view of the paucity of empirical evidence on the features that differentiate developmental *disorders* from normal developmental variations. However, as noted in Chapter 14 of this volume, ICD-10 has gone somewhat further in seeking to specify the criteria to be applied. For example, for specific development disorders of language it is specified that a disorder is suggested by four main features: (1) severity (impairment outside the two-standard-deviation limits), and/or (2) course (so that current impairment may be less than this but there is a history of a previously severe impairment), and/or (3) pattern (deviance and not just delay), and/or (4) associated psychological problems (scholastic, socioemotional, or behavioral). This attempt to make the criteria for disorder more explicit seems worthwhile, but it will be important to put these criteria to the test in future research.

DSM-III-R has also added two more specific developmental disorder categories not in DSM-III: "developmental coordination disorder" and "developmental expressive writing disorder." The first of these, sometimes termed "the clumsy child syndrome," is reasonably well established as a category and its inclusion is well warranted (it was already in ICD-9 and is retained in ICD-10). As the manual makes clear, less is known on the latter and there is a marked paucity of empirical data. The lack of a well-established statistical test of writing may also make for difficulties in diagnosis, but there has been recent interest in writing problems and further studies should determine whether their separate categorization is warranted (frequently they are associated with reading difficulties). ICD-10 has no exactly comparable category, although its "mixed disorder of scholastic skills" would probably include many cases of writing disorder.

ICD-10 has also included "acquired aphasia with epilepsy" (Landau–Kleffner syndrome) and "environmentally determined language disorder" in the broad category of developmental disorders. Both are clinically important conditions (see Yule & Rutter, 1987) that need separate coding. It is arguable whether they are best placed in that category, but it is not clear where they should be coded in DSM-III-R. It could be maintained that Landau–Kleffner syndrome should be in a neurological section on Axis III (physical conditions and disorders) provided that it is covered there. However, it was not in ICD-9, and it is not self-evident that that argument applies any more strongly than it does for, say, specific developmental disorder of receptive language.

MOOD DISORDERS

As in DSM-III, the main subclassification of affective disorders (now renamed "mood disorders") in DSM-III-R remains bipolar disorders, major depression, and dysthymia. This tripartite subdivision has been highlighted by some reorganization of this section, the criteria for melancholic type of depression have been hardened, and a new specification of "seasonal pattern" type has been added to accommodate the growing interest in depressive disorders that appear in the winter months and often seem to respond to light treatment. The organization and subclassification of affective disorders in ICD-9 was both complicated and lacking in empirical validation. That in ICD-10 is much more in line with DSM-III-R, although there are some differences (e.g. schizoaffective disorder is included in this section rather than under "psychotic disorders not elsewhere classified," as in DSM-III-R). ICD-10 has also adopted the general term "mood disorders." For the child psychiatrist, the most obvious lack in ICD-10 is any mention of the occurrence of mood disorders as they are manifest in childhood. DSM-III attempted to specify the ways in which such disorders were manifest in childhood and DSM-III-R does the same. The details are, however, different. Thus, DSM-III-R has dropped the statement that separation anxiety is common in prepubertal children and instead has added the claim that "psychomotor agitation and mood-congruent hallucinations (usually only a single voice talking to the child) are particularly frequent." While, indeed, these symptoms have been reported as common in some inpatient series, it seems very dubious whether they are more frequent than in adult life when like is compared with like; certainly systematic age comparisons using standardized measures are lacking. DSM-III-R also claims that major depressive disorders can begin in infancy. This may be so, but it seems somewhat unlikely that the diagnostic criteria as given can be met in this age period. DSM-III-R has the advantage here over ICD-10 in having tackled the issue of possible age differences in the manifestation of depression, but it rather appears that, in seeking to give definite guidance, DSM-III-R has outreached the empirical data.

OTHER DISORDERS

There are a variety of minor changes in DSM-III-R, most of which constitute improvements over DSM-III. For example, the weight loss criterion for anorexia nervosa has been altered in the light of experience from 25% to 15% of the body weight, and the missing of at least three menstrual cycles has been added as a criterion in females. In DSM-III-R, as in DSM-III, anorexia nervosa is included in the section "disorders usually first evident in infancy, childhood, or adolescence." Curiously, and illogically, in ICD-10 it is not so included, in spite of the very extensive evidence that the age of onset is usually in adolescence. Sensibly, "gender identity disorder of childhood" has been moved to the children's section in DSM-III-R. ICD-10 does not seem to have a place for this disorder as it arises in prepubertal children (although there is a literature documenting both its occurrence and its continuity with adult sexual orientation; see, e.g., Green, 1974, 1985). "Identity disorder" has been retained as a category in spite of the weak evidence in support of its validity.

More extensive changes have been made to the diagnostic criteria for "reactive attachment disorder of infancy or early childhood." Some of the changes constitute improvements, but in many respects these criteria remain rather unsatisfactory. To begin with, this disorder is diagnosed on the presence of only one symptom (either "persistent failure to initiate or respond to most social interactions" or "indiscriminate sociability"). That really does not seem adequate and certainly it does not make optimal use of the growing body of empirical data. A second concern is that the diagnosis requires the presence of "grossly pathogenic care." While certainly that is the circumstance in which the syndrome tends to be diagnosed, to include it as a mandatory feature means that the association between the child syndrome and environmental circumstances cannot be investigated; such investigation is needed because the empirical evidence so far is quite limited. A third issue is the lack of subdivision in spite of the (admittedly limited) evidence that institutional rearing gives rise to a clinical picture that differs from that seen with child abuse or severe maternal depression. The concept in ICD-10 is broadly comparable to that in DSM-III-R but there is, perhaps, a rather more direct tackling of the problems of differential diagnosis.

ICD-10

Throughout this discussion of DSM-III-R, note has been taken of some of the detailed changes in diagnostic concept or criteria in ICD-10 compared with ICD-9 and DSM-III. Although there are some remaining important differences between DSM-III-R and ICD-10, it is encouraging that both seem to have used empirical research findings to move closer together on many syndromes. But by far and away the biggest change is in the diagnostic guidelines provided in ICD-10. These are very much fuller and much more precise than those in ICD-9. It is likely that clinicians will find them much more helpful and it is to be hoped that the increase in precision will also lead to better reliability. It is obvious that the guidelines owe much to the approach pioneered in DSM-III, although they still differ in not being put in the research diagnostic criteria form requiring specific numbers of specific features. The ICD-10 compromise is to have two versions: one in the form of these detailed diagnostic guidelines for general use, and one in the form of diagnostic criteria for research that will be closely comparable in style to DSM-III-R (the latter has yet to be distributed at the time of writing).

CONCLUSIONS

It is encouraging that many of the diagnostic and classificatory issues and challenges noted throughout this volume have been tackled in DSM-III-R, usually with substantial improvements over DSM-III. The same applies to ICD-10 compared with ICD-9, and it is good that the two schemes now have much more in common than they did before. Of course, it would not be realistic to hope that all problems would be solved, and they have not been. In any case, most of the unanswered questions await the knowledge that is needed from future research. Classification cannot be static. As the introduction to DSM-III-R indicates, this revision had the advantage of a more extensive empirical data base than that available to the group preparing DSM-III, and it is to be expected that future research should take matters a further step forward when DSM-IV is developed.

REFERENCES

American Psychiatric Association (1987). *Diagnostic and statistical manual of mental disorders* (3rd ed.—revised). Washington, DC: Author.

Carlson, C.L. (1986). Attention deficit disorder without hyperactivity: A review of preliminary experimental evidence. In B.B. Lahey & A.E. Kazdin (Eds.), *Advances in clinical child psychology* (Vol. 9, pp. 153–175). New York: Plenum.

Chick, J., Waterhouse, L., & Wolff, S. (1979). Psychological construing in schizoid children grown up. *British Journal of Psychiatry, 135,* 425–430.

Corbett, J., Harris, R., Taylor, E., & Trimble, M. (1977). Progressive disintegrative psychosis of childhood. *Journal of Child Psychology and Psychiatry, 18,* 211–219.

Evans-Jones, L.B., & Rosenbloom, L. (1978). Disintegrative psychosis in childhood. *Developmental Medicine and Child Neurology, 20,* 462–470.

Folstein, S., & Rutter, M. (1987). Autism: Familial aggregation and genetic implications. In E. Schopler & G. Mesibov (Eds.), *Neurobiological issues in autism* (pp. 83–105). New York: Plenum.

Green, R. (1974). *Sexual identity conflict in children and adults.* New York: Basic Books; London: Duckworth. (1975. New York: Viking/Penguin.)

Green, R. (1985). Atypical psychosexual development. In M. Rutter & L. Hersov (Eds.), *Child and adolescent psychiatry: Modern approaches* (2nd ed., pp. 638–649). Oxford: Blackwell.

Hagberg, B., Aicardi, J., Dias, K., & Ramos, O. (1983). A progressive syndrome of autism, dementia, ataxia, and loss of purposeful hand use in girls: Rett's syndrome: Report of 35 cases. *Annals of Neurology, 14,* 471–479.

Harris, T., Brown, G.W., & Bifulco, A. (1986). Loss of parent in childhood and adult psychiatric disorder: The role of lack of adequate parental care. *Psychological Medicine, 16,* 641–660.

Hill, A.E., & Rosenbloom, L. (1986). Disintegrative psychosis of childhood: Teenage follow-up. *Developmental Medicine and Child Neurology, 28,* 34–40.

Hetherington, E.M., Cox, M., & Cox, R. (1982). Effects of divorce on parents and children. In M.E. Lamb (Ed.), *Non-traditional families* (pp. 233–288). Hillsdale, NJ: Erlbaum.

Kerr, A.M., & Stephenson, J.B.P. (1985). Rett's syndrome in the West of Scotland. *British Medical Journal, 219,* 579–582.

Leckman, J.F., Weissman, M.M., Merikangas, K.R., Pauls, D.L., & Prusoff, B.A. (1983). Panic disorder and major depression: Increased rate of depression, alcoholism, panic, and phobic disorders in families of depressed probands with panic disorder. *Archives of General Psychiatry. 40,* 1055–1060.

Lotter, V. (1978). Follow-up studies. In M. Rutter & E. Schopler (Eds.), *Autism: A reappraisal of concepts and treatment* (pp. 475–495). New York: Plenum.

Parker, G. (1983). *Parental overprotection: A risk factor in psychosocial development.* New York and London: Grune & Stratton.

Pauls, D., Cohen, D., & Caparulo, B.K. (1983). A longitudinal study of patients with severe developmental disorders of language learning. *Journal of the American Academy of Child Psychiatry, 22,* 525–534.

Robins, L. (1978). Sturdy childhood predictors of adult antisocial behaviour: Replications from longitudinal studies. *Psychological Medicine, 8,* 611–622.

Rutter, M. (1981). *Maternal deprivation reassessed* (2nd ed.). Harmondsworth, England: Penguin.

Rutter, M. (1984). Psychopathology and development. I. Childhood antecedents of adult psychiatric disorder. *Australian and New Zealand Journal of Psychiatry, 18,* 225–234.

Rutter, M. (1987). Temperament, personality and personality disorder. *British Journal of Psychiatry, 150,* 443–458.

Rutter, M. (in press). Attention deficit disorder/hyperkinetic syndrome: Conceptual research issues regarding diagnosis and classification. In T. Sagvolden, H.M. Borchgrevink, & T. Archer (Eds.), *Attention deficit disorder and hyperkinetic syndrome.* Hillsdale, NJ: Erlbaum.

Rutter, M., & Shaffer, D. (1980). DSM-III: A step forward or back in terms of the classification of child psychiatric disorders? *Journal of the American Academy of Child Psychiatry, 10,* 371–394.

Volkmar, F.R., Stier, D.M., & Cohen, D.J. (1985). Age of recognition of pervasive developmental disorder. *American Journal of Psychiatry, 142,* 1450–1452.

Wing, L. (1981). Asperger's syndrome: A clinical account. *Psychological Medicine, 11,* 115–130.

Wing, L., & Gould, J. (1979). Severe impairments of social interaction and associated abnormalities in children: Epidemiology and classification. *Journal of Autism and Developmental Disorders, 9,* 11–30.

Wolff, S., & Barlow, A. (1979). Schizoid personality in childhood: A comparative study of schizoid, autistic and normal children. *Journal of Child Psychology and Psychiatry. 20,* 19–46.

Wolff, S., & Chick, J. (1980). Schizoid personality in childhood: A controlled follow-up study. *Psychological Medicine, 10,* 85–100.

World Health Organization (1987). *ICD-10 1986 draft of Chapter V. Categories F00–F99: Mental, behavioral and developmental disorders.* Geneva: Author.

Yule, W., & Rutter, M. (Eds.). (1987). *Language development and disorders: Clinics in developmental medicine, Nos. 101/102.* London: MacKeith/Blackwell.

INDEX